Legal Systems & Skills

Judith Embley

To my husband, Greg, and my son, Oliver, with thanks for their help and invaluable insights into today's legal profession, as well as my daughter, Charlotte, and son, Edward, for all their support, and also to my grandson, Sebastian.

Catherine Shephard

For Jack, who happily still loves books despite having to live with me when I'm writing; my parents; and James. Your good humour, cheery support and late-night kitchen make all the difference.

Peter Goodchild

To my long-suffering and usually tolerant family, and in memory of my parents. Thanks also to my cat for her 'assistance' in updating my parts of the book.

Legal Systems & Skills

FOURTH EDITION

Consultant editor: Scott Slorach

Judith Embley

Peter Goodchild

Catherine Shephard

OXFORD
UNIVERSITY PRESS

OXFORD

UNIVERSITY PRESS

Great Clarendon Street, Oxford, OX2 6DP,
United Kingdom

Oxford University Press is a department of the University of Oxford.
It furthers the University's objective of excellence in research, scholarship,
and education by publishing worldwide. Oxford is a registered trade mark of
Oxford University Press in the UK and in certain other countries

© Oxford University Press 2020

The moral rights of the authors have been asserted

First edition 2013
Second edition 2015
Third edition 2017

Impression: 3

Public sector information reproduced under Open Government Licence v3.0
(http://www.nationalarchives.gov.uk/doc/open-government-licence/open-government-licence.htm)

Published in the United States of America by Oxford University Press
198 Madison Avenue, New York, NY 10016, United States of America

British Library Cataloguing in Publication Data
Data available

Library of Congress Control Number: 2020932955

ISBN 978-0-19-883432-8

Printed in Great Britain by
Bell & Bain Ltd., Glasgow

Contents

Detailed contents

About the authors

© Rebecca Slorach

Scott Slorach (consultant editor) is a Professor and Director of Teaching & Learning at York Law School at the University of York. He holds Visiting roles at the University of Strathclyde and the College of Law Australia. A qualified solicitor with City experience, he was author of *Corporate Finance* (OUP) and is currently co-author of *Business Law* (OUP). Scott now specializes in the design, delivery, and assessment of legal education at all levels; he has held various roles with the SRA, including membership of the SQE working group, Chief External Examiner for business law, LPC assessor, and training committee member. He was recently part of a team reporting to the Irish LSRA as part of its statutory review of legal practitioner education.

Judith Embley is Associate Professor at the University of Law. She qualified as a solicitor in 1980, practising in a Lincoln's Inn firm and began teaching law in 1999 as a Visiting Lecturer at Bellerby's College and then Anglia Ruskin University in Cambridge. She joined the University of Law in 2001, where she has taught contract, commercial, and business financial law. She is now Module Lead for the LPC commercial law and practice module, the LLB 'companies, governance, tax and insolvency' module, and the LLB transactions module. She is joint author of *Commercial and Intellectual Property Law and Practice* and *Legal Foundations*, two of the University of Law's Legal Practice Guides.

Peter Goodchild is an Associate Professor and Programme & Student Lead for the GDL and MA Law at the University of Law. He read Politics, Philosophy and Economics at St. Anne's College, Oxford, then attended the University of Law and qualified as a solicitor in 1997, into commercial practice. He joined the University of Law in 2000, where he has taught the English legal system, contract, tort, ethics, commercial, IP and business structures law. In addition to over nineteen years of teaching experience, he has wide experience of designing programmes and has been an author of texts on tort, commercial law, IP law, and the English legal system.

Catherine Shephard is Senior Lecturer and Subject Leader of corporate practice, company law, and professional skills in practice at Manchester Law School. She read law at Emmanuel College, Cambridge, and practised as a solicitor in corporate finance. Catherine has extensive experience of designing, teaching, leading and assessing law, skills and management programmes across academia and practice. Catherine is a Fellow of the Higher Education Academy, a qualified civil and commercial mediator, and a resilience trainer for the Social Mobility Business Partnership charity.

Preface

From the first edition of this text, prefaces have underlined the importance of an holistic understanding of:

- legal systems, law, and lawyers;
- academic, vocational, and professional skills; and
- commercial awareness, in its widest sense.

At the time of this fourth edition, there is an environment of change which makes such an understanding of even greater importance.

The changes in question can be organized using the strategic analysis tool PESTLE. This scans Political; Economic; Social; Technological; Legal; and Environmental factors across a particular environment.

The **political** landscape has been dominated by Brexit which will have a major impact on UK law, legal services and, potentially, legal education.

The **economic** impact of Brexit has been the subject of many and varied reports. However, the global financial crisis and a period of austerity have already resulted in law firms of all sizes focusing on efficiency and providing greater value to clients. We have seen new resourcing and process models, and increased use of technology

Social inclusion and diversity factors are also influencing change: university contextual admission policies to encourage more socially diverse student cohorts; the Solicitors Regulation Authority's (SRA) proposals for the Solicitors Qualifying Examination (SQE) to encourage a more diverse profession by providing more routes to qualification; the solicitors' profession having to respond to gender pay imbalance.

Technology is, arguably belatedly, having an increasing impact on the legal profession, with applications being developed to increase efficiency, reduce cost, and potentially improve quality of legal processes previously carried out 'by hand'. The title of Richard Susskind's 2008 work on *The End of Lawyers?*[1] suggested a *Rethinking the Nature of Legal Services* and appears to have been prescient.

We have noted the likely **legal** impact of Brexit. The SQE is already having an impact on legal education with some universities announcing changes to undergraduate law degrees to prepare students for the exams, and SQE preparation programmes being announced by traditional LPC providers and newcomers to the market.

All these factors are bringing change to the legal education and professional **environments**. Law curricula face the twin challenges of the SQE and the professional demands for multi-skilled recruits. There are more modules to develop legal practice skills, and some law schools offer learning around law and technology. Varied routes to employment and professional qualification are increasing, alongside varied roles within legal services providers including specialised paralegal and technology-related roles. Technology has underpinned development of new legal services providers and new functions within a number of existing firms.

It is within this environment of change, increasing demands and development, that this text has been developed. Each part individually addresses its themes and issues raised

---

[1] Susskind, R. (2008) *The End of Lawyers? Rethinking the Nature of Legal Services*. Oxford: OUP.

within this context. Together, they provide insight into the holistic development of knowledge, skills, and understanding required both at law school and in looking ahead to legal practice and other careers.

Professor J Scott Slorach

York Law School

Spring 2020

New to this edition

- Legal skills: each skill is now explained in the context of its development and application, first during legal studies, and then in legal practice.
- Analysis and guidance on each of the skills proposed to be assessed in SQE2, including case and matter analysis, persuasive oral communication, and negotiation.
- New contemporary case studies to demonstrate commercial awareness.
- Consideration of the impact of technology and AI on business and legal services, and the increasing changes in the legal services environment.
- Additional material on professional conduct and ethics.
- Updated Brexit coverage.

Getting the most out of *legal systems & skills*

A truly innovative resource combining coverage of legal systems with academic and professional legal skills. *Legal Systems & Skills* is a rich learning resource, enhanced with a range of features designed to help you get the most out of your studies and to help support a practical approach to learning. This guided tour shows you how to fully utilize the content. Throughout the text you will find prompts to continue your development via the **online resources**.

www.oup.com/he/slorach4e

Slorach, Embley, Goodchild and Shephard, Legal Systems & Skills 4e Student Resources

Description

Student resources can be used to consolidate your learning after each lecture, to prepare for seminars, as a starting point to research a coursework essay, and of course during your revision. The resources available include:

- Self-test questions to assess your understanding of the key concepts and skills
- The authors' guidance to answering the practical exercises in the book
- Sample interview questions to help students identify which areas of commercial awareness they need to focus on
- A library of web links that direct students to useful websites and relevant media

⬇ CC v1.0 (Single)

Resources by Chapter ⌄
Chapter 01
Chapter 02
Chapter 03

Chapter 01

Chapter 1 Self-test questions
Introduction to law

Chapter 1 Guidance to answering the practical exercises
Introduction to law

To focus your learning

Learning objectives

After studying this chapter you should be able to:

- Explain the importance of law as a concept.
- Develop an awareness that law can (and should) be studied in its wider context.
- Relate law to its underpinnings in ethics.
- Explain in outline selected aspects of philosophies of law, known as jurisprudence.
- Discuss the importance of legitimacy in law, and in particular the idea of sovereignty.
- Understand the theoretical and practical importance of the rule of law.

Learning objectives

A bulleted outline of the main concepts signposts what you can expect to learn from each chapter.

Summary

- Law is a system of rules by which a state operates.
- Law touches on every aspect of our day-to-day lives.
- Law cannot be viewed in isolation from other related areas.
- Morality is difficult to define and analyse, but this is a worthwhile exercise as it helps us understand the relationship between law and ethics. This relationship should be viewed in the context of values.
- Jurisprudence is the study of key concepts in law, and has developed over time.
- One important issue in legal theory is the legitimacy of law, and a common means of providing legitimacy is to find an acceptable mindroom (or basic rule)

Summary of key points

The central points covered in each chapter are gathered into summaries, providing a useful tool to help reinforce your understanding.

Helping you become more confident with new concepts

Essential explanation boxes

> **① Essential explanation**
> Law
>
> What is law?
> *The Shorter Oxford English Dictionary* defines 'law' in 17 different ways, but the first definition is most relevant here.
>
> The body of rules, whether formally enacted or customary, which a particular state or community recognizes as governing the actions of its subjects or members and which it may enforce by imposing penalties.[1]
>
> The significant words are 'rules' and 'state': the rules by which a state operates.

Quickly understand unfamiliar terminology and concepts with these useful jargon-busting explanation boxes.

Diagrams and tables

Numerous diagrams and flowcharts provide a visual representation of concepts and processes.

Example boxes

> **Example 1**
>
> Here are two contemporary examples of the uneasy relationship between legal, social, and moral values:
>
> • Should discrimination be illegal against employees on the ground of their being overweight? In the UK the Equality Act 2010 protects persons from discrimination on the grounds of certain protected characteristics—e.g. race or sex. Body type is not (of itself) one of those characteristics. An employee might perceive an overweight employee as lazy or unhealthy. Many would perceive this behaviour as unjustified and immoral, but it is not legally regulated.
>
> • What about same-sex marriage? While civil partnerships between gay couples are legal in the UK,[7] marriage has only been legal since the Marriage (Same Sex Couples) Act 2013, which came into force in 2014. In only 26 countries and jurisdictions is same-sex marriage legal.[8] In the US, same sex

Frequent examples and short case studies throughout the book provide legal and real-life illustrative examples to help you fully understand concepts.

Self-test questions

Chapter 01	☑	Chapter 1 Self-test questions
Chapter 02		Introduction to law
Chapter 03	☑	Chapter 2 Self-test questions
Chapter 04		Legal system and sources of law
Chapter 05	☑	Chapter 3 Self-test questions
Chapter 06		The court system of England & Wales
Chapter 07	☑	Chapter 4 Self-test questions
Chapter 08		Legislation
	☑	Chapter 5 Self-test questions
		Case Law

On the **online resources** you will find multiple-choice questions arranged by chapter to assess your understanding of the key concepts and skills.

To help you think critically about the law

Essential debate boxes

> **② Essential debate**
>
> There are two general views on how ethics works:
>
> • Objectivism: objectivists believe that it is possible for there to be one absolute set of moral values, although precisely what this set of values is, is clearly extremely controversial.
>
> • Relativism: relativists argue that morals are the function of human thought and are therefore the reflection of the beliefs of people themselves, either as a society, or individually. This means that morality can change over time (e.g. the example of homosexuality referred to in 1.2) and can vary between societies, or even people. Some relativists claim that social values and morality are intertwined
>
> [3] An Act To Render The Laws More Effective For The Preventing The Stealing And Destroying Of Sheep

Quickly grasp the essential debates you need to know about legal systems with these concise boxes, and start to develop your own critical thinking.

Practical exercises

> **③ Practical exercises**
>
> 1. Why do you think law is important?
> 2. Should law-makers have a moral agenda?
> 3. Is jurisprudence relevant in practice?
> 4. Is the Rule of Law an intellectual construct, designed to justify the Western democracies?
> 5. Is the Separation of Powers appropriate in the modern world?
>
> ⟳ *Visit the **online resources** for the authors' reflections and to check your progress*

Challenge your thinking about legal systems and skills with these practical exercises and thought-provoking questions, great for exam and interview preparation. Guideline responses from the authors are available on the **online resources**.

Further reading

Extend your knowledge with these annotated further reading sections. You will also find on the **online resources** a library of links to useful sites and relevant media to facilitate research into areas of interest.

To apply knowledge and skills

Annotated documents and templates

Familiarize yourself with the format of important legal documents with these annotated resources and document templates, great for use in study and preparing for subsequent employment.

'What the professionals' say boxes

Enhance your employability by following the advice of top legal services and other professionals, as found throughout Parts II and III.

Practice tip boxes

Relevant aspects of the realities of legal practice are introduced to provide context for your skills development.

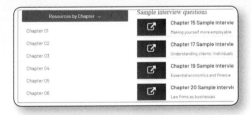

Sample interview questions

On the **online resources** you will find sample interview questions used by law firms in recent graduate interview processes to help you to practise for those all-important interviews.

LEARN HOW LAW WORKS > DEVELOP THE ESSENTIAL SKILLS > APPLY THEM TO SUCCEED

Acknowledgements

Judith Embley wishes to thank colleagues (past and present) at the University of Law at Bloomsbury, particularly Jacqui Kempton, Susan Sang, Stuart Roberts, Judith Pothecary, Louise Mawer, and Jane Vandervlies, for their helpful suggestions and invaluable support.

Catherine Shephard is grateful to Nicola Beck, Natasha Choolun, Zachary Clough, Sarah Cook, Andrew Francis, Dan Hill, Mark Keith, Tom Laidlaw, Wendy Laws, Nick Poole and Corryn Walker for their advice and support in making this book a success. Thanks also to all her students, past and present, for their inspiration, and to everyone named in the chapters who took time out of their busy schedules to listen to her and provide such illuminating quotations.

Peter Goodchild wishes to thank colleagues past and present at the University of Law for their help, ideas and patience. In particular, thanks to Judith Pothecary, Martin Norris and Stuart Roberts for shedding light on the niceties of public law and criminal law. Finally thanks to his students, who make all this so enjoyable.

Publisher acknowledgements

Grateful acknowledgement is made to all the authors and publishers of copyright material which appears in this book, and in particular to the following for permission to reprint material from the sources indicated:

- The Incorporated Council of Law Reporting for England and Wales—the special permission to reproduce in Chapter 7 extracts from the headnotes of *Donoghue v Stevenson* [1932] AC 562, is gratefully acknowledged.
- Every effort has been made to trace and contact copyright holders prior to publication. Where this has not proved possible, if notified, the publisher will undertake to rectify any errors or omissions at the earliest opportunity.

Introduction

Legal Systems & Skills comprises three parts, which focus on:

1. legal systems, sources of law, legal institutions, the legal profession, and the role of lawyers;
2. the skills required for both the study and practice of law, and for other professions and vocations; and
3. individuals and businesses affected by the law, and the economic and commercial context within which this occurs.

The aim, to misquote Aristotle, is that the whole textbook should be greater than the sum of these parts. The parts in themselves have a dual role.

First, they support core individual modules or activities, such as English legal system, legal skills, and employability. In addition to supporting development of understanding through substantive content, the design of the textbook also supports the development of a more critical mind-set and a wider skill-set. This is achieved by the inclusion of essential debate features and a range of practical exercises. The former aim to challenge students' thinking on law and society; the latter require application of academic and practical legal skills.

Second, the individual parts provide underpinning for all aspects of a law programme. That is, they are reference points for students to return to throughout their degree on the fundamental aspects of legal systems, academic and legal skill, and commercial awareness, which underpin myriad modules, themes, and tasks.

However, taking the sum of the parts, there are interrelationships to explore. Each part is better understood in the context of the other, and cross references are provided to enable and encourage readers to develop an holistic understanding.

This understanding is more important than ever due to the coincidence of recent, current, and expected changes in: legal education—including the proposed SQE, the legal profession, and the wider environment. These have brought sharp focus to the need for successful law students and practitioners to be multi-skilled, commercially savvy, client-focused and, perhaps above all, adaptable: And that is not to forget the need to have excellent academic credentials and the ability to translate these into the practical application of law for clients. The challenges are considerable; this textbook has been developed to support students in taking steps to meet them.

Within *Part I: Legal Systems*, we explore the development and forms of legal systems and law; the specific legal system of England and Wales, and its institutions, including the courts; and the sources of law. This includes consideration of common law and civil law systems, not only explaining the differences but also encouraging students to analyse their own legal system. The potential impact of Brexit is discussed in the latter, as well as other, contexts. There is a detailed chapter on legislation, helping students to understand not only its purpose and effect, but also the processes involved in the introduction of new legislation.

In addition, this part considers legal services and the legal profession. In the latter context, particular attention is given to the regulation of legal services and the professions, and the concomitant ethical standards required of lawyers.

The overall intent, within *Legal Systems*, is to provide a focused and practical guide to the purpose and application of law. Contemporary and holistic in approach, essential topics are considered from social, moral, ethical, and jurisprudential perspectives. Taking learning further, it helps students to evaluate critically legal systems and law, and their implications for individuals, businesses, and commerce. It also provides students with an initial insight—developed further in the third part—into the individuals and entities who advise individuals and businesses on the implications of law.

Part II: Legal Skills has been expanded to include negotiation; mediation; case/matter analysis; and persuasive oral communication skills. These add to the skills of research, reading law, writing, drafting, interviewing, presentation, mooting, and advocacy. This expansion of the ambit of the legal skills content is reflective of changes within: law schools—as more skills modules are introduced; the legal profession—as firms' expectations of their new recruits continue to grow; and the process of qualification as a solicitor—with the proposed mandatory assessment of legal skills by the Solicitors Regulation Authority. The legal skills chapters in Part II are therefore structured to reflect skills development requirements from commencing legal studies through to professional or other employability.

A law student's initial focus is to develop research skills, become practised at reading and understanding law and related academic materials, then apply these to solve problems, and produce written, well-referenced discourse and argument on the law. In addition, a law student may be involved in activities involving oral discourse and argument: debates, presentations, and moots. Each legal skill is therefore introduced and developed in the context in which readers are likely to experience it as practised at law school.

When students begin to think about employability, whether in the legal profession or another vocation, the focus and context of application of each skill will change. To reflect this, each legal skill is then explored further in the context of professional legal services to provide this additional insight into the competencies required and client-focused application of skills.

A sound understanding of legal systems and skills underpins employability and commercial awareness. Part III of the text builds on this understanding, helping students to see how their knowledge and skills can be practically applied. It also considers the range of further competencies required for employment, whether in legal services or in other vocations and professions. These include an understanding of basic economics, and the finances and interests of individuals and businesses. Students are encouraged to reflect on and improve their skills and commercial awareness through case studies and activities.

This part of the text also provides guidance on how best to present personal competencies to potential employers when developing a CV, and in the context of interviews. Given the overall ambit of the text, specific focus is given to law firms, linking back to the consideration of the legal profession in the first part of the book. However, students are reassured as to the transferability of both skills and commercial awareness, whatever their career aspirations may be. Overall, the aim is to help students approach a future career with confidence, and to communicate their competencies effectively.

The text as a whole has been designed not only to offer the explanation and guidance as described above, but also to provide insight through demonstrations, exemplars, and case studies. In addition, it provides scope for wider discussion and further consideration of issues, by regular presentation of topics for debate, and setting a series of thought-provoking questions. Specific topics and themes are also continued through into the **online resources** which accompany the text.

Legal Systems

It is important that law students develop an holistic and contemporary understanding of the purpose and practical application of the law. This goes beyond a basic knowledge of the English legal system.

This section therefore considers the rationale for law from social and moral perspectives, and reflects on further jurisprudential perspectives, considering a number of legal and ethical theories. It then focuses on the development of legal systems, illustrated with practical examples from a range of jurisdictions, and compares common law and civil law systems. Within the context of the English legal system, there is coverage of the courts, and the civil and criminal justice systems. The various sources of law are explained, with specific coverage of case law and the doctrine of precedent, and statutes.

Throughout this section, there is a theme of contemporary application: the current function of legal systems and their effect on individuals, businesses, and commerce. This leads to consideration of why and when legal services are required; the range of ways in which these are provided and by whom; the regulation and ethics of legal services provision; and the changing nature of the legal services market.

1 Introduction to law

Learning objectives

After studying this chapter you should be able to:

- Explain the importance of law as a concept.
- Develop an awareness that law can (and should) be studied in its wider context.
- Relate law to its underpinnings in ethics.
- Explain in outline selected aspects of philosophies of law, known as jurisprudence.
- Discuss the importance of legitimacy in law, and in particular the idea of sovereignty.
- Understand the theoretical and practical importance of the rule of law.
- Describe the central principles relating to the doctrine of Separation of Powers, and understand its importance in maintaining the rule of law.

Introduction

In this chapter we consider law as a concept and law in its wider context.

The concept of law, in its simplest sense, is straightforward.

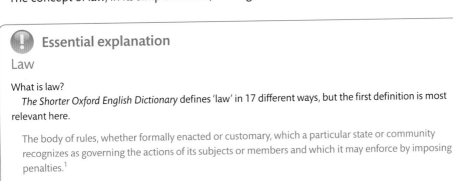

Essential explanation

Law

What is law?

The Shorter Oxford English Dictionary defines 'law' in 17 different ways, but the first definition is most relevant here.

The body of rules, whether formally enacted or customary, which a particular state or community recognizes as governing the actions of its subjects or members and which it may enforce by imposing penalties.[1]

The significant words are 'rules' and 'state': the rules by which a state operates.

Chapters 1 to 6 on Legal Systems are about the law, and how it works. They aim to underpin all your legal studies and lay the early groundwork for your professional life. Specific legal rules will be referred to by way of illustration and example.

[1] *Shorter Oxford English Dictionary* (2007) Vol. 2. Oxford: OUP, 6th edn.

In Chapter 1 we consider law as a concept and in its context. We examine key legal concepts such as law and morality, jurisprudence, the legitimacy of laws, the Rule of Law, and the Separation of Powers, looking at these in both theory and practice. Chapter 2 examines how these concepts are manifested in England & Wales. Chapter 3 outlines the court system, and the general principles of its operation. Chapters 4 and 5 consider the two main types of law in England & Wales, statutes and case law, respectively. These chapters will therefore give you the framework to underpin all your legal studies.

To give access to legal rights, we need people who can help citizens use the law. This is where lawyers come in. In Chapter 6 we look at the development of the legal profession and whether, in the light of recent reforms, it provides efficient access to law.

1.1 Law in context

Law is important.

This may seem obvious, but it is easy to lose sight of how significant law is in a modern society. As law students or lawyers become absorbed in their work, they will understandably focus on the particular area they are involved in. They may reflect less on the importance of the law as a whole—practically and culturally. It is a vital element of so many disciplines, including politics, history, and economics. Equally, other fields impact significantly on the law and on lawyers. This context is important. In this section we look at how law relates to all citizens and how it relates to other academic subjects.

1.1.1 Law and the citizen

Evidence of the importance of law is all around us. Imagine your typical day, and think about how it involves the law. What follows is a day in the life of an imaginary citizen somewhere in England. Note the variety of laws involved in guaranteeing that our lives run smoothly. Note also the variety of institutions involved in implementing and adjudicating on the rules, including the different political entities involved:[2]

- You wake up in the morning. Your phone alarm works. If it is faulty then this is a breach of your contract with whomever sold the phone to you, under a term of the contract implied by a statute. A statute is a law passed by Parliament.

- You go to the bathroom and take a shower. The water is uncontaminated and drinkable partly because it is regulated by UK and European legislation. If the company that provides the water breaches this legislation then the government will take action via the Department for Environment, Food and Rural Affairs, and its agency Ofwat. The company is a large Public Limited Company which is subject to extensive statutory rules and law developed by courts to protect the public if they invest in it.

- You live in a house or flat. The right to use it is governed by many different legal rules, either in statutes, or case law, or both.

[2] The UK left the EU on 31 January 2020 (as a result of a referendum of 23 June 2016). Any references to the EU in this section should be read with this in mind. For information relating to the continuing importance of EU Law, refer to Chapter 2, and in particular the Essential explanation of 'Brexit' at 2.2.3.

- Then you go down some stairs. If built in recent decades, the stairs and in fact all of the dimensions and infrastructure of the building will have been subject to building regulations passed under the authority of Parliament.

- To make your morning coffee, you switch on a kettle that must be sold in conformity with UK legislation deriving from EU regulations. The coffee beans may be imported from Brazil, under a series of contracts, governed by English and international commercial law. You add some milk—Parliament has passed legislation to ensure that all food and drink is safe. Kellogg's Cornflakes are subject to similar regulation. No other manufacturers of cereals can call their product 'Kellogg's' because of the Kellogg's trade mark, under UK and EU legislation (and related case law). You can be relatively confident that the food matches the labelling on the packet because of legislation.

- You take a quick look at the news, streamed onto your phone. Statutes passed by Parliament regulate the broadcasts, along with further case law and non-binding codes of practice involved in the regulation of media. Without the WiFi connection supplied by your phone provider, this would not work. There is a contract, subject to significant regulation, plus a body of legislation regulating telecoms providers and internet service providers. This regulation exists to protect you from wrongs like overcharging, poor service, wrongful use of your data (e.g. via cookies), and so on.

- As you go outside, you lock the door and leave with the expectation that your property and goods will remain secure. You hope not to be burgled while you are out. This would constitute a crime. There are statutory penalties for people who steal from other people. These statutes are interpreted by case law.

- You get to the station and wait for your train. It is delayed. Half an hour later, there is still no train. On the platform your fellow travellers are impatient. This is likely to be a breach of contract by the rail operator and will normally trigger its compensation scheme, required by the Office of Rail Regulation under statute. There is also a large amount of UK and EU legislation relating to public transport, cars, trains, streets, etc.

- While you are waiting, you send a message to a friend on Facebook and read a tweet with a photo of you from last night's party. Surely there are rules to protect your privacy? But then again, there must be rules to protect freedom of expression. There are both, and the Human Rights Act is at the centre of them. Thankfully no one has tweeted anything derogatory about you, but if they did, the law of defamation might provide you with help.

Your day is not even two hours old, and hundreds of laws of various types from several institutions and different eras have been relevant. The law, then, includes an astonishingly wide spectrum of rules and institutions. Human activity is enormously creative but without formal regulation is open to open-ended abuse. We need law.

Imagine a society without law. There would be no binding rules to live by. Only vague social values, religion, and family would provide any guidance on acceptable behaviour in society. The state would not be able to organise itself. Much of what we take for granted—government, taxes, utilities, infrastructure, medicine, welfare—would never have been developed. At 1.2 we consider the critical but also sometimes troubled relationship between law, social values, and morality. At 1.5 we see that the concept of the Rule of Law is critical to maintaining the rules by which society lives.

The example above illustrates the variety of issues that arise in the law. The word 'law' describes a huge and diverse body of rules and skills, involving many different people. It describes both the substance of rules, but also the procedures by which people access and use it. We have seen that it can be local, national, or international law. It can regulate the affairs of anyone from individuals to large companies. When it is applied by courts the people concerned can be subject to many types of sanction, from prison to orders that they compensate someone they have wronged. Rulings by courts can be challenged, but as we will find out in Chapter 3, few of them are. Some areas of law constantly change, and yet some remain largely the same as they were centuries ago.

There are some fundamental aspects of the question 'what is law' that all lawyers need to consider.

1.1.2 Law and its boundaries

It is often counterproductive to view law in isolation. Of course, if you are in the thick of focused academic study, or advising a client on a subtle aspect of (say) patent law, you may need to immerse yourself in the subject matter to some extent. But to understand law as a discipline, we must consider it in context, as part of a suite of subjects that work together and impact on each other. This contextual approach is sometimes referred to as the 'empirical' study of law.

Figure 1.1 shows law at the centre of a range of subjects. This is not to say that law is the most important of these areas, but that, as lawyers, we must have our main focus on law (for an historian, history would be at the centre of a similar range of disciplines, and so on). Law must be seen in context, and this means that when we start to study it, we should dispense with boundaries.

Law regulates people and institutions in a society and develops to reflect a combination of needs and influences. In Chapter 2 we consider its development against the background of society and history in England & Wales. There is an interplay between society's values and the law, along with ethics and religion. We examine this in 1.2. All statutes are enacted by Parliament, and Parliament is the product of politics. So much of the law you will encounter is the product of the political process. There is an example of this in Chapter 6 on the regulation of the legal profession.

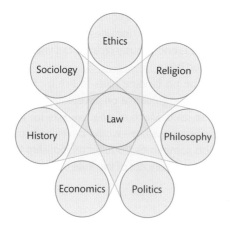

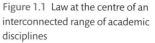

Figure 1.1 Law at the centre of an interconnected range of academic disciplines

Politics, philosophy, and law have always been natural bedfellows in the sense that political dogma is often implemented through law. Moreover, a lawyer should be aware, in theoretical terms, how and why law works as it does; this will educate the lawyer's understanding of how ideas like natural justice impact on practice, in the development and application of legal rules. The study of this is called jurisprudence, and is addressed in 1.3.

1.2 Law, morality, and society

We saw in the Introduction that law is a system of rules by which a state operates. We have also seen that it overlaps with other disciplines. It must provide some kind of guidance about behaviour, a benchmark against which people are judged. This standard must reflect the views of the majority of the population to ensure it can be enforced. As a result, the law incorporates moral issues and also social values (which may be distinct from ethical principles).

This necessity may be illustrated by examples from history. Some laws acceptable in a different era would now be unpalatable. Until 1831 it was a capital offence to steal a sheep.[3] Over a thousand people were hanged between 1825 and 1831 for this offence. By contrast, today it would be unusual even to go to prison for theft of a sheep.

An illuminating example is the law relating to sexual offences. Homosexual behaviour was a criminal offence in England & Wales until 1967.[4] Oscar Wilde was famously sentenced to two years' hard labour for gross indecency, partly because of his own testimony that, "'The love that dare not speak its name" in this century is such a great affection of an elder for a younger man . . . such as you find in the sonnets of Michelangelo and Shakespeare.'[5] The age of consent for homosexuals was only brought into line with heterosexuals in 2003.[6]

To address the interplay between law, morality, and society, we must first clarify what is meant by 'morality'.

1.2.1 What is morality?

Whole books have been written on this complex subject; however, a basic understanding will suffice to allow us to address its interplay with law. Two vital terms here are ethics and metaethics. Philosophers often refer to ethics as being the study of morality. Metaethics looks at the nature of morality.

> ### ⊛ Essential debate
>
> There are two general views on how ethics works:
>
> - Objectivism: objectivists believe that it is possible for there to be one absolute set of moral values, although precisely what this set of values is, is clearly extremely controversial.
> - Relativism: relativists argue that morals are the function of human thought and are therefore the reflection of the beliefs of people themselves, either as a society, or individually. This means that morality can change over time (e.g. the example of homosexuality referred to in 1.2) and can vary between societies, or even people. Some relativists claim that social values and morality are intertwined.

[3] An Act To Render The Laws More Effective For The Preventing The Stealing And Destroying Of Sheep 1741.
[4] Criminal Law Amendment Act 1885, Sexual Offences Act 1967.
[5] *R v Wilde* (1895) unreported. [6] Sexual Offences Act 2003.

1.2.2 **Examples and analysis**

1.2.2.1 Introduction: legal, moral, and social duties

We have seen that there are two (much generalised) views of morality. So a moral duty is a duty owed by people to each other as a function of whatever moral or ethical system is being used; by contrast, a legal duty is a duty created by law, rather than by any system of moral values. Different again is a social duty, which is a more informal category of duties that help society work on a day-to-day basis. These are not necessarily backed up by legal sanction, and are not seen as 'moral' duties.

Example **1**

Here are two contemporary examples of the uneasy relationship between legal, social, and moral values:

- Should discrimination be illegal against employees on the ground of their being overweight? In the UK the Equality Act 2010 protects persons from discrimination on the grounds of certain protected characteristics—e.g. race or sex. Body type is not (of itself) one of those characteristics. An employer might perceive an overweight employee as lazy or unhealthy. Many would perceive this behaviour as unjustified and immoral, but it is not legally regulated.

- What about same-sex marriage? While civil partnerships between gay couples are legal in the UK,[7] marriage has only been legal since the Marriage (Same Sex Couples) Act 2013, which came into force in 2014. In only 26 countries and jurisdictions is same-sex marriage legal.[8] In the US, same sex marriage was illegal in 31 states until the US Supreme Court intervened to legalise it nationwide.[9] But the Church of England, as well as other religious bodies, is opposed on moral grounds, as is the Campaign For Marriage. Social values, moral values, and legal reality in this area are currently in a state of flux around the world.

Figure 1.2 shows an overlap between legal, moral, and social duties. They overlap but are not the same. It is arguable that the greater the overlap between these categories of duty, the easier it is to enforce them all, because they are more comprehensively justifiable.

Let's draw out some themes and examples.

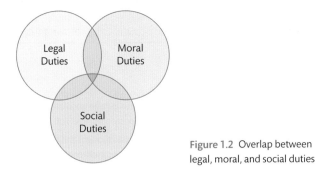

Figure 1.2 Overlap between legal, moral, and social duties

---

[7] Civil Partnership Act 2004.

[8] *Same-Sex Marriage: Global Comparisons*, Claire Felter and Danielle Renwick, Council on Foreign Relations, https://www.cfr.org/backgrounder/same-sex-marriage-global-comparisons (accessed 24/06/2019).

[9] *Obergefell* v *Hodges* 576 US (2015).

1.2.2.2 Legal vs moral

Not all moral duties are legally enforceable. Adultery is not illegal in the UK (although it is against the law in some other countries, e.g. Pakistan and Saudi Arabia), but many people would contend that under most (if not all) circumstances, it is immoral.

Exclusively moral duties may not be given legal protection either because some moral rules are difficult to police, or because for whatever reason such behaviour is seen as beyond the sphere of state intervention. When a legal duty diverges too much from morality it runs the risk of becoming unenforceable without resorting to heavy-handed or violent enforcement. Statistics bear out the relationship between speeding and an increase in the risk of serious injury.[10] In 2018 in the UK, 48 per cent of motorists exceeded 70mph in free-flowing motorway traffic.[11] All of these motorists were committing a criminal offence. Do they feel morally responsible when they do so?

This brings us to the first case study:

Example 2

The Enabling Act and the Nuremberg Laws

Hitler became German Chancellor in January 1933. In February the German *Reichstag* (Parliament) building burned down and civil liberties were suspended. The Nazis used the state of panic as a pretext to force the passing of the Enabling Act, which allowed the Cabinet (mainly composed of Nazis) to enact legislation without reference to the *Reichstag*. The *Reichstag* became a cipher for propaganda, especially after the banning of all political parties bar the Nazi party in July that year. Between 1933 and 1945 the *Reichstag* passed only four laws, all other regulation being by decree.

Within four months of Hitler coming to power, the first laws curtailing the rights of Jewish citizens were enacted. By 1935, the political climate in Germany had been transformed by Hitler's rule.

In September 1935, the 'Nuremberg Laws' were enacted by the *Reichstag*, comprising The Law for the Protection of German Blood and German Honour, which prohibited marriages and intercourse between Jews and Germans, and The Reich Citizenship Law, which declared those of Aryan blood to be citizens and those not of Aryan blood to be merely subjects.

The Nazis had so engineered the social prejudices of a significant proportion of the German population in the 1930s that it was possible to bring in laws that were clearly amoral. There were two factors which enabled this. First, severe penalties were threatened for those seen to flout or evade the Nuremberg Laws. Second, it is possible for a state to manipulate and distort social attitudes, often through the medium of legislation.

1.2.2.3 Legal vs social

A government will not be able to enforce a law which is too divergent from social attitudes. The importance of social norms is often downplayed, but it is society that collectively determines good and bad behaviour.

In early societies it was natural for legal rules to reflect social values. In India, Hindus adhered to values epitomised in *Manu Smriti (Laws of Manu)*, poems of the 1st century BC, about social obligations (set out by caste or class) and the consequences of their breach. There was no differentiation between 'legal' and 'social'.

---

[10] Royal Society for the Prevention of Accidents, *Inappropriate Speed* Factsheet (June 2018).

[11] Department for Transport, *Free Flow Vehicle Speeds: Great Britain 2017* (September 2018).

In a modern society, for laws to match social values so precisely would be problematic. If you steal something, you would expect to be punished under the criminal law. However, you would be surprised to be arrested for pushing in front of someone in a supermarket queue. It is probably a social wrong creating mild annoyance. It may or may not be a moral wrong, but it is unlikely to be a legal wrong.

The illustration of the Nuremberg Laws shows how important it is for legal rules to shadow social attitudes. Hitler had to 'prepare the ground' for his anti-Semitic legislation. Legal rules therefore need to attract some legitimacy from the degree to which they reflect important social values, even if these have been manipulated.

1.2.2.4 Moral vs social

One would hope that the social values of all societies reflect morality. To a relativist, morality will always (logically) coincide with such values.

Social values include, but are much more extensive than, mere etiquette. Etiquette would, however, seem to occupy a lower domain than morality. Take this extract from a Victorian magazine:

> Again I must conduct you back to the dining-room. Observe how highly-bred people eat asparagus. They feel with the knife where the soft part ends, and dividing the stems, they eat with the fork. It is a disgusting spectacle to see people draw out a mangled end from their mouths reduced to a ragged fringe.[12]

But social values are more important than passing the salt to the left at supper. They are at the root of major issues affecting a society, such as whether immigration is a good thing, and what a welfare state should provide. Most moral philosophers draw a distinction between morality and social values. It is possible for social values to be amoral. Anyone who believes that right and wrong exist at least to some extent separately from society would agree with this. This chapter contains many possible examples.

Referring back to Oscar Wilde, although homosexuality has become part of the mainstream in many modern moral cultures, Wilde also referred to a practice which remains unacceptable according to the values of most societies in the 21st century. It was common in ancient Greece for adult men to engage in sexual relations with pubescent or adolescent boys (see e.g. *Phaedrus* by Plato). Were the ancient Greeks amoral as a society?

Those who believe in an objective morality would point out that in some societies, morals and social values diverge, and where this happens, there is an opening for the law to follow malign social pressures.

Hitler's Germany again provides a chilling example. A British writer living in Germany (Christopher Isherwood) witnessed the arrest of a Jew in a Berlin café where German citizens turned away. Of course, it is likely that many of these citizens were not unwilling to act; merely that they were unable to act, for fear of reprisals.

1.2.2.5 Conclusion: reconciling legal, moral, and social duties

An ideal society would be one where law reflected social customs, and these in turn were morally justifiable. But because people are different this is virtually impossible. Whether we regard morality as objective or relative, people have different views on right and wrong, so it

---

[12] 'On Dinner', *Girl's Own Paper*, 1880.

is difficult to see how this utopian vision would ever work. Because of cultural, technological, and industrial progress, society develops and with it opinions on morality.

However, governments and legislators do often try to translate their own ethical preferences, and society's developing customs, into law. The next section is about the degree to which real legal rules have reflected this.

1.2.3 Law and morality in practice

1.2.3.1 Ethical underpinnings of law

Ethical systems divide into three broad categories:

- virtue theories (e.g. Aristotle in his Nicomachean Ethics), which focus on developing good traits of character (these are sometimes referred to as character-based theories of ethics);
- duty theories (e.g. John Locke, Immanuel Kant), which seek to set out fundamental obligations or rights (these are sometimes referred-to as deontological theories of ethics); and
- consequentialist theories (e.g. John Stuart Mill, Jeremy Bentham), which evaluate the consequences of our actions (these are sometimes referred-to as outcomes-based approaches to ethics).

All of these theories have been manifested to a greater or lesser extent in political and legal reality.

Virtue theories

Virtue theories focus on developing good traits of character.

Aristotle viewed personal virtue and happiness as being mutually reinforcing. He and like-minded philosophers believed that the ideal political unit for reflecting and fostering these virtues was the city state. The aim of Aristotle's ideal city state was the 'good life', rather than making money or conquests. Modern societies do not reflect this view of morality (although there are city states today, such as Singapore, Vatican City, Monaco, and San Marino, these are some way from the ancient cities Aristotle had in mind).

While not the subject of 'hard law' (i.e. enforceable by courts), it is common for politicians and organisations to espouse nebulous concepts of social responsibility, and the value of volunteering to help others individually and in society generally.

Example 3
The Fairtrade movement

You may have bought or used 'Fairtrade' products. In return for the right to apply their trade mark to products, producers must show that they are sourcing products in a virtuous and sustainable way. According to the Fairtrade website, 'By requiring companies to pay sustainable prices (which must never fall lower than the market price), Fairtrade addresses the injustices of conventional trade, which traditionally discriminates against the poorest, weakest producers. It enables them to improve their position and have more control over their lives.' It could be said that although the standards to be met are set by the Fairtrade movement, their aim is to instil in producers a set of virtues which they will then choose to follow and become second nature in their daily working lives. Happiness will be achieved by adhering to the standards and achieving success. It is quite likely that a number of these values were already held by the producers, but they did not necessarily always act upon them because they did not previously have the backing and support of the Fairtrade organisation. A Fairtrade trade mark licence can be revoked if the producer falls short of these standards.

Thomas Hobbes was far more pessimistic about human nature. He saw that individuals were fundamentally self-seeking. He saw morality as an artificial framework constructed by society for everyone's mutual advancement. In his 'social contract', deviation from social norms was discouraged by punishment.

Duty and consequentialist theories do, however, find manifestation in modern legal systems.

Duty theories

Duty theories seek to set out fundamental obligations, and their flip-side, 'rights'.

Legal theorists from the Roman era onwards have referred to the importance of 'Natural Law', a set of duties whose validity does not depend on human concepts like sovereignty (see 1.4.3). This contrasts with 'Positive Law', being the 'real' law of the land. St Augustine stated: 'An unjust law is not a law'.[13] Thomas Aquinas (in the 13th to 14th centuries) argued that there was no duty at all to obey a law contravening Natural Law. Over time such concepts were refined: Hobbes and Locke (in the 17th century) developed concepts of Natural Rights alongside duties under Natural Law.

Sir Edmund Coke, a lawyer, judge, and legal theorist in the 16th to 17th centuries, explicitly linked Natural Law and legal theory:

> this law of nature is part of the laws of England . . . the law of nature was before any judicial or municipal law in the world . . . the law of nature is immutable, and cannot be changed.[14]

Only sometimes are judges free to align Positive Law and Natural Law. Two common law (i.e. case law—see Chapter 5) examples follow:

- A recurring theme in ethics has been the 'Golden Rule' that we should do to others what we would want them to do to us. This traces its lineage back to Ancient Babylon, via Egypt, Greece, China, and Rome. In the Parable of the Good Samaritan, Jesus said, 'You shall love . . . your neighbour as yourself'.[15]

  This is often expressed as 'Love Thy Neighbour'. In Chapters 2 and 5 we shall consider one of the most important cases in English law, *Donoghue* v *Stevenson*,[16] in which Lord Atkin expressly refers to this rule and places it in legal language to formulate the Neighbour Principle that underpins the modern law of negligence. It is not common for the law so clearly to reflect morality—an important theme as you continue your legal studies.

- Judges and lawyers in common law jurisdictions such as England, the US, and Australia (see Chapter 5) often refer to something called 'natural justice'. This is an attempt to reflect basic tenets of morality in the law and its execution. In England, natural justice is epitomised by the rule against bias, and the right to a fair hearing; in the US, by the principle of Due Process.

Most legal systems incorporate either a written constitution or a statement of rights, or both. All (or most) actors within these systems are bound by such duties and rights. Here are some examples:

- The European Convention on Human Rights 1950 as incorporated into UK law by the Human Rights Act 1998, and EU law by the Treaty of Lisbon 2007.

---

[13] St Augustine (387–95 AD) *On Free Choice of the Will*, 1.5.33. Indianapolis: Hackett Publishing Co., 1993.
[14] *Calvin's Case* (1608) 7 Co Rep 1a, 77 ER 377. [15] Luke 10:25–29.
[16] *Donoghue (or M'Alister)* v *Stevenson* [1932] AC 562.

- The United States Constitution 1789 as amended, in particular, by the (so-called) Bill of Rights 1791. This sets out fundamental rights and obligations among other provisions.
- The French Constitution (in its various forms) has always included the Declaration of the Rights of Man and the Citizen of 1789.

Such documents explicitly reflect 'duty'-based morality. The lineage of the US Constitution is clearly traceable to Hobbes, Locke, and Baron de Montesquieu (see 1.6.1). Arguably they also epitomise 'Rule Utilitarianism'.

Consequentialist, or utilitarian, law?

Consequentialist theories (including Utilitarian theories) evaluate the consequences of our actions.

Bentham's 'felicific calculus'[17] (or 'utilitarian calculus') is perhaps the most notable of these theories. He, Mill, and their successors maintained that the moral worth of an action could be determined by a calculation of the total goodness of its consequences.

Many modern statutes are detailed in focus and contain provisions which contribute to what the government of the day sees as the greater good. These can be explained in utilitarian terms, and many ambiguities in them will be addressed on a case-by-case basis by courts in a narrow literal analysis (see 4.4.4, statutory interpretation). This is often justified using a utilitarian evaluation (or calculus)—essentially 'a means to an end'.

Example 4

The Coinjoined Twins

An emotive example of consequentialist law was the 'conjoined twins' case heard in the Court of Appeal in 2000.[18] The parents of conjoined twins, Mary and Jodie, appealed against a decision to allow an operation to surgically separate them. The operation would result in the death of Mary, but Jodie's continued survival. Without the operation it is likely that both would have died. The parents were devout Catholics, who believed that the operation should not take place because the doctors would be taking a life by operating. The court needed to decide whether the doctors were guilty of murder, or (alternatively) whether a defence of necessity could apply. For the court, this was a choice between a rules-based approach, and a consequentialist approach, to law. The doctors chose to apply the defence of necessity by allowing the separation of the twins, the death of one, and the survival of the other.

According to Ward LJ, 'The respect the law must have for the right to life of each must go in the scales and weigh equally but other factors have to go in the scales as well. For the same reasons that led to my concluding that consent should be given to operate so the conclusion has to be that the carrying out of the operation will be justified as the lesser evil and no unlawful act would be committed'.[19]

---

[17] Set out in Bentham, Jeremy (1789) *An Introduction to the Principles of Morals and Legislation*, ch. 4. Reprinted many times, e.g. in Burns, J.H. and Hart, H. L. A. (1996) *The Collected Works of Jeremy Bentham*. Oxford: Clarendon Press.

[18] *Re A (Children) (Conjoined Twins: Surgical Separation)* [2001] Fam 147

[19] *Re A (Children) (Conjoined Twins: Surgical Separation)* [2001] Fam 147, at 203

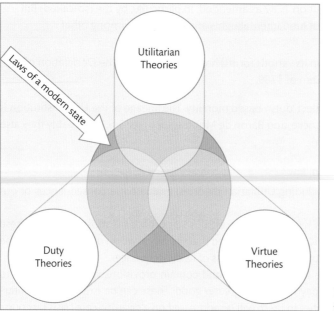

Figure 1.3 Moral ancestry of the modern state

Conclusion

Modern law, especially in England & Wales, can derive its justification from several different moral traditions.

Figure 1.3 summarises the degree to which these moral systems have been reflected in the laws of a generalised modern state. Some laws lie outside the moral sphere; others are justified by duties, or by utilitarian calculation, or both. Very few are classically virtue-based—a theme that will become increasingly familiar throughout your legal studies.

1.2.4 Can all law be morally justified?

Murder and rape are universally condemned, but what about more controversial areas? For instance, euthanasia and abortion. These two cases, about the beginning and end of human life respectively, demonstrate how emotive the moral/legal nexus can be.

1.2.4.1 Abortion

In the US, one of the defining political issues for several decades, upon which any politician must have a view, is abortion. The issue is far more politicised in the US than in the UK. The 1973 US Supreme Court case *Roe* v *Wade*[20] is arguably one of the three most significant cases in that court over the last century. In it, a liberal court stated that the right to privacy derived from the US Constitution[21] extended to a woman's decision to have an abortion, but was qualified by the state's interests in protecting the health of the mother and the life of the foetus as it matured.

---

[20] *Roe* v *Wade*, 410 US 113 (1973).   [21] US Constitution, Amendment XIV.

To be taken seriously, American politicians must have an opinion on this—they must be either 'pro-life' or 'pro-choice'. It is the barometer by which the political make-up of the Supreme Court is tested, and its initial 7 to 2 majority ruling in 1973 has been subject to fluctuation in later cases reconsidering the issue. These fluctuations have, by-and-large, reflected public opinion, as measured in polls.[22] At the time of writing (2019), this decision is likely to be reviewed as the balance of the US Supreme Court has swung decisively in favour of a general ban on abortion.

So in the US the law, at least as enunciated by the Supreme Court, tends to reflect social values. This is even more the case in state (as opposed to federal) courts, where the population is often more homogenous than in the US as a whole.

1.2.4.2 Euthanasia/'mercy killing'

Example 5
Diane Pretty

Diane Pretty suffered from motor neurone disease, an illness making it impossible for her to move or communicate easily. Despite having full mental capacity, she required round-the-clock care. She wanted her husband to be able to help her die, as she was unable to take her own life. On her website, she said, 'I want to have a quick death without suffering, at home surrounded by my family so that I can say goodbye to them'. Under s. 2(1) of the Suicide Act 1961, this would make her husband guilty of assisted suicide.

The House of Lords refused to order the Director of Public Prosecutions to undertake not to prosecute under the Act.[23] They reasoned that the right to life under the Human Rights Act 1998 did not include the right to choose to live, and that therefore it was not discriminatory (under the Human Rights Act) to prevent assisted suicide of the incapacitated by loved ones. To allow this would open the door to doctors being pressurised to accelerate the demise of elderly or infirm patients by unscrupulous relatives. In parallel litigation, the European Court of Human Rights refused to declare that the actions of the UK government violated the European Convention on Human Rights.[24]

It is currently against the law in the UK to help someone to commit suicide, which suggests that society places a supreme moral value on the preservation of life. Maybe you believe this is wrong and that it should be left to individuals to decide whether or not they wish to live.

As suggested at 1.2.2.5, an ideal society would be one where individual morality and social values coincided and were reinforced by legal duties in all cases. The two examples here have shown that this is unlikely ever to be possible.

1.3 Jurisprudence

1.3.1 Justifying jurisprudence

'Laws are like sausages. It's better not to see how they are made', Otto von Bismarck (the First Chancellor of Germany) is reputed to have said in 1849. To any lawyer, the opposite must be

---

[22] Harris Interactive, *Support for Roe v. Wade Increases Significantly, Reaches Highest Level in Nine Years* (9 November 2007).

[23] *R (Pretty) v DPP and Secretary of State for the Home Department* [2001] UKHL 61.

[24] *Pretty v UK*, App. no. 2346/02 (2002) 35 EHRR 1.

true. To make sense of the law we need to know exactly how and why it is made; it is important that a lawyer comprehends how ideas like natural justice impact on law in practice.

> **(!) Essential explanation**
>
> Jurisprudence
>
> Jurisprudence (sometimes known as 'legal theory', or the philosophy of law) constitutes the formal study of themes of law, including the nature of law as a concept. This may seem very academic, but hundreds of books have been written on the subject. It is important to any lawyer, academic or vocational, because it aims to show how and why law is created as it is. It places law in its historical, political, social, and philosophical context. The discussion in which we engaged in 1.2, on law, society, and morality, was a jurisprudential one.
>
> The term 'jurisprudence' is occasionally used in another sense, meaning the body of law created by a court or judge, for example the jurisprudence of the European Court of Justice or of Lord Bingham. In this section we are using the term in the wider sense, namely the nature of law as a concept.

In 1.5 we consider the Rule of Law, a very important concept within jurisprudence. Lord Bingham (a former Master of the Rolls, Lord Chief Justice, and Senior 'Law Lord') made it very clear why it is important for practising lawyers to understand key legal theories like the Rule of Law: 'we are not, as we are sometimes seen, mere custodians of a body of arid prescriptive rules but are, with others, the guardians of an all but sacred flame which animates and enlightens the society in which we live'.[25] Jurisprudence allows lawyers to reflect on why the law is so important in the real world.

Jurisprudence is not a mere theoretical or mystical exercise, as it is sometimes portrayed. It is motivated by and focuses on the value of law in itself and (in many views) as an instrument for the promotion of moral values. It also assists both aspiring and practising lawyers to understand that the law is a constantly changing and developing entity.

1.3.2 **An overview of jurisprudence**

There are many ways to characterise jurisprudence. Focusing on four of the main philosophies in roughly chronological order, there have been the following approaches to legal theory, that is the way people have thought about law:

- Natural Law.
- Positivism.
- Realism.
- Critical Legal Studies.

These are clearly labels, and many theories of law defy such neat categorisation. These theories draw out different aspects of the law and of legal systems. It might be said that to evaluate, for instance, Positivism against Realism or Feminist Critical Legal Studies, is like comparing the merits of lychees with the benefits of ladders. Figure 1.4 summarises this view.

We can now draw out a few general themes.

---

[25] Lord Bingham 'The Sixth Sir David Williams Lecture: The Rule of Law' (16 November 2006). Cambridge: Centre for Public Law, Faculty of Law, University of Cambridge. Available online at: http://www.cpl.law.cam.ac.uk/.

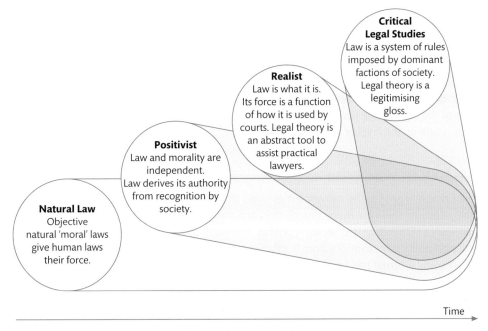

Figure 1.4 The historical development of approaches to jurisprudence

1.3.2.1 Natural Law

We saw in 1.2 that there is a complex relationship between law and morality. Early theorists like Aristotle and Aquinas thought that law derived its authority from having moral underpinnings. This is the Natural Law model of jurisprudence.

Natural Law remains a significant element of judicial reasoning, for instance in human rights law. Modern contemporary theorists like Dworkin still promote principles of Natural Law, and argue that contemporary views of legal authority cannot be complete without acknowledging the importance of moral force.

Islamic Law can be related to this model. *Fiqh* constitutes much of the practical legal principles of Islamic jurists, but it is based on *Sharia* (taken from the Qu'ran), expressed to be the moral principles underlying *fiqh*. We examine legal systems that use sharia law at 2.8.1.

1.3.2.2 Legal Positivism

By the 19th century, another school of thought was developing. Positivists believed that the search for a relationship between law and morality was of secondary importance, and that more significant was an understanding of how law obtained its authority in society.

Initially, philosophers like Bentham and Mill (drawing from Hobbes) saw the threat of sanctions as the incentive for people to do what was good for them. More recently, writers like HLA Hart and Hans Kelsen have seen law as deriving authority as a system of rules. These rules draw legitimacy from fundamental laws accepted as basic to a society. The discussion at 1.4 uses this reasoning. Natural Law—giving law moral underpinnings—and Legal Positivism—giving law authority because it is a set of rules recognised by society—are generally seen to be difficult to reconcile.

1.3.2.3 Legal Realism

Realists emerged in the 20th century. They felt that all this theorising was rather missing the point. The celebrated American judge Oliver Wendell-Holmes said: 'The life of the law has not been logic, it has been experience.'[26] The law is what it is, and is determined by factors as prosaic as who represented the parties, who was on the bench, and, most importantly, the facts of the cases being heard or appealed. Karl Llewellyn (a famous realist), stated: 'The real rules . . . are on the level of *isness* and not *oughtness* . . .'[27] (italics added).

1.3.2.4 Critical Legal Studies

The Critical Legal Studies movement evolved during the 1970s, and is difficult to define, partly because there are many strands to it, and partly because it is still evolving. One of the themes is a recognition that 'all law is politics', in other words it is difficult or impossible to dis-entangle political motivations from legislative and judicial acts. A second theme is an agenda of removing external bias from the creation and administration of law.

By the mid-20th century, politically active philosophies such as feminism and communism took centre stage, and provided critiques on legal rules as inherited from the *ancien régime*. To feminists, law was created in patriarchal societies and reflected this; to Marxists, law has been one of the tools of the bourgeoisie, and the nobility before them, in reinforcing eco-nomic relationships favourable to them, and detrimental to the proletariat. In your study of contract law, for instance, you will find that many early cases were decided in favour of the employer and not the employee. Marxists would find such outcomes more than coinciden-tal. Indeed the fact that domestic and European employment law was significantly reformed in the second half of the 20th century, reflecting the political mood of the time (discussed in more detail at 2.3.3 and 6.3) would serve to confirm that at least some 'law is politics'. This more socially responsible legal environment can be identified not just in employment law, but elsewhere, for instance in consumer law.

1.3.2.5 Summary

Jurisprudence is important in the development of the law. An understanding of why the law is as it is, is an important tool in developing and analysing legal principles.

This can be reflected in many of the subjects you will study throughout your legal education. In criminal law, for example, the viability of life sentences has been put under scrutiny from a human rights perspective. Under what circumstances and for what reasons should individuals be deprived of their liberty? This issue is frequently in the news. Is the sentence for punish-ment, retribution, rehabilitation, or some other aim? Restorative justice, for instance, gives victims and perpetrators the opportunity to talk about the crime committed. Is this desirable?

Jurisprudence is far from a dead or arcane subject. It educates and illuminates legal and judicial practice.

---

[26] Wendell-Holmes, Oliver (1881) *The Common Law*. Montana: Literary Licensing LLC, 2014, p. 461.

[27] Llewellyn, Karl N. (1962) *Jurisprudence: Realism in Theory and Practice*. New Jersey: Transaction Publishers, 2008.

A simplified summary of the development of jurisprudence would be as follows: over time analysis of the law has moved from placing law within its moral context, to an acknowledgement that law is one of many social constructs, and need not necessarily be elevated to such an ethical level. Many of the features of each movement have been adopted by successive scholars over time, so that many theorists now use a variety of analytical tools taken from a jurisprudential toolbox. This is reflected in disciplines such as statutory interpretation, which we examine in Chapter 4.

1.4 How legitimate is law?

1.4.1 Importance of the question

We have seen that law has some moral underpinnings, but that law and morality do not always coincide. So why are laws obeyed? This is a key jurisprudential question. Is it just that, as Hobbes said, if we didn't obey the law, we would be punished? Is it laziness, a lack of imagination, or an inherent respect for order?

A more common contemporary view is that, irrespective of the morality of a given rule of law, we need to respect the *legitimacy* of the law. Senior lawyers earning over £1 million per annum may well not agree that they should pay high levels of tax on most of their income, but they will usually respect their legal obligation to do so.

In the following example, we shall trace the *legitimacy* of this tax rule.

There are two themes here: one is that we can (in theory) trace the legitimacy of all law in a jurisdiction back to one fundamental legal rule. We explore this at 1.4.2. The other is that, usually as a result of that rule, an actor (or combination of actors) in a political system is given something called 'sovereignty', which entitles them to make law unconstrained by other actors. We first (at 1.4.2) examine the idea that there might be a fundamental legal rule, and then (at 1.4.3) the importance of sovereignty.

Example 6

Legitimacy of legal rules

Assume it is 2014. Frank Mackworth, chairman of Valuebank plc, has failed to pay his £1 million-plus tax bill, on the ground that he morally objects to the imposition of the additional rate of tax at 45 per cent on all income above £150,000.

Figure 1.5 shows how one might establish that Frank's conduct runs contrary to legitimate legal rules.

1.4.2 One solution: the *gründnorm*

1.4.2.1 The importance of the *gründnorm*

Legal theorists sometimes give a name to a law which provides legitimacy to subsequent laws: the term *'gründnorm'*.

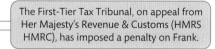

The First-Tier Tax Tribunal, on appeal from Her Majesty's Revenue & Customs (HMRS HMRC), has imposed a penalty on Frank.

The Tribunal derives its authority to impose penalties from the Tribunals, Courts and Enforcement Act 2007.

Under the authority of the Taxes Management Act 1970, s. 59(B)(3) Frank is liable to a penalty for not paying his income tax to HMRC by the due date.

Income tax is charged under the Income Tax Acts, including the key statute, the Income and Corporation Taxes Act 1988, and the Income Tax Act 2007 as amended by the Finance Acts 2009, 2011.

These are all statutes passed by Parliament, comprising the House of Commons, the House of Lords, and the Monarch.

The Enrolled Act Rule states that no court can challenge the validity of an Act.

Parliament is given soverignty (see 1.4.3) by the Bill of Rights 1688, enacted by the revolutionary Convention Parliament.

Because the Glorious Revolution of 1688 replaced the sovereignty of the Monarch alone, it is the Bill of Rights that gives all subsequent statutes their legitimacy.

Figure 1.5 Legitimacy of legal rules: example

> ### 🛈 Essential explanation
> #### The *gründnorm*
>
> '*Gründnorm*', coined by Kelsen[28] means 'basic rule'.
>
> The idea is that all law in any jurisdiction can be characterised as 'norms'—in English this means 'rules'. Each can be quite specific, for example the application of case law to a specific narrow circumstance. Each norm derives its legitimacy from a wider and more basic principle until one can legitimise no further. This rule is called the *gründnorm*.

It is argued that in any jurisdiction where there is a rule of law (see 1.5) there will be a *gründnorm*. In the US, the *gründnorm* is the US Constitution, which gives each actor in the legal and political system its authority, and defines basic principles.

[28] Kelsen, Hans (1934) *Pure Theory of Law*. Translation from the Second German Edition by Max Knight. Originally published: Berkeley: University of California Press, 1967. Reprinted: New Jersey: The Lawbook Exchange, Ltd, 2005.

Even the example of Nazi Germany illustrates this. The Rule of Law was increasingly a sham in the Third Reich but Hitler paid lip-service to the legitimacy of his regime. You will remember from Example 2 that it was the *Reichstag* that in 1933 passed the Enabling Act, devolving its powers to the Cabinet. The Act was renewed in 1937 and 1941, giving a theoretical legitimacy to his regime. The Enabling Act was passed by the *Reichstag* under the constitution of the Weimar Republic that preceded Nazi rule. The Weimar Constitution of 1919 ended a year of constitutional uncertainty after the demise of the German Empire. It is arguable, therefore, that the *gründnorm* in Nazi Germany was this document.

The *gründnorm* will usually change if there is a revolution, and a different regime is recognised. This occurs when society begins to acquiesce to the new legal and political order.

This process is illustrated in Figure 1.6. Time is important in this analysis, as we must look back in time to find the rules (or 'norms') that legitimise any given legal rule. So, starting from the most recent legal rules on the right of Figure 1.6, we can trace their legitimacy back, until we arrive at the *gründnorm*. In the case of the Frank Mackworth example (Example 6), the intricacies of tax legislation and case law occupy the area on the right of Figure 1.6. They are dependent on earlier norms for their legitimacy.

As we saw in Example 6, the *gründnorm* from which many legal rules in the current UK political settlement derive their legitimacy is the Bill of Rights 1688.[29] This created parliamentary sovereignty (sovereignty is defined at 1.4.3 and parliamentary sovereignty is explored at 4.1). All previous norms (laws) are no longer considered automatically legitimate. The slate is wiped clean at that point.

The gründnorm in practice

The UK (for simplicity we will restrict our discussion here to England) is a special case. While England's political settlement was the Glorious Revolution, so that the Bill of Rights 1688 is the *gründnorm*, there is a significant amount of prior law that also has legitimacy.

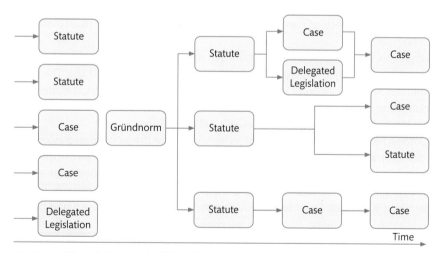

Figure 1.6 Role of the *gründnorm* in justifying subsequent law

---

[29] Enacted in 1689.

This is either because the *gründnorm* as a concept does not suit a country that has developed organically like post-1066 England; or it is because the concept of the *gründnorm* is flawed because it attempts to impose an intellectual framework on an enormous variety of realities.

> ### (*) Essential debate
>
> Is the concept of the *gründnorm* flawed?
>
> Kelsen advanced the theory that in any jurisdiction the current body of law could be traced back to one fundamental rule or norm, called the *gründnorm*. Does this work?
>
> Should we regard the idea of the *gründnorm* as a useful analytical tool? Or is it an interesting but flawed attempt to impose a logical structure on complex and sometimes arbitrary historical and legal developments?

One conclusion is this:

Provided the *gründnorm* permits it, courts are free to adopt previous laws, but only under the authority of the *gründnorm*, and their legitimacy now flows from that *gründnorm*, and not any previous one. This has occurred in the UK where some very old cases and statutes remain good law. So the relationship between *gründnorm* and dependent law is not necessarily one that flows with time.

So, for instance, parts of Magna Carta 1215[30] (e.g. s. 1, confirming the liberty of freemen in England) are still recognised as good law, but only because post-1688 cases have done so. In your study of contract law, you will encounter a case from 1602, *Pinnel's Case*,[31] which remains central to the study of the doctrine of consideration in this way.

Many of the US states enacted 'reception statutes' under the Declaration of Independence (and then the US Constitution) which formally incorporated relevant prior English case law. Hong Kong retained English case law in the same way when it reverted to China in 1997. This formal adoption of aspects of previous law is more common than the unusual piecemeal approach taken in the UK.

Another conclusion is that a country can have more than one *gründnorm*, depending on the area of law concerned. Between 1973 and 2020 the UK adopted EU law. The European Communities Act 1972 incorporated it into UK law, and in such matters, it is the Treaty on the Foundation of the EU (originally the Treaty of Rome 1957) that is the *gründnorm*.[32] It is possibly by similar reasoning that Magna Carta still has legitimacy.

It is important for laws to have legitimacy. One view about the *gründnorm* concept is that it helps demonstrate this legitimacy. An analogy might be that of a family. You can demonstrate that you are part of your family by listing all the people you are descended from, all the way to (say) your great-great-grandfather. The *gründnorm* is like the first identifiable member of your family. It is because you can identify this person that you (and everyone descended

---

[30] Originally issued in 1215, but the version now in force is Magna Carta 1297.

[31] *Pinnel's Case* (1602) 5 Co Rep 117.

[32] The UK left the EU on 31 January 2020 (as a result of a referendum of 23 June 2016). Any references to the EU in this section should be read with this in mind. For information relating to the continuing importance of EU Law, refer to Chapter 2, and in particular the Essential explanation of 'Brexit' at 2.2.3.

from this person) can legitimately claim to be in that family. Likewise, it is because (say) the Companies Act 2006 is created within a system derived from the 1688 *gründnorm*, that it has legitimacy in the UK.

1.4.3 The importance of sovereignty

Sovereignty is a very complex concept and the subject of much debate among constitutional and legal scholars. Its importance is that law made by a sovereign actor in a state has legitimacy.

! Essential explanation

Sovereignty

A notoriously difficult concept to pin down. Here we use it in the following sense: sovereignty (sometimes called 'supremacy') is the characteristic of an actor in a state who can impose its will on all the other actors without constraint.

Although a sovereign power can devolve authority to make rules, that power is always given with the authority of the Sovereign.

Positivists like Hobbes believed that the idea of laws that were legitimate by virtue of nature was misguided. They believed it to be more important to recognise that the law was given legitimacy simply because it was the law prevailing in that jurisdiction at that time. In Hobbes' state of nature, each person has complete freedom to do what they want—so everyone is sovereign. In such a situation, it would be impossible to resolve disputes—there would be anarchy. We consider this further in the context of the Rule of Law at 1.5. Hobbes (in his *Leviathan*[33]) and others reasoned that at some point in the distant past, individuals gave up their sovereignty for a degree of protection and support from the state and its machinery. This was called the 'social contract'.

Many legal and political theorists say that the necessary consequence of sovereignty is that a sovereign body cannot irrevocably bind its future self. This is because to do so would undermine its own later freedom to do what it wants.

In the UK, sovereignty is said to be vested in 'The Queen in Parliament', namely the Queen, the House of Lords, and the House of Commons. This is called 'parliamentary sovereignty' or 'parliamentary supremacy' (see 4.1).

Some theorists refer to '*de facto* sovereignty', as distinct from '*de jure* sovereignty'. *De jure* sovereignty resides in the body that has formal authority to make laws; *de facto* sovereignty resides in those people who *actually* make the decisions. In the UK *de facto* sovereignty normally resides in the Cabinet—when the government has a working majority.

Historically, sovereignty vested in monarchs; it was generally accepted that by 'divine right' God had vested His authority in the King or Queen, so the monarch had sole sovereignty. The monarch in the UK is still referred to as the 'Sovereign', though in practical terms the monarch

---

[33] Hobbes, Thomas (1651) *Leviathan*, in Malcolm, Noel (ed.) (2014) *Thomas Hobbes: Leviathan: The English and Latin Texts (Clarendon Edition of the Works of Thomas Hobbes)*. Oxford: OUP.

is no longer sovereign because he or she cannot make law independently of other actors in the system.

Any powers exercised by local authorities in the UK do not give them legal sovereignty. This is because these powers are granted (or devolved) by Parliament. The UK is said to be 'unitary' in this respect.

In contrast, the US and Germany are examples of countries where sovereignty is shared federally, that is to say it is shared between federal (national) institutions and those of the 50 states/16 *länder*. The US Constitution[34] states that any powers not expressly conferred on the federal government are reserved for the states. So some powers are reserved for the states and some are ceded to federal institutions. This has a profound impact on the consciousness of citizens in that their political loyalty is in many circumstances to their state more than to their nation. It also affects the degree of acceptance they may or may not have for decisions made (and politicians) at a federal level.

Sovereignty is often shared between different institutions within a state. Sometimes it is difficult to pin down exactly where sovereignty lies. For instance, in the US, there is a true Separation of Powers, with different powers vested (by the Constitution) in the three branches of the federal government (executive (President), legislature (Congress), and judiciary (Supreme Court)). Indeed it is arguable that in the US, it is the citizens, through the Constitution, who are sovereign. In theory, the people created the Constitution and it is the people who can amend it. Famously, the US Constitution opens with the words, 'We, the People . . .'.

1.5 The Rule of Law

'The Law is King', wrote Thomas Paine.[35] He meant that in a free country the law itself must be sovereign, and not any one individual or body. Nobody is 'above the law'.

To many lawyers, one of the vital ingredients of civilised society is something called the 'Rule of Law'. To an academic lawyer the idea of the Rule of Law is notoriously difficult to pin down. To the politician, it is an easy rhetorical shortcut to the moral high ground. Dwight D. Eisenhower, President of the US 1953–61 (and famous World War II general) opined: 'The clearest way to show what the rule of law means to us in everyday life is to recall what has happened when there is no rule of law.'[36] Eisenhower was referring to the terror of the 'knock on the door in the middle of the night' in Nazi Germany, and warning about what he saw as the future in Communist states. These were states where the regimes aimed to exert total power, without reference to the niceties of legality. At the other extreme are states or ghettoes within states where there is no law at all, and people revert to what Hobbes would call a 'brutish' state of nature.[37]

---

[34] US Constitution, Amendment X.

[35] Paine, Thomas (1776) *Common Sense*. London: Everyman's Library, 1994, p. 279.

[36] Eisenhower, Dwight D., Speech, Law Day (5 May 1958).

[37] Hobbes, Thomas (1651) *Leviathan*, in *Malcolm*, Noel (ed.) (2014) *Thomas Hobbes: Leviathan: The English and Latin Texts (Clarendon Edition of the Works of Thomas Hobbes)*. Oxford: OUP, chs. XIII–XIV.

1.5.1 Defining the Rule of Law

The Rule of Law is therefore a concept used to describe a group of characteristics necessary for a functioning and civilised state. Lord Bingham was noted for his advocacy of human rights and the Rule of Law. Among many proponents he was one of the most influential. In his seminal lecture on 'The Rule of Law',[38] he identified eight 'sub-rules':

1. The law must be accessible, intelligible, clear, and predictable.

2. Questions of legal right and liability should ordinarily be resolved by application of the law and not the exercise of discretion.

3. The laws of the land should apply equally to all, save to the extent that objective differences justify differentiation.

4. The law must afford adequate protection of human rights.

5. Means must be provided for resolving, without excessive cost or delay, civil disputes which the parties cannot resolve themselves.

6. Ministers and public officers must exercise the powers conferred on them reasonably, in good faith, for the purpose for which the powers were conferred and without exceeding the limits of such powers.

7. The adjudicative procedures provided by the state should be fair.

8. The state must comply with its obligations in international law.

A more concise definition was given by theorist John Finnis, who said the Rule of Law is 'the name commonly given to the state of affairs in which a legal system is legally in good shape . . .'.[39]

Referring back to Eisenhower's statement, there are various factors which prejudice the Rule of Law:

- arbitrariness;
- lack of protection for some or all citizens;
- lack of an independent judiciary; and
- legitimacy replaced by coercion.

1.5.2 Absence of the Rule of Law

Imagine a state with no laws at all. Sovereignty would vest in the individual. Freedom would be complete. Hobbes painted a dire picture in his seminal work, *Leviathan*, a key source for all modern political and legal theorists.

> In [the state of nature] . . . where every man is enemy to every man; . . . men live without other security, than what their own strength, and their own invention shall furnish them with all. In such condition, there is no place for industry; because the fruit thereof is uncertain; and consequently no culture of the earth; no navigation, nor use of the commodities that may be

---

[38] Lord Bingham 'The Sixth Sir David Williams Lecture: The Rule of Law' (16 November 2006). Cambridge: Centre for Public Law, Faculty of Law, University of Cambridge. Available online at: http://www.cpl.law.cam.ac.uk/.

[39] Finnis, John (2011) *Natural Law and Natural Rights*. Oxford: OUP, 2nd edn, p. 270.

imported by sea; no commodious building; no instruments of moving, and removing such things as require much force; no knowledge of the face of the Earth; no account of time; no arts; no letters; no society; and which is worst of all, continual fear, and danger of violent death. And the life of man, solitary, poor, nasty, brutish, and short . . .[40]

The state would not be a 'state' in the conventional sense. The weak would be at the mercy of the strong, and everyone would fight to assert themselves over all but their immediate family. Hobbes wrote that we had to give up much of our personal sovereignty in return for the state guaranteeing us a structured society. This was his 'Social Contract'. Figure 1.7 shows how the Rule of Law occupies a middle ground between anarchy and totalitarianism (i.e. where the state seeks to exert total control over its subjects); and how the individual gives up some personal sovereignty in exchange for a system of laws.

The following passage is taken from *Dangerous Society (Detroit's Inner City Gangs)*,[41] by Carl Taylor:

In the Third City, you have citizens, noncitizens—people who participate in an underground economy, but not in mainstream civic life—and anticitizens—people who defy authority and accept criminal activity as normative.

There's a strong identity of 'us' against 'them'—the white power structure and the black bourgeoisie.

The Third City is held together by common values often at loggerheads with mainstream ones.

The thug is perceived as the underdog. I was taught to walk away from a fight. In the Third City, parents are likely to tell kids to never back down—even to carry a gun. Their biggest resentment is hypocrisy. When major systems fail it only affirms the feeling that everything is rigged to favour whites and the rich.

This is a modern day version of anarchy. In theory, Detroit is governed, maintained, and policed by the Detroit City Council at local level, the state of Michigan at state level, and the US government at a federal level. In practice, the apparatus of state has disintegrated in some parts of Detroit and the Rule of Law has disappeared from areas of the city, as graphically portrayed in the film *Eight Mile*, starring Eminem.

In the wider world today, there are some states that are said to have 'failed', in that many of the indicators of the Rule of Law are absent. A 'fragile state' index is generated annually[42] by analysing

Figure 1.7 Relationship between personal freedom and types of state

---

[40] Hobbes, Thomas (1651) *Leviathan*, in Malcolm, Noel (ed.) (2014) *Thomas Hobbes: Leviathan: The English and Latin Texts (Clarendon Edition of the Works of Thomas Hobbes)*. Oxford: OUP, ch. 13, para. 9.

[41] Taylor, Carl S. (1990) *Dangerous Society (Detroit's Inner City Gangs)*. Michigan State University Press.

[42] Fund for Peace, *Fragile States Index*. Available online at: https://fragilestatesindex.org/.

social, economic, and political components, many of which overlap with factors of the Rule of Law (e.g. adherence to human rights, and the security apparatus being above the law). In 2016, the three most failed states were listed as Somalia, South Sudan, and the Central African Republic.

There have been societies where the Rule of Law was shunned or had not yet developed. Evidence suggests that Iron Age societies were organised around survival and, where necessary, cooperation and barter. After the disintegration of the Tsarist regime in 1918, the Ukraine was proclaimed (by Nestor Makhno) as an anarchist community on similar principles. The instruments of state control and the Rule of Law were eschewed. The experiment was extinguished by Lenin's communists after four years.

At the other extreme are totalitarian systems (such as Lenin's in the Soviet Union) where state control aims to be absolute. Many would say that the Rule of Law is suffocated under these regimes. However, some theorists like Raz[43] argue that, on the contrary, the Rule of Law in these states is strong. Raz refers to the 'sharp knife' of the Rule of Law, in that it can be used for both good and bad ends.

In Figure 1.7, at the totalitarian end of the spectrum, there is no freedom, where all sovereignty is vested in an individual: an autocracy (one person has ultimate power) is one type of totalitarian approach.

Example 7

President Niyazov of Turkmenistan

After the dissolution of the Soviet Union in 1990, Suparumat Niyazov became President of Turkmenistan. He attempted to fill the legal and cultural vacuum left by communism with a quasi-dictatorial rule combined with a cult of personality. His regime was noted not only for these features but also for its idiosyncracy. Among his many decrees, Niyazov:

- banned the use of sound recordings at cultural events on the ground that they stifled creativity;
- forbade opera, ballet, and the circus on account of their being 'decidedly unturkmen-like';
- excluded dogs from the capital because of the smell;
- ordered the building of a 'palace of ice', so that those living in the desert country could learn to skate;
- ordered that men should no longer wear beards or long hair;
- prohibited television personalities from wearing make-up because he believed Turkmen women were already beautiful enough;
- outlawed gold teeth to encourage dental health; and
- renamed months and days of the week after notable Turkmens, including himself.

One of the characteristics of the Rule of Law is that laws must not be arbitrary. Citizens must be able to anticipate the nature of the obligations they have to the state. The situation in Example 7 is an illustration of the exercise of arbitrary power. There are many examples from history where such exercise of power has been used to more malign ends.

If we generalise different systems into a spectrum from total control, through various types of democracy, to anarchy, we can broadly conclude that the Rule of Law probably typifies any

---

[43] Raz, Joseph (2009) 'The Rule of Law and its virtue' in *The Authority of Law*. Oxford: OUP, 2nd edn, pp. 210–32.

system where laws are created and administered in a democratic and fair context. This is a generalisation as it is culturally slightly blinkered to equate democracy with the Rule of Law; many cultures do exhibit many of the characteristics outlined by Lord Bingham, but are not necessarily democracies.

1.5.3 The nature of the Rule of Law

While the Rule of Law is absolutely central to the self-image of a modern state, Lord Bingham warned of the dangers of the concept becoming so misappropriated and watered-down that it becomes 'the jurisprudential equivalent of motherhood and apple pie'.[44]

Here we need to refer back to the discussion of jurisprudence at 1.3. You may recall that Natural Lawyers (see 1.3.2.1) regard law as deriving its underpinnings from moral arguments. They would say that the Rule of Law must depend for its legitimacy on minimum standards of morality and predictability. Many of Lord Bingham's 'sub-rules' would seem to reflect this.

But positivists would claim that a clear and consistent body of rules does not necessarily need to be moral, or conform to certain social or political ideals. This is Joseph Raz's 'sharp knife' argument again.

They would say that the main virtue of the Rule of Law is to allow subjects (not necessarily called 'citizens') to plan their lives. The philosopher and economist Freidrich von Hayek most clearly summarised this position:

> Stripped of all technicalities this means that government in all its actions is bound by rules fixed and announced beforehand—rules which make it possible to foresee with fair certainty how the authority will use its coercive powers in given circumstances, and to plan one's individual affairs on the basis of this knowledge.[45]

In the light of this, the positivist view would mean that it does not really matter how fair a system of law is, merely that it exists and conforms to its own clear rules. Thus, all systems but anarchic systems or arbitrary tyranny would conform to the Rule of Law.

1.5.4 The Rule of Law in practice

1.5.4.1 'Window dressing'?

For the purposes of this work, we will adopt the more ambitious ideal of the Rule of Law, as set out by Lord Bingham at 1.5.1. Lord Bingham's concern that the term is used as 'window dressing' (i.e. to distract from a less wholesome state of affairs) remains valid. The Rule of Law might be termed an aspiration, rather than a reality.

Governments do openly aspire to follow the Rule of Law. Leaders as polarised as ex-US President Barack Obama and Robert Mugabe, President of Zimbabwe, seek to adopt the

---

[44] Lord Bingham 'The Sixth Sir David Williams Lecture: The Rule of Law' (16 November 2006). Cambridge: Centre for Public Law, Faculty of Law, University of Cambridge, p. 4. Available online at: http://www.cpl.law. cam.ac.uk/.

[45] Hayek, Freidrich (1944) *The Road to Serfdom*. London: Routledge, 2nd edn, 2005, p. 72.

legitimacy of the term 'the Rule of Law', but these states can fall short (in the view of academics and journalists) because aspects of the Rule of Law are not adhered to, for instance because laws are applied arbitrarily or because human rights are disproportionately compromised. In the debates over whether the invasion of Iraq in 2003 was legal, the then British Prime Minister Tony Blair expended a great deal of effort to show that, in his view, the invasion was legally justified—because he was following the Rule of Law.

By contrast, governments sometimes adopt a more pragmatic attitude to observing the doctrine. When Anthony Eden (British Prime Minister 1955–57) ordered the invasion of Suez in Egypt, he stated: 'We should not allow ourselves to become involved in legal quibbles . . . .'[46]

Equally, legal academics critically evaluate the approach of governments observing the rule of law. For example, in 2006 a scholar stated, 'the Rule of Law has yet to be reinstated in the US battle on terror. The problem started when the Bush administration rejected the Geneva conventions which are intended to apply to every armed conflict in the World.'[47]

1.5.4.2 Cultural considerations

The Rule of Law may seem like a basic constituent requirement of a state, but it is arguable that it is (like democracy, which so frequently accompanies it) a construct of Western academics. This links with sociology because different cultures have different approaches to rights and obligations—even on the need for laws.

Here is one example. Contract law is an absolutely central element of law in Western countries and in many others. But it is not an entirely familiar idiom in parts of the world where barter and bribery have historically been more commonplace forms of business. In the Middle East, Africa, and the Far East it was long acknowledged that reciprocal gift-giving and trade were perfectly acceptable bedfellows.[48] The idea that a bribe is culpable was alien in some cultures. Squeamishness about gifts and incentives is sometimes seen as a view held only in certain Western democracies.

For instance, some societies have been more recently tribal. Many tribes existed on a smaller scale to Western societies and so did not need the machinery of state that has typified the latter in the last few centuries. This is closer to the Hobbesian state of Nature (see 1.5.2) where administrative creations such as legally binding obligations are unfamiliar. To individuals in such societies, replacing long-established customs with laws might seem unnecessary and inappropriate. Many studies have focused on Africa as an example, where the number of tribes (over 3,000 according to one study[49]), languages, or ethnic groups, far exceeds the number of countries (54). Even the idea of a country or state was (it is argued) superimposed on these societies by European empires. All the apparatus that comes with a state (including legal systems) could be said to be unsuitable.

---

[46] Marston, Geoffrey (1988) Armed Intervention in the 1956 Suez Crisis: The Legal Advice tendered to the British Government. *International and Comparative Law Quarterly* 37, pp. 773, 777.

[47] Olshansky, Barbara (2006). Deputy Legal Director, The Center for Constitutional Rights (now a consultant at Public Health & Human Rights).

[48] For more on this issue, see e.g. Mauss, M. (1954) *The Gift. The Form and Reason for Exchange in Archaic Societies*. New York: W. W. Norton, 1990.

[49] The Joshua Project. Available online at: http://www.joshuaproject.net/.

An analogy might be drawn with the idea of cultural imperialism. This is a term used by sociologists, among others, to characterise the spread of (usually) Western culture into other civilisations. This extends to the adoption of the English language, and the incorporation of Western popular culture, be it sporting, musical, or cinematic. This has accelerated with the stimulus of information technology. Whether the Rule of Law is an aspect of 'cultural imperialism' is a matter of opinion.

The alternative view is that, as the world shrinks and becomes interconnected, so it is more important to have common ground in doing business and politics; hence essential legal concepts such as legally enforceable contracts and internationally comprehensible law have to be projected on to local cultures.

1.5.4.3 Compliance with the Rule of Law today

Studies have been made of the degree to which modern states comply with the Rule of Law. An organisation called the World Justice Project has attempted to rank states by conformity with indicators of the Rule of Law, which by and large mirror those of Lord Bingham at 1.5.1.

While the Rule of Law Index[50] breaks down the indicators into factors, some general observations are sufficient to provide us with evidence of the Rule of Law in practice:

- Even the top-ranked nations (Denmark, Norway, Finland) fell some way short of the ideal, with around 15 per cent shortfall overall using the factors in the report.
- There is a strong correlation between prosperity and the indicators, but not a necessary one. One view is that the Rule of Law is a luxury for states who can afford it. Alternatively, it could be said that the Western democracies with higher scores have a culturally different attitude to the role of the law and the status of the citizen.
- The most common limitations on the Rule of Law (even in otherwise high-scoring nations) were the prevalence of police discrimination, and the difficulty (owing to expense) of accessing civil justice.
- China scored highly in criminal justice and security, and absence of corruption, but low in fundamental rights and judicial independence.
- Corruption and high crime rates were rife in South America and the Caribbean, as well as lack of government accountability.

1.6 The Separation of Powers

1.6.1 Separation of Powers in theory

Many of the indicators or sub-rules (to use Lord Bingham's language) of the Rule of Law can be safeguarded to some extent by a simple constitutional device, the Separation of Powers. This division of powers within a state will prevent accumulation of too much power in the hands of one body or person. It is necessary to give a brief account of this doctrine, although a fuller discussion is properly the preserve of public law.

---

[50] http://worldjusticeproject.org/rule-of-law-index.

> ## ⓘ Essential explanation
> ### The Separation of Powers
>
> The Separation of Powers doctrine was first advocated by the Ancient Greeks, but was given its modern expression by Baron de Montesquieu in the 18th century. He believed that a division of the roles of the state between three branches would provide a safeguard to the tyranny of one of them, most especially the executive branch.
>
> Under the doctrine, each 'branch' of government has a different role to play in the idealised constitution. In its purest form, there should be no overlap between the branches, either in function or personnel. If overlap occurs, then power will concentrate; this will open the door to arbitrary or oppressive government.
>
> Normally powers are divided between three functions of state (as in Figure 1.8):
>
> - the legislature makes law;
> - the executive (the government) implements law; and
> - the judiciary resolves disputes relating to the law, between the state and its citizens.

1.6.2 Separation of Powers in practice

It is difficult, if not impossible, for a real jurisdiction to match the theoretical ideal of the Separation of Powers. There are many reasons for this, but one is that real states involve real people and institutions. These actors rightly or wrongly guard their historical authority. Although the normal model has three branches, there are variations around the world: China, for instance, has five branches.

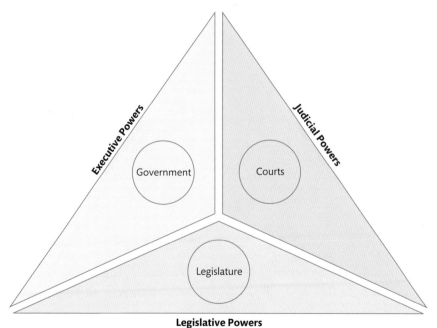

Figure 1.8 The Separation of Powers

The doctrine also states that the branches cannot operate in isolation and that there should be a system of 'checks and balances' so that each branch can keep the others in check and maintain a balance of power. So, for instance, in England & Wales, the doctrine of judicial review allows courts to ensure that public bodies (formally within the 'executive' branch) act within the powers they have been granted and do not exceed or abuse those powers. In England & Wales judicial review does not extend to questioning the merits of the decisions of the state (unlike in the US, for instance) but merely that the decisions are made in the right way.

The US Constitution was conceived deliberately to reflect Montesquieu's doctrine, and the success of the Constitution in this respect is the source of sustained debate among political and legal theorists. The repeated 'budget impasses' where a President from one party refuses to sign into law the budget drawn up by a Congress with majorities of the other party, are evidence of these checks and balances at work. Periodic rebalancing occurs if one branch sustains political primacy for too long, usually with the US Supreme Court (the judiciary's highest court) moderating the behaviour of the President or of Congress.

In the UK at national level, the executive is Her Majesty's Government, the legislature is Parliament, and the courts constitute the judiciary. The Separation of Powers is not so formally delineated as in the US, though the Constitutional Reform Act 2005 tidied up many of the loose ends (e.g. the anomaly that the Lord Chancellor was at the same time a senior member of all three branches). The Queen remains at the head of all three branches but is by convention unable to exert any real power in any capacity. Because the UK is a parliamentary democracy, ministers in the government sit in the legislature; hence the government straddles the executive and legislative branches. By contrast, in the US only the Vice-President has any role to play in Congress. In Chapter 5 we see that some courts have a quasi-legislative (as well as judicial) role in England & Wales. Figure 1.9 summarises the Separation of Powers within the UK at national level.

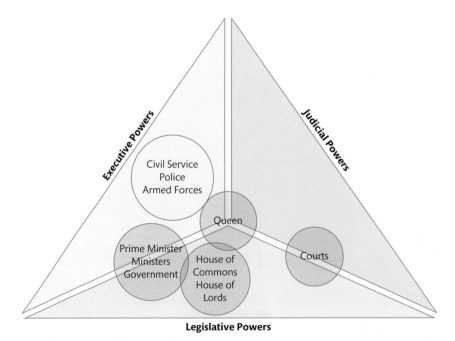

Figure 1.9 The Separation of Powers in the UK

In several of the Examples, the ideal has broken down. President Niyazov of Turkmenistan (in Example 7) perpetuated the Soviet concentration of power in the hands of the President, notionally the executive. There was no legislature, and the judiciary was staffed by political appointees.

In Nazi Germany (Example 2), the position was summarised in this extract from the Nuremberg War Trials:

> Independence of the judiciary was destroyed. Judges were removed from the bench for political and 'racial' reasons. Periodic 'letters' were sent by the Ministry of Justice to all Reich judges and public prosecutors, instructing them as to the results they must accomplish. Both the bench and bar were continually spied upon by the Gestapo and SD [intelligence agency], and were directed to keep disposition of their cases politically acceptable. Judges, prosecutors and, in many cases, defense counsel were reduced in effect to an administrative arm of the Nazi Party.[51]

It is quite clear that 'successful' states depend on the embodiment of various characteristics of the Rule of Law, importantly including a separation of powers. Without clearly delineated and balanced participants, it is unfortunately human nature that power will be abused. 'Power tends to corrupt, and absolute power corrupts absolutely.'[52]

Summary

- Law is a system of rules by which a state operates.
- Law touches on every aspect of our day-to-day lives.
- Law cannot be viewed in isolation from other related areas.
- Morality is difficult to define and analyse, but this is a worthwhile exercise as it helps us understand the relationship between law and ethics. This relationship should be viewed in the context of social values.
- Jurisprudence is the study of key concepts in law, and has developed over time.
- One important issue in legal theory is the legitimacy of law, and a common means of providing legitimacy is to find an acceptable *gründnorm* (or basic rule).
- Sovereignty is important in a legal system—it describes which actor in that system has power over other participants.
- Another important legal concept is the Rule of Law, by which we can analyse certain characteristics of a healthy state. If the Rule of Law disappears, the individual will usually suffer.
- The Separation of Powers is a central doctrine in preserving the Rule of Law, and with it the rights of citizens.

---

[51] *United States* v *Altstotter*, Nuremberg Military Tribunals case no. 3 p. 7 indictment count 1 (1947).
[52] Dalberg-Acton, John. *Letter to Bishop Mandell Creighton* (5 April 1887).

Practical exercises

1. Why do you think law is important?
2. Should law-makers have a moral agenda?
3. Is jurisprudence relevant in practice?
4. Is the Rule of Law an intellectual construct, designed to justify the Western democratic state?
5. Is the Separation of Powers appropriate in the modern world?

 *Visit the **online resources** for the authors' reflections and to check your progress.*

Further reading

Lord Bingham 'The Sixth Sir David Williams Lecture: The Rule of Law' (16 November 2006).
Cambridge: Centre for Public Law, Faculty of Law, University of Cambridge. Available at:
http://www.cpl.law.cam.ac.uk/.
—This is one of the definitive modern statements on the importance of the Rule of Law.

Finnis, J. (2011) *Natural Law and Natural Rights.* **Oxford: OUP, 2nd edn**
—Includes authoritative discussions on the Rule of Law.

Hobbes, T. (1651) *Leviathan,* **in Malcolm, Noel (ed.) (2014)** *Thomas Hobbes: Leviathan: The English*
and Latin Texts (Clarendon Edition of the Works of Thomas Hobbes). **Oxford: OUP**
—A text demonstrating early concepts of the social contract.

Kelsen, H. (1934) *Pure Theory of Law.* **Translation from the Second German Edition by Max Knight.**
Originally published: Berkeley: University of California Press, 1967. *Reprinted:* **New Jersey: The**
Lawbook Exchange, Ltd. 2005
—One of the important texts incorporating the idea of the *gründnorm*.

Raz, J. (1979) *The Rule of Law and its Virtue in The Authority of Law: Essays on Law and Morality.*
Oxford: OUP, 2nd edn, pp. 210–32
—Where it is argued that the Rule of Law can be taken to undesirable extremes.

 For the authors' reflections on the practical exercises, additional self-test questions, sample
*interview questions and a library of links to useful websites, visit the free **online resources** at*
www.oup.com/he/slorach4e.

2 Legal systems and sources of law

Learning objectives

After studying this chapter you should:

- Understand the concept of a 'legal system' and some significant manifestations.
- Differentiate key jurisdictions relevant to lawyers in England & Wales.
- Be familiar with sources of law relevant to lawyers.
- Demonstrate a basic understanding of the development of case law and statutes.
- Show a comprehension of key actors in EU law.
- Understand the impact and typical operation of international law, including ECHR law.
- Distinguish between important legal cultures, focusing mainly on the common and civil law traditions.
- Be aware of important classifications and terms used by English lawyers.

Introduction

In Chapter 1 we looked at general theories of law, and placed the law in its political, cultural, and historical context. In this chapter we look at how this is manifested in legal systems, focusing on England & Wales.

The first thing that might surprise you is the term, 'England & Wales'. This is not a function of any bias among lawyers in relation to Scotland or Northern Ireland, merely that their legal systems are largely different from those of England & Wales.

This chapter also addresses the basic 'language' of law in the jurisdiction of England & Wales. ('Jurisdiction' is defined at 2.1.) An understanding of the essential terms introduced in this chapter is essential for any lawyer.

Lawyers need to know *where* they are practising. Section 2.1 concerns the fundamental issue of which law a lawyer in England & Wales will be working with. Section 2.2 deals with the issue of where that law comes from: that is, sources of law. You will not be surprised that there is no single source of law in England & Wales, and that it is a fascinating hybrid of different types of law, not all of which are wholly compatible with the others. Section 2.3 examines the development of case law and statutes in the English legal system, and its wider importance. This groundwork is essential before we explore in more detail the court system, statutes, and case law, in Chapters 3, 4, and 5 respectively. We then widen the focus at 2.4 and 2.5 to look at EU and international law, their status and operation. Section 2.7 draws out key classifications used by lawyers within England & Wales, and introduces some further important terminology. At 2.8 we examine the distinctions between different legal cultures around the world. The final section reviews some of the key terms introduced in the chapter.

2.1 Legal systems

2.1.1 What is a 'legal system'?

A lawyer's ability to practise is limited by matters of 'jurisdiction'.

> **Essential explanation**
>
> Jurisdiction
>
> 'Jurisdiction' is a term you will come across often.
>
> It is most commonly used to refer to a political entity where a particular law has application. This could be the EU, the UK, Greater London, the London Borough of Camden, or even a local parish. This is the context in which this book will use the term.
>
> The term is sometimes used in another sense, that of a body or court having 'jurisdiction', or, conversely, lacking 'jurisdiction', over a particular issue. What this means is that it does, or does not, have the power to make law or settle disputes in that area of human endeavour. So, for instance, a particular court may not have jurisdiction to decide on certain issues of immigration. Indeed, later in this chapter we distinguish between courts with 'criminal' jurisdiction, and courts with 'civil' jurisdiction.
>
> Legal system
>
> In many ways, a 'legal system' is synonymous with a 'jurisdiction'. The legal system describes the body of institutions that make, execute, and resolve disputes on the law of a jurisdiction, together with the law they deal with. You may encounter the term 'legal system' in a narrower sense, meaning the courts of a jurisdiction.
>
> The boundaries between the legal and the political frames of reference are very blurred. We saw at 1.1.2 that this is by no means an inappropriate analysis.

These key concepts are not merely academic. They have practical significance to lawyers in many situations. For instance, in a modern contract two important common clauses are about 'jurisdiction' (where litigation happens if there is a dispute in relation to the contract) and 'choice of law' (which country's law applies to that dispute).

2.1.2 Legal systems in Britain

The legal system in the 'British Isles' (this very loose term is used deliberately) is idiosyncratic and complex. There are overlapping jurisdictions for different types of law. What is peculiar is the variety of combinations of states and nations which have, to varying degrees, been associated with, or unified with, England. As a result, there is a multiplicity of different forums. This is very much an accident of history.

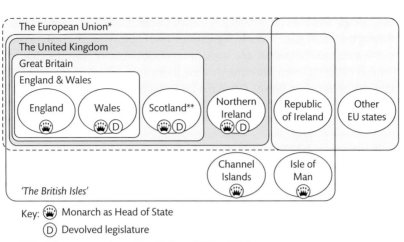

Key:  Monarch as Head of State

ⓓ Devolved legislature

* The UK was a member of the EU from 1973 to 2020.

** It is possible that Scotland may leave in the UK in the near future, partly as result of the UK's exit from the EU.

Italics denote a geographical (rather than legal or political) entity.

Figure 2.1 Jurisdictions within the British Isles

This is not unusual; for instance many nations like Germany or the US have several layers of law. But the legal systems in the 'British Isles' do have a quirkiness that bemuses even some practising lawyers.

Another eccentricity is the continuous, evolutionary, and extended development of the political system. Each change has left a legacy in the legal system. Figure 2.1 summarises the key distinctions.

We start by looking at all the British Isles, and gradually narrow the focus. At 2.2.3 we broaden the focus again, to place these jurisdictions in the (post-) EU context.

2.1.2.1 'The British Isles'

The British Isles is a geographical, rather than legal or political, term. It is made up of two sovereign states: the Republic of Ireland and the United Kingdom. The Monarch (currently Queen Elizabeth II) (symbolised by a crown in Figure 2.1) is Head of State in all of these islands, except the Republic of Ireland. The Republic gained independence in 1922, ending a state of affairs that had existed from 1801, when the formerly separate kingdoms of Great Britain and Ireland were united.

The Republic of Ireland (also known as Eire in the Irish language) is therefore entirely separate from the rest of the UK in political and legal terms; Ireland remains a member of the EU, the UK having left on 31 January 2020.[1] The summary in Figure 2.14 places some of these changes in historical context.

---

[1] The UK left the EU on 31 January 2020 (as a result of a referendum of 23 June 2016). Any references to the EU in this section should be read with this in mind. For information relating to the continuing importance of EU Law, refer to Chapter 2, and in particular the Essential explanation of 'Brexit' at 2.2.3.

Guernsey, Jersey, and the Isle of Man are Crown Dependencies, and are independent of the UK, having their own governments, legislatures, and court systems. They are usually represented internationally by the UK, and the latter is responsible for their defence. None was ever a member of the EU (even when the UK was), though some trading aspects of the EU did apply to these islands before Brexit.[2] Often the UK Parliament is asked to extend the jurisdiction of statutes to these dependencies, but it has no formal sovereignty there.

2.1.2.2 The United Kingdom

The United Kingdom (formally, 'The United Kingdom of Great Britain and Northern Ireland') is the state in which 'British' people live and which acts on the international stage. The default position for any legislation produced by Parliament is that its jurisdiction is the whole of the UK. It includes the countries of England, Northern Ireland, Scotland, and Wales.

Northern Ireland, Scotland, and Wales all have devolved legislatures (shown with a 'D' in Figure 2.1) which have varying degrees of competence or jurisdiction (i.e. power) independently of the UK Parliament.

Had the referendum on Scottish Independence of 18 September 2014 decided 'Yes', Scotland would have ceased to be part of the UK. This issue may be re-examined in the aftermath of the UK's withdrawal from the EU. Scotland's First Minister, Nicola Sturgeon, put Scottish Independence back 'on the table' as a result of Scotland's voters' strong preference to remain in the EU during the 2016 EU referendum.

2.1.2.3 Great Britain

Great Britain does not include Northern Ireland. 'Great Britain' is not a commonly used term (except in international sport). Because of the political situation in Northern Ireland during 'the Troubles', legislation for Northern Ireland was often created separately from that applying to Great Britain.

Northern Ireland and Scotland are said to have separate 'legal systems', in the sense of the forum in which legal disputes are settled. This means that a citizen living in Northern Ireland would be tried in Northern Ireland or make civil claims in the courts of Northern Ireland. Likewise a citizen living in Scotland would be tried or make civil claims in the Scottish courts. Although the Northern Irish system resembles that of England & Wales, and is common law in nature (see 2.3.2 for more on the contrast between common law and civil law), the Scottish system does not mirror that of England & Wales. The court system is particular to Scotland, and the law itself is an amalgam of civil, common, and customary law, with certain academic publications having almost the force of law.

2.1.2.4 England & Wales

This leaves England & Wales—the 'English legal system'. References to 'English' normally imply 'Welsh' too in this context. Wales was annexed to England in 1282. The law English lawyers

---

[2] Treaty on the Functioning of the European Union, Art. 355(5)(c).

use is that of England & Wales, and is administered by the English courts. The main focus of this book is the law applicable in the English legal system, although viewed in a wider context.

2.1.2.5 Summary

The map in Figure 2.2 offers what is perhaps a more familiar summary. Table 2.1 provides a key to the map as well as drawing out important features of each jurisdiction highlighted.

Figure 2.2 Legal map of the British Isles

Table 2.1 Key to Figure 2.2: Legal and political systems within the British Isles

	Entity	Legal system	Political system
1.	England	England & Wales	Part of the UK (and formerly the EU pre-Brexit)*.
2.	Wales	England & Wales	Part of the UK (and formerly the EU pre-Brexit)*; devolved legislature.
3.	Scotland	Scottish	Part of the UK* (and formerly the EU pre-Brexit)*; devolved legislature.
4.	Northern Ireland	Northern Irish	Part of the UK (and formerly the EU pre-Brexit)*; devolved legislature.
5.	Bailiwick of Guernsey	Guernsey, Privy Council is final court of appeal	Crown dependency. Adopts some UK legislation. Has dependent territories of its own—Alderney and Sark; never part of the EU.
6.	Bailiwick of Jersey	Jersey, Privy Council is final court of appeal	Crown dependency. Adopts some UK legislation; never part of the EU.
7.	Isle of Man	Isle of Man, Privy Council is final court of appeal	Crown dependency. Adopts some UK legislation; never part of the EU.
8.	Republic of Ireland	Irish	Republic of Ireland, part of the EU.

*The UK left the EU on 31 January 2020 (as a result of a referendum of 23 June 2016). See the Essential explanation on Brexit at 2.2.3 for further discussion of the consequences, including the possibility of revisiting Scottish independence.

2.2 Sources of law in England & Wales

English legal tradition places a lot of emphasis on the 'sources' of law. It is important to find which institution 'made' or 'recognised' a legal rule, and to identify exactly when it was made, so that you can decide which rule takes precedence.

In England & Wales, by an accident of history, the legal system has a varied combination of sources. This is not unique. Most countries possess a blend of legal cultures. As an example, in Norway civil law has been superimposed on common law and customary law.

Figure 2.3 summarises the current situation: there are four main sources of law in England & Wales—statutes, case law, EU-derived law, and ECHR law (which is a type of international law). This was not always so, and, is continuing to develop as a result of Brexit (see the Essential explanation at 2.2.3). For a long time, the two principal institutions which were said to 'make' law in the English legal system were Parliament and the courts, although (as we saw in 1.4.3) Parliament was ultimately sovereign. In 2.5 we explore the separate status of international law.

2.2.1 Statutes

Parliament consists of the House of Commons, the House of Lords, and the Queen, although the monarch's role is largely ceremonial. The government usually has a majority in the House of Commons, and is responsible for introducing most of the laws made by Parliament, called 'Acts of Parliament', 'statutes', or 'legislation'. Legislation can be divided into primary legislation made by Parliament, and secondary (and tertiary) legislation made with the authority of Parliament, but not by it. It is discussed in detail in Chapter 4.

2.2.2 Case law

The courts consist of independent, non-elected judges. By contrast, in some jurisdictions, judges have a more political focus, the epitome being in the US, where they are commonly appointed by politicians.

Senior judges create case law by reaching decisions on the cases before them. This is often referred to as the 'common law' to distinguish it from legislation; at 2.3.2 we see that the term

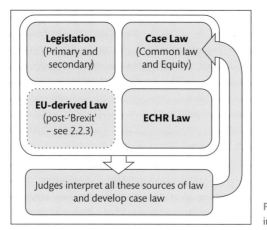

Figure 2.3 Sources of law
in England & Wales

'common law' can be used in different ways. Case law also includes equity, which is a largely separate body of case law with different historical origins from common law. We explore case law in more detail in Chapter 5.

We saw at 1.6 that the functions of the state are divided into distinct roles: the legislature, the executive, and the judiciary. The judiciary is sometimes said also to have a quasi-legislative role when it produces case law. We examine this idea in more detail in Chapter 5.

Judges have a law-making role: they develop law in areas where legislation is sparse (e.g. the law of negligence), and, if necessary, fill the gaps in legislation. Figure 2.3 summarises the sources of law in England & Wales, focusing on the operation of case law.

2.2.3 EU law, ECHR law, and international law

In the modern English legal system, both Parliament and the courts have been obliged to take into account EU law, incorporated into UK law (until Brexit) by the European Communities Act 1972, and the European Convention on Human Rights (ECHR) (via the Human Rights Act 1998). The UK is also part of the international community, so is also bound by international law. We look at international law at 2.5.

It is vital to understand that EU law and ECHR law are entirely separate from each other, and also that their judicial branches, the Court of Justice of the EU, including the European Court of Justice (CJEU and ECJ) and the European Court of Human Rights (ECtHR) are entirely distinct.

Both areas of law have had a profound effect on the English legal system. We look in detail at the former and current status and impact of EU Law at 2.4 and the Human Rights Act (derived from the ECHR) at 4.6. Law emanating from the European Court of Human Rights is a type of international law—we look at its status at 2.5. Although both areas of law govern relations between states, both also create rights enforceable by individuals. The status of each of the ECJ and ECtHR is examined in Chapter 3 and the effect of their judgments in Chapter 5.

🛈 Essential explanation

Brexit

The UK left the EU on 31 January 2020. This was a consequence of a referendum on 23 June 2016 in which the UK voted by 52 per cent to 48 per cent to leave the EU. There is a Withdrawal Agreement, the product of negotiations with two UK Governments under Theresa May and Boris Johnson. At the time of writing several important aspects are unresolved, including the nature of the UK's future political and trading relationship with the EU.

The legal effects of Brexit can be aniticpated in part. After Brexit, domestic legislation derived from EU law will continue in force,[3] although EU legislation passed after Brexit will no longer have direct effect in the UK. Brexit will not mean that EU law has vanished from the UK legal system. Further, as many UK statutes and statutory instruments enacted EU law, many court decisions will be made by reference to EU law or jurisprudence.[4] This means that interpreting and using this law will require reference to the law of the EU, some of it post-dating Brexit. It is quite possible that many provisions of EU law will have the status of international law (see 2.5) post-Brexit, rather as they do in Switzerland.

On a practical level, British businesses continue to trade in the EU, so EU law remains directly relevant to them.

(continued)

---

[3] European Union (Withdrawal Act) 2018, s. 7.   [4] European Union (Withdrawal Act) 2018, s. 6.

EU law therefore continues to have relevance in the UK, for lawyers and businesses alike.

The Brexit vote has many ramifications, some of which are still unclear. One is the re-examination of Scotland's relationship with the rest of the UK. In the EU Referendum, 62 per cent of Scots voted to remain in the EU; as mentioned at 2.1.2.2: this has led many Scots to believe that independence from the UK will need to be revisited to allow Scotland to rejoin the EU.

Brexit is placed in historical context in the summary diagram at Figure 2.14.

2.2.4 Other sources of law in England & Wales

Beyond the law identified in 2.2.1–2.2.3, there are some specialised areas of law concerning discrete areas of activity. Ecclesiastical and military law both have their own forums for litigation, with their own procedures. In this context, any law not within the relevant specialist area of law is called 'civil law'.

The legal implications of actions by members of a body such as the clergy or the military can be the subject both of litigation in the specialist courts (e.g. courts Christian and courts martial), and if necessary the 'civil' courts, which are those courts that have jurisdiction over citizens generally.

Ecclesiastical courts derive their authority directly from the Crown, as the monarch is the Supreme Governor of the Church of England, and courts martial derive theirs from the Armed Forces Acts 2006[5] and 2016[6]

2.3 Development of the English legal system

2.3.1 Why study the history of the English legal system?

In Chapter 1 we looked at the concept of the *gründnorm*. The origins of a body of law are significant because they relate to its legitimacy.

In addition, the development of case law has wide significance because all 'common law' legal systems (as distinguished from 'civil law'—see 2.3.2) can trace their origins back to the pre-Victorian English legal system. Most were at one time colonies of Great Britain. The development of English case law is consequently of broad relevance.

Finally, we have seen that the law does not operate in isolation; it is one of a suite of disciplines. History has impacted directly on how the law has developed. Politics has, and continues to, weigh heavily on how the law develops. Throughout this section you may wish to keep track of this interaction using the timeline in Figure 2.14. In this section we look at the development of the two 'traditional' sources of law in England & Wales—case law and statutes.

2.3.2 Case law

2.3.2.1 Development of the common law

The development of English case law is important to any lawyer dealing with the law of a common law jurisdiction.

---

[5] Armed Forces Act 2006, s. 50.   [6] Armed Forces Act 2016.

Essential explanation

'Common Law' and 'Civil Law'

The vast majority (but not all) of the world's legal systems fall into one of two categories—'common law', or 'civil law'—as illustrated in Figure 2.4. A common law jurisdiction has a system of binding judicial precedent which generates a body of case law. Examples are England & Wales, the US, Australia, and others in the same tradition. In these jurisdictions, legislation is not the only source of law; principles of law stated in some courts will bind many later judges. Legislation grows organically to meet demands and deal with problems as they arise, so in a given area there may be many relevant statutes.

By contrast, civil law (sometimes called, 'civilian') jurisdictions, tend not to have binding case law. Notable examples are France and Germany. Civil law jurisdictions do, of course, have litigation, but cases do not coalesce into a self-standing system of legal principles. Instead civil law systems usually adopt one or more comprehensive 'codes' which attempt to define all the rules in a given area. The foundation of many codified civil law systems is Roman law, which was for a long time a staple of university courses. It is important to note that many English legal principles (in particular those in equity) also borrow from Roman law. The standardisation of rules within the EU also owes much to the ideas of codification within Roman law.

Figure 2.4 illustrates common law and civil law jurisdictions; at 2.8 we look in more detail at the distinction between common and civil law states.

We shall now examine how English case law has developed over time. You may wish to refer to Figure 2.14 as you read on to help keep each feature in context.

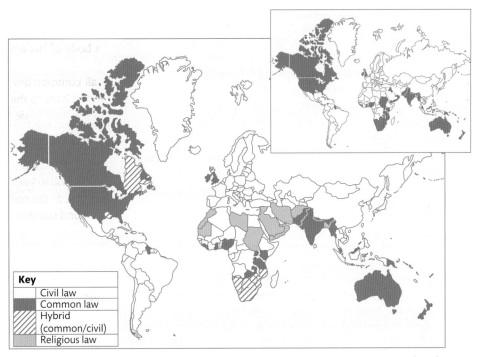

Figure 2.4 Legal systems of the world, compared with states formerly within the British Empire (inset)

William the Conqueror invaded England from Normandy in 1066. He realised that it would be easier to control the country if he also controlled the legal system. He imposed his authority by travelling around the country accompanied by his court, listening to and then ruling upon his subjects' grievances. The King would literally sit on a bench to hear these cases, which is why the most important court became known as the Court of King's Bench. This name is still used today, although it is currently called the Queen's Bench.

Later monarchs were less conscientious and this role was gradually delegated to Justices, who held 'Assizes' (sittings) of the royal courts. There was no unified or national set of laws. Local customs were applied. The local sheriff and later justices of the peace would deal with less serious offences. The King's courts gradually achieved ascendancy over local courts as the preferred forum for resolving disputes, when litigants (the parties) had a choice.

The system was formalised under Henry II (1154–89). Henry divided the country into 'circuits' or areas for the judges to visit on a regular basis. Judges as a group began to adopt the best of the local customs, and eventually a 'common' law emerged. If you turn to the timeline in Figure 2.14, you can see this interaction between Norman high politics and the need for legal uniformity.

This system of circuit judges from the King's Bench and the Assizes was not abolished until 1971, and a version of this system still exists in the US. The Rule of Law was so well entrenched by Henry's reign that, when he was accused of ordering the death of his Archbishop of Canterbury, Thomas Becket, the King accepted the punishment of a public whipping.

Respect for the Rule of Law required some consistency, and the 'common law' gradually coalesced into a body of binding case law. This doctrine of *stare decisis*, which means 'standing by previous decisions', still exists.

2.3.2.2 Drawbacks of the common law

A person could only litigate in the King's courts if a 'writ' was available, covering the facts of the case (e.g. a writ for entry onto land). By the 13th century, the number of writs became limited. The writs themselves were extremely formulaic and inflexible, and the slightest error by the plaintiff (now the 'claimant') would lead to the collapse of the case.

For example, there were particular problems with mortgages: in common law, once the loan repayment date had passed the land became the property of the lender and the borrower had no title to the land. It was common for lenders deliberately to make themselves unavailable on the date for payment, so the borrower lost the land.

In addition, only one remedy was available for civil wrong: damages (compensation). This was not always appropriate, for instance if the plaintiff wanted the defendant to stop doing something, or to perform his obligations.

! Essential explanation

Equity

The word 'equity' has several meanings. You may have used it in the past to mean 'fairness'. Alternatively, you may have encountered the word in a financial context, to refer to the property held by a person in a house (once a mortgage is paid off), or a shareholding in a company (once any liabilities are paid off). Both senses are related to the legal meaning, which we explore in this section.

Equity began as an alternative system of legal rules, which morphed over time into a body of rules supplementing the common law with rights based on fairness. You will often read that 'Equity follows the law'. Today this means that the common law position is normally considered before any equitable rules. Many of the rules relating to 'equity' finance derive from equity's status as 'supplementing' the common law.

2.3.2.3 Emergence of equity

By the 14th century the common law had become distorted and entrenched. The number of dissatisfied litigants was growing, and claimants started to petition the King in person to exercise his royal prerogative as the 'fountain of justice'. This function was gradually delegated to the Lord Chancellor, who became known as the 'Keeper of the King's Conscience'. The Court of Chancery evolved and the Chancellor began issuing decrees in his own name by 1474, separately from the King and the common law courts.

The Chancellor (as the Court of Chancery) developed the law of equity (see Figure 2.14). No writ was necessary and cases were determined purely on grounds of fairness. Remedies were not limited to damages, and procedure was simple—litigants made their claim to the Chancellor.

To take the example of the trust (which is explained in the next Essential explanation), in common law no writ was available in respect of a trust, a vital concept in law today. But equity recognised trusts very early in its development, during the Crusades (1095-1291). Nobles would leave the country for years at a time to fight holy wars in the Middle East. Often, landowners would transfer their property to a trusted friend, on the understanding it would be used for the crusader's family if he did not return. The legal interest in the land vested in the 'friend'. This is known as 'legal title', and was enforceable at common law. The family did not have legal title, and therefore had no rights at common law.

Until equity developed, crusaders' families were frequently left homeless. Equity imposed a 'trust' where the friend held the land as trustee for the benefit of the crusader and his family as beneficiaries. They had 'equitable title'. The friend was obliged to transfer legal title to the crusader or his family on request.

Essential explanation

A trust

A trust arises when one person (the 'trustee') is obliged to hold property on behalf of another person (the 'beneficiary') so that the benefit of the property is ultimately given to the beneficiary.

A trust allows the separation of administration and enjoyment of property. The trustee has management and control of the property subject to the trust (the 'trust property'), but the beneficiary is the 'real' owner in the sense that he will eventually enjoy the benefit of the property.

The trust is still a significant element of most common law legal systems. It is used by individuals in tax planning, the shared ownership of property, or in making provision for dependants. It is also important in matters of corporate or public interest, such as pension funds and charities.

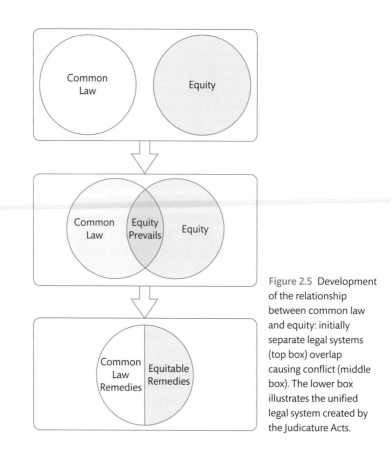

Figure 2.5 Development of the relationship between common law and equity: initially separate legal systems (top box) overlap causing conflict (middle box). The lower box illustrates the unified legal system created by the Judicature Acts.

Paradoxically, one criticism of equity was that it was simply too erratic:

> Equity is a roguish thing: for law we have a measure, know what to trust to; equity is according to the conscience of him that is Chancellor, and as that is larger or narrower, so is equity. 'Tis all one as if they should make the standard for the measure we call a foot, a Chancellor's foot; what an uncertain measure would this be? One Chancellor has a long foot, another a short foot, a third an indifferent foot: 'tis the same thing in a Chancellor's conscience.[7]

Take a look at Figure 2.5. In the top box you will see that principles of equity gradually emerged and equity became a separate branch of the law with its own rules and procedure, rather than simply being the application of natural justice to a case.

2.3.2.4 Equitable maxims

You will read about equitable 'maxims'. These were developed by the Court of Chancery and remain relevant when using equity today. There are at least 20, but important ones include:

- Equity looks on that as done which ought to be done: this means that equity will observe the parties' intention instead of rigid procedure. This means that it is more flexible and litigation less formulaic.

[7] Selden, J. (1689) *Table Talk*. London: JR Smith, 1856.

- He who comes to equity must come with clean hands: an equitable remedy is not available to a claimant who is not acting in good faith.
- Delay defeats equity: a claimant cannot wait too long before making a claim as this may prejudice the other party. This is frequently a problem for litigants who seek injunctions to stop others from doing something.
- Equity will not suffer a wrong to be without a remedy.

2.3.2.5 Equitable remedies

Equitable remedies developed because receiving damages in common law was not always adequate to meet the claimant's needs. These remedies still have a vital role in English law. They remain discretionary: the court has discretion as to whether litigants deserve the exercise of equity on their behalf. This contrasts with common law remedies, which are available as of right to those who can prove their case. Two significant equitable remedies today are:

- An injunction: here the court orders someone to perform an action or to refrain from an action, for example to stop using the claimant's trade mark. Injunctions can be issued in a matter of hours if they are equitable. For instance, if a celebrity seeks to prevent a newspaper from publishing a defamatory story, or if someone wants to prevent the publication of confidential information about them, they may seek an injunction to prevent publication. The BBC, for instance, failed to obtain an injunction preventing publication of Ben Collins' memoirs revealing his identity as 'The Stig' from *Top Gear*.[8]
- A decree of specific performance: here the court orders someone to perform their obligations under a contract or trust. The following fictional example illustrates a situation where an order of specific performance might be appropriate: Andrew makes a contract to sell a famous painting to Ben, and then changes his mind. If Andrew refuses to sell the painting, he will be in breach of contract. Money (in the form of damages) may not be an appropriate remedy for Ben—it may be more suitable for a court to order the transfer of the painting itself from Andrew to Ben. This would be an order of specific performance.

2.3.2.6 Discord between common law and equity

Equity developed to supplement the common law, often as an alternative forum for settling disputes. Conflicts arose between it and the common law. By the 16th century, equity did not merely supplement the common law, but directly challenged it.

In 1615, James I personally decided that in cases of conflict, equity should prevail over common law.[9] You can see this stage in the development of the relationship illustrated in the middle box in Figure 2.5.

This resolution lost much of its value as equity itself hardened into a system of law with rules which sometimes became as inflexible as those of the common law. Both jurisdictions needed reform by the 19th century. There were too many courts with overlapping jurisdictions and it was expensive and slow to obtain justice.

---

[8] 'Top Gear court case: The Stig revealed as racing driver Ben Collins', *The Telegraph* (1 September 2010).
[9] *Earl of Oxford's Case* (1615) 21 ER 485, 1 Rep Ch 1.

2.3.2.7 Amalgamation of courts of common law and equity

The courts of common law and equity were merged by the Supreme Court of Judicature Acts of 1873 and 1875. Both systems of law remained but these were administered by all courts when it was necessary to discuss equity. Some significant effects were:

- Civil courts can now grant both common law and equitable remedies in the same action, which you can see in the lower box in Figure 2.5. For example, an injunction to stop unlawful behaviour can be ordered, in addition to damages for losses accrued to date. In a classic Lord Denning case,[10] it was found that the repeated hitting of 'sixes' out of a cricket ground into neighbours' gardens constituted a private nuisance. The court was happy to award damages for losses, but (and this romanticism was a theme of Denning's judgments) used its discretion not to award an injunction to stop the cricket. Rights in common law and in equity are recognised by the same courts, for example an equitable right of way over land held at common law by someone else, or an equitable interest in shares held at common law by another.

- Equity sometimes provides defences to common law claims. In contract law, for instance, you will read about a defence to a common law debt claim, called promissory estoppel. It was developed almost singlehandedly by Lord Denning, to prevent creditors going back on promises to ease repayments by debtors.

Equity may have developed in England & Wales, but it was inherited by most of the common law jurisdictions, and in many, most notably the US, it continues to play an important role in the courts.

2.3.2.8 Summary

In summary, the English legal system has developed from largely local customs, into law 'common' to the country ('common law'). We have seen the development of equity in the 14th century to mitigate the worst problems with the common law. Until the mid-19th century equity comprised a system of law entirely separate from the common law. While this is no longer the case, there remain two distinct bodies of case law—common law and equity—the latter being considerably more flexible than the former.

2.3.3 Statutes

In England & Wales, there are records of the formal enactment of statutes from the accession of William the Conqueror in 1066, and written evidence of laws purporting to be statutes going back to Anglo-Saxon times (around 600). The legislation.gov.uk website reveals a trickle of statutes in force starting in 1262, and increasing significantly in volume after the 'Glorious Revolution' in 1688. If you look at the timeline in Figure 2.14, you can appreciate the historical context to this development. But this is only part of the story. Incredibly, the early statutes listed on that website are still in force. As the role of the state has increased, so statutes have replaced the common law as the primary source of law in England & Wales.

[10] *Miller v Jackson* [1977] QB 966.

Until the 15th century, however, a 'statute' was merely a law passed with Royal authority. Try to look at old statutes today, and you may find the variety surprising and content often unfamiliar.

In the 15th century, the consent of the House of Commons became necessary when a statute was passed, a process formalised by the Tudors in the 16th century.[11] The 17th century saw a struggle for supremacy between the Monarchy and Parliament, resolved initially by the *Case of Proclamations*[12] in which it was declared that 'The King has no prerogative but that which the law of the land allows him', and eventually confirmed by the 'Glorious Revolution' of 1688 (see Figure 2.14). This was a key moment in English law, as it confirmed (via the Bill of Rights 1688) that Parliament was the pre-eminent law-making body in the UK—it created parliamentary sovereignty.

As the country expanded, so the territorial extent of statutes also grew. Social and industrial development (particularly associated with the industrial revolution of the 18th and 19th centuries) required a significant expansion in regulation—it is difficult to believe that until the mid-19th Century social provision was limited to the medieval Poor Laws and that there was hardly any regulation of workplace conditions. Bigger cities and more dangerous workplaces combined with an antiquated electoral system to create pressure for social and political reform. Look again at Figure 2.14; the Reform Acts of 1832, 1867, and 1884 were reactions to the clamour for greater representation of the growing middle and working classes. The same pressures, along with rapidly evolving attitudes within the House of Commons, led to early workplace safety legislation.

The 20th century saw further significant changes in society and politics. Up to 900,000 servicemen perished and a further 1,700,000 were wounded in World War I (1914–18) (see Figure 2.14). Resentment grew against the ruling elites around Europe that were seemingly out of touch and unwilling to countenance wholesale changes to the structure and politics of their countries. Revolutions occurred around mainland Europe as a reaction to these related factors. Without recognition of the sacrifices of ordinary people, there would almost certainly have been revolution in the UK. Parliament passed unprecedentedly interventionist housing, health, and welfare legislation, including the establishment of a state pension. Many women got the vote in 1918.[13] The apparatus of the state grew: the civil service numbered only around 50,000 in 1910, rising to 221,000 at the end of World War I in 1918,[14] to a peak of 733,800 in 1977.[15] A larger state needed more regulation.

In the 19th and 20th centuries, Parliament, and hence also statutes, reflected the democratisation of society. World War II (1939–45) witnessed another terrible death toll (around 400,000 UK military deaths) and an enormous growth of the state to drive forward war production and the control of infrastructure. In 1945, a Labour government was elected on a platform of extensive state intervention, including the establishment of the National Health Service, and the extension of welfare 'from the cradle to the grave'. By the 1950s largely Keynesian theories of economics (named after John Maynard Keynes—see also 19.1.2) became the default in most Western economies. This meant a social democratic model, incorporating state ownership of utilities and central planning. Wide-ranging legislation was

---

[11] Plucknett, T. F. T. (1956) *Concise History of the Common Law*. London: Butterworth, 5th edn, p. 322.

[12] *Case of Proclamations* (1611) 12 Co Rep 74.   [13] Representation of the People Act 1918.

[14] Civil Service (2014) *Civil Service Statistics*. Available online at: https://www.gov.uk/government/statistics/civil-service-statistics-2014.

[15] Lowe, Rodney R. (2011) *The Official History of the British Civil Service: Reforming the Civil Service, Volume I: The Fulton Years, 1966–81 (Government Official History Series)*. London: Routledge.

necessary in the short term[16] to provide the complex legal framework for this, and the need for these rules continues to this day.

Eventually even primary legislation could not keep up with the demand for regulation, and secondary legislation (i.e. not passed directly by Parliament) such as statutory instruments (see 4.2.2) grew in importance.

Some rather sensationalist headlines have bemoaned a jump in regulatory legislation in recent years, allegedly burdening businesses with red tape; others lament the torrent of criminal legislation overwhelming the justice system with new offences.[17] Lord Phillips of Sudbury has said, 'We legislate more than any other major democratic country. I'm talking 200–300 per cent more. And you don't need to be a soothsayer to see that the downstream consequences of all that law-making are parlous—more bureaucratisation, centralisation, more demoralisation.'[18]

You might be surprised to learn that the number of statutes has decreased consistently since the 1960s. This is arguably a result of two factors: first, a significant increase in the amount of statutory instruments; and second, that the complexity and comprehensiveness of Acts has increased. This is supported by looking at the number of pages of legislation per year. Figure 2.6 shows how the volume of legislation has increased since the early 20th century[19]—an average for each decade is set out in the graph. Until the 1950s, the pages

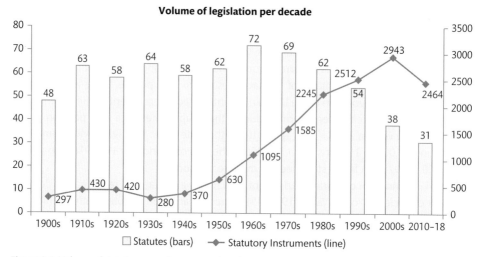

Figure 2.6 Volume of statutes, annual mean per decade

[16] E.g. Family Allowances Act 1945, National Insurance Act 1946, National Insurance (Industrial Injuries) Act 1946, National Health Service Act 1946, Town and Country Planning Act 1947, National Assistance Act 1948, Children Act 1948, Housing Act 1949.

[17] See Hope, C. 'Lord Judge tells Jack Straw: the UK has too many crime laws', *The Telegraph* (15 July 2009).

[18] Lord Phillips of Sudbury, quoted in *The Times* (31 May 2012).

[19] Statistics derived from (for 1950–2007) Crackness, Richard R. (2008) *Acts & Statutory Instruments: Volume of UK legislation 1950–2007*. London: House of Commons Library; (for pre-1950 Acts) (2010) *Chronological Table of Statutes*. London: TSO; (for pre-1950 statutory instruments) *Halsbury's Statutory Instrument Citator 2012* (N.B. numbers estimated according to statutes cited); for average number of pages per piece of legislation prior to 1950, figures derived from Crackness. Mean figures for statutory instruments 1900s and 1910s, figures extrapolated from mean for 1920s.

of legislation emanating from Parliament numbered in the low hundreds; since the 1950s there has been a steady (and seemingly inexorable) rise to the 2000s level of roughly 3,000 each year. The Companies Act 2006 is an illuminating example of the increasing complexity of primary legislation. It was passed to bring together the content of several preceding statutes and to give statutory footing to common law and equitable principles. It also amended the law in some areas. It runs to 1,300 sections, divided into 47 parts. It also includes 16 schedules. The Act totals 571 pages. This is before we consider the 32 statutory instruments relating to its implementation, passed by mid-2012.

A study[20] examined the length of companies legislation since 1844, providing an excellent illustration of the increased volume of law passed by Parliament. Figure 2.7 shows that the volume of legislation in this important field has increased each time it has been legislated. The Companies Act 2006 contains twice as many sections as the 1985 Act.

✱ Essential debate

In India, equity was a key element of the law until independence from Great Britain in 1947. In 1963, the Indian Parliament abolished and replaced most equitable rights and remedies with statutory rights.[21]

Is there an argument for replacing the idiosyncratic principles of equity in England & Wales with a statement of rights and remedies in a statute? Would this be more open and authoritative? What drawbacks would there be?

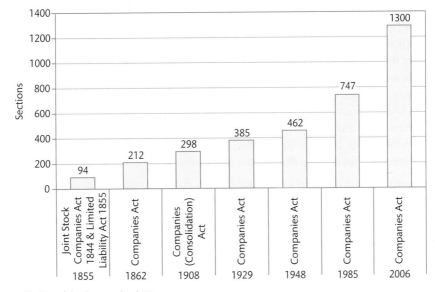

Figure 2.7 Size of the Companies Acts

---

[20] Armour, John J. (2008) 'Codification and UK Company Law'. In Association du Bicentenaire du Code de Commerce (ed.) *Bicentenaire du Code de Commerce 1807–2007: les Actes des Colloques*. Paris: Dalloz, pp. 287–310.

[21] Specific Relief Act 1963.

2.4 EU law

2.4.1 EU law: Introduction

The UK left the EU on 31 January 2020 (as a result of a referendum of 23 June 2016). As a result, you might justifiably ask why this book addresses EU law. At 2.2.3 we examined Brexit. You will therefore recall that the following section has continuing relevance in the UK, especially for lawyers.

The UK became a member of the European Economic Community (EEC) on 1 January 1973 (having signed the Treaty of Rome 1957 in the previous year). When the UK was a member of the EU, EU law applied throughout the UK. The EEC (as it was then) was created in 1957 to promote trade within the European common market (then constituting six member states) by seeking to create a level playing field for commercial activity in Europe. The EU's role is now significantly greater, incorporating a wide range of economic matters (notably monetary union), justice, education, health, and foreign relations. Since the UK left, the EU has had 27 member states.

It is important to remember that the jurisdiction and institutions of the EU are entirely separate from those of the ECHR (although the EU is a signatory to the ECHR).

Because international law is not regarded as part of our legal system (see 2.5) it was necessary to enact the European Communities Act 1972 (the 'ECA 1972'). As a result of the ECA 1972, EU legislation was (under some circumstances) incorporated into UK law without Parliament having to legislate on each separate occasion. The ECA 1972 was repealed on 31 January 2020 (Brexit day) by virtue of the European Union (Withdrawal) Act 2018,[22] so EU law is no longer incorporated directly into UK law. The UK system in this context was known as a 'dualist' system because EU law was not automatically binding; it needed to be incorporated into domestic legislation by Parliament, via the European Communities Act. This is why Parliament needed to abolish the ECA 1972, and with it the automatic incorporation of EU law into UK law. In contrast, some other jurisdictions (e.g. France) are 'monist' in that, on ratification of the EU Treaty (then the EEC Treaty) by the French government, (French) domestic legislation was not needed for EU law to become part of domestic law.

Some of our national law (e.g. land law) was not affected by membership of the EU, but certain highly significant areas were, for example, commercial and consumer law, employment law, the environment, and freedom of movement. These areas remain heavily influenced by law carried over from the EU era, and may well shadow developments within the EU for the foreseeable future. Three examples will help illustrate the direct impact EU law had on the life of a UK citizen:

- Article 102 TFEU prohibits the abuse by a party of its dominant market position. There are various practices that can constitute abuse, but one is called 'tying', whereby a consumer is strongly encouraged to use one product because it is tied to another. This happened in the *Microsoft* case, where certain programs (e.g. Internet Installer and Windows Media Player) were 'bundled' into the Microsoft Windows operating system, so inhibiting take-up of competitor products. A series of cases before the ECJ resulted in Microsoft being found to be in breach of Article 102 (then Article 82) fined nearly €300 million and being ordered to change its contracts and products to prevent continued abuse. This has had tangible benefits for any consumer who uses Windows PCs.[23]

- The Transfer of Undertakings (Protection of Employment) Regulations were made in the UK to implement an EU Directive which dealt with protection of employment when one

[22] European Union (Withdrawal Act) 2018, s. 1.
[23] *Microsoft v Commission* (Case T-201/04) [2007] ECR II-3601.

business is sold to another.[24] The House of Lords (now the Supreme Court) has interpreted the Directive and therefore the UK regulations to mean that workers whose employment had been terminated by reason of a business transfer should still be considered as employed as at the date of the transfer, and should therefore be able to enforce their accrued employment rights even if they were sacked just before the transfer itself.[25]

- The Consumer Rights Directive 2011/83/EU required member states to implement extensive protections for consumers. One of many changes in UK law was that consumers now have a 14 day 'cooling off' period once they have bought goods over the internet.[26]

Since its creation in 1957 the EU has passed well over 100,000 pages of statute law.[27]

Essential explanation

EU terminology

There are several terms that are, or have historically been used to, describe fundamental features of what is now the EU and its law.

- The EEC, or European Economic Community, created by the Treaty of Rome 1957.
- The EC, or European Community, created under the Maastricht Treaty 1992.
- The EU, or European Union, also established under the Maastricht Treaty 1992.

There have been key differences in the jurisdiction of each body.

Under the Maastricht Treaty in 1992, the EC replaced the EEC, and also the EU was created. The EU at this stage comprised three 'pillars'—the EC, which had a legal system; the Common Foreign and Security Policy; and Police and Judicial Cooperation in Criminal Matters. The EU did not itself have a legal system, so the law within the EU was called 'EC law'.

The Lisbon Treaty, signed in 2007, and which came into force on 1 December 2009, unified the three 'pillars' of the EU into one legal entity. At this stage 'EC law' became 'EU law'. The Lisbon Treaty had many effects; importantly in this context, the Treaty of Rome was at the same time retrospectively renamed the Treaty on the Functioning of the European Union.

In the context of the legal system, we will examine the institutions of the EU. In Chapter 4 we will look in more detail at the legislation they produce, and its effect.

2.4.2 **EU institutions**

2.4.2.1 The institutions identified

To understand how EU law is made, it is important to have an understanding of the EU institutions. These descriptions should be read in conjunction with Figure 2.8, which places them in a traditional framework of Separation of Powers.

- The Council of Ministers (formally, the Council of the European Union) consists of a government representative from each member state. It has a legislative role—the

---

[24] The Business Transfers Directive 77/187/EC, since replaced by the Transfers of Undertakings Directive 2001/23/EC.

[25] *Litster* v *Forth Dry Dock and Engineering Ltd* [1989] 1 All ER 1134.

[26] Consumer Contracts (Information, Cancellation and Additional Charges) Regulations 2013 (SI 2013/3134).

[27] In 2009, the EU's estimate was 80,000 pages, although some pressure groups have put the figure a lot higher, e.g. Open Europe, who estimated around 670,000 pages of legislation, which, laid end-to-end, would equate to 120 miles of legislation, enough to stretch from London to Birmingham.

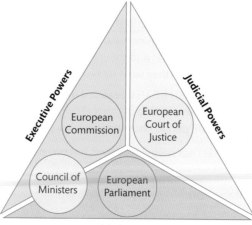

Figure 2.8 Separation of powers within the EU

'co-decision' procedure (formally, the 'ordinary legislative procedure')—in tandem with the Parliament, and it approves the EU budget. It also has an executive role, being the main decision-making body of the EU, most significantly for economic policy.

- The European Commission develops and implements policy. It consists of independent Commissioners appointed by national governments, but who must work independently of national loyalties, and who make proposals for legislation and oversee implementation of legislation.

- The Parliament has a limited legislative role including the ability to veto some types of legislation. This is called the 'co-decision' procedure (with the Council of Ministers). With the Council of Ministers, it approves the EU budget. It also has oversight over the Commission. It is made up of elected members.

- The Court of Justice of the European Union, the senior court of which is the ECJ, consists of judges nominated by each of the member states. Its role is to ensure that EU law is observed throughout the EU. It has the power to judicially review the actions of the other institutions. Be careful not to confuse the ECJ with the European Court of Human Rights.

- The European Council, not to be confused with the Council of the European Union, is a label given to the heads of government (or heads of state) of the member states, meeting on an *ad hoc* basis (around six times each year). Their role is to give overall impetus to the EU.[28]

2.4.2.2 The institutions compared

In this context, we need only look at what legislation emanates from which EU institutions. However, this is also an appropriate point at which to compare their key features (summarised in Table 2.2). We look in detail at the different types of legislation at 4.5.1. Figure 2.9 summarises the legislative process within the institutions of the EU.

[28] Art. 15 TFEU.

Table 2.2 Summary of EU institutions

Institution	Composition	Overall role	Legislative role	Legislation produced/ decisions taken
European Commission	One Commissioner per member state,[29] each with a portfolio approved by Council of Ministers and Parliament.	One of two executive branches: implements and enforces policy.	Makes formal proposals for legislation; drafts the EU budget.	Decisions (in competition law). Recommendations and opinions. Regulations are sometimes passed by the Commission alone.
Council of Ministers (Council of the EU)	One member per member state, normally votes by qualified majority voting.	One of two executive branches for some issues, e.g. foreign policy. Coordinates economic policies of member states.	Can request Commission to propose legislation. Co-decision procedure with Parliament.[30] Approves the EU budget.	Regulations and directives. Some decisions. Recommendations and opinions.
European Council	Heads of government.	Gives overall impetus to the EU.[31]	None.	None.
European Parliament	754 MEPs directly elected in proportion to member states' population.	Supervises Commission and legislates.	Can request Commission to propose legislation. Co-decision procedure with Council in many areas of competence. Approves Commission's draft budget.	Regulations and directives.
European Court of Justice	One judge per member state in both the General Court and ECJ.	Preliminary rulings:[32] references from national courts on EU matters. Judicial review of validity of the acts of other EU institutions.[33] Actions against member states by the Commission[34] or other member states.[35]	Rules on EU law.	Rulings.

[29] Art. 245 TFEU.   [30] Art. 294 TFEU.   [31] Art. 15 TFEU.   [32] Art. 267 TFEU.
[33] Art. 263 TFEU.   [34] Art. 258 TFEU.   [35] Art. 259 TFEU.

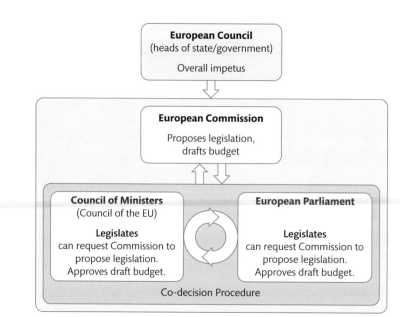

Figure 2.9 Creation of EU legislation

2.5 International law

> ### 🛈 Essential explanations
>
> 'International law', 'public international law', and 'private international law'
>
> International law comprises rules governing relations between different states or people within them. Usually 'international law' refers to public international law, rather than private international law. Both are explained here, and in Figure 2.10. National (sometimes 'Federal') law, by contrast, is the law governing actors within a state.
>
> Public international law comprises a system of rules and principles that govern the international relations between sovereign states in addition to some other institutions such as the United Nations (UN). With a very few isolated exceptions it does not concern individuals, organisations, or lower levels of government.
>
> By contrast, private international law comprises international legal relations between private individuals and organisations. It usually (but not exclusively) relates to commercial endeavour and how to determine which rules apply to transnational trade.
>
> EU law is an example of *supra*national law (as contrasted with international law), under which sovereignty is genuinely ceded to institutions comprising more than one state.

2.5.1 **Public international law**

2.5.1.1 Nature of international law

In Chapter 1 we saw that law is a body of rules that a state recognises as governing the actions of its subjects. Some legal theorists therefore argue that 'international law' is a misnomer because there is no sovereign body that legislates to bind states to international law in the same way that a sovereign body in a state binds its subjects to that state's laws. However, this is a minority

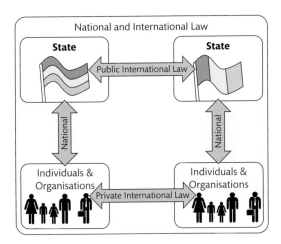

Figure 2.10 National and international law compared

view, because in reality all states conduct themselves on the assumption that the rules comprising international law are in some sense binding, even if they choose to flout or sidestep them.

Much of international law is executed under the auspices of the United Nations (itself a creature of an international treaty, the UN Charter of 1945[36]), often via one of its 17 specialised agencies. These include e.g. UNESCO (the UN Educational, Scientific and Cultural Organization), the WHO (World Health Organization), the ILO (International Labour Organization), the IMF (International Monetary Fund), and WIPO (the World Intellectual Property Organization). There are 560 multilateral treaties and conventions deposited at the UN, although this is a fraction of the treaties in force around the world.

The International Court of Justice also recognises other sources of international law, including custom (which occupies a more significant role than in UK national law), its own judicial decisions, and other 'general principles'[37]—globally accepted standards of behaviour. One hundred and fourteen states, including the UK, have ratified the Vienna Convention on the Law of Treaties 1969, which regulates the entry into and conduct of treaties. This gives treaties even more of the characteristics of 'hard' national law.

There are different academic analyses of why international law is binding, but most rest on the idea of consent. In much the same way as individuals enter a contract by consenting to be bound, states consent to be bound by treaties. This mechanism is summarised in Figure 2.11. It is important to reflect on this, and to note that international law is not part of the UK or English legal systems.

2.5.1.2 Example

International law governs areas as diverse as the Law of the Sea, the Antarctic, the environment, space law (which purports to govern the rights and obligations of Earth's states in space),[38] armed conflict, and war crimes. Among the variety of international rules, there is a strong emphasis on human rights.

---

[36] *Charter of the United Nations*: Mikazuki Publishing House, 2012.
[37] Art. 38, Statute of the International Court of Justice.
[38] E.g. 1967 Treaty on Principles Governing the Activities of States in the Exploration and Use of Outer Space, including the Moon and Other Celestial Bodies.

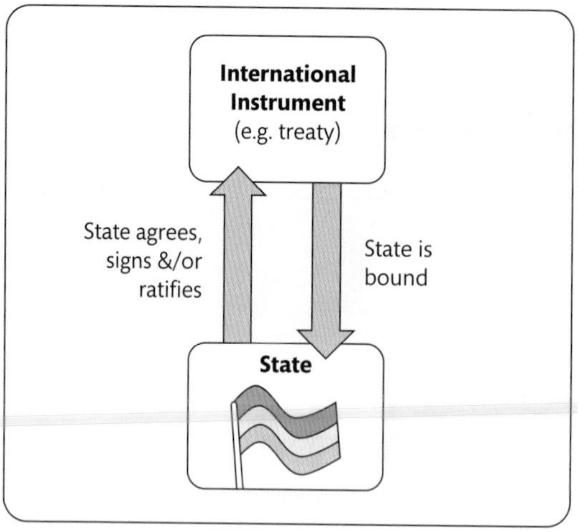

Figure 2.11 Bindingness of international law

In the aftermath of the human carnage of World War II it was felt that only international action would suffice to prevent a repeat of the atrocities of the 1930s and 1940s. This pressure spawned the UN's Universal Declaration of Human Rights 1948 (UDHR) and the European Convention on Human Rights 1950 (ECHR, as developed by the Council of Europe). Both have been developed since with the addition of Protocols (not all of which the UK has signed) and an expansion of signatories. To this day the Council of Europe actively promotes democracy, human rights, and the rule of law.[39] Forty-seven states are members including the UK and all EU states, plus others including EFTA (European Free Trade Area) states, Russia, and other eastern European states. Other states have observer status, and Belarus is a candidate member. Like many international institutions, whilst it purports to make international law, enforcement of ECtHR judgments depends on political pressure being applied by other states on transgressor members.

The UN lists nine core international human rights instruments, including its International Bill of Rights (the UDHR, the International Covenant on Economic, Social and Cultural Rights 1966, the International Covenant on Civil and Political Rights 1966, and its two Optional Protocols).

There are other regional (rather than worldwide) instruments too, for instance the American Convention on Human Rights 1969 and the African Charter on Human and Peoples' Rights 1979 (signed and ratified by all African states bar South Sudan).

2.5.1.3 Enforcement

International law is enforceable in various international courts, most notably the UN court, the International Court of Justice (ICJ). The ICJ may be the UN court but there are other international courts of note. Table 2.3 lists notable international courts by way of example.

There may be courts mediating between states but there are few institutions to enforce international law. There is no police force and no army (the UN peacekeeping force is not an army). The powers of the ICJ are limited, and normally enforcement is via the threat of sanctions or international and regional condemnation. Once again we can draw a parallel with the

---

[39] For further information visit the Council of Europe website at www.coe.int/en.

Table 2.3 Selected International Tribunals and Courts

Court	Instrument establishing	Nature
European Court of Human Rights (also see 3.5.2)	European Convention on Human Rights 1950	Located in Strasbourg, a European-based court regulating human rights conduct of 47 member states of the Council of Europe, including the UK. Claims made by private individuals against states.
International Court of Justice	UN Charter and Statute of the ICJ 1945	Located in the Hague, the principal judicial organ of the UN, settles disputes submitted by states and gives advisory opinions on legal questions referred to it by UN organs and agencies. Has jurisdiction over member states.
International Criminal Court (also see 3.5.3)	Rome Statute 1998	Sitting in the Hague, set up under the auspices of the UN, but not part of the UN, 124 states are party to the Rome Statute. Individuals of such states are subject to the court, if they are suspected of war crimes, etc. At the time of writing 39 individuals had been indicted since 2002. In cases referred by the UN all UN states are subject to the ICC's decision. There are also *ad hoc* criminal tribunals set up by the UN to bring justice to victims of international crimes.
International Tribunal for the Law of the Sea	UN Convention for the Law of the Sea 1982	Based in Hamburg, an independent judicial body to adjudicate disputes arising out of the UN Convention for the Law of the Sea.
International Court of Arbitration		Based in Paris, part of the International Chamber of Commerce, the ICA deals with international disputes between commercial parties from 85 states. It handles roughly 500 cases a year.
Permanent Court of Arbitration	Hague Convention for the Pacific Settlement of International Disputes 1899.	Located in the Hague, it is an organisation (not a court) providing dispute resolution services to the international community. 119 countries including the UK. 138 cases in 2015. Disputes can concern states or individual entities.

law of contract. In most circumstances an alleged breach of contract is settled by a negotiation process backed up by the threat of litigation; alleged breaches of international rules are usually the subject of negotiation (often through mediation in international courts) backed by the threat of international censure. For instance, Art. 46 of the European Convention on Human Rights obliges member states to abide by the judgments of the court—but even compliance with the judgments of the court is patchy.

In 2016 China came before the Permanent Court of Arbitration as a result of its practice of artificially augmenting islands in the South China Sea to form the basis of a claim to sovereignty. The court found China to be in breach of the Law of the Sea; China's response via its newspaper *The Peoples' Daily* was: 'The Chinese government and the Chinese people firmly oppose [the ruling] and will neither acknowledge it nor accept it.' This is a powerful illustration of the difficulties of enforcing international law against all comers.

Despite these limitations the European Convention on Human Rights, in particular, has led to impressive improvements in the lives of ordinary people. The ECtHR has required Bulgaria to care properly for people with mental and physical disabilities, France to legislate to protect domestic servants, and Austria to allow same-sex couples to adopt each other's children. It has obliged the UK to regulate the monitoring of employees' communications, forced Cyprus to take action against sex trafficking, and Moldova to halt state censorship of TV. Its judgments have compelled improvements in Russian prisons, and more effective punishment of domestic violence in Turkey.

Example 1

The ILO and workers' rights in Burma

The International Labour Organization was formed as part of the Treaty of Versailles 1919 (you may recognise this as the Treaty that formally ended World War I) and is now a specialised agency of the UN. It brings together governments, employers, and workers' representatives of 187 states, 'to set labour standards, develop policies and devise programmes promoting decent work for all women and men.'[40] These are contained within 190 conventions ranging from the Forced Labour Convention 1930 to the Domestic Workers Convention 2011. These conventions must be opted into by each ILO state. But its limitations are typical of international rules. It has three compliance mechanisms: it can give technical assistance to ministries and agencies, it can shame countries into improving working conditions, and under Article 33 of its constitution it can punish countries who do not comply by requesting member governments and other UN organisations to take appropriate action.

In post-colonial Burma, successive governments, and most particularly the military junta that seized power in 1988, had routinely forced civilians to work on state infrastructure projects, e.g. building roads and even towns. The junta would demand villages supply labour under threat of fines if households were unable to meet the required quota. On occasion villagers would be forced to act as human minesweepers to clear the way for the safe passage of soldiers. Many prisoners would be sentenced to terms which also included hard labour, often in labour camps.

The ILO had been monitoring this situation, but the Burmese government refused to comply with the ILO's recommendations. In 2000 intense negotiations among the ILO's members, including Burma and its neighbours, attempted to forestall punishment under Article 33. Eventually the governing body of the ILO asked the International Labour Conference to take measures to lead Burma (at the time called Myanmar) to end the use of forced labour. Even after two years, however, no government, organisation, or workers' or employers' group had taken any action against Burma under the resulting resolution.

Example 1 illustrates the 'toothless tiger' syndrome common to much of international law. Only consistent pressure from the outside world coupled with economic incentives forced the junta to change its practices as part of a much wider raft of reforms in the 2010s.

2.5.2 **Private international law**

The commercial world is increasingly transnational in nature, with parties doing business across borders between states. A significant body of law concerns how such relationships are legally regulated. Like public international law it comprises a body of conventions, model laws, national laws, and other instruments that regulate private relationships across borders. Also, like public international law, it rests on the concept of consent for its bindingness. This consent can either be that of the parties' states or of the parties themselves.

---

[40] International Labour Organization website (http://www.ilo.org/global/lang--en/index.htm), accessed at 14/07/2016.

Table 2.4 Three instruments allowing trade across borders

Instrument Convention/Treaty	Originating Institution	Nature
United Nations Convention on Contracts for the International Sale of Goods (CISG or Vienna Convention) 1988	UNCITRAL—the UN Commission for International Trade Law	A treaty containing default terms for the sale of goods—these terms fill gaps in contracts between parties of different contracting states. The UK is not a party. 85 parties (18 additional signatories). It is based on the Uniform Commercial Code of the United States.
Principles of International Commercial Contracts (PICC)	UNIDROIT (International Institute for the Unification of Private Law)	Parties can opt into these model rules on the sale of goods and provision of services. There are 63 members of UNIDROIT, including the UK, and the institute has ten international conventions under its auspices.
Incoterms	International Chamber of Commerce	A series of pre-defined commercial terms published by the ICC, reflecting common trade practices, most particularly in shipping contracts. Parties commonly opt into one of a variety of packages of terms.

An important part of private international law concerns 'the conflict of laws': it is normally very easy for parties to stipulate the laws which apply to a contract and the courts (or arbitrators) which will resolve disputes. Sometimes, however, it is less clear which laws apply or which bodies have jurisdiction to settle disputes. This area occupies whole modules of legal study.

Another key area is how parties do business across borders. Commercial parties like certainty, so it is in their interests to have rules stipulating contract terms where they have failed to do so. There are therefore many treaties and instruments which help regulate this. Much of EU Law concerns this issue, but outside the EU it is arguably even more important to have rules of this nature. Table 2.4 lists three such instruments by way of an example.

2.6 Sources of law: conclusions

In 2.2–2.5 we have seen that there are several distinct sources of law that impact on the lives and operations of citizens and organisations in the UK. It is clear that, after decades, and even centuries of comparative inertia, these sources are in a state of continual change. This makes the job of the lawyer ever more crucial in advising clients on their legal rights and obligations in a changing world. One way lawyers make sense of these many concepts is by classifying legal rules.

2.7 Classifications of law in England & Wales

You will probably have realised from the discussion of the development of the English legal system earlier in this chapter that lawyers have gradually classified the law into a number of broad areas. Every lawyer needs to be aware of the most important classifications. They impact on the nature of legal rules, and on the practice of law and litigation.

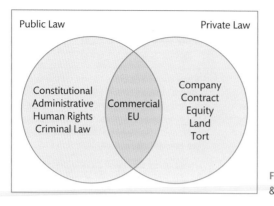

Figure 2.12 Categorisation of law in England & Wales: public and private

2.7.1 Public law and private law

Possibly the most fundamental is the distinction between public law and private law.

> #### ⚠ Essential explanation
>
> #### Public law
>
> Duties owed to or by the state are matters of public law. Public law is often said to include not only things like administrative law, constitutional law, and human rights, but also criminal law.
>
> #### Private law
>
> Duties owed to or by individuals (including corporate individuals like companies) are generally matters of private law. Private law includes (among other things) tort, contract, land, and equity. Company law is mainly private because it concerns relations between private people (a company is a legal person, as opposed to a natural person) rather than the state.
>
> Figure 2.12 offers a simple summary of this categorisation of law in England & Wales.

The division between public and private law is not always clear-cut; for example, EU law was a hybrid, as it covered relations between individuals, relations between states, and relations between individuals and the state.

The importance of distinction between public and private law can be illustrated by Example 2, which illustrates the differences in approach in the two areas.

Example 2

Police duties

Between 1975 and 1980, 13 young women were murdered (plus eight attempted murders) by the notorious 'Yorkshire Ripper'. By 1980 it was clear from the evidence available that the Yorkshire Ripper was a man called Peter Sutcliffe, and that it was likely he would kill more young women if not apprehended. In April 1980, he was arrested on a driving offence and released, awaiting trial. In November 1980, in Leeds, he murdered his last victim, Jacqueline Hill. He was arrested and charged with murder only in January 1981. It was claimed that the police had not competently investigated the murders, and that, had they done so, Jacqueline Hill would not have been murdered.

Jacqueline Hill's family sued the police in the civil courts for damages in the tort of negligence. This was a private law claim. The House of Lords[41] confirmed that no duty of care in negligence was owed by the police to the general public as potential victims of crime, because this would impose prohibitively demanding burdens on police officers. This is now called 'the Hill Principle'. When you study negligence in Tort, you will read that this is a developing area of law, where negligence claims are now possible in narrow circumstances, and also where the Human Rights Act is engaged.

By contrast, it has long been the case that police officers owe a duty to the general public to enforce the criminal law.[42] This is enforceable in public law, by 'judicial review' of the relevant police authority by the courts. So if the chief police officer concerned has acted unreasonably, someone with an interest can make a complaint to the Administrative Court (a specialist court within the High Court—see Chapter 3 for discussion of courts in England & Wales).

2.7.2 **Civil law and criminal law**

The distinction between criminal law and civil law is also central to English law (and many other systems worldwide). It impacts on people's rights and obligations, and on how both are enforced in courts.

Criminal law is a type of public law concerning the right of the state to sanction individuals (and sometimes other legal persons like companies). There are around 9,000 criminal offences in English law. Civil law (in this sense) concerns the rights that individuals (again including companies, etc.) have against each other—it does not directly involve the state.

There is a tendency to believe that most law is criminal in scope, probably because most media coverage of law and most legal dramas concern the criminal law. However, the majority (in terms of pages of legislation) of law is civil. In terms of the number of actions commenced each year, court statistics show that roughly the same number of civil claims is made every year as defendants proceeded against in criminal law.

This distinction is important in your understanding of the court system. You may encounter the terms 'civil jurisdiction' and 'criminal jurisdiction'. This refers to the (mainly) separate courts that administer justice in each area. We look at this in more detail in Chapter 3.

The same set of facts can create liabilities in both areas of law, as illustrated in Example 3.

Example 3

If Ben has stolen a car, and sold it to John, the state (represented by the Crown Prosecution Service—CPS) can prosecute Ben in criminal law under the Theft Act 1968.[43] Then, usually after the prosecution has run its course, John can make a civil claim against Ben in contract, under the Sale of Goods Act 1979,[44] because Ben did not have a right to sell the car.

Table 2.5 sets out some important differences between criminal law and civil law.

---

[41] *Hill v Chief Constable of West Yorkshire* [1987] UKHL 12 (note: the chief constable is named defendant here because he is formally held to be responsible for the actions of any police officer in his authority).

[42] *R v Commissioner of Police of the Metropolis, ex parte Blackburn* [1968] 2 QB 118.

[43] Theft Act 1968, s. 1(1).   [44] Sale of Goods Act 1979, s. 12.

Table 2.5 Key contrasts between criminal and civil law in England & Wales

	Criminal	Civil
Nature of proceedings	**A criminal case is called a prosecution.**	**A civil case is called an action or claim.**
Who will initiate proceedings?	A prosecution will normally be started by the state in the form of the police arresting and charging someone. The victim of a crime does not normally commence proceedings. The prosecution will be continued or discontinued by the CPS (lawyers who are civil servants independent of the police).	Proceedings are commenced by the victim—the person who has suffered damage. Disputes can also involve wills or family matters.
The parties	The CPS is called the 'prosecution'; the accused is called the 'defendant'. See 3.1 for an explanation of these terms.	The person who makes the claim is referred to as the 'claimant' (prior to 1998, the 'plaintiff'), and the person against whom the claim is made is called the respondent. See 3.1.1 for an explanation of these terms.
Standard of proof	Beyond all reasonable doubt: the prosecution will do this by providing evidence of each of the necessary elements of the offence.	On the balance of probabilities.
Onus (or burden) of proof	CPS/prosecution.	Claimant.
Objective of proceedings	Punishment (and sometimes rehabilitation).	The claimant will normally seek compensation for the losses suffered (though in intentional torts, e.g. deceit and defamation, damages may be punitive).
Defendant will be . . .	Guilty: defendant will be convicted. Not guilty: defendant will be acquitted.	Liable. Not liable: case will be dismissed.
Possible outcome	A defendant who is found guilty will be sentenced to e.g. imprisonment, a fine, or a community sentence (e.g. a community penalty order).	A remedy (e.g. damages) will be given to the claimant.

2.8 Legal systems around the world

We started this chapter by asking what a 'legal system' is. A lawyer should be conscious that their colleagues from other countries have their own legal cultures and backgrounds. They should also be aware that legal procedures and rules in other countries may come from a very different tradition to their own. An important theme here is the 'legal tradition' of a legal system. Broadly speaking there are three main legal traditions, with many jurisdictions having hybrids. Around a quarter of the World's legal systems are 'common law', and half are 'civil law' with most of the remainder being religious (below 10 per cent) or hybrid (around 15 per cent) in character.[45]

A disproportionately high number of G20 states are 'common law'. In the US, for instance, however strongly the founding fathers of the US desired independence, they felt that the

[45] *World Factbook 2015–16*, Central Intelligence Agency, United States Directorate of Intelligence, 2016.

legal system of England was suitable at both state and federal levels. Figure 2.4 shows states featuring 'common law' or 'civil law' legal systems, and also shows—for the purposes of comparison—countries formerly associated with the British Empire.

2.8.1 Background

It is important to understand why these two traditions grew as they did. Unlike common law jurisdictions, civil law (sometimes called, 'civilian') jurisdictions, including, for example, France and Germany, tend not to have binding case law. They do, of course, have litigation, but cases do not coalesce into a self-standing system of legal principles.

Instead civil law systems usually adopt one or more comprehensive 'codes' which attempt to define all the rules in a given area. This model, including much of the content of early civil codes, was derived from Roman law, which originated in Ancient Rome.

There is a reluctance in continental Europe to allow judges to develop a leading role in law-making, borne of the revolutions of Europe from the late-18th to mid-19th centuries. Judges were seen as protectors of the ancient regime, so their role was largely restricted to deciding on the merits of the cases before them, rather than developing the law. Instead law-making was seen as the exclusive preserve of legislators. The judiciary was to be given as little room for manoeuvre as possible. This is of course familiar, as it reflects the ideal of the Separation of Powers as defined by Montesquieu.

Civil law jurisdictions also normally use constitutional legislation stating overriding aims and principles by which all subsequent behaviour (including legislation) is to be measured. There is an increasing tendency in common law states (even the UK) for law in some areas to be codified into statutes more resembling civilian codes.

There are therefore clear differences to be drawn between the two types of system. These are set out in Table 2.6.

Although it is common to refer to a common/civil law dichotomy, in reality there is a spectrum of jurisdictions.

England & Wales is probably the jurisdiction with the most extreme common law attributes. In some areas of law, such as negligence or the formation of contracts, there is almost total reliance on binding judge-made law, with little or no impact from statutes or codes. Why? One reason may be that it is so old. The development of the English legal system largely pre-dated the rediscovery of Roman law in Continental Europe.

By contrast, France has an almost entirely codified system. Its code is derived from the *Code Napoleon* (and prior to that the Roman *Corpus Juris Civilis*), created by Napoleon Bonaparte in 1804, and still used in updated form today. To reinforce this, the French *Cour de Cassation*, its supreme court, is not permitted to give decisions supported by written judgments referring to the facts of a case, so there is little scope for the formation of a body of binding or persuasive case law in that jurisdiction.

In between these two extremes, the US, and most of the states comprising it,[46] inherited a heavy reliance on common law and equity. Indeed the states' constitutions expressly refer to pre-independence jurisprudence[47] as surviving. The US has a common law system but

---

[46] Strictly speaking, some of these states are commonwealths, but we will use the generic term, 'states', in this book.

[47] In the context of this chapter, the term 'jurisprudence' will be used to describe a body of case law, rather than the study of legal theory.

Table 2.6 Contrasting features of common and civil law systems

	Common law	Civil (or 'civilian') law
Notable jurisdictions	England & Wales, the US, Australia.	France, Germany, Russia, China.
Legislation & constitutional codes	Legislation grows organically to meet demands and deal with problems as they arise. This means that in a given area there may be many relevant statutes.	Tends to be comprehensive and the subject of continual refinement. The codes are continuously updated and legislators aim to all claims that might be tried in that area of law (e.g. criminal law),
Case law	A system of binding judicial precedent which generates a body of binding case law. Principles of law stated in senior courts will bind many later judges.	No formal role for case law. There is a doctrine of *jurisprudence constant* (whereby a sequence of consistent cases could build an identifiable body of persuasive law to supplement codes) in some jurisdictions (e.g. Germany).
Development	Body of case law built up over time, often from English jurisprudence.	Derived from Roman *Corpus Juris Civilis* and reinterpretations.
Conduct of litigation	Largely 'adversarial', with judge as arbiter. Lawyers drive litigation. They assemble evidence, put together opposing arguments (e.g. a claim or defence and counterclaim in civil law), question and cross-examine witnesses. The judge (occasionally a jury) reaches a decision and then gives a judgment based on the lawyers' arguments.	Largely 'inquisitorial', with judge (in France, the *juge d'instruction*) finding evidence, interrogating witnesses, questioning either side, examining the evidence. The judge investigates the matter fully; the lawyer merely presents arguments when invited to do so by the judge.

with a codified Constitution (of 1789), which incorporates the Bill of Rights (of 1791). The Constitution forms a codified cornerstone on which much US jurisprudence is built. This gives a 'civilian' flavour even to binding US case law.

Another hybrid is the jurisprudence of the European Court of Justice (ECJ), the decisions of which are binding on the courts of member states (almost all of which are 'civil law' jurisdictions), in order to bring consistency to the implementation of EU law.

There are other types of legal system. The most significant by number are those in the Islamic tradition. Islamic law is called 'sharia' and is derived from religious principles. Most countries where there is a Muslim majority adopt various aspects of sharia. The degree of adoption varies, but adherence to sharia has often been in place for many centuries. In its strictest sense, sharia is a divine, not human, law. Its interpretation by humans is called 'fiqh'. As globalisation is embedded, the compatibility of sharia and secular 'western' jurisprudence has become more than an academic debate, and has led to practical issues. These include whether a country with sharia law can legitimately purport to surrender jurisdiction to international institutions like the International Court of Justice, or the degree to which, internally, a country with sharia law can adopt 'western' rules on trade. One manifestation of this is the development of Islamic financial institutions and products—which are compatible with the sharia prohibition on certain

Table 2.7 States, categorised by type of legal system, in order of GDP (G20 states are named)

Common law systems	Civil law systems	Hybrid/other
Around 40 states, including: US (excl. Louisiana—civil), UK (excl. Scotland—hybrid), Canada (excl. Quebec—hybrid), India, Australia.	Around 150 states, including: China, Japan, Germany, France, South Korea, Brazil, Italy, Russia, Mexico, South Korea, Turkey, Indonesia, Argentina.	Around 20 states, including: Saudi Arabia (Islamic), South Africa (hybrid).

investment techniques and markets. Another issue is the degree to which enforcement of rules can entail coercion or retributive violence. Whilst some countries (notably Saudi Arabia and parts of Afghanistan) adopt sharia widely across their competence, others (e.g. Turkey) have chosen to adopt a secular approach. Religious law is not an entirely Islamic phenomenon—the Vatican and Israel adopt elements of religious law alongside secular legal rules.

We will see at 3.7.2 that individuals can chose to abide by sharia law in arbitration. This is not the same as sharia law being part of the relevant legal system, e.g. the UK's, because the determinations of such forums are enforceable by operation of the Arbitration Act 1996, and only insofar as they are not inconsistent with UK law.

There are other legal traditions. The Kyrgyzstan system, for example, places an emphasis on customary law. China, Cuba, Vietnam, and North Korea purport to employ socialist law, which is adapted from the civil law tradition; although in some cases these rules have been adapted by economic and political reforms.

Look at Figure 2.4 to get a sense of the balance between these systems. While the predominant type of system is civil, if we look at *which* systems are common law, a disproportionate amount are economically significant. This is partly because, during the industrial revolution, many of the main trading nations were at some stage part of the British Empire. Table 2.7 sets out which of the G20 states adhere to each system. To put this in practical context, one survey[48] found that 40 per cent of international contracts with arbitration clauses gave English law as the preferred governing law for the contract, and 22 per cent gave a US state.

> **Essential debate**
>
> You have now read about the different legal traditions around the world. Focusing on the two predominant types, which do *you* think most promotes the Rule of Law?

2.9 Summary of important terms in English law

In this section we summarise some of the different concepts introduced in this chapter; in particular, the various senses in which the expressions, 'common law', and 'civil law' are used. These two terms are vital for an English lawyer. In this book we generally use the terms 'common law' and 'civil law' to describe the nature of a legal system, although there are other ways of using both expressions, if the context requires. Lawyers need to be careful to make clear in which context they are referring to such terms.

---

[48] Queen Mary University, 2010 International Arbitration Survey.

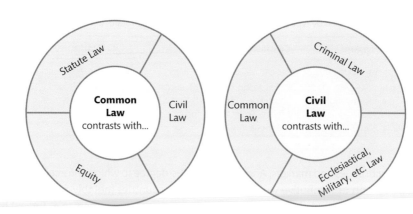

Figure 2.13 Different uses of the terms, 'common law' and 'civil law'

'Common law' is used:

- to differentiate English-based legal systems that use a doctrine of precedent, and civil law systems that use a more codified body of law;
- to distinguish case law (as 'common law') from statute law within England & Wales; and
- to make a distinction between the majority of case law from case law drawing on equitable principles.

'Civil law' is used:

- (as above) to differentiate English-based legal systems that use a doctrine of precedent, and civil law systems that use a more codified body of law;
- to distinguish between law involving criminal liability and other areas of law ('civil law'); and
- to refer to law that is not dedicated to self-governing areas of endeavour (military/ ecclesiastical).

Figure 2.13 summarises the different senses in which these terms are employed, by showing the terms with which they are contrasted in different contexts.

➕ Summary

- A legal system is a body of institutions that makes, executes, and resolves disputes in a jurisdiction.
- Law in England & Wales comes from a variety of sources.
- The 'legal system' is a difficult concept to pin down in the British context. In reality there are several legal systems each involving different geographical entities.
- Lawyers and legal academics categorise the English legal system in various ways. Each brings out important elements and concepts relating to its operation.
- To understand how and why case law operates as it does, we need to look at its historical development.
- To understand the importance of statutes, again, we need to look at their historical development.
- EU law occupies a distinctive place in the English legal system, which will be significantly changed once Brexit is fully implemented (exit from the EU started this process).
- International law is based on consent but in reality it normally imposes rules on a state which are enforceable by political pressure.
- Figure 2.14 summarises the interaction between important events in the political and legal history of England and related jurisdictions. You may wish to use it as a reference source throughout the legal systems chapters.

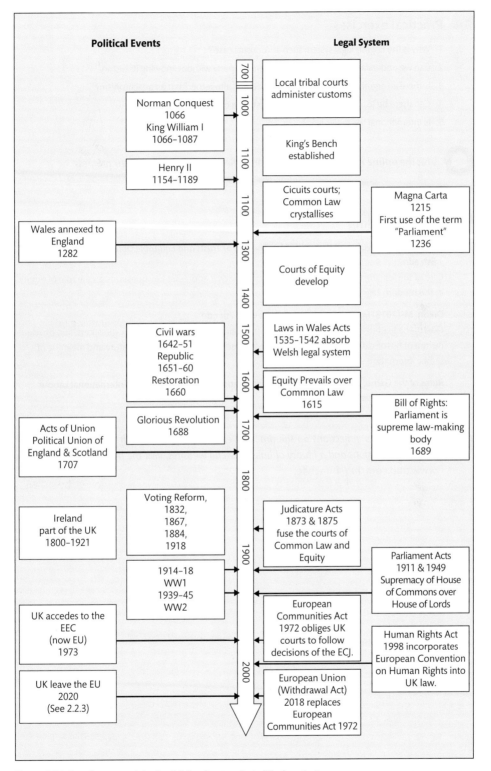

Figure 2.14 Development of the English legal system in political context

Practical exercises

1. Why is the English legal system such an 'unusual case'?

2. Can we understand the English legal system properly without knowing its history?

3. Is there an argument for dispensing with 'equity' altogether? Is it an anachronism?

4. Can there be too much legislation on the statute books?

5. Is International law really 'law'?

*Visit the **online resources** for the authors' reflections and to check your progress.*

Further reading

Pearce, R., Stevens, J., and Barr, W. (2010) *The Law of Trusts and Equitable Obligations.* **Oxford: OUP, 5th edn**
One of the leading modern texts on the law of equity, it addresses key questions on the role of equity in the modern English legal system.

Dixon, M. (2013) *International Law.* **Oxford: OUP, 7th edn**
One of the leading modern texts on public international law. It addresses key questions, and provides pertinent historical and recent examples of detailed jurisprudence on the nature and meaning of public international law.

Rules of the Game: a brief introduction to International Labour Standards, International Labour Office, ILO, revised edn, 2014

*For the authors' reflections on the practical exercises, additional self-test questions, sample interview questions and a library of links to useful websites, visit the free **online resources** at www.oup.com/he/slorach4e.*

3 The court system of England & Wales

Learning objectives

After studying this chapter you should be able to:

- Discuss key themes in the English court system.
- Be familiar with the structure of the court system in sufficient depth to understand the background to case law.
- Understand in outline the criminal and civil court systems, including trial courts and appeals courts.
- Develop an awareness of other courts and tribunals important to the law of England & Wales.

Introduction

The primary function of a court is to administer the law. Any law-making role (as discussed in Chapters 2 and 4) is important, but secondary. Real people need to have real disputes resolved.

There are over 450 different courts at various levels in England & Wales, as well as numerous tribunals and other quasi-judicial bodies. To understand how they administer the law and to give context to the law they create, it is vital to understand the structure of the court system.

Good litigation lawyers will be able to navigate their way through labyrinthine rules of legal proceedings. At this stage in your studies you may not yet have knowledge of these intricacies. However, in this context it is the bigger picture of the system, rather than specific rules, that matters. Considering the wider picture provides a firm and workable foundation for the study of the law. To assist in providing this picture, occasionally some generalisations have been made regarding litigation or court procedure in this chapter; so be aware that some themes covered may involve greater complexity, and may also be, over time, the subject of reform.

First, this chapter examines important themes and concepts that are essential for understanding the structure and mechanics of courts in general, and English courts in particular. We then look at English criminal and civil courts in detail. The chapter ends with an examination of courts and other forums that have significance in the English legal system but which are not part of the court system in England & Wales. You can refer to the Appendix for a summary of the courts discussed with key facts.

3.1 Key themes

Before we go any further with the English court system it would be helpful to make sure you have grasped some key elements:

- the common law 'adversarial' system (and the comparative system in civil law jurisdictions);
- civil vs criminal litigation;
- trial vs appellate courts (including a distinction between facts and law); and
- superior vs inferior courts.

> ### ⓘ Essential explanation
> #### Parties to the case, and the case name
>
> The most important people in any given case are the parties, called the 'litigants'. While lawyers will consider legal principles deriving from a case, it is the parties who are directly affected by the decision.
>
> At 2.3.2 we saw that in the civil jurisdiction, the parties are called the 'claimant' and the 'respondent', but in criminal trials, the equivalents are the 'prosecution' (usually the Crown, represented by the Crown Prosecution Service), and the 'defendant'.
>
> The case name will usually derive from the parties, so:
>
> - A civil case is named after the parties concerned, for example *Donoghue* v *Stevenson*.[1] Sometimes more than one party is claiming or defending the claim. Here, the full case name will have the names of all the parties on each side, often abbreviated to 'and others'. Another example of a civil case name is *Re Vandervell (No. 2)*.[2] This type of case is about ('re') something, such as a trust settlement, a will, or a patent application. Sometimes only one party is involved, such as in a procedural application to court.
> - A criminal case name will normally take the form *R* v *Smith*.[3] 'R' is the Crown, and Morgan Smith was the defendant. Some older criminal cases will use the name of the prosecuting police officer, such as *Fisher* v *Bell*.[4]
> - In public law, a judicial review of the actions of a state body[5] will also mirror the parties' names. In Chapter 4[6] we briefly examine an example in connection with the Hunting Act, *R (Countryside Alliance and others)* v *Attorney General and another*,[7] meaning the Crown, on behalf of the Countryside Alliance (and others), against the Attorney General.

3.1.1 The common law 'adversarial' system

Courts reflect the legal system in which they occupy such an important role. This is most especially true 'at trial'—i.e. at first instance, when the facts of a case are heard and usually settled (see 3.1.3). We saw at 2.8.1 that common law systems use generally uncodified bodies of law, whereas civil law systems use continuously updated legal codes. The role of judges partly reflects this.

---

[1] *Donoghue (or M'Alister)* v *Stevenson* [1932] AC 562, which is discussed in depth in Chapter 5 on case law and in Chapter 7 on reading and understanding law.

[2] *Re Vandervell (No. 2)* [1974] Ch 269.

[3] *R* v *Smith (Morgan)* [2001] 1 AC 146, discussed in Chapter 4 on legislation.

[4] *Fisher* v *Bell* [1961] 1 QB 394.   [5] Examined briefly at 1.6.2.   [6] At 4.4.3.1.

[7] *R (Countryside Alliance and others)* v *Attorney General and another, R (Derwin and others)* v *Same* [2007] UKHL 52.

Consider the following scenarios: Jack White has been charged with murder and is on trial in the Old Bailey (the Central London Criminal Court). Jacques LeBlanc has been charged with murder and is on trial in an Assize Court in Paris.

The Crown Prosecution Service and Jack White's lawyers find evidence to argue either side of the trial, to convince the jury of his guilt or innocence, in accordance with the law of homicide, an amalgam of the case law relating to murder and two statutes relating to defences. The judge will hear these arguments to direct the jury and decide on sentencing.

The French investigating judges will bring formal charges, investigate the circumstances of Jacques LeBlanc's actions, and present their findings in court, with evidence favouring both sides. The judge or judges can interview people and appoint experts among other things. Investigations can take years, but trials can be brief. Witnesses are called and evidence is rehearsed in court. The lawyers will argue according to Article 215-4 of the Penal Code of France. There is no case law to guide judges.

The experiences of Jack White and Jacques LeBlanc are very different and illustrate some of the differences between civil law and common law jurisdictions. England's is a typical common law 'adversarial' system, where litigation is driven more by the parties than by the judiciary.

So, in common law jurisdictions, the role of judges is to moderate the adversaries in a case, and in a civil law system the judge's role is to establish the facts and apply the provisions of a code. There are, of course, advantages to both systems. Proponents of the civil law idiom would generally say that theirs is a more streamlined, efficient, method of determining a just outcome; 'common law' proponents would say that the adversarial system encourages a rigorous examination of facts and law, and is less bureaucratic. Trials in common law jurisdictions tend to be short and involve intensive cross-examination and legal argument by lawyers; in civil law jurisdictions they are often drawn out and lawyers' roles in court will often be confined to short closing statements. As we will see, the English system, whilst adversarial, has been reformed continually over the last few decades, to promote efficient administration of justice and minimise the stresses of litigation. Looking at the Rule of Law index referred to at 1.5.4.3, there does not seem to be an appreciable bias in favour of civil or common law systems in the areas of access to civil and criminal justice, beyond the general trends in relation to the Rule of Law as a whole.[8]

The English system, then, is a common law system, and its court structure and procedure reflects this.

3.1.2 Civil vs criminal litigation

In England & Wales (with some exceptions) criminal trials (and appeals) are usually conducted in different courts from those in which civil proceedings occur. The two types of law are dealt with by court systems which, for the most part, operate independently from each other. These courts have different expertise and, because of the fundamental importance of protecting individual liberty in criminal trials, different procedures. In addition, the civil system includes largely self-contained courts specialising in family and administrative law; areas of law you will come to later in your studies.

In Chapter 2 we explored basic differences between criminal and civil law. The principal objectives of the criminal courts are to decide guilt or innocence according to the criminal law, and then to sanction the wrong-doer. In contrast, the principal objectives of the civil

---

[8] http://worldjusticeproject.org/rule-of-law-index.

courts are to decide disputes between members of society, or between the state and individuals, and to grant an appropriate remedy (usually compensation) to the victim.

The same event, such as a road accident, may lead to proceedings both in the criminal courts (e.g. to punish the careless motorist) and in the civil courts (to compensate the injured pedestrian). Normally the civil case will wait until the criminal proceedings are concluded.

Although it is helpful—as an introductory generalisation—to say that there are two largely distinct streams of court (civil and criminal), some courts do in fact have both criminal and civil jurisdictions. In fact, only the Crown Court (exclusively criminal) and County Court (exclusively civil) conform entirely to this generalisation—even the Family Court has a limited criminal jurisdiction; other courts, like the Court of Appeal, do consider both types of proceeding, but often with separate procedures and administration.

3.1.3 **Trial courts vs appellate courts**

3.1.3.1 The importance of appeals

Another distinction is between a trial (or 'first instance') court, and an appeal (or 'appellate') court.

Essential explanation

Appeal

An important aspect of the Rule of Law is recognition that even courts can make errors. There must be an avenue to correct miscarriages of justice where, for instance, the judge or magistrates misapplied the law, or gave the wrong sentence or remedy. Because adjudicating on legal issues is generally the preserve of the court system, this must comprise access to a different court.

When litigants disagree with a decision of a court, they may try to appeal to a higher court, if they have the resources and a strong enough argument.

This litigant is called the 'appellant' (whether he was claimant, prosecution, or defendant in the case), and the party seeking to prevent the success of the appeal is called the 'respondent'.

Trial courts are contrasted with courts of 'appeal', of which *the* Court of Appeal is only one. In most legal systems there are trial courts, then one or two levels of appeal court (e.g. the Court of Appeal of England & Wales), and finally a supreme court (of which the UK Supreme Court, examined later, is an example). Figure 3.1 summarises this generalised appeals system. There are a number of different procedures to follow depending on the court involved.

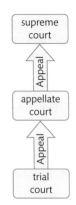

Figure 3.1 Generic appeals system

Normally a trial court will apply law to the facts, deciding mainly on issues of fact or evidence, whereas an appeal court will normally consider appeals from one or other party, to decide whether to reverse the decision of the lower court by interpreting the law differently.

Under most circumstances, litigants will need permission (sometimes called 'leave') to appeal. Normally they will seek leave from the court which handed down the initial decision, and if this is refused, they may instead, under certain conditions, seek leave from the potential appeal court. Frivolous appeals need to be discouraged as they would be expensive and would clog up the court system—for example some appellants may be unwilling to accept the law as it stands, even in cases where the law is well established.

Courts of first instance are where all trials and cases start, and most (around 99.5 per cent) stop. Her Majesty's Courts and Tribunals Service[9] statistics state that the total number of first instance proceedings commenced (most of which will settle or not be tried in full) is annually around 3 million, evenly split between criminal and civil proceedings. The total number of appeals, in any of the courts of appeal, is normally around 26,000 (around 0.5 per cent). This statistic can be viewed in two ways. One might be that 99.5 per cent of proceedings reach a satisfactory conclusion at first instance. A contrasting view would be that for most litigants it is prohibitively expensive to seek justice beyond the initial trial stage.

This generic structure does reflect most jurisdictions. Here we summarise the court stuctures of three significant states; note that some simplifications have been made for clarity:

- In the United States, this structure is reflected through most of the 50 state court systems, with three, and sometimes four, levels of court to the state Supreme Court. Further appeals are to federal courts such as the US Supreme Court. However there is a separate federal court system with a limited US-wide jurisdiction, again culminating in the US Supreme Court.

- In France, the mainstream court system also has three levels, and, like England & Wales, different trial courts for different levels of criminal or civil wrong. However, there are entirely separate systems for administrative law and financial audit. At the top level, there are three courts; the *Cour de Cassation* (roughly equivalent to the UK Supreme Court); the *Conseil d'Etat* (for administrative cases), and the *Conseil Constitutionnel*, which deals with constitutional matters.

- In Germany, there is a four-tier system culminating in the Federal Court of Justice. The extra tier partly reflects the federal nature of Germany's constitution. Even more pervasively than in England & Wales there is a split between criminal, civil, and family courts. Again, like France, there are specialist courts. Like France, at the apex of the court system there is a constitutional court, the *Bundesverfassungsgericht*.

- The US Supreme Court, the *Conseil Constitutionnel*, and the *Bundesverfassungsgericht* all have powers of judicial review over the constitutionality of statutes made by their respective legislatures. This is not the case with the UK Supreme Court.

Note that the law reports—officially reported case law, comprising the bulk of case law studied by lawyers, judges, academics, and students—comprise but a tiny proportion of the overall number of court cases. Only a minority, including appeals, are reported.

---

[9] Ministry of Justice (2016) *Judicial and Court Statistics 2015*. Note that in this chapter the authors have used rounded figures; for precise figures, see the Ministry of Justice website.

3.1.3.2 Fact vs law

The distinction between facts and law is very important in the English legal system. To distinguish between questions of fact and questions of law we will use the case of *Donoghue* v *Stevenson*.[10] This may be the most famous case in the law of England & Wales. Paradoxically, it is a case that originated in Scotland. In Chapter 5 we examine the case in the context of case law.

> ## Example 1
>
> ### *Donoghue* v *Stevenson*
>
> In August 1928, Mrs May Donoghue joined a friend for a drink in the Wellmeadow Café in Wellmeadow Place, Paisley, Glasgow.
>
> The friend bought the drinks. The owner poured some ginger beer from an opaque bottle into Mrs Donoghue's glass (which may or may not have had some ice cream floating in it). She took some swigs and then poured the rest of the contents into her glass. To her horror the remains of a decomposing snail presented themselves to her. Mrs Donoghue later complained of stomach pains and shock, both a result of gastroenteritis.

On appeal, the House of Lords found that the manufacturer would owe a Duty of Care (that is, a duty not to carelessly cause harm) to the consumer. The case was later settled.

Further detail in relation to the case itself can be found at 7.1.5.1, which analyses extracts from the case report.

Questions of fact can be settled without considering the law. These questions can be resolved by looking at the evidence; in other words, issues such as 'was it ginger beer on its own or was it an "ice cream float"?', (a question that remains unresolved) and, 'did Mrs Donoghue suffer any loss of earnings as a result of the gastroenteritis?' These questions are almost exclusively the preserve of courts of first instance.

Unlike questions of fact, questions of law can be answered without reference to the evidence of a particular case, for instance, 'does a manufacturer owe a duty of care to consumers not to cause them unintended physical damage?' Indeed this was an important question of law dealt with in the *Donoghue* case.

When considering appeals, the facts of a case are generally settled in the first instance court. This means that it is very rare that a lawyer would call any witnesses before an appeal court. The higher courts normally accept the facts as found by the first instance court and then focus on issues of law. It is very difficult to show that a trial judge misunderstood or misused the facts presented to the court. It is easier to suggest that the judge misinterpreted the law. However, there may be situations where facts are disputed, so, occasionally, some appeal courts also have jurisdiction to reconsider disputed issues of fact.

Mixed questions of fact and law are the province of first instance courts, for instance, 'did Stevenson cause Mrs Donoghue actionable harm?' This question was never actually answered by a court. While the House of Lords did decide on the question of law, as discussed earlier, this was a preliminary point. The trial, in the Scottish trial court, to determine whether Mr Stevenson had actually caused Mrs Donoghue actionable harm, settled, partly because Mr Stevenson died before the trial commenced. Whole websites are devoted to the niceties of the case.[11]

---

[10] *Donoghue (or M'Alister)* v *Stevenson* [1932] AC 562 (HL).   [11] E.g. https://thepaisleysnail.blogspot.com/.

3.1.4 **Superior court vs inferior court**

Superior courts have unlimited jurisdiction—they can try cases from any part of the country and for claims of any value. Generally, they try the most important and difficult cases. They are: the Supreme Court, the Court of Appeal, the High Court, and the Crown Court. The 'Senior Courts' of England & Wales comprise the superior courts, not including the Supreme Court—the latter having UK-wide jurisdiction in most matters. Before 2005, different terminology was used—anyone researching this issue therefore needs to take care when reading materials from before that date.

All other courts, called inferior (or subordinate) courts, have limited geographical and financial jurisdiction, and deal with less important cases. But inferior courts are important as they try the vast majority of cases. These courts are the Family Court, the County Court, and the magistrates' courts.

3.2 Introduction to the courts of England & Wales

3.2.1 **The courts**

Now that we have the basic concepts, we can develop them. Figure 3.2 sets out the main courts in England & Wales.

Use Figure 3.2 to get a sense of the hierarchy of the courts, and their different names. Courts of High Court level and above are considered 'courts of record', which means that law reporters generally report some of the cases from these courts.

The modern court structure was created by the Supreme Court of Judicature Acts 1873 and 1875 (already encountered at 2.3.2.7). Prior to that, there were separate court systems of equity and common law, which made litigation artificially complex and difficult to access. Key themes in the development of common law and equity were examined at 2.3.2.

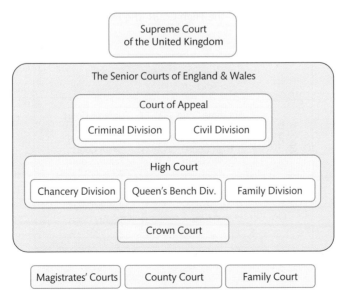

Figure 3.2 The courts of England & Wales

The court structure has seen some reform and streamlining in recent years, generally in an effort to increase access to justice. Highlights include those that follow:

- The replacement of the Lord Chancellor's Department with a Ministry of Justice (also formerly the Department for Constitutional Affairs).
- Bringing together the administration of all courts and most tribunals under one umbrella in Her Majesty's Courts and Tribunals Service.
- The Constitutional Reform Act 2005 removing archaic overlaps between the judiciary, the legislature, and the executive (see Chapters 1 and 4), and creating the Supreme Court of the UK. Its procedures are more open than those of its predecessor, the Appellate Committee of the House of Lords.
- The 1996 Woolf Reforms and the 2013 Jackson Reforms, which revolutionised the way civil claims were pursued in courts. Reflecting attempts to reduce red tape in society as a whole, their express aims included speeding up pre-trial procedure and reducing the cost of litigation—these are discussed further in the context of civil courts at 3.4.
- In 2013, the creation of the unified County Court and the new Family Court.

Her Majesty's Courts and Tribunals Service, an agency of the Ministry of Justice, is responsible for the operation of the courts. The Lord Chancellor (at the time of writing, Robert Buckland) is responsible for this department. Detailed information on the court system, including statistics, can be found on the Ministry of Justice's website.[12]

3.2.2 Jurisdiction and appeals

We can use two of the distinctions set out at 3.1 to create a simplified categorisation of the legal system: see Figure 3.3.

As a general rule, it is the superior courts which are the appellate courts, e.g. the High Court, the Court of Appeal, and the Supreme Court. Three courts have a dual role of being both a trial and an appellate court—the High Court, the Family Court, and the Crown Court.

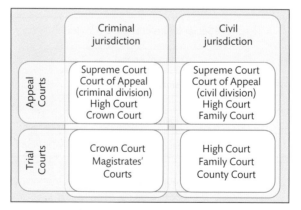

Figure 3.3 Thematic categorisation of courts in England & Wales

[12] http://www.justice.gov.uk/.

The Crown Court hears retrials and some appeals from the magistrates' courts; the High Court hears appeals on points of law from the magistrates' courts and, more commonly, appeals from the County Court. Often appellate courts have more than one judge, and first instance courts usually have a sole judge. Magistrates' courts usually use a bench of three lay magistrates.

It is possible (though rare, because complex cases are normally tried first in the High Court) for a civil case to begin in the County Court or Family Court at first instance and to conclude in the Supreme Court on appeal.

In the detailed description of the court system that follows, reference will be made to the Appendix, which comprises a summary of each of the key courts. The facts are for illustration and background only.

We now look separately at the criminal and civil jurisdictions.

3.3 The criminal courts of England & Wales

3.3.1 The pre-trial stage

To grasp the role of the two criminal trial courts, it is helpful to place the trial in context. While detailed criminal procedure is beyond the scope of this book, it is worth understanding how a criminal case comes to trial.

If the police have reason to believe a criminal offence has been committed, they will arrest the suspect and investigate by questioning them and any witnesses, and by obtaining evidence. There are other agencies with similar powers in specific areas (e.g. Her Majesty's Revenue & Customs, the Health and Safety Executive, or the trading standards departments of local authorities).

The Crown Prosecution Service (CPS), headed by the Director of Public Prosecutions (DPP), is responsible for prosecuting suspects. While the CPS is separate from the police, the two agencies work closely together. The CPS is comprised of around 9,000 employees, a third of whom are lawyers.[13] Solicitors from the CPS are responsible for collating the evidence on which they seek to rely as prosecutors. It is usually the CPS (rather than the police) that will issue a charge if it decides there is enough evidence to ensure a realistic prospect of conviction, and that issuing proceedings is in the public interest.

The controversy over how long a suspect can be held in custody without a charge being issued relates to this stage of proceedings. The current maximum period is three days for most suspects, and 14 days for terrorist offences.

⊛ Essential debate

UK governments have often pushed for extensions to the 14-day period for detention without charge. Between 2006 and 2011, detention without charge could be extended to 28 days. The then Prime Minister, Tony Blair, had originally pushed to extend this to 90 days. The case for such extensions has been backed by assertions that criminal investigations are sometimes complex and, especially in relation to suspected terrorists, sensitive evidence can be difficult to obtain.

By contrast, human rights groups such as Liberty and Amnesty maintain that 14 days is too long, even for complex charges relating to terrorist activities. What are your views on this?

---

[13] For information about the CPS, see http://www.cps.gov.uk.

Once the decision to charge has been taken, the charge will be read out and handed to a defendant in person by the police. Alternatively, if the defendant has not been held in custody, a summons will be sent to the defendant through the post—this method is normally used for driving offences. The defendant will then make their first appearance before the magistrates' court. The magistrates will ask the defendant to confirm their name and ask the prosecution to confirm the offence with which the defendant is charged. What happens next will depend on the classification of offence with which the defendant is charged.

3.3.2 Criminal courts of first instance

In 2018, 1.59 million individuals were dealt with by the criminal justice system, and 1.38 million prosecuted. Of these, 87 per cent were convicted. The criminal courts of first instance are the magistrates' courts (numbering 161 at the time of writing) and the Crown Court (one court, with 77 centres). Many offences, for example ignoring red traffic lights on a bicycle,[14] possession of cannabis,[15] etc., are often dealt with by the use of on-the-spot fines and cautions, issued by police, bypassing the court system altogether.

3.3.2.1 Mode of trial

The key factor determining the forum of the trial is the severity of the offence. Criminal offences are categorised as follows:

- Summary only offences, including driving without insurance and common assault. These are minor offences and must be dealt with in a magistrates' court. Approximately 78 per cent of English trials are summary.

- Indictable only offences, such as murder and robbery. These are serious offences and can be tried only in the Crown Court, because only the Crown Court has the power to sentence defendants accordingly. About 2 per cent of trials are for indictable offences.

- Either way offences, including theft and fraud. These are offences which are capable of being more or less serious depending upon the facts of the case. These can be dealt with in either a magistrates' court or the Crown Court. Theft[16] is the classic either way offence. A shopper snatching a magazine from a shop is committing a theft, as is a company's director using millions from his company's accounts for his own purposes. The former would likely be tried in a magistrates' court, and the latter in the Crown Court. Approximately 20 per cent of trials are for either way offences.

---

[14] Road Traffic Act 1988, s. 361.

[15] Possession of a Class B drug under the Misuse of Drugs Act 1971, s. 5(1), is subject to a warning or an on-the-spot fine of £80.

[16] Theft Act 1968, s. 1(1).

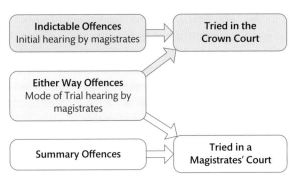

Figure 3.4 Criminal mode of trial

The process for determining the trial court is summarised in Figure 3.4.

For either way offences, there will be an allocation hearing in a magistrates' court, in which the magistrates will decide whether to retain jurisdiction or to commit the trial to the Crown Court. The magistrates base their decision on various guidelines, but most importantly whether the offence, if proved, is likely to lead to a sentence within their sentencing powers (up to six months' custodial sentence). While the magistrates decide on the venue for full trial, the defendant can overrule this decision if the magistrates wish to retain jurisdiction but the defendant elects a Crown Court trial. The defendant cannot elect to stay in a magistrates' court if the magistrates themselves decide the case to be suitable only for the Crown Court.

There is a perception among defendants that the jury in a Crown Court is more likely to acquit than the (allegedly) case-hardened magistrates. There is little evidence for this. Conviction rates in the magistrates courts are high but this is likely to be because the most basic offences are often easy to prove (e.g. speeding). There remains a notion that those who are truly innocent may be more determined to take their case to the higher court than others.

3.3.2.2 The magistrates' courts

The magistrates' courts dealt with 95 per cent[17] (1.2 million) of all criminal prosecutions in 2018. Offences dealt with by magistrates are less serious and more common than those dealt with by the Crown Court. That said, many trials in magistrates' courts fail to reach a full trial, either because the defendant changes their plea to 'guilty' (so-called 'cracked' trials) and goes straight to sentencing, or because the trial collapses, for example through lack of evidence. Many offences tried by magistrates are difficult to defend (e.g. motoring offences) so 98 per cent of magistrates' trials end in conviction. Magistrates' trials are split almost equally between motoring and non-motoring offences.

A panel of three magistrates adjudicates on both matters of fact and law. Most magistrates are 'lay people' who are not qualified lawyers. Although they are given training, lay magistrates are advised on the law by a legally qualified clerk. There are some professional

---

[17] Figures in this section taken from Ministry of Justice (16 May 2019) *Criminal court statistics quarterly: January to March 2019*, and accompanying overview tables, accessible at https://www.gov.uk/government/statistics/criminal-court-statistics-quarterly-january-to-march-2019.

magistrates, district judges, who deal with some more complex cases tried in magistrates' courts. In order to convict a defendant, the magistrates must be satisfied that the prosecution has proved beyond all reasonable doubt that the defendant committed the offence.

Controversially, there has been a programme of court closures over the last decade or so, with some commentators claiming that the administration of justice has been detrimentally affected. Between 2010 and 2019, more than half of the magistrates' courts have been closed, although the volume of trials has remained generally stable.

3.3.2.3 The Crown Court

The 77 Crown Court centres in England & Wales tried around 62,105 cases in 2018. Around 70 per cent of defendants who appear in the Crown Court plead guilty.[18] The Old Bailey is a Crown Court situated in London (formally, the Central Criminal Court), albeit one that often deals with high-profile crimes.

In the Crown Court a judge presides over proceedings, but innocence or guilt (on the facts of the case) is normally decided upon by a jury of 12 citizens chosen at random. The judge directs the jury on the law, but the jury are at liberty to make their own minds up on the verdict. Although the jury must normally reach a unanimous verdict, a majority verdict with one or two dissenters is permitted, if it is taking too long for the jury to reach a unanimous verdict.[19] The conviction rate for these more complex crimes is 80 per cent. Figure 3.5 illustrates the workload of the Crown Court—figures taken from 2018.

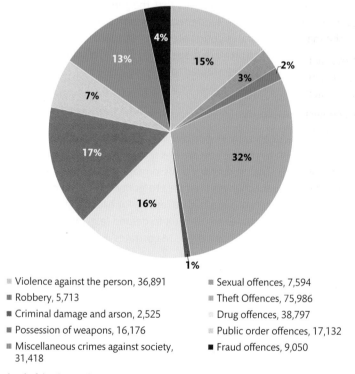

- Violence against the person, 36,891
- Robbery, 5,713
- Criminal damage and arson, 2,525
- Possession of weapons, 16,176
- Miscellaneous crimes against society, 31,418
- Sexual offences, 7,594
- Theft Offences, 75,986
- Drug offences, 38,797
- Public order offences, 17,132
- Fraud offences, 9,050

Figure 3.5 Caseload of the Crown Court, 2018

[18] Ministry of Justice (2019) *Criminal court statistics quarterly: January to March 2019, additional tables.*
[19] Juries Act 1974, s. 17.

3.3.2.4 The importance of the jury

Jury trial is based on the premise that everyone should have the right to be tried by their peers, rather than a judge who (the theory goes) may have a bias towards the establishment.

The jury system has been a valued aspect of the English legal system since the 12th century, and was an important part of Magna Carta in 1215. An alternative to juries was 'Trial by Ordeal'. For instance the defendant would be thrown into the water (often attached to millstones) and if she was guilty, she would sink. If God saw fit to spare the defendant, she was innocent. The law of England and the laws of physics worked together to produce 'justice'. The jury system became subject to abuse as monarchs reasserted their power. Juries were often composed of placemen or were threatened into agreeing the desired result. Only the advent of the English Civil War (1642–51) saw juries restored to their former status.

In a criminal case, the jury merely state that the accused is either guilty or not guilty, and give no reasons. The decision cannot be disputed, as the jury deliberate in secret, and is arrived at on the basis the jury choose, according to the evidence and their conscience. The judge then decides on the appropriate sentence.

The jury trial is a comparative rarity. Only around 8 per cent of all criminal cases are heard in the Crown Court. Of these, less than a third are jury trials, as around 70 per cent of defendants plead guilty without a full trial taking place.[20]

The expense and administrative difficulty of jury trials is significant. The continued use of juries is the subject of detailed, and often passionate, debate. There is extensive literature on the issue.[21] The many perceived problems include:

- in controversial trials (e.g. involving charges of rape) there is a perception that it is difficult for jurors to retain their objectivity;
- some research[22] shows that juries at certain Crown Court centres (e.g. Snaresbrook) have very low conviction rates, suggesting that at least some juries act contrary to objective standards of justice;
- juries may find factual and legal complexity challenging;
- there is a risk of 'jury-tampering'—a practice whereby the independence of jurors is compromised by threats or bribes; and
- a jury sits in secret, so their deliberations are not transparent.

Most commentators consider that the drawbacks of trial by jury are outweighed by the benefits. These include:

- the right of citizens to be tried by their 'peers', namely people like them, with similar values;

---

[20] *CPS Annual Report and Accounts 2015–16.*

[21] E.g. Thomas, C. (2010) *Are Juries Fair?* Ministry of Justice (February 2010).

[22] Thomas, C. (2010) *Are Juries Fair?* Ministry of Justice (February 2010).

- the perception that, even after having been directed by the judge as to the law, juries decide on the basis of 'natural justice';
- the ability of a jury to decide according to perceived common sense, but contrary to unhelpful precedent;
- the ability of the jury to focus on character and facts, and not legal niceties; and
- 800 years of largely successful history.

Because of the potential for problems with the use of juries, in 2003 the law was changed to allow a Crown Court trial by a judge without a jury in cases where there was likelihood of 'jury-tampering', but with safeguards for defendants.[23] The first non-jury criminal trial in the Crown Court commenced in January 2010,[24] after three previous jury trials collapsed (relating to a £1.75 million robbery from a warehouse at Heathrow). Non-jury Crown Court trials are rare—the detailed level of guidance issued by the CPS[25] illuminates the contentious and legally delicate nature of the procedure.

Trial by jury is a sensitive issue, and the recent changes have been controversial. The policy director of Liberty, Isabella Sankey, has said:

> The right to jury trial isn't just a hallowed principle but a practice that ensures that one class of people don't sit in judgement over another and the public have confidence in an open and representative justice system. What signal do we send to witnesses if the police can't even protect juries?[26]

3.3.3 **Criminal appeal courts**

3.3.3.1 Criminal appeals—introduction

If a defendant in a criminal case is convicted she may appeal against conviction. Alternatively, she can accept her conviction but appeal against the sentence if she feels it is unduly harsh. The prosecution may also appeal against the length of the sentence if they feel it is unduly lenient, but may not appeal against an acquittal. The CPS can appeal against decisions of higher courts that favour the defendant. Much depends on where the case was tried—in a magistrates' court or in the Crown Court. Permission (or 'leave') is not always required for a criminal appeal; by contrast, appeals in civil law cases usually require leave.

3.3.3.2 Appeals from magistrates' courts

Figure 3.6 shows the basics of the appeal procedure in relation to summary offences or either way offences tried in a magistrates' court. This section offers an explanation of the key concepts.

---

[23] Criminal Justice Act 2003, Part 7.

[24] *R v Peter Blake, John Twomey, Glenn Cameron and Barry Hibberd*. Trial for armed robbery and firearms offences, Central Criminal Court sitting at Royal Courts of Justice, London before Treacy J sitting without a jury, January–March 2010 (unreported at Crown Court, but reported on appeal as *R v Twomey* [2011] EWCA Crim 8).

[25] Crown Prosecution Service (2019) *Non-Jury Trials*. Available online at: https://www.cps.gov.uk/legal-guidance/non-jury-trials.

[26] BBC News 'First trial without jury approved' (18 June 2009). Available online at: http://news.bbc.co.uk/1/hi/uk/8106590.stm.

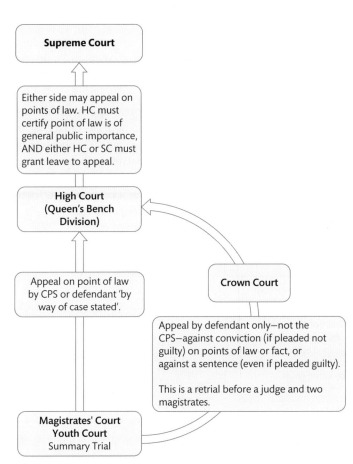

Figure 3.6 Appeals after trial in a magistrates' court

A retrial in a Crown Court (around 11,000 annually) is much more common than an appeal to the High Court (between 50 and 100 annually). The distinction is that in the former there is essentially a retrial of the case, including fresh consideration of factual evidence. In the latter, the Divisional Court of the High Court (Queen's Bench Division) hears an appeal on the ground that the magistrates were wrong in law. This is called an 'appeal by way of case stated', referring to the magistrates, who must state their case. 'Divisional Court' refers to the High Court in its appellate (multi-judge) incarnation. The system is skewed in favour of the defendant, as the CPS can only appeal via the High Court.

Any further appeals in relation to summary offences are rare. Appeals from the High Court (Queen's Bench Division) Divisional Court would be to the Supreme Court, and the appellant must be granted 'leave' to appeal. Often there are no such appeals in a given year.

Details of the High Court and the Supreme Court are set out in the Appendix. The Supreme Court took over the functions of the Appellate Committee of the House of Lords in 2009. You will encounter many cases from the House of Lords—they have the same status and authority as equivalents appealed in the UK Supreme Court.

3.3.3.3 Appeals from the Crown Court

Figure 3.7 shows the basics of the appeals procedure in relation to indictable offences or either way offences tried in the Crown Court. This section offers an explanation of the key concepts.

If a defendant has been tried in the Crown Court, he may appeal to the Court of Appeal, if he has obtained permission. An appeal may be on a point of law or fact, against conviction, or against the sentence imposed. In 2018 there were around 193 appeals against conviction and 1,218 against sentence.[27] While the Court of Appeal refuses to accept most applications for leave to appeal, a slim majority of defendants' appeals are successful.

Thereafter, either side may seek leave to appeal to the Supreme Court. There were only six such appeals from the Court of Appeal (Criminal Division) in 2018.[28]

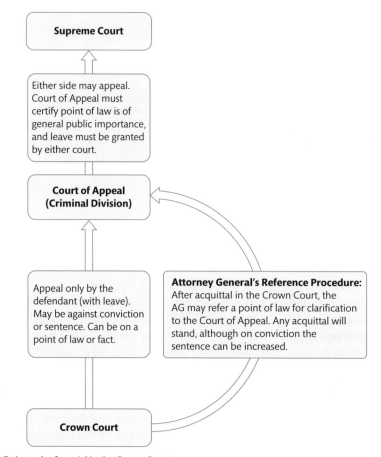

Figure 3.7 Appeals after trial in the Crown Court

[27] Ministry of Justice (2018) *Royal Courts of Justice Annual Tables—2018*, available online at: https://www.gov.uk/government/statistics/civil-justice-statistics-quarterly-january-to-march-2019.

[28] UK Supreme Court: *Supreme Court Annual Report 2017–18*, p. 29.

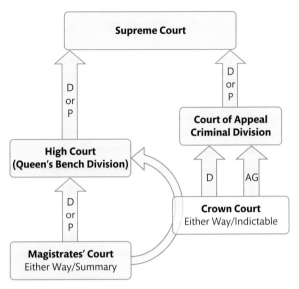

Figure 3.8 Criminal appeals—summary

3.3.3.4 Criminal appeals—summary

Depending on which court was the trial court, the route of appeal follows one of two main routes. The criminal appeal routes are summarised in Figure 3.8.

3.4 The civil courts of England & Wales

In Chapter 1 we saw that access to civil justice is a key indicator of the health of the Rule of Law in a country, and that the US in particular lags behind many other jurisdictions because of the expense of civil litigation.

The UK has a less pronounced, but still sizeable, deficit in access to civil justice. The main factors are the cost of civil litigation (e.g. pursuing a debt) along with the complexity, length, and stress of the process. In recent years, successive reforms have aimed to streamline civil procedure:

- In 1996 Lord Woolf's report *Access to Justice* triggered substantial reforms, via the Civil Procedure Rules[29] and the Access to Justice Act 1999. Central to these reforms is the 'overriding objective',[30] which emphasises putting the parties on an equal footing, saving expense, dealing with cases proportionately and expeditiously, and allocating court resources efficiently.

[29] Civil Procedure Rules 1998 (SI 1998/3132), under the Civil Procedure Act 1997.
[30] Civil Procedure Rules 1998, r. 1.1.

- More recently, a report by Sir Rupert Jackson has made further recommendations intended to promote access to justice at proportionate cost, the bulk of which came into effect in April 2013.[31]

- The Crime and Courts Act 2013[32] and the Children and Families Act 2014 transferred family litigation to a Family Court, the aim being to make family proceedings cheaper, quicker, and less daunting.

- The Crime and Courts Act 2013[33] also simplified the process of making a claim in the County Court, by unifying 173 county courts into one administrative entity, albeit still operating in the same locations as prior to the change.[34]

- Low-value claims are potentially going to be subject to a significant change if plans announced by the Her Majesty's Courts and Tribunals Service reach fruition. Drawing inspirations from the eBay disputes resolution procedure, there are proposals to create an online court for claims up to £25,000 designed for the first time to give litigants effective access to justice without having to incur the disproportionate cost of using lawyers. More details of this potentially revolutionary change can be found on the Judiciary website.

In the next section we examine the courts in which civil claims are made.

3.4.1 An outline of civil litigation

The civil courts of first instance are the County Court (which has over 100 hearing centres) and the High Court (which is based in the Royal Courts of Justice in London but has 137 district registries around the country). Proceedings relating to adoption, divorce, etc. are dealt with by a separate Family Court, usually sitting in buildings shared with other courts around the country. The seniority of judges largely reflects that in other civil courts.

As with criminal litigation, not all claims (let alone disputes) go to trial. In 2018, there were over 2 million claims issued in the County Court. Of these, only 14 per cent were defended, 9 per cent allocated to a 'track', and 3 per cent went to trial.[35]

In real terms, what do we mean by 'civil litigation'? The Ministry of Justice periodically releases statistics to give a sense of the civil courts' workload. Table 3.1[36] gives a summary of the workload of the High Court. In the County Court there is a significantly higher proportion of debt claims (because these are often less technical in nature than some other claims). Personal injury claims have increased in recent years possibly because of the expanding 'claims culture'. Civil litigation also includes family litigation, but remember that in the UK (as in some other jurisdictions like Germany) this is adjudicated by largely separate courts.

Proceedings (in non-family cases) are commenced by a claim form, issued by the relevant court, and served by the claimant on the defendant. If the defendant wishes to contest the claim, she must file a defence at the court and serve it on the claimant. The Woolf reforms attempted to incentivise parties to settle early, or to use Alternative Dispute Resolution (ADR)

---

[31] Jackson, Sir Rupert (2010) *Review of Civil Litigation Costs: Final Report*. London: TSO.

[32] Crime and Courts Act 2013, s. 17.   [33] Crime and Courts Act 2013, s. 17.

[34] Crime and Courts Act 2013, s. 17, Sch. 9; Civil Procedure (Amendment) Rules 2014 (SI 2014/407).

[35] Ministry of Justice (2019), *Ministry of Justice Quarterly Statistics January–March 2019*.

[36] Ministry of Justice (2019) *Ministry of Justice Quarterly Statistics January–March 2019, additional tables*.

Table 3.1 Proportion of claims in the High Court (Queen's Bench Division), by type: 2018

Type of claim	Proportion of claims in the High Court (QBD)
Personal injury	44%
Clinical negligence	22%
Debt action	2%
Breach of contract	6%
Professional negligence	6%
Defamation	6%
Tort (Nuisance & Trespass)	6%
Miscellaneous	9%

(see 3.7), to reduce the cost of civil claims and the burden on the court system. Since the reform, the number of proceedings has indeed declined. There is also now an obligation for parties to family proceedings to consider mediation (see 3.7.1) as an alternative prior to litigation.

If the case does come to trial, it will be before a judge, sitting alone. At the trial, the judge will listen to the evidence from both parties and to any legal arguments. He will then apply the law to the facts to decide whether or not the claimant has proved her claim on the balance of probabilities. The judge will award judgment (note the spelling of 'judgment' in this context) to either party, and the defendant will be found to be either liable or not. 'Guilty' is an unsuitable term in civil proceedings.

In a debt claim, the agreed sum is the main remedy, and in most other actions damages is the most common remedy. You may recall (from Chapter 2) that equitable remedies, such as injunctions, are often appropriate. The court decides who pays the legal costs of the matter. The losing party will usually be ordered to pay the winner's legal costs. Under the small claims procedure (see 3.4.1.4), the loser will only pay court fees, and both parties will normally bear their own costs. While costs are dealt with at the end of the trial, they loom over the proceedings from the start. The fear of paying substantial amounts in costs (not to forget protracted argument and worry) is a major factor in cases being settled or not even being commenced.

Here we describe each court, before examining the basis upon which the case is allocated to one of them.

3.4.1.1 The County Court

County courts were introduced in 1846 so that claims could be heard more quickly and cheaply without using the Queen's Bench (forerunner of the High Court). They deal with the bulk of civil actions—in most years, around 2 million claims are issued, around 97 per cent of civil claims. Since 2014 there has been one national County Court, with 173 County Court hearing centres;[37] previously each county court was administratively separate. While this change has streamlined administration, the physical courts and the judges sitting in those courts are roughly the same as under the pre-2014 system.

---

[37] Crime and Courts Act 2013, s. 17, Sch. 9; Civil Procedure (Amendment) Rules 2014 (SI 2014/407).

Most County Court claims take between six and 12 months from the issue of proceedings to a decision. The cost and expense of this still drawn-out process may help explain why the vast majority (around 90 per cent) settle before the decision is made.

3.4.1.2 The Family Court

In 2014, litigation concerning the protection of children, divorce petitions, violence remedies, and adoption was transferred out of the mainstream civil courts (and magistrates' courts) to a Family Court, so that litigants could be subject to a more open and comprehensible forum for settling disputes.[38] Applications will be made to the appropriate regional Family Court, which will then determine the appropriate seniority of judge, and location of proceedings. This is a procedure known as 'gatekeeping'. In keeping with changes in the court system as a whole, the aim is to make family proceedings cheaper, quicker, and less daunting. The Family Court usually sits in buildings shared with other courts around the country. The seniority of judges largely reflects that in other civil courts. Appeals will be either within the Family Court, or to the Court of Appeal.

3.4.1.3 The High Court

Only complex or higher-value cases are considered in the High Court. Although we have already encountered the High Court in its appellate jurisdiction, its main workload is as a court of first instance. The court is split according to the type of cases considered:

- The Queen's Bench Division: this considers claims in contract and tort, and also incorporates various specialised courts, for example the Commercial Court and the Technology and Construction Court. In 2018, 7,353 claims were issued in the Queen's Bench Division.[39]

- The Family Division: this considers a narrow class of family claims for which the Family Court does not have jurisdiction (e.g. wardship and international child abduction). In 2018, 930 proceedings were started in the Family Division.

- The Chancery Division: this deals with wills and probate, trusts, land and mortgage actions, company law, intellectual property, and bankruptcy. It derives its competence from the old courts of Chancery, the courts of Equity prior to the Judicature Acts. It also incorporates specialised courts, including the Court of Protection (persons under disability), the Patents Court, and the Companies Court. In 2018, 13,704 proceedings were started in the Chancery Division.

Only a small percentage of proceedings in the High Court reach a full trial or decision.

3.4.1.4 Choice of forum—civil claims

Where claimants (termed 'plaintiffs' until 1999) should issue their claim is mainly a matter of value, but also complexity. The Civil Procedure Rules make it clear that the County Court has unlimited jurisdiction to hear all tort and contract cases. Proceedings cannot be started in the

---

[38] Children and Families Act 2014.

[39] Ministry of Justice (2019), *Ministry of Justice Quarterly Statistics January–March 2019*.

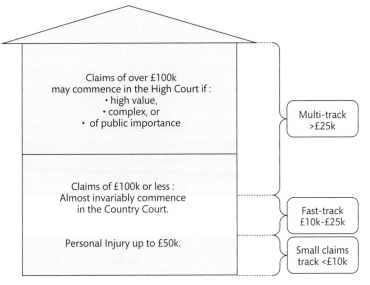

Figure 3.9 Courts of first instance—civil courts

High Court unless the value of the claim is more than £100,000, and *must* be started in the High Court at values over £350,000. The High Court will accept jurisdiction in cases of high value, of greater complexity, or of public importance. So, if the value of the case is £100,000 or less (£50,000 for personal injury), it must be started in the County Court. In some cases, the High Court has exclusive jurisdiction, but those types of cases are beyond the scope of this work. Around 90 per cent of civil claims settle before a trial formally starts.

The Woolf reforms introduced a track system, designed to make the formality and rigour of proceedings proportionate to the nature and size of the claim. A county court will normally allocate a claim of up to £10,000 to the small claims track. Typically, these claims concern consumer disputes and the court does not expect parties to be legally represented. Claims exceeding £10,000 and up to £25,000 are usually allocated to the fast track. While parties will usually have legal representation on this track, the court will tightly control costs, as well as the type and amount of evidence each party can rely on. In particular, the expectation is that a single joint expert should be used by the parties where expert evidence is necessary, and the trial must be conducted within one day (effectively five hours). Claims exceeding £25,000 are usually allocated to the multi-track.

As a claim cannot be started in the High Court unless it exceeds £100,000, all claims in that court are dealt with on the multi-track. The position is set out in Figure 3.9.

3.4.2 Civil appeals

3.4.2.1 Civil appeals—introduction

The civil appeals system was rationalised in 2000 as a result of the Woolf report.[40] Any detailed analysis of the rules and time limits associated with appeals is beyond the scope of this work. However, as a general principle, it is harder to obtain leave to appeal in civil (as distinct

---

[40] Lord Woolf (1996) *Access to Justice*. London: HMSO.

from criminal) litigation because liberty is not at stake. Leave will only be given either if the court considers that the appeal has a real prospect of success or if there is some other compelling reason why the appeal should be heard. This also prevents the system being clogged by implausible appeals.

3.4.2.2 The High Court

We have already looked at the High Court's role as a court of first instance. It is also an appeal court, in which the majority of appeals from the county court will be heard. Very occasionally, appeals from the County Court will be heard in the County Court, and, also very rarely, they may be heard in the Court of Appeal, bypassing the High Court.

An avenue through which the inferior courts can be supervised is the Administrative Court, part of the High Court Queen's Bench Division. Its main role is to supervise public bodies—including courts—by means of judicial review. This is not an appeals procedure. This is a key concept of public law. There are around 4,000 such cases received annually.

Appeals from the High Court will almost always be to the Court of Appeal (Civil Division), but very occasionally will be direct to the Supreme Court under the 'leapfrog' procedure. Some appeals will be made within the High Court. As you have probably realised, there are many variations on the general themes discussed in this chapter.

3.4.2.3 The Court of Appeal (Civil Division)

The Court of Appeal (Civil Division) deals with 1,000–1,500 cases annually (1,163 in 2018). Established by the Supreme Court of Judicature Act 1873, it replaced 12 different courts of appeal. It is exclusively an appeal court. It also considers appeals from the Employment Appeals Tribunal, which itself hears appeals from the Employment Tribunal (tribunals are discussed at 3.6.1).

County Court cases are very rarely appealed beyond the High Court to the Court of Appeal. In exceptional circumstances an appeal can be made straight from the County Court to the Court of Appeal.

3.4.2.4 The Supreme Court of the United Kingdom

The Supreme Court was created by Part 3 of the Constitutional Reform Act 2005, assuming the judicial functions previously held by the Appellate Committee of the House of Lords in October 2009. The change was made to formalise the Separation of Powers between the House of Lords in its legislative capacity and the Appellate Committee of the House of Lords. In reality, Lords who were not legally qualified ceased to take part in judicial matters in 1876.[41] Law Lords, by convention, did not vote at all, and did not speak on controversial matters, though this rule was not well-defined. The Constitutional Reform Act also gave the Supreme Court a separate building and administration commensurate with its status.

---

[41] Appellate Jurisdiction Act 1876.

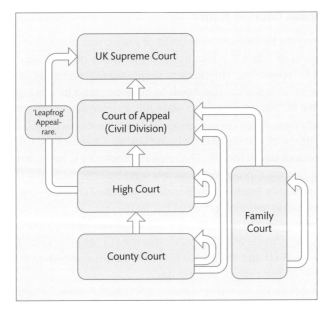

Figure 3.10 Civil appeals—summary

Very few cases go on to the Supreme Court, which is the ultimate court of appeal in the whole of the UK for civil matters and for criminal matters outside Scotland. It only deals with cases of real public importance—in 2018, 78 appeals were heard by the UK Supreme Court.[42] Permission to appeal is required, administered by the Supreme Court. Only around one third of applications are granted. Of the appeals themselves, around half are allowed.

The Supreme Court can hear appeals direct from the High Court under the 'leapfrog' procedure. This procedure is reserved for matters certified by the Supreme Court to be of general public importance—the type of issue which would ultimately be appealed from the Court of Appeal in any event. There are normally a few of these direct appeals from the High Court each year.

3.4.2.5 Civil appeals—summary

We have seen that the civil appeals system can operate at up to four levels. Figure 3.10 summarises the system. Remember that the majority of appeals conform to the 'ladder' of courts, and that appeals bypassing courts and appeals within single courts are rare.

3.5 Other important courts

The UK has many international commitments of different types. Some give supranational courts a degree of jurisdiction within the UK (and therefore England & Wales).

---

[42] Supreme Court of the UK (2019) *Annual Report and Accounts, 2018–2019*.

3.5.1 **The European Court of Justice**

The loss of sovereignty to the European Court of Justice was one of the main complaints made by proponents of Brexit.[43] Whilst the Court of Justice of the European Union (often referred to as the European Court of Justice or simply the ECJ) no longer has a formal role in the UK court system, its historical role needs to be understood by any legal scholar. Based in Luxembourg, the ECJ has jurisdiction to make rulings interpreting law emanating from EU institutions. Usually these rulings were then applied by our national courts. The ECJ has a very limited power to deal with actions brought by individuals. Chapter 4 discusses how decisions of the ECJ had force of law in the UK. The relevant procedure is not strictly an appeal, but instead is called a 'reference' procedure. This role was abolished when the UK left the EU.

The ECJ's role under the Treaty on the Functioning of the EU (TFEU—see 4.5) is 'to ensure that in the interpretation and application of the Treaties the law is observed'. Before Brexit, the EU had competence in the UK in relation to the single market (e.g. trade and competition) and some social policy. Article 267 TFEU states that the ECJ has jurisdiction to give rulings on interpretation of the TFEU and the acts of EU institutions (i.e. including EU legislation—see Chapter 4). For the UK, this ceased on Brexit day.

Until 'Brexit', English courts were able to make an 'Article 267 reference' to the ECJ on matters of EU law. There was no restriction on the level of court that could do this. A significant amount of important jurisprudence resulted from Court of Appeal and House of Lords/Supreme Court references. At the same time, magistrates' courts have jurisdiction in Sunday trading cases, and have made related Article 267 references to the ECJ.[44] The English court would formulate a question of law to be resolved by the ECJ (either the CJEU or the General Court—a 'lower court' set up to deal with the high caseload of the ECJ). The ECJ would then give judgment, and send an answer back to the relevant English court. The English court would then give a judgment. Example 2 gives a famous example of the Article 267 reference at work.

Example **2**

Mrs Murphy vs Sky

In 2006, a pub landlady in Portsmouth was convicted under criminal provisions of the Copyright, Designs and Patents Act 1988 for breach of copyright in using a Greek satellite channel to broadcast Premier League matches. Use of the Greek decoder was significantly cheaper than signing up to Sky's package. The landlady appealed to the High Court on the ground that the Act was discriminatory because it restricted the free movement of cross border services.[45]

The High Court sought a preliminary reference under Article 267 TFEU on matters of EU competition and intellectual property law set out in the TFEU[46]and various EU Directives.[47]

The ECJ decided[48] that the relevant provision of the Copyright, Designs and Patents Act 1988 was unenforceable. The High Court then quashed her conviction.[49]

---

[43] The UK left the EU on 31 January 2020 (as a result of a referendum of 23 June 2016). Any references to the EU and ECJ in this section should be read with this in mind. For more on the status of EU law, refer to Chapter 2, and in particular the Essential explanation of 'Brexit' at 2.2.3.

[44] E.g. Case C-145/88 *Torfaen Borough Council* [1989] ECR 3851.

[45] *Murphy* v *Media Protection Services* [2007] EWHC 3091 and [2008] EWHC 1666 (Admin).

[46] E.g. Art. 101 TFEU.   [47] E.g. Conditional Access Directive 98/84/EC.

[48] Joined Cases C-403/08 and C-429/08 *Football Association Premier League* v *QC Leisure* [2011] ECR I-9083.

[49] *Murphy* v *Media Protection Services Ltd* [2012] EWHC 466 (Admin).

3.5.2 **The European Court of Human Rights**

Based in Strasbourg, the European Court of Human Rights is set up under an international treaty: the European Convention on Human Rights (ECHR). These rights can be enforced in our national courts (under the Human Rights Act 1998—see 4.6). We have already touched upon the nature and status of this court in the context of international law at 2.2.3.

The Convention gives a citizen of a signatory state the right to apply to the European Court of Human Rights for an order for compensation on the grounds that there has been a breach by the state of the Convention, either directly (e.g. by the actions of the police), or indirectly (e.g. because the approach of the courts has constituted a lack of access to a fair trial under Article 6). However, this procedure is both expensive and lengthy, the latter due to the need first to exhaust domestic avenues of justice, and the logjam of cases before the European Court of Human Rights. Certain member states listed in Table 3.2 are the subject of a distressingly high proportion of applications in 2018.[50]

84 per cent of judgments find state violations. The UK government normally shows great attention to detail in observing judgments of the European Court of Human Rights. It is important to realise that the enforceability of the court's judgments is very much a matter of national governments opting in. This is because decisions are binding on states only as a matter of international law (see 2.2.3) under Article 1 ECHR and are not directly binding in domestic law. For instance, the UK government observed the initial judgment of the European Court of Human Rights[51] (under Article 6—right to a fair trial) that the government could not deport the controversial and radical Islamic cleric Abu Qatada to Jordan without specific guarantees from that country that evidence obtained through torture would not

Table 3.2 Number of applications to ECtHR by country: 2018

State	Applications	% applications	applications per 1,000 people
Russia	11,750	21%	0.085
Romania	8,500	15%	0.173
Ukraine	7,250	13%	0.071
Turkey	7,100	13%	0.083
Italy	4,050	7%	0.028
Azerbaijan	2,050	4%	0.032
Armenia	1,900	3%	0.056
Georgia	1,850	3%	0.027
Serbia	1,800	3%	0.304
Poland	1,300	2%	0.051
Other 27	8,800	16%	0.05
(of which, UK)	354	0.6%	0.005
Total	**56,350**	**100%**	

[50] European Court of Human Rights (2018) *Annual Report.*
[51] *Othman (Abu Qatada)* v *UK* App. no. 8139/09 (2012) 55 EHRR 1.

Table 3.3 ECHR – Most violated human rights by percentage of decisions

Article	Right	Percentage of violations found by the ECHR
6	Fair trial	24
3	Prohibition of torture	18
5	Liberty & security	16
13	Effective remedy	12
1st protocol	Protection of Property	9
2	Right to Life	3
	[other]	18

be used against him in trial. By contrast, the Italian government ignored similar rulings four times between 2005 and 2012.[52]

However, the UK government has refused to legislate to change the law, in defiance of a ruling from Strasbourg[53] that, by removing the right to vote from prisoners, the UK government was in breach of Protocol 1, Article 3 ECHR (right to regular, free and fair elections). So, unlike the ECJ (during the UK's EU membership), the European Court of Human Rights has no direct (enforceable) jurisdiction within the UK.

At 4.6.2, we examine the rights protected by the European Convention on Human Rights. Table 3.3 sets out the most violated rights, to give this discussion further context.

3.5.3 The International Criminal Court

Based in The Hague, Netherlands, the ICC has jurisdiction under the Rome Statute of the International Criminal Court (2002)[54] to prosecute individuals for genocide, crimes against humanity, and war crimes. Muammar Gadaffi's son, Saif al-Gadaffi, is among its more notable defendants. As noted in Chapter 2, like the European Court of Human Rights, its jurisdiction is subject to ratification by member states, and their cooperation. Important non-ratifiers include the US and Russia. The ICC has not yet exercised its authority within the UK, but in theory has the right to do so.

3.5.4 The Judicial Committee of the Privy Council

This court, which has largely overlapping membership with the UK Supreme Court, hears appeals from 27 Commonwealth countries, UK overseas territories, and Crown dependencies. The decisions of the Privy Council are not binding on English courts. Nor does the Privy Council have any appellate capacity within the English legal system (except in very rare and particular circumstances, e.g. ecclesiastical courts).

Although not binding, Privy Council decisions are highly persuasive in English case law (see Chapter 5), because of the seniority of the Judicial Committee's personnel. The court

---

[52] Horne, A. and Gower, M. (2012) *Statistics: Deportation of Individuals who may face Torture*. London: House of Commons Library (14 February 2012).

[53] *Hirst v UK (No. 2)* App. no. 74025/01 (2005) 42 EHRR 41.

[54] Rome Statute of the International Criminal Court Rome, 17 July 1998, United Nations Treaty Collection. Entry into force, 1 July 2002, in accordance with Art. 126.

disposed of 44 appeals in 2018. Civil matters recently considered have included a challenge on environmental grounds to the construction of a dam in Belize and an appeal from New Zealand on the extent to which the law of defamation applies to Members of Parliament. Criminal appeals, mainly from Trinidad and Tobago, have related to the mandatory death penalty. Its role is likely to decline in future as more Commonwealth countries (e.g. Belize, New Zealand) establish their own final courts of appeal.

3.6 Other judicial forums in England & Wales

3.6.1 **Tribunals**

While not strictly courts, tribunals have a quasi-judicial role, largely mirroring the lower courts in the court system in specific fields.

Tribunals are established by statute to deal with certain types of claim only; members of tribunals (unlike judges in courts) have specific relevant expertise. They range in jurisdiction from individuals challenging their benefit entitlement in the Health, Education and Social Care Chamber, to multinational corporations arguing over sizeable tax liabilities in the Tax Chamber. They are generally less formal than courts. Bringing claims in tribunals is often cheaper and faster than in the court system. These characteristics are aimed to promote justice.

In 2007, most tribunals were organised into a unified structure,[55] in a move towards accessibility and transparency of access to justice (at 1.5.1 we saw that such characteristics are important to the Rule of Law). First Tier tribunals are equivalent to trial courts (such as county courts) and appeals on questions of law are heard by Upper Tier tribunals. Figure 3.11 draws parallels between the court system and the tribunals system, and gives examples of tribunals at each level.

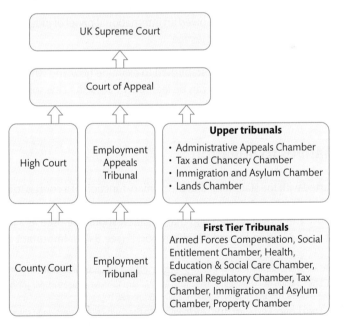

Figure 3.11 Tribunals—summary

---

[55] Tribunals, Courts and Enforcement Act 2007.

Although formally outside the First Tier system, employment tribunals are perhaps the best known tribunal at this level. They hear complaints from employees and former employees who believe that they have been unfairly or wrongfully dismissed, or have been subject to discrimination. Appeals are to the Employment Appeals Tribunal.

Further appeals beyond the tribunal system are to the Court of Appeal. Another way of challenging tribunal decisions is by the judicial review procedure, on the ground that the tribunal's decision-making was in some way flawed. As we saw at 3.4.2, judicial review is not a type of appeal.

3.6.2 Statutory inquiries

Statutory inquiries (not to be confused with judicial inquiries) are established by statute to examine common specific situations where courts may not necessarily have the expertise or appropriate procedures. An example of an inquiry is when the Charity Commission investigates misconduct in the management of a charity. Planning inquiries[56] are a common means of hearing appeals from interested parties in relation to decisions allowing or disallowing the development of land.

3.6.3 Judicial inquiries

Judicial inquiries are established on an *ad hoc* basis to deal with specific issues of public interest, and are often run like court cases, frequently by senior members of the judiciary. However, they do not necessarily reach a 'decision' in the judicial sense—instead they investigate facts and reach conclusions. Many are established by Parliament with wide-ranging powers to call and question witnesses. The Bloody Sunday Inquiry was authorised in 1998 and reported in 2010.[57] This inquiry involved an international panel of judges chaired by Lord Saville, a Law Lord and Supreme Court Justice.

Others are launched by the government, for example, the Chilcott Inquiry (which began in 2009 and reported on 6 July 2016), established to examine how and why the UK's involvement in Iraq started, and what lessons can be learned. In 2012 the Leveson Inquiry reported on the role of the press and police in phone-hacking.[58]

3.7 Alternatives to litigation

This chapter started with the statement that the primary function of a court is to administer the law. Courts (including tribunals) do not, however, have a monopoly on settling legal disputes.

Example 3 illustrates why it is often said that litigation should be used as a last resort. This was an explicit consideration in Lord Woolf's report[59] (see 3.4.2). Important alternatives to

---

[56] Under the Town and Country Planning Act 1990, and related secondary legislation.

[57] The Rt Hon. Lord Saville of Newdigate, The Hon. Mr William L. Hoyt, The Hon. Mr John L. Toohey (2010) *Report of the Bloody Sunday Inquiry*. London: TSO (15 June 2010).

[58] The Rt Hon. Lord Justice Leveson (2012) *An Inquiry into the Culture, Practices and Ethics of the Press*. London: HMSO (November 2012).

[59] Lord Woolf (1996) *Access to Justice*. London: HMSO.

formal litigation include ADR, mediation, arbitration, access to ombudsmen, and negotiation. They are not, however, alternatives to using the law. The rights and obligations created by the law continue to provide the basis of parties' assertions when using these procedures and are observed by the practitioners involved in facilitating them. Indeed, the use of these avenues reinforces respect for the law and the Rule of Law, by making access to the law more feasible to private and commercial parties.

Example 3

Imagine that you are in a dispute over a business contract. You receive a letter from a court together with a document entitled 'particulars of claim' setting out your alleged breach and what is claimed. This formal document sets out the claimant's case, and refers to you as the 'defendant'. There is a list of damage, and then of monetary losses, and a claim for damages. You can see months of expense and stress, and conflict with a once-valuable client. If you lose, you may have to pay all the other side's costs and court fees. The other side is probably mindful of the same issues.

3.7.1 Alternative Dispute Resolution

In its widest sense, ADR is a term used to describe any dispute resolution outside the courts, so it is often said to include arbitration, mediation, and similar schemes. ADR is often used in a narrower sense to describe a procedure where the parties agree that an independent third party should help them reach a solution. It is normally confidential. The decision of the third party is not legally enforceable (with the exception of arbitration, see 3.7.2).

Mediation is a type of ADR often used in matrimonial and commercial matters. Because the independent third party is unable to bind the parties, the proceedings are intended to be less confrontational than litigation or arbitration. The role of mediation was given additional impetus by the Children and Families Act 2014, which obliges a person to attend a family mediation information and assessment meeting before making any relevant application to the Family Court.

3.7.2 Arbitration

Many business contracts contain a clause whereby the parties agree to refer their disputes to a named arbitrator. An arbitrator is an independent third party who considers the parties' arguments and reaches a binding decision on the dispute. The parties can agree to go to arbitration when a dispute arises even without an arbitration clause in their contract. Arbitration proceedings are governed by the Arbitration Act 1996. Crucially, and in contrast to other forms of ADR, the decision of the arbitrator is binding and legally enforceable.

Arbitration is often cheaper and less formal than litigation. Parties have some scope to determine the format of proceedings, with the result that they may be less confrontational. Proceedings may also be private if the parties wish. The arbitrator does not (and cannot) award all the remedies available to a court, but the parties and the arbitrator can formulate more practical solutions, such as agreeing to amend a contract.

Sharia law (see 'Natural law' at 1.3.2.1 and the discussion of Sharia-based legal systems at 2.8.1) is used in some Muslim communities in the UK. In general this does not constitute an attempt to impose an alternative legal system; instead, in certain areas like divorce, civil (not criminal) disputes within the Muslim community can be settled under the Arbitration Act by the Muslim Arbitration Tribunal, a network of Sharia 'courts'. These are not courts in the true sense—they are voluntarily chosen by the parties to give a decision. This means that the rulings of these 'courts' can be enforced by English courts, provided they do not conflict with English law. Other religions have similar practices, such as the Beth Din, which are courts in the Jewish community also operating under the Arbitration Act.

3.7.3 Ombudsmen

Ombudsmen are usually established by statute[60] and given delegated authority to investigate and settle minor complaints. Examples include the Financial Ombudsman Service, and the Property Ombudsman, which provide consumers and businesses with independent advice and investigation relating to disputes with service providers in various sectors.

The template for ombudsmen in the UK was the Parliamentary Ombudsman (officially the Parliamentary and Health Service Ombudsman). The Parliamentary Ombudsman is responsible for considering complaints about poor administration by government departments, made by members of the public via their MPs. Parties are normally free to litigate if they disagree with decisions by ombudsmen.

3.7.4 Negotiation

It is always open to the parties to dispense with third parties altogether, and negotiate a settlement of their disputes. This is, in reality, the most frequent means of dispute resolution without recourse to litigation. As with all forms of ADR, the balance of legal rights and obligations between the parties will exert a strong influence on the ultimate outcome.

 Summary

- Trials take place in different courts depending on the type of law and the degree of harm.
- The appeals systems differ for criminal law and civil law. Within each type of law there are variations depending on the trial court.
- Other bodies also assume judicial or quasi-judicial roles.
- Refer to the Appendix for a useful collection of key facts about all the courts discussed in this chapter.

Practical exercises

1. How long should detention without charge be permitted to last?
2. Should trial by jury be required for all Crown Court cases?

---

[60] The Financial Ombudsman Service was established by the Financial Services and Markets Act 2000 and the Consumer Credit Act 2006; the Property Ombudsman was approved under the Estate Agents and Redress Act 2007.

3. Was it necessary to replace the Appellate Committee of the House of Lords with the UK Supreme Court?

4. Should religious 'courts' be permitted as a form of arbitration? Do they undermine the importance of the English court system?

5. Is the Privy Council an anachronism?

 *Visit the **online resources** for the authors' reflections and to check your progress.*

Further reading

Lord Woolf (1996) *Access to Justice.* **London: HMSO**

—This report highlighted the contemporary barriers to access to justice in England & Wales and triggered the opening-up of litigation procedure.

Thomas, C. (2010) *Are Juries Fair?* **London: Ministry of Justice (February 2010)**

—A very modern take on the old question. This debate extends to the more fundamental question of whether it is desirable to abolish trial by jury.

Ministry of Justice. *Judicial and Court Statistics Quarterly* **(published quarterly by the Ministry of Justice)**

—This puts together useful information relating to the court system in England & Wales, and, in the online version, contains tables of source statistics.

The Rt Hon. Lord Justice Leveson (2012) *An Inquiry into the Culture, Practices and Ethics of the Press.* **London: HMSO (November 2012). Sir John Chilcot (2016)** *The Iraq Inquiry.* © **Crown copyright 2016**

—An illuminating example of a report from a judicial inquiry.

Bowcott, O. and Duncan, P. (2019) Half of magistrates courts in England and Wales closed since 2010, *The Guardian,* **27 January 2019**

—explores the impact on justice of closures of magistrates' courts

 *For the authors' reflections on the practical exercises, additional self-test questions, sample interview questions and a library of links to useful websites, visit the free **online resources** at* **www.oup.com/he/slorach4e.**

4 Legislation

Learning objectives

After studying this chapter you should be able to:

- Explain the concept of parliamentary sovereignty.
- Identify different types of legislation.
- Describe in outline the process by which a statute is created.
- Recognise key issues of statutory interpretation.
- Discuss basic concepts relating to EU and European Convention on Human Rights (ECHR) legislation.

Introduction

At 1.6 we examined the theory of the separation of powers. It is quite clear that laws need to be enforced (by the executive) and legal disputes settled (by the judiciary). This chapter is about the creation of law by the legislature. The most important source of English law is now legislation. Unlike case law, which only applies to England & Wales, and in the absence of specific provisions to the contrary, statutes apply to England, Wales, Scotland, and Northern Ireland.

But why do we actually need laws? Many commentators say that we already have too many laws, too much regulation. This begs the question, why does Parliament need to pass statutes? Here are a few suggestions:

- You might say that statutes are passed to help the government of the day pursue its political objectives, be they the liberalisation of the economy or the strengthening of the welfare apparatus. But this is only partly true. Even manifesto commitments are usually the product of a perceived need to solve a problem or to promote progress.

- Often statutes are passed to address a pressing need, like the regulation of dangerous dogs or the imposition of sanctions on a country perceived to be flouting treaty obligations.

- Public pressure, via the threat of electoral failure, often yields results. There are many examples. The Local Government Finance Act 1992, implemented the replacement of the unpopular Community Charge ('Poll Tax') with the Council Tax. Even more controversial was the European Union Referendum Act 2015, which answered calls for the referendum that would ultimately lead to Brexit. We look at this in more detail at 4.3.1.1.

- Some statutes implement EU law, often Directives that require national legislatures to draft domestic legislation—at 2.4 we examined illustrations of this mechanism.

- Politically neutral factors include the promotion of consumer rights or enterprise—the Consumer Rights Act 2015 being a prime example.
- Many statutes are rather less glamorous, and are passed to facilitate the administration of government, or to promote the national interest or economy. Governments cannot raise money for spending on administration, services, and infrastructure (£680bn in 2015–16)[1] without taxes authorised by Parliament.

Take the Housing and Planning Act 2016. Surely this is just another in a long line of statutes adding red tape and rules to an area already creaking under the weight of legislation. The Act was passed to solve a problem, with the relevant government department stating: 'The Act sets out a clear determination from the government to keep the country building while giving hard working families every opportunity to unlock the door to home ownership. It will give housebuilders and decision-makers the tools and confidence to provide more homes and further streamline the planning system to accelerate their delivery.'[2] This statute, then, reflects several traditional drivers for legislation: promoting business, helping to satisfy consumer demands, regulating business practices, and stimulating home ownership.

In theory Parliament could simply stop legislating and the corpus of legislation would stop expanding. In practice, as society develops, statutes would quickly lose the race against technology and human progress. Modern economies need regulation and stimulation, and statutes are the most efficient and transparent way of doing this.

Essential explanation

'Legislation' is often used as a synonym for 'statutes'. However, strictly speaking, a statute is an Act of Parliament, whereas 'legislation' is a generic term that includes other types of legislation such as secondary legislation (see 4.2.2) and EU legislation.

In this section we use the terms 'Act' and 'statute' interchangeably—this reflects normal practice.

Statute is the primary source of law in England & Wales. This is a key consequence of the doctrine of parliamentary sovereignty, also known as parliamentary supremacy, which gives Parliament an unfettered power to legislate. Therefore, even though the English legal system is a common law jurisdiction, no court may overrule any statute. Unlike in some other jurisdictions (such as the US), a court can do no more than interpret statutes. We examine this in more detail at 4.1.

There have been statutes in one form or another ever since there were governments. Before statutes came customary law (remnants of which survive in some jurisdictions—especially Scandinavian today). All modern states have statutes made by law-making bodies. In contrast with (for instance) case law, a statute has the advantage of being a definitive statement of law, passed with the authority of whatever institution has sovereignty.

This chapter addresses the key issue of parliamentary sovereignty, before looking at the rise of the statute as a source of law in the UK. It then categorises statutes and examines

[1] *Public Spending Statistics July 2016*, HM Treasury.
[2] *Landmark Housing and Planning Bill receives Royal Assent*, Department for Communities and Local Government, 13 May 2016.

the importance of the various types of legislation. We then look at how courts and lawyers interpret statutes before moving on to consider the impact of two of the most fundamental changes in our legal history: the incorporation into our law of EU law (and its disentanglement after Brexit)[3] and the European Convention on Human Rights (ECHR).

4.1 Parliamentary sovereignty

We examined the concept of sovereignty at 1.4.3. In the UK, Parliament is sovereign. The noted constitutional theorist, Professor A. V. Dicey, said:

> The Principle of Parliamentary Sovereignty means neither more nor less than this: namely, that Parliament . . . has, under the English constitution the right to make or unmake any law whatever; and further that no person or body is recognised by the law . . . as having the right to override or set aside the legislation of Parliament.[4]

Parliament is therefore the supreme law-making body in the UK.

Even though England & Wales remains a common law jurisdiction, with a sizeable body of judge-made law, Parliament is at liberty to reverse the common law, and no court can challenge the validity of an Act of Parliament. Courts often shy away from making law in areas deemed too sensitive; they defer to the democratic legitimacy of Parliament. In the Diane Pretty case on assisted dying (discussed at 1.2.4.2), Lord Steyn stated: 'In our Parliamentary democracy . . . such a fundamental change cannot be brought about by judicial creativity.'[5]

The 'Enrolled Act' Rule confirms that courts cannot question the validity of an Act, or disregard it,[6] on any grounds. For instance, the Hunting Act 2004 was challenged on the basis that it had not been passed by the House of Lords. The House of Lords (in their judicial capacity; the forerunner to the Supreme Court) unanimously stated that, because the Act had received Royal Assent (see 4.3.1), its validity could not be challenged in court.[7]

4.1.1 Challenges to parliamentary sovereignty

It has been said that parliamentary sovereignty has been eroded over the last century or so, and that, while Parliament is said to be the 'supreme' law-making body in the UK, it is no longer entirely sovereign. In three areas in particular Parliament has ceded sovereignty, but in each of these there are arguments that formal sovereignty has remained with Parliament.

---

[3] The UK left the EU on 31 January 2020 (as a result of a referendum of 23 June 2016). For more discussion of Brexit, refer to Chapter 2, and in particular the Essential explanation of Brexit at 2.2.3.

[4] Dicey, A.V. (1885) *An Introduction to the Study of the Law of the Constitution.* Liberty Fund Inc., 8th rev. edn, 1982, p. 36.

[5] *R (Pretty) v Director of Public Prosecutions, Secretary of State for the Home Department intervening* [2001] UKHL 61, at [55].

[6] *Edinburgh & Dalkeith Railway Co. v Wauchope* (1842) 8 C & F 710; *Pickin v British Railways Board* [1975] AC 765.

[7] *R (Jackson) v Attorney General* [2005] UKHL 56.

4.1.1.1 Devolution

The Scotland Act 1998, the Government of Wales Act 1998, and the Northern Ireland Act 1998, established the Scottish Parliament, the Welsh Assembly, and the Northern Ireland Assembly, respectively. These statutes devolved certain powers to those institutions. In the medium term, it is clear that devolution is likely to be widened (i.e. to England or parts of it) and deepened (i.e. more powers will be devolved). This is a result of two referendums:

- The 2014 referendum on Scottish independence: although it concluded in a vote against independence, did precipitate a re-evaluation of the balance of powers between national and devolved legislatures. The Scotland Act 2016[8] devolved further powers to the Scottish Parliament and government, including transport, some taxation, and elements of social welfare.

- The 2016 referendum on leaving the EU: whilst the UK as a whole voted 52 per cent/48 per cent to leave, Scotland voted 62 per cent/38 per cent and Northern Ireland 56 per cent/44 per cent to remain. Almost immediately, this raised once more the possibility that Scotland would elect by referendum to leave the UK in order to rejoin (or remain within) the EU. At the time of writing, MPs and Ministers were considering whether to legislate to further devolve parliamentary sovereignty, or even to federalise the UK.

The legislation produced by devolved legislatures and executed by the executive of each country, is limited in its extent by the Westminster Parliament. Strictly speaking, therefore, the Westminster Parliament may repeal or amend the relevant statutes (and has in the past suspended the Northern Ireland Assembly) although it would be politically difficult to do so.

You may note that there is no devolution to any *English* (as opposed to UK) legislature. Whilst it would be consistent to incorporate English devolution into the constitution along-side devolution for the other nations, it would create many issues, including potentially marginalising the role of Parliament itself. The inconsistency remains, however. One consequence of this is the so-called *West Lothian Question*[9]—that Scottish, Welsh, and Northern Irish MPs can vote on matters only affecting England, despite the fact that, since devolution, the reverse is no longer the case in many areas. In 2015 a compromise was reached by Parliament. For Bills or sections of Bills with purely English impact, an England-only committee stage considers the legislation as part of the House of Commons legislative process. This procedure is called 'English Votes for English Laws' (EVEL). EVEL is adopted if the legislation affects only England & Wales, rather than England alone. This is not strictly a form of devolution as the procedure remains within the UK parliamentary process.

4.1.1.2 International treaties

Under the Royal Prerogative the UK government has signed many international treaties, and therefore adheres to many different bodies of international law (see 2.5.1). While the government exercises

---

[8] Scotland Act 2016 cl 11.

[9] This is named after the then MP for West Lothian, Tam Dalyell, who championed the issue during devolution debates in the late 1970s.

these powers, Parliament can take them away, because it is sovereign. Parliament long had the power to ratify treaties, and this was recently codified in the Constitutional Reform and Governance Act 2010. If an international treaty purports to affect citizens within the UK itself, Parliament must legislate to give this legal force. For instance, the UK was a founder signatory to the ECHR, but it only became directly enforceable within the UK after the Human Rights Act 1998 (HRA). Ungoed-Thomas J said in the *Cheney v Conn* case, 'international law is part of the law of the land, but it yields to statute'.[10]

4.1.1.3 The European Union

Possibly most controversially, the European Communities Act 1972 incorporated into UK law the Treaty on the Functioning of the European Union (then the Treaty of Rome). The UK became a member of the European Union (then the EEC—see 4.5 in relation to EU terminology). In the *Factortame*[11] case, the House of Lords (after consulting the European Court of Justice (ECJ)) confirmed that, in any area of EU competence, EU law would take precedence over conflicting UK legislation. The UK voted on 23 June 2016 to end this state of affairs.[12]

4.2 Types of legislation

We saw in 2.3.3 that the state has grown considerably in the last two centuries. This has required a prodigious amount of statutory implementation, with the consequence that the body of legislation has grown enormously. Every year the UK Parliament enacts around 3,000 pages of statutes in the form of Acts. Although it is the job of Members of Parliament to legislate, there is a limit to how much work they can do. They certainly cannot debate and consider all of the thousands of pages of legislation necessary to provide the framework for regulation of the UK, extending to welfare, tax, health, education, etc. Parliament cannot legislate for every aspect of our lives in intricate detail, nor would anyone want it to.

There are therefore several types of domestic legislation in the UK. Figure 4.1 summarises the main types of legislation in the UK; you may wish to refer to it as you read about each type of legislation.

4.2.1 Primary legislation

4.2.1.1 Public and private Acts

Acts are known as primary legislation to distinguish them from secondary legislation, also known as delegated legislation. Before it is enacted, a statute is called a 'Bill', rather than an 'Act'. Public Bills are introduced to Parliament by Members of Parliament (usually government ministers) and concern matters affecting the public as a whole, whereas private Bills are submitted to Parliament by a person or body who needs parliamentary authority to get something done.

---

[10] *Cheney v Conn (Inspector of Taxes); Cheney v Inland Revenue Commissioners* [1968] 1 All ER 779.

[11] *R v Secretary of State for Transport, ex parte Factortame (No. 2)* [1991] AC 603.

[12] For more discussion of Brexit, refer to Chapter 2, and in particular the Essential explanation of Brexit at 2.2.3.

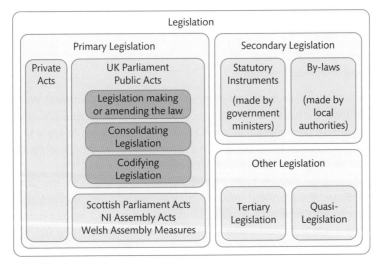

Figure 4.1 Types of legislation in the UK

A well-known public statute is the Human Rights Act 1998, which is in the news virtually every day. All public statutes proceed through Parliament as Bills, either government Bills, introduced by a minister as part of the government's legislative programme, or private members' Bills, which are non-government sponsored Bills introduced by backbench MPs.

Private members' Bills are public Bills, but they are not introduced on behalf of the government, and so do not benefit from the weight of any government majority. The Hunting Act 2004 illustrates the distinction neatly. It eventually passed as a government Bill, but was preceded by at least six private members' Bills on the same subject, unsuccessfully introduced in Parliament since 1949.

Private Bills are quite distinct from private members' Bills. Private Bills (including a category called local Bills) affect particular persons or a particular locality, such as a Bill to build a new section of railway line or a reservoir. They were more prolific in the 19th and early 20th centuries before statutory instruments became the preferred method of legislative micro-management. A memorable example was an Act of 1727,[13] giving George Händel (the composer) citizenship of Great Britain. Outdated as they may seem, private Bills have performed an important role as society has developed:

> Every citizen of this country, whenever he mounts an omnibus or tram or gets into a railway train, whenever he turns on a water tap . . . ignites a gas burner . . . whenever he walks in a well-paved and lighted street, saunters on an esplanade, or listens to a band playing in a municipal bandstand . . . is profiting from the results of private Bill legislation.[14]

While this role has diminished, many major infrastructure projects still require (and benefit from) parliamentary authority as private Bills. For instance, the London Local Authorities

---

[13] Act of Naturalisation of George Frideric Händel and Others 1727.

[14] Cyprian Williams, O. (1948) *The Historical Development of Private Bill Procedure and Standing Orders in the House of Commons*. London: HMSO, p. 1.

and Transport for London Act 2008 concerned parking penalties and rail penalty charges in Greater London.

4.2.1.2 UK and devolved legislation

It is a presumption that all primary legislation will apply throughout England, Wales, Scotland, and Northern Ireland unless the statute specifically states that it does not apply in any of these jurisdictions. (A presumption in law is a rule that is presumed to apply in certain situations. Presumptions are often rebuttable. A presumption is rebuttable when the legal rule concerned can be disapplied if there is enough evidence to the contrary.)

Since the devolution statutes were passed (the Scotland Act 1998, the Government of Wales Act 1998, and the Northern Ireland Act 1998), each of the devolved legislatures has had the power to pass primary legislation in its jurisdiction, in a limited number of areas of competence (including health, education, the Scottish legal system, and transport, but notably not raising taxes). The range of competences is likely to expand in the near future, as discussed at 4.1.1.1. Also note the discussion on English Votes for English Laws at 4.1.1.1.

4.2.1.3 Categories of public Act

Most legislation makes or changes law. The Hunting Act 2004 is an example of a statute creating new law. It created the offence of hunting wild mammals with dogs, where no such law existed beforehand. The Welfare Reform Act 2012 is an example of amending legislation. It purported to simplify the welfare benefits system and improve work incentives. You will encounter some statutes which attempt to do neither; instead they are 'tidying-up' exercises.

Consolidating Acts

Consolidation occurs where one statute re-enacts law which was previously contained in several different statutes. There is a presumption that consolidation does not materially change earlier legislation (the presumption is rebuttable by an express statement in the Act or by the promoter of the Act).

This is sometimes of great importance. The last Labour government embarked on a project to rewrite tax law, the aim of which was stated to be 'to rewrite the UK's primary direct tax legislation to make it clearer and easier to use, without changing the law'.[15] In 2010, it proudly announced that the project was complete, with ten statutes having been enacted since 2001. The law was changed only to a limited extent by these statutes.

Codifying Acts

Codification occurs where all the law on a topic, which may previously have been covered by common law, custom, and even statute(s), is brought together in one new statute. The codifying statute may, if necessary, change the pre-existing law (e.g. the Theft Act 1968).

The law relating to the sale of goods is an illuminating example. The law originated in medieval mercantile custom, which eventually crystallised into case law. The law was then

---

[15] Her Majesty's Revenue & Customs (2009). Available online at: http://webarchive.nationalarchives.gov.uk/+/http:/www.hmrc.gov.uk/rewrite/index.htm.

codified by the Sale of Goods Act 1893. Over the course of nearly a century, this Act was the subject of a number of statutory amendments, which changed and repealed parts of it. These were then consolidated into the Sale of Goods Act 1979. The 1979 Act, amongst other things, makes a seller of goods liable to the buyer if the goods supplied are not of satisfactory quality. However, that Act has since been the subject of further amendment, notably by the Sale and Supply of Goods Act 1994. The Sale of Goods Act still applies to businesses in the UK. The Consumer Rights Act 2015,[16] consolidated the Sale of Goods Act and other related consumer legislation, for instance regarding distance selling, but also purported to streamline the law in this area.

4.2.2 Secondary legislation

> **(!) Essential explanation**
>
> Secondary legislation
>
> Also called 'delegated' or 'subordinate' legislation.
>
> Any law not made directly by Parliament or a devolved legislature is called secondary legislation. It is typically made with the authority of Parliament by local authorities, the Crown (i.e. the government), or ministers.

The authority to make secondary legislation is usually contained in a 'parent' Act, which creates the framework of the law, but then delegates the power to add the detailed provisions to others.

4.2.2.1 Statutory instruments

As mentioned earlier, it would be impractical for Parliament to be expected to consider and debate every detail of each Act. To overcome this, ministers and their departments are given authority to make regulations and orders (i.e. statutory instruments) in areas for which they are specifically responsible. For example, in 2014, the Chancellor of the Exchequer exercised his authority under the European Communities Act 1972 to extend sanctions against Russia.[17]

Parliament has always had this power, but it is now used to such an extent that the amount of secondary legislation far exceeds Acts of Parliament. In the early decades of the 20th century around 1,200 statutory instruments were made each year; by the middle of that century, the number was around 2,100, and by the beginning of the 21st century, around 3,000 each year, that is around 90 times more statutory instruments than statutes (totalling a yearly average of around 10,000 pages). Thus the balance has shifted from statutes to statutory instruments over time. According to http://www.legislation.gov.uk, in 2018, 1,387 UK statutory instruments (or SIs) were made compared with the passing of just 34 Acts of Parliament. Why is this?

---

[16] Consumer Rights Act 2015, c.15.
[17] Ukraine (European Union Financial Sanctions) (No. 3) Regulations 2014 (SI 2014/2054).

As the state has expanded, the need for extremely technical secondary legislation has increased. Statutory instruments enable Parliament to call upon technical expertise to assist in drafting regulations such as those relating to health and safety or road traffic matters. Delegation can be extremely useful in dealing quickly with emergencies, such as the outbreak of foot-and-mouth disease in 2000.

It might seem that statutory instruments run contrary to the spirit of parliamentary sovereignty, except in so far as they are created under the authority of Parliament. But all statutory instruments are subject to the approval of Parliament and to judicial review, under which courts can strike down a statutory instrument if it is outside the scope of the parent statute.

The move toward delegating legislative functions has culminated in secondary legislation occasionally being made without specific parliamentary delegation. Since 1994, ministers have had limited powers to legislate without specific prior parliamentary authority. Most controversially the Legislative and Regulatory Reform Act 2006 extended these powers significantly, so that a minister can make a regulatory reform order changing existing primary or secondary legislation if reform is needed, or to implement recommendations by the Law Commissions. Although there are limitations on this power (e.g. it cannot be used to amend the taxation regime, and must be used proportionately), it can extend even to creating new minor criminal offences.

⊛ Essential debate

Legislative and Regulatory Reform Act 2006

Look at Example 2 at 1.2.2.2 on the Enabling Act 1933, under which the *Reichstag* in Germany delegated its authority to Hitler's cabinet. Then read s. 1 of the Legislative and Regulatory Reform Act 2006, in addition to the contents page.

During the debates leading to the Act, David Howarth MP called the Bill the 'Abolition of Parliament Bill'. The main criticism of the Act is that it is anti-democratic in that it undermines parliamentary power. Former parliamentary draftsman Daniel Greenberg wrote, 'if an anti-democratic and dictatorial regime were to acquire significant political power in the United Kingdom, it would be able to bypass Parliament and legislate in an extreme and controlling way on a troublingly wide range of subjects, all through reliance on powers that have been duly granted by Parliament, with very little controversy'.[18]

The very existence of these powers, it is alleged, is a problem. The contents page reveals that the powers are currently heavily circumscribed. Even acknowledging that they are used responsibly in the current political climate, if a less well-meaning government were ever to take power, critics argue that they might be able to take advantage of the Act to force undesirable policies into law without parliamentary scrutiny.

Do you think the Act—like the Enabling Act—is an unjustified erosion of democracy?

4.2.2.2 By-laws

Sometimes spelled 'bye-laws', these are made under the authority of parliamentary statute. They are usually made by local authorities to deal with issues within their own area. For example, public bathing is regulated by local councils under the authority of s. 231 of the Public

---

[18] Greenberg, D. (2011) *Laying Down the Law*. London: Sweet & Maxwell, pp. 214–15.

Health Act 1936. In 2014 Norwich City Council controversially considered a by-law banning skateboarding. Occasionally other bodies make by-laws, such as public transport operators, utilities, or the National Trust.[19] For instance, queuing (among many other activities) on the London Underground is regulated by by-law.[20]

By-laws cannot take effect until they are confirmed by the appropriate minister. As government control of local matters has increased, so the need for by-laws has reduced.

4.2.3 Other legislation

Primary and secondary legislation are both created with some degree of legislative scrutiny. Government is so complex that some rules need to be made by government departments without any formal parliamentary examination. This is sometimes categorised as tertiary legislation. For instance many tax forms have the force of law but, although they are made with parliamentary *authority* they have not necessarily had any *scrutiny* by the legislature. Important examples include:

- codes of practice made by the Home Secretary under s. 66 of the Police and Criminal Evidence Act 1984, which regulates police procedure; and

- rules and guidance of the Financial Conduct Authority (FCA), the body created by the Financial Services Act 2012 to supervise all firms to ensure that business across financial services and markets is conducted in a way that advances the interests of all users and participants. The Financial Services and Markets Act 2000, as amended by the Financial Services Act 2012, delegates powers and functions to the FCA. Rules made by the FCA are therefore delegated legislation.

Yet another, even less formal, category of rules exists. Quasi-legislation (sometimes called 'soft law') is a category of rules passed with the authority of Parliament, but in the form of guidance, for example some codes of practice. It often has force of law. If you have read the Highway Code, then you have already encountered 'quasi-legislation'.

4.3 The creation and enforcement of statutes

A statute becomes law when it receives Royal Assent. The Bill becomes an Act. The Act is then brought into force, often at a later date, and is enforced by the executive. This is often the end of an arduous process. The legislature (Parliament) creates statutes, but it is the executive (the government) that enforces them.

4.3.1 The creation of statutes

Parliament consists of the Queen, the House of Commons, which is democratically elected, and the House of Lords, which is not. The UK is a constitutional monarchy, which means that,

---

[19] Under the National Trust Acts 1907, 1919, 1937, 1939, 1953, and 1971.

[20] The Transport for London Railway Byelaws were made under para. 26 of Sch. 11 to the Greater London Authority Act 1999, confirmed by authority of the Secretary of State for Transport on 6 September 2011.

although it has the machinery of a democratic state, the monarch still has a formal role as Head of State—this is why Bills are signed into law by (or on behalf of) the Monarch.

Both Houses are involved in the process of creating statutes. An Act will begin its life as a document known as a Bill. Only when it has passed through all the stages set out below will it eventually become an Act of Parliament. There are three clear phases in the creation of a statute: the pre-parliamentary stage; the debates in Parliament; and finally its enactment and commencement. You may wish to refer to Figure 4.2 as you digest the description that follows.

4.3.1.1 Before Parliament

Before a Bill starts its progress through Parliament, there is usually an extensive gestation period. In the introduction to this chapter we saw that there are many reasons for Parliament to pass statutes.

Governments are formed after general elections. Historically these have occurred every four or five years unless an emergency election is needed (e.g. there were two elections in 1974 because the first failed to yield a decisive result). As a result of the passing of the Fixed Term Parliaments Act 2011 general elections will normally be held every five years. The political parties campaign using a platform of policies contained in a manifesto. The manifesto is key to democratic legitimacy. Regardless of whether voters actually read the manifesto or summaries of it in the media, it is important that a government is elected with a mandate to do certain things by introducing appropriate legislation into Parliament. Politically sensitive Bills are often trailed as manifesto pledges.

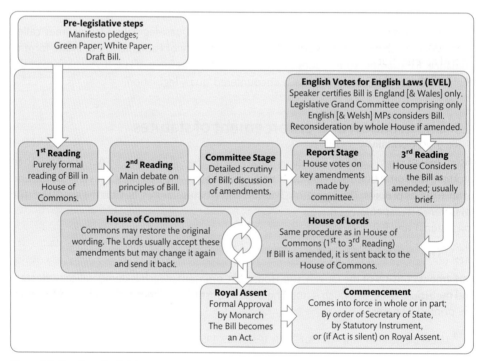

Figure 4.2 Creation of a statute

Example 1

Brexit

On page 72 of the Conservative Party manifesto for the 2015 General Election, was the following statement:

> The EU needs to change. And it is time for the British people – not politicians – to have their say. Only the Conservative Party will deliver real change and real choice on Europe, with an in-out referendum by the end of 2017.

Such a strong manifesto promise pledged the Conservative Party to legislate on the matter. This led to the European Union Referendum Act 2015, s. 1 of which committed the Secretary of State to hold a referendum on EU membership, on the question set out in s. 1 of that Act. This in turn led to the 23 June 2016 vote by the UK electorate to leave the EU. It is clear that the Conservative Party saw this referendum commitment as a vote-winner, possibly in response to the UK Independence Party's surge in popularity among potential Conservative voters in the previous electoral cycle.

In an echo of this, the first words of the Conservative Party manifesto for the December 2019 general election were, 'We will get Brexit done in January and unleash the potential of our whole country.' This undermined much of the appeal of the Brexit Party in that election, and the Conservative victory in that election led to the passing of the European Union (Withdrawal Agreement) Act 2020,[21] leading to withdrawal from the EU on 31 January 2020.

A government Green Paper is a consultation document. It will address an issue with a view to possible reform, inviting responses from interested parties to the relevant government department. A White Paper will then follow. More authoritative, and less open to discussion, it will set out future government policy. The publication of a draft Bill forms an interim stage, allowing examination and consultation on the detail of the Bill before it is formally debated in Parliament. Not all Bills are subject to all (or sometimes any) of these stages. The draft Bill will form the underpinnings of a Bill to be put before Parliament.

4.3.1.2 Debates and readings within Parliament

A Bill must normally pass through all the stages set out here in both Houses, before receiving Royal Assent.

There are some constitutional limits (set out in the Parliament Acts 1911 and 1949) on the House of Lords' ability to delay or prevent passage of Bills that have been passed in the House of Commons, especially in the case of 'money Bills' (e.g. the Finance Acts that contain budget provisions), and Bills that start life as manifesto pledges. Have a look at the Hunting Act 2004. If you read the enacting formula (the words beginning 'Be it enacted . . . ' at the start of the Act) you will see that the Act did not receive the approval of the House of Lords, but became law anyway because it was a Labour manifesto pledge, albeit a very controversial one.

The first reading is purely formal. The Bill is presented to the House and is ordered to be printed. Different types of Bills begin their lives in one or other House. For example, all

---

[21] European Union (Withdrawal Agreement) Act 2020.

finance Bills must first be debated in the Commons, and all Bills relating to the judiciary begin their lives in the Lords. Other Bills can start in either House.

The most controversial stage, where the key plenary debates are conducted, is the second reading, but it occupies only around one-fifth of the parliamentary time for the average Bill.[22] Around two-thirds[23] of Parliament's time on most Bills is spent in committee. This is a more appropriate forum than a plenary discussion of the whole House for detailed, often line-by-line, examination of a Bill, and for consideration of amendments tabled by MPs. Each Bill is allocated a Public Bill Committee (also known as a General Committee), whose membership largely reflects the overall composition of the House. The chairs are also allocated roughly in proportion to political balance.

The Bill is then sent to the whole House for the report stage where key provisions are discussed. The report stage provides an opportunity for MPs who were not on the Public Bill Committee to make amendments to the Bill.

The third reading is usually a brief debate, followed by (usually) a single vote on the Bill. The Bill will then go through the same procedure in the other House. This 'ping pong' stage, when the two Houses try to resolve their disagreements, is frequently the stage at which Bills are amended most substantially. If the two Houses cannot reach agreement, there is deadlock. This is when the House of Commons (subject to procedural limitations) can use the Parliament Acts to force a Bill through to Royal Assent without the approval of the House of Lords.

4.3.1.3 Royal Assent and commencement

All legislation requires Royal Assent to become law. In theory the sovereign has power to refuse Royal Assent, but this has not been done since 1707, and would be unimaginable in today's world. It should be noted, however, that ex-prime ministers have revealed that Queen Elizabeth II has offered advice to them, especially on Commonwealth matters.

A statute may be 'on the books' and 'law' in the formal sense, long before it comes into force. Legislation requires complex implementation, so this is often fleshed out by the use of statutory instruments. Sections of statutes are brought into force in phases, by statutory instrument or directly by the appropriate Secretary of State. The most extreme example is the Easter Act 1928, which was an Act to regulate the date in the UK of Easter Day. The Act, though it received Royal Assent over eight decades ago, has not yet been brought into force.

Debate is essential to democracy; the word 'Parliament' itself comes from the Norman French meaning 'talking shop'. Controversial Bills can therefore take a considerable amount of time to become Acts. For example, it took five years and 700 hours of parliamentary time before the Hunting Act 2004 received Royal Assent.

Rules of parliamentary procedure dictate that most legislation takes less than a year from first reading to Royal Assent. Parliament can, however, respond quickly to crisis. In the recent banking crisis, the Banking (Special Provisions) Act 2008, giving the government power to nationalise banks (in particular, Northern Rock), made the journey through Parliament in a day. One of the most infamous statutes is the Dangerous Dogs Act 1991, which took only two

---

22 Griffith, J.A.G. et al. (2003) *Griffith & Ryle on Parliament*. London: Sweet & Maxwell, p. 17.

23 Griffith, J.A.G. et al. (2003) *Griffith & Ryle on Parliament*. London: Sweet & Maxwell, p. 17.

months from first reading to commencement, including all three readings in the Commons in one day's sitting. This Bill was generated after a very brief period of drafting against a background of tabloid fury at maulings of children by certain breeds of dogs. These breeds are now effectively banned or severely restricted. There has been a swathe of criticism in relation to this Act. Critics cite this 'knee-jerk' legislation as being overly restrictive, as a result of insufficient debate within Parliament.

4.3.2 The implementation of statutes

By the time a statute is in force, the means to implement the statute should be in place. This is the role of the executive, namely the government. The executive is split into 45 government departments, 25 of which have an appointed government minister, and all of which are run by civil servants. Most of these departments delegate enforcement to various agencies. For a criminal statute this often means the police, with the Crown Prosecution Service (CPS) providing lawyers to act for the Crown. Her Majesty's Courts and Tribunals Service is an agency of the Ministry of Justice. In the civil context, 'enforcement' is often simply a matter of individuals using the rights created within a statute, such as a consumer claiming against a producer for burns caused by an exploding hairdryer under s. 2 of the Consumer Protection Act 1987.

Certain executive powers are devolved by Parliament (mainly under the Local Government Act 1972) to various levels of local government:

- devolved Administrations (in Scotland, Wales, or Northern Ireland);
- county, then district, then parish councils; and
- unitary authorities.

Local government (especially in England & Wales) is very complex in structure with many regional variations. All of these local authorities have some sort of election, and many have a split between legislature and executive.

4.4 Statutory interpretation

Statutes set out laws which regulate a population. People live complex lives, constantly creating new legal issues which require laws to be interpreted and applied. Over time, judges and lawyers have developed a set of rules by which statutes can be interpreted to apply to millions of individuals living real lives in a constantly changing country.

This section starts by focusing on the nature of the problem of statutory interpretation. Next, we look at the tools available to the lawyer in resolving ambiguities. We then use a case study to apply some of those rules, before drawing some conclusions on statutory interpretation in general.

4.4.1 The problem

Statutes are required to give legal effect to what often starts as loose political rhetoric. Politicians create policy. Government lawyers (in the Government Legal Service) then advise the politicians on how to give policies legal effect, and instruct parliamentary draftsmen. These draftsmen give concrete statutory shape to government policy. The draftsmen and the lawyers have to turn the results of debate and compromise into unambiguous, consistent, and adaptable form. The detailed wording of the statute is critical—this is what the courts will pore over in difficult cases. The slightest drafting error can have great ramifications, and statutes regularly need to be applied in a world beyond the imagination of the most far-thinking of draftsmen. Sometimes legislation is deliberately drafted loosely, in an attempt to avoid confrontation, but this may lead to ambiguity.

Although Parliament is the source of the statutes, the courts play a vital role. When the courts apply the statutes, they will have to ascertain the intention of Parliament. This can be extremely difficult. There are a number of actors in the process that might be able to personify Parliament's intention:

- The minister: the passing of a Bill involves the minister who initiates the new law. But that person's intention may have changed or the wording may have been changed by the amendments introduced so that the Bill, as finally enacted, is very different from the one originally submitted to Parliament.

- The lawyers in the Government Legal Service who advise the minister on the legal implementation of their policies: they are the interface between the politicians and the draftsmen. They also directly draft some legislation, most commonly statutory instruments.

- The draftsmen: the draftsmen are the people who write the words of the statute at every stage from Bill to Act. If anyone knows what the words mean, surely they do. But they are not part of the decision-making process and, in theory, just translate the intent of others into print.

- The legislators: MPs debate the Bill in the House of Commons, and some of the MPs will discuss the Bill in detail in committees. Their deliberations reveal why the Bill is changed before it becomes law. But their deliberations are politically motivated, and perhaps are not appropriate as a source of assistance in statutory interpretation.

So the intention of Parliament emerges as an artificial and elusive concept which can pose all sorts of problems. Even straightforward phrases can have more than one meaning. Take this example from s. 1(1) of the Street Offences Act 1959:

> It shall be an offence for a common prostitute to loiter or solicit in a street or public place for the purpose of prostitution.

In *Smith v Hughes*[24] the defendant was inside her home, tapping on the window, to attract the attention of potential clients. Did the prostitute need to be in the street, or did the soliciting need to be there? The High Court (Queen's Bench Division) decided that only the soliciting had to be in the street and that therefore the defendant was guilty under the Act. They decided this to reflect the reason behind the passing of the statute. We look at this technique under 'The mischief rule' at 4.4.3.1.

---

[24] *Smith v Hughes* [1960] 2 All ER 859.

4.4.2 Drafting legislation in the UK

Statutory interpretation is especially important in the UK because Parliament was created in a common law (as opposed to civil law) tradition. We examined the interaction of statute law and case law in Chapter 2.

In most civil law jurisdictions, legislators aim for statutes to be comprehensive and continuously updated legal codes. These combine very general core principles with often exhaustive codification of detailed rules. There are many variations on this picture, but possibly the most extreme is in France, where all national level law is contained within 40-plus codes in specific areas (e.g. a criminal code), each amended frequently. The basic version runs to over 3,000 pages. It has existed in some form since the *Code Napoleon* in 1804. Statutes in these jurisdictions attempt to specify all matters that may be litigated, including procedure and remedy (or punishment). English lawyers find this rationale difficult to visualise:

> In a judicial utopia, every statute . . . would be expressed with such clarity and would cover every contingency so effectively that interpretation would be straightforward and the only task of the courts would be to apply their terms. Utopia has not yet arrived . . . and judges facing the interpretation of ambiguous or obscure provisions must use the well-worn tools of statutory construction to arrive at a result.[25]

In common law jurisdictions, the body of legislation (like case law) tends to grow organically. There is rarely an attempt in English law to create a comprehensive 'code' in any area, and there are no overriding written constitutional principles. It is rare for a statute to attempt to provide an answer for every situation in which a statute may be relevant. The common law frequently fills the gaps left (intentionally or not) by the legislators. Consequently, legislators can legislate in the knowledge that they can leave some issues (in many areas of law) to the courts to resolve.

Four examples (Examples 2–5) draw out key ramifications of this 'common law' style of drafting.

Example 2
Reasonableness and exemption clauses—letting the courts fill in the gaps

A typical example is the concept of 'reasonableness' which is central to the Unfair Contract Terms Act 1977 (UCTA). Under this Act, certain attempts to exclude liability in contract and tort are enforceable only if they are 'reasonable'.

While there is some guidance in the statute as to what constitutes a 'reasonable' exclusion of liability, subsequent case law has fleshed out the concept considerably, including the seminal case of *Smith* v *Bush*,[26] consideration of which is usually essential in any discussion of UCTA reasonableness.

Example 3
Companies Act 2006—reliance on an established body of case law

Even the Companies Act 2006, which was drafted to be comprehensive and to codify the law (in the civil as distinct from common law tradition), leaves key concepts open to judicial interpretation, by

---

[25] Lord Carswell in *Smith* v *Smith* [2006] UKHL 35, at [79].
[26] *Smith* v *Bush (Eric S) (A firm); Harris* v *Wyre Forest District Council* [1990] 1 AC 831.

explicitly relying upon accepted case law. The key area of directors' duties epitomises this approach. See, for example, s. 178:

Civil consequences of breach of general duties

(1) The consequences of breach . . . are the same as would apply if the corresponding common law rule or equitable principle applied.

(2) The duties in these sections . . . are, accordingly, enforceable in the same way as any other fiduciary duty owed to a company by its directors.

Example 4

Hunting Act 2004—letting courts deal with controversial issues?

This statute consumed a significant amount of parliamentary time. It would seem important, in legislation regulating the hunting of foxes, to define the word 'hunt'. The draftsmen deliberately avoided providing a definition, perhaps conscious of the ability of courts to fine-tune the law to suit complex situations.

It has been suggested that the draftsmen were striving to give effect to a key election pledge without making the legislation so draconian that it would be unenforceable. According to a leading text,[27] an early private member's Bill on the subject demonstrated the problems associated with attempts to draft too specifically. Had that Bill become law, courts would have been invited to determine the intention, not of the huntsmen, but of the dogs.

Example 5

Copyright, Designs and Patents Act 1988—an example of 'future-proof' drafting?

Partly because UK statutes are not all-encompassing codes, their wording becomes strained when society and technology develop. The Copyright, Designs and Patents Act 1988 ('CDPA') was drafted at a time when widespread use of computers was in its infancy, and digital file sharing (and so-called 'format-shifting') was science fiction for most people. The statute (with some modification) is still the primary source of law in the area, thanks to some flexible drafting and imaginative judges in key cases.

For instance, s. 16 of the Act states that the owner of copyright in a 'work' (e.g. a book, a photograph, or a painting) has the exclusive right to copy the work or any substantial part of it. In 1988, whether 'a substantial part' could be construed to include the overall structure of a computer program (its 'architecture') was still a question that could not be accurately legislated for. But the words 'substantial part' have since been found to include a program's architecture.[28]

However, even so, there are still limitations, and increasing demands for amendment of this particular statute only serve to show how difficult is the balancing act for draftsmen.[29] The CDPA has indeed been amended on numerous occasions to help the law adapt to the digital age among other things.

---

[27] Greenberg, D. (ed.) (2008) *Craies on Legislation*. London: Sweet & Maxwell, 9th edn, p. 359.

[28] E.g. *Cantor Fitzgerald* v *Tradition (UK)* [2000] RPC 95.

[29] See Hargreaves, I. (2011) *Digital Opportunity: A Review of Intellectual Property and Growth*. London: TSO. Available online at: http://www.ipo.gov.uk/ipreview-finalreport.pdf.

So a UK statute attempts to provide general rules but also seeks precision when necessary. Taxation statutes tend to leave little to the discretion of courts, whereas others (like the Hunting Act, see Example 4) may adopt a looser style. A parliamentary draftsman seeks to create rules that are 'justiciable', that is to say that the courts can apply to everyday situations.

The result of this is that, as drafted, statutes may often contain ambiguities. What are the techniques used for resolving these ambiguities?

4.4.3 **Rules of interpretation**

Just as a mechanic might have boxes containing tools with which to fix cars, so a lawyer (and, in particular, a judge) has a mental box of tools with which to interpret statutes. These are called rules of interpretation, although they are not 'rules' in the strictest sense of the word. They are very much tools of the trade from which lawyers can choose, if there is an ambiguity, to help interpret the provision concerned. They are free, within reason, to choose the means they believe most appropriate for the task.

There is no particular order of priority, though each type of rule has a different role to play, and the rules of construction usually drive the judge's reasoning.

Essential explanation

Key rules of statutory interpretation

- Rules of construction: what meaning to give words, and why.
- Rules of language: how to read specific words in context, especially when used in lists.
- Presumptions: at 4.2.1.2 under 'UK and devolved legislation' presumptions were defined as rules that are presumed to apply in certain situations. Statutory presumptions are rebuttable, but they can be used to settle finely balanced arguments about meaning.
- Statutory aids: sources of guidance on the meaning of words in a statute both inside and outside the statute itself.

Lawyers rarely refer to the various rules of interpretation by name. The list of techniques here, however, is given to allow you to familiarise yourself with the tools at a lawyer's disposal. Continuing the analogy, a mechanic rarely sets out all of his tools while working on a car, but he does need to know instinctively which sort of tool will suit a given job.

4.4.3.1 **Rules of construction**

For this section we use the Hunting Act 2004 as an example. The primary offence created by this statute is as defined in s. 1:

> A person commits an offence if he hunts a wild mammal with a dog, unless his hunting is exempt.

Imagine that you have been charged with this offence by the CPS after riding a horse in the countryside with a pack of terriers. You were carrying a gun to shoot any foxes that might be pursued by the hounds. Your lawyer would challenge the CPS to explain why it had construed the statute so that 'hunts' included your activities. The CPS lawyer would justify its interpretation by using a rule of construction.

The literal rule

The court will always look first at the literal rule, applying the language of a statute using the ordinary and natural meaning of the words. A dictionary often helps with this.

Here, a terrier is a dog, and you were riding with hunting dogs and a gun. *The Oxford English Dictionary* defines 'hunt' to include, 'pursue (wild animals or game . . .) for sport or food; . . . use (horse or hounds) for hunting'. You were hunting.

The golden rule

Sometimes, as we saw in relation to *Smith* v *Hughes*[30] at 4.4.1, the literal rule may give rise to an ambiguity. The golden rule is designed to mitigate some of the problems which can arise with the literal rule. So, if the literal rule leads to manifest absurdity or an offensive result, the court will depart from the literal meaning—but only if there is any ambiguity. A lawyer may also argue that the golden rule can be used even if the literal interpretation is clear, but this 'wider' approach is not universally accepted.

Here, your defence lawyer might argue that the literal interpretation argued by the CPS is manifestly absurd. Its argument was that because you had a pack of dogs and a horse, you were clearly hunting; but this could mean that any person walking a dog, while on horseback (possibly irrespective of the presence of a gun) could potentially be caught by the Act. Horse-riding is, after all, a sport, as included in the dictionary definition of 'hunting'. As this is absurd, this interpretation should not be used and therefore you should not be guilty.

The mischief rule

The mischief rule strives to allow interpretation of a statute in line with the intent of Parliament. The court tries to ascertain why the legislation was introduced with this wording. It asks itself, 'what was the mischief which Parliament was trying to address?' and then seeks to resolve any ambiguity in the wording to reflect the legislative intention. One of the ways it can do this is by looking at *Hansard*, the official record of proceedings in Parliament.

In 4.4.1, we examined the problems of trying to divine the intention of Parliament. *Hansard* may help. So your lawyer might argue (using a *Hansard* report) that Alun Michael, then a minister at the Department for Environment, Food and Rural Affairs, had maintained during debates in the Hunting Bill Committee on 4 February 2003 that:

> The intentions or actions of the hunter determine what is going on. Hunting has an ordinary meaning: 'to hunt' is the intention to pursue a wild mammal. Without that intent, a person is not hunting and is not covered by the offence.

However the circumstances in which *Hansard* can be used in court are limited: see *Pepper* v *Hart* under 'Extrinsic aids', at 4.4.3.3.

The purposive approach

The purposive approach involves the court interpreting legislation bearing in mind its purpose. It often yields similar results to the mischief rule but by a different means. Judges look

---

[30] *Smith* v *Hughes* [1960] 2 All ER 859.

at the reasons why the statute was passed and its purpose, even if it means distorting the ordinary meaning of the words. This approach has been influenced by our historical membership of the EU as it is widely used in European law, which is drafted with the expectation that judges will consider the policy behind the words. However, the principle is not confined to EU law and UK judges frequently adopt a purposive approach when considering all types of statute.

In relation to EU law: under s. 2(4) of the European Communities Act 1972, the court must adopt a purposive approach in construing EU-related legislation, and in particular UK provisions implementing EU law. Section 6 of the European Union (Withdrawal) Act 2018 preserves this approach for retained EU legislation.[31] The purposive approach[32] is normally taken in civil law jurisdictions.[33]

EU legislation is drafted in a very different way from English statutes. It follows the civil law tradition—although it is exhaustive, there is an emphasis in key parts of EU legislation on a high degree of generalisation. For instance, an EU Directive often starts with a summary of the policy behind the legislation, including its aims. This means that a purposive approach is vital when interpreting legislation, so that questions of wider economic or social aims are often considered by the courts, including in the UK post-Brexit.

Example 6

Litster v Forth Dry Dock and Engineering Co. Ltd

A statutory instrument[34] had implemented the EU Employee Rights on Transfer of Business Directive.[35] It provided that a transferee (the new owner of a business) should not terminate the contract of any person employed 'immediately before the transfer'.

In *Litster v Forth Dry Dock and Engineering Co. Ltd*,[36] dockworkers were dismissed one hour before a business was transferred to a new owner. The employees claimed they were unfairly dismissed.

The House of Lords (now the Supreme Court) read into the provision the additional words 'or would have been so employed if he had not been unfairly dismissed before the transfer'. This was necessary to achieve the purpose of the EU Directive, which was to protect the employees on the transfer of a business.

In relation to the Human Rights Act: the purposive approach is also used in relation to human rights law. The HRA incorporated into UK law most of the rights set out in the ECHR. Under s. 3 of the Act, legislation must be read, so far as it is possible to do so, in a way compatible with the rights enshrined in the Convention.

---

[31] The UK left the EU on 31 January 2020 (as a result of a referendum of 23 June 2016). The statute mentioned here is part of the raft of statutes implementing this referendum. Any references to the EU in this section should be read with this in mind. For information relating to the continuing importance of EU Law, refer to Chapter 2, and in particular the Essential explanation of 'Brexit' at 2.2.3.

[32] European Union (Withdrawal) Act 2018, s. 6.

[33] For more discussion of Brexit, refer to Chapter 2, and in particular the Essential explanation of Brexit at 2.2.3.

[34] Transfer of Undertakings (Protection of Employment) Regulations 1981 (SI 1981/1794), reg. 5.

[35] Employee Rights on Transfer of Business Directive 77/187.

[36] *Litster v Forth Dry Dock and Engineering* Co. Ltd [1989] 1 All ER 1134.

In our 'hunting' example, your lawyer might argue that the Hunting Act 2004 as a whole is incompatible with citizens' rights (e.g. the right to privacy,[37] and to freedom of assembly[38]) under the Act. This was argued—albeit unsuccessfully—in the *Countryside Alliance*[39] case that tested the enforceability of the Act in the House of Lords.

Analysis: because very broad principles are set out in these areas of law, courts can interpret legislation in line with these principles. This is sometimes called a 'teleological' approach. As a consequence UK courts have to adopt an explicitly aims-based or policy-driven approach to EU-derived legislation, and also where the ECHR is involved. This approach is incrementally superseding the 'mischief' approach traditionally used by English courts in interpreting legislation. Although the purposive approach is strongly reminiscent of the mischief rule, there are differences:

- When using 'traditional' principles of statutory interpretation, courts are unable to change (or 'do violence to', as judges often say) the wording of the legislation. Parliament, remember, is sovereign. With the purposive approach, even where there is no ambiguity in the wording for the courts to play with, courts may do some violence to the statutory provision, by adding or substituting words, as they bring it into line with the perceived aims of the legislation.

- The two rules also operate differently: the purposive approach looks forwards (or even upwards) at the aims of the original legislation. By contrast, the mischief approach looks backwards to the root of the problem before the relevant statute was passed.

4.4.3.2 Rules of language

Rules of language are technical tools to help you use the language in a statute to resolve any ambiguity. You will often use them in the context of lists. We examine four of the key rules of language, by translating them, discussing them, applying each of them to a sample statute, and then looking at an example of their application from case law. The rules have Latin names, but the techniques are quite straightforward and in practice you rarely need to use the Latin expressions.

To illustrate these rules we use the Dangerous Wild Animals Act 1976 (DWAA).

Example 7

Dangerous Wild Animals Act 1976

The Dangerous Wild Animals Act 1976 (DWAA)[40] was enacted to regulate the import and keeping of exotic pets. The aim was to reduce the risk of injury to the public and maltreatment of the animals concerned. The regime requires anyone who wishes to keep such an animal to obtain a licence from the local authority.

---

[37] Art. 8 ECHR. [38] Art. 11 ECHR.

[39] *R (Countryside Alliance and others) v Attorney General and another, R (Derwin and others) v Attorney General and another* [2007] UKHL 52.

[40] Text available online at http://www.legislation.gov.uk.

Section 1(1) states, 'no person shall keep any dangerous wild animal except under the authority of a licence granted in accordance with the provisions of this Act by a local authority'. The animals concerned are listed in a schedule to the DWAA.

Imagine you have a spider in your possession, very similar to the notorious Black Widow spider. It is however of a different genus and unlike any other spider. Like the Black Widow, it can kill or paralyse with its bite. Section 1 creates the obligation to keep a licence if a person keeps a dangerous wild animal. What is such an animal? Do you need a licence? We look next at how each of the chosen rules of language applies to the DWAA and could assist in interpreting the statute, and answering these questions.

Expressio unius est exclusio alterius

Translation: to say one thing is to exclude the others.

Explanation: sometimes a court will decide that a list is clearly intended only to include all the relevant items, and so if something (e.g. a mouse in a list of mammals) is not specifically listed, then it must be excluded. This is a very literal and often common-sense approach, and could certainly be used in tandem with the literal rule.

Application to DWAA: most statutes have an interpretation section, usually towards the end of the statute. Longer legislation may have a series of sections, forming a distinct part of the statute. These sections contain definitions of important terms in the relevant statute. Part II of this book gives more detail on techniques of reading statutes.

Section 7(4) states that '"dangerous wild animal" means any animal of a kind for the time being specified in the first column of the Schedule to this Act'. This incorporates the schedule into the Act. Schedules are frequently used to contain lengthy detail that might undermine the clarity of the main (or operative) parts of the Act.

Go to the end of the schedule and you will find a list of spiders which require a licence. At the end of the list is 'Theridiidae of the species of the genus Latrodectus', explained in the second column as, 'The black widow spider (otherwise known as redback spider) and its close relatives'. The list, therefore, does not expressly include your spider. Indeed, the Secretary of State has not seen fit to amend the list in the schedule under powers conferred by the statute. Are you therefore entitled to keep this spider outside the protective regime of the DWAA? Using the *expressio* rule, yes. It is not on the list, so you do not need a licence.

Example from case law: in *R v Secretary of State for the Home Department, ex p Crew*,[41] *expressio* was used to exclude the father of an illegitimate child from rights under immigration law, because the definitions section mentioned the mother alone. (The law has since changed.)

Noscitur a sociis

Translation: known by the company it keeps.

Explanation: the meaning can be taken from the surrounding words and context; this could extend as far as all relevant parts of the statute. It is usually used to interpret words in an *exhaustive* list (i.e. where there is a list of specific things to which that provision of the statute applies, with no general words to allow the inclusion of unforeseen alternatives). This is often used in conjunction with the mischief rule, because the context of the statute is important. The rule is often used in opposition to an *expressio* argument.

[41] *R v Secretary of State for the Home Department, ex parte Crew* [1982] Imm AR 94.

Application to DWAA: you would be ill-advised not to apply for a licence for keeping your spider. The argument used by the local council (and then the CPS) would be that, while not expressly mentioned in the Act, the spider should be taken to be a 'close relative of' the Black Widow. It would therefore be a dangerous wild animal because all the other spiders listed, indeed the scorpions too, are potentially very harmful. The CPS might also use the mischief rule to help reinforce this argument, namely that regulating animals like yours was exactly what this statute was designed for.

Example from case law—*Pengelly v Bell Punch Co. Ltd*:[42] the Factories Act 1961 required that all 'floors, steps, stairs, passageways and gangways' had to be kept free from obstruction. The court had to decide whether a floor used for storage came under the provisions of the Act. It held that as all the other words were used to indicate passage, a floor used exclusively for storage did not fall within the Act. This was a negative use of the rule; but note how the rule goes further than *expressio*, because it examines the context of the words to help interpretation.

Eiusdem generis

Translation: of the same type.

Explanation: this rule is used where general words need interpretation. This is usually the case with *non-exhaustive* lists, where the list allows for as yet unforeseen possibilities, often using general words. (Compare this with *noscitur a sociis*, earlier, which is useful when dealing with *exhaustive* lists.) If a general word follows two or more specific words, that general word will only apply to items of the same type as the specific words. There is a considerable overlap in application between *eiusdem* and *noscitur*.

Application to DWAA: the 'cat' section of the schedule is more appropriate as an example here, because it contains general words that may need interpretation. A client has acquired a Bengal cat, a hybrid breed of cat, formed by the cross of a domestic feline and an Asian leopard cat. It is not a pure domestic cat, though many are kept as pets. Do they need a licence? Looking at the schedule the relevant provision states that a keeper needs a licence for '*Felidae*, except the species *Felis catus*': that is, all cats except domestic cats.

The explanation clarifies this as: 'The bobcat, caracal, cheetah, jaguar, lion, lynx, ocelot, puma, serval, tiger and all other cats (the domestic cat is excepted)'. So we need to look at the rest of the provision. 'All other cats' seems quite unequivocal—it includes the Bengal cat. The client might argue that the list of cats is a list of potentially dangerous cats not commonly kept in the home. This list reflects the mischief the Act was designed to address. The general words, 'all other cats', require interpretation. Does this include domestic/wild hybrids? These general words need to be construed *eiusdem generis*. The list of cats includes dangerous wild undomesticated cats. 'All other cats' (you might argue) means 'all other wild undomesticated cats', and therefore not your Bengal cat. Bengal cats are not dangerous wild cats like the others.

You may wish at this stage to look at how the statute has been updated. The Dangerous Wild Animals Act 1976 (Modification) (No. 2) Order 2007[43] was enacted to deal with this exact problem, and the exception has been explicitly expanded to include so-called hybrid cats.

Example from case law—*Woods v Commissioner of Police of the Metropolis*:[44] the Vagrancy Act 1824 was enacted to deal with a sudden influx of 'ne'er-do-wells', including soldiers

---

[42] *Pengelly v Bell Punch Co. Ltd* [1964] 1 WLR 1055.   [43] SI 2007/2465.
[44] *Wood v Commissioner of Police of the Metropolis* [1986] 1 WLR 796.

discharged from the Napoleonic Wars and refugees fleeing hostile absent landlords in Scotland and Ireland. Section 4 of the Act defined offensive weapons as 'any gun, pistol, hanger, cutlass, bludgeon or other offensive weapons'. Mr Wood was charged with an offence under this Act after using a piece of broken glass, which had fallen out of his front door, as a weapon. It was held that the words 'other offensive weapons' were to be construed as being confined to articles made or adapted for use for causing injury to the person. The glass was no such article, so it was not *eiusdem generis* with the specific items caught by the statute and therefore no offence was committed by the defendant.

In pari materia

Translation: upon the same matter or subject.

Explanation: the meaning of an ambiguity in a statute can be determined in light of other statutes on the same subject matter, provided the ambiguous statute concerned does not expressly mention another statute. This promotes consistency and transparency of law.

Application to DWAA: s. 5 of the Act exempts certain keepers from the requirement to license, mainly because they are subject to alternative regimes. The section states:

The provisions of this Act shall not apply to any dangerous wild animal kept in:

(1) a zoological garden;

(2) a circus;

(3) premises licensed as a pet shop under the Pet Animals Act 1951;

(4) a place registered pursuant to the Cruelty to Animals Act 1876 for the purpose of performing experiments.

The rule of language does *not* apply to s. 5(3) and (4) because these refer explicitly to other statutes. But s. 5(1) does not refer to another statute. The proprietors of a zoo could however (in the event of doubt) point to the Zoo Licensing Act 1981. Section 1(2) of this Act defines the term 'zoo' (the definition is quite lengthy and does not need to be repeated here). If they are within this definition, then they are likely to be within the definition of a 'zoological garden' for the DWAA.

Example from case law—*R (ZA (Nigeria)) v Secretary of State for the Home Department, R (SM (Congo)) v Secretary of State for the Home Department*:[45] a claimant's asylum claim under a statute[46] was denied on the basis that previous asylum claims under earlier secondary legislation[47] had also been denied.

Rules of language—conclusion

It is worth remembering that these rules often reiterate common sense, and sometimes it is better to ignore their Latin labels. They are not 'rules' in the normal sense of the word in that there is no obligation to use them. It may be better to think of them, along with principles of construction—with which they overlap—as a set of techniques and tools that you can use in

---

[45] *R (ZA (Nigeria)) v Secretary of State for the Home Department, R (SM (Congo)) v Secretary of State for the Home Department* [2010] EWCA Civ 926.

[46] Borders, Citizenship and Immigration Act 2009, s. 53.

[47] *Statement of Changes in Immigration Rules* (1994) (HC 395), r. 353 (as inserted by *Statement of Changes in Immigration Rules* (2004) (HC 1112)).

any combination to support interpretation of statutes. You should also remember that these rules apply to most legal documents, from a residents' association constitution, through contracts, to Acts of Parliament. Therefore, it is also important to bear in mind how these rules could affect the potential interpretation of a legal document when you are drafting.

4.4.3.3 Aids to interpretation

These are resources inside and outside statutes which can help the courts in interpreting meaning. The courts can in theory use anything to ascertain the intention of Parliament, although they place greater reliance on some sources than others.

Intrinsic aids

Anything in the same Act is 'intrinsic'; therefore the first port of call is always the relevant statutory provision. Definitions will usually be at the start of the relevant part of the Act, or towards the end in an interpretation section. Chapter 7 contains a detailed explanation of the structure of a typical Act.

Other parts of the Act are helpful but not binding in the same way, so, for instance, headings and marginal notes or the Long Title—if the Act has one—may help determine its meaning. While the Long Title is formally part of the Act, it cannot be used to displace the text of provisions themselves in the statute. The Short Title, and any headings used in the Act are not considered operative parts of the statute but are helpful for reference. Chapter 7 examines the Long and Short Titles in more detail.

Extrinsic aids

Courts can look beyond the statute using an almost limitless array of extrinsic aids. In particular:

- The Interpretation Acts: these supply general assumptions for interpreting statutes, for example that the masculine includes the feminine in the absence of a contrary express statement in a specific Act.
- Dictionaries: a lawyer or court might use a dictionary to provide a meaning of a word.
- Explanatory notes: these are guidance on the majority of statutes passed since 1999 prepared by the Government Legal Service to make the Act accessible to non-lawyers.
- Other statutes: the use of other statutes can change depending on the circumstances, indeed sometimes depending on the point the advocate is trying to argue. Often a statute will expressly refer to definitions in previous statutes, but sometimes this helpful approach may not be taken. Courts may be obliged to interpret a statute in line with an earlier one if instructed expressly by the statute, or if a court considers the Acts to constitute a 'package' of measures.[48] Alternatively courts may be compelled not to follow the earlier legislation, again either expressly within the later statute, or where each statute clearly needs different application. For instance, different statutes define 'groups' of companies in different ways. Alternatively it may be a matter of discretion, and left for lawyers to argue.

[48] E.g. the concept of 'honest practices in industrial or commercial matters' is used as part of a defence to infringement of the Olympic Association right in the Olympic Symbol etc. (Protection) Act 1995. It is clear from case law that courts should follow jurisprudence developed in relation to the same phrase as used in the Trade Marks Act 1994.

- *Hansard*: as seen earlier, this is a record of the proceedings of Parliament, and helps to determine the intention of law-makers. It is particularly helpful when applying the mischief rule. In *Pepper v Hart*[49] the House of Lords set out some rules relating to the use of *Hansard*—it may only be used in relation to speeches by the relevant minister or promoter of a Bill, and even then only when the statute itself is ambiguous.
- Academic know-how: a court may refer to articles or books written on controversial areas of law by legal academics.
- Previous cases: under the doctrine of precedent one court is bound to follow the reasoning of some previous courts on a particular statute, and may be persuaded by the reasoning of others (see Chapter 5).

The list of extrinsic aids is endless, and the lawyer's skill is to give due weight to any resources used or encountered.

4.4.3.4 Presumptions

At 4.2.1 we saw that a presumption is a rule that is presumed to apply in certain situations. Presumptions are often rebuttable. A presumption is rebuttable when the legal rule concerned can be disapplied if there is enough evidence to the contrary. A statutory presumption is one about the intention of Parliament. Presumptions help clear up ambiguities in relation to common or fundamental issues. All these presumptions (there are many more than the most important ones listed in the following bullet list) are rebuttable if the Act under consideration has express statements to the contrary. Indeed there are some statutes with retrospective effect.

Certain presumptions in relation to statutes are important to the mechanics of England's legal system:

- There is a presumption against statutes altering the common law. The theory is that these two sources of law—statute and case law—should sit comfortably alongside one another. This is sometimes difficult when statute is superimposed upon existing areas of law.
- It is presumed that no statute applies retrospectively, otherwise something which was lawful when you did it might be rendered unlawful after the event. This presumption is rebutted very rarely, especially in criminal or tax matters. Occasionally, legislation is specifically stated to have retrospective effect, such as the War Crimes Act 1991, which allows the prosecution of those suspected of committing acts of atrocity during World War II.
- In criminal statutes it is presumed that any ambiguity be construed in favour of defendants as it is their liberty which is at stake—this is of course rebuttable in the face of conflicting arguments. It is also presumed that commission of an offence requires a 'guilty mind' (intent) unless it is stated that no intent to commit the crime is needed on the part of the defendant.
- There is a presumption against ousting the jurisdiction of the courts.

You should always keep the major presumptions in the back of your mind when considering ambiguities in statutes.

---

[49] *Pepper v Hart* [1993] AC 593.

4.4.4 Statutory interpretation–conclusion

Issues of interpretation are sometimes quite difficult. Mr Justice Donaldson said: 'The duty of the courts is to ascertain and give effect to the will of Parliament as expressed in its enactments . . . the interpretation of statutes is a craft as much as a science.'[50] As we have seen, the intention of Parliament is a critical concept; over time techniques for interpreting this intention have evolved.

A lawyer has many different tools to call on when interpreting a statute.

4.4.4.1 Case study

There have been few ambiguities in statutes more controversial than that in s. 3 of the Homicide Act 1957, now repealed because the deliberate ambiguities in its wording created so many problems. After the extract from the statute we summarise two cases which tested it (literally) to destruction.

Example 8
Homicide Act 1957, s. 3 (now repealed)

The Homicide Act put on a statutory footing various defences to a charge of murder.

> Where on a charge of murder there is evidence on which the jury can find that the person charged was provoked (whether by things done or by things said or by both together) to lose his self-control, the question whether the provocation was enough to make a reasonable man do as he did shall be left to be determined by the jury; and in determining that question the jury shall take into account everything both done and said according to the effect which, in their opinion, it would have on a reasonable man.

Scenario 1: *R v Smith (Morgan)*

In *R v Smith (Morgan)*[51] the defendant killed his friend, by stabbing him several times with a carving knife, after spending the evening 'in drinking and recrimination'. He claimed he had been provoked into doing so as a consequence of a number of grievances, the latest being his belief that the victim had stolen his carpentry tools. The defendant suffered from a depressive mental condition which had the effect of reducing his self-control below that of an ordinary person. He pleaded provocation as a defence to the charge of murder.

Scenario 2: *Attorney General for Jersey v Holley*

In *Attorney General for Jersey v Holley*[52] the defendant killed his girlfriend with an axe, after spending the afternoon 'drinking heavily and arguing'. They were both alcoholics. She told him she had just had sex with another man. He picked up the axe, intending to leave the flat and chop wood. When the deceased said, 'You haven't got the guts', he struck her with the axe seven or eight times. He pleaded provocation.

---

[50] *Corocraft Ltd v Pan American Airways Inc.* [1969] 1 QB 616, at 638.
[51] *R v Smith (Morgan)* [2001] 1 AC 146.   [52] *Attorney General for Jersey v Holley* [2005] UKPC 23.

In both cases the stakes were very high. The reason it was so important to the defendant to succeed in establishing provocation was because the murder charge would then be reduced to one of manslaughter. Whereas murder attracts a mandatory life sentence, the sentence for manslaughter is discretionary. These two cases produced very different results because of the way the courts approached the ambiguity in the section.

The first step is to identify the ambiguity. What is the ambiguity in s. 3 of the Homicide Act 1957? The main uncertainty which required interpretation was the term 'reasonable man'. In assessing the reasonable man can we take into account any medical conditions or personality traits?

> ### Essential explanations
> #### The 'reasonable man', the objective test
>
> You will encounter the so-called reasonable man frequently in legal discourse, particularly in the contexts of criminal, contract, and tort law. The normal use of the term is as a means of measuring a person by purely objective, dispassionate, and neutral standards.
>
> This objective standard is to be contrasted with a subjective standard. The latter is a standard matched to the characteristics of the person being discussed.

In the case study, if we are able to adapt the reasonable man to reflect the characteristics of someone with a depressive mental condition with reduced levels of self-control (as in *R v Smith (Morgan)*[53]), then the defendant in that case would be more likely to reach that standard, and be able to use the defence of provocation under the Homicide Act. He would be found guilty only of manslaughter. In *Holley*,[54] if we are able to adapt the reasonable man to reflect the characteristics of someone suffering from alcoholism (in the sense of the recognised medical affliction), then (again) Holley would be found not guilty of murder, and guilty only of manslaughter.

In these circumstances we need to use principles of statutory interpretation. In Table 4.1 are just a few of the rules that we might use (some of which were used by the Lords of Appeal in the cases).

Both the case decisions surprised academics and lawyers, albeit for different reasons.

In *R v Smith (Morgan)*,[55] the House of Lords confirmed the Court of Appeal's decision that Smith was not guilty on the ground that juries could take into account any circumstances which they regarded as relevant, including any personal characteristic of the defendant which made him particularly susceptible to losing his self-control.

In *Attorney General for Jersey v Holley*[56] the Privy Council decided that juries could not take account of the personal characteristics of defendants when deciding the issue of provocation. The standard was an objective one (would the *reasonable* man have lost control in these circumstances), not whether this defendant had.

---

[53] *R v Smith (Morgan)* [2001] 1 AC 146.
[55] *R v Smith (Morgan)* [2001] 1 AC 146.
[54] *Attorney General for Jersey v Holley* [2005] UKPC 23.
[56] *Attorney General for Jersey v Holley* [2005] UKPC 23.

Table 4.1 Use of statutory interpretation: Homicide Act 1957, s. 3

Rule	Type of rule	Favours murder or manslaughter?	Reasoning
Literal	Construction	Murder	Defendants with such medical conditions are not acting as reasonable persons if they kill people. The reasonable man does not suffer from depression, nor is he an alcoholic.
Golden	Construction	Either	It is arguably absurd that provocation is limited only to such provocation as would provoke mentally 'normal' people.
			Equally, it might be absurd to say that provocation can be adapted to suit the person provoked. There is a contradiction in terms—schizophrenics do not come within the usual definition of a 'reasonable man'.
			Taken too far, the concept could become meaningless. It would lead to absurd questions such as: would the reasonable 50-year-old overweight schizophrenic who had suffered abuse as a child have lost control when taunted about his inadequacies? A jury would find this a very difficult question to answer.
Mischief/ Purposive	Construction	Neutral	The purpose of the legislation was to mitigate the harshness of the death penalty for murder in certain circumstances. The section recognises the fact that everyone has a breaking point if they are provoked far enough.
			However, perhaps this exception was not designed to help people who have mental impairments—see argument for '*noscitur*' next.
Noscitur a sociis	Language	Murder	In view of the wider context—including the presence of other exceptions (like diminished responsibility)—this exception was not designed to deal with defendants with mental impairments.
Interpretation Act 1978	Extrinsic aid	Neutral	Section 6 states that (in all legislation) unless expressly stipulated otherwise, the masculine includes the feminine. The 'reasonable man' thus becomes the 'reasonable person'.
Presumption against deprivation of liberty	Presumption	Manslaughter	In the event of an ambiguity, it must be presumed that Parliament did not intend to deprive defendants of liberty (in this case by increasing the sentence).

The first decision was surprising because it seemed to make a mockery of the objective test. The second was surprising because, despite being more justifiable, it ran counter to the doctrine of precedent (see 5.1). The literal rule had effectively won the day; Lord Nicholls in *Holley*, impliedly restated its importance:

> Their Lordships consider there is one compelling, overriding reason why this [*Smith*] view cannot be regarded as an accurate statement of English law. It is this. The law of homicide is a highly sensitive and highly controversial area of criminal law. In 1957, Parliament altered the common law relating to provocation and declared what the law on this subject should henceforth be. In these circumstances, it is not open to judges now to change ('develop') the common law and thereby depart from the law as declared by Parliament.[57]

He went on to state there should be a uniform, objective standard of behaviour which everyone is expected to meet. If there are mental health reasons as to why a person cannot meet this standard, he would have to use the alternative defence of diminished responsibility. This ambiguity created so many problems that eventually Parliament legislated to change the defences to murder, and abolish the defence of provocation.[58]

4.4.4.2 A possible approach to statutory interpretation

We can see from Example 8 that the tools at the disposal of a lawyer when considering statutory ambiguity are varied and flexible. Aside from starting with a literal interpretation it is vital to remember that there is no particular order of priority, and that you can use these rules whenever you feel they will benefit your legal argument relating to a statute. There are no absolute rules.

Having said that, while getting used to using techniques of interpretation you might wish to adopt the following approach:

1. Start with a literal interpretation of the provision.

2. Use an alternative rule of construction either:
   - if the literal rule produces unsatisfactory results, or,
   - in relation to EU or ECHR law, when a purposive approach is required.

3. Support your interpretation. Tools for this include:
   - rules of language (in particular for lists), and
   - aids to statutory interpretation.

4. If the statute is still ambiguous, use presumptions.

4.5 EU legislation

At 2.4 we examined EU law as a source of law in the UK. We also looked at some possible effects of the vote on 23 June 2016 to leave the European Union. Here we look in more detail at the effect of EU legislation, both pre- and post-Brexit.[59] In this section we look first at EU

---

[57] *Attorney General for Jersey* v *Holley* [2005] UKPC 23, at [22] (Lord Nicholls).

[58] Coroners and Justice Act 2009, ss. 54–5.

[59] For more discussion of Brexit, refer to Chapter 2, and in particular the Essential explanation of Brexit at 2.2.3.

legislation (see 4.5.1). The effect of that legislation (see 4.5.2) is then examined before looking at how this impacts on each type of legislation (see 4.5.3).

4.5.1 EU legislation identified

EU legislation can be split into primary and secondary legislation.

The primary legislation comprises the founding treaties, such as the Treaty on the Functioning of the European Union (TFEU), the Treaty on European Union (often known as the Maastricht Treaty), and the Lisbon Treaty. These treaties are agreed by member states in various ways. Although formally signed by heads of state or prime ministers, they are normally subject to ratification by national legislation, or referendums, both of which have historically been fraught processes (the European Constitution failed in 2005 as a result of two adverse national referendums). The European Communities Act 1972 approved the UK's accession to the EEC.[60] Primary legislation is binding on member states and EU institutions, and it cannot be challenged in national courts or the ECJ.

The secondary legislation which emanates from the institutions described earlier takes the form of regulations, directives, and decisions. For a complete picture we can also include non-binding recommendations and opinions emanating from the Commission and Council, particularly in competition law. Despite being non-binding, these are classified as legislation. Lawyers will usually use the TFEU in combination with secondary legislation. They will also often refer to ECJ rulings in the same area.

Figure 4.3 summarises the main types of EU legislation, including how they are created and their legal effect.

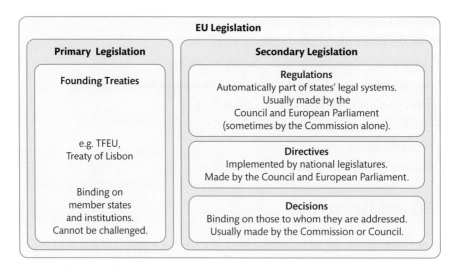

Figure 4.3 Binding EU legislation

[60] The then Prime Minister, Theresa May, notified the President of the European Council (then Donald Tusk) of the UK's intention to withdraw from the EU under Article 50(2) TFEU. Parliament granted the Prime Minister permission to do this under the European Union (Notification of Withdrawal) Act 2017.

4.5.2 The effect of EU legislation

The enforceability of EU legislation is complex, because of the variety of legislation emanating from the EU. It is crucial to understand some key terminology, even for a basic understanding of the functioning of EU law in the UK before Brexit, and possibly beyond. The terms below describe various characteristics of EU legislation; they are not necessarily mutually exclusive.

4.5.2.1 Direct effect

Directly effective legislation gives rise to rights and obligations which individuals may enforce in their national courts. There are two categories of directly effective legislation:

- Vertical direct effect: this describes a situation where EU legislation allows an individual (i.e. a legal person including companies, etc.) to make a claim in a national court against the state (or its 'emanations', i.e. public bodies).
- Horizontal direct effect: this allows individuals to make claims against each other in EU law.

There are strict criteria to determine whether a piece of EU legislation has direct effect, set out in the *Van Gend en Loos*[61] case. By virtue of the European Union (Withdrawal) Act 2018, EU legislation which is directly effective before withdrawal, remains operative after withdrawal until it is revoked. EU legislation postdating Brexit will not be enforceable in the UK, although the UK Parliament may selectively legislate to shadow EU legislation in areas where the UK is aligned with EU law.

4.5.2.2 Direct applicability

Some directly effective legislation is also said to be directly applicable. This means that the legislation becomes part of the national legal system without the need for further implementation by national legislatures (e.g. Parliament). If EU legislation requires implementation (e.g. by an implementing statute) then it is not directly applicable to EU citizens. If you think this is complex, you are not alone. The ECJ commonly uses the terms 'direct effect' and 'direct applicability' interchangeably.

4.5.2.3 Indirect effect

Under Art. 4(3) TFEU, member states must take all appropriate measures to ensure the fulfilment of their EU obligations. This requirement falls on all member state authorities including, importantly, courts. This means that courts must interpret national law in line with the relevant EU legislation.

Any EU legislation which requires national implementation will need to be legislated by the national legislature. If an individual believes the legislature has failed to legislate correctly (e.g. by giving them insufficient rights, or by failing to legislate at all within the EU time limits) then that individual can ask the national court to interpret domestic legislation in line with the relevant EU legislation. This is called 'indirect effect'. The extent of this principle is still unclear. What is clear is that this concept ceases to have an effect in the UK post-Brexit.

---

[61] *Van Gend en Loos* v *Nederlandse Administratie der Belastingen* [1963] ECR 1.

4.5.3 **EU legislation in detail**

Let us now look at each type of EU legislation in the light of how it affects an individual in a member state (both natural and legal, i.e. companies, etc.). For each type of legislation we describe it, look briefly at how that type of legislation becomes part of UK law, give a fictional illustration, and then an historical example. We use the fictional illustration to provide a direct comparison between the effects of the legislation in the same factual context.

4.5.3.1 **Treaty articles**

- Treaties are the EU's primary legislation, and are often (but not always) framed in very general, teleological (aims-based) terms.

- Articles of the TFEU form part of the legal systems of all member states. They are directly applicable. They may also be directly effective, which means an individual can rely upon rights granted by treaty articles and enforce them, if necessary, in the national courts.

- A fictional example might be the EU adopting a treaty article stating, 'Anyone working within the EU must wear clothing appropriate to their employment, because it ensures workers around the EU are equally protected.'

- For example, Art. 157 TFEU states: 'Each Member State shall ensure that the principle of equal pay for male and female workers for equal work or work of equal value is applied.' In *Defrenne* v *SABENA*,[62] SABENA paid its female flight attendants less than comparable male flight attendants. Ms Defrenne was able to use Art. 119 (now 157) TFEU to claim equal pay from her employer.

4.5.3.2 **Regulations**

- Regulations are detailed secondary legislation made under the co-decision procedure by the Council and Parliament, or by the Commission alone. At the time of writing, there were 9,159 regulations in force.

- Once a regulation has been passed, it automatically becomes part of the legal systems of all member states. It is directly applicable. Like treaty articles, regulations may also be directly effective.

- A fictional example might be a regulation directly requiring anyone working on a building site to wear appropriate protective clothing, including a hard hat and footwear with protective toecaps.

- One example of an important regulation is Commission Regulation (EC) No. 2790/1999, which deals with competition law. It permits a supplier to appoint distributors and to accept restrictions on their activities, despite the fact that restricting market behaviour is potentially anti-competitive and in breach of the TFEU. Like many regulations it is very complex and requires advanced understanding, not only of EU law but also economics.

---

[62] Case 43/75 *Defrenne* v *SABENA* (No. 2) [1976] ECR 455.

4.5.3.3 Directives

- Directives are detailed secondary legislation that the EU believes is best left to member states to implement because of the wide variety of national characteristics. They are made by the Council and Parliament under the co-decision procedure. At the time of writing, there were around 2,000 directives in force. They are binding as to the result to be achieved on each member state but leave implementation (e.g. how it is to be administered and the range of remedies available) to the national legislature. In the UK (pre-Brexit), Parliament usually (but not always) implemented directives into national law by passing secondary legislation containing the provisions specified in the relevant directive. Because they give individuals rights and obligations, directives have direct effect. However, if a member state does not implement a directive, or implements it incorrectly, it may then have indirect effect, and an individual can rely on it in the national courts, but only against the state or a state body.

- A fictional directive might require member states to legislate in line with EU policy on building site protective clothing, including their requirements in relation to hard hats and protective toecaps.

- You will encounter statutes like the Consumer Protection Act 1987 and the Trade Marks Act 1994 where national implementation has been via primary legislation. Citizens of member states are sometimes sceptical about regulation emanating directly from the supra-national EU; this may have been a factor in the UK's vote to leave the EU. If implementation of EU law is via the national legislature, the legislation concerned may have greater 'legitimacy' in the eyes of a sometimes sceptical public. This process has inherent drawbacks—both these statutes have been the subject of debate in the courts in relation to whether the implementing legislation truly reflected the parent directive.[63]

4.5.3.4 Decisions

- Decisions are made either by the Commission or the Council (sometimes by co-decision procedure with the Parliament). They are secondary legislation, binding on those to whom they are addressed—specified member states or individuals. They are very common in competition law. They are very focused in their ambit. At the time of writing, more than 16,000 decisions have been made by the Commission or Council over the lifetime of the EU.

- EU decisions are directly effective and directly applicable.

- A fictional example of a decision might be the EU telling the UK, or even a building contractor in the UK, what their policy on hard hats should be.

---

[63] Council Directive 85/374/EEC of 25 July 1985 on the approximation of the laws, regulations and administrative provisions of the Member States concerning liability for defective products; Council Directive 89/104/EEC of 21 December 1988 to approximate the laws of the Member States relating to trade marks.

- In 2007, attention in the UK focused on a series of Commission decisions relating to the export of British beef during the foot-and-mouth crisis.[64] Another famous example is the EU Commission decision under the TFEU[65] that Microsoft had abused its dominant economic position by preventing interoperability elements of its Windows bundle with rivals' products. The Commission ordered Microsoft to disclose relevant information to competitors, and levied a fine of €497,196,304.

4.5.3.5 Summary of EU legislation

Key aspects of EU legislation are summarised in Table 4.2.

4.5.4 Interpreting EU law

Because the original EU (then EEC) member states all had civil law systems (see 2.3.2 on civil vs common law), EU law was based on civil law traditions. The ECJ therefore uses an inquisitorial, rather than adversarial, system. This means that the court is aiming for the truth, as well as a winner, and the court will be more active in respect of evidence and witnesses. There are no minority judgments or dissents—for more details of the ECJ see 3.5.1.

The ultimate source of law in a civil system is a Code—in the EU this is the EU Treaty (TFEU). This sets out the principles on which the rest of the law is based. The ECJ then interprets the law by applying those principles in the circumstances of each particular case.

Table 4.2 Summary of EU legislation

Type of legislation	Directly applicable?	Directly effective?	Capable of indirect effect?	Institution
	Automatically part of legal system	Gives enforceable rights to individuals	Reinterpretation of domestic legislation by national courts	
Treaty article	Yes	Sometimes	N/A	N/A
Regulation	Yes	Often	N/A	Commission, or Council and Parliament
Directive	No	Yes	Yes	Council and Parliament
Decision	Yes	Specific addressees only	No	Commission or Council (sometimes with Parliament)

---

[64] E.g. Commission Decision 2007/663/EC of 12 October 2007 amending Decision 2007/554/EC concerning certain protection measures against foot-and-mouth disease in the United Kingdom (notified under document number C(2007) 4660).

[65] Commission Decision 2007/53/EC of 24 May 2004 relating to a proceeding pursuant to Art. 82 of the EC Treaty and Art. 54 of the EEA Agreement against Microsoft Corporation (Case COMP/C-3/37.792—Microsoft) (notified under document number C(2004) 900).

The ECJ would (like an English court) normally start with a literal approach (see 4.4.3), but it may (even if there is no ambiguity) depart from this with a purposive approach. In the *SABENA* case mentioned at 4.5.3.1 a literal interpretation would only have protected the air hostess had she been a state employee. The ECJ purposively interpreted the article to include private employers as being subject to the obligation.

The ECJ does not adopt a strict system of precedent, but, rather like the UK Supreme Court, it will try to follow a principle of consistency. All EU national courts are bound by the rulings of the ECJ—although some national courts (particularly the German and French constitutional courts) have been reluctant to follow ECJ jurisprudence when it was not consistent with their domestic codes.

4.5.5 EU law and UK law—revisiting parliamentary supremacy

During the Brexit campaign, leading 'Brexiteer' (and future Prime Minister) Boris Johnson stated, 'you cannot express the sovereignty of Parliament and accept the 1972 European Communities Act'[66]—see 2.2.3 for the 'Essential explanation' of Brexit. Sections 2(1) and 3 of the European Communities Act 1972 obliged all UK courts to give effect to any EU law which is directly effective and to follow decisions of the ECJ. UK courts were required to apply directly effective EU law in preference to domestic law and to interpret all domestic law to comply with EU law, as far as possible. While the TFEU does not state that EU law is supreme over national law, the ECJ has developed key principles that have entrenched this supremacy. Until Brexit, it was increasingly recognised in the English legal system that EU law had supremacy over Parliament and was therefore a limitation on parliamentary sovereignty. This was a central issue in the campaign that ultimately led to the vote to leave the EU.

An example of the way in which the UK courts acknowledged the supremacy of EU law can be seen in Example 9.

Example 9

R v Secretary of State for Transport, ex parte Factortame (No. 2)

Some Spanish fishermen set up a UK company to operate trawlers with the intention of exploiting the UK fishing quota in the North Sea. The Merchant Shipping Act 1988 was enacted to prevent this practice. The Spanish fishermen who found themselves excluded by this rule argued that the Act was contrary to the TFEU.

The ECJ agreed that the Merchant Shipping Act was indeed contrary to the TFEU. This case was significant because the ECJ stated that national courts were to ignore any national law which ran contrary to directly effective EU law. The House of Lords[67] was given no choice by the ECJ but to ignore the relevant provision of the UK statute, and grant the injunction.

This was clearly a watershed decision, but it is worth noting that the House of Lords (and now the UK Supreme Court) never declared UK statutes void in whole or part, as happens under the doctrine of judicial review in the US.

---

[66] Boris Johnson MP, *Andrew Marr Show*, BBC 1, 6 March 2016.

[67] *R v Secretary of State for Transport, ex parte Factortame (No. 2)* [1991] 1 AC 603.

During the UK's EU membership, it was argued (see 4.1.1.3) that Parliament remained sovereign in that it had the power to abolish the European Communities Act 1972 and with it EU law supremacy. This formerly academic argument was vindicated by Brexit. This is only an option for 'dualist' systems like the UK, where, international and/or EU law is not automatically part of domestic law. By contrast, in 'monist' systems, such as the Netherlands, all international law to which the state in question is party is given constitutional supremacy. In the last edition of this book, we stated, 'Abolition of the European Communities Act 1972 and withdrawal from the EU would, however, be politically exceedingly controversial, so we can conclude that in areas of EU competence, EU law is in practice supreme.' It is fair to say that circumstances have changed since then.

4.6 The Human Rights Act 1998

The HRA was passed to give UK citizens protection of certain rights in the UK courts. It was a key pledge in the manifesto of the Labour Party before its landslide victory in 1997. The White Paper that preceded this Act contained a foreword by the then Prime Minister, Tony Blair, which shows how important the Act was to the government:

> The Bill marks a major step forward in the achievement of our programme of reform. It will give people in the United Kingdom opportunities to enforce their rights under the European Convention in British courts rather than having to incur the cost and delay of taking a case to the European Human Rights Commission and Court in Strasbourg. It will enhance the awareness of human rights in our society. And it stands alongside our decision to put the promotion of human rights at the forefront of our foreign policy.[68]

The issue of human rights is contentious in British politics. Ex-Prime Minister David Cameron said in 2011 (a day after widespread riots had caused extensive damage):

> But what is alien to our tradition—and now exerting such a corrosive influence on behaviour and morality, is the twisting and misrepresenting of human rights in a way that has undermined personal responsibility. The interpretation of human rights legislation has exerted a chilling effect on public sector organisations, leading them to act in ways that fly in the face of common sense, offend our sense of right and wrong, and undermine responsibility. We're working to develop a way through the morass by looking at creating our own British Bill of Rights.[69]

Statutory interpretation had hit the headlines. David Cameron was referring to certain defensive administrative practices that may have developed such as, for instance, police needing to keep one eye on duties under the HRA towards suspects and witnesses, or (the example David Cameron used in the interview concerned) a prison van being driven nearly 100 miles to transport a prisoner 200 yards when the prisoner was willing to walk. It is interesting to note that the 'British Bill of Rights' has been de-prioritised since the vote to leave the EU.

The HRA is unique in its pervasive effect on the operation of the English legal system, and sits alongside the European Communities Act 1972 as one of the most important statutes of recent times. This book does not look in detail at the substance of human rights law, but instead gives an outline of its effect on the English legal system.

---

[68] *Rights Brought Home: the Human Rights Bill* (1997). London: HMSO, Cm. 3782.
[69] David Cameron, speech (15 August 2011).

4.6.1 Before the Human Rights Act

Prior to the coming into force of the HRA, the UK was a (founder) member of the Council of Europe, meaning that it was a signatory to the ECHR, adopted in 1950. The Convention was a response to the atrocities of World War II and Nazi Germany, and also intended as a barrier against the totalitarian practices of the Soviet bloc. The aim was to prevent large-scale violations of human rights.

The rights specifically defined in the Convention include the rights to life, freedom from torture or inhumane or degrading treatment or punishment, and the right to a fair trial by an impartial tribunal. Schedule 1 to the HRA lists the 'Convention Rights'. The Convention gives a citizen of a signatory state the right to apply to the European Court of Human Rights for an order for compensation on the ground that there has been a breach by the state of the Convention, either directly (e.g. by the actions of the police) or indirectly (e.g. because the approach of courts has constituted a lack of access to a fair trial under Art. 6). However, this procedure is expensive, and lengthy, because of the need to exhaust domestic avenues of justice, and because of the logjam of cases before the European Court of Human Rights. It is said to take five years to get a case to the court, and cost on average £30,000.[70]

The HRA was passed to give citizens remedies for breach of their human rights without having to go to the European Court of Human Rights. The key mechanisms are:

- making it unlawful for a public body to act incompatibly with the Convention rights;
- ensuring courts take into account European Court of Human Rights jurisprudence in their decision-making; and
- ensuring courts interpret legislation compatibly with the Convention.

4.6.2 The rights protected

The protection of key rights and freedoms is an important attribute of the Rule of Law (see 1.5). The rights are classified in three ways:

- Absolute rights: these do not allow for any exception at all. For instance, it is always a breach of the Convention for a signatory state to use torture against its citizens (Art. 3).
- Limited rights: these can be suspended in times of war or emergency, for example the right to a fair trial (Art. 6).
- Qualified rights: these require a balance between the rights of individuals and (if the state is involved) the needs of the state. So, for instance, while a newspaper may claim that revealing private information about a celebrity is an important aspect of freedom of expression (Art. 10), the individual concerned would counter that it is an infringement of her right to privacy (Art. 8). Many of the sensationalist headlines of newspapers tend to ignore that many rights within the Convention (and HRA) are subject to the principle of 'proportionality'. This means that the impact of the HRA must not be out of proportion to the importance of the allegedly infringing action by the state.

Some of the key rights are listed in Table 4.3.

---

[70] *Rights Brought Home: the Human Rights Bill* (1997). London: HMSO, Cm. 3782, para. 1.14.

Table 4.3 The Convention rights

Absolute rights	Qualified or limited rights
Art. 2: Right to life	Art. 5: Right to liberty and security
Art. 3: Prohibition of torture	Art. 6: Right to a fair trial
Art. 4: Prohibition of slavery	Art. 8: Right to respect for private and family life
Art. 7: No punishment without law	Art. 9: Right to freedom of thought, conscience and religion
	Art. 10: Right to freedom of expression
	Art. 11: Right to freedom of assembly and association
	Art. 12: Right to marry
	Art. 1 of the 1st Protocol: Right to protection of property
	Art. 2 of the 2nd Protocol: Right to education
	Art. 3 of the 2nd Protocol: Right to free and fair elections

4.6.3 Using the Human Rights Act

The HRA gives additional rights to UK citizens using two mechanisms: vertical and horizontal effect. It also affects statutory interpretation and the operation of case law. In this section we look at how individuals can use the HRA; an understanding of this will help in many different areas of law.

4.6.3.1 Vertical effect

A rule of law with 'vertical' effect can be used by a person against the state (we have already seen this in the context of EU law at 4.5.2). Section 6 of the HRA states that it is unlawful for a public authority (e.g. the police) to act in a way that is incompatible with Convention rights unless it is left with no choice to do so by statute. In public law there has long been a doctrine called 'judicial review'. This is a mechanism which enables the courts to ensure that the government and other public bodies exercise the powers which they have been granted in the proper way and so do not breach the rule of law. The HRA has given a significant impetus to the doctrine of judicial review.

4.6.3.2 Horizontal effect

This is perhaps the most radical effect of the Act in terms of its effect on the English legal system. As we have seen in the context of EU law (see 4.5.2) any rule of law that has 'horizontal' effect can be used by one person against another. This means that in some contexts a person can say that another private person or organisation has infringed his rights. There is no express statement to this effect in the HRA. The process is indirect.

It has already been said that s. 6 of the HRA requires public authorities to act compatibly with Convention rights. This, crucially, includes the courts. Baroness Hale has said: 'The

1998 Act does not create any new cause of action between private persons. But if there is a relevant cause of action applicable, the court as a public authority must act compatibly with both parties' Convention rights.'[71] So the Convention right needs to 'piggyback' on another claim.

On 30 March 2008, the *News of the World* published an article, the 'sting' of which was that Max Mosley (former President of the Federation Internationale de l'Automobile and leading contemporary Formula 1 figure) had employed five prostitutes to act out allegedly pseudo-Nazi prison camp sex scenes. He successfully sued the paper.[72] The claim was made under what Mr Justice Eady called an 'old fashioned breach of confidence'. 'Breach of confidence' is a tort. However, Mr Justice Eady used Art. 6 of the Convention (respect for private life) to help him come to the conclusion that the tort had been breached. Prior to the HRA, this avenue would not have been available to him. Some commentators felt that (despite Mr Justice Eady's protestations to the contrary) this let a new tort of privacy in through the back door.

This mechanism has been used in many other important areas of law, including defamation and negligence.

4.6.4 The impact of the Human Rights Act on statutes

4.6.4.1 The purposive approach under s. 3

We saw in 4.5.3 that the European Communities Act 1972 requires UK courts to give effect to any EU law which is binding. Likewise, s. 3 of the HRA provides that 'so far as it is possible to do so, primary and secondary legislation must be read and given effect in a way which is compatible with the Convention rights'. If a court cannot achieve this, it may make a declaration of incompatibility in respect of the relevant piece of legislation.

Section 3 of the HRA implies that a purposive approach must be adopted by courts in relation to the Convention rights (as listed in Table 4.3). This purposive approach was alien to English courts, except in the context of EU law. Lady Justice Arden has said that courts have been 'feeling their way towards a set of rules and canons of construction that will apply where section 3(1) is in point'.[73] The application is less strict than for EU law and the words 'so far as it is possible to do so' in s. 3 of the HRA clearly envisage that some statutes are beyond compliance with Convention rights and cannot be adapted.

An example of the application of the purposive approach in this context is seen in *R (Sim) v Parole Board*[74] in which s. 44A of the Criminal Justice Act 1991 (no longer in force) was considered in the light of the obligation under s. 3 of the HRA. The Criminal Justice Act set out circumstances in which a prisoner might be brought back into custody after having been

---

[71] *Campbell* v *Mirror Group Newspapers* [2004] UKHL 22, at [132].

[72] *Mosley* v *News Group Newspapers Ltd* [2008] EWHC 1777 (QB).

[73] Rt Hon. Lady Justice Arden (2004) The Interpretation of UK Domestic Legislation in the Light of European Convention on Human Rights Jurisprudence. *Statute Law Review* 165, p. 179.

[74] *R (Sim)* v *Parole Board* [2003] EWHC 152 (Admin).

released on parole. It required that further release was required when 'it is no longer necessary for the protection of the public'. The court needed to determine the construction of the word 'necessary'. This was done flexibly to allow release of the prisoner, giving effect to Art. 5(4) ECHR (Right to liberty—continued detention).

Because of s. 3 of the HRA and the court's obligations as a public authority under s. 5, the doctrine of precedent under which case law develops has also been modified—see 5.1.1.3 for more on this effect of the HRA.

4.6.4.2 Procedural requirements of the Human Rights Act

Section 4 of the HRA gives judges at the level of the High Court and above the power to make a declaration of incompatibility, if it is found that an Act of Parliament cannot be used consistently with the relevant Convention rights. This has occurred roughly four times a year since the passing of the HRA.[75]

To guard against this possibility, s. 19 of the HRA requires the minister who introduces the draft legislation into Parliament to state whether or not the Bill is compliant with the Act. This mechanism, called a 'statement of compatibility', can stimulate early debate on human rights issues inherent in proposed legislation. Ministers almost always state legislation to be HRA-compatible, even if the compatibility is subject to some debate. For instance, much of the anti-terrorism legislation passed since 2001 is arguably very restrictive of human rights, especially with regard to privacy and detention. But ministers have often stated such legislation to be HRA-compatible. This requirement can be suspended under the Convention in the context of an emergency.

Under s. 10 of the HRA, if a court makes a declaration of incompatibility with Convention rights in relation to a statute, the government can (under parliamentary scrutiny) enact statutory instruments (called 'remedial orders') to amend primary legislation in order to remove any incompatibility. Between 2000 and 2007, only 24 declarations of incompatibility were made by courts.[76] The Joint Committee on Human Rights is a select committee comprised of members of both Houses of Parliament with a remit to consider human rights issues in the UK. It scrutinises government Bills for human rights implications, and also examines government remedial orders.

4.6.4.3 Summary of effect of the Human Rights Act on statutes and interpretation

The HRA therefore contains many procedural protections of the Convention rights, which impact on elements of parliamentary sovereignty and the doctrine of precedent. These are summarised in Figure 4.4.

---

[75] Houses of Parliament Joint Committee on Human Rights (2007) *Sixteenth Report* (HL86/HC111), part 4.

[76] Houses of Parliament Joint Committee on Human Rights (2007) *Sixteenth Report* (HL86/HC111), part 4.

HRA, s. 19
Statement of Compatibilty
Minister obliged to state whether proposed Bill is compatible with Convention rights.

HRA, s. 3
Interpretation
Courts must (if possible) read legislation in a way compatible with Convention rights.

HRA, s. 4
Declaration of Incompatibilty
If this is not possible, Courts must make a 'Declaration of Incompatibilty'.

HRA, s. 10
Remedial Orders
The government has an option (not an obligation) to make fast-track 'Remedial Orders' to amend or repeal offending legislation.

Figure 4.4 HRA process in relation to statutes

Summary

- Statutes are the primary source of law in the UK.
- Legislation is passed by or with the authority of Parliament.
- Parliament is said to be 'sovereign', meaning that it is the supreme law-making body, and that no other institution can unmake laws passed by it.
- Parliamentary sovereignty has been subject to challenges, especially in the context of law derived from the EU (pre-Brexit) and the ECHR.
- Statutes can be ambiguous, and lawyers have developed techniques of interpretation to help resolve these ambiguities.
- As discussed in Chapter 2, EU Law will continue to have an impact post-Brexit, both by operation of law and economic necessity.
- EU law can be broken down into several different types, and the impact of this legislation varies.
- The HRA has had profound implications for parliamentary sovereignty and the interpretation of statutes.

Practical exercises

1. Should statutes made by the UK Parliament apply to all the UK by default?
2. Does the Regulatory Reform Act have a place in a democracy like the UK?
3. Is Parliament still sovereign?
4. Are human rights adequately protected by the mechanisms of the HRA?
5. Will UK legislation shadow EU legislation post-Brexit?

 *Visit the **online resources** for the authors' reflections and to check your progress.*

Further reading

Dicey, A. (1885) *An Introduction to the Study of the Law of the Constitution*. **Liberty Fund Inc., 8th rev. edn, 1982**

—This contains the definitive statement of parliamentary sovereignty by one of the earliest modern constitutional theorists.

Greenberg, D. (2011) *Laying Down the Law*. **London: Sweet & Maxwell**

—An accessible account by a legislative draftsman of the realities of drafting legislation in the UK.

Greenberg, D. (ed.) (2012) *Craies on Legislation*. **London: Sweet & Maxwell, 10th edn**

—A detailed guide to the interpretation of statutes.

Houses of Parliament Joint Committee on Human Rights (2007) *Sixteenth Report* **(HL86/HC111), part 4**

—Analyses the constitutional, legislative, and judicial impact of the HRA in the first decade since its coming into force.

Zander, M. (1980) *The Law Making Process*. **Cambridge: CUP, 6th edn**

—The definitive critical analysis of the law-making process.

For the authors' reflections on the practical exercises, additional self-test questions, sample interview questions and a library of links to useful websites, visit the free **online resources** *at* **www.oup.com/he/slorach4e**.

5 Case law

Learning objectives

After reading this chapter you should be able to:

- Describe the distinction between common law and civil law jurisdictions.
- Explain in outline the operation of the doctrine of precedent.
- Use basic terminology relating to the case law of England & Wales.
- Develop an opinion on whether judges should make law.

Introduction

To most people, a court is where issues of law are tried by judges. But in many countries, courts and judges have an additional role. Courts, especially appeal courts, are also called upon to make law, either where statutes leave room for interpretation, or where there is no statutory coverage.

'Someone must be trusted. Let it be the judges.'[1] Most commentators agree that judges make law because they reach verdicts or make decisions. And yet, every four or five years, in the UK, we elect a House of Commons to lead the law-making process. Indeed, roughly two-thirds of countries today are democracies[2]—so why should judges make law?

In Chapter 2, we looked at the distinction between common law and civil law jurisdictions, and at 3.1.1 we compared the roles of courts in civil and common law jurisdictions. Here we examine the operation of the doctrine of precedent, so integral to common law countries. Finally, we address the arguments for and against the development of judge-made law.

5.1 The doctrine of precedent

The doctrine of precedent exists wherever there is case law, whether or not that law is binding. But in England & Wales there is a doctrine of binding precedent, or *stare decisis*, as it is sometimes called—literally, 'to stand by [previous] decisions'.

One way of formulating it is as follows: a statement in one case will be binding on a later case if it is a statement of law, which is part of the *ratio decidendi* (reasoning) of the earlier case, decided in a court which binds the present court, where there are no relevant factual distinctions between the cases. To help understand this formulation, let's look at Figure 5.1. You can see that the doctrine of precedent can be broken down easily into its constituent parts.

---

[1] Lord Denning (1982) *What Next in the Law* Oxford: OUP, p. 330.
[2] World Forum on Democracy, Warsaw (25–7 June 2000).

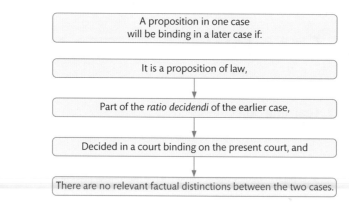

Figure 5.1 The doctrine of precedent

This chapter now examines each aspect of the doctrine in turn. We first look at each aspect of the doctrine before drawing out some important themes.

To help us with this, we use the case study introduced in Chapter 3, *Donoghue* v *Stevenson*.[3] Here are the key case facts again:

Example 1

Donoghue v *Stevenson*

In August 1928, Mrs May Donoghue joined a friend for a drink in the Wellmeadow Café in Wellmeadow Place, Paisley, Glasgow.

The friend bought the drinks. The owner poured some ginger beer from an opaque bottle into Mrs Donoghue's glass (which may or may not have had some ice cream floating in it). She took some swigs and then poured the rest of the contents into her glass. To her horror the remains of a decomposing snail presented themselves to her. Mrs Donoghue later complained of stomach pains and shock, both a result of gastroenteritis.

On appeal, the House of Lords found that the manufacturer would owe a duty of care (that is, a duty not to carelessly cause harm) to the consumer. The case was later settled.

There is also an annotated extract from this case at 7.1.5.1, should you wish to look in more detail at the legal themes referred to here.

Why should this quaint-sounding case be so important in English law, and indeed in many jurisdictions? It is because the case addressed the fundamental question, 'Who is my neighbour?'

We are using *Donoghue* here as an example to aid the study of the doctrine of precedent; you will cover the law of negligence itself in detail in your study of tort law. The case was never decided on the facts—it was settled after the House of Lords decided on the preliminary issue of whether a duty of care was owed.

---

3 *Donoghue (or M'Alister)* v *Stevenson* [1932] AC 562.

5.1.1 Basic elements of the doctrine of precedent

5.1.1.1 A statement of law . . .

A statement of law can be distinguished from a statement of fact. We have already seen that the difference between questions of fact and law is a key concept in the study and operation of legal systems.

Fact: from the information we have in the Scottish Law Reports, we know that Mrs Donoghue contracted gastroenteritis after drinking contaminated ginger beer. This is a statement of fact and cannot form part of any body of law.

Law: from the *Donoghue* case it is possible to derive many statements of law, for instance:

1. You must not injure your neighbour.
2. 'You must take reasonable care to avoid acts or omissions which you can reasonably foresee would be likely to injure your neighbour', as stated by Lord Atkin in his speech.[4]
3. A duty of care does arise when the person or property of one person is in such proximity to another that, if due care is not taken, she might suffer physical and consequential damage.[5]
4. ' . . . a manufacturer of products, which he sells in such a form as to show that he intends them to reach the ultimate consumer in the form in which they left him with no reasonable possibility of intermediate examination, and with the knowledge that the absence of reasonable care in the preparation or putting up of the products will result in an injury to the consumer's life or property, owes a duty to the consumer to take that reasonable care . . . '[6]
5. A manufacturer of ginger beer must take care to prevent molluscs from entering and contaminating its products, thus causing gastroenteritis in anyone resident in Glasgow.
6. A duty of care should not extend to everyone injured by a defect in a product, irrespective of proximity. It would be difficult for trade to be carried on.

All of these are statements of law. Only some of them are of importance. In fact, *Donoghue* is unusual in that there are so many statements of law that are of general importance. You may note that only (2) and (4) are quotations (from Lord Atkin's leading speech).

When you study tort law, you will find that statements (2), (3), and (4) are vital to an understanding of the modern law of negligence.

5.1.1.2 . . . part of the *ratio decidendi* . . .

Ratio decidendi, usually abbreviated as *ratio*, means 'the reason for the decision'. The *ratio* is the most important statement of law in the case. Every statement in the case which is not part of the *ratio* is called *obiter dictum*, which means 'said in passing'.

---

[4] *Donoghue (or M'Alister)* v *Stevenson* [1932] AC 562, at 580.
[5] This statement of law is adapted from a quote made in Lord Atkin's speech, from *obiter* comments in an earlier Court of Appeal case, *Heaven* v *Pender* (1883) 11 QBD 503.
[6] *Donoghue (or M'Alister)* v *Stevenson* [1932] AC 562, at 599.

The Judgment

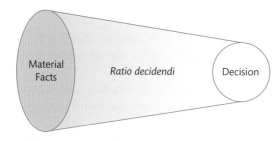

Figure 5.2 *Ratio*: the reasoning necessary to get from the material facts to the decision

Look at Figure 5.2. The decision in a case is guilty/not guilty in criminal proceedings, or liable/not liable in a civil case. This is the outcome of the case, and is what the litigants and their lawyers want to know. In a civil law system, as contrasted with common law, it is common for the decision to be the only information reported, with no reasoning. However, observing lawyers want to know the reasoning or *ratio*. This is the 'law' in 'case law'. This reasoning derives from the court's application of the law to the material facts.

A case may have more than one *ratio*, either because the law is complex and requires lengthy reasoning, or because the *ratio* is disputed, or because different judges reached their decisions in different ways. We explore these issues at 5.1.2.

Statements (2), (3), and (4) in *Donoghue* have all been accepted as *ratios* (or *rationes*) arising from the case. Statement (6) summarises part of Lord Atkin's reasoning, but is only a statement made *obiter*.[7] Note that the *ratio* does not need to be a quotation from a judgment. The *ratio* is the underlying principle of law. This helps give the concept its flexibility.

5.1.1.3 . . . decided in a court binding on the present court . . .

Most legal systems divide their courts into three types (see 3.1.3). Trial courts deal with all litigation and most of it stops there. Issues of law can then go to appeal. Most legal systems have one level of appeals court, although in England & Wales we have both the High Court in its appellate capacity and the Court of Appeal. Finally there is a final court of appeal, often called a supreme court. Until 2009 in the UK this was the House of Lords; it is now the Supreme Court of the UK.

In general:

- All courts are bound by superior courts (i.e. courts above them in the court hierarchy)— vertical *stare decisis*. The reason for this is to ensure consistency and reinforce the case law-making primacy of the supreme courts.

- Some courts are usually bound by previous decisions of their own court (or their predecessors)—horizontal *stare decisis*. The reason for this is to reinforce consistency in their jurisprudence unless absolutely necessary for reasons of justice.

- Courts are never bound by courts of a lower level.

---

[7] *Donoghue (or M'Alister) v Stevenson* [1932] AC 562, at 576.

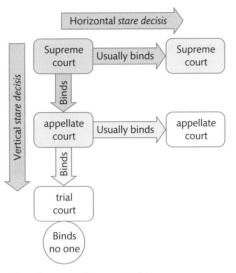

Figure 5.3 Generic representation of common law *stare decisis*

A generic representation of common law *stare decisis* (i.e. not specific to England & Wales) is set out in Figure 5.3.

In England & Wales this situation is manifested as follows (see also Figure 5.4):

Vertical stare decisis

All courts are 'bound' by higher courts; this means they must follow the higher court's reasoning. So the law made by the House of Lords in *Donoghue* would bind any High Court or Court of Appeal judge considering questions relating to product liability in negligence.

Only appellate courts are called 'courts of record', which means courts where the case is reported in a recognised series of law reports (see 7.1.5.1). Some decisions of lower courts are however reported in newspapers or on legal databases like Lawtel. Partly as a consequence of this, only statements from appellate courts have binding effect. The position of the Family Court is as yet unclear as the reforms which created the court are so recent, but is likely to reflect the position of equivalent High and County Court decisions.

The jurisprudence of the ECJ is binding (in all 27 member states, now that the UK has left) on matters of EU law, even though it is a court founded on civil law principles under EU law. ECJ (the CJEU is part of the ECJ, strictly speaking) jurisprudence is likely to be very highly persuasive on matters of ex-EU law now that the UK has left the EU.[8] As at the time of writing, there is some discussion of the right of any UK court to depart from retained EU case law—it is unclear how this will work in practice.

There is in theory one limitation on vertical *stare decisis*. Under s. 6 of the Human Rights Act 1998 it is unlawful for any public authority (including courts) to act inconsistently with the Convention rights (see 4.6.3). This means that a court has a strong (though not binding) obligation to ignore

---

[8] The UK left the EU on 31 January 2020 (as a result of a referendum of 23 June 2016). Any references to the EU in this section should be read with this in mind. For more on the current and likely future status of EU law, refer to Chapter 2, and in particular the Essential explanation of Brexit at 2.2.3.

precedent case law which is incompatible with Convention rights, even if it would otherwise be bound. There have not yet been any reported cases where this has occurred. It has, so far, been possible to interpret binding case law compatibly with Convention rights.

Horizontal stare decisis

In the past the House of Lords bound itself. While this led to consistency, it also caused its jurisprudence to become embedded and inflexible. So since 1966 the House of Lords (now the Supreme Court) has been able to depart from its own earlier decisions.[9] It does so rarely, in what is estimated to be only around 25 times since 1966.[10] This extract from the Practice Statement of 1966 pertinently summarises the merits and drawbacks of the strict application of the doctrine of precedent:

> Their Lordships regard the use of precedent as an indispensable foundation upon which to decide what is the law and its application to individual cases. It provides at least some degree of certainty upon which individuals can rely in the conduct of their affairs, as well as a basis for orderly development of legal rules. Their Lordships nevertheless recognise that too rigid adherence to precedent may lead to injustice in a particular case and also unduly restrict the proper development of the law. They propose therefore, to modify their present practice and, while treating former decisions of this house as normally binding, to depart from a previous decision when it appears right to do so.[11]

For reasons of consistency the Court of Appeal also tends to follow its own earlier decisions, although the Criminal Division is more liable to change its approach, because the liberty of individuals is at stake. In *Young v Bristol Aeroplane Co Ltd* [1944] KB 718, a 'full' court of six members was convened to decide whether the Court of Appeal (Civil Division) is bound by its own decisions. It decided that it is normally so bound, but subject to three (infrequently applied) exceptions:

(a) where its own previous decisions conflict; or

(b) where its previous decision has been implicitly overruled by the Supreme Court; or

(c) where its previous decision was made *per incuriam* (a synonymn for an error in reasoning).

Since this decision, two further exceptions have been added:

(d) where it was an interim decision by two judges; or

(e) where one of its previous decisions is inconsistent with a subsequent decision of the European Court of Human Rights.

All the exceptions which apply to the Civil Division apply to the Criminal Division. However, in addition, the Court of Appeal has a wider discretion where the liberty of the individual is at stake. It is generally thought that the two divisions of the Court of Appeal do not bind each other, though courts do in general try to be consistent on similar points of law.

The same approach applies to the High Court—remember that only its appellate decisions have binding authority.

---

[9] Practice Statement [1966] 3 All ER 77

[10] A figure of 20 occasions is quoted for 1966–2005 in Martin, Jacqueline (2005) *The English Legal System.* London: Hodder Arnold, 4th edn, p. 25.

[11] Lord Gardiner, statement to the House of Lords, 26 July 1966.

Other courts

It should not be thought that other courts' decisions are irrelevant. Statements of law in other courts, either lower in the hierarchy, or in other jurisdictions, are persuasive. A persuasive authority is not binding but may be used in reasoning.

Case law of the Privy Council is only persuasive authority unless it expressly states other-wise.[12] Also persuasive is the reasoning of the European Court of Human Rights (under s. 2 of the Human Rights Act 1998). However, it would be a brave court to decide contrary to the jurisprudence of either court where English law was similar to the law applied in the earlier authority. Another example of a persuasive authority is the Old Bailey. It is nominally a Crown Court, yet some of its decisions involve consideration of important issues of law, and have been variously reported.

Decisions of foreign courts are frequently important. The laws of tort and contract in the US and England & Wales have developed in parallel, and authority from one jurisdiction is frequently highly persuasive in the other. *Shuey v US*[13] is a US Supreme Court case which is important in English contract law. Much of the reasoning in *Donoghue v Stevenson* is derived from a New York state Supreme Court case.[14] *Donoghue* is itself highly persuasive authority in the US.

Figure 5.4 sets out the full hierarchy of courts in England and Wales. Note that the court hierarchy echoes the appeals system discussed at 3.1.3, but describes a separate mechanism.

5.1.1.4 ... where there are no relevant factual distinctions between the cases ...

We have already learned that if the earlier case was decided in a higher court, its *ratio* is bind-ing on lower courts. However, you will recall that the *ratio* is the application of the law to the material facts; it is the later court which determines both what is the *ratio* of the earlier case and the material facts of both cases.

If a court considers a case before it to be different in some material way from the precedent cited, either on the facts or the law, that earlier case need not be followed. The new case will then be said to be 'distinguished' from the earlier case and, as a consequence, the court can decide not to apply the prior *ratio*. Indeed, where the court is anxious not to be bound by a particular precedent, some distinctions are drawn which are very fine.

Therefore, the more a case is distinguished, or confined to its facts, the narrower its *ratio* is likely to be. We explore this technique next.

5.1.2 **Key themes in the doctrine of precedent**

5.1.2.1 Alternative *ratios*

As we saw at 5.1.1.2 there may be many possible *ratio*s. Some are unworkably narrow and others are impossibly wide. The importance of this is that the *ratio* will be used by lawyers in later cases to promote their arguments about the impact of the earlier authority.

---

[12] Expressly confirmed in *Willers v Joyce & Anor* [2016] UKSC 44.

[13] *Shuey v US* 92 US 73 (1875).

[14] *MacPherson v Buick Motor Co.*, 217 NY 382, 111 NE 1050 (1916) (New York Court of Appeals, equivalent to the Court of Appeal in England & Wales).

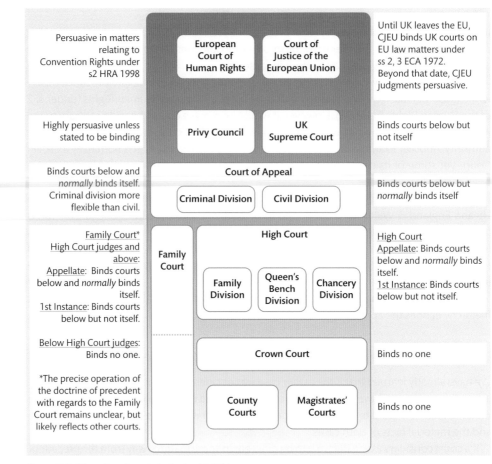

Figure 5.4 Hierarchy of courts in England & Wales

It is the number of facts considered to be material which will make the *ratio* either narrower or wider. These are the concepts of narrow and wide *ratio*. The more general the statement of facts, the greater the number of subsequent cases which will be 'caught' by the principle. You can see from Figure 5.5 that this effect makes the *ratio* 'wider'. The formulation of the judgment will be an important factor. It would be unlikely in many cases that the narrowest and widest statements would actually be considered to be *ratios*.

An advocate seeking to employ too wide a *ratio to* bring his argument within the ambit of a previous line of authority will find his arguments are likely to be too spurious to have any impact. Likewise using too narrow a *ratio* in order to distinguish authority will be unlikely to succeed.

The example of *Donoghue* brings this out well:

1. You must not injure your neighbour.

    This would be an unmanageably wide *ratio*, and would apply to any two people when any harm occurs. Any advocate seeking to use this would be going beyond the realm of law into statements hitherto the province only of morality. If this were accepted as a *ratio*, the floodgates would be wide open to indeterminate litigation.

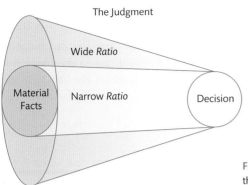

Figure 5.5 Wide and narrow *ratio*: the more general the facts considered relevant, the 'wider' the *ratio*

2. 'You must take reasonable care to avoid acts or omissions which you can reasonably foresee would be likely to injure your neighbour', as stated by Lord Atkin in his speech.

   This statement of law seems quite wide: the material facts are that there are two parties, who are legally proximate, with damage causing foreseeable harm. This is however the accepted statement of the neighbour principle in *Donoghue*, and is called the 'wide rule', the wide *ratio* of the case. It has since been refined slightly by case law, and in particular the crucial *Caparo*[15] case.

3. A duty of care does arise when the person or property of one person is in such proximity to another that, if due care is not taken, she might suffer physical and consequential damage.

   Here, the material facts are that there are two parties with no contract and some injury with consequential economic losses. This statement of law is important in defining the limits of the neighbour principle as Atkin saw it. Importantly, negligence could only cover physical damage, and its consequences. Purely 'economic' damage, not arising from physical damage, was properly the province of contract law and not negligence. Such a *ratio* would now be considered too restrictive, based on too narrow an interpretation of *Donoghue's* material facts.

4. '. . . a manufacturer of products, which he sells in such a form as to show that he intends them to reach the ultimate consumer in the form in which they left him with no reasonable possibility of intermediate examination, and with the knowledge that the absence of reasonable care in the preparation or putting up of the products will result in an injury to the consumer's life or property, owes a duty to the consumer to take that reasonable care . . .'

   Here, the material facts narrow again—a manufacturer has caused a foreseeable consumer physical injury or property damage and consequential harm. This statement of law is the accepted 'narrow rule' from *Donoghue* and this *ratio* has generally recognised importance in the area of product liability law. No lawyer would attempt to distinguish this rule.

5. A manufacturer of ginger beer must take care to prevent molluscs from entering and contaminating its products, thus causing gastroenteritis in anyone resident in Glasgow.

   Here, the material facts are that there was a manufacturer of ginger beer, a snail, a stomach-related illness, and the events occurred in Glasgow. A statement of law derived from this would be far too narrow to form the basis of useable precedent. No lawyer would attempt to confine the impact of *Donoghue* to its facts in this way.

[15] *Caparo Industries plc v Dickman* [1990] 2 AC 605.

In conclusion, using the example of *Donoghue*, we can see that one person's reading of the judgments in a case may yield a subtly different *ratio* from another's, although the statements (2) and (4) set out above have become accepted in respect of the case. This can be quite liberating for the lawyer or legal scholar seeking to use a precedent case in argument. It is critical at an early stage of your study to realise that to some extent *ratio* is, like beauty, in the eye of the beholder.

5.1.2.2 Finding a *ratio*

When we look for a *ratio*, we are trying to distil the legal reasoning in the case which is essential for the decision. Sometimes, it is straightforward to determine the *ratio* of a case. One can ask a rhetorical question, 'What's the key legal question being asked?' The answer to that legal question will be the *ratio*.

For instance, if we refer back to Example 8 in Chapter 4, summarised below, the question is: 'In judging the actions of a reasonable man for the purposes of provocation under s. 3 of the Homicide Act 1957, can we take a subjective view, reflecting relevant characteristics of the defendant?' The answer was 'yes', and then became 'no', before legislation put a stop to the debate. The legal principles derived from these answers were the *ratios* of the cases in which they were considered.

> ### Example 2
> ### Homicide Act 1957, s. 3 (now repealed)—summary
>
> **The Homicide Act put on a statutory footing various defences to a charge of murder.**
>
> Where on a charge of murder there is evidence on which the jury can find that the person charged was provoked (whether by things done or by things said or by both together) to lose his self-control, the question whether the provocation was enough to make a reasonable man do as he did shall be left to be determined by the jury; and in determining that question the jury shall take into account everything both done and said according to the effect which, in their opinion, it would have on a reasonable man.

But often it is not quite so hard and fast. *Ratios* are sometimes difficult to find. There are four main difficulties:

- The first problem is that often judgments are lengthy and judges say many things. So the *ratio* may be buried amongst a mass of other statements, and is not often highlighted or labelled in any way.

- Second, and at the other extreme, occasionally judges take care to highlight the key parts of their reasoning. Even this raises issues. If a judge purports to state the law in any definitive way, this should sometimes be viewed with caution, as the judge concerned may have a policy agenda. She may be going beyond the reasoning necessary to reach a decision. One possible example—depending on your interpretation of the case—is the principle of law claimed to be decisive by Glidewell LJ in the *Williams v Roffey*[16] case in

---

[16] *Williams v Roffey Bros. & Nicholls (Contractors) Ltd* [1991] 1 QB 1.

contract law. In that case, Glidewell LJ legitimised the idea that contracting parties could agree to raise the price of a contract, even if the customer did not receive anything more from the contractor. This was heretical to many lawyers and staked out new ground in this area of law. Not all judgments are definitive like Lord Atkin's in *Donoghue*.

- A third issue is that judges frequently have more than one reason for their decision: it can often be hard to determine which their main line of argument is.

- Finally, there may also be more than one judge, not necessarily giving the same reasons. Where multiple-judge courts are concerned, one needs to distinguish between the reasoning of the individual judge and the *ratio* of the court as a whole. Each judge must have a reason for her decision, but it does not follow that there is any single reason for the decision of the court as a whole, since each of the judges may give different reasons which may be inconsistent. In one infamous contract law case,[17] of the five judges in the House of Lords, one dissented from the final judgment (which was therefore a majority decision of 4:1) and no more than two of the other judges delivered similar *ratios* on any point. In other words, the court as a whole produced no discernible *ratio*. The case has since been written off as inconclusive.

5.1.2.3 *Obiter dicta* and dissent

We have already seen that if reasoning is part of the majority reasoning but is not necessary for the decision of the court as a whole, then this is not *ratio* but *obiter* instead. *Obiter dicta* means 'said by the way'. *Obiter* is, like decisions of foreign courts, persuasive in value. There is no magic formula for the strength of persuasive authority. You simply give the persuasive authority the weight it deserves.

In 1946, a High Court judge of two years' seniority heard a case involving the lease of some flats in High Trees House in Clapham. The landlord promised to lower the rent for the duration of World War II, and then went back on his promise. In *obiter* the judge contradicted unhelpful unanimous House of Lords authority. Without any prior knowledge of the judge involved, one might give the authority little value. This *obiter*, in the *High Trees* case,[18] has since formed the basis of the equitable doctrine of 'promissory estoppel' (which is a defence to a contract debt claim), which survives today. The judge later became Lord Denning, whose jurisprudence in private law is given great weight; the doctrine of promissory estoppel has been approved by the Court of Appeal on numerous occasions (sometimes, admittedly, by Denning himself).

Judges in multi-judge courts, who do not agree with the decision, give a dissenting opinion. In *Donoghue* v *Stevenson*,[19] of the five Lords of Appeal, two disagreed with the majority decision. Some of these dissents carry persuasive weight in later cases. They may be approved or referred to when the law subsequently develops. For example, Lord Denning dissented from decisions early in the development of the law of negligence (relating to purely economic damage) after *Donoghue*. His dissents gave impetus to later developments in the law in this area. In *Donoghue*, the reasoning in Lord Buckmaster's dissent (he was the senior Law Lord at the time) helps lawyers analyse the background to Lord Atkin's leading judgment (see 7.1.5 for more on how to read cases).

---

[17] *Esso Petroleum Co. Ltd* v *Commissioners of Customs and Excise* [1976] 1 WLR 1.

[18] *Central London Property Trust Ltd* v *High Trees House Ltd* [1947] KB 130.

[19] *Donoghue (or M'Alister)* v *Stevenson* [1932] AC 562.

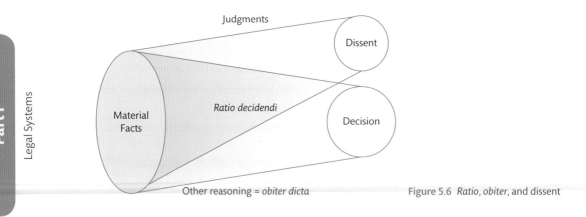

Figure 5.6 *Ratio, obiter,* and dissent

Figure 5.6 illustrates the status of *obiter* and dissent. Neither is part of the *ratio* of a case, although dissenting reasoning does stem from the material facts and leads to an alternative decision.

You may well have realised that what one lawyer states to be *ratio*, to another is *obiter*, and non-binding. Lawyers are free to make any sensible interpretation. Eventually, a later court will decide which one is correct.

5.1.2.4 Evolving *ratios*

Zhou Enlai, the first Premier of the People's Republic of China, was once asked to assess the impact of the French Revolution, nearly 200 years previously. He replied, 'It's too soon to say' (this story is sometimes said to be apocryphal).

Likewise, the *ratio* often crystallises with time and perspective. A case may be analysed by academics and lawyers, and considered in later cases. Eventually, like a picture coming into focus, the reasoning of a case becomes refined and clear.

Figure 5.7 illustrates this. In your study of tort law you will see that the law of negligence has evolved in this way in several areas. One example was the area of product liability developing from the *Donoghue* case study. The so-called 'narrow rule' (described earlier) has been applied and refined in many different contexts—including cars, lifts, and even irritant chemicals in undergarments. Another, closely related, example is where courts have refined principles relating to economic losses when they result from statements rather than from physical damage. The case law in this area has witnessed many twists and turns.

5.1.3 Terminology of the doctrine of precedent

When reading about how courts deal with precedent, it is important to understand the terminology used. The explanations given below can be read in conjunction with Figure 5.8.

5.1.3.1 Distinguishing, applying, or following

A lower court must normally **apply** or **follow** an earlier ruling of a higher court. The only way to disagree is to **distinguish** that ruling.

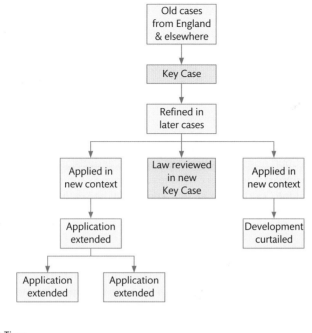

Figure 5.7 Evolution of *ratio*—generic diagram

For example, a litigant could find himself in court, faced with unhelpful precedent. We have seen that a statement in one case will bind a court in a later case unless there are relevant distinctions between the two cases. Therefore, the litigant could argue that the facts of the case at hand are materially different to those from the problematic precedent, and consequently that the court is not bound to follow the earlier precedent. That is, the litigant would be asking the court to distinguish the earlier ruling from the instant case.

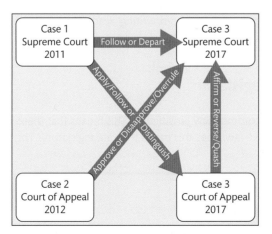

Figure 5.8 Precedent terminology: what can a later court do with an earlier precedent?

5.1.3.2 Overruling, disapproving, and approving

A higher court can **approve** the decision of a lower court or it may **disapprove** or **overrule** it, if it disagrees.

The latter occurs when a principle laid down by a lower court is declared incorrect and not followed by a higher court in a different later case. The higher court will set a new 'correct' precedent.

5.1.3.3 Departing or following

A court can follow or depart from an earlier case.

The Supreme Court normally **follows** its own earlier decisions (and those of the House of Lords) but it can **depart** from them if it wishes to change its approach to the law in a particular area. This is what the Court did when departing from the *Smith* decision in *Holley*, which we looked at in Example 8 in Chapter 4.

5.1.3.4 Reversing, quashing, or affirming

If a case is appealed from a lower court to a higher court, then the higher court can **confirm**, or **affirm**, the decision of the lower court, if the appeal is dismissed. However, if the appeal is allowed, the decision of the lower court will be **reversed**, and if it is a criminal case, the sentence may be **quashed**.

Reversing therefore occurs where the decision of a court in the same case is altered by a higher court on appeal. It is thus different in nature from the other terms considered, because it does not relate to the doctrine of precedent. For example, the Court of Appeal may come to a different conclusion from the High Court on a point of law; in this situation, it will reverse the decision made by the High Court.

5.1.4 Practical application of case law

We have seen in this chapter that case law occupies a significant role in England & Wales. In particular we have looked at the importance of finding principles of law, both binding and non-binding. In Chapter 7 we will develop these themes using practical skills of case analysis. These skills have wide application, from writing academic legal essays, through providing legal opinions, to giving client advice.

5.2 Judges as legislators

England & Wales is a common law jurisdiction. This means that there is a significant role for case law. If judges make law, does this mean they are legislators? This section discusses this controversial issue.

5.2.1 Do judges legislate?

5.2.1.1 Yes, judges do legislate

At the most basic level, judges clearly make law. According to the American legal theorist John Chipman Gray, 'in truth all law is judge-made law . . . the courts put life into the dead words of the statute'.[20] So even first instance judges such as district judges or magistrates make law.

The main debate is not about law-making in this literal sense. The main academic discussion in this area concerns whether judges make law in the sense of legal principles that can be used in the future by other lawyers and courts.

It is clear that certain areas of law, such as formation of contracts, negligence, and equity, are largely judge-made, with little statutory intervention. It is also clear that other areas are mainly created by statute, such as tax law and health and safety legislation. There are other areas where the two types of law-making sit alongside each other, such as land law, where a large body of case law sits alongside and around certain key statutes like the Law of Property Act 1925. In such areas case law predating statutes still applies, if it has not been expressly replaced by the statute, and is sometimes expressly referred to in the statute.

An example is the codification of directors' common law and equitable duties to a company in the Companies Act 2006.[21] Section 170(4), for instance, states that: 'The general duties shall be interpreted and applied in the same way as common law rules or equitable principles, and regard shall be had to the corresponding common law rules and equitable principles in interpreting and applying the general duties.'

An alternative situation is where judges make law to 'fill the gaps' in statutes, especially by interpreting them (see 4.4 for a full discussion of statutory interpretation). This is sometimes called 'interstitial' law-making.

In other countries, judges' law-making takes on a different character entirely. Perhaps the most extreme example is in the US, where the Supreme Court can declare Acts of Congress unconstitutional.[22] It has done so over 160 times since the early 19th century.[23] Partly this is a function of the fact that the US has a written Constitution, and that the Supreme Court quickly assumed a role as its guardian. This role is common to many US state Supreme Courts, and courts around the world. This process is more common in civil law jurisdictions, where a court is frequently given power to protect the code or constitution, although this court is usually a separate constitutional court, such as the *Bundesverfassungsgericht* in Germany or the *Conseil Constitutionnel* in France.

In England & Wales, the UK Supreme Court does not have power to overrule any legislation. It does, however, have the ability to make a declaration of incompatibility under s. 3 of the Human Rights Act 1998, although this has no formal effect on the legislation concerned. During the UK's membership of the EU, the House of Lords/Supreme Court had on occasion ignored UK statutes that are ruled by the ECJ as incompatible with EU law, as we saw at 4.1.1.3 in the *Factortame*[24] case.

5.2.1.2 No, judges do not legislate

An alternative analysis of English judicial law-making is the now largely defunct 'declaratory theory', in which it is maintained that judges merely *declare* the law as it subsists at the time

---

[20] Gray, John Chipman (1909) *The Nature and Sources of the Law*. New York: Colombia University Press, pp. 119–20.

[21] Companies Act 2006, ss. 170–81.   [22] *Marbury* v *Madison*, 5 US (1 Cranch) 137 (1803).

[23] US Government Printing Office Database, 2002.

[24] *Secretary of State for Transport, ex parte Factortame* (No. 2) [1991] AC 603.

of the events in question. This is reminiscent of the civil law approach where judges decide on the facts of a case. But this is clearly not the case in England & Wales. Lord Reid, a famous House of Lords judge, once said, 'We do not believe in fairy tales any more, so we must accept the fact that for better or worse judges do make law.'[25]

5.2.1.3 Judges do legislate, but they are not legislators

It is, however, arguable that the extent of judicial law-making in many common law countries is overstated, and that in civil law countries it is understated.

Many commentators view judicial law-making as increasingly 'interstitial', that is to say filling in the gaps left by or between statutes. The most common view is that because statutes are made by legislators in Parliament they are the primary source of law. Statutes necessarily leave room for interpretation; they cannot, and indeed should not normally, seek to provide for each and every scenario explicitly. Look again at Figure 2.3 summarising how judges make law in England & Wales.

You may recall, for instance (as in Example 8 in Chapter 4), that the defence of provocation was replaced by the defence of 'loss of self control' after the confusion of *Smith* and *Holley*. Section 54 of the Coroners and Justice Act 2009 still requires that, for the defence to be available, 'a person of D's sex and age, with a normal degree of tolerance and self-restraint and in the circumstances of D, might have reacted in the same or in a similar way to D'. Against this background, it is quite clear that the legislators saw the courts as qualified to fill in the gaps in relation to concepts like 'normal'. The techniques of statutory interpretation examined in Chapter 4 were developed by judges and are a pivotal part of law-making in England & Wales.

What about civil law jurisdictions? The term 'civil law' is a broad term for many varied legal systems. The key distinction we are examining here is the nature and impact of judicial law-making.

While in general there is no doctrine of *binding* precedent in civil law jurisdictions, there is a doctrine of *non-binding* precedent, often called the doctrine of judicial consistency. It would be seen as erratic if a court changed its approach to a legal question too much. Without this dependability it would be more difficult for people to rely on the decisions of courts.

An extreme example is the French *Cour de Cassation* (its supreme court), which adopts an approach of 'imperial brevity', ruling only on narrow legal questions, an approach which constrains its ability to set useable precedent. Most other French courts give decisions without revealing their reasoning—this means that a body of case law based on judicial reasoning cannot emerge at all. By contrast, the jurisprudence of the ECJ is frequently lengthy and comprehensive. It is rare for the ECJ to amend or overrule its earlier reasoning. Further, the jurisprudence of the ECJ is binding on national courts in member states.

It is therefore evident that judges do have some sort of law-making function in the UK and in other parts of the world, including most 'civil law' systems. Is this a desirable outcome?

---

[25] Lord Reid (1972) 'The Judge as Lawmaker'. *Journal of the Society of Public Teachers of Law* 12, p. 22.

> ⊛ **Essential debates**
>
> Should judges legislate?
>
> There are several criticisms of judicial legislating, or 'activism' as it is sometimes known. These are that:
>
> - legislating is the job of legislatures such as Parliament, and no branch of state should have more than one function;
> - courts are somehow 'undemocratic', and should not be legislating;
> - judges are 'out of touch', or worse still, make arbitrary or immoral decisions; and
> - judge-made law is inflexible and prone to paralysis.
>
> Would you agree with these criticisms?

5.2.2 Criticisms of law-making by judges

Let's take these criticisms in turn. In each we set out a challenge to the legitimacy of judges' law-making role. This will be followed by an answer to that challenge:

5.2.2.1 That judicial law-making offends the principle of Separation of Powers

In Chapter 1 we saw that many constitutional theorists regard the doctrine of Separation of Powers as the cornerstone of a modern state. Let's examine the courts' role in a little more detail.

In a 'pure' theory of Separation of Powers, the role of the courts would be limited entirely to resolving legal disputes. Taking this to extremes, the role of an appeals court would simply be to rule on ambiguities in the law on a case-by-case basis. There would be no point in reporting judgments because they would have no future value. This hypothetical situation was set out in Figure 1.8.

In a common law system like England & Wales, the role of the courts is more ambiguous. When the courts of a common law jurisdiction hear appeals, the reasoning leading to their decisions becomes binding precedent. Not only are they acting in their judicial capacity, they are arguably also adopting a legislative role. This situation was summarised in Figure 1.9. To the casual observer, this would seem to be an encroachment by the courts on a role properly the province of Parliament.

The answer to this challenge is that the Separation of Powers is a theoretical concept and that no legal and political system can hope to reflect it fully. The US Constitution was drafted explicitly to reflect Montesquieu's doctrine of the Separation of Powers, but even this incorporates overlaps between the roles of each branch, called 'checks and balances'. This means that each branch has a limited role outside its core powers, to prevent too much power accumulating in one 'branch' of the system.

Further, modern courts are arguably aware of the limitations of their role, and bear in mind some of the criticisms levelled at their law-making role. At 1.2.4.2 we looked at the case of Diane Pretty, and saw that the House of Lords refused to order the Director of Public Prosecutions not to prosecute under s. 2(1) of the Suicide Act 1961. Lord Hope, in his judgment, said, 'In the present uncertain climate of public opinion, where there is no consensus in favour of assisted suicide and there are powerful religious and ethical arguments to the contrary, any change in the law which would make assisted suicide generally acceptable is best seen as a matter for Parliament.'[26]

There are also rare examples where courts have gone too far in their law-making function, and it is clear that Parliament does legislate to limit this. A line of tort cases concluded[27] with liability being imposed on employers for compensating workers for certain diseases where it was impossible to determine when the disease was caused, and therefore by whom. This was unfair on employers as it was impossible to determine whether they were at fault. The Compensation Act 2006[28] put an end to the courts' law-making in this area. At 4.4.4.1, we saw another instance when Parliament stepped in to prevent further judicial confusion on the issue of provocation as a defence to murder.

5.2.2.2 That judicial law-making is undemocratic

In the UK General Election of 2017, roughly 32 million people voted for 650 Members of Parliament to represent them in the House of Commons. In India (the world's largest democracy), roughly 600 million voted in their 2019 General Election. Whatever objections one might have to the electoral systems adopted by modern democracies, there is no disputing that the laws passed by legislatures in such nations are, to a significant extent, legitimate.

By contrast, in England & Wales, there are 154 judges serving in appellate courts, comprising 94 High Court Judges, 38 Lords Justice of Appeal, and 12 Supreme Court Justices.[29] They are appointed by the Judicial Appointments Commission, comprised of 15 members. They are drawn from a very narrow background—only 7 per cent of judges are non-white, and only 29 per cent of judges in England & Wales, and only two of the 12 current Supreme Court Justices, are female[30]—though both proportions are increasing. It is true to say that the selection of the judiciary is undemocratic, and that judges do not have a popular mandate.

In answer to this assertion, it is worth asking whether judges *should* have a mandate. Certainly in their judicial capacity, it is strongly arguable that this is not a relevant consideration. Mere arbiters of legal liability should not need to be elected. The problem is, the more that we conclude that judges make law, the more it is arguable that they should be accountable to the people who are subject to those laws, namely elected. Much of the discussion reduces to an evaluation of the nature of the judges' law-making (see 5.2.1). An instructive case study is that of the judiciary in the United States, epitomised by the US Supreme Court. Judges are politically appointed (indeed, they are elected at some levels). Some experts in the US argue that the politicised judiciary in the US is far from impartial and not capable of applying or developing law objectively. In England & Wales, the fact that judges are independently appointed might be said to add to their legitimacy. The argument is that people who arbitrate disputes should be appointed on a meritocratic basis, rather than because of their politics.

Another counter-argument is that the comparison with legislatures is not as unflattering as it might at first seem. There are many arguments about how truly democratic legislatures are around the world. While it is not the aim of this chapter to discuss the merits of democratic institutions, we can at least acknowledge that Parliament in the UK, the European Parliament, and the US Congress are frequently cited as suffering from a 'democratic deficit'.[31] The latter in particular is said to be stymied by 'pork barrel politics'. This happens when the interests of powerful pressure groups or voters in marginal districts dictate the positions of some key congressmen during consideration of legislation in committee. In return, pet projects are given funding out of proportion to their public value.

5.2.2.3 That judicial law-making is out of touch, arbitrary, and immoral

Jeremy Bentham, a philosopher mentioned in Chapter 1, was an ardent critic of judicial law-making, about which he wrote sarcastically:

> But King, Lords and Commons are a dull and slow set determining nothing about facts till after they been poring over as well as prying into facts. How more easily are these things managed by a learned Judge! When at any time he *thinks* it worthwhile to make a law it need cost him but a word nor is it necessary even to that word to contain *thought* or any such heavy matter at the bottom of it.[32]

The implication was that judges can make law, if they wish, arbitrarily or by whim.

One of the most infamous examples of judicial activism in the face of the opposition of a legislature is the *Dred Scott* case in the pre-civil war US.[33] The Missouri Compromise, an Act of the US Congress, had partitioned the states of the US into states where slavery was, and states where it was not, permitted. Dred Scott (a slave) had lived in so-called 'free' states for some time and sued for his freedom, when it was denied to him. The US Supreme Court, in *obiter*, stated that the Missouri Compromise was unconstitutional, much of the impetus coming from the activist Supreme Court Chief Justice, Roger Taney. This is seen as one of the most politically motivated, immoral, and controversial decisions in US legal history.[34]

In England, Lord Denning, a popular champion of private rights, had a notorious reputation in the area of public law. In his 1982 book, *What Next in the Law*, he seemed to suggest that immigrants were unsuitable to serve on juries because they had different moral standards to a native Englishman.

An answer to this challenge also comes from the US. In Chapter 1 we saw that the US Constitution is the archetype of constitutions drafted to preserve the Separation of Powers. Much of its content was based upon reasoning by the 'Founding Fathers' in the *Federalist Papers*. Alexander Hamilton insisted:

> the independence of the judges may be an essential safeguard against the effects of occasional ill humors in the society.[35]

---

[31] See e.g. Wintour, P. 'European Parliament should be abolished, says Jack Straw', *The Guardian* (21 February 2012), quoting a poll by the Institute for Public Policy Research, and *Report of the Independent Commission on the Voting System (the Jenkins Commission)* (1998). London: HMSO, Cm. 4090.

[32] Bentham, Jeremy (1821) *The Elements of the Art of Packing: As Applied to Special Juries, Particularly in Cases of Libel Law*. London: Effingham, p. 157.

[33] *Dred Scott* v *Sandford*, 60 US 393 (1857).

[34] Finkelman, Paul (2007) Scott v. Sandford: The Court's Most Dreadful Case and How it Changed History. *Chicago-Kent Law Review* 82, p. 3.

[35] Hamilton, Alexander (1788) *The Federalist Papers No. 78*. New York: J. & A. McLean.

So the 'arbitrary' argument can be turned on its head. Indeed, Hamilton went on to say:

> To avoid an arbitrary discretion in the courts, it is indispensable that they should be bound down by strict rules and precedents, which serve to define and point out their duty in every particular case that comes before them; and it will readily be conceived from the variety of controversies which grow out of the folly and wickedness of mankind, that the records of those precedents must unavoidably swell to a very considerable bulk, and must demand long and laborious study to acquire a competent knowledge of them. Hence it is, that there can be but few men in the society who will have sufficient skill in the laws to qualify them for the stations of judges.[36]

So the very weight of precedent lends gravitas to the case law it generates, because it demands interpretation by experts.

5.2.2.4 That judicial law-making is inflexible

If we accept that significant swathes of law are still judge-made, then we meet a problem. Common law systems adhere to a binding doctrine of precedent (see 5.1). Because of this, it is not open to courts to develop law if they are faced with awkward precedents.

It is very unusual in England & Wales for a case to be stated as the definitive statement of the law in a given area. One rare example was a case[37] which sought to state comprehensively the law on 'undue influence' in contract law. This relates to how mortgages could be set aside, on the ground that a person had unduly influenced their spouse into guaranteeing their debts.

In general, case law in a given area needs to be refined as issues are litigated. Only rarely will these issues be appealed to courts that have the power to depart from earlier decisions, and even then only the part of the decision which is directly relevant to the material facts will be accepted as *ratio* and therefore binding law. Figure 5.9 summarises the process.

You will recall from Chapter 2 that equity is a largely separate body of case law with different historical origins from common law. Equity provides a little more flexibility, for example with the creation by Lord Denning of the doctrine of promissory estoppel, in the face of countervailing House of Lords authority. However it is often argued that case law all too often moves too slowly to meet the needs of an evolving society.

By contrast, it is theoretically easy for a new statute to be passed if there is enough pressure. Figure 5.10 illustrates how public mores and morality are sometimes reflected in legislation.

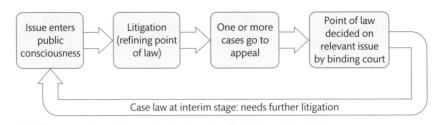

Figure 5.9 The process by which case law develops to reflect changes in society

---

36 Hamilton, Alexander (1788) *The Federalist Papers No. 78*. New York: J. & A. McLean.

37 *Royal Bank of Scotland plc v Etridge (No. 2)* [2001] UKHL 44.

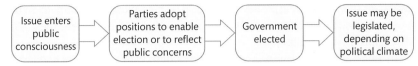

Figure 5.10 The process by which legislation develops to reflect changes in society

Given enough impetus, a government can implement important manifesto planks or pressing social needs. A good example is the swift implementation in 1945–7 of the comprehensive welfare state (requiring several significant Acts of Parliament). Public pressure led to the passing of the Dangerous Dogs Act 1991, which made it illegal to own certain breeds of dog; however that piece of legislation is often cited as an example of a rushed and botched law.[38]

So is judicial law-making inflexible? In practice, many proposed statutes are victims of lack of parliamentary time, insufficient political will, or decaying mandate. A commonly cited example is the further reform of the House of Lords, which has been part of the manifestos of all three major UK parties, but is as yet still unlegislated, despite taking up much parliamentary time.

The interstitial nature of case law allows principles to be refined in situations too narrow to be legislated, in either primary or secondary legislation. Also, case law allows legislation to be applied in circumstances beyond the contemplation of legislators, such as applying rules of contract, or in creating duties in tort in a new world of instantaneous and detailed communication.

Bearing in mind the justification for the role of interstitial judicial law-making, any democratic deficit might be argued to be an irrelevance in the modern political world.

5.2.2.5 That judicial law-making is unclear or uncertain

At 5.1.1 we looked at the challenges of finding a *ratio*. Judgments in case law are infamous for using too many words to get to a decision, and for being difficult to interpret. In addition, it is sometimes difficult to reconcile two cases in the same area. This leads to uncertainty. In contract law, some of the rules relating to 'consideration', or the price paid for the other party's promise, are difficult to reconcile.

It is straightforward to counter this argument. The flip-side of the inflexibility encountered above is certainty: it is no coincidence that much of contract law in the Anglo-Saxon world is based on clear legal principles, creating the backdrop for making bargains with predictable consequences. Benjamin Cardozo, the esteemed US Supreme Court justice, declared:

> The judge . . . is not to innovate at pleasure. He is not a knight-errant roaming at will in pursuit of his own ideal of beauty or of goodness. He is to draw his inspiration from consecrated principles. He is not to yield to spasmodic sentiment, to vague and unregulated benevolence. He is to exercise a discretion informed by tradition, methodized by analogy, disciplined by system, and subordinated to the primordial necessity of order in the social life.[39]

[38] See, e.g. Low, Colin. 'Lords reform: the Lords is more diverse and democratic than the Commons', *Daily Telegraph* (13 April 2004); Hollingshead, Ian. 'Whatever happened to dangerous dogs?' *The Guardian* (5 November 2005).

[39] Cardozo, Benjamin N. (1921) *The Nature of the Judicial Process*. Universal Law Press, 2010.

Clear law means that contracting parties can bargain with confidence. Commercial contracts are often given jurisdiction in England & Wales, or New York or Delaware, as the law of contract in these forums is so robust.

In defamation and privacy law, newspapers can publish with a degree of certainty about the boundaries of what is legally acceptable, though it is instructive that the goalposts have moved with the more 'civil law', codified approach of the Human Rights Act 1998, and the certainty provided by the common law has been somewhat vitiated.

5.2.3 Judges as legislators: conclusions

Because England & Wales is a common law jurisdiction, case law has a significant role to play. While judges make law in most (but not all) jurisdictions, their role in England & Wales is comparatively substantial. Many criticisms have been levelled at the practice of judges contributing to the body of law to which all citizens are subject.

Lord Reid, a notable Law Lord, once wrote:

> There was a time when it was thought almost indecent to suggest that judges make law—they only declare it. Those with a taste for fairy tales seem to have thought that in some Aladdin's cave there is hidden the Common Law in all its splendour and that on a judge's appointment there descends on him knowledge of the magic words Open Sesame. Bad decisions are given when the judge muddles the password and the wrong door opens. But we do not believe in fairy tales any more.[40]

But most of those criticisms can be countered or at least put into perspective. The reality is that the courts have a limited but important role to play in the law-making system in England & Wales, and that it would be very difficult to remove this role without undermining the whole apparatus.

Summary

- Judges and courts are given different roles in different countries; the degree to which they are given power to make, as opposed to only adjudicating on, law is a controversial issue.
- Case law operates via a doctrine of (usually) binding precedent. A statement of law from one case will bind lower courts provided there are no relevant factual distinctions between the cases.
- Skilled lawyers can feel liberated to use case law in many ways to argue points for their clients.
- It is possible to argue that the existence of binding case law offends the principle of Separation of Powers, but history shows us that case law has many benefits and can be flexible if times change.

Practical exercises

- Should judges be restricted to the role of adjudication between litigants?
- Should law be generated by cases, or just by Parliament?
- Lord Denning famously thought that the Court of Appeal should be free to depart from unhelpful House of Lords (now Supreme Court) precedent (see *Broome v Cassell*).[41] Would you agree?
- After Brexit, how should UK courts treat the jurisprudence of the ECJ, both past and current?

 *Visit the **online resources** for the authors' reflections and to check your progress.*

---

[40] Lord Reid (1972) 'The Judge as Lawmaker'. *Journal of the Society of Public Teachers of Law* 12, p. 22.

[41] *Broome v Cassell* [1971] 2 QB 354.

Further reading

Lord Denning (1982) *What Next in the Law.* **Oxford: OUP**
—This is widely regarded as one of the definitive statements of Lord Denning's jurisprudence, including, controversially, on the rights of immigrants. At the time, Lord Denning saw the book's publication as a rallying cry for change.

Hamilton, A. (1788) *The Federalist Papers No. 78.* **New York: J. & A. McLean**
—Hamilton, as one of the 'founding fathers' of the US Constitution, used this paper to explain why he felt that judges should have some law-making powers in a democracy.

For the authors' reflections on the practical exercises, additional self-test questions, sample interview questions and a library of links to useful websites, visit the free **online resources** *at* **www.oup.com/he/slorach4e.**

Chapter 5

Case law

6 Legal services and the ethical lawyer

Learning objectives

After reading this chapter you should be able to:

- Explain the importance of a strong legal profession.
- Understand the central role played by professional ethics in a lawyer's work.
- Understand the potential ethical dilemmas faced by lawyers.
- Describe the basic structure of the legal profession in England & Wales.
- Gain an awareness of the changing legal profession in the context of a changing society.
- Discuss how the increased importance of market forces has been reflected in the legal profession.

Introduction

We have looked at the law as a concept (Chapter 1), how it is created (Chapter 2), and where it is litigated (Chapter 3). We have seen that a key factor in entrenching the Rule of Law was the ability of the individual to access justice effectively. But this entire framework lacks impact without an accessible and effective legal profession.

In this chapter we focus on the legal profession in the UK, where major regulatory changes have been made to the provision of legal services. In the changing context in which lawyers operate, we look at why it remains important to have a robust legal profession with strong values. We look at how these values are compatible with the pressures of delivering professional services in the contemporary world.

This chapter is designed to complement Chapter 20. While this chapter looks at the importance of legal services, and their evolution, Chapter 20 focuses on law firms as businesses and the commercial challenges they face as a result of the changing economic and regulatory environment.

6.1 The importance of lawyers

We have already noted the importance of access to justice. 'Justice' should be seen in the widest sense: not only enforcing rights but also establishing rights, obligations, and relationships within the legal framework adopted by society.

Because they concern people's rights, obligations, and freedoms, the legal services that assist individuals' access to justice are qualitatively different from other services. Over the years, a mystique has built up around them—in popular culture the law provides powerful drama derived from its traditions and significance; countless novels and films feature lawyers as role models, heroes, or villains.

The legal profession has also developed a mixed reputation outside legal circles: it can be expensive to use the law, and lawyers' fees are an obvious (if often unjustified) target. The press are quick to make generalisations on the rare occasions that lawyers are found to be guilty of breaches of professional ethics, or, more challengingly, perceived abuses of society's morals. Also, what for some may epitomise the gravitas of a profession, may appear to others (rightly or wrongly) arcane or insular: the complexity of the law, professional traditions, even the architecture of the Inns of Court.

However, the fact remains that a healthy legal profession providing accessible legal services is vital to the Rule of Law and to the wider economy. This is what we shall explore in this section.

6.1.1 Lawyers and the Rule of Law

In Chapter 1 we saw that a key factor in entrenching the Rule of Law was the ability of the individual (including legal persons like companies) to access justice effectively. Lord Bingham's definition included: 'Means must be provided for resolving, without excessive cost or delay, civil disputes which the parties cannot resolve themselves.' In a study undertaken by the World Justice Project, the UK ranked 18th in access to civil justice, with a 73 per cent score using their methodology—a significant drop since the last edition of this book.[1] Denmark ranked first with 87 per cent, and the US ranked 30th with 64 per cent. For criminal justice the UK ranked 9th with 75 per cent, Finland first with 84 per cent, and the US 23rd with 63 per cent.

Recent history has shown that the winds of change that have blown through the wider economy, in the shape of market forces, have also affected the legal profession. While this has created significant challenges, it must also be hoped that, in opening up the profession, it will allow non-lawyers to understand a little more the importance of lawyers. A healthy legal profession is very important in the functioning of a modern state.

We saw in Chapter 1 that anarchy is undesirable for anyone who wants a stable framework within which to live their lives. Societies need rules. The daily actions and rights of individuals and businesses are governed and regulated by the law. It follows that anyone acting within a society needs to know what those rules are. In a mature society, legal rules are necessarily detailed and very carefully formulated; we have seen in Chapter 2 that the law is extensive, varied, and frequently complex. Laws are often difficult to find and interpret.

Consider, by analogy, the rules of a sport. Football has something called 'the Laws of the Game'. There are 17 rules, and most football players know most of these rules. However, the detail of the rules is set out in a book occupying 50 pages. Not many footballers would profess to an intimate understanding of everything written in that book. In a modern society, 'the rules of the game' are not 50 pages long. A visit to a law library will reveal how long 'the rules of the game' in England & Wales are. Whole walls are filled with so-called black letter law, namely the statutes, statutory instruments, and law reports, as well as commentary on those sources. (In Chapter 8 we discuss the role of paper legal resources in a digital world.)

The stakes are higher in law than in football. In civil law, there could be billions at stake. For most people, if they are presented with a claim for £1,000, this is a major issue. A convicted

---

[1] World Justice Project (2019) *Rule of Law Index 2019*. Available online at: http://worldjusticeproject.org/.

criminal might be sentenced to decades of incarceration. In international law, people's lives, and the fate of whole countries is in the balance.

Some areas of law are familiar to most people and do not require legal advice. For instance, most people know that if they drive at over 70 mph on a UK motorway, they are committing an offence. But in many other areas, people require expert help. The lawyer is this expert.

Example 1

Why people need lawyers

Imagine you are a newspaper editor. You have found out that a prominent MP, Norbert Samm, is making money from operating a pensions scam via a company. You think it is important that you expose this potentially illegal conduct by a public servant. You also need to sell newspapers, and the headline, 'MP Samm's Pension Scam' would certainly increase the paper's circulation.

Which areas of law might be relevant? How much time would it take to research them? Could you understand all the nuances while doing your normal day's work? What if you get something wrong?

We can see from this relatively simple example that some legal rules need a professional to find, interpret, and enforce them.

Thus lawyers are important because they assist in maintaining the stable framework and Rule of Law by providing individuals and businesses with access to justice. The lawyer will know where to take the argument, to which court or tribunal. She will be able to tell the client whether it is worth spending any money to argue his case, or whether instead it is a lost cause.

At a more pragmatic level, lawyers can provide a valuable expert service by interpreting and applying the law to assist individuals and businesses in maintaining rights, complying with regulation, creating legal relationships, and protecting property, etc. A lawyer will know where to look to find the relevant rules (or 'law'); the lawyer will know which issues are open to interpretation, and what the best arguments are for the client.

6.1.2 Lawyers and the economy

Kenneth Clarke, who, among many other positions, has held the office of Secretary of State for Justice, stated in 2011: 'The UK may no longer be able to boast it is the workshop of the world, but the UK can be a lawyer to the world.'[2] Indeed UK firms account for 10 per cent of global law firms' revenue.[3]

Legal services contribute significantly to the UK economy, generating £27 billion[4] (or 1.5 per cent of the UK's Gross Value Added (GVA)) in 2018–19. The profits of the 100 largest law firms together amount to around £8 billion. Around £1.5 billion is spent on legal aid by the government each year,[5] and £6.5 billion is generated through the export of legal services. Law firms therefore make a significant contribution to the country's economy.

[2] Kenneth Clarke MP, speech at CityUK Future Litigation event (14 September 2011).

[3] TheCityUk, July 2019. *Legal Services 2019*. Available online at: https://www.thecityuk.com/assets/2019/Report-PDFs/294e2be784/Legal-excellence-internationally-renowned-UK-legal-services-2019.pdf.

[4] TheCityUk, July 2019. *Legal Services 2019*. Available online at: https://www.thecityuk.com/assets/2019/Report-PDFs/294e2be784/Legal-excellence-internationally-renowned-UK-legal-services-2019.pdf.

[5] House of Commons Library, Alison Pratt, Jennifer Brown, and Georgina Sturge, 31 October 2018: *The Future of Legal Aid*, CDP-2018/0230.

6.2 Lawyers as professionals

Service industries generate 79 per cent of the UK's GVA.[6] Lawyers make a major contribution to this—we have already noted the magnitude of the legal services market. However, while lawyers are one of the UK's service industries, they are also members of a profession. First we examine the idea of a profession, before focusing on lawyers as professionals.

6.2.1 What is a professional?

> **Essential explanation**
>
> A **professional** is someone who works in a profession. The Royal Commission on Legal Services 1979 defined a 'profession' as an occupation that:
>
> - requires central organisation;
> - is self-regulated (this has been replaced in recent years by independent regulation);
> - has required minimum standards of training;
> - places significant importance on duty to the client; and
> - involves the giving of specialist advice.
>
> To this list one might add social prestige and a sense of calling (see Herring: *Legal Ethics*[7]). It is arguable that underlying several of these characteristics is a recognition of the importance of ethics in the delivery of these services. Indeed the *quid pro quo* for their exalted status might be said to be the observance of an ethical code.
>
> Other 'professions' include accountants, architects, dentists, doctors, engineers, pharmacists, and teachers. The list is open-ended, but these are good examples.

Lawyers are legal professionals. In the recent past there have been many initiatives aimed at removing lawyers' monopolies in areas such as domestic conveyancing and will drafting. Despite the erosion of lawyers' monopolies (see 6.2.2 and 6.6), lawyers remain professionals.

6.2.2 What is a legal professional?

In the widest sense, this includes:

- judges at all levels (although magistrates are said to be 'laypeople', so not practising lawyers);
- solicitors and barristers, who are qualified lawyers entitled to practise law by offering their advice professionally;
- paralegals, trainee solicitors, and pupil barristers, none of whom have yet qualified to offer their services; and
- academic lawyers, who write about or teach the law.

Traditionally, the legal profession in England & Wales has been made up predominantly of solicitors and barristers, both of whom exhibit the traits of a profession. They are centrally

[6] House of Commons Library, Lorna Booth, Philip Brien and Matthew Ward: *Economic Indicators, June 2019*: Briefing Paper 8606, 28 June 2019.
[7] Jonathan Herring (2017) *Legal Ethics* (2nd edn) Oxford: OUP, chapter 2.

organised and regulated—solicitors by the Solicitors Regulation Authority (SRA), and barristers by the Bar Standards Board (BSB). Each body places substantial emphasis on high standards of training and qualification, and on professional ethics (which we examine at 6.4). Both carry out statutorily defined[8] areas of work such as litigation and representing clients in court.

Other legal services providers, such as legal executives, patent attorneys, and trade mark attorneys, are also regulated by their own regulatory bodies. All of these bodies are approved by the Legal Services Board (a 'super regulator'). However, this chapter focuses mainly on solicitors and barristers. We will also look at the expanding role of legal executives.

Over time, changes have impacted upon the work of both professions, such as solicitors getting rights of audience in superior courts (see Chapter 3 on the court system), and the opening up of traditional solicitors' monopolies (such as domestic conveyancing and the drafting of wills) to non-lawyers. Arguably the principal change has occurred recently, as a result of the Legal Services Act 2007 (LSA), with the creation of ABSs (Alternative Business Structures). We examine these changes at 6.6.

Although it is perhaps artificial to create an exhaustive list of legal services, a lawyer will provide some or all of the legal services listed in Table 6.1. One column lists legal services

Table 6.1 Legal activities

Reserved Activities	Not Reserved Activities
advocacy in court;	commercial law, including international trade (including contract drafting, competition law, and marketing agreements)
administration of oaths;	corporate finance (including banking, debt finance, and capital markets)
the conduct of litigation;	corporate regulatory compliance (including company procedure, directors' duties, shareholders' rights, and mergers and acquisitions)
handling probate matters;	domestic conveyancing
notarial activities; and	employment law (including workplace safety, redundancy, unfair and wrongful dismissal, and discrimination)
reserved instrument activities.	environmental and planning law
	family law (including non-contentious aspects of divorce, abuse, rights of children)
	financial services law (although advising on specific financial products is itself regulated)
	housing law (including eviction, housing benefit, and private and public sector lettings)
	immigration law (including asylum and deportation)
	insurance law (including claims handling, reinsurance, the Lloyd's market)
	media and intellectual property law (including licensing and media finance)
	professional negligence
	tax compliance by individuals and businesses
	the legal aspects of new media and the internet.

[8] Legal Services Act 2007, s. 12.

which are 'Reserved Activities'. These must be undertaken by a qualified lawyer under the LSA.[9] The other column contains examples of legal services which are not reserved activities. Historically, they were almost always provided by qualified lawyers; however, this monopoly is being eroded.

As you can see, legal practice involves a vast range of disciplines. Yet beyond this, some lawyers' work is non-legal, for example advising on the merits of transactions, acting as 'wise counsel' to clients, etc. In addition, many non-lawyers,[10] such as licensed conveyancers, accountants, Citizens Advice Bureaux, Legal Advice Centres, etc., provide legal services, including some of the 'legal' services identified above.

At 6.6 we look at the continuing changes to the regulation and character of the legal profession and its work: the nature of lawyers' work, the structure of the profession, and those permitted to undertake work formerly the sole preserve of solicitors and barristers, are all changing.

6.3 The legal profession in England & Wales

The legal profession has changed beyond recognition since the Victorian era. Charles Dickens wrote in *Bleak House*: 'Mr. Vholes's chambers are on so small a scale that one clerk can open the door without getting off his stool, while the other who elbows him at the same desk has equal facilities for poking the fire'. He wrote of an office, 'blending with the smell of must and dust, the fretting of parchment forms and skins in greasy drawers'.[11] Multinational, multidisciplinary, firms are a world away from this cramped, stuffy picture of a bygone age. They operate from elegant space-age glass towers, and their websites proclaim worldwide practices offering one-stop legal services for huge corporate and banking clients. Still further removed is the emerging *virtual* lawyer, where the lawyer and client communicate online and may never meet; there may even be, for some services, no lawyer at all, but instead, AI enabled by lawyers.

We will examine the structure of the legal profession first, before focusing on the importance of ethics and regulation. At 6.5 we will look at the development of legal services in England & Wales, focusing on the changes currently sweeping through their regulation and delivery.

6.3.1 Structure

Only a minority of jurisdictions have a 'divided' legal profession, including England & Wales, Scotland, and Hong Kong. Solicitors traditionally constituted only one branch of the legal profession; barristers (collectively, 'the Bar') formed the other. This is a historic division in the profession, and has been likened to the division between general practitioners and specialist doctors in medicine. This analogy is increasingly inaccurate as more solicitors specialise in a

---

9 Legal Services Act 2007, s. 12.

10 In this context, we refer to 'lawyers' as those licensed to perform reserved activities under the LSA.

11 Dickens, Charles (1852–53) *Bleak House*. London: Wordsworth Editions Ltd, 1993, p. 626.

particular field of law or take up rights of audience in courts. In addition, there are several other, less numerous, types of lawyer in England & Wales.

These two branches of the profession are organised separately. The General Council of the Bar—the Bar Council—is the governing body for the Bar, and barristers are regulated by the BSB. The Law Society represents the interests of solicitors, and the SRA regulates their conduct. Both barristers and solicitors have detailed Codes of Conduct (see 6.4). Each branch of the legal profession (including legal executives, patent and trade mark attorneys, etc.) has an Approved Regulator. The ten Approved Regulators are overseen by the Legal Services Board under the LSA.[12]

6.3.2 **Barristers**

Traditionally, the Bar was viewed as the senior branch of the profession, both for its historic roots and because almost all the senior judges were appointed from barristers. 'The Bar', incidentally, is derived from a physical bar that separated the public (including solicitors) from those in the 'well' of the court—that is, the barristers and judges.

The Bar is comparatively small—there are 16,598 practising barristers,[13] with the majority based in London, compared with 146,092[14] practising solicitors. Barristers operate as consultants, offering specialised services as advocates in court and giving opinions and advice on specific areas of law. Clients do not normally go directly to barristers (although this situation is changing—see 6.6.2); rather it is the solicitor who instructs 'counsel', as lawyers usually call barristers (see Figure 6.1).

Until 1990, only barristers were entitled to appear in the superior courts (the High Court, the Court of Appeal, and the Supreme Court) and, for most purposes, the Crown Courts. Now, rights of audience—as the right to appear in court as an advocate is known—depend instead only on ability and qualification as an advocate.

| | Client finds appropriate solicitor to undertake all 'legal tasks' for extended period | | Preferred barristers take instructions from solicitors but not from clients | |

Figure 6.1 Roles of solicitors and barristers

[12] Legal Services Act 2007, s. 2 and Sch. 1.

[13] Practising Barrister Statistics, Bar Standards Board: https://www.barstandardsboard.org.uk/news-publications/research-and-statistics/statistics-about-the-bar.html, accessed at 19/06/2019.

[14] Solicitors Regulation Authority (December 2019) *SRA Regulated Population Statistics*. Available online at: https://www.sra.org.uk/sra/how-we-work/reports/statistics/regulated-community-statistics/data/population_solicitors/.

Unlike solicitors, barristers are not permitted to enter into a professional partnership with other barristers. Instead, they are members of Chambers, a form of association which is less formal than a partnership and which provides, among other things, for the sharing of office expenses and other resources with fellow barristers. Practising barristers have to be members of one of the four Inns of Court: Lincoln's Inn, the Inner Temple, the Middle Temple, and Gray's Inn.[15] Each Inn's main function is to maintain a collegiate framework for the Bar, and foster legal education and standards of professional conduct. To qualify, a barrister has to be 'called to the Bar' by one of the Inns.

6.3.3 Solicitors

Historically, there was a formal distinction between the roles of solicitors and barristers, the solicitors' role being to advise the client and to instruct a barrister, if advocacy was necessary on behalf of the client (as in Figure 6.1). In addition, the work of most solicitors was more general than that of many barristers, who commonly performed the role of experts, giving opinions to solicitors who needed specialist advice in given areas of law. This is still the most common situation—a solicitor is the first point of contact for most individuals or organisations seeking legal advice. Solicitors may have to deal with a wide variety of problems; however, they do increasingly specialise in particular areas of legal work, and the formal distinction between the roles of solicitors and barristers is no longer as clear cut (see 6.6.2).

Unlike barristers, solicitors are entitled to practise in partnership with other solicitors. Most of them do this, although sole practitioners still make up almost half of the total number of solicitors' practices.

The structure and size of the solicitors' profession in England & Wales can be seen from the following statistics, released by the SRA.[16] Of around 200,000 qualified solicitors, approximately 146,000 have practising certificates (around 50,000 solicitors do not practise). There are around 10,000 law firms. Every year roughly 5,500 people begin training contracts and 6,500 new solicitors qualify.[17]

Chapter 20 examines the range of firms in which solicitors work. Not only is the solicitors' profession distributed among many different types of firm, it is also changing rapidly in composition. An increasing proportion of lawyers do not work for a firm, but directly 'in house', for example exclusively for a large company or for the government, as an employee of that entity. The number of solicitors employed outside private practice has more than doubled between

---

[15] Formally, the Honourable Society of Lincoln's Inn, the Honourable Society of the Inner Temple, the Honourable Society of the Middle Temple, and the Honourable Society of Gray's Inn.

[16] Solicitors Regulation Authority (accessed January 2020) *SRA Regulated Population Statistics*. Available online at: https://www.sra.org.uk/sra/how-we-work/reports/statistics/regulated-community-statistics/data/population_solicitors.

[17] The Law Society (2018) *Annual Statistics Report 2018*.

2000 and 2018. Just under one third of solicitors is employed outside private practice; as a proportion of total solicitors, this has nearly doubled since 2000.[18]

In the period 2000–18, the number of women practising as solicitors went up by over 80 per cent (although their average age is much lower than their male counterparts, suggesting that the profession may not yet uniformly accommodate women seeking to balance the pressures of a career in practice with the demands of family life). Around half of all solicitors are women, although there remains a 'pay gulf' between the genders—only 30 per cent of partners in the top 20 UK law firms are women.

Figure 6.2 shows the proportion of solicitors in 2019 in each of these important groups. It also shows the proportion from 2000, to illustrate how quickly the profession is changing its composition. At 6.6.2 we examine the considerable structural changes also occurring in the delivery of legal services.

6.3.4 Legal executives

Legal executives are increasingly recognised as being one of three (rather than two) branches of the legal profession, alongside barristers and solicitors. This enhanced status is largely a result of regulatory changes—see 6.6. The legal executive branch grew from the law clerk profession in the 19th century. In 1963, the Law Society created what is now the Chartered Institute of Legal Executives (CILEx) to bolster the legal profession at a time when there were too few qualified lawyers to serve the legal services market—this is because there are fewer barriers to qualification as a Fellow of CILEx. Legal executives should not be confused with paralegals—the latter is not a route to status as a qualified lawyer. Solicitors and legal

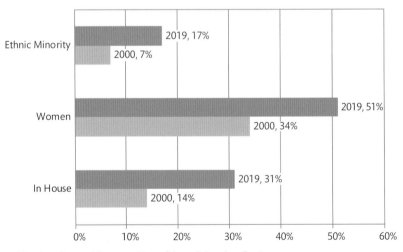

Figure 6.2 The changing social composition of the solicitors' profession

[18] Statistics derived from figures in TheCityUK, 2019. *Legal Services 2019*. Available online at: https://www. thecityuk.com/research/legal-excellence-internationally-renowned-uk-legal-services-2019/, and the Law Society, *Annual Statistics Report 2019*.

executives often work together. Legal executives have a different route to qualification from that of solicitors, but once qualified, their position is similar—indeed, they have rights of advocacy, they can be partners in law firms, and since 2014 have been able to practise independently of solicitors in some areas. According to CILEx, by 2019 there were 20,000 legal executives in England & Wales, of whom around 7,500 were chartered[19] (i.e. qualified), and over 250 were partners in law firms.

6.4 Professional ethics and regulation

In this section, we will look at the importance of ethics and regulation to lawyers and the public who use them (at 6.4.1). We will then examine the regulatory framework that has developed to reinforce professional ethics and safeguard the public (at 6.4.2). We then explore the role of professional ethics in ensuring competing ethical pressures are reconciled (at 6.4.3). Finally, we look at the manifestation of these pressures in a case study (6.4.4) before, then, stress-testing this framework using some practical examples.

6.4.1 The importance of professional ethics and regulation

In Henry VI Part 2, Shakespeare wrote, *'The first thing we do, let's kill all the lawyers.'* Why are lawyers such an easy target? And is this fair?

At 1.2 we touched on the important but occasionally uneasy relationship between law and morality. Because of this, ethics assumes an even more acute role when considering legal services. Lawyers are intimately involved with some of the most important decisions people make in their lives and must confront many interesting ethical challenges. Almost all activities carried out by lawyers have ethical implications. The legal profession is special not merely because (like other professions) it demands probity from its members, but also because its work is *about* probity. So, just as doctors adhere to ethical codes (e.g. the 'four principles', and the Hippocratic Oath, to practise honestly and ethically), lawyers also have comprehensive rules about ethical behaviour.

There is plenty of cynicism about lawyers, especially in the tabloid press, but the vast majority do adhere to the very high ethical standards which the profession sets itself. A lawyer's probity and competence will have a critical impact on a client, for example:

- Will the client succeed in business deals?
- Will the client be able to have contact with his children?
- Can the client avoid going to prison?
- Will the client receive compensation for her injuries?

The lawyer is often in a position of great power: entrusted with enormous sums of money and with confidential information about the most important and delicate aspects of people's lives. This brings great responsibility. Much of the time, certainly in the tabloid press, the

---

[19] CILEx, *Facts, Figures, Statistics,* accessed at https://www.cilex.org.uk/media/interesting_facts/facts__figures.

impression is of a profession profiting from people's problems, so-called 'ambulance chasers'. It is safe to say that this is, in general, inaccurate.

Professional ethics, then, are necessary to ensure that the public is protected by (and occasionally, from) lawyers, and also to ensure that the public knows that this is the case. Let us start with a quote from the introduction to the SRA's Standards and Regulations (explained at 6.4.3). Solicitors must, '. . . *safeguard the wider public interest (such as the rule of law, and public confidence in a trustworthy solicitors' profession . . .)*'.[20] This seems very straightforward. As we will see, the quote is taken (deliberately) out of context. A more contextual description is that the ethics of a professional overlap with, but do not coincide with, more general principles of ethics. For a lawyer this means that they have additional ethical obligations to the lay person (e.g. to keep things they are told in confidence), and that they may be excused from some general ethical obligations imposed on others—for instance an obligation to report a crime (due to a duty of confidentiality).

6.4.2 The regulation of lawyers and law firms

We have seen how important it is that lawyers must act ethically, and also be seen to do so. We have also seen that lawyers are professionals, so they must be regulated. The LSA made many profound changes to the legal sector, and one was to the way lawyers were regulated. It was felt that lawyers should not be self-regulated, so that the public felt their interests were being served, rather than lawyers' own interests. This is in keeping with changes in the utilities sector, and in banking. The outcome was that any legal profession authorised to carry out some or all regulated activities must now be regulated by an independent regulator. In turn, these regulators have to be approved by the Legal Services Board under the LSA. Hitherto, professional bodies, like the Law Society and the Bar Council, performed two functions: both regulating and representing their professions. After the LSA, they were recast as bodies that were limited to representing their professions; the independent regulators are the Solicitors Regulation Authority ('SRA') and the Bar Standards Board ('BSB') respectively. One of the aims of this change was to give the public greater confidence in lawyers, knowing that they were objectively regulated and subject to independent oversight. Figure 6.3 summarises the position.

6.4.3 The Codes of Conduct

As a result of the critical nature of ethics in a lawyer's role, the lawyer must abide by a rule book. The existence of a transparent and demanding set of rules is vital therefore to ensure that they meet the highest standards, and also to preserve the reputation of lawyers. For barristers, this is BSB Handbook, which includes the BSB Code of Conduct. For solicitors, this is the SRA Standards and Regulations, which includes the SRA Principles and the Codes of Conduct for Solicitors and for Firms.

These provide for disciplinary action to be taken against any member of the profession who does not comply. Sanctions range from a reprimand, a fine through to suspension or even striking-off (removal from the profession).

---

[20] *SRA Standards and Regulations, Introduction to the Principles*, Solicitors Regulation Authority, November 2019.

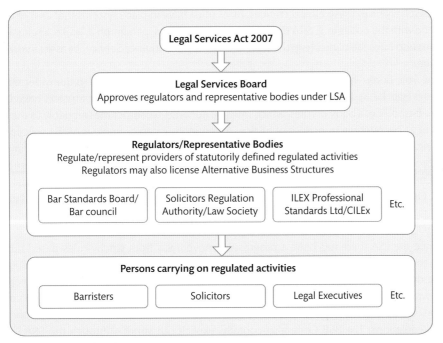

Figure 6.3 Regulation of legal services

The SRA Principles have an introduction (mentioned at 6.4.1 but now used in context) which bears repetition as it explicitly addresses this key demand:

> Should the Principles come into conflict, those which safeguard the wider public interest (such as the rule of law, and public confidence in a trustworthy solicitors' profession and a safe and effective market for regulated legal services) take precedence over an individual client's interests.[21]

Here is a list of some key professional conduct responsibilities to be aware of that provide a flavour of the ethically intensive nature of legal practice:

- a duty to act in the client's best interests (even if the effect is to reduce your own fees, because it is not in the client's interests to proceed);[22]

- a duty to keep a client's affairs confidential (think of the sensitivity of the personal, commercial, or financial information lawyers will keep in relation to their clients);[23] and

- a duty not to deceive the court or the other side (e.g. if your client tells you half-way through a trial that they are guilty after all)[24, 25].

[21] *SRA Standards and Regulations, Introduction to the Principles*, Solicitors Regulation Authority, November 2019.

[22] *SRA Standards and Regulations, Principle 7*, Solicitors Regulation Authority, November 2019, and *BSB Handbook, Code of Conduct: Core Duty 2*, BSB, 15 October 2019.

[23] *SRA Standards and Regulations, Code of Conduct for Solicitors, RELs and RFLs: Paragraph 6.3*, Solicitors Regulation Authority, November 2019, and *BSB Handbook, Code of Conduct: Core Duty 6*, BSB, 15 October 2019.

[24] *BSB Handbook, Code of Conduct: gC9*, BSB, 15 October 2019.

[25] *SRA Standards and Regulations, Code of Conduct for Solicitors, RELs and RFLs: Paragraph 1.4*, Solicitors Regulation Authority, November 2019, and *BSB Handbook, Code of Conduct: rC9*, BSB, 15 October 2019.

To assist lawyers in these ethical choices, firms must have in place systems that ensure compliance with the codes (e.g. SRA Code of Conduct for Firms, paragraph 2.1(a)).[26] Professional bodies also have 'helplines' (e.g. the Bar Council Ethical Enquiries Service) to assist inidivdual lawyers.

The 'rule books' have never existed in a vacuum. They can be placed in the wider ethical context (see 1.2.3). Historically, the codes of conduct for solicitors and barristers have been 'rules-based'—i.e. a book of rules, which must be adhered-to, sometimes arguably to the detriment of overarching principles of justice. A frequently-cited example is of the solicitor for the victims of the Ladbroke Grove rail crash (which in 1999 killed 31 people and injured hundreds), who told the press that their evidence would '. . . reveal shocking evidence of total mismanagement and utter callous disregard for safety . . .' on the part of the defendants. One of the defendants, Railtrack, complained to the Law Society (the then regulator of solicitors), who found that the solicitor had not breached professional rules—he Solicitors' Publicity Code.[27]

Since the LSA there has been a progressive move away from strictly rules-based regulation, towards more outcomes-based regulation, focusing on giving lawyers the discretion to meet overarching outcomes—this is designed to address concerns that professional regulation was as much about box-ticking as about meeting higher aims. There are now ten mandatory Core Duties in the BSB Code of Conduct, and seven Principles in the SRA Standards and Regulations. The BSB Code also contains explicit outcomes. Although the SRA Codes no longer explicitly contain outcomes, they are short enough (the SRA Code of Conduct for Solicitors, RFLs and RELs is just seven pages long in printed form) to leave many decisions open to the individual's discretion, guided by the high-level Principles and the provisions of the Codes.

Lawyers in both professions generally take complaints and ethics very seriously, but if clients are unhappy with their lawyer they will normally complain first to the firm or barrister concerned. In the event that this does not produce the required result, or is inappropriate, the client can then contact the Legal Ombudsman who will consider the complaint. If the lawyer or firm is in breach of professional rules, the case is then referred to the SRA or BSB as appropriate.

6.4.4 Dilemmas in professional ethics

Professional ethics are not straightforward, as professionals are sometimes faced with dilemmas caused by conflicting ethical priorities. The practising lawyer owes ethical obligations not only to the client, but also to the court, and to other lawyers. This places the lawyer's priorites under strain. Because lawyers are among the custodians of the Rule of Law, and because they represent the law as an entity, they also owe non-formal ethical obligations to the world at large. Lawyers earn their living by acting for clients. Ethical issues can arise over whether you as a lawyer are willing or able to act for a specific client. Paedophiles, rapists, fraudsters, traffickers, terrorists, torturers, and murderers all look for lawyers to represent them.

[26] *SRA Standards and Regulations, Code of Conduct for Firms, paragraph 2.1(a),* Solicitors Regulation Authority, November 2019.
[27] A.Boon and J.Levin (2008) *The Ethics and Conduct of Lawyers in England and Wales,* Oxford: Hart, 287.

Example 2
Defending the Yorkshire Ripper

In 1981 Peter Sutcliffe was convicted of murdering 13 women and attempting to murder seven others. His attacks were generally brutal—involving hammer strikes to the head and multiple stabbings. In court he was represented by barrister James Chadwin. The latter was beloved of his family and friends, and known for his warmth and generosity—he was much mourned on his death in 2006. How is it that Mr Chadwin could reconcile his own morals with representing Sutcliffe, known also as The Yorkshire Ripper? The answer must be because of the ethical requirement for defendants in criminal trials to be given legal representation.

A choice to represent a mass murderer is justified—indeed it is sometimes mandated—by the professional codes. How is this justified using ethical principles?

Under a rules-based system, it is hard to justify the defence of a killer, but, given clear enough rules, it is apparent that lawyers can promote the interests of their clients. The codes for solicitors and barristers both allow for this with unambiguous rules:

The BSB Code of Conduct:

You must not withhold your services or permit your services to be withheld:

1. on the ground that the nature of the case is objectionable to you or to any section of the public;
2. on the ground that the conduct, opinions or beliefs of the prospective client are unacceptable to you or to any section of the public . . .[28]

Similarly, a solicitor must also ignore their personal views when advising clients.[29]

Under an outcomes-based system, defending murderers can be more easily justified (as above) on the basis that legal representation must be given to defendants in criminal trials, in order to promote the right to a fair trial, and thus the Rule of Law. This is set out as a priority in the quote from the SRA Standards and regulations at 6.4.1.

It is more difficult to justify the defence of Peter Sutcliffe under a virtue-based theory. Promoting the interests of serial killers does not seem virtuous. However, James Chadwin might have argued that his instinctive sense of justice would be best served by providing representation to Sutcliffe.

From this, we can see that sometimes professional ethics can conflict with an individual lawyer's ethical values, and a given course of action may be demanded by professional ethical codes but may not be compatible with traditional ethical values as discussed at 1.2.3.

6.4.5 Would you act?

To conclude this discussion of the importance of professional ethics to a lawyer, let us take a few examples of the nuanced situations lawyers often face in practice. Think about whether you should, would, or could act in these situations.

---

[28] BSB, *BSB Handbook, version 4.3*, Part 2, *Code of Conduct: Core Duties* (BSB, 15 October 2019).
[29] *SRA Standards and Regulations, Solicitors, RELs and RFLs, paragraph 1.1* (SRA, 25 November 2019).

⊛ Essential debate

Would you act?

Example 1

Imagine you are a solicitor specialising in criminal law. A potential client comes to see you, in your capacity as an advocate. He asks you to appear for him in court. He has been charged with rape. He says that the woman consented. You instinctively don't believe him.

Would you represent him, notwithstanding your suspicions, or would you refuse to act?

Example 2

Imagine you live in a small town in rural Herefordshire. You are the only local solicitor, a sole practitioner. You handle much of the town's legal work. Your sister is looking to buy a house near you, and one of your existing clients (for whom you have acted on various matters over ten years) has one for sale. You are of course impartial and would have no problem (in your mind) acting for your client in the sale of the house to your sister.

Example 3

You are an experienced litigation solicitor. You have recently managed to secure a large settlement in respect of your client's recent litigation matter. The client tells you that he wishes to invest this money in buying shares in a technology company, and asks you which company he should invest in.

Answers

In the Example 1, a solicitor or barrister must not knowingly mislead the court. This is part of the so-called 'duty to the court'. Provided the lawyer does not know that the client is guilty, she can continue to represent the client. If the client (even privately) admits his guilt, then the lawyer can no longer represent the client on a 'not guilty' plea, without breaching her duty to the court. The lawyer would be obliged to tell the court of the client's guilt, or cease to act.[30]

In the Example 2, a lawyer (here a solicitor) has a duty to act in the best interests of their client. The SRA Standards and Regulations prohibit a solicitor from acting where this duty conflicts, or (as here) there is a significant risk that it may conflict, with his own interests in relation to that matter. This would likely extend to any loyalties he would have to his sister.[31]

Example 3 is less obviously an ethical issue, but it shows how widely a lawyer's conduct duties are drawn. There is legislation to prevent investors from giving poor or dishonest advice. In giving advice on the merits of an investment, you fall within the ambit of the Financial Services and Markets Act 2000 (which has recently been tightened up in light of the banking crisis). Giving investment advice is illegal under that Act, unless the adviser is authorised to do so by the Financial Conduct Authority. Lawyers can be authorised, but need to pass FCA examinations to do so, which is rare. So there are complex rules concerning when it is permissible to give 'investment advice' in the context of legal services. The scenario is unlikely to fall within these rules. If you provide this advice outside these rules you will commit a criminal offence under the Act. In addition, you must only advise if you are competent to do so.[32]

These are just a few of the many ethical issues engaged in a lawyer's job. You can see, therefore, that the ethical dimension can be construed very widely indeed, and that lawyers need clear and comprehensible professional regulation to ensure that their actions are ethically justified and justifiable.

---

[30] *SRA Standards and Regulations, Code of Conduct for Solicitors, RELs and RFLs: Paragraph 1.4*, Solicitors Regulation Authority, November 2019, and *BSB Handbook, Code of Conduct: rC9 and gC9*, BSB, 15 October 2019.

[31] *SRA Standards and Regulations, Code of Conduct for Solicitors, RELs and RFLs: Paragraph 6.2*, Solicitors Regulation Athority, November 2019.

[32] *SRA Standards and Regulations, Code of Conduct for Solicitors, RELs and RFLs: Paragraph 3.2*, Solicitors Regulation Athority, November 2019.

6.4.6 Professional ethics: conclusion

We have seen that lawyers are collectively a vital element of the legal system, and so they must abide by a robust but workable system of professional ethics. We have looked at how this is manifested in the professional codes of the SRA and BSB. We have examined how these codes mandate and guide the behaviour of lawyers in real situations where moral dilemmas present ethical challenges.

In one of the seminal reported cases in this area, *Bolton* v *The Law Society*,[33] Lord Bingham (mentioned in the context of the Rule of Law at 1.5) confirmed the pivotal character of professional ethics for lawyers as they execute their obligations to clients and society at large. In confirming a relatively draconian sanction (two years' suspension), he said that, '. . . the reputation of the profession is more important than the fortunes of any individual member. Membership of a profession brings many benefits, but that is a part of the price'. He concluded that the purpose of such sanctions is not solely to sanction the individual but, '. . . to maintain the reputation of the solicitor's profession as one in which every member, of whatever standard, may be trusted to the end of the earth . . .'. The discharge of a professional duty with less than complete integrity would attract severe sanctions (and mitigating factors will assume a lesser role than in criminal law).

We have seen that, because lawyers' activities so innately concern ethics, it is vital that lawyers act in accordance with professional ethical principles. This is why the modern professional codes emphasise the public interest so fundamentally. Since 2007 it has become clear that the codes require lawyers to think ethically and to aim to promote the interests of their clients and of the public at large; and also be seen to promote these interests.

6.5 History of the legal profession in England & Wales

The size and organisation of the solicitors' profession has changed out of all recognition in recent decades, and probably not even Charles Dickens could have imagined the changes which have produced the typical law firm (if there is one) of the 21st century. Why?

In this section we look at how the 'traditional' model of legal services provision evolved. This is vital for an understanding of the impetus for the fundamental changes that have occurred in the recent past.

Legal practice does not exist inside a bubble. Radical changes affecting lawyers and the legal system today are a reflection of wider changes in society and politics, touched upon at 2.3.3. The next section puts changes to the legal profession in the context of society, politics, and the legal system. While reading it, you may find it helpful to refer to Figure 6.4 as an overview.

6.5.1 Development up to the late 20th Century

Like the country, legal services in England & Wales was decentralised until the Elizabethan era (1558–1603). You may remember (from 'Development of the common law' at 2.3.2.1) that the circuit courts historically travelled around the country to dispense justice. The courts were

---

[33] *Bolton* v *The Law Society* [1993] EWCA Civ 32.

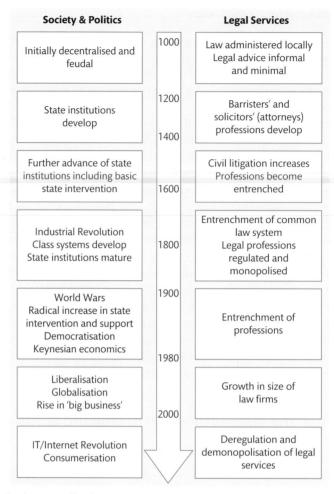

Figure 6.4 The development of legal services in context

accompanied by a retinue of lawyers, to act for those who needed representation—these lawyers evolved into barristers, and most judges were drawn from their ranks. Originally, solicitors were court officers (called 'attorneys'), who helped their clients bring their case before the local courts only. It was useful for litigants to engage a solicitor to find the appropriate barrister. Over the centuries this crystallised into the rule that an attorney did not have rights of audience before a court, while a barrister did. In London, lawyers performing a mainly clerical role 'solicited' actions in the Court of Chancery.

In 2.3.3 we saw that in the late 19th Century the state grew to deal with industrial and social pressures. In the law this gradual process of formalisation was reflected by the requirement for legal practitioners to be regulated, and monopolies were established for solicitors and barristers. The Law Society (which still represents solicitors) was created in 1845.

By the mid-1970s, because of the ballooning of the state and its machinery, many of Britain's institutions had become monopolies, sheltered from the pressures of competition. Both public and private sectors were perceived to be complacent, overregulated, and unwieldy. The 'Winter of Discontent' of 1978–9 was the culmination of this process, as the country was crippled by a series of strikes. Something had to change. In 6.6.1 we describe what happened. It could be argued that even the legal system was stultified by the rigid system of precedent and an unreformed court system.

This entrenchment was echoed by the monopolies within the law. Only solicitors and barristers could practise law. Only barristers had rights of audience in the courts. Under the Solicitors Act 1974[34] unqualified persons were prohibited from acting as solicitors, commencing litigation, or preparing documents relating to probate (handling the administration of a person's estate after their death). These monopolies were significant and long-standing, and were justified by the need to prevent fraud and maintain high standards of service and probity. Barristers' rights of audience in superior courts (now 'senior courts'—see 3.1.4) had been entrenched since the Bar emerged in the 12th century.

In this period, a client would use a very rigid mechanism to obtain legal advice. If a client already had a reliable solicitor, he would normally continue to employ that solicitor. If not, then he would research an appropriate solicitor, either by word of mouth, or by using published directories. Advertising was not permitted for the provision of legal services. The client would retain that solicitor, who would then, if necessary, instruct a barrister (usually a preferred counsel, with an established relationship with the solicitor's firm) for any expert advice or representation in a higher court. This traditional position is summarised in Figure 6.1.

It might be contended that lawyers, schooled in entrenched case law, become naturally conservative and resistant to change. These lawyers rose up the career ladder to manage their firms, with the effect that managers in the profession were arguably focused on maintaining the status quo, rather than embracing any changes developing within society and the wider economy.

Other professions also became entrenched by monopolistic or anti-competitive regulation. Accountants, engineers, and architects were prime examples. In 2001, the Office of Fair Trading (OFT),[35] investigated the regulation and deregulation of professions in the UK and around the world. It highlighted certain restrictions which were characteristic of the traditional regulation of professions:

- entry restrictions (i.e. the requirement for professionals to have undergone a formal professional training course like the Legal Practice Course or the Bar Professional Training Course);

- price regulation;

- the prohibition of certain business structures (e.g. not allowing limited liability for professions);

- prohibition of joint practices combining more than one profession (e.g. lawyers and accountants); and

- restrictions on advertising, placing emphasis on word of mouth recommendation.[36]

---

[34] Solicitors Act 1974, s. 21.   [35] Now largely replaced by the Competition and Markets Authority.
[36] Office of Fair Trading (2001) *Competition in Professions—A Report by the Director General of Fair Trading* (March 2001, OFT328).

The OFT's survey concluded that in most professions, many of these restrictions were generally negative in their effect on quality of service. Since that report, things have moved on.

6.6 The free-market revolution in legal services

6.6.1 Background: the free market

Here, we focus on two (linked) themes: the growth in very large companies, and the loosening up of key features of the post-war social democratic state.

Very large companies became ever more important to Western economies. Many developments came together to encourage this expansion:

- globalisation of markets as transport and information improved;
- liberalisation of stock markets allowing a surge in demand for publicly tradable shares, and the rise in investment opportunities (e.g. taking over rivals);
- increased relevance of economies of scale in relation to infrastructure (e.g. information technology, buildings, and plant), and employment;
- greater ability of larger companies to meet regulatory requirements;
- the need to meet manufacturing challenges from the Far East;
- the increased role of marketing triggered by technologically-driven advances in media, most especially the intelligent mining of big data by tech and social media companies;
- expansion of companies' portfolios horizontally (i.e. by taking over or merging with rivals) and vertically (i.e. by expansion into new fields); and
- lowering of taxes (particularly in the US) to encourage the growth of businesses and investment.

Chapter 19 discusses the economics behind these market changes in more detail.

The UK was the first major European economy to embrace 'free market' or 'laissez-faire' principles (see 19.1.4) as an alternative to social democracy, most emphatically during the administrations of Prime Minister Margaret Thatcher in the period 1979–90. Free market theorists (such as Milton Friedman and Freidrich Hayek)[37] believed that a market would find its own equilibrium, most typically through the mechanisms of supply and demand rather than national planning. One means by which services can be provided efficiently (according to free market theories) is by removing barriers to entry into markets. Increased competition forces existing suppliers to reduce prices and/or improve quality. The counter-argument is that the free market forces most actors to prioritise short-term gains over longer-term investment and quality.

The emphasis on state monopolies was replaced by a mixed economy. The balance between state and private ownership of utilities was significantly tilted in favour of 'private' by the progressive privatisation of utilities in the 1980s, opening these utilities up to market investment and market pressures. The theme, then, is the opening up—or liberalisation—of the economy to the involvement of private institutions and the removal of institutional and

---

[37] Particularly in Hayek, Friedrich (1944) *The Road to Serfdom*. London: Routledge, 2014.

economic restrictions on participation. Successive governments sought to reduce inefficiencies based on procedure and regulation, and to modernise the machinery of state, with an emphasis on transparency where possible. Roles hitherto the preserve of the state (even the National Health Service) were contracted out to private service providers, such as service industries providing the government with IT, etc. As of 2018, the Civil Service had shrunk to 440,000.[38]

Liberalisation has been further stimulated by the information and communications technology revolution over the past 30 years. The growth of internet-based commerce is transforming all parts of the economy. Information is readily available to consumers and businesses at all levels, and decision-making is thus more informed. In many areas this has led to increased competition and greater consumer choice.

We can see the results of these changes today, with hyperactive financial markets, an often wide-ranging array of choices for basic services and utilities, and a consumer-led market economy. Market transparency and information transparency have become increasingly important to allow businesses and consumers to make informed choices. In turn, those more traditional professions that advise businesses and consumers have had to respond and adapt their services, often adopting artificial intelligence (AI) to assist professionals in focusing on high-level advice, whilst more mundane work is facilitated by AI, saving on fees.

6.6.2 The free market in legal services

6.6.2.1 Changes to the legal system

Any changes to the profession must be seen not only in the wider context of society, but also in the context of the law as a whole. This liberalisation process has been mirrored by parallel changes in both the efficiency of the legal system and the provision of legal services; changes which overlap and cross-fertilise. The courts of England & Wales and their procedure have been radically overhauled—see 3.2.1. So the legal *system* is more open and clearly defined than before. Neither can we ignore the fact that elements of this drive for efficiency include the widespread closing and consolidation of courts (mentioned in Chapter 3), and the rapid restriction of availability of legal aid under the Legal Aid, Sentencing and Punishment of Offenders Act 2013 ('LASPO'). But what have these wider changes meant for the legal *profession*?

6.6.2.2 Changes to legal services—background

There have been two key changes in delivery of the law and legal services, roughly in parallel with the changes in society and politics described at 6.5.1.

First, large law firms have mushroomed in size since the 1980s. The advantages of scale in exploiting IT, training, marketing, and premises have largely mirrored those available to large companies in mainstream industries. As clients grew, so did the need for large (often international) law firms that could cope with the demands of huge multinational clients, for example in the growth area of corporate finance. Mergers among law firms are very common, often for similar reasons as in the mainstream economy, such as diversification or the strengthening of market share. In 1986, the Law Society allowed its members to advertise directly to the public,

---

[38] Office for National Statistics (2018), Civil Service Statistics. Available online at: https://www.ons.gov.uk/releases/civilservicestatistics2018.

following the more market-driven pressures of the economy as a whole. The largest law firms in the UK employ thousands of lawyers, with even more support staff. These trends continue and developments in IT and marketing are adopted by smaller firms as they also grow.

Second, the trend to liberalisation has been echoed in the legal profession. The Courts and Legal Services Act 1990, the Access to Justice Act 1999, the LSA in 2007, and LASPO in 2013 have changed the landscape of legal services (see Table 6.2). Indeed it is arguable that they created a concept of 'providers of legal services', built around the existing core legal profession. To give a flavour of the context of these statutes, the Courts and Legal Services Act 1990 has a stated objective:[39]

> The general objective . . . is the development of legal services in England and Wales (and in particular the development of advocacy, litigation, conveyancing and probate services) by making provision for new or better ways of providing such services and a wider choice of persons providing them, while maintaining the proper and efficient administration of justice.

Remember that this statute was not drafted in isolation, but as an element of the continuing liberalisation of western economies. Milton Friedman (the intellectual figurehead of free market capitalism) stated:

> So that the record of history is absolutely crystal clear, that there is no alternative way so far discovered of improving the lot of the ordinary people that can hold a candle to the productive activities that are unleashed by the free-enterprise system.[40]

Table 6.2 summarises the key relevant statutes in this transformation, and these trends are drawn out by Figure 6.4.

Table 6.2 Summary of reforms to legal services

Solicitors Act 1974	Puts existing solicitors' monopolies on a formal footing.
Administration of Justice Act 1985	Breaks solicitors' monopoly in conveyancing.
1986	Law Society permits solicitors to advertise their services to the general public.
Courts and Legal Services Act 1990	Rationalises civil courts. Allows solicitors higher rights of audience.
Access to Justice Act 1999	Increases flexibility on funding access to law.
	Allows other professions the right to litigate.
Limited Liability Partnerships Act 2000	Permits the LLP as a medium of business organisation.
2004	Bar Council permits barristers to accept direct instructions from the public (rather than via a solicitor) ('public access').
Legal Services Act 2007	Redefines professional bodies approved to authorise several aspects of key legal work (e.g. trade mark and patent attorneys, licensed conveyancers, legal executives, law costs draftsmen).
	Allows alternative business structures (ABS) for lawyers, i.e. beyond partnerships, including multi-disciplinary practices where lawyers and non-lawyers (e.g. accountants) are in partnership.
Legal Aid, Sentencing and Punishment of Offenders Act 2012	Restricts availability of legal aid, reducing significantly the work available to legal aid firms and barristers.

[39] Courts and Legal Services Act 1990, s. 17.
[40] Friedman, Milton (1979). Interviewed by Phil Donaghue on *The Phil Donaghue Show*.

All of these regulatory changes have the aim of liberalising the provision of legal services and making access to justice more transparent. The most far reaching is the LSA, which implemented elements of the Clementi Report of 2004.[41] The LSA has stated objectives, which are worth repeating:

(a) protecting and promoting the public interest;

(b) supporting the constitutional principle of the rule of law;

(c) improving access to justice;

(d) protecting and promoting the interests of consumers;

(e) promoting competition in the provision of services . . .;

(f) encouraging an independent, strong, diverse and effective legal profession;

(g) increasing public understanding of the citizen's legal rights and duties;

(h) promoting and maintaining adherence to the professional principles.

All of these objectives echo key themes in this chapter.

The LSA made many changes, including bringing regulation of legal services into line with other service industries (see 6.4.2). The Act put regulation of all branches of the profession on a more consistent footing, promoting openness to client complaints, among many other benefits. For solicitors, though, the other significant change was permitting new ways of organising their businesses. This reflects the drive, in a market-led world, for businesses, including legal businesses, to appeal to consumers, and to offer them a comprehensible choice. Any business, legal or not, must respond to such pressures. This freeing up of regulation has led to the provision of legal services being marketed in more varied and entrepreneurial ways.

This started with the inception of legal disciplinary practices (LDPs) in which different types of lawyers, such as solicitors, barristers, and foreign lawyers, can enter into partnership. More than 500 LDPs were registered with the SRA, although they are progressively being relicensed as ABSs (see next bullet point).

The most far-reaching change made by the LSA was the ability for Alternative Business Structures to offer legal services. In an ABS, non-lawyers can manage or own law firms. England & Wales is very much in the vanguard of this change, one of only five jurisdictions permitting ABSs. By May 2018 more than 1,130 ABSs had been licensed to carry out reserved legal activities, including trade unions, accountancy firms, local authorities, and insurers (e.g. Allianz). Only 60 per cent of these licences were issued by the SRA[42]—there are eight authorities who can issue licences, including, significantly, the ICAEW (Institute of Chartered Accountants of England & Wales).

Earlier reforms to the permitted ownership models for law firms had allowed them to operate as companies and LLPs, as well as the more traditional but exposed partnership model (see Chapter 20)—these helped pave the way for more varied ownership structures.

ABSs have many potential advantages beyond opening up the legal sector to outside players. The intention was to allow non-lawyers to invest in, as well as be partners of, law firms. This, it was hoped, would increase investment and incentivise investors in law firms. In 2017

---

[41] Clementi, Sir David (2004) *Review of the Regulatory Framework for Legal Services in England and Wales— Final Report.* London: TSO.

[42] Langdon-Down, Grania, *New model armies*, Law Gazette, 26 March 2018.

the Legal Services Board confirmed that outside investment in law firms had not yet been significant, at 12 per cent. Another aim of permitting ABSs was to allow talented non-lawyers (e.g. finance directors, human resources) to become partners, giving law in general a bigger pool of talent. There is some evidence to suggest that this development has indeed had the desired effect.

6.6.2.3 Changes to legal services—the new marketplace

What have these changes meant 'on the ground'? The intention was to incentivise external investment and liberalise business rules to foster a 'Big Bang' in legal services. The Legal Services Act has most certainly had an impact, but it remains difficult to make any definitive analysis as the market is so sophisticated. Whilst he was Justice Minister, Lord Faulks said, however, the changes have already driven a diversification possibly unforeseeable even a decade ago. We can divide these into several overlapping categories:

- *External ownership*: Remember that this was one of the main vehicles of reform—the idea being to stimulate broader and stronger investment in legal practice. Minster Law, a personal injury claims firm, was acquired by the financial services company, BGL Group. Law firms can invite external investors (just as companies can issue shares to people who are not directors—see Chapter 18). The Australian firm Slater & Gordon, which was the world's first practice to have publicly traded (listed) shares, entered the fray with its purchase of the London firm Russell Jones and Walker for £53.8 million in April 2012.

- *Diversified practices*: the move to ABSs has allowed some diversifcation, in theory providing the public with a more meaningful choice of legal services providers. A pertinent example is the University of Law, which was the first University to be granted an ABS licence by the SRA, whereby trainee solicitors provide legal advice on a pro bono basis to members of the public in various areas of social welfare law, supervised by experienced solicitors.

- *New avenues of litigation funding*: At 6.1.1 we saw how access to justice is at a premium, and that, via legal aid, or otherwise, access to justice in the UK is poor. This is to a significant extent a function of the high cost of lawyers. An important object of the liberalisation of legal services is to improve this access. One of the most significant trends in the late 2010s has been the growth of 'litigation funding' as a phenomenon. It involves a specialist entity financing a claimant's legal fees incurred in a dispute, in exchange for a share of the damages, via a DBA (Damages Based Agreement). Hitherto this would have offended centuries-old rules in relation to third party influence in litigation (called 'champerty'). If the litigation succeeds, the funder recovers their investment plus a success fee. Otherwise, the funder loses their investment. Alternatively a lawyer can insure against the possibility of losing, with the lawyer and insurer bearing the risk that might otherwise burden the client.

- Linked with these developments, some *local authorities* have started outsourcing their legal work, the first such ABS being Buckinghamshire Law Plus (owned by Buckinghamshire County Council and the Milton Keynes Fire Authority). Although this venture is no longer active, it trailblazed the sector for others like Invicta Law, owned by Kent County Council, which is an ABS specialising in public sector law.

- *'Tesco law'*: is an umbrella term for the provision of legal services to the public by organisations that have traditionally provided non-legal services. This was made possible by the creation of ABSs. Paradoxically, Tesco itself has not (at the time of writing) created an ABS. The Co-op, though, which historically provided retail services, has expanded into banking and financial services. It now offers legal services to its customers. One of its core businesses, funeral services, has a natural fit with certain legal services, including advice on probate law, which deals with a person's assets on death. The offer to consumers is a combination of a trusted brand and value for money. Note that this mode of delivering legal services is very different from that of in-house lawyers, who provide legal advice exclusively *within* non-legal businesses. BT Law (owned by the BT Group) is another notable recent example. This model was given a boost recently by further deregulation of ABSs as Multi-Disciplinary Practices ('MDPs').

- *MDPs* are a category of ABS in which lawyers can practise in partnership with non-lawyers such as accountants, with obvious economies of scale and efficiencies of service, especially for corporate clients. Parts of these MDPs can be regulated by regulators from outside the legal profession (e.g. the ICAEW). By 2018 all the 'Big 4' accountancy firms (PWC, Ernst & Young, KPMG, and Deloitte) had formed or acquired legal practices. Some law firms had in turn created accountancy practices. The advent of 'Big 4' is significant—these are global players with portfolios that dwarf the world's largest law firms, and a combined employee count of over 1 million.

- *'Uberisation'*: further deregulation by the SRA in 2019 has the potential to open the door to freelance solicitors, doing non-reserved legal work within firms which are themselves not legally-regulated (e.g. business advisors, employment advisers, will-writers, and even large supermarkets like Tesco—see earlier in this list).

- *'Factory law'* (which overlaps with 'Tesco law'): Some areas of legal work can be comparatively routine, such as insurance claims, road traffic accident claims, and debt recovery. Legal services businesses have been developed to manage high volumes of these types of work at low cost. The typical model will have low numbers of qualified lawyers supervising large numbers of paralegals either in the UK or, increasingly, outsourced paralegals or lower-cost qualified lawyers based overseas. 20.1.9 examines the threat which businesses like this pose to traditional firms. Certainly, the advent of AI may help commoditise relatively straightforward legal work, making it more accessible to the public at a lower cost.

- *Cloud-based legal services*, such as Keystone Law, which provides a wide range of legal services online—individual lawyers share 'back office' support and branding. Keystone Law was also one of the first firms to be listed on the AIM (Alternative Investment Market).

- *Franchised legal services*: The development of 'franchise' schemes where firms or even individual solicitors buy into a franchise to help give small players market access, and to help consumers easily find expertise for their issues. Quality Solicitors[43] is an example of existing firms operating under one 'tent'. Visit their website and you will be met with

---

[43] http://www.qualitysolicitors.com/.

testimonials from customers (rather than clients) about the quality of service provided. Administrative intermediaries match the lawyer to the client. This is a very different business model from the traditional high-street law firm.

- The *opening up of some reserved legal activities* (see 6.2.2) to defined groups beyond solicitors and barristers, such as registered foreign and European lawyers, notaries, legal executives, licensed conveyancers, patent agents, trade mark agents, and law costs draftsmen. Legal executives, in particular, have been successful in offering probate and conveyancing services without supervision by solicitors.

- The marketing of barristers on a *direct access* basis, sometimes through specialist intermediaries like Clerskroom Direct, and BriefaBarrister.

A key word here is 'marketing'—the legal sector increasingly resembles other service industries, for example the financial services sector. For more on the impact of advertising and marketing on lawyers, see 20.1.5. The consumer is now in a much more powerful position. According to the former President of the Law Society, 'Today people shop smarter and differently from before. They expect to be able to shop around for the best value and most convenient service for them.'[44]

You will note the sheer variety of business media now offering legal services.

6.6.2.4 Changes to legal services—taking stock

Read again the statement of objectives in the LSA. An October 2018 study by University College London, and written by Professor Stephen Mayson, has reviewed the changes made by the LSA. According to the study, 'Many would suggest that the Legal Services Act 2007 has led to the positive developments and outcomes intended ... It is doubtful, though, that those intentions have been realised as quickly or as fully as their initiators would have wished.'[45] In 2014, the then President of the Law Society made the following observations, based on research undertaken by the Legal Services Board:[46]

- ABSs created an environment that fostered innovative practices (not just in the way firms do business);

- ABSs generate higher fees-per-fee-earner than LDPs, which, in turn generate higher fees than traditional firms;

- ABSs (often with a culture of consumer service inherited from their owners) are better at resolving consumer complaints; and

- ABSs make greater use of information technology than other firms.

---

[44] Speech by then Law Society president, Nick Fluck 'Non-lawyer ownership of law firms: the view from here and there' (9 January 2014).

[45] *Independent Review of Legal Services Regulation—Assessment of the Current Regulatory Framework*, Working Paper LSR-0, Stephen Mayson, UCL Centre for Ethics and Law, March 2019.

[46] Speech by then Law Society president, Nick Fluck 'Non-lawyer ownership of law firms: the view from here and there' (9 January 2014).

Table 6.3 Types of legal practice

Traditional model of legal services	New legal services landscape
Self-employed barristers instructed by solicitors.	Self-employed barristers sometimes operating through intermediaries on a direct access basis.
Solicitors' firms (partnerships or sole practitioners, latterly limited liability partnerships)	Solicitors' firms Partnerships or sole practitioners, latterly limited liability partnerships.
	Legal Disciplinary Practices Different types of lawyers in legal practice together as a partnership or LLP. Can have up to 25% non-lawyer ownership. Being replaced by Alternative Business Structures Legal practices with non-traditional ownership structures—non-lawyers have stakes over 10%. Includes 'Tesco Law'.
	Multi-Disciplinary Practices Overlaps with ABSs—deliver legal services with other professional services, e.g. accountancy.
	Freelancing solicitors—can offer services to legal and non-legal businesses.

Table 6.3 sets out the types of legal practice in the marketplace, contrasting the traditional model with the new legal landscape.

In a written statement to Parliament,[47] Justice Minister Lord Faulks offered the following appraisal of these changes, 'These new, innovative providers have increased competition in the market, which we believe encourages a wider variety of legal services in the market that are more accessible and affordable to consumers'. The SRA is pressing for further liberalisation of the rules applying to ABSs.

The liberalisation of the legal marketplace has not been an unalloyed success for lawyers brave enough to embrace the changes. This is not to say that the new media are any less secure for lawyers than the traditional model; merely that not every venture that has embraced these reforms has been successful in running a profitable business. High profile examples of less successful innovations have included:

- Slater & Gordon was forced to undergo a painful restructuring in late 2017 after its initial investment model failed to support the firm.
- Parabis, an ABS which went into administration in 2015.
- Stobart Barristers[48]—direct access barristers, dissolved in 2014, was run by the Stobart Group (of transport fame), offering the public direct access to appropriate counsel.
- Buckinghamshire Law Plus, given ABS approval by the SRA in summer 2014, but wound up in 2019.
- Even the Cooperative Legal Services, now a mainstay in the legal marketplace, initially sustained significant losses, before stabilising after some retrenchment.

---

[47] Legal Services Regulation: Written statement-HCWS69, 7 July 2016.
[48] http://www.stobartbarristers.co.uk/.

Table 6.4 Types of law firm ownership structure

44%	Limited Company
23%	Sole Practitioner
17%	'Traditional' Partnership
15%	Limited Liability Partnership

It should also be noted that these changes have not displaced the traditional model of legal access—they have provided an alternative. This is reflected by the ownership structure of law firms. A recent survey found that the distribution was as in Table 6.4.

In Chapter 20 we set out the characteristics of these different business media. It is however pertinent that of all the Top 50 Law Firms, only Slaughter & May remains a traditional partnership.

6.6.2.5 The other side of the fence—legal aid

Finally, in exposing the legal profession even more acutely to market forces, whilst the strong thrive, some sectors have suffered—simply because the model upon which they were built has become unsustainable. Probably the most controversial area is legal aid. LASPO in 2013 introduced funding cuts to legal aid and narrowed the scope and financial eligibility criteria, with the result that fewer people could access legal advice and representation for problems in areas such as family, employment, and welfare benefits law. The knock-on effect is that many legal advice centres and legal aid firms have been starved of fees and some have closed (e.g. TA Law in April 2019 and the Lambeth Law Centre in July 2019). At the Bar, many barristers are leaving legal aid work because the work is no longer financially viable, with some fees barely covering travel costs. Meanwhile, pupils and aspiring barristers are being put off legal aid work, decreasing the supply of capable barristers to represent some of the poorest and neediest clients.

6.6.2.6 Conclusions

So, does this mean 'The End of Lawyers?', a concept being discussed actively by academics?[49] Most probably not. It can be analysed, again, against the wider backdrop. Privatisation of utilities has not dispensed with the need for gas, electricity, water, or trains; they are merely provided in a different and, some would say, more efficient way. Equally, legal services have been liberalised. They are provided, still mainly by lawyers, in a different, and evolving, way. It is worth noting that (at the time of writing) no further liberalisation is planned. In Chapter 20 we discuss the challenges these changes are likely to present to lawyers of the future.

There is still a role for law firms in the traditional image (from high-street to City firms), especially in more complex contentious and commercial areas where the advice of an experienced and expert lawyer is essential; but increasingly they need to market and structure

---

[49] E.g. Susskind, Richard (2008) *The End of Lawyers?* Oxford: OUP.

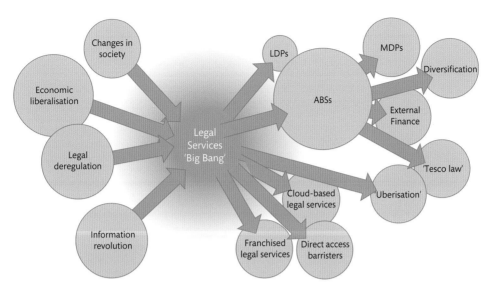

Figure 6.5 The developing legal market

themselves imaginatively in response to the freeing up of the market. It is quite clear that law firms must adapt quickly or face an uncertain future.

Figure 6.5 summarises the impetus for, and some of the outcomes of, the 'Big Bang' in legal services.

6.6.3 Arguments

Over the last few decades, governments and regulators have performed a difficult balancing act between freeing up lawyers to market efficiencies, and maintaining standards through tight regulation of lawyers' business practices. Former President of the Law Society, Joe Egan, has said, 'It is important that solicitors are able to operate on a level regulatory playing field and that client protections remain prioritised'.[50]

There are arguments for, and against, the liberalisation of legal services. The balance of these arguments is clearly shifting as society becomes less entrenched in its structure. These arguments[51] are summarised in Table 6.5.

You may have noticed a tension in the process of liberalisation. Giving firms and lawyers more freedom does not necessarily sit well with the ethical obligations outlined in 6.4.1. The SRA has been careful to free up the legal market whilst preserving important aspects of regulatory compliance. The 2019 reforms focused on streamlining regulation, so, for instance, the SRA Handbook was halved in length, giving greater scope for professional judgement. One key reform is in keeping with the theme of liberalisation: there will be (from November 2019)

---

[50] Quoted In Langdon-Down, Grania, New model armies, *Law Gazette*, 26 March 2018.
[51] E.g. Susskind, Richard (2008) *The End of Lawyers?* Oxford: OUP.

Table 6.5 Arguments for and against the liberalisation of legal services

	In favour of the traditional model	In favour of deregulated provision of legal services
Probity	Lawyers should feel able to be selective about the work that they do, and in decisions relating to ethics, their only concern should be integrity; profit should not be a factor. Multi-disciplinary practices in particular risk exposure to conflicts of interest.	Regulation will be more in line with other industries. A Legal Ombudsman takes initial legal complaints handling away from the professions, promoting probity in a more open way. A properly regulated service will prevent a drop in ethical standards.
Quality of service	Market pressures may force lawyers and their firms to 'cut corners' in the search for short term profit.	Specialised knowledge is often joined with a high degree of exclusivity, jargon, and impenetrability. Bringing non-lawyers into management improves quality of service. Larger pool of talent.
Cradle to grave service/one stop shop	A highly defined marketplace allowed people to know where to look for advice. Solicitors were the people you went to for legal advice: that was all they did.	ABSs allow law firms to employ non-lawyers, and non-law firms to employ lawyers, e.g. accountants and solicitors working together, or lawyers providing services to the public, working for banks in the high street (like the Co-op). Another alternative is solicitors and barristers working together in partnership. These structures prevent duplication of costs. The ideal is a 'one stop shop' for legal and related services.
Consumer focus	The established model of the law firm, though it has its problems, is very good at providing a tailored or personal service, with emphasis on strong bonds between solicitor and client, e.g. in the high street.	The express objectives of the LSA (s. 1) included improving access to justice and protecting and promoting the interests of consumers. The market will of necessity promote transparency and value for money.
Independence	An independent legal profession promotes democracy and liberty, by giving lawyers, and hence the law, special status. External ownership of firms may expose lawyer to pressures compromising quality of service.	There is no reason why liberties should be endangered by (for instance) changing business structures. Bringing management professionals into ownership and management will increase efficiency and quality of service.

a separate code for individual solicitors, and a separate code for firms. 'We want to make sure that every solicitor is absolutely clear about their personal obligations and responsibility to maintain the highest professional standards, whether they work in-house, or within or outside an LSA regulated firm. By having a separate code for firms, they will have clarity about the systems and controls they need to provide good legal services for consumers and the public.'[52]

[52] SRA, *Response to Consultation*, June 2017.

This brings us back to the foundational theme of ethics. The LSA's aims included promoting competition in the provision of services. Recent changes have certainly addressed this desire. But the LSA had several aims, another being improving access to justice. In some sectors, with diversification, and the advent of AI, this has been promoted. But in others, like legal aid, and more 'traditional' areas, some commentators are concerned that the ability of lawyers to perform their role has been restricted.

Summary

- A legal system cannot be analysed in isolation from history or society, and neither can lawyers.
- Lawyers, whatever their formal role or job description, are vitally important to the maintenance of the Rule of Law. A legal profession must (in theory) provide access to high-quality legal advice when it is needed.
- An important part of a lawyer's job is dealing with ethical dilemmas. Professional ethics seeks to give lawyers clear rules that reconcile client service with wider ethical standards.
- The legal profession has largely developed as a reflection of wider trends in society and politics. Figure 6.4 summarises this process.
- Recent reforms have sought to improve market efficiency in the provision of legal services, also in the name of quality.
- At this point, these changes have yet to permeate the profession fully. Only time will tell whether the new freedoms are compatible with the integrity which is so important to the Rule of Law.

Practical exercises

1. Are legal services just like any other service?
2. Should legal services be regulated just like any other service?
3. Should all defendants, no matter how odious, have legal representation?
4. How much freedom should professional codes give lawyers, to make the 'right' ethical decision?
5. Is it only a matter of time before solicitors and barristers disappear?
6. Should the solicitors' and barristers' professions merge?

 *Visit the **online resources** for the authors' reflections and to check your progress.*

Further reading

Roper, S., Love, J., Rieger, P., and Bourke, J. (July 2015) *Innovation in Legal Services: A report by the Enterprise Research Centre for the SRA and the LSB in Legal Services*
—Commissioned by the SRA and LSB, this 74-page report puts together some detailed evidence to reach some conclusions about the effects of the Legal Services Act.

Clementi, Sir D. (2004) *Review of the Regulatory Framework for Legal Services in England and Wales—Final Report.* **London: TSO**
—Commissioned by the Department for Constitutional Affairs in 2003, the Clementi report triggered the LSA. It contains discussion about the possible extent of legal services reform.

Herring, J. (2017) *Legal Ethics*, Oxford: OUP
—An overview of legal ethics with a strong focus on professional and technological challenegs facing the legal profession.

Mayson, S. (2019) *Independent Review of Legal Services Regulation—Assessment of the Current Regulatory Framework*, UCL Centre for Ethics and Law
—An independent report on whether the reforms under the LSA 2007 have had the effects intended by lawmakers and under the Clemeti Report (as above).

Office of Fair Trading (2001) *Competition in Professions—A Report by the Director General of Fair Trading* (March 2001, OFT328)
—A report by a government department which symbolised a perceived need to identify restrictions within professions (including the legal profession) that prevented, restricted, or distorted competition to the detriment of consumers.

SRA (2019) *SRA Code of Conduct for Firms.* Available at: https://www.sra.org.uk/solicitors/standards-regulations/code-conduct-firms/
—The SRA Code of Conduct for Firms, in effect from 25 November 2019.

SRA (2019) *SRA Code of Conduct for Solicitors, RELs and RFLs.* Available at: https://www.sra.org.uk/solicitors/standards-regulations/code-conduct-solicitors
—The SRA Code of Conduct for solicitors and overseas lawyers in effect from 25 November 2019.

SRA (2019) *SRA Principles.* Available at: https://www.sra.org.uk/solicitors/standards-regulations/principles/
—Sets out the SRA's seven principles it requires solicitors to comply with on a continuous basis, including honesty and integrity.

SRA (2019) *Standards and Regulations resources.* Available at: https://www.sra.org.uk/solicitors/standards-regulations-resources/
—Resources and guidance, including videos, on the new SRA Standards and Regulations, which replaced the SRA Handbook on 25 November 2019.

Susskind, R. (2008) *The End of Lawyers?* Oxford: OUP
—This attention-grabbing question crystallises a series of issues identified by the author, which together present the challenges for the legal profession in the current environment. Susskind argues that the concept of 'legal work' is changing quickly, and that lawyers need to adapt equally fast.

World Justice Project (2014) *Rule of Law Index 2015–2016.* Available at: http://worldjusticeproject.org/
—An organisation set up in 2006 by the American Bar Association to promote the Rule of Law, and to draw attention to examples of states exhibiting the presence or absence of these characteristics. In the context of this chapter there is extensive discussion and analysis of access to lawyers and justice.

 *For the authors' reflections on the practical exercises, additional self-test questions, sample interview questions and a library of links to useful websites, visit the free **online resources** at* www.oup.com/he/slorach4e.

Legal Skills

The skills which you are required to practise and demonstrate on undergraduate programmes are fundamental to the development of your professional legal skills too. This section will help you to develop these skills and build foundations for your future in a structured manner.

This Part II is structured to help by giving you effective strategies to research, read, and understand law; to analyse and apply the law to solve legal problems; and to communicate legal concepts and solutions in writing and orally. It will advise 'what' is good practice and 'how' you can develop this into your own practice.

Each chapter begins by providing advice, guidance, and strategies that you can use immediately to good effect in your undergraduate studies. The chapter then continues to help you develop those skills into those you will need as a professional, whether in a legal or other graduate role, with examples of how core skills are later employed in professional practice. You will learn how to enjoy succeeding with the skills you are learning now, and how to transfer those skills into a professional context with relative ease.

7 Reading cases and legislation

Learning objectives

After studying this chapter you should be able to:

- Understand that legislation comprises both statutes and statutory instruments, and that legislation and case law are our primary sources of law.
- Appreciate that your approach to reading cases and legislation will differ from your approach to reading in general.
- Develop your own practical strategies to help you to read cases and legislation more effectively.
- Follow guidance to read and understand cases and legislation effectively.

Introduction

It used to be a rite of passage for a law student to walk into a law library for the first time and be overawed by the sheer volume of law and commentary on that law, all in books, some ancient, all beautifully bound and displayed, volume by volume, shelf by shelf. Now that these sources of law are available electronically, and physical law libraries are shrinking, this is an experience modern law students might miss. So before we begin, it is useful to reflect on the simple fact that there really is a huge amount of law. Chapters 2, 4, and 5 examine the sources of this law in some detail; you will recall that our primary sources are legislation (comprising statutes and statutory instruments) and case law. This chapter focuses on how to read these sources most effectively.

After a moment's reflection, you may feel relieved to learn that you will not be expected to read all of the primary sources of law at any stage in your legal career. This can often come as a surprise and slight disappointment to a non-lawyer, who might ask you a question about a speeding fine, divorce, and a company director's duties all in the same breath, and look puzzled when you cannot answer all three questions immediately without looking anything up. A lawyer knows that law is diverse, and it is also changing constantly. For that reason, it is usual for a lawyer to specialise, either in one particular area of law, or several related areas of law. It would be unusual, for example, for the same lawyer to be advising on a catastrophic injury claim one day and a stock market flotation the next. However, it is in fact at the beginning of your career, as a student (and, later if you decide to go into the legal services sector), when you will be exposed to the most diversity in terms of the areas of law you will be expected to read and understand. You need, therefore, to hone your skills of reading and understanding cases and legislation at an early stage in your legal career. If you decide to pursue a legal career these skills will become time critical (because, as Chapter 20 explains, you will charge clients based on the time you spend on their work).

Let's now consider how we can make the process of reading cases and legislation as efficient and enjoyable as possible. We will then examine how we can make sure you understand what you have read, because it is rarely enough for any lawyer simply to *know* what the law is, whether in academia or in practice. You must also *understand* it so that you can *analyse* and *apply* it to solve legal problems.

Once you have mastered the art of reading and understanding primary sources of law, you will have developed your skills of analysis, synthesis, and summarising to a point where you will notice that your reading and understanding of other everyday reading material, be it newspapers, history books, or political manifestos, seems considerably easier. Conversely, you will find that you can adopt an approach to your everyday reading material in a way which will assist your reading and understanding of law. This is a skill for life.

7.1 Reading and understanding primary sources

7.1.1 Practicalities of reading

Lawyers spend quite a lot of time reading primary sources (and secondary sources, and generally). It is fair to say that legal text can be quite dense and reading it can be relatively heavy going. In light of this, it is helpful to consider what practical steps we can take to make this process as effective and enjoyable as possible.

Increasingly, lawyers are accessing electronic sources of law, because they have advantages in terms of being updated on a timely basis, and they are portable on a laptop, tablet, or smartphone. You should consider whether you have any particular issues with reading on a screen. Adjusting the brightness of the screen, the font size, and colour can help you to focus more clearly on your reading. Use the accessibility settings on your device to address any specific needs you may have in this regard (see Further Reading).

If you are using paper sources of law or decide to print your online sources in order to read them more comfortably, then there are also steps you can take to help with your reading. If the source is photocopied, make sure you adjust the contrast settings so that the print is clear. It is not uncommon for people to find that reading copious amounts of black text on a stark white background can be difficult. In this case you may find that printing onto coloured paper, or simply putting a sheet of coloured perspex over the white page, can help to stop the text jumping around. However, sometimes all that is needed is a break, and so in that regard you should make sure you set aside enough time to read. Of course, time is money in a law firm, so you also need to be able to navigate sources of law effectively, and understand which parts, if any, you can skim read or not read at all, and which you must read in detail.

Make sure you are free from distractions when you are reading. You will not read effectively if you are checking your email or social media accounts every five minutes. If possible, move to a quiet place where you will not be distracted.

Practice tip

Do not assume that in practice your desk will be a quiet place. Law firms are busy places and lawyers are often discussing cases and transactional matters, either face to face with their colleagues or over the telephone with others. Increasingly lawyers work at **hot desks** (not allocated to them alone) in open plan offices with lots of other lawyers in the same room. Most firms however, and particularly those which have chosen to have an open plan office layout, will provide work spaces which are suitable for and can be used for quiet work, e.g. the library or a room referred to as a **breakout room** or **space**.

7.1.2 Sources of law

Your strategy for reading law effectively will depend on the nature of what you are reading. Chapters 4 and 5 explained that there are two primary sources of law in England and Wales, namely legislation (statutes and statutory instruments) and case law, and that there are numerous secondary sources of law which comment on these primary sources. We will now take each source in turn and consider how it is likely to be set out, and the best approach to reading and understanding the law it contains.

7.1.3 Statutes

Chapter 4 considers the nature of a statute in some detail. Broadly, you will remember that Parliament produces statutes and that statutes set out our *rights*, or alternatively impose *obligations* on us (and often set out the *sanctions* we will face if we fail to comply).

7.1.3.1 Structure of a statute

Helpfully, most statutes are set out in a similar way, so once you are familiar with this structure you should be able to navigate around any statute, regardless of the subject matter.

Let us consider the layout of a statute called the Unfair Contract Terms Act 1977 (the 'UCTA'). As with any statute this chapter might feature, the UCTA will be subject to continuous change and, eventually, repeal. Some of it has been repealed, for example, by the Consumer Rights Act 2015. So, while clearly you must not rely on its content being up to date, happily it remains entirely fit for our purpose of examining it to achieve an understanding of the generic structure of any statute. The UCTA is set out in Figure 7.1. We have added our own guidance (in the blue boxes) to help you navigate and understand it. This guidance is transferable, and is included not only to help you understand the UCTA, but to be of use to help you read and understand any statute. Read Figure 7.1 and the guidance on it now and, when you have done that, continue your reading at 7.1.3.2.

7.1.3.2 How to read and understand a statute

You can feel proud that you have mastered the art of reading sufficiently well to allow you to progress to where you are now. However, you are about to learn that your approach to reading law will differ quite significantly to the approach you will have adopted in your reading to date. It is a common error for junior lawyers to attempt to read a statute like a book.

Unfair Contract Terms Act

1977[1]

1977 CHAPTER 50[2]

An Act to impose further limits on the extent to which under the law of England and Wales and Northern Ireland civil liability for breach of contract, for negligence or other breach of duty, can be avoided by means of contract terms and otherwise, and under the law of Scotland civil liability can be avoided by means of contract terms.[3]

[26th October 1977][4]

Table of Contents[5]

PART I [6]

AMENDMENT OF LAW FOR ENGLAND AND WALES AND NORTHERN IRELAND

Introductory[7]

PART II

AMENDMENT OF LAW FOR SCOTLAND

Figure 7.1 Annotated version of the UCTA

(continued . . .)

1 Short Title

This is the short title of the statute and its year of publication, the 'Unfair Contract Terms Act 1977'. It is the normal way to describe a statute, but it is common for lawyers to refer to the most regularly used statutes using an abbreviation. For example, the Unfair Contract Terms Act is often referred to as the 'UCTA' (pronounced 'uc-ta') and sometimes the year is also referred to, e.g. 'UCTA77'. The Sale of Goods Act 1979 is often referred to as the 'SoGA' (pronounced to rhyme with yoga) or 'SoGA79'. You will learn from experience which statutes tend to be referred to by abbreviated names.

2 Citation

This is the official citation for the statute. Each statute passed in any one year is given its own number, known as the chapter number. The UCTA is the 50th Act of 1977. The citation 1977 Chapter 50 refers to this statute alone. In the official citation, 'chapter' is often abbreviated to 'c'.

3 Long Title

The long title gives some indication of the statute's general purpose. Here the long title is the wording, 'An Act to impose . . . can be avoided by means of contract terms' and it indicates that the purpose of the UCTA is to impose further limits on the extent to which liability for breach can be avoided, and gives some indication of how the statute differs in scope between the different jurisdictions within the UK.

4 Royal Assent and Commencement

This date at note 4 is the date when the statute received Royal Assent. The default position is that a statute will take effect on the date that it receives the Royal Assent. If it does not (as is the case with the UCTA and many other relatively recent statutes) then a commencement section near to the end or beginning of the statute will state the date the statute comes into force. Here you can see (see note 18) that s. 31(1) provides the UCTA will come into force just over three months following its Royal Assent, namely on 1 February 1978. (Note that the year in the short title is the year the statute received Royal Assent, not the year it came into force.) Alternatively, a statute can grant power to a government minister to decide when it should become law. In this case the minister would bring the statute (or part of it) into effect by issuing a commencement order, which is a form of delegated legislation. If it is intended that the statute should apply to anything that pre-exists the statute itself, then the statute must specifically provide for this. This reflects the principle that a statute does not take effect retrospectively.

5 Table of Contents

The table of contents provides a useful summary of what you will find in the statute.

6 Parts

You can see that the statute is subdivided into different parts, and that each part has a heading which indicates what that part deals with. Here, the parts are divided according to which jurisdiction within the UK the provisions apply to.

7 Headings

Within each part, there are headings which group together certain sections of the statute. For example, ss. 5–7 all deal with liability arising from the sale or supply of goods, so they are grouped together under an appropriate heading. Sections 2–4 deal with other types of liability and so are grouped together under another heading, and so on. The headings are part of the statute.

8 Sections

Within each part, and grouped together under appropriate headings, are the sections of the statute. Each section contains a different rule of law and is given a number and a useful heading to let you know what it is about. When you refer to a rule of law contained in a statute, you should identify where it can be found. It is usual to abbreviate 'section' to 's.' so that s. 1 refers to section 1. If you are referring to more than one section, it is usual to refer to 'ss.', e.g. 'see ss. 6–7 of the UCTA'. You will see when we consider the body of the statute that the sections are subdivided into:

- subsections, e.g. s. 1(2)
- paragraphs, e.g. s. 1(1)(a)
- subparagraphs, e.g. s. 3(2)(b)(i) (however the table of contents does not drill down into this detail).

9 Definitions

The definitions (sometimes referred to as interpretation or explanatory provisions) provide an explanation of the meaning of certain words to which the statute refers. The meaning will not necessarily be the meaning that a non-lawyer would understand to be the meaning of a word (and indeed you should assume that a definition in a statute applies only to that statute unless it states otherwise). It is very important to find and read any definitions in order to understand the legislation.

Figure 7.1 *Continued*

Part II

Legal Skills

PART III

PROVISIONS APPLYING TO WHOLE OF UNITED KINGDOM

Miscellaneous

26 International supply contracts.
27 Choice of law clauses.
28 ...
29 Saving for other relevant legislation.
30 ...

General

31 Commencement; amendments; repeals.
32 Citation and extent.

SCHEDULES[10]

SCHEDULE 1—Scope of Sections 2 to 4 and 7

1 Sections 2 to 4 of this Act do not extend . . .
2 Section 2(1) extends to—(a) any contract of marine salvage . . .
3 Where goods are carried by ship or hovercraft in pursuance . . .
4 Section 2(1) and (2) do not extend to a contract . . .
5 Section 2(1) does not affect the validity of any discharge . . .

SCHEDULE 2—'Guidelines' for Application of Reasonableness Test
     The matters to which regard is to be had in . . .

SCHEDULE 3—Amendments of Enactments

. . .

     In the Supply of Goods (Implied Terms) Act 1973 . . .

SCHEDULE 4—Repeals
     The repeals in sections 12 and 15 of the Supply . . .

PART I[11]

AMENDMENT OF LAW FOR ENGLAND AND WALES AND
NORTHERN IRELAND

Introductory[12]

1 **Scope of Part I[13]**
    (1) For the purposes of this Part of this Act, 'negligence' means the breach—
        (a) of any obligation, arising from the express or implied terms of a contract, to take
            reasonable care or exercise reasonable skill in the performance of the contract;
        (b) of any common law duty to take reasonable care or exercise reasonable skill (but not any
            stricter duty);
        (c) of the common duty of care imposed by the [M1] Occupiers' Liability Act 1957 or the [M2]
            Occupiers' Liability Act (Northern Ireland) 1957.
    (2) This Part of this Act is subject to Part 111; and in relation to contracts, the operation of
        sections 2 to [, 3] and 7 is subject to the exceptions made by Schedule 1.

Figure 7.1 *Continued*

(3) In the case of both contract and tort, sections 2 to 7 apply (except where the contrary is stated in section 6(4)) only to business liability, that is liability for breach of obligations or duties arising—

   (a) from things done or to be done by a person in the course of a business (whether his own business or another's); or

   (b) from the occupation of premises used for business purposes of the occupier; and references to liability are to be read accordingly but liability of an occupier of premises for breach of an obligation or duty towards a person obtaining access to the premises for recreational or educational purposes, being liability for loss or damage suffered by reason of the dangerous state of the premises, is not a business liability of the occupier unless granting that person such access for the purposes concerned falls within the business purposes of the occupier.

(4) In relation to any breach of duty or obligation, it is immaterial for any purpose of this Part of this Act whether the breach was inadvertent or intentional, or whether liability for it arises directly or vicariously.

Marginal Citations[14]

M1   1957 c. 31
M2   1957 c. 25 (N.I.)

Avoidance of liability for negligence, breach of contract, etc

2   Negligence liability.

(1) A person cannot by reference to any contract term or to a notice given to persons generally or to particular persons exclude or restrict his liability for death or personal injury resulting from negligence.

(continued . . .)

Reading cases and legislation

Chapter 7

10 Schedules

Some statutes have schedules to them. This can be for several reasons, but it is often to separate reference or administrative material from the detail in the body of the statute. For example, a schedule can contain specific detail relating to provisions in the main body of the statute, it can expand or define phrases in the statute, or it can contain detailed amendments of any earlier legislation. Typically the final schedule will set out which earlier statutes it repeals. Schedule can be abbreviated to 'Sched.' or 'Sch.' and the terminology is to refer to a schedule 'to' (not 'of') the statute. The schedule itself may be divided into paragraphs, which can be abbreviated to 'para.' and the correct terminology is a paragraph 'of' a schedule.

11 Parts

See note 6.

12 Headings

See note 7.

13 Sections

See note 8. Following the table of contents, this is the first section of the statute

14 Marginal Citations or Notes

There may be short marginal citations or notes by each section explaining its contents. Unlike headings, the marginal notes are not part of the statute. Here, for example, the marginal citations provide the citations for other statutes referred to in s. 1(1)(c) of the UCTA.

Figure 7.1 *Continued*

(2) In the case of other loss or damage, a person cannot so exclude or restrict his liability for negligence except in so far as the term or notice satisfies the requirement of reasonableness.

(3) Where a contract term or notice purports to exclude or restrict liability for negligence a person's agreement to or awareness of it is not of itself to be taken as indicating his voluntary acceptance of any risk.

(4) This section does not apply to-

    (a) a term in a consumer contract; or

    (b) a notice to the extent that it is a consumer notice,

    (but see the provision made about such contacts and notices in sections 62 and 65 of the Consumer Rights Act 2015).

3 Liability arising in contract.

(1) This section applies as between contracting parties where one of them deals as consumer or on the other's written standard terms of business.

(2) As against that party, the other cannot by reference to any contract term—

    (a) when himself in breach of contract, exclude or restrict any liability of his in respect of the breach; or

    (b) claim to be entitled—

        (i) to render a contractual performance substantially different from that which was reasonably expected of him, or

        (ii) in respect of the whole or any part of his contractual obligation, to render no performance at all,

    except in so far as (in any of the cases mentioned above in this subsection) the contract term satisfies the requirement of reasonableness.

(3) This section does not apply to a term in a consumer contract (but see the provision made about such contracts in section 62 of the Consumer Rights Act 2015).

4 ...

Liability arising from sale or supply of goods

5 ...

6 Sale and hire purchase.

(1) Liability for breach of the obligations arising from—

    (a) section 12 of the Sale of Goods Act 1979 (seller's implied undertakings as to title, etc.);

    (b) section 8 of the **M3** Supply of Goods (Implied Terms) Act 1973 (the corresponding thing in relation to hire-purchase),

    cannot be excluded or restricted by reference to any contract term.

(1A) Liability for breach of the obligations arising from—

    (a) section 13, 14 or 15 of the 1979 Act (seller's implied undertakings as to conformity of goods with description or sample, or as to their quality or fitness for a particular purpose);

    (b) section 9, 10 or 11 of the 1973 Act (the corresponding things in relation to hire purchase),

    cannot be excluded or restricted by reference to a contract term except in so far as the term satisfies the requirement of reasonableness.

    (2) ...

    (3) ...

    (4) The liabilities referred to in this section are not only the business liabilities defined by section 1(3), but include those arising under any contract of sale of goods or hire-purchase agreement.

    (5) This section does not apply to a consumer contract (but see the provision made about such contracts in section 31 of the Consumer Rights Act 2015).

    (2) ...

Figure 7.1 *Continued*

Marginal Citations

M3   1973 c. 13.

7   Miscellaneous contracts under which goods pass.
[*omitted for the purposes of this work*]

Other provisions about contracts

[*omitted for the purposes of this work*]

Explanatory provisions[15]

11   The 'reasonableness' test.[16]
(1) In relation to a contract term, the requirement of reasonableness for the purposes of this Part of this Act, section 3 of the [M6] Misrepresentation Act 1967 and section 3 of the [M7] Misrepresentation Act (Northern Ireland) 1967 is that the term shall have been a fair and reasonable one to be included having regard to the circumstances which were, or ought reasonably to have been, known to or in the contemplation of the parties when the contract was made.
(2) In determining for the purposes of section 6 or 7 above whether a contract term satisfies the requirement of reasonableness, regard shall be had in particular to the matters specified in Schedule 2 to this Act; but this subsection does not prevent the court or arbitrator from holding, in accordance with any rule of law, that a term which purports to exclude or restrict any relevant liability is not a term of the contract.
[*The remainder of this section omitted for the purposes of this work.*]

(continued . . .)

15 Explanatory provisions
See note 9.

16 This section sets out the reasonableness test referred to in several sections of the UCTA. Section 11(2) makes clear that you also need to refer to Sch. 2 in relation to ss. 6 and 7.

Marginal Citations

M6   1967 c. 7
M7   1967 c. 14(N.I.)

12   . . .

13   Varieties of exemption clause.
[*omitted for the purposes of this work*]

14   Interpretation of Part I.[17]
In this Part of this Act—
'business' includes a profession and the activities of any government department or local or public authority;
'consumer contract' has the same meaning as in the Consumer Rights Act 2015 (see section 61);
'consumer notice' has the same meaning as in the Consumer Rights Act 2016 (see section 61);
'goods' has the same meaning as in the Sale of Goods Act 1979;
'hire-purchase agreement' has the same meaning as in the [M8] Consumer Credit Act 1974;
'negligence' has the meaning given by section 1(1);
'notice' includes an announcement, whether or not in writing, and any other communication or pretended communication; and
'personal injury' includes any disease and any impairment of physical or mental condition.

Marginal Citations

M8   1974 c. 39

Figure 7.1 *Continued*

PART II

[omitted for the purposes of this work]

PART III

[omitted for the purposes of this work]

PROVISIONS APPLYING TO WHOLE OF UNITED KINGDOM

Miscellaneous

[omitted for the purposes of this work]

General

31   Commencement; amendments; repeals.[18]

(1) This Act comes into force on 1st February 1978.

(2) Nothing in this Act applies to contracts made before the date on which it comes into force; but subject to this, it applies to liability for any loss or damage which is suffered on or after that date.

[X2](3) The enactments specified in Schedule 3 to this Act are amended as there shown.

(4) The enactments specified in Schedule 4 to this Act are repealed to the extent specified in column 3 of that Schedule.

(continued . . .)

17 Interpretation

See note 9. Definitions for Part 1 are included here, in s. 14, in addition to the explanatory provisions in eg s. 11, and definitions within sections (eg s. 1(1)).

18 Commencement

See note 4. This statute did not come into force on the date it received Royal Assent (1977—the date in its short title), but over three months later, in 1978.

Annotations:

Editorial Information

X2   The text of s. 31(3)(4) is in the form in which it was originally enacted: it was not reproduced in Statutes in Force and does not reflect any amendments or repeals which may have been made prior to 1.2.1991.

32   Citation and extent.[19]

(1) This Act may be cited as the Unfair Contract Terms Act 1977.

(2) Part I of this Act extends to England and Wales and to Northern Ireland; but it does not extend to Scotland.

(3) Part II of this Act extends to Scotland only.

(4) This Part of this Act extends to the whole of the United Kingdom.

Figure 7.1 *Continued*

SCHEDULES [20]

SCHEDULE 1   Section 1(2).

SCOPE OF SECTIONS 2 [, 3] AND 7

1   Sections 2 [and 3] of this Act do not extend to—
     (a) any contract of insurance (including a contract to pay an annuity on human life);
     [Remainder of Schedule 1 omitted for the purpose of this work.]

SCHEDULE 2   Sections 11(2) and 24(2).

'GUIDELINES' FOR APPLICATION OF REASONABLENESS TEST

The matters to which regard is to be had in particular for the purposes of sections 6(1A), 7(1A) and (4), 20 and 21 are any of the following which appear to be relevant—
     (a) the strength of the bargaining positions of the parties relative to each other, taking into account (among other things) alternative means by which the customer's requirements could have been met;
     (b) whether the customer received an inducement to agree to the term, or in accepting it had an opportunity of entering into a similar contract with other persons, but without having a similar term;
     (c) whether the customer knew or ought reasonably to have known of the existence and the extent of the term (having regard, among other things, to any custom of the trade and any previous course of dealing between the parties);
     (d) where the term excludes or restricts any relevant liability if some condition was not complied with, whether it was reasonable at the time of the contract to expect that compliance with that condition would be practicable;
     (e) whether the goods were manufactured, processed or adapted to the special order of the customer.

SCHEDULE 3   Section 31(3).

AMENDMENTS OF ENACTMENTS

SCHEDULE 4   Section 31(4).

[omitted for the purposes of this work]

19 Citation
This section reiterates the short title provided at the beginning of the statute.

20 Schedules
See note 10. In the UCTA, Schedules 1 and 2 provide detail, Schedule 3 sets out which earlier statutes it amends, and Schedule 4 sets out the earlier statutes it repeals.

Figure 7.1 *Continued*

When you have finished reading Figure 7.1 you should return to your reading at 7.1.3.2.

The temptation to turn to the first page and start reading is great. Although technically this may work with some statutes, usually it is not the most effective approach. When you consider that, for example, the Companies Act 2006 comprises over 1,000 sections, in some cases it is just not a workable option at all. Instead, you should aim to read the *relevant* parts of the statute. The skill is to determine which parts of the statute are relevant to your needs.

You have just learned, from reading Figure 7.1, how most statutes are structured. This knowledge will help you to navigate around any statute effectively, to find the law which is relevant to your needs at any particular time. The following approach will help you to read any statute effectively.

Read as part of a wider research strategy

You should not expect to obtain a holistic understanding of the statute simply by reading it. Your reading is likely to form part of a wider research strategy to ensure you have a sound understanding of the relevant law, and this is explored in Chapter 8.

If you turn to Figure 8.1, which summarises the legal research strategy in a flowchart, you will note that 'analysing the primary source', such as a statute, is just one aspect of finding all relevant law. In particular, where available you should first have read an up to date secondary source, such as *Halsbury's Laws*, which describes the key aspects of the law enshrined in the statute.

Read the long title of the Act as a guide to its general purpose

For example, if you have found a term in an employment contract which appears to be unfair, and you have chosen to read the UCTA because it sounds like it might be relevant, the long title will explain that the unfair terms it is seeking to address are certain terms which avoid liability. If the reason your term appears unfair is because it obliges your client to work for 18 hours a day without a break, then reading the long title will have helped you to identify at the earliest opportunity that the UCTA is unlikely to help you.

Check whether the statute is in force, in part or as a whole

A statute may not yet have come into force, or it may even have been repealed. Bear in mind that some sources give the text of statutes as originally passed by Parliament, while others give the text as amended by later provisions and statute, and some offer both, so you should check that you are reading the version you wish to read.

Identify the sections you may need

You should begin by analysing the table of contents. The headings and titles of each section in particular will help you to find what is most likely to be relevant. While a statute itself does not include an index, typically a publisher will publish a text which includes the most common statutes in a subject area, and it will include a helpful consolidated index for those statutes. For example, corporate lawyers will usually have a copy of *Butterworths Company Law Handbook* which includes an indexed collection of the main primary sources of law that are relevant to corporate lawyers. If you access a statute using an electronic database, you will be able to search the statute on screen to find a specific word.

Skim read the sections that you have identified as possibly relevant, to check whether they do appear to be relevant.

Locate the definition or interpretation sections

Again, the table of contents may help here, but some definitions are hidden within sections and this may not be evident from the title of any section. There is no general rule as to where you will find the definitions section (sometimes called the interpretation section), although often you will find it in one or more of the following places:

- near the beginning of the statute;
- near the end of the statute;
- within the section where the term(s) feature;
- near the end of the part of the statute where the term(s) feature.

In the UCTA the definitions for Part I are in s. 14 (at the end of Part I) and there are also separate explanatory provisions in ss. 11 and 13. The definitions for Part II are in s. 25 (at the end of Part II). There are also some definitions within the section where the terms feature (e.g. s. 1(1) sets out the meaning of 'negligence' which features in s. 2). Note that the meaning of a word in a statute will not necessarily be the meaning that a non-lawyer would understand to be the meaning of that word. Nor can you assume that the definition of a word in one statute will be the same as the definition of the same word in another statute. It is very important to find and read any definitions in order to understand the legislation.

Carefully read the relevant parts of the statute

Once you have used this approach to identity the relevant sections, you should now re-read the sections with care, having attended to the practicalities of reading referred to at 7.1.1. The general rule is that a statute means precisely what it says, so each word of the statute is important. You must focus and pay attention to what you are reading. The following guidance will help you.

Rights, obligations, and prohibitions

1. Is the statute granting a right; that is, saying someone **can do** something?

The statute might use words such as 'can' or 'may' to do this. In fact, the UCTA does not do this. It prefers to use 'cannot' (eight times) to impose negative obligations instead (see (3) below). However, in places, it does limit the scope of the negative obligation, so in this way grants some notion of a right. The statute might use words such as 'except in so far as', 'subject to', or 'provided that' to do this. For example, s. 6(1A) of the UCTA grants a limited negative obligation ('cannot . . . except in so far as . . . satisfies the requirement of reasonableness') applying to a contract term to exclude liability for breach of various obligations. In other words, in some circumstances, provided there is compliance with the UCTA (for example in terms of satisfying the requirement of reasonableness), there does exist a limited right for a contract term to exclude or restrict liability for some breaches.

2. Is the statute imposing a positive obligation; that is, saying someone **must do** something?

The statute might use words such as 'must', 'shall', or 'will' to do this. Again, the statute might limit the scope of the obligation, or render it subject to the court's discretion. For example, s. 11(2) of the UCTA states that, when considering whether a contract term satisfies the requirement of reasonableness under s. 6 of the UCTA, there is an obligation on the court ('regard shall be had') to consider 'the matters specified in Schedule 2'. The statute also makes clear that this obligation would not prevent a court or arbitrator 'in accordance with any rule of law' from striking out a term even if it appears to be reasonable in light of Sch. 2. In other words, while the court must consider Sch. 2, it then has an element of discretion.

3. Is the statute imposing a negative obligation, or prohibition, that is, saying someone **must not do** something?

The statute might use words such as 'cannot', 'must not', 'shall not', or 'will not' to do this. For example, s. 2(1) of the UCTA prohibits a term of a contract from excluding or restricting liability for death or personal injury resulting from negligence.

4. What are the consequences of failing to comply with a positive or negative obligation?

You will need to find the consequence of any non-compliance. You might find them in a separate section of the Act, which may or may not be helpfully cross-referenced, or have a useful heading which you can see clearly in the table of contents. Sometimes, however, you may have to 'read in' this information from related relevant case law.

Cross-references

It is common for a section of a statute not to 'stand alone' but instead to require reference to another section of or schedule to that statute, or even to another statute entirely. This adds to the complexity of your reading, as you need to read the section in conjunction with something else. We have already seen examples of this, such as that the reference in s. 6(1A) to the requirement of reasonableness needs to be read in light of s. 11 which sets out the 'reasonableness' test, which in turn must be read in light of Sch. 2, which sets out the guidelines for the application of the test. While s. 11(2) clearly signposts back to s. 6 and forward to Sch. 2, in fact s. 6 is silent even as to the existence of s. 11 and Sch. 2.

A further example is the reference to 'that party' in s. 3(2). This can only be explained by looking at the previous subsection. Reading s. 3(1) it becomes clear that the reference to 'that party' in s. 3(2) is a reference to a party to a contract who deals on the other party's 'standard terms of business'.

Another example is the cross-references in s. 6(1A)(a) to various obligations arising under a different act entirely to the UCTA, namely the Sale of Goods Act 1979.

You can see why some students actually never get round to reading the sections, having given up trying to navigate their way to an answer. Chapter 8 explains how reading an up to date secondary source of law, such as *Halsbury's Laws*, before you read the statute itself, can really assist your reading and understanding of a particular statute, understand the jargon it contains, and find out how best to navigate around it.

Section structure

The sections of a statute are often drafted as subsections of a central 'stem', and the subsections may end with 'and', 'or', or nothing at all. It is important to understand this structure in order to understand fully the meaning of the section. To take s. 3 as an example, you can see that the central stem in s. 3(2) is 'As against that party, the other cannot by reference to any contract term' and this stem then needs to be read in front of two subsections, (a) and (b). The word 'or' at the end of s. 3(2)(a) clearly shows that there are two things that the 'other party' cannot do, one set out in (a) and one set out in (b). These are in the alternative; that is the 'other party' will be in breach if she does (a) or (b), not just if she does (a) and (b). You will then note that there is an exception at the end of s. 3(b), 'except in so far as (in any of the cases mentioned above in this subsection) the contract term satisfies the requirement of reasonableness'. When reading this exception, you need to be clear that it applies just to s. 3(2)(b) and definitely not to s. 3(2)(a). How can you ascertain this? The exception wording alludes to this by referring to 'in any of the cases mentioned above in *this subsection*'. However, even if it did not say so, you can tell by the alignment of the exception. Can you see that the word 'except' is aligned under 'claim'? Contrast that with s. 6(1).

There the final part of the section, 'cannot be excluded or restricted by reference to any contract term', is aligned under the stem 'Liability for breach of the obligations arising from', indicating that those words must be read onto the stem, not just a subsection.

'Reading in' the facts

Clearly a statute uses generic wording and will not refer to the specific facts of the legal issue you are facing. Example 1 illustrates that it is for you to 'read in' to the statute the facts of your legal issue, in order to understand better the statute you are reading.

> ### Example 1
>
> If Customer Ltd buys an item from Retailer Ltd on Retailer's Ltd standard terms, you might therefore read s. 3(2) as 'As against Customer Ltd, Retailer Ltd cannot by reference to any contract term . . . (a) when Retailer Ltd is in breach of contract, exclude . . ., or (b) (i) claim to be entitled to render a contractual performance substantially different from that which was reasonably expected of Retailer Ltd', and so on.

Case law

Chapter 4 details how to interpret a statute and how case law can affect this interpretation. For example, it may be that case law has interpreted and refined the guidelines which are set out in Sch. 2 to the UCTA regarding the application of the reasonableness test. This may not be obvious from the statute itself; it may not be annotated anywhere on the page. This is why it is not enough simply to read the statute in isolation, but instead as part of a wider legal research strategy, including to find out if there are any related cases you need to read, and this is explored further in Chapter 8.

Updating information

You may have noticed that the statute contains . . . or other punctuation or text formatting that you were not expecting to see. This is likely to relate to the updating of the statute, and is code to tell you whether something is in force, pending, or has become obsolete. Check the user guide for the database you are using. Chapter 8 provides further guidance on this.

7.1.4 Statutory instruments

Chapter 4 considers the nature of a statutory instrument in some detail. As a reminder, statutory instruments are secondary legislation made under powers delegated by Parliament, usually to government ministers. There are various reasons for their use. Statutes can progress more quickly through Parliament if some of the detail is left to be set out in a statutory instrument at a later date. Sometimes statutory instruments are needed to bring statutes up to date with modern life (e.g. to include reference to civil partners alongside existing references to spouses and other family members).

7.1.4.1 Structure of a statutory instrument

Helpfully, as with a statute, most statutory instruments are set out in a similar way. Figure 7.2 sets out the Health Protection (Coronavirus, Business Closure) (England) Regulations 2020. As with the UCTA, you should not rely on this statutory instrument for legal content. It was intended to be in force only for a limited time and has been revoked, but it is a valuable template to use for our purposes of understanding how any statutory instrument is structured. To help with this, the statutory instrument is annotated with some explanations about its structure, which in turn will allow you to follow the basic structure of any other statutory instrument. You should read Figure 7.2 before returning to read 7.1.4.2.

7.1.4.2 How to read and understand a statutory instrument

Generally, you should read a statutory instrument in the same way as a statute. However, there are some minor differences in the approach you should adopt. As Chapter 4 explains, a statutory instrument is secondary legislation, made under powers conferred by an Act of Parliament (often referred to as the **parent statute** or the **primary legislation**). You should expect to see references in the statutory instrument to the parent statute and some-times to other relevant statutory instruments, some of which may have been made under the same parent statute. To understand the statutory instrument fully, you must understand the context in which it was made. This means that you must be prepared to refer back to the parent statute and across to any other relevant statutory instruments and cases which relate to it.

Part II

Legal Skills

2020 No. 327[1]

PUBLIC HEALTH., ENGLAND[2]

The Health Protection (Coronavirus, Business Closure) (England) Regulations 2020[3]

Made	*at 2.00 p.m. on 21st March 2020*
Laid before Parliament	*23rd March 2020*
Coming into force	*at 2.00 p.m. on 21st March 2020*[4]

Table of Contents[5]

1.   Citation and commencement
2.   Requirement to close premises and businesses during the emergency[6]
3.[7] Offences and penalties
4.   Enforcement of restrictions and prosecution
5.   Expiry

SCHEDULE

PART 1

PART 2

EXPLANATORY NOTE

The Secretary of State[8] makes the following Regulations in exercise of the powers conferred by sections 45C(1), (3)(c), (4)(d), 45F(2) and 45P of the Public Health (Control of Disease) Act 1984.[9]

Figure 7.2 Annotated version of the Health Protection (Coronavirus, Business Closure) (England) Regulations 2020

These Regulations are made in response to the serious and imminent threat to public health which is posed by the incidence and spread of severe respiratory syndrome coronavirus 2 (SARS-CoV-2) in England.

The Secretary of State considers that restrictions and requirements imposed by these Regulations are proportionate to what they seek to achieve, which is a public health response to that threat.

In accordance with section 45R of that Act the Secretary of State is of the opinion that, by reason of urgency, it is necessary to make this instrument without a draft having been laid before, and approved by a resolution of, each House of Parliament.

Citation and commencement

1.   (1) These Regulations may be cited as the Health Protection (Coronavirus, Business Closure) (England) Regulations 2020 and shall come into force at 2.00 p.m. on 21st March 2020.

         (2) These Regulations apply in relation to England only.

Requirement to close premises and businesses during the emergency

2.   (1) A person who is responsible for carrying on a business which is listed in Part 1 of the Schedule must—

         (a) during the relevant period—

            (i) close any premises, or part of the premises, in which food or drink are sold for consumption on those premises, and

            (ii) cease selling food or drink for consumption on its premises; or

         (b) if the business sells food or drink for consumption off the premises, cease selling food or drink for consumption on its premises during the relevant period.

         (2) For the purposes of paragraph (1)(a), food or drink sold by a hotel or other accommodation as part of room service is not to be treated as being sold for consumption on its premises.

         (3) For the purposes of paragraph (1)(a)(ii) and (b), an area adjacent to the premises of the business where seating is made available for customers of the business (whether or not by the business) to be treated as part of the premises of that business.

         (4) A person responsible for carrying on a business which is listed in Part 2 of the Schedule must cease to carry on that business during the relevant period.

         (5) If a business listed in the Schedule ("business A") forms part of a larger business ("business B"), the person responsible for carrying on business B complies with the requirement in paragraph (1) if it closes down business A.

         (6) The Secretary of State must review the need for restrictions imposed by this regulation every 28 days, with the first review being carried out before the expiry of the period of 28 days starting with the day after the day on which these Regulations are made.

         (7) As soon as the Secretary of State considers that the restrictions set out in this regulation are no longer necessary to prevent, protect against, control or provide a public health response to the incidence or spread of infection in England with the coronavirus, the Secretary of State must publish a direction terminating the relevant period.

         (8) A direction published under paragraph (7) may terminate the relevant period in relation to some of the businesses listed in the Schedule, or all businesses listed in the Schedule.

         (9) For the purposes of this regulation— [10]

         (a) "coronavirus" means severe acute respiratory syndrome coronavirus 2 (SARS-CoV-2);

         (b) a "person responsible for carrying on a business" includes the owner, proprietor, and manager of that business;

         (c) the "relevant period" starts when these Regulations come into force and ends on the day specified in a direction published by the Secretary of State under paragraph (7).

(continued . . .)

Figure 7.2 Continued

Offences and penalties

3.　(1) A person who, without reasonable excuse, contravenes regulation 2 commits an offence.

(2) A person who obstructs, without reasonable excuse, any person carrying out a function under these Regulations commits an offence.

(3) An offence under these Regulations is punishable on summary conviction by a fine.

(4) If an offence under paragraph (1) committed by a body corporate is proved—

(a) to have been committed with the consent or connivance of an officer of the body, or

(b) to be attributable to any neglect on the part of such an officer,

the officer (as well as the body corporate) is guilty of the offence and liable to be prosecuted and proceeded against and punished accordingly.

(5) In paragraph (4), "officer", in relation to a body corporate, means a director, manager, secretary or other similar officer of the body corporate.

Enforcement of restrictions and prosecution

4.　(1) A person, designated by the Secretary of State, may take such action as is necessary to enforce a closure or restriction imposed by regulation 2.

(2) Proceedings for an offence under regulation 3 may be brought any person designated by the Secretary of State.

Expiry

5.　(1) These Regulations expire at the end of the period of six months beginning with the day on which they come into force.

(2) This regulation does not affect the validity of anything done pursuant to these Regulations before they expire.

Matt Hancock[11]

Secretary of State for Health

Department for Health and Social Care

2:00 p.m. on 21st March 2020

SCHEDULE

Businesses that must close

PART 1

1.　Restaurants, including restaurants and dining rooms in hotels or members clubs.

2.　Cafes, including workplace canteens, but not including—

(a) cafes or canteens at a hospital, care home or school;

(b) canteens at a prison or an establishment intended for use for naval, military or air force purposes or for the purposes of the Department of the Secretary of State responsible for defence;

(c) services providing food or drink to the homeless.

3.　Bars, including bars in hotels or members' clubs.

4.　Public houses.

PART 2

5.　Cinemas.

6.　Theatres.

7.　Nightclubs.

8.　Bingo halls.

9.　Concert halls.

10.　Museums and galleries.

11.　Casinos.

12.　Betting shops.

13.　Spas.

14.　Massage parlours.

15.　Indoor skating rinks.

16.　Indoor fitness studios, gyms, swimming pools or other indoor leisure centres.

Figure 7.2 *Continued*

EXPLANATORY NOTE[12]

(This note is not part of the Regulations)

These Regulations require the closure of businesses selling food or drink for consumption on the premises, and businesses listed in the Schedule, to protect against the risks to public health arising from coronavirus. The closure lasts until a direction is given by the Secretary of State. The Secretary of State is required to keep the need for these restrictions under review every 28 days.

No impact assessment has been prepared for these Regulations.

1 Citation
The year and serial number of the statutory instrument. SI 2020 No. 327 means that this was the 327th statutory instrument of 2020, and this is the definitive way to identify it. The serial numbering reverts to '1' at the start of each calendar year.

2 Subject matter
This SI is about public health in England.

3 Title
The Health Protection (Coronavirus, Business Closure) (England) Regulations 2020.

4 Date
The SI was made on 21 March 2020. It was laid before Parliament two days later. By reason of urgency, very unusually, this SI came into force before the draft was laid before, or approved by, Parliament. It clearly states the commencement date of 21 March 2020 here and also in s. 1. Note that the year in the title is the year the SI was made, not the year it came into force (here, both are 2020).

5 Table of Contents
The table of contents provides a useful summary of what you will find in the statutory instrument (SI) and can help you to navigate around the SI.

6 Interpretation
This SI does not have a specific regulation dealing with interpretation. Instead, this regulation provides an explanation of the meaning of certain words (sometimes referred to as Definitions) which the SI refers to. The meaning will not necessarily be the meaning that a non-lawyer would understand to be the meaning of a word (and indeed you should assume that a definition in a SI applies only to that SI unless it states otherwise). It is very important to find and read any definitions in order to understand the legislation.

7 Structure
The body of a SI is divided. The names of these divisions depend on the form of the title. If (as here) it is entitled 'Regulations', the divisions are also known as regulations. If it is an 'Order', the divisions are known as articles. If it is entitled 'Rules', the divisions are also known as rules. A subdivision of a regulation, article, or rule is always referred to as a paragraph.

8 Minister
The minister who signed the SI (in this case the Secretary of State for Health). You will find the name of the minister at the end of the SI. Here it was Matt Hancock.

9 Authority
The authority under which the statutory instrument is made, which in this case is the Public Health (Control of Disease) Act 1984.

10 Interpretation
See note 6.

11 Minister
This is the name of the minister who signed the SI and who is referred to, but not by name, at the beginning of the SI.

12 Explanatory Note
As stated in this explanatory note, it does not form part of the SI. As here, it may summarise the purpose and context of the SI.

7.1.5 Case law

As Chapter 5 explains, case law is a primary source of English law. That chapter also explains the doctrine of precedent (concerning when courts are bound to follow previous decisions) and various other information you need to be aware of if you are to read and understand case law effectively. This chapter considers the practice of reporting a case, the structure of a case report, and how to read and understand that case report effectively.

7.1.5.1 Reporting cases

Where cases are reported

Cases are published in various places. Higher courts will keep a record of the cases they hear, which are often referred to as **transcripts**. The Supreme Court publishes transcripts of its judgments on its website, and the British and Irish Legal Information Institute (BAILII) publishes transcripts of judgments from a variety of courts in the UK (details of both websites are set out in the Further Reading section of this chapter). Electronic databases such as Lawtel and Lexis®Library also publish transcripts of judgments.

Commercial publishers will choose to report some judgments which they consider to be of particular interest, perhaps because they changed the law or applied it differently. These cases are likely to be ones heard in the higher courts and typically it is these reported cases which you will be reading as a student or junior lawyer. A publisher will help you to read and understand a case by providing useful navigation tools and summaries such as a headnote. You will find these law reports in a variety of places. Three general series report the most significant cases across all areas of the law: the Law Reports (divided into Appeal Cases, Chancery, Family and King's/Queen's Bench), the Weekly Law Reports, and the All England Law Reports. There are also specialist reports (e.g. the Road Traffic Reports and the Family Law Reports), reports in weekly practitioners' journals (such as *New Law Journal* and the *Solicitors' Journal*), and reports in newspapers including *The Times*.

Case citation

You can find cases by using the case citation. This is a list of abbreviations which are used in citations to refer to the most well known series of law reports. You can look up other abbreviations in the Cardiff Index to Legal Abbreviations, further details of which are set out in the Further Reading section at the end of this chapter.

AC	Appeal Cases (Law Reports)
All ER/AER	All England Law Reports
CL	Current Law
CLJ	Cambridge Law Journal
CLY	Current Law Year Book
CMLR	Common Market Law Reports
Ch	Chancery (Law Reports)
Cr App R	Criminal Appeal Reports
Crim LR	Criminal Law Review
ECR	European Court Reports
ER	English Reports
FLR	Family Law Reports
Fam	Family Division (Law Reports)
ICR	Industrial Cases Reports
IRLR	Industrial Relations Law Reports
KB	King's Bench (Law Reports)
LJR	Law Journal Reports
LQR	Law Quarterly Review
LR	Law Reports
LS Gaz	Law Society's Gazette
LT	Law Times
LTJ	Law Times Journal
Lloyd's Rep	Lloyd's List Reports (1951 onwards)
MLR	Modern Law Review
New LJ/NLJ	New Law Journal
P	Probate, Divorce & Admiralty (Law Reports)

QB	Queen's Bench (Law Reports)
RTR	Road Traffic Reports
SJ	Solicitors' Journal
WLR	Weekly Law Reports

An example and explanation of a case citation is provided in the extract from the *Donoghue* v *Stevenson* case set out in Figure 7.3.

A new system of neutral citation of judgments was introduced in 2001. The court gives a neutral citation to every judgment, and numbers every paragraph of the judgment. This citation should then feature in every subsequent publication of that judgment, whether online or in hard copy, and paragraphs of the judgment can be referred to by number.

The neutral citation takes the form:

| [year in square brackets] | Abbreviation of the name of the court | Serial number (which reverts to 1 each calendar year) |

Examples of abbreviations of the name of the courts are:

UKSC	Supreme Court
EWCA Civ	Court of Appeal (Civil Division)
EWCA Crim	Court of Appeal (Criminal Division)
EWHC Admin	High Court (Administrative Division)

Example 2

Smith v *Jones* [2012] EWCA Crim 3 at [49].

This is a reference to paragraph 49 in the judgment of *Smith* v *Jones*, which was the third judgment of the year 2012 in the Court of Appeal (Criminal Division).

Example 3

R (Miller) v *The Prime Minister* [2019] UKSC 41 at [1].

This is a reference to paragraph 1 in the judgment of *R (Miller)* v *The Prime Minister*. This is the constitutional law case brought against the Prime Minister, concerning the suspension (prorogation) of parliament, which the Supreme Court found to be unlawful. The citation shows the case was the 41st judgment of the year 2019 in the Supreme Court. An extract is set out at Figure 7.4.

7.1.5.2 Structure of a case

As with a statute and a statutory instrument, the layout of a case follows a particular convention. Again, this means that the more familiar you are with this layout, the easier it will be for you to navigate, read, and understand the case effectively. The case of *Donoghue* v *Stevenson* is set out in Figure 7.3, together with guidance as to how the case is set out. You may recognise this case; it is 'the one about the snail and the ginger beer' and is one of the most famous cases in British legal history. The case concerns the law of tort, and in particular the law of negligence. It is introduced and analysed in Chapters 3 and 5.

Figure 7.4 is an excerpt from *R (Miller)* v *The Prime Minister* (the Supreme Court's judgment about The Prime Minister's prorogation of parliament), cited at Example 3.

The entire judgment is available in the 'decided cases' section of the Supreme Court's website (www.supremecourt.uk/decided-cases/index.html). You are encouraged to access it using this link and the neutral citation provided, and compare and contrast the structure and style of the report of this Supreme Court case with that of the older report of *Donoghue* v *Stevenson* at Figure 7.3. You will note the similarities, in terms of content, and also some differences which will make your reading easier, including paragraph numbers.

[1932] A.C. 562[1]

[HOUSE OF LORDS.][2]

M'ALISTER (OR DONOGHUE) (PAUPER)...APPELLANT

AND

STEVENSON...RESPONDENT[3]

1932 May 26.[4]

Lord Buckmaster, Lord Atkin, Lord Tomlin, Lord Thankerton, and Lord Macmillan.[5]

Negligence - Liability of Manufacturer to ultimate Consumer - Article of Food - Defect likely to cause Injury to Health.[6]

By Scots and English law alike the manufacturer of an article of food, medicine or the like, sold by him to a distributor in circumstances which prevent the distributor or the ultimate purchaser or consumer from discovering by inspection any defect, is under a legal duty to the ultimate purchaser or consumer to take reasonable care that the article is free from defect likely to cause injury to health:-[7]

So held, by Lord Atkin, Lord Thankerton and Lord Macmillan; Lord Buckmaster and Lord Tomlin dissenting.[8]

George v. Skivington (1869) L. R. 5 Ex. 1 approved.

Dicta of Brett M.R. in Heaven v. Pender (1883) 11 Q. B. D. 503, 509-11 considered.

Mullen v. Barr & Co., Ld., and M'Gowan v. Barr & Co., Ld., 1929 S. C. 461 overruled.[9]

APPEAL against an interlocutor of the Second Division of the Court of Session in Scotland recalling an interlocutor of the Lord Ordinary (Lord Moncrieff).

---

1 Case citation

This tells you that the report of the case of Donoghue v Stevenson starts at page 562 of the Appeal Cases series of the Law Reports for 1932.

Each series of law reports has its own abbreviation. A list of the most common abbreviations is set out in this chapter.

Note that in this citation the year is in square brackets. This is code to show that the year is essential information for finding this case, because volumes of the Law Reports are consecutively numbered within each year. In some citations the year is in round brackets, which is code to show that the information about the year is superfluous as the other information in the citation will allow you to find the case.

This case was reported before the neutral citation system was implemented.

2 Court

It is important to understand which court heard the case, in this instance the House of Lords, because of the doctrine of precedent explained in Chapter 5. A House of Lords (now the Supreme Court) decision is really significant, a Court of Appeal decision still important, but less so, and so on.

3 Case name

This is a civil matter, so you should pronounce the case name as 'Donoghue **and** (not 'v' 'vs' or 'against') Stevenson'. This is an appeal case, so

Donoghue, who is bringing the appeal, is referred to as the appellant, and Stevenson, who won in the last hearing, is called the respondent. As Chapter 3 explains, the first time a civil case is heard the person bringing the claim is referred to as the **claimant** (formerly the plaintiff) and the person against whom the claim is brought is referred to as the **defendant**.

Criminal cases are set out as 'R v [Name of person being prosecuted]'. You pronounce these case names as 'The Crown against [Name]'. Until 1985, in the magistrates' court, the name of the senior police officer was used instead of 'R'. The person bringing the criminal claim is called the prosecution and the person defending the claim is called the defendant.

Figure 7.3 Annotated extract from *Donoghue* v *Stevenson*

By an action brought in the Court of Session the appellant, who was a shop assistant, sought to recover damages from the respondent, who was a manufacturer of aerated waters, for injuries she suffered as a result of consuming part of the contents of a bottle of ginger-beer which had been manufactured by the respondent, and which contained the decomposed remains of a snail. The appellant by her condescendence averred that the bottle of ginger-beer was purchased for the appellant by a friend in a café at Paisley, which was occupied by one Minchella; that the bottle was made of dark opaque glass and that the appellant had no reason to suspect that it contained anything but pure ginger-beer; that the said Minchella poured some of the ginger-beer out into a tumbler, and that the appellant drank some of the contents of the tumbler; that her friend was then proceeding to pour the remainder of the contents of the bottle into the tumbler when a snail, which was in a state of decomposition, floated out of the bottle; that as a result of the nauseating sight of the snail in such circumstances, and in consequence of the impurities in the ginger-beer which she had already consumed, the appellant suffered from shock and severe gastro-enteritis. The appellant further averred that the ginger-beer was manufactured by the respondent to be sold as a drink to the public (including the appellant); that it was bottled by the respondent and labelled by him with a label bearing his name; and that the bottles

4 Dates

Here the date indicates that the judges heard the case and gave judgment on it on the same day, 26 May 1932. If, after the hearing, the judges left to consider the issues and present a full written judgment at a later date (referred to as **deferring judgment**), then this date would also be stated here. Note that the date of the report can be different from the date of the decision (it might not even be the same year as the decision).

5 Judges

These are the names of the five House of Lords judges who considered this case. This is useful information as the seniority or reputation of judges can affect how a decision is regarded. The judges deliver their judgments in order of seniority so you can tell that Buckmaster was the most senior Law Lord (although, as discussed at summary of the judgments below, he was in dissent).

6 Subject matter

The editor of the report will choose some words to put here (in italics) as a guide to the subject matter of the case.

7 Headnote

The editor of the report will prepare a summary of the facts of the case and put it here as a headnote. The headnote should summarise

the case accurately and if you read this in conjunction with a secondary source of law (e.g. a textbook or *Halsbury's Laws*) it will be extremely helpful in allowing you to ascertain the key points of the case. During legal research (see Chapter 8) the headnote can also help you to consider whether you have found a case which is relevant to the issue you are researching. So there is no doubt that the headnote is useful. However, you will soon hear the mantra, if you have not already, that you really should not read the headnote as an alternative to reading the case itself (which is of course precisely what law students with long reading lists are tempted to do). The reason for this is that the headnote will state what the reporter considers is the decisive legal principle in the case, but a later case may take a different view or place a different emphasis on the case. The headnote is not authoritative, it is only a summary, and cannot capture the detail of the legal arguments that you will need to understand and apply as a lawyer. A good strategy is to use the headnote and secondary sources to shortlist relevant cases in order of priority, but then make sure you proceed to read those relevant cases (following the guidance set out below). It is interesting, for example, that the headnote of *Donoghue* v *Stevenson* does not really do anything to highlight that the case had the potential to be seen as groundbreaking. You would really have to have read a secondary source of law to ascertain

this before proceeding to read the case itself.

8 Summary of the judgments

This says that Lords Atkin, Thankerton, and Macmillan agreed with each other and their judgment prevailed. Lord Buckmaster (the most senior judge) and Lord Tomlin agreed with each other but not with the other judges, so their judgments are referred to as **dissenting**. It is important to read and understand not only the prevailing judgments, but also the dissenting ones. You can tell that this case was controversial, as the judges only reached a 3:2 majority decision.

9 Relationship with existing case law

The headnote will often indicate what the effect of the decision of this case is on existing case law. We can see here that *Donoghue* v *Stevenson* approved one case, considered one case, and overruled another. Other terms which could be used to describe the effect of a case on existing case law are explained at 5.1.3.

Approved: the House of Lords is stating that this case was correctly decided.

Considered: the House of Lords simply discussed this case.

Overruled: The House of Lords overturned this decision of another court in a different case.

Figure 7.3 *Continued*

were thereafter sealed with a metal cap by the respondent. She further averred that it was the duty of the respondent to provide a system of working his business which would not allow snails to get into his ginger-beer bottles, and that it was also his duty to provide an efficient system of inspection of the bottles before the ginger-beer was filled into them, and that he had failed in both these duties and had so caused the accident.

The respondent objected that these averments were irrelevant and insufficient to support the conclusions of the summons.

The Lord Ordinary held that the averments disclosed a good cause of action and allowed a proof.

The Second Division by a majority (the Lord Justice-Clerk, Lord Ormidale, and Lord Anderson; Lord Hunter dissenting) recalled the interlocutor of the Lord Ordinary and dismissed the action.[10]

1931. Dec. 10, 11. George Morton K.C. (with him W. R. Milligan) (both of the Scottish Bar) for the appellant. The facts averred by the appellant in her condescendence disclose a relevant cause of action . . . [omitted for the purposes of this book]

W. G. Normand, Solicitor-General for Scotland (with him J. L. Clyde (of the Scottish Bar) and T. Elder Jones (of the English Bar)) for the respondent. In an ordinary case such as this the manufacturer owes no duty to the consumer apart from contract . . . [omitted for the purposes of this book]

George Morton K.C. replied.[11]

The House took time for consideration.
1932. May 26.
LORD BUCKMASTER (read by LORD TOMLIN).
LORD ATKIN.
LORD TOMLIN.
LORD THANKERTON.
LORD MACMILLAN.[12]

[The full text of each judgment is made available for you on this book's online resources or you could choose to look up the case yourself on sites such as BAILII. You are recommended to read this text in conjunction with the guidance below. Chapter 5 considers the judgments and the ratio of the case in some detail and 7.1.5.4 summarises the key points.]

Interlocutor of the Second Division of the Court of Session in Scotland reversed and interlocutor of the Lord Ordinary restored. Cause remitted back to the Court of Session in Scotland to do therein as shall be just and consistent with this judgment. The respondent to pay to the appellant the costs of the action in the Inner House and also the costs incurred by her in respect of the appeal to this House, such last mentioned costs to be taxed in the manner usual when the appellant sues in forma pauperis.

Lords' Journals, May 26, 1932.[13]

Agents for the appellant: Horner & Horner, for W. G. Leechman & Co., Glasgow and Edinburgh.

Agents for the respondent: Lawrence Jones & Co., for Niven, Macniven & Co., Glasgow, and Macpherson & Mackay, W.S., Edinburgh.[14]

10 Details of the Appeal
This provides some background information about the case. It often also includes a short summary of the facts, as here (where the facts are particularly intriguing). It ends with a summary of all the courts that have previously considered this case. It is important to understand this. The first time this case was heard, the Lord Ordinary (the first instance judge for this case in Scotland) found for Donoghue, who had drunk the ginger beer. Stevenson, the manufacturer of the ginger beer, then appealed against this decision to the Second Division, and won. This case is an appeal by Donoghue against the decision of the Second Division. (Do not worry if the court names appear unfamiliar; remember this case was heard in Scotland.)

Figure 7.3 *Continued*

11 Counsel's submissions

Here are the names of the barristers (also referred to as counsel) who represented each party. Senior barristers are called QCs (Queen's Counsel) when the monarch is female and KCs (King's Counsel) when the monarch is male. At the time of this case George V was King.

As a solicitor it can be useful to know which barristers appeared in a particular case, as you might wish to instruct them in future. However clearly this is no help when the case was decided in 1932.

There is a summary of the legal arguments each barrister put to the court, together with the names of previous cases that they asked the court to consider. (These summaries are omitted in this extract.)

12 Judgment

The judgment is the most important part of any case. (Note that 'judg-ment' is the correct spelling to use in a legal context, not 'judgement'.)

Judges are each entitled to deliver their own judgment, however here Lord Tomlin reads Lord Buckmaster's judgment. The senior judge usually gives the first judgment, or decides who should. The judges following may give a brief concurring judgment (which can be 'I agree', or a full judgment of their own) and will either support the decision of the other judges, or dissent.

The decision of each judge is key and will be summarised towards the end of their judgment.

(The book *Final judgment: the last law lords and the Supreme Court*, referred to in the Further Reading section below, provides further insight and considers the recent trend of the Supreme Court towards providing more collegiate judgments.)

Of course before you read these judgments you already know that two of the judges dissent, from the summary of the judgments provided earlier in the report.

13 Decision

The overall decision of the court is stated here. You need to make sure you understand what this is, as it can be less than clear in appeal cases. Here, Donoghue's appeal is being allowed. The original judgment of the Lord Ordinary finding, in favour of Donoghue, that Stevenson owed Donoghue a duty of care, is restored. The appeal decision of the Second Division, finding in favour of Stevenson, is reversed.

14 Solicitors

The names of the solicitors who represented each party are set out here.

[2019] UKSC 41
On appeals from: [2019] EWHC 2381 (QB)
and [2019] CSIH 49

Note the spelling of this word in a legal context.

JUDGMENT

R (on the application of Miller) (Appellant) v The Prime Minister (Respondent)
Cherry and others (Respondents) v Advocate General for Scotland (Appellant) (Scotland)

before

Lady Hale, President
Lord Reed, Deputy President
Lord Kerr
Lord Wilson
Lord Carnwath
Lord Hodge
Lady Black
Lord Lloyd-Jones
Lady Arden
Lord Kitchin
Lord Sales

Figure 7.4 Annotated extract from *R (Miller)* v *The Prime Minister*

JUDGMENT GIVEN ON

24 September 2019

Heard on 17, 18 and 19 September 2019

Appellant	*Respondent*
(Gina Miller)	*(The Prime Minister)*
Lord Pannick QC	Sir James Eadie QC
Tom Hickman QC	David Blundell
Warren Fitt	Christopher Knight
	Richard Howell
(Instructed by Mishcon de	(Instructed by The Government
Reya LLP (London))	Legal Department)
Appellant	*Respondents*
(The Advocate General)	*(Joanna Cherry MP and others)*
Lord Keen of Elie QC	Aidan O'Neill QC
Andrew Webster QC	David Welsh
	Sam Fowles
(Instructed by Office of	(Instructed by Balfour and
the Advocate General for Scotland)	Manson LLP (Edinburgh))
	1st Intervener
	James Wolffe QC, Lord Advocate
	James Mure QC
	Christine O'Neill
	(Instructed by the Legal Department
	of the Scottish Government)
	2nd Intervener
	Ronan Lavery QC
	Conan Fegan BL
	Richard Smyth
	(Instructed by McIvor Farrell Solicitors)
	3rd Intervener
	Michael Fordham QC
	Celia Rooney
	Hollie Higgins
	(Instructed by Welsh Government
	Legal Services Department)
	4th Intervener
	Lord Garnier QC
	Tom Cleaver
	Anna Hoffmann
	(Instructed by Herbert Smith
	Freehills LLP (London))
	5th Intervener
	Deok Joo Rhee QC
	Catherine Dobson
	(Instructed by Howe and Co)
	6th Intervener
	Thomas de la Mare QC
	Daniel Cashman
	Alison Pickup
	(Instructed by Public Law Project)

Interveners:-

(1)   The Lord Advocate

(2)   Raymond McCord

(3)   Counsel General for Wales

(4)   Sir John Major KG CH

(5)   Baroness Chakrabarti CBE, PC (written submissions only)

(6)   Public Law Project (written submissions only)

Figure 7.4 *Continued*

LADY HALE AND LORD REED GIVING THE JUDGMENT OF THE COURT:

Note that paragraphs are numbered

1. It is important to emphasise that the issue in these appeals is not when and on what terms the United Kingdom is to leave the European Union. The issue is whether the advice given by the Prime Minister to Her Majesty the Queen on 27th or 28th August 2019 that Parliament should be prorogued from a date between 9th and 12th September until 14th October was lawful. It arises in circumstances which have never arisen before and are unlikely ever to arise again. It is a "one off". But our law is used to rising to such challenges and supplies us with the legal tools to enable us to reason to a solution.

Subheadings provide structure and clarity

What is prorogation?

2. Parliamentary sittings are normally divided into sessions, usually lasting for about a year, but sometimes less and sometimes, as with the current session, much longer. Prorogation of Parliament brings the current session to an end. The next session begins, usually a short time later, with the Queen's Speech. While Parliament is prorogued, neither House can meet, debate and pass legislation. Neither House can debate Government policy. Nor may members of either House ask written or oral questions of Ministers. They may not meet and take evidence in committees. In general, Bills which have not yet completed all their stages are lost and will have to start again from scratch in the next session of Parliament. In certain circumstances, individual Bills may be "carried over" into the next session and pick up where they left off. The Government remains in office and can exercise its powers to make delegated legislation and bring it into force. It may also exercise all the other powers which the law permits. It cannot procure the passing of Acts of Parliament or obtain Parliamentary approval for further spending.

[Paragraphs 3-22 omitted for the purposes of this work.]

These proceedings

23. Meanwhile, on 30th July 2019, prompted by the suggestion made in academic writings in April and also by some backbench MPs, and not denied by members of the Government, that Parliament might be prorogued so as to avoid further debate in the run-up to exit day, a cross party group of 75 MPs and members of the House of Lords, together with one QC, had launched a petition in the Court of Session in Scotland claiming that such a prorogation would be unlawful and seeking a declaration to that effect and an interdict to prevent it. This was met by averments that the petition was hypothetical and premature and that there was no reasonable or even hypothetical apprehension that the UK Government intended to advise the Queen to prorogue the Westminster Parliament with the intention of denying before Exit Day any further Parliamentary consideration of withdrawal from the Union. This denial was repeated in revised Answers dated 23rd and 27th August. On 27th August the Petition was amended to claim that it would be unlawful to prorogue Parliament with the intention to deny "sufficient time for proper consideration" of withdrawal. On 2nd September, the Answers were amended to deny that there was any reasonable apprehension of that.

[Paragraphs 24-51 omitted for the purposes of this work.]

Conclusions on justiciability

52. Returning, then, to the justiciability of the question of whether the Prime Minister's advice to the Queen was lawful, we are firmly of the opinion that it is justiciable. As we have explained, it is well established, and is accepted by counsel for the Prime Minister, that the courts can rule on the extent of prerogative powers. That is what the court will be doing in this case by applying the legal standard which we have described. That standard is not concerned with the mode of exercise of the prerogative power within its lawful limits. On the contrary, it is a standard which determines the limits of the power, marking the boundary between the prerogative on the one hand and the operation of the constitutional principles of the sovereignty of Parliament and responsible government on the other hand. An issue which can be resolved by the application of that standard is by definition one which concerns the extent of the power to prorogue, and is therefore justiciable.

The alternative ground of challenge

53. In addition to challenging the Prime Minister's advice on the basis of the effect of the prorogation which he requested, Mrs Miller and Ms Cherry also seek to challenge it on the basis of the Prime Minister's motive in requesting it. As we have explained, the Prime Minister had made clear his view that it was advantageous, in his negotiations with the EU, for there to be a credible risk that the United Kingdom might withdraw without an agreement unless acceptable terms were offered. Since there was a majority in Parliament opposed to withdrawal without an agreement, there was every possibility that Parliament might legislate to prevent such an outcome. In those circumstances, it is alleged, his purpose in seeking a prorogation of such length at that juncture was to prevent Parliament from exercising its legislative functions, so far as was possible, until the negotiations had been completed.

[Paragraphs 54-70 omitted for the purposes of this work.]

71. Thus the Advocate General's appeal in the case of Cherry is dismissed and Mrs Miller's appeal is allowed. The same declarations and orders should be made in each case.

Figure 7.4 *Continued*

7.1.5.3 How to read and understand case law

Chapter 5, 5.1 gives guidance on how to find the *ratio* of a case and how to identify what is *obiter dicta*, and considers this specifically in the context of *Donoghue* v *Stevenson*. This chapter focuses on the practical skill of how to approach your reading of a case.

Read as part of a wider research strategy

As with a statute, you should not expect to obtain a holistic understanding of a case simply by reading the case. Again you can refer to the helpful research strategy provided at Figure 8.1, which makes clear that 'analysing the primary source' such as a case is just one aspect of finding all relevant law. In particular, where available you should first have read a secondary source, such as a textbook or *Halsbury's Laws*, which describes the key aspects of the case.

Preparing to read the judgments

The key to reading and understanding the judgments effectively is to prepare for your reading of those judgments. You should not read the judgments, wondering, as you do when you read a novel, what the ending will be. Instead, you should have 'done your homework' first, and use the information set out before and after the judgments before you become embroiled in the detail of the case.

The *Donoghue* v *Stevenson* example shows where you can find this information. To recap, the headnote provides a significant amount of important basic information about the case. You should read this first and digest that information. You should also read the important information that, as the example highlights, you can find at the end of the case, particularly the overall decision of the court. This means that, when you begin reading the judgments, which can be heavy work, you are reading from an informed position. You will already know, for example, before you start reading any judgment, the basic facts of the case, the area of law it concerns, what the decision of the case is, which judges agreed with the decision, and which judges dissented from it. You should also have worked out whether it is a decision at first instance, or on appeal. You need to know who the parties are, and have worked out which party actually won the case. In an appeal case this can take a little concentration, as the report might simply say 'appeal dismissed' or 'appeal granted'. When you know what the ending is, and what the starting point is, it is so much easier to concentrate on reading through the judgments and searching for the *ratio* of the case.

Engaging with the court process

Cases will mean much more to you when you are familiar with the court process through which they progress. For an explanation of how you can arrange to visit court to observe case hearings see 13.1.3.4. Since 2019, the Supreme Court has recorded hearings; you can view these under the 'reported cases' or 'current cases' part of its website. You are encouraged to find and watch your selection from the six recordings (of the morning and evening hearings over three days) of *R (Miller)* v *The Prime Minister* [2019] UKSC 41, (where the Supreme Court found the Prime Minister's prorogation of Parliament to be unlawful) which is cited at Example 3 (www.supremecourt.uk/cases/uksc-2019-0192.html). You will learn so much from watching the hearings, as well as reading (as suggested at 7.1.5.2) and watching (as suggested in Practical Exercise 5 of Chapter 10) the subsequent judgment in this key constitutional law case. It will help to familiarise you with the court process and bring to colourful life the words you have read (see Georgiadis et al, Further Reading). This in turn, will not only inform your understanding of that case, but also of any subsequent case you read, because it will ignite your curiosity to understand the human element, to look closer at the inflexions, turns of phrase, and nature and background of the judges who are opining, and at the context of the times. For example, Lady Hale's choice of brooch in the shape of a spider quite captured the public's imagination, but you would not have caught that detail from reading the case itself (see Sleigh, Further Reading). Watching the hearings will also help you understand how an ongoing familiarity with key Supreme Court cases will give you an excellent opportunity to show commercial awareness at interview (as explored at 15.3).

7.1.5.4 How to focus, capture, assimilate, and synthesise your reading of case law

Preparing a case note

You need to use your analytical skills when you read a case. The following list of questions will help you to capture the essential facts in context and you can enjoy using them to prepare an effective case note. The case note at Figure 7.5 uses the *Donoghue v Stevenson* case as an example of how these questions can identify the key points in your reading. Explanatory guidance notes are provided in italics. You will be able to answer some of the questions from the information set out before and after the judgments, but you will not be able to answer all of the questions comprehensively until you have read the judgments too. Referring to these questions before, during, and after your reading can help you to remain focused and analytical and avoid drifting into reading them as a narrative story.

Name:	Donoghue v Stevenson
Citation:	[1932] A.C. 562
Judges:	Lord Atkin, Lord Thankerton and Lord Macmillan; Lord Buckmaster and Lord Tomlin dissenting
Council:	George Morton K.C (with him W.R. Milligan) for the appellant. W.G. Normand, Solicitor-General for Scotland (with him J.L Clyde and T. Elder Jones) for the respondent.
Acting Solicitors:	Horner & Horner, for W. G Leechman & Co., for the appellant. Lawrence Jones & Co., for Niven, Macniven & Co., and Macpherson & Mackay, for the respondent.

1. **To what area of law does this case relate?**
The law of tort.

2. **What principles of law are considered?**
The law of negligence and in particular the duty of care.

3. **What level of court did this case reach?**
The House of Lords.

4. **What are the relevant facts of the case?**
[Note: The facts were summarised for you at 3.1.3.2 as follows:]
   In August 1928, Mrs May Donoghue joined a friend for a drink in the Wellmeadow Café in Wellmeadow Place, Paisley, Glasgow.
   The friend bought the drinks. The owner poured some ginger beer from an opaque bottle into Mrs Donoghue's glass (which may or may not have had some ice cream floating in it). She took some swigs and then poured the rest of the contents into her glass. To her horror the remains of a decomposing snail presented themselves to her. Mrs Donoghue later complained of stomach pains and shock, both a result of gastroenteritis.

Figure 7.5 Case note on *Donoghue v Stevenson*

On appeal, the House of Lords found that the manufacturer would owe a duty of care (that is, a duty not to cause harm carelessly) to the consumer. The courts were considering the issue of whether a duty of care was owed as a preliminary point of law which needed to be established. The case was never tried on its facts as it later settled out of court, so the court did not, for example, ever even consider the issue of whether it was actually the snail which caused Donoghue's gastroenteritis.

[Note: sometimes you will not need to refer to the actual facts of a case; all that you will need will be the principle established in the case. However, sometimes it can be very helpful to know the facts to compare or contrast with the facts of a problem you are considering. Chapter 9 explores this further in giving guidance on how to answer problem questions.]

5. Why is this case important?

It forms the basis of the law on the duty of care between a manufacturer and a consumer. Before this case, the law of negligence had evolved piecemeal to impose liability in the absence of a contract, but there had been no attempt to state generally when a duty of care would arise. Instead it had been examined and extended on a case-by-case basis and largely confined to situations where there was a pre-existing relationship between the parties. This case was notable because it established that a duty of care could arise between two parties in the absence of a pre-existing relationship, in any situation where two very general criteria were satisfied (namely that the parties are legally 'proximate' and the damage is 'reasonably foreseeable'). Most think that the wide and general nature of this decision reflects that the majority of the judges were attempting to encourage a more general approach to establishing a duty of care than had gone before.

6. What decisions did the Court reach?

That the manufacturer, Stevenson, owed a duty of care to Donoghue as the consumer and end user of his products.

7. Who gave the lead judgment?

Lord Atkin.

[Note: this is sometimes not immediately obvious. For example, Lord Atkin's judgment is not the first judgment set out in the case. You should look for the judgment with which the majority of other judges agree (or 'concur'). Sometimes the other judges simply say 'I agree' or 'I concur' with the judge giving the leading judgment, but sometimes, as in this case, they will set out their judgments in more detail. In Donoghue v Stevenson it was with Lord Atkin's judgment that the majority of the other judges, that is Lord Thankerton and Lord Macmillan, agreed.]

8. What was the *ratio decidendi* of the case, that is, the reason for the decision?

[Note: you may recall that this was discussed in some detail at 5.1. It is not always clear what the ratio decidendi of a case is, and you should use the Chapter 5 guidance to help you.]

In *Donoghue* v *Stevenson* the *ratio decidendi* is very clear, because Lord Atkin made it so. He said (at 580, emphasis added):

You must take reasonable care to avoid acts or omissions which you can *reasonably foresee* would be likely to injure your neighbour. Who, then, in law is my neighbour? The answer seems to be—persons who are so closely and directly affected by my act that I ought reasonably to have them in contemplation as being so affected when I am directing my mind to the acts or omissions which are called in question.

Most think Lord Atkin was seeking to establish a more general approach to a duty of care, which was consistent with the case-by-case approach adopted previously, but which in future might make it easier to anticipate when a duty might be found. He also said (at 599):

A manufacturer of products, which he sells in such a form as to show that he intends them to reach the ultimate consumer in the form in which they left him with no reasonable possibility of intermediate examination, and with the knowledge that the absence of reasonable care in the preparation or the putting up of the products will result in an injury to the consumer's life or property, owes a duty to the consumer to take that reasonable care.

Both of these quotations are accepted as *ratios* arising from the case (the second being narrower than the first). However [Note: as explained at 5.1], a *ratio* does not have to be quoted from a judgment. A further *ratio* arising out of *Donoghue* v *Stevenson* which is not directly quoted from Lord Atkin's judgment, but which might be implied from his definition of 'who is my neighbour', is that a duty of care arises when the person or property of one person is in such *proximity* to another that, if due care is not taken, she might suffer physical and consequential damage.

9. Were there any other notable majority judgments?

As already noted, Lord Thankerton and Lord Macmillan did not simply state 'I concur'. When Lord Macmillan states (at 619) 'the categories of negligence are never closed', this can be interpreted to support the view that the majority of judges were seeking to use this case to establish a more general approach to duty of care.

Figure 7.5 *Continued*

10. **Were there any notable dissenting judgments?**
Yes, two of the five law lords dissented, which is significant dissent.

[*Note: In fact, the first judgment you read is Lord Buckmaster's dissenting judgment (his is first because he is the most senior law lord amongst the judges). His judgment is read by Lord Tomlin who also dissented. However, you should have been aware before you started reading, from the information provided before the judgments, that Lord Buckmaster's judgment was dissenting. It is easy to see how you would not have a hope of understanding what happened in this case if you had not prepared properly for reading the judgments and had given up after reading the most senior law lord's (Buckmaster's) judgment. Unlike Lord Atkin, Lord Buckmaster was very dismissive of Donoghue's case and cautioned against extending the reach of a duty of care.*]

11. **How old is this case?**
The parties made their submissions in 1931 and judgment was passed in 1932.

12. **Why is this case relevant today?**
This case is still relevant to the law of negligence and is the basis of the law on duty of care between a manufacturer and a consumer. Although the 'wide *ratio*' has been refined by *Caparo Industries plc* v *Dickman* (see 5.1), the case has not been overruled and, due to the doctrine of precedent, the law in *Donoghue* v *Stevenson* would bind any High Court or Court of Appeal judge considering questions relating to product liability in negligence.

Figure 7.5 *Continued*

Preparing a summary of cases on a specific topic

You need to develop a good technique to capture what you have read and understood in a way that will help you assimilate the information logically, put it into context and, crucially for a student, help you to revise effectively. Your answers to the questions just considered will focus your reading and ensure you extract essential information from a particular case. However, you then need to place what you have read into the wider context and assimilate it with other relevant law in the same area. You can use a spreadsheet very effectively to do this.

Let's consider how you might create a spreadsheet which collates the cases you have read and makes sense of them. We will take as an example the area of contract law, but of course this technique can apply equally well to any other area of law. You could create a separate sheet for each topic of contract law you cover, and label the tabs of the sheets with those topics, such as agreement and intention, consideration and agency, damages, remedies, frustration, pre-contractual terms, duress, and undue influence. Within each sheet, you could summarise the key findings from your reading of each case you have read on that topic. How much information to capture is up to you, but for most cases the basics would be name, date, facts, and key findings. For key cases you may wish to include the other information covered by the questions already considered. One of the distinct advantages of using a spreadsheet to record this information is that you can then easily re-order and collate the cases logically under headings. Consider, for example, the sheet on exemption clauses. Most cases in this area are on incorporation, construction, or reasonableness of the clause. Some cases cover third party liability. You could use these as headings, and order the cases beneath those headings. Creating the spreadsheet in itself will therefore help you to identify the relevant legal issues in relation to each topic (e.g. exemption clauses) within an area of law (e.g. contract). It also means that if you subsequently read another case on that issue, you can slot it in at the correct point with ease, e.g. under the reasonableness heading, which of course you cannot do with handwritten notes. You can also easily annotate and amend your work throughout the course as your understanding increases and clarifies. Working with the spreadsheet in this way will familiarise you with the relevant material and make your revision easier.

The example at Table 7.1 is an excerpt from a basic exemption clause spreadsheet that a student might create on contract law. It covers just the name and key principle learned from the student's reading of the case. The student can develop this using the guidance above, and could also abbreviate words to make it more concise.

Being able to distil complex reading into a summary of key facts is a skill which will benefit from practice, so the sooner you start a working spreadsheet, the earlier you can start to hone this particular skill. Of course, you can practise this skill in other ways too. Even trying to summarise the newspaper article you read over breakfast, and identifying its key message, will help you on your way to an effective method of reading and under-standing law.

Table 7.1 Excerpt from a basic exemption clause spreadsheet

Incorporation	
Chapelton v Barry	Clause must be in document of contractual nature (deckchair ticket is not)
L'Estrange v Graucob	If clause signed, even if not read, is incorporated . . .
Curtis v Chemical Cleaning	. . . provided no misrepresentation
Parker v SE Railway	If clause unsigned, 'reasonable notice' test—by time contract signed
Olley v Marlborough	Exemption clause in hotel bedroom—too late (in absence of regular course of dealings)
Thornton v Shoe Lane	The more onerous the clause, the more needs to be done to bring to notice (here, excluded liability for personal injury)
Interphoto v Stiletto	Applying above. Very high penalty for late return of photos
Hollier v Rambler	Car serviced 3/4 times in 5 yrs is not 'continuous course of dealings'
Kendall v Lillico	Risk of incorporation if seen clause before
Construction	
Houghton v Trafalgar	Ambiguity construed against person who suggested the wording ('*contra proferentem*')
Stewart Gill v Horatio Myer	Won't blue pencil within one term; immaterial if some parts of clause might have been reasonable in isolation
	So draft discrete clauses e.g. *Watford* (and more liberal approach taken there)
Thomas Witter v TBP	Excluding misrepresentation would mean fraudulent misrepresentation also excluded, so unreasonable.
	Cf (contrast) *Phillips Products* v *Hyland, Skipskredittforeningen*
Phillips Products v Hyland	Excluded liability for negligence, which would include death and personal injury. But case turned on other loss.
Skipskredittforeningen	Court should not focus too much on fact clause would fail by reference to unlikely situations

Table 7.1 *Continued*

Reasonableness	
Watford Electronics v Sanderson	Court reluctant to find unreasonableness when bargaining power equal e.g. Business 2 Business
	Saw price cap term as distinct from other unreasonable term, so would 'blue pencil' one term.
Smith v Bush	Negligence other than death/personal injury. House buyer brought negligence claim against building society's surveyor. Had signed disclaimer. Guidelines:
	● bargaining power?
	● reasonably practicable to obtain from alternative source?
	● how difficult was task?
	● practical consequences?
Third party liability	
Adler v Dickson	Cannot rely on contract if not party to it.
	Exception in Contract (Rights of Third Parties) Act 1999

7.1.6 European Union law

Chapter 4, 4.5 provides an analysis of EU law and how it affects law in the UK. Guidance follows to help you find, read, and understand EU legislation and cases.

7.1.6.1 European Union legislation

As 4.5 explains, the primary legislation of the European Union (comprising the founding Treaties that established the European Communities, along with later amending treaties) is very much a framework. It is the secondary legislation which contains the detail. The authoritative text of both primary and secondary legislation appears in the Official Journal of the European Communities (OJ) L-series (for 'legislation').

The most common types of secondary legislation you are likely to have to read are:

● Regulations (directly applicable in member states): these are cited by running number then year, so that 1/99 is the first Regulation of 1999.

● Directives (require member states to pass implementing legislation within a certain time frame): these are cited by year then running number, so that 99/1 is the first Directive of 1999.

You can find EU legislation on the Europa website and the EUR-Lex website (see the Further Reading section at the end of this chapter) as well as the commercial databases such as Lawtel, Lexis®Library, and Westlaw UK.

7.1.6.2 Reporting of European Union case law

The European Court Reports contain the authoritative reports of EU judgments. In the UK the monthly Common Market Law Reports also publish some decisions of the European Court of

Justice and some decisions before courts of other member states that have a bearing on EU law. There is also a European Cases series of the All England Law Reports.

Cases before courts in the EU can proceed differently from cases in courts in the UK, and this in turn affects the reporting of case law. For example, judgments are preceded by an 'opinion' of the Advocate General which, although not binding, is usually followed. Applications to the court that concern the same area of law may be joined together. This means that the names of parties can be very long, and so lawyers often abbreviate the case name when referring to those cases. Law reports, however, may use the full name rather than the abbreviated name by which the case has come to be known.

Citations also differ. Cases have a case number, comprising a running serial number followed by the year of application or reference to the Court. A full citation comprises:

Case number	Parties	Citation of the authoritative report in the European Court Reports

Example 4

Case C-295/95 *Farrell v Long* [1997] ECR I-1683.

Since 1989, when the Court of First Instance was created, cases are prefixed by 'C-' (Court of Justice, or 'Cour' in French) or 'T-' (Court of First Instance, or 'Tribunal' in French).

7.2 Reading and understanding primary sources for practice

The advice and guidance in 7.1 about reading and understanding law applies equally to practice. Your law degree provides plenty of opportunity to practise these skills so you will be adept in them before you arrive. During practice you will develop your expertise. You will find it helpful at this point to read the short summary by the Law Society about practice (see Further Reading), which will provide some context for this section (and all the practice-focused skills sections in the other chapters of Part 2). In particular, note that, depending on your area of practice, you might be undertaking:

- contentious legal work, which involves resolving disputes between two or more parties (for example, litigation), or
- non-contentious legal work, which involves dealing with the legal aspects of a client's business or personal matter (for example, drafting a sale and purchase agreement in corporate, or drafting a will in private client), or
- both contentious and non-contentious work (for example, in employment law, where you might be representing an employer company in a dispute and drafting the terms of the company's service contracts).

There follows some guidance to help inform and tailor your approach to reading specifically in the context of practice.

7.2.1 Why am I reading?

You will be reading, and need to understand, primary sources of law in order to prepare something. This may be:

- a piece of written work (e.g. a guidance note, a letter to progress the answer to a client's legal problem, a letter of advice to a client, or a research report or email for your supervisor (see Figure 8.2) so that they can write such a letter); or
- a form of oral communication (e.g. advocacy, negotiating, presenting, or interviewing a client).

Pay attention to the purpose of your reading, and keep it front of mind while you are reading. For example, if you are reading to inform a fellow solicitor about the law, then you may not need to 'translate' any jargon in the primary source, depending on the familiarity of that solicitor with the subject matter. However, if you are reading to inform a client, then you may need to 'translate', and to do so with care, in line with any definitions in the primary source. (In both cases, you must fully understand the law and every word you use to describe it, before you even begin to draft any communication in relation to it.)

7.2.2 What am I reading?

7.2.2.1 Sources

You might be reading primary sources (legislation and case law), or secondary sources which provide commentary on those primary sources of law, both of which will be familiar from your studies. In practice, however, you may be exposed to reading a wider range of source material in some respects, such as procedural rules or guidance from a regulatory body, which is likely to feel less familiar. In other respects, your range of reading material may be narrower: for example, you may have fewer opportunities to read purely academic or theoretical journal articles, than you enjoyed during your studies.

7.2.2.2 Identifying the general area of law

You may have to pay more attention to identifying the general area of law covered by the source you are reading in practice, compared to during your studies, because you no longer have the benefit of reading it as preparation for a seminar which a lecturer has helpfully structured and labelled for you (for example 'Tort: duty of care', or 'Contract: exemption clauses'). Instead, expect the possibility that you might encounter both *Donoghue* v *Stevenson* and the UCTA in one day, and you may do so whether you are working in the corporate team or the litigation team, and you will be expected to be able to have some memory of the basics, from your studies. In turn, let this knowledge inform your approach to your studies now, and ask yourself (or your lecturer if you are stuck), what are the key core areas of learning in each subject you have studied, that would be useful to a practising lawyer and so which you might be expected to have committed to memory long after you have graduated.

> ### Example 5
> #### Non-contentious
>
> As a corporate lawyer, you will need a working knowledge of the following core key areas of contract law, on a daily basis, to understand how to draft and advise on a basic share sale agreement:
>
> - the measure of damages in contract (and how this differs from the measure of damages in tort);
> - the legal requirements for formation of a valid contract;
> - the difference between a warranty and an indemnity;
> - the key issues in *Hadley* v *Baxendale*.

> ### Example 6
> #### Contentious
>
> Your client company tells you they have not been paid for goods they have sold, and mentions the buyer company has not paid because it considers the goods were sub-standard. Rather than jump to the conclusion it can be solved simply by bringing a claim against the buyer to pay its debt to the seller, you consider whether the buyer may have a valid case that your client has breached the terms implied by the Sale of Goods Act 1979 as to satisfactory quality.

7.2.2.3 Research strategy

You may have to find your sources yourself, using a successful research strategy you have practised and have faith in during your studies (and Chapter 8 provides one for you, with helpful guidance on how to use it), or alternatively your supervising solicitor, or a client, may give you a source or sources. In both cases, you will need to consider whether all the sources you find, or a given, are relevant, and also whether there is any hierarchy of importance between them. This will inform your decision as to which source to read first, which you should prioritise, and which you might not need to read at all, or can skim read. Chapter 8 gives you what you need to know about this, including how to use sources effectively, and how to evaluate their relative strengths, weaknesses, reliability, and relevance.

7.2.3 How should I be reading?

The guidance in this chapter, and Figures 7.1 to 7.4 will help you to read any primary source of law. Figure 7.5 and Table 7.1 will help you to digest what you read. For practice, you will need to pay particular attention, while reading, to the following matters.

7.2.3.1 Precedent

Chapter 5, 5.1 explained the importance of finding the *ratio decidendi* of a case, because it is the reason for the court's decision and generally it will be binding on lower courts and later judgments (unlike *obiter*). In practice, in contentious work, you will be particularly interested in which specific parts of a previous case will bind the court in a case or transaction you are preparing, so you can determine the limits within which your argument must operate, and evaluate your client's chances of success. You can see from your reading of *Donoghue* and *Miller* that the courts consider previous cases and must decide how free they are to choose whether to follow those cases, or not. If they must follow them, for example because they are from a higher court, then the court will consider whether they can distinguish the current case, on its facts, from the previous case. So you will need to apply what you know about the law of precedent to decide if you need to persuade the court it is bound, not bound, or can distinguish this case from, any previous relevant case. In non-contentious work you will want to identify and understand relevant cases which inform how to draft a clause in a way which the courts would be most likely to support as valid (for example, specific wording which has been held to be reasonable in a restrictive covenant in a director's service contract, and why).

7.2.3.2 Case and matter analysis

You will need to be able to read lengthy cases in a way where the detail of the facts does not escape you, so you can feed this into case analysis and determine the arguments available in your client's case (in contentious work) or matter analysis, and identify the solutions and procedures available to your client to best progress the matter (in non-contentious work). Techniques you learned in academia, such as being able to summarise a case and determine its *ratio* (see Figure 7.5), will be particularly helpful here, as will reading decent secondary sources (see Chapter 8) which analyse the primary source for you. Chapters 9, 12 and 13 will explain case and matter analysis in more detail, building on what you will have learned about finding and reading the law in Chapters 7 and 8.

7.2.3.3 *Ratio* and *obiter*

If lawyers begin to treat *obiter* comments as if they were part of the *ratio*, it can cause problems, because the law may begin to move in a direction which cannot be supported. This can result from the temptation to quote something a judge has said, but which actually is *obiter dicta*. Quotations may be useful, but make sure you clarify whether you are quoting binding *ratio*, or non-binding *dicta* (see Chapter 5 and Figure 7.5 for helpful guidance. Examples of how this has affected family court proceedings is set out in the Further Reading section (see Masson).

7.2.3.4 Legislation

The advice in 7.1.3.2 and 7.1.4.2 remains good advice for your reading of statutes and statutory instruments in practice. The focus on the need for precision and attention to definitions, cross-referencing, words conveying rights, obligations and prohibitions, and compliance will continue to be important in your reading and understanding, and you will need to track this level of detail into your own communications about what you have read and understood, whether in writing or otherwise.

The article by Ashurst (see Further Reading) provides an illustration of why and how as a practising lawyer you may need to read the UCTA (set out at Figure 7.1). You may be drafting limitation and exclusion of liability clauses which you need to ensure comply with the requirements of the statute (in non-contentious work), analysing them in a dispute (in contentious work), or tasked with writing a guide for clients to publish on your firm's website, like this one. Read the article, and reflect on how the writer focuses on the key practical issues, using headings, examples, definitions and short paragraphs, and avoiding unnecessary legalese and jargon, to give clarity and structure. They write in a way which interprets the statute faithfully, however, and do not shy away from mirroring the language used by the statute itself, and referring to specific sections where necessary. Detail is kept out of the body of the article, but is there, in footnotes for refence if required, so the reader can 'see the wood for the trees'. The article names and explains relevant cases, showing specifically how those cases have provided practical guidance and interpretation of the statute. You are encouraged to subscribe to this website (and other firms' websites), to receive regular updates in areas of law you are study- ing and/or interested in practising. Reading practitioners' own summaries of their reading and understanding of the law will inform and improve your own understanding and practice.

Be particularly keen to pay attention to definitions. For example, if you are a non-contentious lawyer, tasked with providing training to directors on their duties under the Companies Act, you will need to pay particular attention as to whom, specifically, those duties apply, when you are reading this piece of legislation. For example, does the Act impose the same duties on execu- tive directors, non-executive directors, former directors, someone who acts like a director and who the company responds to as if they were, but actually they are not appointed as a director, someone who is about to become a director imminently, and so on. You would want to find any applicable definition in the legislation, check case law for interpretation, and then mirror what you find in your own use of language in your written training document and accompanying presentations. Otherwise, the risk is that your training could be excellent in terms of content, but not be received by everyone in the company who needs to hear and read it.

7.2.4 **When?**

You will need to read efficiently and effectively, because you will be charging for your work, and the client will not want to pay too much, and your employer will (in most cases) want to make a profit. You can expect to have to work to a deadline. The techniques in this chapter certainly will make your reading of primary sources more efficient and effective, and you will have also learned how to assimilate and summarise information quickly. Practice will polish this skill, so practise reading and summarising as much as possible, be it newspaper articles, fiction, or the articles in your reading lists. Students like highlighting, but beware highlighting everything just to prove to yourself that you have read something (even though you might not be able to recall doing so). Instead, enjoy experimenting with different techniques, such as summarising each page or section, or distilling each article or primary source you read into three key points (see, for example, Figure 7.5) to develop your ability to read, retain, and com- municate the material you have read. There are also techniques that can help you to speed up your reading (see Levy, Further Reading). With practice, you might be able to skim-read down the middle of the page, and 'read in' the surrounding areas using your peripheral vision; or look for key words. In providing preparatory questions on your reading, your lecturer will have given you some helpful key words for an initial skim-read. Technology might also help you; ask Siri to read electronic articles to you, or use your device's accessibility features, such as Microsoft's Learning Tools, if you are experiencing reading fatigue (see articles by Barbosa and Microsoft, in Further Reading). Lawyers read, and they read a lot, so ask your lecturer and your learning community now what works for them, research effective reading techniques, and enjoy experimenting now how to hone this skill.

Summary

- Reading law requires a structured approach.
- The primary sources of law are a statute, a statutory instrument, and a case.
- There are practical steps you can take to enhance your reading skills.
- Do not read a statute from beginning to end, but navigate the statute to find the relevant law.
- Before you read judgments in a case, make sure you have a good understanding of the basic facts.
- Bring to life your reading of cases by watching them, in person or online.

Practical exercises

Consider how you would answer the following questions.

1. What was your experience of reading (online) the judgments in the *Donoghue* v *Stevenson* case? If you lost focus, consider why you did and what you might be able to do differently next time to read them more effectively.

2. Compare and contrast your experience of reading (online) the judgment in *Donoghue* v *Stevenson* with the *R (Miller)* v *The Prime Minister*. What, specifically, did you note about the new (post-2002) reporting structure? Which do you prefer, and why? How did the accompanying recordings of the hearing, and summary, inform your reading of *Miller*?

3. How would you describe what (i) a statute and (ii) a case look like in terms of structure and layout?

4. Can you summarise the guidance in this chapter into three tips you would give to someone about to read (i) a statute and (ii) a case for the first time?

5. Use Figure 7.5 to prepare a case note for *R (Miller)* v *The Prime Minister*, the case you were recommended to read at 7.1.5.2. Reflect on which parts of the case were most difficult to summarise. Which secondary source did you choose to read, to clarify your understanding of the *ratio decidendi*?

6. Read Coleman's article for BBC News, and listen to his broadcast for Radio 4 if available to you (both about *Donoghue* v *Stevenson*) and read the Ashurst article (about the UCTA), all of which are referred to in the Further Reading section. Reflect on the audiences for whom these written and oral communications were made. How would the authors' reading and understanding of the primary sources of law have differed from (a) a law student's and (b) a lawyer in practice needing to advise a client on these primary sources of law?

 *Visit the **online resources** for the authors' reflections and to check your progress.*

What the professionals say

No-one finds reading a case for the first time an easy task. The key is to approach your reading in an analytical way, looking beyond the particular facts of the case and identifying the principles of law that are being discussed. Visiting court to see how practising lawyers deploy their research and apply legal principle to argue their client's case can really help you to understand what you are aiming to achieve from your reading. Putting these observed skills into practice during a moot will help you further in identifying the principle rather than unnecessary detail. Then read, read, and read some more. It will get easier. The hard work put in at this stage will equip you with a range of analytical skills which will prove invaluable wherever your career may take you.

Katherine Pierpoint, Criminal Barrister, Lincoln House Chambers, Manchester

Further reading

Ashurst.com (2019) *Quickguide: Limitation and exclusion of liability*. Available at: https://www.ashurst.com/en/news-and-insights/legal-updates/quickguide-limitation-and-exclusion-of-liability/
—A practical guide written by law firm Ashurst and published on its website. The guide sets out the principles to be considered when drafting limitation and exclusion of liability clauses (in non-contentious work) or analysing them in a dispute (in contentious work). This illustrates why you might need to read and understand the statute in Figure 7.1 (the UCTA) in practice, including draft guidance notes on it. It also illustrates the depth in which you need to understand it, in order to communicate it clearly, in detail and with practical application. As is common practice, you can subscribe to this (and other) law firm websites, to receive regular developments, updates, and news. You are encouraged to do so, as this will give you essential practice-focused context for your reading and understanding of law.

Barbosa, G. 'How to get Siri to read articles to you on ios', Available at:
https://9to5mac.com/2017/03/10/how-to-get-siri-to-read-articles-to-you-on-ios-macos/
—As you increasingly access your reading electronically, this articles sets out one way to relieve reading fatigue, and allow you to work more flexibly (even during your commute using only your iPhone), by letting Siri read to you.

British and Irish Legal Information Institute (BAILII). Available at: http://www.bailii.org
—A good source for case transcripts.

Cardiff Index to Legal Abbreviation. Available at: http://www.legalabbrevs.cardiff.ac.uk
—An online index of the abbreviations used in citations to refer to law reports.

Coleman, C. (2019) *The legal case of the snail found in ginger beer*. Available at:
http://news.bbc.co.uk/1/hi/business/8367223.stm.
—A BBC news feature summarising *Donoghue* v *Stevenson* for reading for interest by a general readership. If your school subscribes to Box of Broadcasts, you can also listen to the Coleman's accompanying broadcast here, **The Cases That Changed Our World, 05:45 29/11/2009, BBC Radio 4, 15 mins. https://learningonscreen.ac.uk/ondemand/index.php/prog/01276CCB?bcast=37685862**.

EUR-Lex. Available at: http://eur-lex.europa.eu/en/index.htm
—A good source of European legislation.

Europa. Available at: http://europa.eu/eu-law/index_en.htm
—General information on EU law.

Georgiadis, P., McCormick, M., Rutter Pooley, C., and Samson, A. (2019) Brexit chaos deepens after Supreme Court rules against Boris Johnson's prorogation of parliament—as it happened, *Financial Times*. Ft.com. Available at: https://www.ft.com/content/c1ae7f0c-8bca-39b5-91a5-02a1a9494732.
—The FT's coverage of The Supreme Court's judgment in *Miller*, as it happened.

The Law Society (2019) *Becoming a solicitor*. Available at: https://www.lawsociety.org.uk/law-careers/becoming-a-solicitor.
—This page on The Law Society's website provides helpful context to inform your understanding of how the skills you learn during your studies will be relevant in practice. In particular it outlines the difference between contentious and non-contentious work, and what solicitors do on a daily basis.

Levy, J. (2016) *Three Steps to Becoming a Faster Reader*. Time. Available at: https://time.com/4484634/speed-reading-tips/.
—An article discussing strategies to improve your reading speed.

Masson, J. 'Dicta . . . dictators and law'. Available at:
https://legalresearch.blogs.bris.ac.uk/2017/02/dicta-dictators-and-law/#more-511
—A short article from the University of Bristol Law School Blog, exploring the effect, in the family courts, of lawyers citing *obiter dicta*.

Microsoft (2019) *Improve Reading & Writing—Microsoft Education*. Available at:
https://www.microsoft.com/en-gb/education/products/learning-tools.
—Information about Learning Tools accessibility features in Microsoft Word, Edge, and Outlook, including features that reduce visual crowding, highlight text, break words into syllables, read text aloud, and provide visual references.

OUP online resources (2019) *Blackstone's Statutes Series. Video: A Guide to Reading and Interpreting Statutes*. Available at: https://oup-arc.com/access/content/statutes-resources/statutes-video-a-guide-to-reading-and-interpreting-statutes.
—A video by Mr Justice Sales, High Court Judge and Member of The Statute Law Society Council providing guidance about reading and interpreting statutes.

Paterson, A. (2013) *Final Judgment: The Last Law Lords and the Supreme Court*. Oxford: Hart Publishing
—A readable insight into the workings of the House of Lords during its final decade and into the formative years of the Supreme Court.

Sleigh, S. (2019) *Lady Hale's spider brooch causes a stir on social media*. Evening Standard. Available at: https://www.standard.co.uk/news/politics/lady-hales-causes-a-stir-as-she-wears-giant-spider-brooch-to-hand-down-supreme-court-ruling-a4245041.html
—One of a flurry of articles to discuss Lady Hale and the brooch she chose to wear while handing down her judgment in *Miller*.

Supreme Court website. Available at: https://www.supremecourt.uk
—For transcripts of Supreme Court judgments since August 2009, and recordings of current and decided hearings, and summaries of some of the judgments, since 2019. (For judgments handed down before 31 July 2009, transcripts are available on the House of Lords (https://publications.parliament.uk/pa/ld/ldjudgmt.htm) or BAILII (http://www.bailii.org/uk/cases/UKSC/) websites.)

*For the authors' reflections on the practical exercises, additional self-test questions, sample interview questions and a library of links to useful websites, visit the free **online resources** at www.oup.com/he/slorach4e.*

8 Research

Learning objectives

After studying this chapter you should be able to:

- Analyse what your research task is and why you are being asked to undertake it.
- Describe different types of sources and appreciate when they might be useful (or not).
- Explain the main features of primary and secondary sources of law.
- Follow an appropriate legal research strategy.
- Apply appropriate techniques to ensure that sources are up to date, and relevant.
- Record and report effectively on the process and results of your legal research.

Introduction

All lawyers need good legal research skills. Your research provides the content you need to produce high quality written work (such as essays, dissertations, and providing answers to problem questions) and oral communication (such as mooting, negotiating, presenting, or client interviewing). For lawyers in practice, the skills are a fundamental requirement to advise clients and solve their problems. In both cases, the skill is much more than simply 'finding and citing the law'.

For that reason, much of the content of this chapter is relevant to both academia and practice. We give you an effective legal research strategy (Figure 8.1), and guidance on it (8.1.1–8.1.12), to help you succeed with your research. 8.2 then discusses how you might use legal research specifically for practice. While we hope the signposting is helpful, we do encourage you to read the entire chapter, to gain a useful overview of the topic, and the difference between (but, overall, the striking similarity in) how you might use this skill to good effect in academia and in practice.

Our aim in writing this chapter is to help you with the 'what', 'why', and 'how' of legal research. You will learn the importance of identifying precisely what is being asked of you in terms of research, the purpose of your research, and, crucially, our research strategy guidance will give you all you need to make a start and complete the task with confidence. Chapter 7 provides further detail about where to find UK case law and legislation, and EU law. To compliment this, we encourage you to engage with your law librarian, and the training they and your faculty will deliver. They will provide you with comprehensive guidance on the specific content and location of the various and numerous sources of law (see Chapter 2), and how to access them.

Since the first edition of the book, electronic databases and sources have become more widely available to students and practitioners alike. While they provide many advantages over traditional paper resources in physical libraries, you need to learn to use them discerningly and with skill and care and we include information and guidance to help you with this.

8.1 Legal research

Students report as a common problem not understanding what a task is expecting of them, which results in the frustrating feeling of simply not knowing how to begin research. In response, we have developed a flowchart at Figure 8.1 which provides a strategy to take you from beginning to end of the legal research process. It will help you begin, and it will help to give you confidence that the answer you have found is likely to be correct (avoiding another common research-induced worry). It summarises the essential steps for conducting effective and efficient legal research and we will examine how to use each component part of it in 8.1.1 to 8.1.12. When you read Chapter 9 you will see that this legal research strategy is incorporated into Figure 9.1, to create a comprehensive problem-solving strategy, with worked examples, so make sure you read both chapters.

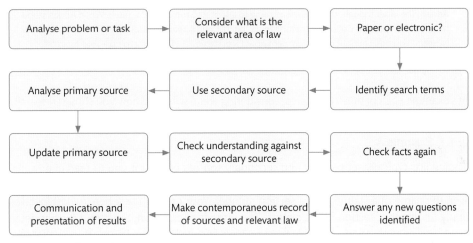

Figure 8.1 Legal research strategy

8.1.1 Analyse problem or task

It is tempting to embark prematurely on finding the law, just to feel relief at actually having made a start. This is not a good idea. You risk wasting time in taking notes, printing and reading law which is wholly irrelevant to your research task. Once you have taken this route, it can be quite difficult to go back and start afresh. Now that you have the strategy (Figure 8.1), you can enjoy a better start, with the comfort of having a clear idea of *what* you are looking for, *why*, and *how* you are going to find what you need. So, however tempting it may be, delay your search for the relevant law until you have first analysed effectively your problem or task.

Effective analysis will always involve considering *what* the task or problem is expecting you to research, the purpose (*why*) of your research, and that in turn will affect *how* you research, including the sources you first consult, and what you will do with your findings. One variable is your level of knowledge: how well you know the law in an area, and the specific sources of that law, will differ between research tasks.

A helpful way to illustrate this is to consider some examples of legal research tasks and problems you may encounter as a student. Useful background information follows. All of them require some research into s. 4 of the Public Order Act 1986. You will remember from Chapter 7 that legislation (statutes and statutory instruments) is a primary source of law (case law being the other primary source of law). Section 4 of this statute deals with the specific offence of causing fear or provocation of violence.

Example 1

A. Your criminal law reading list states: 'Read section 4 Public Order Act 1986'.

B. You are given the following essay question: 'There is an overlap between the types of conduct required for offences under section 91 Criminal Justice Act 1967, and sections 4, 4A and 5 Public Order Act 1986. Discuss.'

C. You are given the following problem question: 'Adrian is working as a steward at a football match. At the end of the match, Colin, a supporter of the losing side, ran down the steps of the stand towards Adrian. The latter thought that Colin was going to attempt to run on to the pitch. When Adrian stood his ground, to prevent Colin from getting to the pitch, Colin screamed abuse at Adrian, including the words: 'if you don't get out of my way right now, I'll make you . . . I'm going to take your head off . . .'. Adrian wants Colin arrested. Advise Adrian.

Let's examine each of these examples, considering *what*, *why*, and *how* you should research.

8.1.1.1 Example A

Reading lists typically set primary and secondary sources of law for you to read in advance of class contact. Some may be marked optional and some compulsory. Here, you have been given the name of a statute, and a section number. Your research task here (*what*) involves simply finding that section of the statute. The intended result (*why*)—without further detail about facts or application—is simply that you have *knowledge* of the law created by that section. You need to look up the legislation (see Chapter 7) and most likely, you will either print, screenshot, or photocopy the section, or otherwise make a note of its provisions, so you can discuss it in the related criminal class.

8.1.1.2 Example B

Here, as in Example A, you are given the name and section of the legislation you need, so your first research task (*what*) is to find these statutes (primary sources of law). Again, you will print, screenshot, photocopy, or make notes of the relevant provisions. However, the intended result (*why*) is not simply for you to have *knowledge* of the law. In your legal essay you will need to practise meeting your school's stated assessment criteria. They will differ between schools, but are likely to include not only *knowledge* of what the law is, but also other criteria, often featuring *communication*, *structure*, *sources*, *application*, and *analysis*. So, you will also need to undertake research at a level which will enable you to evidence that your essay meets these criteria at the grade band you are aiming for (e.g. first class). To meet the *application* and *analysis* criteria you will need to show your wider understanding of the purpose and effect of the law, and be able to discuss and analyse the law critically. Critical analysis involves showing that you understand, have thought about, and have your own view on any discussion, arguments, and counter-argument about how the law has developed, been interpreted, and applied (see 14.1).

So, considering the *how*, Example B requires you to research:

(a) what is the law (*primary source*: legislation); but also

(b) how has the law developed, been interpreted and applied (by reading *secondary source commentary* on the law, e.g. textbooks, encyclopaedias, journal articles, practitioner texts, parliamentary debate), focusing on the areas of overlap mentioned in the question; and

(c) what have been the views, arguments, and counter-arguments of academics and other experts on (b), and are there calls for reform (*secondary source opinion* on the law, e.g. as above).

To develop and demonstrate a broader understanding, you might also wish to research:

(d) sources *relating to* the law (e.g. official and 'think tank' reports, trustworthy websites (see 8.1.5.5), law firm publications). Finding and citing some data about how the law has been applied, such as statisics on the number of convictions for each of the offences created under each of the sections, could further support your argument and help your essay meet the higher grade descriptors for *analysis and sources*, such as demonstrating 'unique argument' or 'highly independent research'.

8.1.1.3 Example C

The problem analysis required here is set out in more detail in Chapter 9, which deals specifically with problem-solving. It involves the I (issue) of the IRAC model (see Figure 9.1):

Parties:	Adrian and Colin. We are advising Adrian.
What is your task?	Advise Adrian if Colin can be arrested
Relevant facts:	Adrian: A steward at a football match; stood his ground when Colin ran at him down steps; thought Colin was going to attempt to run on to the pitch; abusively screamed at by Colin.
	Colin: supporter of losing side at same match; ran down steps towards Adrian; impeded by Adrian; screamed abuse at Adrian, including 'if you don't get out of my way right now, I'll make you . . . I'm going to take your head off . . .'.
Missing facts:	How did Adrian feel and why? How did Colin feel and why? Where was Colin going and why? What happened just before/after the incident? Why was he running? What else did he say? Are there witnesses? Will they agree the facts above are correct? What reason does Colin say explains his actions? Was anyone else involved?
Parties' objectives:	Adrian wants Colin arrested. Colin presumably disagrees.
Legal issues raised:	Do Colin's actions above amount to an arrestable offence?

This analysis will help clarify that you need to find, analyse, and apply the relevant law to determine whether Colin's actions amount to an arrestable offence (*what*) because you are advising Adrian and his objective is to have Colin arrested (*why*). As to *how*, you can go on to identify the relevant area of law (public order offences) and apply a series of search terms (see 8.1.4) within which to research (e.g. public; order; threats; words; abuse; arrest). Then, within that area, you can use secondary sources to both (i) identify the relevant primary sources of the law that cover the offence in question (the R (rule) in IRAC), and (ii) understand how the law applies to the facts (see 9.1.3), and any differing views about this (the A (application) in IRAC). Only then should you proceed to read the primary source, armed with the benefit of having read the secondary source description of how it works, in order to advise Adrian (the C (conclusion) in IRAC).

Depending on the particular issues posed by the problem, you might then consider additional sources, if relevant on the facts.

8.1.1.4 Sources of law

If we summarise the various types of sources which featured in the examples, we can see that, depending on the research task, you will be looking for sources which provide:

- the relevant law (*primary source*: legislation and case law);
- commentary on the relevant law (*secondary source*—e.g. textbooks, encyclopaedias, journal articles, practitioner texts, parliamentary debate);
- opinion on the relevant law (*secondary source*—e.g. as above); and
- 'non-legal' material relating to the relevant law (*secondary source*—e.g. official and 'think tank' reports, *trustworthy* websites (see 8.1.5.5), law firm publications).

These sources can be in paper format or electronic format (see 8.1.3) and further information is provided at 8.1.5 (secondary sources) and 8.1.6 (primary sources).

8.1.2 Consider what is relevant area of law

This refers to the good practice of identifying and naming, for your own clarity, the broad relevant area of law that your analysis of the task or problem has revealed. It could be 'public order offences', or 'sale of goods', or 'directors' duties'.

In Examples A and B, note that you were given details of the primary source of law. Example C differs in that you were not given any details of the source. (The essay at Example B could have been set without specific reference to the sections, perhaps referring more broadly to 'public order offences'. In this case, you would first have had to identify the primary source of law, as with Example C.) You might, however still know that the relevant area of law is 'public order offences', perhaps because the problem (or task) was set at the time of teaching on public order offences or, if part of an assessment on criminal law, through having revised the subject. If so, you at least know the relevant area of law (public order offences) within which to narrow down your search to find the specific source of the offence in question. If not, then you have neither knowledge of the relevant area of law, nor the source of that law.

8.1.3 **Paper or electronic?**

The trend in academia, as with practice, is towards favouring electronic sources and data-bases to conduct research. University libraries remain popular; it is what students are doing in the library (using the library computers and Wi-Fi to access electronic, rather than paper, resources) that has changed. Increasingly, students are digital natives, accustomed to and adept at using technology to find information in daily life. This is both an advantage (you already have digital skills) and a disadvantage (you have easy access to many sources which fail to meet the high standard of accuracy and reliability required for legal research). While in your daily life it is advisable, in your legal research it is essential to pay attention to the quality of your sources. During your studies, you must ensure your sources have academic credibility and are of a suitable standard. As you will read in Chapter 14, for example, lecturers tend to expect you to cite a rich mix of primary and secondary sources in an essay or dissertation, including academic journal articles. If you are selecting an authority to support an argument in court, then you would still follow your strategy to read a secondary source before the pri-mary source to inform your own understanding of the primary source, and to identify it in advance. However in the majority of cases, in court itself you would be citing just the primary source and not, for example, any textbook or academic journal even if they have informed your understanding of that primary source.

8.1.3.1 Electronic sources

How, then, do you know which electronic sources are appropriate and have enough academic credibility to use during your studies? On the one hand, it is safe to say that you should not be relying on a Google search result, Wikipedia, a student essay-writing site (which, aside from accuracy issues, also raise serious issues of plagiarism—see 14.1.7), or a tabloid newspaper to prove facts, however helpful and supportive of your legal argument they may appear to be, and however easy they are to find. On the other hand, there are some excellent, authoritative electronic sources, such as the electronic version of Halsbury's Laws of England ('Halsbury's Laws') (see 8.1.5.1). Between the two lies a greyer area, of websites (see 8.1.5.5), news reports, and other electronically available information, which will require you to apply your common sense as to the likely factual accuracy of the information they contain, and whether and how you might use them in your research. If in doubt (and you will be while you gain experience), ask your law librarian or lecturer their opinion about the appropriateness of citing a source.

The aforementioned are all electronic *sources*. A distinction should be drawn between electronic *sources* and electronic *databases*.

8.1.3.2 Electronic databases

An electronic database is in effect a library, just not a physical one. It is not a source of law; you should not put it in your source list; you would reference it as a database that you used to find your sources. An electronic source is something which you would find in an electronic library (database) and would feature in your source list. There are numerous electronic data-bases, and we do not seek here to list them all. However, there are two which generally will be useful for you to locate secondary and/or primary sources while following our research strategy, whatever your subject, and they are Westlaw UK and Lexis®Library. The providers of these databases update them regularly, not only as to the law, but also with new features and functionality. The Westlaw UK database has undergone a comprehensive update relatively recently to include a more modern interface, enhanced search facilities, and a more seamless interface with the Practical Law electronic database (both are owned by Thomson Reuters).

For this reason, we do not think it will be helpful to include detailed user guides for these databases in our textbook, because they will update, as an electronic source, before we do, as a paper source. It is, however, important that you learn how to use these main databases, and we encourage you to familiarise yourself with the excellent and comprehensive user guides (including videos), FAQ sheets, and online training, which the main database providers produce and update, including to the point of certification, together with attending the regular training on them which will be offered by your law librarian. Links to the user guides of Lexis®Library, Practical Law, and Westlaw UK are all provided in Further Reading, as are links to the information about certification from Lexis®Library and Westlaw UK.

The advantages of using electronic databases rather than visiting a physical library are numerous: they are updated more regularly; provide you with more flexibility as to the time and place that you conduct your research; you can screenshot your findings and collate your contemporaneous note without having to photocopy lots of pages; and you can delete your notes without the guilt of throwing away lots of paper if what you have found happens not to be relevant in the end. Some databases also allow you to collate content into your own personalised collection. For example, Lexis®Library allows you to 'customise your bookshelf', and Westlaw UK to 'personalise your folders', as explained in their respective user guides (see Further Reading). However, our experience is that students must learn to use them with care as they are not without their disadvantages. However subconsciously, students seem disinclined from 'reading around' the subject, restricting themselves instead to reading just what is on the screen, and not what comes before or after, nor reading footnotes and annotations in the same way as they seem to be inclined to do with paper sources in a physical library. It is possible quite easily to find yourself with too many browser tabs open at the same time, or losing track of how you reached the point you have. Particular skills are needed (we give you them at 8.1.4) to find search terms that are effective, and neither too narrow, so excluding relevant sources, nor too wide, so returning more hits than is manageable. It can feel to some like an isolating way of working, compared to the camaraderie of being in a physical library. The temptation to dispense with a decent legal database and just use Google instead also appears to be strong. As is the distraction of social media, while online. As with all skills, practice and making and learning from mistakes, will help you succeed, and so we are encouraging you to make an appointment with your law librarian sooner rather than later to iron out any specific issues you may be facing. Law librarians are a valuable resource and, in the authors' experience, without exception extremely knowledgeable, approachable, and happy to help. Feel reassured, they have seen and heard it all before. So do not wait until you have an assessment involving research looming, because they are likely to be embargoed from helping you at that stage, in the interests of fair assessment.

The guidance below continues to include reference to paper resources (for reasons made clear by the author in her answer to a thought-provoking question at the end of this chapter). It also includes some information on Westlaw UK and Lexis®Library, including how to use them to update your primary sources (see 8.1.7). Ask your lecturer which other electronic databases they might recommend. For example, for business law, Practical Law is an excellent database to find clearly written explanations of law and practice, and while originally intended for practice, universities are increasingly subscribing because of the quality, clarity, and depth of the content, and its compatibility with Westlaw UK (see Further Reading).

8.1.4 Identify search terms

As illustrated in Example C, you need to consider which search terms will best assist you to find the relevant law. Search terms should be key words relevant to the issues of law you are seeking to research. The wording of a question or facts of a problem will help you to identify some of these key words. You should then use these key words to search in the search engine of a legal database (for electronic resources), or in an index (for paper resources), using the following techniques to narrow your results.

Example 2

Consider a problem where you are asked to advise someone who has bought a domestic washing machine about their rights. The door seal of the appliance was faulty and the buyer's kitchen flooded. As a result, the buyer has had to replace two adjoining kitchen units, the bases of which had become saturated with the water from the washing machine. The appliance had been sold on the basis of a standard form contract, which included a term purporting to exclude any liability for damage other than to the appliance itself.

Examples of search terms which will help are:

- Sale
- Goods
- Consumer
- Faulty
- Liability
- Exclusion
- Rights
- Remedies

You may be able to think of others. Be prepared to try variations of your original search terms if they prove fruitless. For example, if 'faulty' does not return any helpful material, try 'poor quality', 'defective', 'unsatisfactory quality', and so on.

The following techniques will improve the effectiveness of your search of electronic resources to help you to reduce your results to a manageable number without missing anything important.

8.1.4.1 Truncation

Typing 'excluding' into a search engine will only find examples of that particular word. It will not look for 'exclude' or 'exclusion'. For example, if a leading case on excluding liability did not actually include the word 'excluding' at all, but referred throughout to 'exclusion', using phrases such as 'exclusion of liability', 'exclusion clauses' and so on, then your search using the term 'excluding' would not find this case at all. A search with a truncated word is better because it will extend your search to find all permutations of that word. The technique will vary from database to database; however, a common way is to type 'exclu*', or 'exclu!'. The following further examples demonstrate how truncating search terms can keep open your search options:

- pollution (Pollut*—finds pollute, pollutes, pollution, polluting, and pollutants);
- penalties (Penalt*—finds penalty and penalties);
- taxation (Tax*—finds tax, taxes, taxation);
- infestation (Infest*—finds infest, infests, infestation);
- injury (Injur*—finds injury, injuries).

8.1.4.2 Wild card characters

Wild card characters work within a word just as truncation works at the end of a word. For example, 'm*n' would search for both 'men' and 'man'. They can be useful for searches where there may be alternative spellings or missing letters, for example recognise/recognize (search 'recogni*e') or colour/color (search 'col*r').

8.1.4.3 Connectors

The words 'and', 'or', and 'not' are such common words that they are not useful as search terms. Electronic databases recognise this, and generally will not use them as search terms but will instead take them to be commands as follows:

- Joining two search terms with:
  - 'and' will retrieve results only where both words appear;
  - 'or' will produce results where either of the search terms appear.
- Using 'not' will exclude results in which the search term appears.

8.1.4.4 Phrase searching

If you consider that a source will likely use words in a phrase (such as 'sale of goods' or 'exclusion clause'), then you should search for that phrase. The most common technique is to put the phrase in quotation marks, so, for example, you would search for 'exclusion clause' rather than search for 'exclusion' and 'clause'. Using this guidance, we might refine our search terms from Example 2 as follows:

- 'Sale of Goods' and Fault*
- 'Consumer rights'
- Limit* and liability
- Exclu* and liability
- 'Exclusion clause'
- Remed* and 'sale of goods'

8.1.5 **Use secondary source**

'Secondary sources' of law are so-called because they are not the original, primary source of the law (that is, legislation—statute and statutory instrument—and case law). Secondary sources of law provide commentary or opinion on the primary sources of law. This is useful in two ways. First, the secondary source should identify the primary source(s) of the relevant law. Second, the secondary source should help to give you an initial understanding of the primary source, how it applies (see 9.1.3) and any differing views about this, and hence its relevance to your particular task.

The legal research strategy in Figure 8.1 uses a **funnel approach**. This involves casting a wide net to begin with by *first* reading a secondary source overview of the area of law in question. Beginning with a secondary source is valuable even if you have been directed to the relevant primary source of law (as in Examples A and B (see 8.1.1)), because of the information it provides about *application* and *analysis*. If you have not been directed to the relevant primary source of law (as in Example C (see 8.1.1)), then a secondary source will of course identify it for you much more effectively, however hopeful you may be of success using a random Google search (which is just as likely to find American law/old law/completely fictitious law . . . all of which, unhelpfully for you, are readily available electronically).

For more common legal issues, students like to research using their undergraduate textbooks (which are secondary sources of law). However, bear in mind that the law described in a textbook will only be up to date as at the publication date of the textbook. The moment a textbook is published, it risks being out of date. If the legal issue you need to research is not common and is quite niche, there may not even be a textbook which covers the issue. For these reasons, whether used alone, or in conjunction with a textbook, we encourage you to start your research with *Halsbury's Laws* (see 8.1.5.1), a legal encyclopaedia, and a secondary source of law, because it avoids both of these potential disadvantages of relying on your textbook.

8.1.5.1 **Halsbury's Laws**

This is a really useful secondary source to use to begin your research. It differs from most other legal encyclopaedias in the comprehensive nature of its commentary on the law of England & Wales. It is available as an electronic source (using the Lexis®Library electronic database) and a paper source. Using the electronic version has definite advantages in terms of updating the law. However, the disadvantages outlined at 8.1.3 also apply, particularly that you may feel less inclined to read around a subject when accessing it electronically, sticking to the screenshots returned in your results and not realising you can click on footnotes or annotations to read them. Beginning with the electronic version and then cross checking your answer in the paper version will help to give you confidence that consistently your research is returning the same answer and that you have found all that is relevant. How you can access both the paper and electronic version is explained below.

Access Halsbury's Laws *as an electronic source*

You can access *Halsbury's Laws* (reminder: a secondary source) through Lexis®Library (reminder: an electronic database) where it is listed as a source. The following steps will help to familiarise yourself with this source, and you are encouraged to watch the tutorial on Lexis®Library (see Further Reading).

1. You can choose to search across the entire encyclopaedia, or within specific parts of it, such as one volume, depending on how familiar you are with the legal issue you are researching.

2. Input your search terms to return a list of results. You can select to sort this list by source order (the default) or by relevance.

3. If your search returns too many hits, you may need to refine your search terms further.

4. Clicking into one item on the list will display a numbered paragraph of *Halsbury's Laws*.

5. When you read the paragraph, it will provide a commentary on the law, and there are likely to be lots of footnotes. It is essential to read these footnotes, which can contain key detail (for example, about the primary sources of law). You must remember to click on the 'footnotes' button to reveal this essential material.

6. You must also click on the UPDATE button, towards the bottom of the page, to check if there has been any change to the law since the volume you have read was published (this button is the electronic equivalent of both the *Cumulative Supplement* and the *Noter Up* in the paper version of *Halsbury's*).

Access Halsbury's Laws *as a paper source*

The electronic version has significant advantages in terms of updating. However, it can be very helpful to familiarise yourself with the paper version, to help you to understand exactly what you are seeing when you use the electronic version (for example, a volume, or a paragraph within a volume, of an encyclopaedia). Again, the following steps will help familiarise you with the paper source, but you are encouraged to read the Lexis®Library *Halsbury's Laws* user guide for the paper source (see Further Reading).

1. You should search against the broad legal context in the index to find the volume, edition, and paragraph number.

2. You will then read the paragraph, and the footnotes (which are more obvious in the paper version, being on the page without you needing to remember to reveal them).

3. You then need to consult the *Cumulative Supplement* to check if there has been any change to the law since the volume you have read was published. The *Cumulative Supplement* cross-refers to the volume you have just read. It will note any changes that have been made to any paragraphs of that volume. If there have been no changes, there will be no listing in the *Cumulative Supplement*, so do not worry if there is no update for the paragraph you have read.

4. Finally, you should check the *Noter Up*, again by volume then paragraph, for any changes to the law since the *Cumulative Supplement* was published.

In addition to an undergraduate academic textbook or *Halsbury's Laws*, which can provide a good starting point when researching a particular area of law, you should also consider the following secondary sources.

8.1.5.2 Journal articles

Legal journals are a valuable secondary source of opinion on the law. They are an excellent resource when carrying out research for a legal essay or dissertation. They are published by academic schools and commercial publishers on a periodic basis. Many are also available in electronic form. They may be general in nature, such as the *Law Quarterly Review*, or more specialised, such as the *Journal of International Banking Law & Regulation*. Depending on its target readership, a journal may adopt an academic or more practical approach to the law. Journals may also provide a source of commentary on the law. Westlaw UK (reminder: electronic database) has the best coverage of full text and abstracted legal journal articles in the UK.

8.1.5.3 Encyclopaedias

You should consider consulting this type of secondary source for detailed explanation of and commentary on the law. As discussed, *Halsbury's Laws* is in the form of an encyclopaedia. It differs from most other legal encyclopaedias in the comprehensive nature of its contents: commentary on the law of England & Wales. Other encyclopaedias tend to focus on a single area of law: for example, Sweet & Maxwell publishes encyclopaedias on employment law and competition law which are updated periodically throughout the year. Although a secondary source, some may also include relevant primary legal materials. Given their depth, they are often compiled and kept up to date by a team of authors and editors, which may include both academics and practitioners, providing a rounded and detailed explanation of the law in an area.

8.1.5.4 Practitioner texts

These secondary source texts provide guidance, explanation, and commentary on how the law in a particular area is applied in practice. Commonly used by practitioners (as the description suggests), they can also be a very useful resource when dealing with problem-solving questions. Practitioner texts may vary in depth and complexity: some may resemble encyclopaedias (e.g. Butterworth's Property Law Service), while others may be in a handbook (e.g. The Family Court Practice (Red Book)) or electronic format (e.g. articles on Practical Law or the Lexis®PSL service). Depending on the subject matter in question, practitioner texts may also include guidance on legal procedures, such as court actions and company administration matters.

8.1.5.5 Websites

Certain websites are very good for finding and reading primary and secondary sources of law. Examples of government websites which give access to law, commentary, and guidance are provided in Table 8.1. Outside the government websites, there are a host of other sources of legal material, and other material that might be useful to support legal analysis, including websites and blogs hosted by law firms, practitioner groups, and interest or campaigning groups (examples are also included in Table 8.1).

Table 8.1 Examples of government and other websites providing legal material and material to support legal analysis

Website type	Website address	Description
Government	http://www.legislation.gov.uk	Provides access to UK legislation, some of it dating back to 1267, with the ability to track new UK legislation.
	https://www.gov.uk/government/organisations/hm-revenue-customs	HMRC. Provides information on revenue law.
	https://www.gov.uk/government/organisations/companies-house	Companies House. Provides information about company formation and administration.
	https://www.gov.uk/government/organisations/department-for-business-energy-and-industrial-strategy	BEIS. Provides a range of guidance on business law and employment.
	http://www.cps.gov.uk	Crown Prosecution Service. Provides a range of legal resources, including guidance on the application of a number of criminal statutes. You can also find data on prosecutions on this website, an example of material which is not law but which you might use in an essay to support your analysis.
Practitioner group	http://www.step.org	The Society of Trust and Estate Practitioners. Provides various publications including a series of leaflets explaining wills and trusts matters to the public.
Law firm	https://www.cliffordchance.com/insights.html	Clifford Chance Insight. Shares knowledge and expertise through briefings, blogs, podcasts, and events.
Interest group	https://www.citizensadvice.org.uk/	Citizen's Advice Bureau. Information on a range of topics including consumer rights, debt, housing, family, law and the court system, and work. Includes policy publications in areas including pensions and domestic abuse.
Campaigning groups	https://www.amnesty.org.uk/	Amnesty International UK. Includes information about campaigns such as free speech and children's rights.
	https://thecircle.ngo/about/	The Circle. Founded by Annie Lennox in 2008, an organisation of women working together to achieve equality. Includes the lawyers' circle, whose campaigns include a living wage for garment workers.

It is very important to understand that, while websites can be a rich source of material, you should use them with care. It is, generally, neither good practice nor efficient to rely on general internet search engines such as Google for legal research. You should have a rationale—being clear as to what particular type of material you are searching for—before searching. You should also consider the reliability of any website: is it a trustworthy, up-to-date reference source which has academic credibility, and which is reliable (see 8.1.3)? As mentioned, websites hosting American law, old law, and even completely fictitious law are all readily accessible from a Google search. Government websites and those belonging to major and well-respected organisations are likely to be more reliable, but it is still advisable to cross-check against legal sources the law you find referred to in these sources. In other words, if you start your research using Google, check what you find by using your trusted legal research strategy set out at Figure 8.1. Then, when it comes to reporting any research, refer to those legal sources instead of any Google search (which you would not mention at all). This is explained further under 'research trail' at Figure 8.2.

8.1.6 **Analyse primary source**

As explained in Chapter 2, the original source of law will be legislation and/or case law. These are referred to as 'primary sources' of law. Reading a secondary source first will help you both to identify and understand the primary source. However, if you are to develop both your general skills as a lawyer and your specific research skills, you should not rely solely on secondary sources. To be a good lawyer you must develop the confidence and the skills to read and interpret the primary source of law. It is very obvious to an experienced lecturer if you are writing abut law that you have not actually read. Similarly, they will spot quite easily if you use someone else's language from a secondary source (and see also plagiarism at 14.1.7).

You will find *legislation* in a variety of sources including *Halsbury's Statutes* and *UK Parliament Acts*, which you can find using electronic databases including Westlaw UK, and Lexis®Library. *Case law* is found by undertaking a case search, using sources such as *Current Law Case Citator*, which again you can access using electronic databases. See 7.1.6 for where to find European Union law. Guidance on finding current legislation and case law is set out at 8.1.7.

To a new user, these sources can feel impenetrable. Wording may appear complex, definitions from one section of a statute have to be 'read in' to other sections, and there is no denying that many pieces of legislation are long. Attempting to read a statute or even a part of a statute in its entirety will be difficult. That is why we recommend reading a secondary source overview first, and it is also why we have provided guidance in Chapter 7 on how to read primary sources. When you follow that guidance, you will find you are able to read the law more effectively, and the entire process is significantly easier, than you first imagined. Before you read any statute, statutory instrument, or case law, make sure the relevant pages of Chapter 7 are open in front of you to help you.

It is not uncommon for students to struggle to understand the meaning of the term 'relevant' law, particularly when researching case law. When looking for relevant case law, you are looking first and foremost for cases which feature the same *legal principles* which you think are relevant to your task. Many students will search only for cases with the same, or strikingly similar, *facts* as the problem they have been asked to research. Although any such cases with similar facts are likely to be relevant and helpful, in practice you are unlikely always to find a case which is factually similar to the legal problem you are researching.

To illustrate what we mean about featuring the same legal principles, we shall look at the case of *Donoghue* v *Stevenson*, set out in Chapter 7. The *facts* in that case are both memorable and specific, featuring a decomposing snail and ginger beer. To the authors' knowledge, there have been no reported cases with the same *facts*. However, this key case in tort established a *principle*, namely that a manufacturer owes a duty of care to the consumer and end-user of its products. It is therefore a relevant case to consider in relation to *any* problem where a consumer wants to sue a manufacturer, *regardless of the type of goods manufactured*. It is not restricted to applying to similar *factual* cases involving a snail and ginger beer. In fact, the legal *principles* established in *Donoghue* on owing and measuring a duty of care are not limited even to cases where the *facts* involve manufacturing and product liability. The *principles* of this one case have been applied in numerous other cases where the *facts* concern something completely different, (for example, personal injury or occupiers' liability). The *principles* in *Donoghue* v *Stevenson* may be *relevant law* to consider when dealing with a range of matters in tort completely unrelated to the original *facts* of the beer and the decomposing snail.

8.1.7 Update primary source

The law continues to change and evolve, and this makes legal research particularly challenging. It is all too easy to find law which is out of date. The challenge is to find out whether changes have been made to the version you have found and are reading and, if so, to identify those changes. The following guidance will show you how to check that the law you find is current and in force.

8.1.7.1 Legislation

Potential problem 1: is it in force?

Figure 7.1 contains guidance about where you can find the commencement date of legislation. It explains that the short title of the legislation refers to the date of Royal Assent, and the default position is that the statute will take effect and come into force on that date. However, it also explains that it may come into force later, either in its entirety or in part. Therefore, when you are researching legislation, it is vital to check whether the version you are referring to has actually come into force yet.

Consider the following example, an extract from the Treasure Act 1996. Section 8(3) of this statute sets out the penalty which can be imposed on someone who finds treasure (as defined elsewhere in this statute) but fails to comply with the obligation to notify the coroner (as set out earlier in the statute, s. 8(1)).

> ### Example 3
>
> 8. Duty of finder to notify coroner
>
> > (3) Any person who fails to comply with subsection (1) is guilty of an offence and liable on summary conviction to—
> >
> > (a) imprisonment for a term not exceeding *three months* [51 weeks];
> >
> > (b) a fine of an amount not exceeding level 5 on the standard scale; or
> >
> > (c) both.
> >
> > *Sub-s (3): in para (a) words 'three months' in italics repealed and subsequent words in square brackets substituted by the Criminal Justice Act 2003, s 280(2), (3), Sch 26, para 48.*
> > *Date in force: to be appointed: see the Criminal Justice Act 2003, s 336(3).*
> > *This statute contains public sector information licensed under the Open Government Licence v1.0.*

The question is: what is the maximum term of imprisonment under the statute? The answer to this depends on whether para. 48 of Sch 26 to the Criminal Justice Act 2003 is in force. Given that the commencement date of a statute can be after the date it receives Royal Assent, it is perfectly possible that a statute with the year 2003 in the title, or part of that statute, is not yet in force. (For example, much of the Companies Act 2006 came into force in 2009.) The words 'to be appointed' indicate that para. 48 was not in force at the time this version of s. 8 was printed; however, it could have been printed some time ago. You would need to use your legal research skills to check the position using an electronic database or paper resource (See 'Locating current legislation using electronic databases'). If para. 48 is in force, it will have repealed the words 'three months' and imposed the new maximum sentence of 51 weeks. If it is not yet in force, the maximum sentence remains at three months.

Potential problem 2: has it been amended or repealed?

Statutes are amended over time, or even repealed altogether. Again, you need to check before relying on the source.

Locating current legislation using electronic databases: Lexis®Library and Westlaw UK

The most common general electronic databases are Lexis®Library and Westlaw UK. Both databases employ techniques to highlight updating issues, but the techniques they use are different.

At the time of writing, Lexis®Library uses text formatting such as square brackets, italics, underline, and ellipsis to identify issues such as prospective repeals, repeals, prospective insertions, and insertions, although it is beginning to use more status icons. An explanatory document is maintained on its website to 'translate' the text formatting you will see (see Further Reading). Lexis®Library also features UK Legislation Status Snapshots, a click through button which provides all the applicable information available about the statute in one place. These include commencement details from *Halsbury's 'Is It In Force?'* (so useful to find the answer to Example 3), amendment details from *Halsbury's Statutes*, a 'stop press' feature to alert you to any pending amendments, and 'related cases/commentary' to highlight case law relevant to, and descriptions of, the law you have found.

At the time of writing, Westlaw UK uses status icons to indicate whether the law is in force, whether amendments are pending or prospective, or whether the provision has been superseded or repealed. These icons are explained in a glossary document maintained on its website (see Further Reading). Westlaw UK also uses click-through buttons such as 'Commencement', 'Key Cases Citing', and 'Commentary', as well as an interface with Practical Law to provide related practitioner-related material.

You may develop a preference for one database over another, and your preference may differ depending on whether you are searching for legislation or case law, or due to the differing content (for example, only Lexis®Library has *Halsbury's Laws*). Regular practice will help you to establish your preference, and it can then be helpful to begin your research using your preferred database, and cross-check your findings using the other (and then, cross-checking again in the paper source, will really help to reassure you that your answer is correct, if all three provide the same information consistently).

Locating current legislation using paper sources

Halsbury's Statutes and *Halsbury's Statutory Instruments* are paper sources you can use to find legislation. The steps to follow are:

1. Look up the legislation in the index. This will give you the volume and page you need.

2. When you find the legislation in the volume, check the commencement date (see Figure 7.1) not only for the legislation as a whole, but also for the particular sections you are reading. You cannot assume every part of the legislation is in force.

3. Next, consult the *Cumulative Supplement* to check whether there have been any changes since the volume you have just read was published. The *Cumulative Supplement* is an annual volume that updates all the main volumes up to the end of the previous calendar year.

4. Then, check the *Noter Up* for changes made since the date of publication of the *Cumulative Supplement*. The *Noter Up* is issued monthly and updates the *Cumulative Supplement*.

In both the *Cumulative Supplement* and the *Noter Up* you will search against the name of the Act then against the section you are using. If the section is not referred to, you can assume that the legislation in the volume is up to date.

8.1.7.2 Case law

Potential problem: has the case been reversed or overruled?

Chapter 5 explains that a higher court can reverse cases, on appeal, or overrule them in a subsequent case (see 5.1.3). The potential problem is that in the course of your research you might encounter a judgment that is no longer current law. The following guidance will ensure that you are able to identify this, and feel confident you are using only current case law.

Locating current case law using electronic databases: Lexis®Library and Westlaw UK

Lexis®Library has a Case Search function, and at the time of writing uses status icons to indicate whether a decision has been reversed, disapproved, overruled, had doubt cast on it, received positive treatment, and whether or not it has been considered.

Westlaw UK has a Case Analysis function which uses a different set of status symbols, to indicate how a case has been treated and its currency. For example, a green tick indicates positive or neutral judicial consideration.

Both databases maintain icon glossaries of their respective status symbols and icons (see Further Reading).

Locating current case law using paper sources

Current Law Case Citator provides information on all English cases which have been judicially considered since 1947. It is set out as an alphabetical index of cases in volumes according to the period indicated on the spine. For each case, there will be provided details of when and where it was reported, together with any articles or journals in which the case was commented upon. There will also be a reference to a digest of the case in the *Current Law Yearbook*. The *Citator* will also indicate whether the case has been applied, considered, distinguished, or overruled, and, if so, in which case or cases. A reference to the location of these cases in the relevant *Current Law Yearbook* will also be provided. When considering more recent cases, the *Current Law Monthly Digest* provides similar information.

8.1.8 **Check understanding against secondary source**

A good way to check your understanding of a primary source is to sanity-check your interpretation of it against a secondary source *after* you have analysed the primary source. As this is a verification stage, it may be helpful to use an alternative secondary source (e.g. an encyclopaedia or practitioner text—see 8.1.5.3 and 8.1.5.4) rather than the original secondary source (e.g. an academic textbook or *Halsbury's Laws*) which you may have used at the outset. This verification process will also help to consolidate your understanding of the relevant area of law.

8.1.9 **Check *facts* again**

If you are dealing with problem questions or advising, you should continue to check the facts as you carry out your research. This is for two reasons:

1. It is easy to forget about an important fact when you have been researching another issue for a while. It is a surprisingly common error in legal research to overlook an important fact. In Example 2 about the washing machine, for instance, it would be possible to become consumed by the purported limitation on liability and to forget to consider the central issue of the defective product. A mind map, setting out the main facts and issues (see Figure 9.3), can help to avoid this problem.
2. Sometimes you will not have realised the importance of a fact until you have read the law. For example, if you discover that a penalty applies only to someone who is over 18, you may need to go back to the facts if, at the time you originally considered them, you had not realised that age would be a relevant factor.

8.1.10 **Answer any new questions identified**

Often the answers you find to one question will raise further questions of their own. You must learn to enjoy approaching the answers you find with a curious mind, and leave no relevant question unanswered (starting your research early will help). By way of example, let's return to the Treasure Act 1996 at Example 3 and assume you have found that there has been an offence under s. 8(1). If you answered that the offender would be liable on conviction to 'a fine of an amount not exceeding level 5 in the standard scale', you have not progressed the matter as far as you are able to on the facts provided. Whoever reads your answer will have more questions for you. Avoid that by researching further what the 'standard scale' is, and then find out what 'level 5' means. Stating in your answer the precise maximum fine that can be imposed will make it stand out, for all the right reasons.

8.1.11 **Make contemporaneous record of sources and relevant law**

You will want to make a contemporaneous record of:

- the sources of your research;
- the date your research was carried out (this is particularly important when working with online sources, where content can change daily);
- the titles of the sources consulted;
- search terms used during searches;

- page references or website addresses for important pieces of information;
- dates of publication (including the date of the latest release for a loose-leaf source);
- any dates to which the law as stated is claimed to be up to date by the publisher;
- how you made sure the law you found was up to date.

This will help you to (a) easily locate the material again should you wish to check a point or an additional question arises from later research; (b) correctly reference your final piece of work (see 14.1.8); and (c) remind yourself to take steps to ensure that your primary sources are up to date (see 8.1.7).

A contemporaneous record involves noting what you do, and when you do it, as you do it. As it is initially for your own reference and benefit, you can choose how to do this. You may wish to annotate a written or diagrammatic record of the facts with the source material information, produce a separate written record, or simply save screenshots as you go (you can also link screenshots, for example, to a Dropbox account (see Further Reading), so they automatically save, and you can simply delete anything if ultimately it proves not to be relevant). Alternatively use referencing software such as Endnote or Cite This For Me (see 14.1.8), which can help you create an electronic database of sources with the added advantage that you can also use it to insert references in the preferred style (usually OSCOLA in law schools) into your word-processed work when the time comes.

8.1.12 Communication and presentation of results

As an undergraduate, usually you will need to incorporate the results of your research into either a piece of written work (e.g. an essay, dissertation, answer to a problem question or preparatory questions for a seminar or, perhaps for a legal skills or practice module, a research report), or an oral communication (e.g. a moot, negotiation, presentation, client interview, or discussion in a seminar). The remaining chapters of Part 2 of this book provide specific guidance for you on such written and oral communications, and you are encouraged to read Part 2 from beginning to end. Once you have done so, Table 8.2 will help you navigate your reading, depending on how you intend to use your research:

Table 8.2 Navigating your reading of Part 2 for academic output

Use	Chapter
A legal practice or skills module including stand-alone research skills tasks	8.2
An answer to a problem question	8.2 (because there is a commonality of skills required as between practice and, in particular, dealing with problem-solving questions on an undergraduate programme) then Chapter 9.
A dissertation	8.1.13, then Chapter 14
A presentation	Chapter 10
A client interview	Chapter 11
A negotiation	Chapter 12
A Moot, criminal advocacy competition, or advocacy	Chapter 13
An Essay	Chapter 14

However you are intending to use the results of your research, the following guidance will help you produce your best work.

8.1.12.1 Do:

- **Before** you start to communicate and present your results, be sure to (i) read carefully and understand the question and any resources you have been given to help you answer the question (e.g. a template to structure your answer) and (ii) then complete the steps covered in 8.1.1–8.1.11, to find the answer to the question you have been asked.

- Use what you already know about the law. You are expected to have a working knowledge of the foundation subjects you have already studied (e.g. the law of contract, so you can establish if there is a contract and if there is a potential breach), techniques (e.g. the importance of setting out the constituent parts of an offence before exploring any exceptions to that offence), and how the courts work (e.g. that some cases may not be reported, and recent cases may not yet have been judicially interpreted simply because not enough time has passed). This may call for a timely refresher of some of your previous areas of study.

- Motivate yourself to be curious enough to start your research early.

- When you do come to communicate and present your results, be selective and include only information that is *relevant* to the task and to your reader.

- Communicate with clarity and a decent structure so your reader can understand what you are communicating.

- Consider any learning outcomes and/or assessment criteria against which your work will be judged (remember they tend to include not just knowledge and sources, but typically also communication, structure, application, and analysis).

- Undertake a hard edit at the end, where you delete any and all irrelevant information, unnecessary repetition, and check that your writing style is not too verbose (this is more likely to happen if you have made the recommended early start to your research).

- Consider who will be reading your communication and presentation of the results of your research and how to best communicate to meet their needs. If in any doubt, ask your lecturer about this. For example, if you are answering a problem question, in a substantive law subject, which asks you to advise a fictional client, are they expecting you to use language appropriate for that client (as in practice, so no jargon), or for the lecturer marking it (so it is a practice based question but testing academic skills only, and so jargon is acceptable), or something else (e.g. use jargon but make sure you explain it)?

- Take any and all opportunities for practice and formative feedback.

If you or your lecturer identify any particular issues in your communication or presentation (and common issues include a lack of clarity of expression in written English, the inclusion of ir-relevant material, and/or an over-reliance on description rather than application), then take on board this feedback (not failure) and make sure you use all resources available to you in good time to address them effectively. Student support officers, faculty writing projects, and reading a good quality broadsheet newspaper regularly (where complex information is summarised concisely), are all examples of steps you can enjoy taking early in your studies to improve your work in time for when you need it (in a summative assessment, or in a graduate role).

8.1.12.2 Do not:

- Present every last detail you found, no matter how irrelevant, or how it might detract from your readers' understanding or indeed enjoyment. Simply accept as part of the process that you are likely to have spent some time working to find law that does not make it into your communication or presentation of results.

- 'Hedge your bets' by including information you think is irrelevant, just in case you are wrong and it happens to be relevant after all. If you are at this stage, you are not yet ready to communicate and present your results, you need to obtain further clarity as to what the question is asking and what, specifically, is the answer.

- Spend too much time researching, at the expense of planning enough time to think about how to communicate and structure your answer well.

- Exceed any word limit. If you are struggling with this, the hard edit referred to at 8.1.12.1 will provide a solution.

- Rely on simply copying out answer guidance you have been given previously, instead of properly reading, understanding, and researching the new question you have been asked. Lecturers may use similar questions, but bear in mind a change to just a few key facts can completely change the content of the correct answer.

- Let any template tempt you to complete it as you go. This would be allowing the tail to wag the dog. While it will help you to read it before you begin, and to structure your answer once you start writing, you should avoid writing up anything formally until you have finished your research and know the answer for certain and with clarity (by following the research strategy at 8.1.1–8.1.11).

8.1.13 Academic research methodology and methods

If you are undertaking a dissertation, you will be asked to set out your research methodology and research methods.

8.1.13.1 Legal methodology

Methodology in this context has a specific meaning; it is 'concerned with the discussion of how a particular piece of research should be undertaken . . . the term refers to the choice of research strategy taken by a particular scholar'.[1] In other words, your *legal methodology* is your philosophical and investigative *approach*, which may be one or more of those explained in Table 8.3.

---

[1] Grix, J. 2018. *The Foundations of Research*. 3rd edn. London: Macmillan International Higher Education.

Table 8.3 Academic legal methodologies table

Approach	Concerned with ...
Comparative	The comparison of laws from different jurisdictions
Doctrinal	The formulation of legal doctrines through the analysis of legal rules
Socio-legal	The relationship between law and society
Theoretical	Theoretical perspectives on legal issues

(Note that this differs from referring to 'methodology' in a practical context to describe your research trail, which is explained at 8.2.2.1 and Figure 8.2.)

8.1.13.2 Legal method

In academic dissertation writing, your *legal methods* are the processes you use to gather your data. They may be (and at undergraduate, or as part of a professional top-up postgraduate, level are very likely to be) desk-based, where you proceed through the analysis of primary and secondary legal sources (and this is covered by the research strategy at Figure 8.1). Alternatively they may be (and at MPhil and PhD level are likely to be) based on empirical research, which is 'the study of law, legal processes and legal phenomena using social research methods, such as interviews, observations or questionnaires'.[2] The detail of this method of legal research is beyond the intended scope of our undergraduate textbook (see Further Reading). The further guidance as to how to structure an essay, in Chapter 14, will also be helpful to inform your writing of any undergraduate or professional top-up postgraduate dissertations.

8.2 Research skills in practice

The good news is that, with the exception of 8.1.13, all of the preceding content in this chapter about legal research is essential work for the research you may undertake in legal practice (or indeed a legal skills or practice module). The difference really lies in the context. In practice, you may be researching in order to prepare a piece of written work (e.g. a letter to progress the answer to a client's legal problem, or a research report for your supervisor (see Figure 8.2)) so that they can write such a letter), or to prepare for oral communication (e.g. advocacy, negotiating, presenting, or client interviewing).

As Chapter 20 explains, law firms are businesses, and so make no mistake, they will not be asking you to research as a 'test' to which they already hold the answer. Instead, more senior lawyers will be asking you to research instead of them because it is more cost effective (because you will have a lower hourly rate, so can spend longer on research while still delivering a profit for the firm). For that reason, expect a large amount of legal research tasks early in your career, and that they will tend to feel challenging (because if they were easy, the likelihood is that a fee-earner would already know the answer). Some of the most challenging

---

[2] Burton, M. (2017) 'Doing Empirical Research' in *Research Methods in Law*. London: Routledge.

questions are along the lines of, 'is there anything that would stop the client from doing X'. If you find nothing, you need to have faith in your research strategy, to reassure you that there is nothing to be found, rather than you have missed something.

8.2.1 Analyse problem or task

Let's revisit lozenge 1 of our research strategy in Figure 8.1. You will remember that we agreed the wisdom of delaying your search for the relevant law until you have *first* analysed your task and any related facts and clearly identified the legal issues it raises.

We established that a good analysis will consider the *purpose* of your research, and that in turn will affect the *sources* you first consult, why, and what you will do with your findings. The other factor involved is your level of *knowledge*: how well you know the law in an area and the specific sources of that law will differ between research tasks. We then considered some examples, all of which required some research into s. 4 of the Public Order Act 1986. Practice has a degree of commonality with the problem-solving questions you answer on an undergraduate programme, so it will be useful for you to re-read Example C (8.1.1), and the analysis of the problem (8.1.1.3). Reading Chapter 9 will also be helpful in due course. Let's now consider some more examples of research, this time in the context of legal practice.

8.2.1.1 Example D

You have graduated and are now in practice as a trainee solicitor in a busy suburban criminal practice. Your supervisor sends you an email asking you to summarise the offence of coercive behaviour in an intimate relationship. She has a client who has not been harmed physically by her partner, but appears to have been harmed psychologically. Your supervisor recalls this is now an area covered by the Serious Crime Act 2015.

- Here, you are given information about the nature of the offence and the relevant primary source of law (the statute). You have been asked to summarise the offence.
- Your supervisor will use your summary to begin to explore whether her client's partner has committed the offence.
- You are not familiar with the offence and neither is your supervisor.
- You will need to find the statute, identify the relevant section(s) and read the precise wording of the offence, *and* which words are most important in defining and establishing the offence, *and* how these important words have been interpreted in previous cases.
- From the information given, you might expect that you will find some detail about both the behaviour (what constitutes coercive behaviour?) and the relationship (what constitutes an intimate relationship?).
- Before you read the primary source, you will want to find and read *secondary source commentary*—most likely a practitioner text, (e.g. here, Blackstone's Criminal Practice—see 8.1.5) to identify the specific section of the statute which contains the offence, and to find out how the wording has been applied, and then refer to the primary source to check the precise wording.

- Using electronic databases will have advantages in terms of updating. As this law is relatively recent, this will affect how many related reported cases you might expect to find. (There may be no related reported cases when a statute is very recent.)

- You then need to assimilate all that you have read, and record it in a concise way, which is not too verbose, but which does not exclude any necessary detail, in order to summarise the offence. It will help your reader to structure your answer clearly (perhaps using headings and sub-headings and bullet points) to highlight where you are summarising different elements of the offence (e.g. the behaviour; the relationship).

- You will need to reassure your supervisor that you have used a sound research strategy, so they can feel confident to rely on your summary.

8.2.1.2 Example E

Your supervisor has read your summary of the offence created in 2015 by s. 76 of the Serious Crime Act 2015, informed by related reported cases. She then gives you some more detailed facts specifically about the alleged behaviour, including the nature and timing of it and the nature of the relationship, including how long they have been in a relationship. She asks you to email her your conclusion and advice, supported by your reasoning as to how the law you summarised applies to the facts she has just given you. She tells you she will use the content of your email to write a letter of advice to her client, to advise whether to commence proceedings against her partner.

- Here you will benefit from the work you did earlier to structure your summary of the law well. This will make your application of that law to the facts clearer. In turn, that will help your supervisor lift parts of your email to use directly in the letter she needs to write to her client.

- Your reader is your supervisor, her reader is the client, so there may be a few elements of jargon or detail which you need to include and which your supervisor does not. However, she will want to be able to cut and paste significant parts of your well-written and clearly expressed conclusion, advice, and reasoning.

- You will need to outline the application of the law to the facts first regarding the main offence, before then considering any exceptions or defences, and then draw as clear a conclusion as is possible, and identify any missing facts that you would need to progress the matter further.

- Sometimes, you will not be able to advise clearly yet as to whether the client should be advised to commence proceedings; it may be premature. All you may be able to do at this stage is identify further facts you need to know first.

- As a professional, you need to be aware of conduct issues too see 6.4. In this example, you would need to check that the client's partner is not also a client of the firm, because this would raise conflict and confidentiality issues under the Codes of Conduct (see 6.4.3).

8.2.1.3 Example F

You have graduated and are now in practice. Your client has been charged under s. 4 of the Public Order Act 1986. You recall you may be able to argue that she did not commit this offence by reason of having committed a lesser offence.

Research

Chapter 8

- Here, you are familiar with the offence and the relevant law under which the client has been charged. You also appear to have some knowledge about a lesser offence that you believe you can argue was the *actual* offence committed. Presumably, then, you know where to find the relevant primary source of law (the relevant statute and section).

- You might imagine that, as a practitioner, you would also already know the precise wording of each statute, *and* which words are most important in defining and establishing the offence, *and* how these important words have been interpreted in previous cases. However, except in the most basic of scenarios, in practice even experienced lawyers will take a prudent approach and refer to *secondary source commentary*—most likely a practitioner text (see 8.1.5.4) to find out how the wording has been applied, and then refer to the primary source to check the precise wording.

The remainder of the research strategy remains equally applicable to practice as it does to academia, until we reach the final lozenge; communication and presentation of results.

8.2.2 Communication and presentation of results

The remainder of the chapter provides help to identify how you might report the results of your research. You should read it until the end, and then Table 8.4 will help you navigate your reading, depending on how you intend to use your research.

Table 8.4 Navigating your reading of Part 2 for practice-based output

Use	Chapter
A letter to progress the answer to a client's problem.	Chapters 9 and 14
A presentation	Chapter 10
A client interview	Chapter 11
A negotiation or mediation	Chapter 12
For advocacy	Chapter 13
An email to your supervisor	Chapter 14

8.2.2.1 Reporting the results of your research

Once you have completed your research, you need to communicate what you have found in a way which the recipient of your communication will find helpful. In undergraduate skills or legal practice modules, you might be asked to produce a formal written report of your research, or aspects of it. In legal practice, you might be asked to produce a formal report or, less formally, summarise your research to your supervisor by email or memorandum. You might even be asked to produce the first draft of a letter of advice or a legal opinion to a client, based on your research. The remainder of this chapter will guide you as to how to prepare a research report. This will prepare you well in terms of analysing the content you will need to communicate effectively your research results, even if you are asked to draft that content, or parts of it, into a different format from a report, such as an email, letter, memorandum, or other form of communication.

Your contemporaneous record will help you to report the results of your research, albeit the latter (for the attention of another reader) will look very different to the former (which is for your own benefit). It is important that you do not include anything in your report which you do not fully understand, as it is also common to be asked to explain the results of your research, or any part of it, verbally.

Purpose

A report of your research results is normally required only for internal purposes. Usually, once reviewed by your supervising lawyer, it will then be used as the basis for written or oral advice, or some other action. Any report of your results should therefore fulfil two purposes. It should:

- highlight and summarise the main issues and your key findings in terms of your conclusion and advice. The person you have undertaken research for is likely to be busy. A wordy, lengthy research report with the answers buried within it may demand time to digest that the recipient simply cannot spare (or justify from a fees perspective—see Chapter 20). Your advice must be correct, comprehensive, and tailored specifically to the needs of your reader; and

- provide enough detail so that the reader could replicate your research if necessary, and check that your conclusions are properly supported. A report that is too brief will leave the recipient with no way of verifying its accuracy. For this reason, as a junior lawyer initially at least, you need to be ready to explain precisely how you found your answer. This might be referred to as your 'research trail', 'research method', or 'methodology' (not to be confused with the purely academic definition explained at 8.1.13). Some practitioners and practice-based units insist on including it, and others do not, so check if you are unsure whether you should include a research trail. If you do need to include it, your research trail will include identifying and evidencing that you have read the key relevant primary source(s) and have checked it is/they are up to date. It will provide reassurance not only to you (because your sound research strategy will give you confidence in your answer) but also to your supervisor. It also shows your supervisor how you found your answer, using a level of detail that they could follow to find the same information as quickly and efficiently as possible.

Content and structure

The research report template in Figure 8.2 provides guidance about how to communicate your research results in practice. As you study for a skills or practice unit, you may be asked to produce a full report, or certain elements of it (see Examples D and E (8.2.1.1 and 8.2.1.2)). Of course, law firms are likely to have their own preferred format which they will recommend you use. Equally, your lecturer may recommend a template incorporating their own preferred format for recording and reporting research (perhaps related to the module's assessment criteria). For example, some might prefer you to *begin* the report with the conclusion and advice (that summarises the main issues and your key findings), followed by the detail of the research, the facts, application, and your reasoning which supports that conclusion. This may seem counter-intuitive, but it has the advantage for your reader that they will know immediately what the result of your research is, before moving on to the more detailed rationale. You might summarise your conclusion and advice in a covering email or memorandum instead of, or in addition to, the report itself.

Figure 8.2 provides an example of the content and structure to include in any report of your research, with useful suggested headings. Note that it does not put the advice and conclusion first, but you can cut and paste into that format once you have completed your report if you are persuaded by its merits or are asked to do so. Similarly, if you are given a template with different headings, they are not likely to be introducing new content not dealt with here; they probably will correspond with those in Figure 8.2, albeit using different words. While templates change, the principles of reporting research remain constant.

Be flexible in your approach. You can use the headings to prepare only parts of an answer, or to set out your research findings in an alternative format such as an email or memorandum (see Chapter 14). It also illustrates various elements commonly required in practice, such as client details.

RESEARCH REPORT

CLIENT: CHL
MATTER: Purchase of 1 Dove Lane
FILE REFERENCE: 1234–5678
DATE: 1 October 20XX

CLIENT'S OBJECTIVES

Your list of the client's known objectives (see 9.2.1.4 for a practice-based example of this).

LEGAL ISSUES

Your own summary of the legal issues that you cover in your report. You may have been given these issues to research or you may have had to deduce them yourself by analysing the facts and the legal problems arising out of them (again, see 9.2.1.5 for a practice-based example of this, and how the 'legal issues' differ from the 'client's objectives').

HOW THE LAW APPLIES TO THE FACTS OF THE PROBLEM

This is where you explain your legal reasoning; how you reached the 'answer' that you will be setting out in your conclusion. This is the main part of your report where you will detail how the law applies to the facts of the legal issue. You should follow the guidance in 9.2.3 as to how to apply the law to the facts effectively, and the guidance in 14.2.1.11 as to how to write clearly and concisely. Your explanation should be easy to read and it should refer expressly to the facts of the question.

> In practice, each client and each matter for that client will be given a reference, which might be numerical or some letters derived from the client's name, or a combination of those. It is helpful to include these references here (e.g., Client: CHL, Matter: 1234–5678) so it is clear where to file your report and to ensure that any time spent on this report, for example reading it, can be recorded against the correct file. For a professional appearance, use the 'tab' key to align the information that you type here.

> This heading is prompting you to apply rather than just cite the law.

Figure 8.2 Legal research report template

You must identify the primary source(s) of law here. It is good practice to include details of the relevant ratio of a case (see 5.1 and figure 7.5) and/or the text of the relevant parts of the legislative provision. Do not simply copy out chunks of legislation or judgment though: cite only that which is relevant. Occasionally it may be helpful to attach extracts of the primary source, but again only attach relevant extracts. In general, however, be cautious about attaching extracts. Practitioners, with some displeasure, recount tales of junior lawyers having been asked to undertake research and presenting their supervisor with a sheaf of photocopied extracts from primary and secondary sources. Legal research is not limited to finding sources of law: it is about identifying which sources of law are *relevant* for the purpose of a specific task. If you have been asked to report the results of your research, expected that it should feature not only *knowledge* and refer to *sources* but also *analysis* and *application* of the law (with regard to *structure* and *communication*). These words will be familiar to you from undergraduate assessment criteria, and they remain important in practice.

There is little value in providing a chronological guide as to how you conducted your research. In following our recommended research strategy (Figure 8.1) you will have used the 'funnel approach' (see 8.1.5) when conducting your research, starting with a secondary source then progressing to the primary source. This will have helped your understanding. However your report should take the opposite approach and detail the primary sources first, as they are the main source of law, in which your reader will be interested, as would any judge in court. This might be case law only, or legislation only, or it may be both. (You can reference the secondary sources later, in your *research trail*, to support your citation and application of the primary source here.)

Subheadings can be used well here, for clarity and structure. For example, if you have a Sale of Goods business-to-business question, you could use three separate subheadings, one for s13 SGA 1979 – correspondence with description, one for s14(2) SGA – satisfactory quality, and one for s14(3) SGA – fitness for particular purpose, assuming they are all relevant to the question asked. Consider how best to format your subheadings consistently (for example, if your headings are in bold, consider using underline for subheadings. There is no set way to format, but each level should be consistent).

CONCLUSION AND ADVICE

Here you provide 'the answer' to the client's problem (see 9.2.4 for a practice-based example of this). You should aim to provide as unequivocal a conclusion as you can. It takes confidence to do this. Do not 'hedge your bets' or be inconsistent if a clear answer is available on the facts. Students often use language such as 'it seems that it might' or 'probably'. If this is to express a *genuine* doubt that exists, having applied the law to the facts correctly, then identify what further information you need in order to advise definitively, and resist the temptation to advise prematurely. However do not use evasive language simply because you are not confident that your answer is correct. Make sure you use the facts properly here too. Do not say '*If* X is Y' if the facts are clear that X is Y; say '*As* X is Y' instead. To avoid these pitfalls, resist the temptation to start writing up your research using the template until you have fully researched the matter and have found the answer.

Figure 8.2 *Continued*

Your conclusion as to the effect of the law must be clear, complete and progress the matter as far as is appropriate:

- It should be clear enough so that your supervisor (or you) could cut and paste substantial parts of it into an email or letter to the client (with appropriate changes to accommodate the different needs of the new recipient).
- You should not include explanatory detail, such as citing your authority, here in the conclusion. Supporting detail is very important, but you will have included the main primary sources in the 'How the law applies to the facts' legal reasoning section, and will include the detail of your successful research strategy in the 'Research Trail' section.
- Your conclusion should be complete, such that you neither leave anything unanswered, nor make a point that raises further questions that you do not address (as illustrated by the 'standard scale' example at 8.1.7.1 above).
- Your conclusion should progress the matter as far as is appropriate; resist any need to feel obliged always to 'solve' the client's problem for good; you may be at an earlier stage where this is impossible and instead you succeed in your goal of progressing the matter by identifying further information you need first from the client, or a third party. For example, if you have been ask to research whether your client has a remedy, and they have identified facts which you consider constitute a potential breach of contract, then you will need some further information (eg, does the other party agree or dispute the facts, what evidence exists) before you can advise whether the client is likely to succeed with a breach of contract case against the other party.
- Your report must form the basis for advising a client, so it should set out your overall advice here, including any practical advice. This is where you need to evaluate the options (see 9.2.4.1) and provide advice on which might be the most appropriate (see 9.2.4.3).
- The difference between conclusion and advice is explored in section 9.2.4.4; however, to give an example, you might *conclude* that the client has a legal right to sue, but *advise* not to sue because, for example, it would be too expensive for your client in terms of cost or time, or they need to preserve a working relationship with the other party. This is another reason why it is so important to avoid the temptation to advise prematurely until you have all of the facts.
- In practice, few initial research reports lead to a straightforward letter advising a client they should proceed directly to court and are likely to win, although you may have had that impression from your undergraduate studies (where typically you are asked to advise fictional characters with a limited backstory, for free, in the context of a short problem question).

RESEARCH TRAIL

Here you should provide enough detail about how you conducted your research and found the relevant law, so that your supervisor or lecturer (i) could easily replicate your research in your absence, and (ii) is reassured that you have followed a sensible research strategy. If your supervisor has given you the sources of law and assured you they are up to date, then you would simply note this (the Figure 8.1 strategy would still be useful here, in helping you decide which source to read first, using the funnel technique). Otherwise, you should be prepared to give a brief description of how to find your sources again quickly. For example, include the search terms you used (if the

Figure 8.2 *Continued*

search produces quick results), the electronic database, or the path or URL that your supervisor can use to browse straight to the relevant material.

However, note that you do not need to detail every step you actually took while conducting your research, providing a blow-by-blow account of 'what I did yesterday afternoon'. While you may not have taken the most direct route to the answer, you should only detail here the most direct route which you are now aware of, in hindsight. This is not 'cheating' or seeking credit for something you did not do, it is simply reflecting the practical reality that whilst you may have taken an indirect route to the answer, the recipient of your report should not have to. The reader should be able to follow this part of your report and directly find the relevant material that you found.

It can be useful to reassure your supervisor by stating that you have checked that secondary sources are consistent with your conclusion, and identify those sources. However, if you started your research by using a very basic source such as a legal dictionary, and this adds nothing now that you have progressed on to more reliable legal sources, then there is no merit in including a reference to this source. In other words, recognise that there may be some sources which helped you make a start, but would not now help your supervisor because they add nothing to your report. This applies equally to internet search engines. You may well have started your research with a Google search, but once this led you into decent secondary and primary sources of law, they are what you should cite, and you should not be mentioning Google anywhere in this report, because your supervisor cannot put it to any use at all in advising a client or making a case in front of a judge.

One of the most important parts of your research trail is where you show you have checked that your research is up to date. You will need to explain how you made sure that you have used sources of law which are current and in force (see 8.1.7). Give the date to which the research is up to date (which may be the date of your report).

As electronic databases are kept up to date by the suppliers and usually updated daily, they tend not to provide the specific date on which they were last updated. If you have used an electronic database, then explain which one you used and the steps you took to make sure that there are no further relevant points of law. Refer to the symbols and text formatting of electronic databases to evidence that you have checked the law is up to date. You should also detail here whether any changes to the law are imminent, if relevant.

If you have used paper resources, then references to the *Cumulative Supplement* and *Noter Up* will help you to show that you have ensured paper versions of *Halsbury's* (Laws, Statutes or Statutory Instruments) are up to date. You should mention you have checked these even if all they showed was that the law you found had not been amended.

If your research has led you to legislation then you must check that the legislation has come into force and not been repealed, and give the date of commencement (again, see 8.1.7).

TIME TAKEN

In practice this would be required to be recorded to assist time management and be used in calculating the overall cost of the matter for the client (see Chapters 6 and 20). Your supervisor should be encouraging you to state the actual time you took; remember that as a trainee (at, say £75ph) you can spend much longer on this (in this example, over three and a half times longer) than a more senior fee earner with a higher charge-out rate (at, say £275ph), and still deliver more profit.

Figure 8.2 *Continued*

Summary

- Legal research is seldom conducted in isolation. It is usually undertaken to provide content for a particular task, such as solving a legal problem.

- You should consider the purpose (the 'why') of the research *and* task (the 'what') to assist you to identify the types of material you need to locate.

- Before starting your research, take a strategic approach (the 'how') by following our suggested research strategy at Figure 8.1, and plan which secondary and primary sources are most likely to provide the material you need, and consider the appropriateness of any electronic source you plan to use.

- Read a reliable secondary source first; *Halsbury's Laws* is a universally good starting point and is available through Lexis®Library. Westlaw UK also provides access to good secondary source commentary on the law.

- Use appropriate techniques to ensure that the law you refer to is in force, up to date, and relevant to the issues in hand.

- Avail yourself of the user guides, FAQ sheets, and training provided by Lexis®Library, Practical Law, and Westlaw UK (see Further Reading) and those of any other electronic databases recommended to you by your lecturer and your law librarian.

- Keep a contemporaneous record of your research as you progress.

- Consider the recipient of your research, and use appropriate written and oral communication skills to provide them with your conclusions and advice.

What the professionals say

Any future lawyer must be able to research efficiently, summarise effectively and communicate accurately. In my position as a junior lawyer, I can be asked to research anything, from breach of contract to the tax implications on settlement monies. It is having a clear research strategy, and versatility in using several different databases, that makes me succeed in what I do. No matter the route to qualification future lawyers take (whether that be the LPC, SQE, CILEx, Solicitor Apprenticeship) legal research skills should be at the forefront of any aspiring lawyer's mind. These skills need to be learned early, so that they can be practised and developed throughout an academic career and then transitioned into practice. To any aspiring lawyer reading this: enjoy researching, enjoy writing, and most of all, enjoy learning and embedding these skills. You are going to be using them a lot over the next 40 years as a lawyer. Remember while artificial intelligence can process 400 contract clauses in mere seconds, it cannot understand the nuances, complexity, and consequences of those clauses as they apply to each individual circumstance; make sure it is no replacement for you by honing your research skills to become an excellent lawyer.

Zachary Clough, LLM, LLB—Paralegal at Knights plc

Don't underestimate just how many research tasks you will be given in practice. Law firms pay anything up to tens of thousands of pounds a month for their legal research searches and resources. Your employer will want to know that you can find the relevant law as efficiently as possible and they need to have confidence that what you find is current and that you have not missed anything. They will judge you on that. If you can show that you can use resources well then you will become the 'go to' person for research and will be given the best work to do. My advice would be to appreciate the freedom you have as a student, from the pressure of time recording and having to justify search costs and your salary. Now is the time to practise these skills, to make mistakes and to learn from them. Apply for certification using online schemes such as those provided by Westlaw UK and Lexis®Library. As the routes into the legal sector evolve, it is vital that your skills such as legal research are as good as they possibly can be to improve your chances of employment. Your first legal role may not be as Trainee or a Pupil, rather you may be a paralegal carrying out research tasks. Your chances of progressing into the role you want will be greatly improved if you can show effective and efficient research skills.

Corryn Walker, Law Librarian, Manchester Metropolitan University, and former Librarian at Freshfields LLP and the Inner Temple

Research

Chapter 8

Practical exercises

1. What criteria would you apply to decide whether a case you have found is relevant to your legal problem?

2. Should today's law student still be required to learn how to research using paper resources?

3. Explain the difference between primary and secondary sources of law, giving examples.

4. What are the benefits of starting (rather than ending) a research report with your conclusion and advice?

*Visit the **online resources** for the authors' reflections and to check your progress.*

Further reading

Albon, E. (2019) *Legal Research: A Practitioners Handbook*. **London: Wildy, Simmonds and Hill Publishing, 3rd edn**

—Provides practical advice on legal research: problem analysis, selecting and finding the best sources; and presenting results effectively.

CiteThisForMe (2019) *Save Time and Improve your Marks with CiteThisForMe, The No. 1 Citation Tool*. Available at: http://www.citethisforme.com/
—An app and web page to help you format and generate citations in various referencing styles, including OSCOLA and Harvard.

Dropbox.com (2019) *Save screenshots to your Dropbox account*. Available at: https://help.dropbox.com/installs-integrations/photos/screenshots
—A guide explaining how to save screenshots to Dropbox, which can be helpful to make your contemporaneous record referred to at 8.1.11.

EndNote (2019) *EndNote|Clarivate Analytics*. Available at https://endnote.com/
—An electronic research and reference manager.

Grix, J. (2018) *The Foundations of Research*. (3rd edn). London: Macmillan International Higher Education
—For undergraduate and postgraduate students interested in undertaking academic research for dissertations and research degrees. This text will help you explore the language and nature of research and further develop your understanding of different research methods and the role of theory in research which are beyond the scope of this book.

Lexisnexis.com (2019) *LexisNexis® Help—Case Overview Signals*. Available at: http://help.lexisnexis.com/tabula-rasa/rosetta/citationsignals_ref-reference?lbu=GB&locale=en_GB&audience=legal
—Status icon glossary, for use with case law on Lexis®Library.

Lexisnexis.com (2019) *LexisNexis® Help—Text Formatting in Legislation*. Available at: http://help.lexisnexis.com/tabula-rasa/rosetta/legislationtextformatting_ref-reference?lbu=GB&locale=en_GB&audience=legal
—Explanatory document to 'translate' the text formatting in legislation on Lexis®Library.

Lexisnexis.com (2019) *LexisNexis® Help—Tutorial: Using Halsbury's Laws of England*. Available at: http://help.lexisnexis.com/tabula-rasa/rosetta/tutorialusinghalsbury_utube_cpt-concept?lbu=GB&locale=en_GB&audience=legal
—An online tutorial for using *Halsbury's Laws* as an electronic source.

Lexisnexis.com (2019) *How to use Halsbury's Laws of England*. Available at: https://www.lexisnexis.co.uk/halsburyslaw/downloads/how2halsburyslaws.pdf
—A user guide for using *Halsbury's Laws* as a paper source.

Lexisnexis.com (2019) *Law Students|LexisNexis*. Available at: https://www.lexisnexis.co.uk/academic-law/students
—Information for students about Lexis®Library, including how you can become certified, and a student ambassador.

Lexisnexis.com (2019) *LexisNexis Help and Support|Lexis®Library*. Available at: https://www.lexisnexis.co.uk/help-and-support/lexis-library
—Lexis®Library user guide.

Lexisnexis.com (2019) *LexisNexis Help and Support|LexisPSL*. Available at: https://www.lexisnexis.co.uk/help-and-support/lexis-psl
—Lexis®PSL user guide.

Thomson Reuters (2019) *Practical Law Tutorials*. Available at: https://legalsolutions.thomsonreuters.co.uk/en/products-services/practical-law/tutorials.html
—Practical Law user guide.

Thomson Reuters (2019) *Get Certified in Westlaw UK*. Available at: https://legalsolutions.thomson-reuters.co.uk/en/products-services/uk-law-student/get-certified-westlaw-uk.html
—An interactive walk-through of Westlaw UK with the option to then test your skills and become certified.

Thomson Reuters (2019) *Icon Glossary*. Available at: https://uk.westlaw.com/Browse/Home/WestlawUK/AboutWLUK/WestlawUKUserGuideIconGlossary?comp=wluk&transitionType=Default&contextData=%28sc.Default%29
—Icon glossary for Westlaw UK cases and legislation.

Thomson Reuters (2019) *User Guide*. Available at: https://uk.westlaw.com/Browse/Home/WestlawUK/AboutWLUK/WestlawUKUserGuideVideos?comp=wluk&transitionType=Default&contextData=(sc.Default)&firstPage=true
—Westlaw UK user guide.

 For the authors' reflections on the practical exercises, additional self-test questions, sample interview questions and a library of links to useful websites, visit the free **online resources** *at* **www.oup.com/he/slorach4e.**

Chapter 8

Research

9 Problem-solving and case/matter analysis

Learning objectives

After studying this chapter you should be able to, in relation to legal problems:

- Apply and develop Figure 9.1, a problem-solving strategy expanding the IRAC model to incorporate case/matter analysis and your legal research strategy.
- Identify and analyse relevant facts, and the legal and practical issues arising from them.
- Identify and analyse the law relevant to solving the problem.
- Apply the relevant law to the relevant facts.
- Identify and advise on the legal remedies and other options.
- Evaluate options with reference to a client's personal, commercial, and financial situation.

Introduction

A good lawyer is a problem-solver; someone who not only *knows* what the relevant law is and where it comes from, but also *understands* it and can *analyse* and *apply* it, to *structure* and *communicate* clear advice on possible solutions. Problems can arise in contentious cases, for example where there is a dispute, or in non-contentious matters, for example where there is a compliance issue to be worked through.

In your legal studies, your first encounter with problem-solving is likely to be when you are asked to answer 'problem questions', a common form of assessment. Figure 9.1 gives you a simple, effective problem-solving strategy, incorporating and expanding the IRAC model to include helpful detail for case analysis (in contentious cases) and matter analysis (in non-contentious matters), and incorporating the legal research strategy from Figure 8.1. 9.1 will help you understand it and learn how to use it to answer problem questions effectively.

Problem-solving questions will also help you to develop key skills for practice. The Bellwether Report, *The Good Solicitor's Skill Set* (see Further Reading) revealed that solicitors consider 'identifying the real problem, and the result the client wants', as the most important skill in today's marketplace. However, the same report revealed that solicitors perceive a skills gap; it is those very problem-solving skills ranked high (fourth) on the list of skills that solicitors believe are most lacking in the profession. So, learn these skills well and you will distinguish yourself. 9.2 shows how you can use Figure 9.1 to do just that. The chapter will give you examples of problems of increasing complexity, and helpful guidance about how you can develop your skills and use Figure 9.1 to succeed in answering them with relative ease.

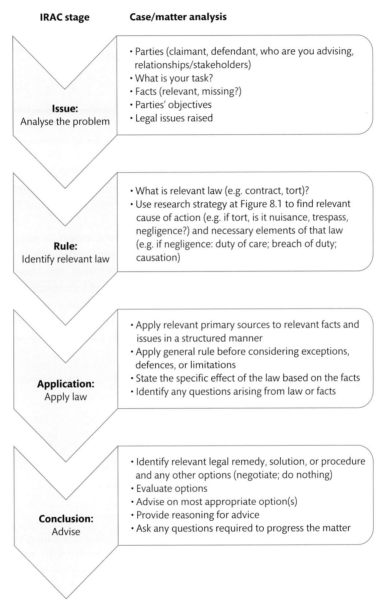

IRAC stage   **Case/matter analysis**

Issue:
Analyse the problem
- Parties (claimant, defendant, who are you advising, relationships/stakeholders)
- What is your task?
- Facts (relevant, missing?)
- Parties' objectives
- Legal issues raised

Rule:
Identify relevant law
- What is relevant law (e.g. contract, tort)?
- Use research strategy at Figure 8.1 to find relevant cause of action (e.g. if tort, is it nuisance, trespass, negligence?) and necessary elements of that law (e.g. if negligence: duty of care; breach of duty; causation)

Application:
Apply law
- Apply relevant primary sources to relevant facts and issues in a structured manner
- Apply general rule before considering exceptions, defences, or limitations
- State the specific effect of the law based on the facts
- Identify any questions arising from law or facts

Conclusion:
Advise
- Identify relevant legal remedy, solution, or procedure and any other options (negotiate; do nothing)
- Evaluate options
- Advise on most appropriate option(s)
- Provide reasoning for advice
- Ask any questions required to progress the matter

Figure 9.1 Case/matter analysis for problem-solving strategy

Problem-solving in its widest sense, whether as part of your studies or in practice, incorporates a range of skills considered throughout this part of the book. You will need a sound legal research strategy (see Chapter 8), and a strategy for reading the law you find in the most effective way (see Chapter 7). You will be presenting your analysis of, and solutions to, problems in oral and/or written form, using communication skills covered in Chapters 10 to 14. In practice, the background to legal problems can be complex, and you might need to assimilate and analyse a great deal of factual information first, before applying the law and finding a solution. Case/matter analysis, and how to advise clients, are other, vital skills required for the problem-solving process. The other chapters in Part 2, and Chapters 15 and 17 of Part 3, will further develop aspects of these skills, which can then be applied to the relevant personal, business and economic contexts of problems, which contexts are explored in Part III.

9.1 Solving legal problems

9.1.1 The purpose of problem-solving questions

Problem-solving questions and essays do share some common purpose; they can both test at least some shared criteria, including attention to structure, communication, knowledge, and sources. Some schools will use the same criteria for both types of question, others will have separate criteria for each (essay questions might test analysis, for example, and the focus of problem questions may be on application).

However, the main difference in purpose lies in the format of the question. An essay either presents a proposition for critical analysis, or an instruction or question to be dealt with in the context of a particular law, case, or topic. Chapter 14 provides helpful guidance about how to answer essay questions. In contrast, a problem question is based on a set of facts describing particular events, and asks you to 'advise' a particular party (in practice, this would be your client).

On first reading, the facts and events may appear complex. They are likely to involve more than one party. Whatever the scenario you are presented with, the underlying purpose is to develop, and then assess, your ability to:

1. analyse the facts of the problem to identify who you are advising, their objective, and the legal issues;
2. identify, find, understand, and analyse the relevant law;
3. apply the relevant law to the facts of the question; and
4. structure advice to the party you are asked to advise, and communicate it effectively to complete the task set.

9.1.2 A simple problem-solving model: IRAC

A simple model which you will apply to solve legal problem questions during your undergraduate studies is IRAC. It applies the following titles to steps 1 to 4 at 9.1.1, to help you to memorise them.

1. **I**ssue
2. **R**ule
3. **A**pplication
4. **C**onclusion.

These steps are incorporated into Figure 9.1, and we will look at them in more detail below.

9.1.3 **Using Figure 9.1 to answer problem questions**

Figure 9.1 expands the IRAC model (in column one) into a problem-solving strategy, with column two adding the detail of the specific case analysis (for contentious problems) or matter analysis (for non-contentious problems) you will need to undertake at each stage, and incorporating the legal research strategy from Figure 8.1. This means you can use Figure 9.1 to help you solve contentious and non-contentious problems through traditional academic units, into practice-focused units, and beyond into professional practice.

Figure 9.1 encourages you to follow *a process*. This has two benefits. First, you can break down your task into a series of manageable steps. Once you understand what each step involves, you will feel able to enjoy the process of tackling any problem presented to you. Second, you have a structure for your answer, and the more you practise using that structure, the more familiar it will become to you. By following Figure 9.1, you will set out the results of your thinking at each stage in a way that demonstrates very clearly to your reader your problem-solving skills (and your ability to meet related assessment criteria).

To demonstrate how you can apply Figure 9.1 in traditional academic units, let's consider an example of a very simple problem. The answer provided has also been simplified for the purpose of this example, to allow you to see more easily the process Figure 9.1 encourages you to follow when answering problem questions. Following the example, we shall look in more detail at each stage of the process, which will show you how to use Figure 9.1 to complete your answer to the question.

Example 1

Facts: Nina was driving through Manchester city centre behind a pick-up truck owned and driven by Sema, an independent contractor. Nina could see that the tailgate of the truck had been left down. As the truck rounded a bend, a large container of paint slid along the bed of the truck, before falling out. The container hit the road directly in front of Nina's car, and burst open, spraying the front of Nina's car (a two-year-old silver Mercedes A Class) with paint. The container hit and then cracked the front bumper of her car. The estimated cost of replacing the bumper, and cleaning, then respraying, the affected areas of her car is £1,800.

Advise Nina whether she has a legal right to claim the cost of repair from Sema.

Issue: The potential parties are Nina (potential claimant) and Sema (potential defendant) who owns and was driving the truck. Our task is to advise Nina whether she has a legal right to claim the cost of repair from Sema. The relevant facts are: Nina's car has been damaged by paint and a paint container, which fell from Sema's truck. The tailgate had been left down. The estimated cost of repair to Nina's car is £1,800. We do not know if there was a witness, or what Sema's view is of the incident. Nina's objective is to have her car repaired in full and recover the cost of that repair from Sema. Presumably (but need to check), Sema's objective is to avoid any liability for paying for the repair. The legal issue is whether Sema's actions provide Nina with a remedy to recover the costs of repair.

Rule: While Figure 9.1 incorporates legal research, so you can find any law you need to find, in the context of traditional undergraduate units you are likely to have been taught the law that you need, and will have lecture notes, a textbook, and class notes. Here, for example, the relevant *area* of law is the law of tort and the relevant *cause of action* is negligence. You are likely to know this, and what follows, from your studies. As covered in Chapters 5 and 7, the general principles of the law of negligence were established in the leading case of *Donoghue* v *Stevenson* (1932), and have been developed through a number of subsequent cases. The necessary elements of law to consider are:

(a) establish that a *duty of care* exists;

(b) consider what *standard of care* is required;

(c) assess whether that standard was observed, or the duty was *breached*; and

(d) if the duty was breached, the question of damages arises, where the elements to consider are:

    (i) actual damage must occur;

    (ii) the damage must be caused by the breach of duty of care; and

    (iii) any damages must be reasonably foreseeable as resulting from the breach.

The general purpose of damages in tort is to put injured parties back into the position they were in before the relevant event occurred.

Application: Applying the law to the facts means that we have to establish the following:

(a) Did Sema owe Nina a duty of care?

(b) If so, what standard of care was owed by Sema to Nina?

(c) Did Sema fail to meet the required standard?

(d) Did actual damage occur?

(e) Was the damage caused as a result of Sema's breach of duty?

(f) Was the damage a reasonably foreseeable result of Sema's breach of duty?

(g) What amount of damages would be required to put Nina back into the position she was in before her car was damaged by the container and paint?

Conclusion: Assuming that each of questions (a)–(f) was answered in the affirmative, you would conclude that Nina would have a claim in negligence against Sema. Her legal remedy would be in tortious damages, and the amount of those damages would be based on the answer to (g).

Reflecting on the example reveals the benefits you will gain by using Figure 9.1 to solve legal problems:

- It gives you a logical order for working: only when you identify the issue can you consider the relevant law; and only when you have the relevant law can you apply it to the facts of the question; and only when you have done that can you conclude with the appropriate advice.

- This logic extends into the narrative of your answer to provide clarity: each subsequent point is the one that the reader would want to come next.

- It helps you produce a structured plan or 'skeleton' for your written answer. Your *introduction* will set out the I (Issue) and signpost the structure of your work; the *body* of your writing will deal with the R (Rule) and the A (Application to the facts of the question); and then you will set out a clear C *(Conclusion)*. You might then want to go back to your *introduction* and signpost for your reader what the *Conclusion* is going to be. You can use headings and sub-headings to make clear your structure for the reader.

- It clarifies what, specifically, you need to cover at each stage.

- Perhaps best of all, by breaking down the task into these chunks, you will feel that the overall task is much easier to tackle.

- It ensures you deal with each of the typical assessment criteria for solving legal problems, for example, *knowledge, understanding, application, structure, communication*, and *sources*.

Look back at the answer given in the example. All that you now need to do is expand your work through a combination of: explanation; citing authorities; applying the law to the facts to answer the questions you have posed; and tailoring your advice based on the facts of the question. More detailed guidance follows, which will help you use Figure 9.1 to answer any problem question with success.

9.1.3.1 Issue

The facts of the question, and the legal issue raised, were relatively easy to identify in the example. You may be presented with problems which are based on more complex facts and which raise more than one issue. Be aware that, as a first year law student, you have an advantage that the problems you will be set will be based on the current areas of law you are studying. You should be familiar with the areas of law that are likely to be raised in a specific subject area. By the time you are assessed, you should be familiar with all of the areas you have studied in each subject, and have developed an instinct for the type of facts and scenarios that give rise to them. For example, you will recognise facts that present a negligence issue when you see them in a tort assessment. It is important to adopt a deep approach to your learning (as opposed to a shallow approach which involves memorising in the short term to pass an exam), so that as you progress from one year to the next, you understand and can remember (at least enough to research further) the basic principles of each of the subjects you study. Examples of key principles that any law graduate might be expected to show understanding at some level (whether they decide to practise law or not) include: the measure of damages in tort and in contract; the basis of negligence; what is necessary to form a valid contract; the standard of proof in criminal and civil cases, the concept of *mens rea*; the relevance of the year 1966 on the law of precedent and the House of Lords; and so forth. You can ask your lecturer what they consider to be the key principles in their own subject that you might be expected to recall years from now.

Adopt the approach in the example: summarise the *facts* which give rise to the issue; then summarise the legal *issue*, with reference to those facts. This involves analysing only the facts you have identified as *relevant*, that is, they *give rise to the issue* in the summary. In our example, the issue arose because of damage to a car resulting from a container falling from an open truck. These are the relevant facts. The make and colour of Nina's car, for example, are irrelevant facts as far as the legal issue is concerned.

9.1.3.2 Rule

Once again, the subject areas you are studying and your developing instinct as a lawyer will provide you with a good indication of both the relevant area (in our example, tort) and specific cause of action (negligence). Clearly indicate these in your answer. You will need to apply your legal research strategy to identify the specific primary source(s) of law which is relevant to the issues identified. This strategy, which was set out in Figure 8.1 and explained in Chapter 8, is now referred to in the expanded 'Rule' section of Figure 9.1. In Example 1, the primary source of the law relating to negligence is case law (*Donoghue* v *Stevenson*) rather than legislation (see Example 4). Remember that as you carry out your research, you should not only summarise the relevant law but make a contemporaneous record of its source. That will allow you, when stating a rule in your answer, to support it with relevant authority, and to reference your work properly (see 14.1.8). Remember to follow any required referencing style.

Summarise and order the applicable law giving thought to clarity and structure. This will make your task easier when you come to apply it in the next step. Example 1 illustrates how to do this well, in this case following the standard order of the tests and definitions that must be met to establish negligence.

9.1.3.3 Application

Your task here is to apply the law to the particular facts and issue in hand. The approach illustrated in Example 1—posing a series of questions—can work well when you need to apply a series of tests or definitions to analyse whether a claim, or particular rights, exist. You are effectively mirroring the court process, where judges will decide each case based on what they think is the effect of the law on the facts, evidence, and argument before it. You should spend some time considering the application stage of Figure 9.1, as this will be both the largest and most important part of your answer. You will be using higher-level intellectual skills. For example, we have already seen that you will be:

- reading, assimilating, and summarising facts and law, showing that you *know* and *understand* them;
- *applying* law and principles to the facts of the problem;
- *critically analysing* the application of law in similar cases and comparing to and contrasting with the current situation; and
- clearly *structuring* and *communicating* all of the above, and drawing preliminary conclusions as a result.

Let us consider some common areas where you can distinguish your application.

The facts

Be clear that you are applying the law to the facts. You might feel inhibited, because you assume mentioning the facts is stating what you consider to be obvious, or 'non-law' and surplus to requirements. On the contrary, the relevant facts are important and you should be referring to them explicitly (for example, names and dates, the fact that the tailgate of the truck had been left open, that the damage was caused by paint and the paint container), to show your answer is tailored to the question and not simply generic. If your interpretation of how the law applies to the facts is that, for example, because of particular words during a phone call, X made an offer to Y for the purchase of goods at a set price, then say exactly that. Do not be tempted to make up facts. If you are sure that you have not been told a fact that you would need to know in order to advise definitely, then identify what that is and how you suggest you can best progress the matter. Speak to your lecturer about this. They may say they will be giving you all you need to answer the question. Or they may say they would want you to advise, 'if X=Y, then . . .; but if X=Z, then . . .'(where X is the missing fact, and Y and Z the possible answers). In practice, if you invent or assume a fact, you risk advising prematurely. Your advice may then turn out to be incorrect once you do have all the facts you should have had before advising.

Applying the law

When applying the law to the facts, you need to support your argument (i.e. explain *why*) with reference to primary sources. They could be case law, or legislation.

Applying cases

You can use cases to support your argument in two main ways:

- As authority for a legal principle. Here you are unlikely to need to refer to the facts of the supporting case. For example, citing *Donoghue* v *Stevenson* as authority for what you say are the principles of negligence (see 9.1.3.2).

- As a comparison with the facts of the legal problem on which you are advising, for example, if the facts are similar to a case, or similar but with a significant difference. Here you will need to refer to the facts of the supporting case, for instance 'case X is relevant, as it is very similar on the facts, however in that case the defendant was a business and in this case the defendant is a consumer . . . so will the court apply the same principles here, or distinguish this case on its facts?'

Applying legislation

While citing the legislation, then citing the facts, then applying the legislation to the facts is not incorrect, it can be a time-consuming approach and feel repetitive to read. Consider instead using brackets to cite and apply as you go, as demonstrated in Example 2.

> ## Example 2
>
> 'There has been a breach of s. 177 Companies Act 2006. This is because a director (Nihal) of a company (Elite Limited, "Elite") is directly interested (his sister, Sonia, is the Seller) in a proposed transaction with the company (the proposed purchase by Elite of an Aston Martin Valkyrie for £2.5M). Nihal should have declared (and he did not) the nature and extent of his interest (as set out above) to the other directors (Lauren, Ash, and Jas).'

However you choose to cite and apply, be aware that generally the passive voice will not be as helpful as the active voice when you are discussing the law. Compare, for example, 's. 177 has been breached' with, 'Nihal has breached s. 177'.

You will also need to give thought to the rules of statutory interpretation (see 4.4.3).

Applying the general rule before considering exceptions

If you think an exception applies, you must still state the general rule first, before you explore whether the exception applies. For example, if someone has posted an acceptance, you should state the general rule—that acceptance must be communicated—*before* you consider any exceptions to that rule, such as whether the postal rule applies.

Applying only relevant law

As with the facts, you should be discussing only what is *relevant* in the law. Writing all you know about a topic is not application and is not what is required in response to a problem question. It will not help you succeed in meeting the criteria at a high level because, while you might be able to demonstrate *knowledge*, *structure*, and *sources* this way, you will not be evidencing *understanding*, *application*, or effective *communication*. Consider in particular who you have been asked to advise, and read the question carefully to determine whether it ring-fences the law that you need to discuss in any way.

At the end of this section on problem-solving questions, there features Example 3, with two answers to compare, and some further guidance on how best to apply the law and structure your answer (see 9.1.5). There is a further demonstration of the application of law in Example 4.

9.1.3.4 Conclusion

It is a common error, during the application stage, to drift off course and begin inadvertently to rephrase the question in your head as you compose your answer. Before finalising your conclusion, read the facts and the question again, and check that your conclusion will answer *that* question.

Most questions require you to advise, so make sure that your conclusion (a) clearly advises the relevant party on the legal remedies (and, if relevant) other options available and (b) provides, concisely, your reasoning behind your advice. In Example 1, the first part of your conclusion could be that, based on the facts, Nina has a strong case in tort to bring an action for negligence against Sema, seeking a remedy in damages, and you should explain that this would be on the ground that Sema had breached her duty of care to Nina to take reasonable steps to avoid damage resulting from her trade activities.

If your analysis is that there are two possible answers (for example, you may be unable to conclude categorically whether a general rule or the exception applies) you should consider the effects of both possibilities before stating, as far as possible, which option you are most persuaded would be the most appropriate outcome, and why. You must not do this purely to 'hedge your bets' however, if on the facts given you should be able to draw a clear conclusion. It will provide your reader with most clarity if you also signpost your conclusion in your introduction (where you will be dealing with the 'Issue'), for example, 'This answer will conclude that Nina has a strong case in tort to bring an action for negligence against Sema and seek a remedy in damages'. 9.2.4.1 explains that, in real life, clients have other options too, including to do nothing, or negotiate. However, often in traditional undergraduate units your lecturer is not expecting such a practical level of advice. Speak to your lecturer if they are using practical, problem-solving questions in a traditional academic unit, to clarify how far they expect you to take the practical aspect. You can use Figure 9.5 as a basis for your discussion.

9.1.4 Structuring and communicating your answer to a problem question

Consider carefully how you can structure and communicate your answer most effectively and efficiently, so your work avoids verbosity, repetition, and irrelevant material, and has flow. Your approach should differ from your approach to structuring an essay question (see 14.1). To answer any problem-question effectively, your introduction will consist of the Issue stage of Figure 9.1, and signpost your conclusion; the body of your answer will be identifying the Rule and Application stages, where you will identify the relevant law and how it applies to the facts of the question. You will end with the Conclusion stage, where you identify legal remedies (and, if relevant) other options, and evaluate them.

With single-issue or otherwise simple problems, this structure will be straightforward. If you identify multiple issues, you should consider whether following the RAC stages for each I (Issue) at a time would produce a clearer, more structured answer than attempting to deal with all of the issues at each stage. Equally, if there are several parties, or a chain of several different events, you may be encouraged to deal with each separately. In all 'multiple aspect' cases, use headings to make clear which issue, character, or event you are discussing. This will signpost your structure and give clarity to your reader, and prevent you from mixing up different issues or revisiting an issue you have already dealt with. Clarify with your lecturer how they prefer you to deal with 'multiple aspect' cases, and whether they require anything else from you when answering a problem question for their particular unit (for example, some may require you to track the history of the law that you have cited, or consider reform in some detail). They may already have provided you with some answer guidance, in which case scrutinise how they have structured their own guidance, and let that inform your discussions with them about structure.

9.1.5 **Further practice**

Example 3 provides you with further guidance on problem-solving questions and, in particular, application of the law. It gives you an example of application of regulation (as opposed to case law) in a non-contentious matter (as opposed to a contentious case such as a dispute). The problem involves advising on procedure and compliance. The specific regulations applicable to the facts have been summarised and simplified, and are expressed as 'Rules', so you need no prior knowledge of the subject area and can focus on the process, which is transferable to any area of law you might be studying. Before reading the examples of good and poor Application and Conclusion stages, attempt to answer this problem question yourself. You can then compare your answer to the example answers.

Example **3**

Problem question

Predator plc ('Predator') wants to buy all the shares in Target plc ('Target'). Both companies' shares are traded on the London Stock Exchange. Currently Predator does not own any shares in Target. It decides to buy the shares in Target gradually, in the hope that it can buy as many as possible in secret without having to disclose to Target that it is gradually building a stake in it, with the intention of buying all its shares (in case Target does not want to be bought by Predator). Predator will buy Target shares on the Stock Exchange from the existing shareholders of Target. It intends to build its stake as follows:

- On 9 September Predator will buy 2 per cent of Target's shares.
- On 28 September it will buy a further 0.9 per cent.
- On 2 October it will buys another 7.1 per cent.
- On 31 October it will buy another 0.9 per cent.

This will brings Predator's total shareholding in Target as at 31 October to 10.9 per cent.

(Continued)

Advise Predator whether it can keep these share purchases secret from Target, or whether it must disclose them.

Issue

The parties here are the buyer and potential defendant (Predator), the sellers (the shareholders of Target) and the potential claimant, the company whose ownership will be changing (Target). We are advising Predator. Our task is to advise Predator specifically about the need to disclose to Target any or all of four different purchases it intends to make. Predator's objective is to buy all the shares in Target, build its stake gradually, and keep its purchases secret from Target for as long as possible. The legal issue is whether any disclosure will be required, and if so when and how, when one public company listed on the stock exchange buys shares in another such company.

Rule

The relevant law is company law and the cause of action to be explored arises from the disclosure obligations in relation to public companies listed on the stock exchange. A sound research strategy (see Figure 8.1) revealed Rules 1 to 5 which are relevant to the issue:

Rules:

1. *Rule 2 applies only to shares that you have bought or sold in a company which is a public company that trades on a UK stock market.*

2. *You must tell a company the percentage of shares you own if, having bought or sold shares, the percentage of shares you own either reaches or exceeds each of 3 per cent, 4 per cent, 5 per cent, 6 per cent, 7 per cent, 8 per cent, 9 per cent, 10 per cent, and each 1 per cent threshold thereafter up to 100 per cent.*

3. *You must comply with Rule 2 as soon as possible and in any event no later than two days after you bought or sold shares.*

4. *When you calculate percentages for Rule 2, you should round down any fractions.*

5. *If you breach Rule 2 the Regulator will fine you an amount at their discretion (maximum £X), and/ or publicly name you on its website as being in breach of these Rules.*

Good example

Good Application

Applying the Rules to Predator's share purchases:

Does Rule 2 apply to Predator?

Yes, because:

- Predator owns shares in Target;
- Predator has bought shares in Target (on four separate occasions);
- Target is a public company ('plc' stands for public limited company) and trades its shares on the London Stock Exchange, which is a UK stock market.

Rule 2 therefore applies as a result of Rule 1.

Each of the four purchases will now be analysed in turn, with reference to the relevant percentages at each stage, to establish if and when Predator would have to tell Target about them.

9 September: purchase of 2 per cent

Predator can keep this purchase secret from Target. This purchase will not take Predator's shareholding to the minimum threshold of 3 per cent referred to in Rule 2.

28 September: purchase of 0.9 per cent

Predator can keep secret. Following this purchase Predator will own only 2.9 per cent of Target shares. This fraction will be rounded down to 2 per cent under Rule 4, and so still will not reach the 3 per cent threshold in Rule 2.

2 October: purchase of 7.1 per cent

Predator cannot keep secret. Following this purchase Target will own 10 per cent of Target shares, and 'reaching 10 per cent' is one of the thresholds referred to in Rule 2. Predator will have to tell Target about this purchase. Under Rule 3, Predator must tell Target as soon as possible after the purchase on 2 October. 'As soon as possible' is not defined, but it cannot be longer than two days after that day. So we can be certain that Predator would have to disclose its 10 per cent shareholding to Target by 4 October at the latest, and by 2 October at the earliest.

31 October: purchase of 0.9 per cent

Predator can keep secret. This is because this purchase takes its shareholding to 10.9 per cent which, under Rule 4, would be rounded down to 10 per cent. This purchase would not take the shareholding through another 1 per cent, which would be the triggering event for another disclosure under Rule 2.

Good Conclusion

Predator will not be able to meet its objective of keeping all of its share purchases secret from Target, as under Rule 2 Predator must disclose to Target when Predator's shareholding in Target reaches 10 per cent. This will occur following the purchase of 7.1 per cent on 2 October, and Predator will have to disclose the purchase to Target as soon as possible, and no later than two days after the purchase, namely 4 October. If Predator fails to do so, the Regulator can impose a fine at their discretion (maximum £X) and/or publicly name Predator on its website as being in breach of these Rules. Predator will not have to disclose to Target its further purchase on 31 October, because the resulting shareholding does not exceed the relevant threshold for a further notification.

Note that this answer is good for the following reasons:

- It does not just cite the law. At each stage, it refers to the relevant facts of the problem (for example, to the percentages of shares Predator bought and to actual calendar dates and deadlines).

- As there are four purchases, it analyses each one, in chronological order, using appropriate headings to signpost the structure to the reader. This is a good approach whenever a problem details a series of events (or parties, or is in some way 'multi-issue').

- No time has been wasted in copying out the law first in its entirety, then repeating it when applied to the facts. Instead, efficiently, it refers to the law (in this case by reference to Rule numbers), and applies it to the facts, as it goes along.

- The structured, consistent application of the law to the facts means that, if there were an error at any point (there is not), causing the wrong conclusion to be drawn, then an experienced reader (a lecturer marking an assessment, or a supervising solicitor checking your work in practice) is likely to be able to identify this and possibly infer what the correct answer should have been. This means that the answer is still useful to the reader, and will attract a better mark which reflects that, compared to an answer comprising only wrong conclusions with neither explanations nor references to the relevant law and facts.

- It uses active language, for instance it does not just say Predator needs 'to disclose', or that Target needs to 'be disclosed to'; it identifies that Predator should notify Target.

- It provides a clear, reasoned conclusion, and outlines the remedy that the Regulator may impose on Predator.

Compare this with the following, poorer, answer.

Poor example

Poorer Application

Rule 2 states that Predator must tell a company of the percentage of shares it owns if, having bought or sold some shares, the percentage of those shares reaches, exceeds, or falls below certain thresholds, one of which is 10 per cent.

Poorer Conclusion

As the company now holds 10.9 per cent, it must disclose within two days.

This answer is poorer in several respects:

- The majority of it is copying out the law (i.e. the Rules).

- The only fact against which the writer has applied the law is the final shareholding of 10.9 per cent. It does not analyse each chronological event. As a result, the answer is vague as to the exact date which Predator must disclose, and specifically which of the four purchases crosses the Rule 2 10 per cent threshold and triggers notification.

- Compared to the first example, there is far less evidence of application of the law to the facts. This has resulted in an imprecise conclusion.

- It lacks detail. For example, it does not identify who must disclose, or to whom, or consider the actual dates of notification. Predator would need to know these practical issues.

- It does not clearly conclude, by reference to the question, that Predator cannot build its stake in secret.

- It does not refer to the remedy that Predator may face for breaching Rule 2.

For these reasons, this answer would be awarded a lower mark in an assessment compared with the example above of a good answer. In legal practice, it would amount to unhelpful, imprecise advice.

9.2 Solving legal problems in practice

At 9.1, we considered how to deal with problem-solving questions, as traditionally set for students on undergraduate law programmes. The skills developed by working on these problems are transferable to legal practice (that is one of the reasons for the use of these questions). The majority of scenarios used in problem-solving questions are at least derived from actual events, if not based directly on them.

However, it is fair to say that these questions cannot replicate all of the aspects of problem-solving in practice. Increasingly, law programmes are including commercial awareness in their curriculum, integrating elements of this into problem-solving questions, sometimes in specifically practice-focused units. For these problem-solving questions you have to think like practising lawyers, taking into account clients' personal and commercial considerations when advising on options to solve problems (see Chapters 17 and 18), such as the effect on ongoing relationships, or weighing the financial risk of pursuing court action as against the likelihood of success. (For a specific example on advising in practice, see Example 5.)

The rest of this chapter therefore considers these wider aspects of case/matter analysis for problem-solving in practice. It also provides guidance as to how you can use and develop Figure 9.1 to accommodate these differences.

9.2.1 **Figure 9.1 in practice: the Issue stage**

9.2.1.1 **Case/matter analysis**

Example 4 is used to illustrate case/matter analysis at the 'Issue' stage of Figure 9.1 in a more practice-focused context. The guidance here includes some diagrammatic techniques which you can use to assist with your case/matter analysis. Example 4 is an illustration of the benefits (both in practice and in dealing with complex problem questions and scenarios) of investing time early on in case/matter analysis. Your return on this investment is the focus that it will give your legal research, application of the law to these facts, and advice.

In practice, a client may not always provide all the facts required, and may provide many facts that are irrelevant to the matter in hand.

As a lawyer, you may identify the additional facts required early on, or might only do so after an initial analysis of the problem based on the facts in hand at that time. Even then, you may need to undertake some initial research to identify the issues. Thus, while as a lawyer the stages of Figure 9.1 still apply, typically you should expect the process to be less structured and more iterative; you may have to go back and forth between the stages. It is often necessary to spend more time on case/matter analysis at the Issues stage *before* carrying out research into the law, applying that law, and advising. There will also be both personal and commercial considerations and objectives of the client that have to be factored in (to both identifying issues and ultimately providing advice). For example, you need to consider how much resource your client has in terms of money and time. Finally, there may also be additional parties (sometimes referred to as 'stakeholders') whose interests need to be considered, even though they may not be directly involved in the matter as parties.

Example 4

It is August. You act for Stentor Limited ('S'), a company that manufactures and sells high-quality brass hardware, including buckles and locks. A director of S, Georgia King, has asked your firm for advice.

In the spring, S was approached by Britbag plc ('B'), which manufactures high-quality handbags. B was interested in buying a large consignment of buckles and locks for its new 'Catherine' handbag, ready for a high-profile advertising campaign to be launched in the autumn. To secure the order, S gave B a 10 per cent discount off the normal list price of the buckles and locks.

(Continued)

S and B entered into a contract for sale of the goods on the basis of S's standard terms and conditions of sale. Clause 9 of that contract is reproduced below.

Extract from contract

9. LIABILITY

9.1 In the event of any defect in the Goods, the Seller shall at its option repair or replace such Goods or refund the price of such Goods. Subject to clause 9.3, the Seller shall have no further liability in respect of the Goods.

9.2 Subject to clause 9.3, the Seller shall not be liable for any claims for damages whether consequential or otherwise, howsoever caused.

9.3 Nothing in clauses 9.1 or 9.2 excludes or limits the Seller's liability for death or personal injury caused by the Seller's negligence or fraudulent misrepresentation.

S delivered the buckles and locks on 1 June and B paid for the goods on 15 June, in accordance with the terms of the contract.

The bags are not yet ready to be sold in shops, but 25 prototypes have been made up and tested by volunteers. This resulted in the buckles and locks discolouring and spoiling the handbags' appearance. Scientific testing revealed a fundamental weakness in the buckles and locks as a result of the poor quality brass used.

B has told S it no longer has faith in S and would not be interested in any replacement goods. B is insisting on returning to S the remaining unused buckles and locks and is demanding a refund from S for those. B has also made clear that it will strip out the buckles and locks it has already used in the prototype bags and wants a refund for those too. B wants S to meet the cost of buying replacement buckles and locks from other suppliers (to the extent that the refunds do not cover that cost).

Georgia has told you that S accepts that the goods are not representative of S's usual standards, although she is a little puzzled because, having read the contract, there does not seem to be anything in it about the standard the goods should meet. Nevertheless S is prepared to replace the buckles and locks 'to honour S's obligations under the contract'. However, S 'refuses to go any further than this' and does not want to give B a refund for any of the buckles and locks, or reimburse B for the cost of buying replacements from any other supplier.

Advise S.

9.2.1.2 Parties

While it may often appear obvious, it is important at the start of any analysis leading to advice to be sure who you are advising. When companies are involved, there can be potential for confusion, as the company and each of its directors are separate persons in law. The parties here are Seller, S (the potential defendant), the Buyer, B (the potential claimant), and Georgia King, a director of S. Although Georgia King is asking your firm for advice, she is asking on behalf of the company of which she is a director. It is this company, S, who you are advising; S, the potential defendant, is your client. Our task is to advise S.

As S is a company, it must consider the interests of others with whom it has a relationship (**stakeholders**), including its owners (called **shareholders**), its employees, and also anyone to whom it owes money (called **creditors**). This is because, if S has to give any remedy to B, S will be worse off than it is now from a financial perspective. However, it may be able to preserve its business reputation, which can bring long-term benefits. The shareholders, employees, and creditors need to be on your radar as wider stakeholders in the context of this problem.

9.2.1.3 Facts

The next stage is to analyse the information received so far from your client and, based on what you currently understand the main issues to be, isolate, summarise, and order the *relevant* facts. This will, in turn, make it easier to focus on what are the legal issues, without being distracted by irrelevant material.

Relevant facts

In this case, the relevant facts are:

- S has sold brass buckles and locks to B at a 10 per cent discount.
- B has used these items on 25 prototype bags and they have discoloured.
- B commissioned testing of the bags: this showed that the discoloration was due to the poor quality brass used in S's product.
- B wants to:
  - reject the unused buckles and locks;
  - claim a refund for all the buckles and locks, used and unused; and
  - be reimbursed for the cost of buying replacement buckles and locks, to the extent that the cost of replacement is more than the refunds it receives from S.
- B does not want any replacement goods from S.
- S accepts liability for any faulty goods, but is willing only to provide replacements.
- Clause 9 of the contract between S and B appears to limit S's liability by giving S the choice of whether to offer a repair, replacement, or refund, and providing expressly that S is not liable for damages.
- S has informed us that it understands that the contract is silent on the standard the bags and locks should have met.

Compare these notes with the initial information set out in Example 4. You have summarised the information and structured it, using bullet points, to give clarity. Let us consider other ways you might wish to do this.

Methods to summarise and structure the relevant facts

Summarising and structuring the relevant facts is a valuable process in embedding these facts in your mind. An initial analysis of the relevant facts has just been set out, using bullet points. Some lawyers find a visual approach valuable, either as an alternative or in addition to words.

> **Practice tip**
>
> In practice, lawyers often distil legal arrangements and transactions into diagrammatic form, to aid understanding of the facts and also to make it easier to explain the problem to other people who may need to understand it.

Diagrams Diagrams can be very useful for setting out transactions and contractual relationships. They are also used to set out corporate structures, showing, for example, a group of companies and their interrelationships. The transaction diagram at Figure 9.2 provides a simple representation of the legal transaction in Example 4.

Figure 9.2 Diagram showing the transaction between S and B

Mind maps A mind map or spider diagram is also a useful visual way to both record facts and set out potential issues. It can be useful in the legal research process: by setting out potential issues and questions, you are providing a focus for your research. Also, if you find law relevant to several areas of the mind map, it can help you to identify that this law is likely to be important. There are several ways of preparing a mind map. Figure 9.3 builds on the transaction diagram at Figure 9.2 to show more of the facts and issues.

You will use the facts you identify at this stage as a basis to start your legal research (when you reach the Rule stage of Figure 9.1). However, as mentioned, once you embark on that,

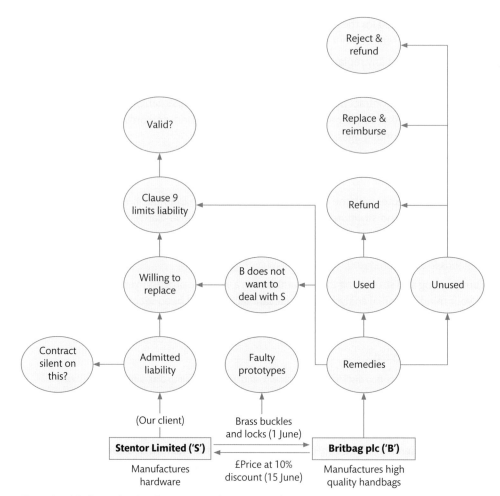

Figure 9.3 Mind map showing the transaction between S and B

you should be open to the fact that you may need to come back to this Issue stage in the near future, based on the results of your research and any additional facts you elicit.

Missing facts

Our case/matter analysis summarised the relevant facts based on the information we have received to date. That process, together with an initial analysis of the issues, may reveal that you need additional facts, or to ask further questions about legal or commercial matters. In this case, for example:

1. Can you have a copy of the signed contract between S and B?
2. Even if there is nothing in the contract about the required standard of the goods, was anything said in this respect before the contract was signed (pre-contract representations)?
3. Is S willing to conduct this claim in a way which might jeopardise the prospect of a good working relationship with B in the future?
4. What is S's financial position?

9.2.1.4 The client's objective

You should now be able to distil what is your client's situation and objective. For example:

> S has accepted liability for the substandard goods and is prepared to provide a remedy in the form of giving replacement goods to B. However, its objective is also to avoid giving B the remedies that B is seeking, namely rejection, refund, and reimbursement.

When you receive the answers to questions 3 and 4, you will be able to add to this summary of the client's objectives, for example, 'S wishes to avoid court proceedings at all costs, for financial reasons and/or due to the overriding need to preserve the possibility of a good business relationship in the future with B, who is an important customer.'

9.2.1.5 Legal issues raised

The process of the fact analysis and setting out the client's situation and objective should, together, raise the legal issues you now have to investigate through research. In this case these include:

- What is the basis of S's liability for providing faulty goods to B if the contract itself is silent on this issue?
- Is clause 9 effective in limiting S's liability to providing replacement goods to B?
- Is B entitled to seek the remedies it is seeking from S (rejection, refund, and reimbursement)?

9.2.2 Figure 9.1 in practice: the Rule stage

The problem questions you might find in traditional units tend not to rely on independent research, but rather to test your understanding of the law you have been taught during that unit. As you switch your focus more towards practice, perhaps on a skills or practice-focused unit, you will be expected to research and find the law yourself. Chapters 7 and 8 provide you with the guidance you need in order to find the relevant law and read it effectively; the Rule stage is based on the legal research strategy set out at Figure 8.1 and explained more fully in Chapter 8. If you have not done so already, you should read Chapters 7 and 8 now, including the more practice-focused material in 7.2 and 8.2.

9.2.3 Figure 9.1 in practice: the Application stage

As with the other stages, it is really just the context that will change in practice. The problem may be more complex; there may be more parties, you may have identified more than one legal issue, the client's objectives may be more nuanced (e.g. involving relationships and finances, which are less commonly raised in traditional unit problem questions) and more than one area of relevant law. You may, therefore, have to structure your Application more carefully, to make clear with which issue or party you are dealing. Using sub-headings for structure can be very helpful here, both for your own clarity, and your reader's. Use different fonts or styles consistently for headings and sub-headings. In Figure 9.4 (9.2.3.1) you will see that the main headings, the causes of action, are in bold type, next level headings are underlined, and further sub-headings italicised. Numbering is also used to separate the application of the different areas of law (contract and tort).

Another, different worked example based on a problem scenario is set out at Example 5, to develop your ability to handle even more complex problem questions, and to inform your understanding of the Application stage (and, in due course, the Conclusion stage) in practice. As you will see, the relevant law involves more than one area: elements of tort, contract, and commercial law are relevant here. To simplify the example and allow you to focus on the Application and Conclusion stages, the relevant law is provided, in the form of rules, and no supporting cases have been cited.

Example **5**

Facts

Jack filled his car with £60 worth of petrol from the petrol station at his local supermarket. However, two days later, ten minutes into a journey to the airport 100 miles from his house, Jack's car seemed to lose power. He was forced to turn the car around and go home, his car misfiring all the way. By the time Jack returned home, he was too late to make alternative plans to travel to the airport and he missed his flight to Dublin where he had planned to spend the weekend visiting friends.

The next day, Jack managed to drive very slowly to the nearest repair garage. They said they had seen several vehicles that day with a similar problem, and there was speculation that there was something wrong with the supermarket's petrol. Later that day, the garage called with a quote for repairing the car of £700.

The garage said that Jack had made the problem worse by driving his car after the power had failed, and they were also having to work 'round the clock' to meet demand, as many cars had been affected locally. Jack was shocked at the amount of the quote but, as he uses his car as a taxi three days a week, he paid the garage the sum, and the next day collected his repaired car. The garage said Jack's car had received the last part they had in stock, and it was going to take them two weeks to take delivery of replacement parts for their other customers whose cars had suffered a similar fate.

Jack has since seen various reports on the television speculating that petrol from one particular terminal had become contaminated and that this petrol had been supplied to several supermarket petrol stations. The contaminated petrol is thought to be causing cars to break down. This has prompted Jack to seek advice from you as to whether he can 'seek compensation' for the £700 he has paid the garage, and 'whether there is anything else he can claim for'. **Advise Jack.**

Law

Using your research strategy at Figure 8.1, you found the following rules in contract, commercial, and tort law:

1. *If a seller sells goods in the course of a business, a term will be implied into the contract that the goods are of satisfactory quality and are fit for purpose.*

2. *It is no defence to a seller who is in breach of Rule 1 that the breach was not the seller's fault.*

3. *A buyer who wants to sue a seller for damages for breach of contract must prove that he has suffered loss or damage as a result of the breach of contract.*

4. *The object of damages for breach of contract is to put the buyer into the position he would have been in if the contract had been properly performed.*

5. *The buyer will not be able to recover damages for any loss which is too remote a consequence of the breach of contract.*

6. *Even if the seller is in breach of contract, the buyer must do what is reasonable to minimise his own loss.*

7. *A buyer can only recover damages for breach of contract from another party to the contract.*

8. *A buyer can recover damages in tort from anyone who owes him a duty of care.*

9. *The object of damages in tort is to put the buyer into the position he would have been in if the tort had never happened.*

9.2.3.1 Application of law to facts in Example 5

Figure 9.4 uses Figure 9.1 to apply the relevant law to the facts of Example 5. The annotations highlight where you can find how the writer has used the case/matter analysis guidance set out in the strategy, and the steps she has taken to ensure her application is structured well and communicated clearly. You can use and adapt this structure to apply the law to the facts of any problem question.

1. Breach of implied terms in sale of goods contract

The relevant primary source is cited and applied efficiently and effectively.

There is a contract here between the seller of the petrol (the supermarket, 'S') and the buyer of the petrol, Jack. As S is selling in the course of its business, there is an implied term in that contract that the petrol is of satisfactory quality and is fit for purpose (Rule 1). If the television reports are correct (this must be verified), and the petrol S has sold to Jack has caused his car to break down, then there has been a breach by S of this implied term as the petrol is not of satisfactory quality and is not fit for its purpose. Jack will have a cause of action against S for breach of contract.

The heading makes clear the relevant general area of law (contract) and the cause of action (breach of implied terms in sale of goods contract)

An appropriate use of the word 'if'. Example 5 does not provide verification of this information.

Identifies questions arising from the facts.

Possible defence?

S will not be able to use the defence that the petrol was contaminated at the terminal before it reached S, and not through any fault by S (Rule 2).

The general rule is applied before considering any defence.

Sub-headings of the main heading are consistently formatted (by underline).

Available remedies in contract

a) Damages

Jack will be able to use this cause of action to recover loss or damage resulting from the breach, that is, the sale of contaminated petrol which caused Jack's car to break down (Rule 3). We can advise Jack that he does have the right to damages. He can seek these from S, the other party to the contract (Rule 7). The measure of damages is to put Jack into a position as if the contract had been properly performed, that is to say had the petrol been of satisfactory quality and fit for its purpose (Rule 4).

Next level headings are also consistently formatted, but differently from headings and sub-headings.

Figure 9.4 An annotated, worked example of the Application stage in practice

Limiting factors: remoteness and mitigation

In advising Jack what he can claim for, we need to consider the two limiting factors of remoteness and mitigation. The effect of Rule 5 is that Jack cannot seek to recover any loss which is too remote. The effect of Rule 6 is that Jack cannot seek to recover any loss which reasonably he could have avoided incurring. Taking each of Jack's losses in turn:

- The £60 Jack paid for petrol which made his car break down is a loss directly related to the breach and so Jack should be able to recover this amount from S.
- If the television reports are correct, and the contaminated petrol caused Jack's car to break down, this is also a loss flowing directly from the breach, and Jack should be able to recover the amount required to repair his car. However, it is likely that S will resist paying Jack the full £700. S should argue that it would have been reasonable to expect Jack to have obtained at least one other quote to check that the figure of £700 was reasonable. Jack may be able to counter this argument by finding out the average repair cost for other cars which suffered similar damage, and he can also point out that garages were busy meeting increased demands on their time as a result of the extent of the contamination (as evidenced by the fact that the garage he used ran out of spare parts). S should also want to analyse the extent of the work done by the garage. It will probably find out that Jack made the problem worse by driving the car after the damage was apparent, rather than calling breakdown services, and may resist compensating Jack for this element of the repair.
- Jack will also be able to claim damages for any other loss directly flowing from the breach, so we should ask him what other expenses he has incurred due to the breakdown. From the facts provided, we know that Jack has missed his flight. We need to advise him that while he could seek to claim this loss from S, S is likely to be advised to resist this, on the basis that it is too remote and does not flow directly from the breach. We also know that Jack is a taxi driver. On the facts it does not appear that Jack missed any work due to the breach. However if he did, again, S is likely to be advised to argue that any loss relating to this is too remote. Unless S and Jack can come to some agreement on these matters, they would have to ask a court to decide.

b) Existence of other contracts which may cover the loss

It may be that Jack is also party to other contracts which could help him to recover his loss. A contract of insurance may give Jack the ability to recover certain costs from the other party to that contract, the insurer. A contract of warranty may give Jack the right to recover certain costs from the other party to that contract, the car manufacturer. Jack should be asked if any such contracts exist.

2. Tortious action in negligence

Under Rule 7, Jack cannot claim for contractual damages against the supplier and distributor ('D') who supplied the contaminated petrol to S, because Jack is not a party to any contract with D. However, if Jack can show that D owed him a duty of care, then Jack could seek 'compensation' from D in the law of tort (Rule 8). Jack would have to prove that by supplying contaminated petrol to S, D breached its duty of care to Jack, the ultimate consumer of that petrol.

Available remedy in tort: damages

The measure of tortious damages would be to put Jack in the position that he would have been in had D not provided the contaminated petrol to S (Rule 9).

Figure 9.4 *Continued*

9.2.4 **Figure 9.1 in practice: the Conclusion stage**

Here we will consider in more detail the Conclusion stage of problem-solving in practice, namely giving advice to your client. We saw at 9.1 that when working on traditional undergraduate problem-solving questions, your aim is to come to a reasoned conclusion on, say, a situation, or rights, or claims. This is likely to conclude by identifying a legal remedy (in contentious cases), solution or procedure (in non-contentious matters). In practice, having concluded as to the effect of the law, it is your responsibility as a lawyer to provide advice to your client. You must take into account the client's objectives, and her personal or business situation and interests. As a lawyer, you should present the client with all of their options, including those other than the legal remedy, but also evaluate those options by weighing up the advantages and disadvantages of each, and what might be most appropriate given the client's objectives. While ultimately it is up to the client to decide which option to pursue, it is your role as a lawyer to ensure that their decision is an informed choice. The following information will help you to develop your ability to advise in this way. We will continue to use Example 5 to demonstrate how to do this.

9.2.4.1 Identifying the relevant legal remedy, solution or procedure, and other options

In most situations, the client's options tend to fall within the following three general categories:

1. Use your legal remedy, solution, or procedure (litigate, end the business, get divorced, sue, make a payment, comply with a procedure)

You will need to explain clearly what these options involve. It is not enough, for example, to say, 'Jack, you could litigate' (in contentious Example 5), or 'Predator, you must disclose your shareholding' (in non-contentious Example 3). Consider, instead the following:

- **Contentious:** You must consider and be clear about the claim Jack would be making, the time and costs involved, and the likelihood of success. The latter two matters also raise conduct issues (see 6.4.3).
- **Non-contentious:** In Example 3, you must consider and be clear about all of the matters included in the 'Good Conclusion', such as when, and how Predator must disclose under the Rules, and the penalties if it does not comply.

2. Negotiate another option and consider bargaining power

Again, the client will need your advice in this regard. Do not be tempted to say, 'one option is to negotiate'. You need to understand and explain what the client might be able to negotiate, and analyse his bargaining power to advise on his chances of success. Consider instead, the following:

- **Contentious:** If the client has a legal right to sue, he could use that as a bargaining chip, along the lines of 'I will agree not to sue you if you agree to do X' (e.g. pay me a sum now which is less than the amount I could sue for, but enough to keep me happy). If the client has a weaker bargaining position, then again you need to advise him of this, so that he is aware he should approach negotiations in a more conciliatory manner.
- **Non-contentious:** In Example 3, Predator will have no bargaining position to negotiate compliance with the Regulator about the Rules. You could, however, test the client's belief that Target does not want to be bought. If the belief remains firm, then you could discuss the different option of buying a reduced number of shares so Predator would not have to disclose its stake to Target, or exploring if there exists a more receptive takeover target. If the belief crumbles, you could explore the concept of negotiating with Target to persuade it to recommend to its shareholders to sell all their shares to Predator.

Chapter 12 explores negotiation in more depth.

3. Do nothing

Take care about how you present this as an option. You should mention it, but you must do so in the context that the client has come to you for help to resolve a problem or find a way to progress a matter. Nevertheless, it may be that when the client receives your advice, they choose not to proceed with it. For example:

- **Contentious:** Often, once a client understands the cost and time involved in resolving or progressing matters, tolerating the current situation seems more attractive than it did previously, or is revealed as the only affordable option, and hence it may be in a client's best interests not to proceed with a specific matter. Again, this point raises conduct issues—see 6.4.3.

- **Non-contentious:** Once it learns that it cannot build its stake in secret, Predator may decide the time is not right to go public with its plans, and halt or postpone building its stake in Target. A client might decide, due to cost, against instructing a lawyer to draft a partnership agreement, despite receiving initial advice that one is necessary to remove risks under the Partnership Act 1890.

While you may have been exposed to the concept that access to justice can be limited, these latter two options may be very unfamiliar if you are a student who has only ever been exposed to traditional problem questions during your studies. Be aware that these questions are often quite restricted to contentious areas of law and tend to encourage you to focus exclusively on whether there is a legal remedy or not.

In practice, even if there is a remedy (or, in non-contentious matters, a solution or procedure) available, 'doing nothing', often due to the cost of legal services, is more common than you might have been led to believe.

The World Justice Project in 2019 (see Further Reading) reported that, globally, 1 in 6 considered it difficult or nearly impossible to find the money required to resolve their problem through legal advice. YouGov research from the previous year found that 61 per cent of those surveyed thought that legal advice was not affordable to the general public in England & Wales (see Legal Services Consumer Panel, Further Reading). In contentious work, even those who do seek advice, and are advised that they have a legal remedy, might yet choose not to pursue it due to their personal, commercial, or financial situation. PwCGlobal observe, 'Very few litigation matters actually end up in court, with the vast majority being settled before reaching that stage' (see Further Reading) (although the threat of litigation, or pursuing it initially can of course help with the negotiation of that settlement).

Walker (see Further Reading) also makes clear that 'doing nothing' is often the chosen option for businesses, including in non-contentious matters too, explaining 'Business owners generally have an antipathy to legal matters that when aligned with a fear of potential cost, means they often try DIY methods rather than seeking out expert advice.' The SRA also report that more than 60 per cent of small businesses they spoke to (including almost 70 per cent of sole traders) thought that the cost of using a solicitor was a barrier preventing some businesses from using one.

Remembering these three general categories will help you with this part of the Application stage in practice, before you go on to be clear about the relative advantages and disadvantages of each.

9.2.4.2 Identifying the relevant remedies and other options in Example 5

Having considered the potential remedies identified in 9.2.3.1, and then combining them with potential practical approaches at 9.2.4.1, we can identify that the options are open to Jack are as outlined in Figure 9.5.

> 1. Use his legal rights in contract law to sue S for damages.
> 2. Use his legal rights in tort law to sue D for damages.
> 3. Do nothing.
> 4. Seek to negotiate with S using the threat of pursuing his legal rights as leverage to obtain a quicker and more cost efficient settlement.
> 5. Seek to negotiate with D using the threat of pursuing his legal rights as leverage to obtain a quicker and more cost effective settlement.
> 6. Rely on any other contract Jack is party to, such as an insurance or warranty contract.

Figure 9.5 A worked example identifing relevant remedies and other options

9.2.4.3 Evaluating the options

Having identified the options, your role as a lawyer is then to inform the client of the advantages and disadvantages of each. Table 9.1 shows you how you can use a table to do this, with reference to the facts in Example 5. It evaluates all of the options open to Jack.

Table 9.1 A worked example of how to evaluate options in tabular form.

Option	Advantages	Disadvantages
Use Jack's legal rights in contract law to sue S for damages.	Jack will be able to seek contractual damages to achieve his aim of being 'compensated'. Jack may be able to use the small claims court which is a quicker and simpler way to pursue his claim than using other parts of the courts system. We need to research what the small claims court thresholds are.	Litigation can be a costly and time-consuming process, and, given the relatively small losses Jack may have incurred, the legal bills alone might outweigh what Jack could seek to recover. The issues of remoteness and mitigation discussed at Figure 9.4 will limit Jack's claim. Jack will have to obtain and provide comprehensive evidence to support his claim.
Use Jack's legal rights in the law of tort to sue D for damages.	Jack will be able to seek tortious damages to achieve his aim of 'compensation'. As previously, Jack may be able to use the small claims court.	Jack would have to prove that D owes him a duty of care. Jack will have to obtain and provide comprehensive evidence to support his claim. As in previous remedy, the costs of litigation might outweigh what Jack could seek to recover.
Do nothing.	This will not involve Jack incurring any further cost or time on this matter.	Jack will not be able to achieve his aim of recovering the losses he has incurred.

Table 9.1 *Continued*

Option	Advantages	Disadvantages
Seek to negotiate with S using the threat of pursuing his legal rights as leverage to obtain a quicker and more cost efficient settlement.	Jack may be able to achieve his aim without recourse to litigation and the related cost and time implications. S may be particularly receptive to this approach, given that it is a consumer-facing business and needs to protect its brand and reputation going forward. It would appear that this is not an isolated incident and this may help to encourage S to provide an accessible solution to all who have suffered loss due to the contaminated petrol, not just Jack.	Jack may require further advice regarding whether to accept any offer S makes. Jack will still have to obtain and provide some evidence to support his claim. S may decide not to enter into negotiations with Jack.
Seek to negotiate with D using the threat of pursuing his legal rights as leverage to obtain a quicker and more cost effective settlement.	As with the previous remedy, this may achieve Jack's aim without recourse to litigation.	As previously, Jack may require further advice. Jack will still have to obtain and provide some evidence to support his claim. D may be less receptive than S to this approach, as it does not rely on consumers like Jack for ongoing custom. D's concern will be to establish its reputation with its own customers such as S.
Rely on any contract of insurance Jack may have, to recover his loss from the insurer.	If suitable cover is in place, Jack may be able to achieve his aim of recovering his loss, even though this is not in the form of 'compensation'.	There may be an excess to pay. Making an insurance claim is likely to result in Jack having to pay more for his insurance next year, and may cause him to lose any 'no claims bonus' he has accrued. The insurance contract is likely to limit the losses for which Jack can claim. It may not cover the damage at all if it was caused by Jack putting contaminated petrol into the car and Jack did not elect to cover 'accidental damage' in a comprehensive policy. Jack will have to obtain and provide some evidence to support his claim.
Rely on any contract of warranty Jack may have with his car's manufacturer.	As with previous remedy, if suitable cover is in place, Jack may be able to achieve his aim of recovering his loss, even though this is not in the form of 'compensation'. Jack may not have to show any link between the breakdown and the contaminated petrol.	As with previous remedy, the warranty is likely to limit the losses for which Jack can claim, and may not cover the damage at all if it was caused by Jack putting contaminated petrol into the car.

9.2.4.4 Advising on the most appropriate option

In practice (and well-designed practice-focused units), unlike in traditional units, you have the ability not only to ask questions of a client, but also to receive a response from them. Advising your client in practice will not be a one-way process. The work you have done so far using Figure 9.1 will have identified some key issues that you can now use to advise on the most appropriate option. This is illustrated by reference to Example 5, and finding the best option for Jack.

It appears that Jack's objective is to recover what he can to cover the losses he has incurred as a result of buying the contaminated petrol. Before advising on the most appropriate option, we would check with Jack that we have correctly understood his aims and objectives.

In Table 9.1 we identified several options which allow Jack to achieve his objective. They involve him seeking payment from S, D, or his insurer. Jack has used the word 'compensation' but it is unlikely that Jack is concerned about the particular source of any reimbursement he can obtain. (We would check this with Jack.)

We have also now checked and know that, currently, the small claims court can be used for claims up to £10,000 but that, even if a claim is within this limit, a judge reserves the right to decide that the case is too complex to be heard as a small claim. The small claims court can still take several months to reach a judgment.

With this in mind, we can begin to discuss with Jack what might be the most appropriate option for him.

The differentiating factors between the options we have identified appear largely to do with: (i) additional costs and (ii) further work required by Jack. In other circumstances, a key factor may be the requirement to preserve a good relationship. Two important questions to ask Jack are:

1. Additional costs vs how much is Jack seeking to recover?

The issue here is balancing what might be the additional costs of taking steps to obtain compensation against the amount he might actually recover. This will involve:

- helping Jack to identify each potential loss following from the sale of contaminated petrol, so we can calculate the total loss Jack thinks he has incurred;
- advising Jack on which losses might not be recoverable (in particular managing his expectations about recovering any loss regarding his missed weekend away and any missed taxi-driving work);
- providing Jack with an estimate of the likely costs of pursuing each option and comparing and contrasting that with the likely amount he stands to recover under each option.

It may be that, as a result of this analysis, Jack decides he no longer wishes to pursue the matter.

If the loss he would be claiming for is relatively low, Jack may also decide he does not wish to affect his future insurance premiums by making a claim under his insurance contract.

However, we could advise that, for relatively little further cost, Jack could make an attempt to negotiate. With whom should he try to negotiate, S or D? Our analysis showed that, as a consumer, Jack has more negotiating power with S than with D. Unless D was a substantially safer proposition financially (unlikely, given that S is a household-name supermarket) it is probably best for Jack to start to negotiate with S. We would advise Jack to gather evidence in support of his claim, such as:

- proof of his purchase of petrol (receipt, credit card, or bank statement);
- anything the repairing garage can provide such as a petrol sample, or any parts it removed from the car;
- any other evidence of loss, such as Jack's flight ticket;
- a written record of events (which Jack should compile while they are relatively fresh in his mind).

Jack would not need to make a decision just yet about whether to pursue his claim in the courts if his negotiation attempt fails, but, if the estimated value of his claim is as low as expected, the possibility of pursuing the claim in the small claims court might offer him further bargaining power in persuading S to settle his claim.

2. Further work: how much time is Jack able to devote to recovering his losses?

This question may be key in helping Jack to make a final decision between (i) doing nothing and (ii) attempting to negotiate a settlement with S.

11.2.1.10 discusses when you may have to use persuasive oral communication, if despite your evaluation of the options, against their best interests a client is ignoring or refusing an option.

9.2.5 Figure 9.1 in practice: Conclusion

The example you have just seen might appear complex, particularly when considering the relative merits of options and what would be the most appropriate course of action. However, both the range of options available to clients, and the considerations which determine a course of action are comparatively generic (see 9.2.4.1). What is important, as with problem-solving in general, is to follow your strategy in Figure 9.1, which you have tested and which you trust. By doing so, you will give consideration at each stage to the pertinent issues, and can make a decision properly informed by both the law and practical factors.

9.2.6 Figure 9.1 in practice: professional conduct issues

When you are advising in practice, you must take care to meet the professional standard set out in the Solicitors Regulation Authority's Codes of Conduct. These are detailed in 6.4.3.

 Summary

- It is the combination of a good knowledge and understanding of the law on the one hand, and sound legal skills on the other hand, which makes a lawyer.
- The legal skills which underpin problem-solving are case/matter analysis, legal research, application of the law to facts, and advising.

- Figure 9.1 gives you an effective strategy to help you use case analysis for problem-solving, and incorporates the IRAC model and your legal research strategy at Figure 8.1. You can use it in academia and practice.

- More complex problems require higher levels of case/matter analysis at an early stage (the 'Issue' stage of IRAC) to make the later stages of problem-solving more efficient and effective.

- When seeking solutions to the problems of clients, lawyers need to consider personal and business factors, and present options.

What the professionals say

As a student you will learn the law and how to apply it to a client's problem. However, practice taught me that while legal acumen is fundamental to the delivery of quality legal advice, it must be underpinned by a true commercial awareness. A lawyer needs to understand the client's objectives and the environment in which they operate, and that the legal options available will not always produce the best commercial solution for that client. As an insolvency lawyer, I dealt regularly with businesses who were in a state of crisis. In order to deliver clear pragmatic advice, it was not enough simply to know and understand the relevant law. I also needed to understand the client, what they did, the market in which they operated, their objectives and the objectives of the other stakeholders such as the bank, directors, and administrators. Only then could we go on to identify the very best solution to the problem they were facing.

Matthew Tomlinson, former Solicitor, DLA Piper

Chapter 9

Problem-solving and case/matter analysis

Practical exercises

Consider how you might answer the following questions:

1. Has your understanding of a lawyer's role in problem-solving changed as a result of reading this chapter, and if so, how?

2. How will you improve your commercial awareness, and your practice so that you can provide a client with all the options, not just those which follow the letter of the law?

3. Do you think a lawyer's fees should relate to the value of the solution provided?

4. What do you think can be done to widen access to legal advice for those with legal problems?

5. How does Figure 9.1 enhance your understanding of IRAC? Consider how you can commit Figure 9.1 to memory, with understanding.

*Visit the **online resources** for the authors' reflections and to check your progress.*

Further reading

Brest, P. and Kreiger, L. H. (2010) *Problem Solving, Decision Making, and Professional Judgment: A Guide for Lawyers and Policymakers*. Oxford: OUP

—This text examines the steps involved in the process of legal problem-solving, in addition to exploring the behavioural aspects of decision-making and exercising professional judgment.

Legal Services Consumer Panel (2018) *Tracker Survey 2018*. Available at: https://www.legalservices consumerpanel.org.uk/publications/research_and_reports/documents/2018/lscp-_infographic_on_how_consumers_are_using_2018.pdf

—YouGov research commissioned by the Legal Services Consumer Panel, exploring how consumers are using legal services.

Lexisnexis.co.uk (2019) *The Bellwether Report 2019: The Good Solicitor's Skill Set*. Available at: https://www.lexisnexis.co.uk/research-and-reports/bellwether-2019-the-good-solicitors-skill-set-bd.html#form

—This report explores whether the human, legal, and business skills which solicitors recognise as the most important ones (including problem-solving and advising), are in fact, the most lacking in the profession. It also considers the tendency of the profession to cling to the status quo, even when beneficial changes, with clearly articulated parameters of success, are identified.

Nathanson, S. (1997) *What Lawyers Do—A Problem-Solving Approach to Legal Practice*. London: Sweet & Maxwell

—This illustrates the key processes which underpin legal problem-solving. It adopts the context of legal practice but is directed very much at law students, to develop their wider understanding.

PwCGlobal 'Litigation can be inefficient and expensive. Why Litigate?' at https://www.pwc.com/gx/en/services/advisory/forensics/dispute-services/litigation.html

—PwCGlobal explore findings that parties want dispute resolution processes that are less costly, less time-intensive, and more aligned to their commercial interests.

Walker, S. (2012) *Small businesses shouldn't be afraid of seeking legal advice. The Guardian*. Available at: https://www.theguardian.com/small-business-network/2012/jun/13/small-businesses-seeking-legal-advice

—Unexpected legal costs can be an unwelcome drain on a business's budget, but with some simple planning they can be prevented says Taylor Wessing's Simon Walker.

World Justice Project. 'Global Insights on Access to Justice 2019: Findings from the World Justice Project General Population Poll in 101 Countries' at https://worldjusticeproject.org/our-work/research-and-data/global-insights-access-justice-2019

—Presents data on how ordinary people around the world navigate their everyday legal problems, highlighting the most common legal problems, respondents' assessment of their legal capability, and sources of help. The study also highlights information on the status of people's problems, the resolution process, and the impact of their justice problems on their life.

*For the authors' reflections on the practical exercises, additional self-test questions, sample interview questions and a library of links to useful websites, visit the free **online resources** at www.oup.com/he/slorach4e.*

Part II

Legal Skills

10 Persuasive oral communication and presentations

Learning objectives

After studying this chapter you should be able to:

- Appreciate why you need good oral communication skills as a student and a professional.
- Understand how both verbal and non-verbal skills will influence the effectiveness of your oral communication.
- Practise and develop these skills during your legal studies and in everyday life, to improve your influence and have your voice heard.
- Learn techniques which will help you to deliver a presentation which is persuasive and well-received, as a student and a professional.

Introduction

This is the first of five chapters on communication skills. Chapter 11 discusses specifically client interviews and meetings, Chapter 12 negotiation and mediation, Chapter 13 mooting and advocacy, and Chapter 14 communication in the form of writing and drafting. This chapter will help you understand the essential foundations for oral communication to be persuasive and influential, and then shows you how to use these skills specifically to give an effective presentation.

As you progress through your legal studies, seek employment opportunities, and then start developing your career, your communication skills will be fundamental to your success. They are the primary means by which you impart what you know and what you think. *How* you communicate will determine the extent to which you will be heard and understood; it will also determine the extent of your influence.

There are a range of situations in which you will need to employ oral communication skills during your studies. In due course, the graduate job interview process will also test your communication skills, and so you will want to have practised and honed these skills by then.

It is a fundamental professional skill to be able to communicate complex ideas in a way that is easy to understand. However, when faced with a real audience, in a situation where there is a little pressure and where you may have to think 'on your feet', you can expect your communication skills to be the first thing to suffer. Unfortunately your audience are likely to

Part II

Legal Skills

notice, too. If you are inclined right now to think the skills in this chapter are all too obvious, then you might like to consider how it was that Ed Miliband in his most important speech as leader of the opposition (at the Labour Party Conference in the year before the General Election), managed to forget to mention the key issue (the UK's significant financial deficit).[1]

Like most skills, developing your communication skills requires preparation, common sense, and subsequent reflection. This chapter aims to refresh you about the skills essential for good oral communication, then help you employ them to deliver a confident and effective presentation during your studies (10.1) and in consideration of practice (10.2). If the thought of this strikes fear into you, show yourself some compassion; fear of public speaking is the biggest phobia worldwide. So, take comfort that you are taking your first steps to certain success in learning a skill, in a supportive environment, that many fear more than snakes or spiders.

10.1 Oral communication skills and presentations: during your studies

10.1.1 What are oral communication skills?

The term 'oral communication skills' can be understood as speaking effectively. However, to really be heard, and to have influence, you are encouraged to understand that this really includes several different skills which you use together to allow you to convey effectively information, opinion, and advice, and to receive the same from others. During your studies, you may be asked to: contribute to class discussion and debate in tutorials and seminars; give presentations, in class and for assessment; compete in a moot or criminal advocacy competition; be involved in pro bono work such as a law clinic or similar initiative; interview for vacation placements, or other work experience schemes.

10.1.1.1 Non-verbal communication

Before you even begin to speak, you communicate through your body language, and very effectively too. Babies are very adept at communicating to get their needs met. Are you as effective, now you have your words? Are you aware how, if at all, your eye contact and body language change when you are dealing with a complex issue or difficult situation, or when you are deep in thought, or nervous? Nerves can have the effect of making even the most naturally pleasant and outgoing people appear hostile, severe, or unapproachable. You may be surprised to find yourself unable to look someone in the eye or offer a firm handshake at interview or assessment—just when you need to be at your most influential. The good news is that much of this can be overcome through self-awareness, preparation, practice, and experience. The first step is to be aware of what you should be aiming for. What follows will help you with your non-verbal communication.

Eye contact

Eye contact is extremely powerful. In Western cultures, avoiding eye contact can be deemed to be a sign of dishonesty. Conversely, good eye contact can be very reassuring, instil confidence,

---

[1] Wintour, P. (2015) 'The Undoing of Ed Miliband—and how Labour lost the election' *The Guardian*, 3 June 2015.

be persuasive, and also allow you to pick up on cues that others are making with their eyes. Therefore eye contact is important. If you struggle with it, and many do, then it is something you can work on to good effect. You can practise making good eye contact in everyday life. Experimenting in situations where you are comfortable can help you develop this skill, so that you can then deploy it when you are outside your comfort zone. A good tip is to focus just behind a person's head to begin with. This helps to practise the habit and gives the other person the impression of eye contact. When you are comfortable doing this, you can progress to looking at their eyes, allowing you to read their cues. Take care to avoid becoming 'locked in'; being able to break off eye contact, then seamlessly re-establish it, is another skill you can practise now.

If you have been diagnosed with, or suspect you may have, Autism Spectrum Disorder, you may find eye contact particularly challenging. Even if you have learned to make eye contact, it may be that you still do not pick up on any cues from other people's eye contact. To take another example, if you are lip reading, your eye contact will reduce. In such cases, simply being aware of the importance of eye contact, and the messages it conveys, can be helpful. For example, you may feel comfortable to explain, where you feel appropriate, that just because you are not making eye contact does not mean you are not listening or paying attention to what someone is saying. This in itself is demonstrating a high level of self-awareness and good communication skills. In other cases, be aware enough to know when you may be reducing eye contact in a way which is avoidable (for example, by taking notes at an inappropriate time, and Chapter 11 explores how to avoid that, and still take a decent note).

Body language

Our bodies can betray feelings that we would prefer to keep to ourselves. To some people, this is not desperately important. If the bass player in a band comes across as surly, hyperactive, or very shy, no one will use this to judge her ability to play guitar. However, in contrast, a lawyer must project a professional persona at all times, and we are professional communicators. As a student, practise paying attention to, and actively manage, the messages your body may be sending to the contrary. Folding your arms, for example, puts a barrier between you and anyone you are speaking to, and you risk looking defensive and hostile, however inadvertently. Persistent habits such as foot jiggling, pen tapping, hand waving, hair flicking, knuckle cracking, fidgeting, or pacing around can be distracting and reduce your power to influence. Consider what messages you might have been communicating to those who have taught or presented to you during your studies. If you are slumped and yawning, or distracted by your phone, throughout a lecture or presentation, the person delivering it will notice. This knowledge is not to shame you, but to become an effective communicator, you will need to become self-aware. We will all do something inadvertently which has a negative effect on our influence, but only some of us will learn to become aware of that fact in order to improve. Painful though it may be, the best way to identify this is to ask someone you trust to be brutally honest, or alternatively record and analyse yourself. This latter technique is an established form of teacher and media training. Smartphones make this process much more accessible than it used to be. Simply recording yourself talking about your favourite subject for five minutes is likely to reveal aspects of your body language of which you were not aware. Even watching yourself present to a mirror will help.

So far, we have discussed inadvertent body language, and it is also worth considering how to use body language deliberately to send messages to others. When presenting in class, formally or otherwise, you will want to influence others, and encourage them to engage with you. This starts by showing, when they are speaking, that you are actively listening and open to hearing what they have to say. Be the audience you would like to have yourself. When it comes to your turn to speak, there will be key points which you will want to make firmly and clearly, so you are certain they are heard and taken seriously. Non-verbal communication can help you here too. Mirroring (see Gorman, Further Reading) is a technique you may be interested to explore during your studies (and practice when you feel it is safe to do so).

Appearance

Consider the interview candidate who wears scuffed shoes or has not washed his hair. Have you made a judgement about them already, before they have started to speak? While encouraging you to learn the skills which will give you the confidence to be your best, authentic self, this chapter also encourages good self-awareness. Any judgement that people may make is, of course, a first impression, which may be refined or even dramatically changed by what you go on to say or do (see the film *Legally Blonde*). You can enjoy reflecting on what impression your current appearance might be conveying to others, and whether that aligns with one you are happy to convey (now, or in the future).

If you have a formal assessment which involves oral communication, such as a presentation, you might be given guidance as to what you should wear, to prepare your expectations for life after graduation. Sometimes students report it can also help you to 'step into' a more professional demeanour if you are wearing different clothes from those you would usually wear in class as a student. If you are at all unsure about what might be appropriate to wear, ask your lecturer and/or, reflect on what professionals have been wearing when you have met them during your studies (another reason to attend careers fairs, or pro bono events). Who have you seen who dresses both professionally and in a way you would feel comfortable dressing? It may be an opportunity for you to start thinking about what you might need to budget for now, to buy and wear for interview and/or assessment (where you can 'road test' your choice to make sure you feel both comfortable and confident while wearing it). Chapter 16 provides further guidance on this.

Listening skills

Most people really appreciate feeling listened to, and in today's busy and technologically driven world, it might be an increasingly rare experience. If you can show someone you are truly listening, they will likely be predisposed towards you. The term 'active listening' refers to the fact that, to do this well, you must be *seen* to be listening too. Body language is clearly important here and nodding and eye contact will convey that you are paying attention and engaged. Similarly, glancing down at your phone, laptop, or watch, or tying your shoelace, and suchlike, will have the opposite effect (and eventually whoever you are listening to will likely stop talking—of course, sometimes this can be useful, but only if you are using it knowingly). Generally, you need to show that you are engaged, and whoever is speaking will appreciate these signs; we tend to remember fondly people who help us to feel comfortable when we might be feeling out of own comfort zones. This is true for large groups as well as for small groups or one-to-one encounters. Any presenter, be it a classmate, your lecturer, or a guest speaker, will appreciate an engaged audience, and your learning community will thrive when those in it are adapting a good practice of active listening.

Conversely, if you are speaking, you are not listening. If you chat through a presentation, whispering or not, the presenter *will* notice you are not listening to them. Interrupting someone is also an error, and common on the part of lawyers, even student lawyers, because we tend to like to be in control of a situation, and to solve problems and, being bright individuals, can be tempted to feel we have thought of a solution or a response before we have really listened properly. Resist this temptation and use Example 1 to practise being open to hearing all that someone is really telling you (and this includes listening to their feelings as well as their words).

Example 1

In a suitable situation, resolve to experiment by concentrating *only* on listening to someone, digesting what they are saying to you, and feeling flexible in terms of your response (rather than listening to respond, which is appearing to listen while actually rehearsing in your head what you are going to say—and were always going to say—next). You will be surprised at the value of the further information which may be revealed to you, and the other person will feel infinitely more valued by being allowed to have his say.

If on occasion you do feel it is appropriate to interrupt (perhaps if someone is clearly upset or nervous and it is best for everyone that they take a break), then reflect now on how you might do this most effectively using body language, and/or the specific words you want to choose to communicate specifically what you are doing and why.

Confidence

The more you have an authentic and well-founded confidence in your own abilities, the more likely you will succeed in persuading others to have confidence in you. Confidence is not the same as arrogance or brashness, however, and the line is a fine one to draw. It will help if you can think now of someone you admire who inspires confidence, and consider them as a role model. What, specifically, do they do which impresses you? How, specifically, do they strike the right balance between confidence and arrogance? What is it, in particular, about their verbal and non-verbal communication that tells you they are a confident person? Consider how you might enjoy incorporating some of the behaviour you have just identified into your own communication skills, and practice until it has become habit.

Feel reassured, those people who come across as truly confident often might not have considered themselves to be naturally confident when they were students of their own discipline. They were, however, astute enough to understand that, to succeed, they needed to project confidence. As with most skills, the earlier and the more you practise looking and sounding confident, even (especially) when you feel nervous, the more adept at it you will become.

10.1.1.2 Verbal communication

It is not just *what* you say, but *how* you say it, that will determine the effectiveness of your oral communication. Your legal knowledge and skills are vital to ensuring that *what* you say is technically correct. However, your communication should not only be correct, it should also be effective. The assessment criteria against which your oral communication will be assessed is likely to include reference to good structure and communication. Let us consider some factors which will affect the effectiveness of your verbal communication during your studies.

Tone

The tone of your verbal communication is very important. It can help you to convey a range of messages: empathy; sympathy; humour; whether something is problematic. If you are not communicating face to face, for example when using the telephone (perhaps during a telephone interview or speaking to a mentor), very subtle changes in tone can be important. Does your tone indicate that you are engaged, or bored? When you are concentrating, what happens to your tone? Do you slip into a monotone? How might that affect your power to influence and persuade? Enjoy exploring the effect of varying the tone of your voice, when it is safe to do so (that is, not during your first formal interview, but perhaps when you are ordering food or buying a newspaper). It is likely to keep others interested and engaged. As explained (and see Gorman, Further Reading) people tend to 'mirror' emotions, and so if you want people to engage with and show interest in what you have to say, then model that behaviour for them.

Pace

You may tend to speed up what you are saying if you are nervous. In one way, this does work because you reach the end of your communication more quickly. Unfortunately, the impact of your message is likely to have suffered as a consequence. Use Example 2 to inform the pace of your communication.

> ### Example 2
>
> Ask a friend to give you some feedback specifically as to how your emotions and feelings may affect your pace, and enjoy experimenting with changing your pace to respond to any such feedback. You may find that your perception does not match your friend's. In particular, you may feel really uncomfortable with what you perceive to be an eternally long pause, only to hear that it was perceived by your friend as a welcome break, effective as providing time to think, or even entirely unnoticeable.

Accent

While the research data about the bias for received pronunciation is far from encouraging (see Smith, Further Reading), provided that you are clear in your speech, there is no good reason that having an accent should pose a problem in communicating (and Eswaran cites data supporting the effects of a diverse workforce on innovation, decision-making, performance, and revenue). During your studies, ensure that you work to avoid any habits you may have developed with colloquialism and regional slang phrases. If you do think that your accent may be causing difficulties with your clarity in class discussion and so forth, you can address this simply by slowing down your speech. The Law Society, the SRA, the Bar Standards Board, and the Judiciary have all spoken of their commitment to inclusion and to promote diversity in the law (including socio-economic diversity), and the Bridge Group Report (see Further Reading) refers to the need for a professional culture that allows candidates from socio-diverse backgrounds to thrive. You might imagine it could be easier to change your accent, and yet note how the Report cites an interviewee lawyer who responded, '..when I am here, I play the middle-class version of me to fit in. I can see the cultural dominance . . . I don't fit in at work, and now I don't fit in at home either.' Whether you perceive 'fitting in' as an issue for you or not, you are encouraged to read the articles under 'Further Reading' about diversity, to inform yourself further about the ongoing debate, and reflect on how, if at all, you might choose to respond to and influence the issues it raises.

Mannerisms

Just as you may *do* things inadvertently which affect your communication, you may also *say* things inadvertently that impede your power to influence others. Asking for feedback or listening to a recording of yourself can also be helpful in revealing these traits. Common examples are saying 'erm' frequently rather than simply pausing. You may have a word you use frequently to punctuate or to fill a gap, such as 'ok', 'yeah?', 'hmm, hmm', 'fine', 'great', or 'like'. Practice eliminating any such habits you may have developed, as soon as you can, because they can irritate whoever you are speaking to, and distract them from hearing the message you want them to hear.

10.1.2 Considering the specific needs of your audience

10.1.2.1 Content

Thinking about your recipient, or audience, is the key to informing the content of any communication, and oral communication is no exception. Throughout, their needs are paramount. Example 3 illustrates how this can affect the content of your presentation.

Example 3

You are asked to deliver a presentation on employment law.
Here, you would need to know who is in your audience.

1. Law students

Students will need to take a good note of the details of the law you are explaining, because it will be useful for their revision and future learning.

2. Students role-playing employees

Employees will be particularly interested in learning about their rights, and how to enforce them against their employer.

3. Students role-playing employers

Employers will be more interested in hearing about how they, as employers, should act in a way that does not infringe those rights of their employees.
So, all three presentations would cover aspects of the same employment law, but your emphasis, as to which particular parts on which to focus, would be informed by the need to engage the different audiences and meet their different needs.

10.1.2.2 Jargon and clarity

While clear and plain English is a good recommendation at all times, some audiences will find jargon easier to deal with than others. Example 4 illustrates the point.

Example 4

Your lecturer has just asked you to present your answer to 'question 2', on restrictive covenants, to the class.

Here, you would need to consider the needs of your audience, which may include the following:

1. **Students who have all prepared an answer to question 2 as part of their preparation for this class.** Question 2 was preparation for everyone. Everyone should be familiar with jargon which was explained in the preparation. They may not have understood it as clearly as you have, however. Conversely, you may have found it tricky to understand all nuances of the question. You can make sure you do your best to meet their need, using the techniques above, including thinking about your audibility, pace and tone, and when to pause, depending on the complexity of the point and jargon you are dealing with, and be willing to invite questions. You might also practise being confident enough to outline the nuance with which you have been struggling and ask if anyone can engage you on that point. They are likely to respond well, and work collaboratively with you, because they are mirroring the support you gave to them with the rest of the question. Your lecturer can correct and add to your understanding, if required.

2. **As with 1 above, however these students did not do their preparation and they are currently engaged in an animated discussion, hurriedly preparing their presentation which they will deliver after yours.** Effective communication is not about people-pleasing, and you will form your own view about how inclined you feel to ensure these students understand your presentation. Nevertheless, here is an opportunity for you, to receive some real-time feedback about your current levels of persuasion and influence, in a supported environment (because your lecturer is present), if you wish to take it. You may or may not manage to instil in these students an understanding of the correct answer, or an enthusiasm to do things differently in their preparation for the next class, but some message is likely to land, if not on this group of students, then on the other students, and on your lecturer, all of whose needs you are showing you have heard and want to meet. You will certainly learn how, if someone is talking, the presenter will definitely notice and will not feel heard (see 10.1.1.1). You may begin to learn what are effective techniques to quieten a room so you can be heard, and what are not. Silence can be effective, to try as a starting point. If not, perhaps consider the specific words you might use to get the attention of these students, so you can begin. In short, even this experience, however uncomfortable, will provide you with valuable feedback (not failure) to inform your future practice.

3. **Students who have not prepared an answer to question 2, because question 2 is an in-class task and each student has a different question to answer.** These students have a greater need for you to be clear and explain any jargon, because (through design, not fault this time), they are entirely dependent on you to help them understand the answer. They are certainly not as familiar with the subject matter as you are (and may be entirely unfamiliar with it). This is an opportunity for you to test the effectiveness of your oral communication, including how approachable they feel you are to ask follow-up questions, while your lecturer is present to support you. These in-class exercises give your learning community a chance to enjoy interacting and teaching each other (which is a very effective method of learning) while it is safe to do so (because your lecturer is present to correct any errors or highlight any omissions).

4. **Your lecturer, who set question 2.** If all is well, your lecturer will know and understand the answer to question 2 in some detail, and be able to explain it herself with structure, application, and analysis. Her need is to test that you not only *know* the law and its *source* but are willing to practice, in class, developing the other skills you need to succeed in law, including *communication*, *structure*, *application*, and *analysis*. If you have not understood her need, you may be tempted to offer a token answer, feeling safe in the knowledge she will happily complete it to give the class the full picture so they all have a good set of notes, and that will certainly feel more comfortable all round. Except she

might not, and after class students might ask you independently what the answer was, and email your lecturer to ask her too. It's not an enjoyable prospect, for anyone in your learning community. Better to have a go and practise providing a full answer, while it is still safe to get it wrong and make mistakes you can learn from before the summative assessment.

Certainly all four categories of audience will benefit from clarity in your expression. Bear in mind that a good approach to jargon and clarity in general, is an inclusive approach; that by being clear (note, not patronising) for everyone, you will meet all of their needs.

10.1.2.3 Specific learning needs

You should consider any specific learning needs of all the individuals in your audience, including any you are aware of, and any you might not be. Adapting a good, inclusive practice, by giving thought to your audience, certainly will improve your presentation for your entire audience, so take the initiative and decide you will do what you can to ensure your oral communication is as clear as it can be for everyone. It is common sense to understand that standing up, moving to the front of the class and if there is a microphone, actually using it, will be helpful for all students, not least anyone who experiences hearing impairment. (It is surprising, however, just how many presenters decide not to use a microphone when it is available, and leave their audience to struggle—and one wonders if it is self-awareness, or confidence, which is lacking. Not a good impression.) Well-structured, clear visual aids will help everyone, and students who may have dyslexia or autism will appreciate them too. Taking care to make sure your pace is not too fast will make sure everyone can follow you and your visual aids, including students with hearing or visual impairment. Asking if everyone can hear and see you and your presentation, while you are still in time to do something meaningful about it, is another technique you can adopt into your own inclusive practice that will be appreciated by all.

10.1.3 Presentations during your studies

During your studies, you are likely to be asked to deliver a presentation at some point. The advice in this chapter (and in Further Reading) will give you what you need to enjoy delivering a presentation more effectively than you can imagine right now. Practice will then help you improve further. You are encouraged to turn any fear into curiosity as to how you can learn, with relative ease, what so many find so difficult.

10.1.3.1 Purpose

The purpose, as with essays, problem questions, and other written pieces of work, is for you to demonstrate your understanding of and opinions on a particular topic. You may be asked to present a pre-prepared answer in class, or you may be asked to prepare a presentation for an assessment. This may be individually, or in a group, which also tests your team-working skills. As you study, you are likely also to be applying for a graduate role, and it is common for graduate employers to ask candidates at interview to deliver a presentation too. This helps them to compare all candidates objectively, assess your communication and time-management skills, observe how you perform under pressure, and generally assess your self-awareness.

The following guidance will help you to prepare for a presentation during your studies. Of course, nothing will enhance your presentation skills more than actually practising presenting. The more familiar and comfortable you become with presentation skills, the more you will be able to concentrate on the subject matter of that presentation without losing your audience. So, whenever appropriate, take the opportunity to speak up and be heard. There is no failure only feedback (at least, until you reach the point of assessment, by which time, if you follow the advice in this chapter, you will be well prepared for success).

10.1.3.2 Title

You may be given your title, or you may be able to choose it, either freely, or in relation to a particular topic. If you are able to choose your title, make sure that it is broad enough to fill the time and meet all of the assessment criteria you have been given, but narrow enough so you will not overrun. Be prepared to revise your title as you progress with your preparation, and can make a more informed decision about content and timing.

10.1.3.3 Research

Before you begin planning your presentation, you need to identify the relevant law on which you have been asked to present. You may already have this from your lecture notes, or you may need to use the Rule stage of Figure 9.1, and the guidance in Chapters 7 to 9, to identify the relevant law, relevant cause of action, and necessary elements of that law.

10.1.3.4 Timing

You will be given a target time frame for delivery of the presentation. There are likely to be others presenting before and after you, so your timing does matter. You must make sure that you do not run significantly under or over. Practise in advance to check your timing. Is an amendment to the title required, to narrow (or broaden) the subject matter you will cover? If not, you can add some flexibility to your final presentation by preparing some extra items that you can bring in, and identifying some items that you can cut out, if necessary. Note that the more interactive your presentation, the longer it is likely to take, and the more flexibility you will need to build in. Twenty minutes passes very quickly when you are delivering a presentation. So make sure you have a technique to keep an eye on the time. This could be taking off your watch and placing it directly in front of you, or knowing from your preparation that you should advance one slide every five minutes. One key stipulation given to all TED talk speakers is that they have a maximum of 18 minutes to present their material, based on an understanding that this is long enough to have a serious presentation but short enough to hold a person's attention.[2] You are encouraged to watch some, on topics in which you are interested, paying particular attention to how the presenters manage their timing and content, and how the period of 18 minutes feels for you as the audience.

10.1.3.5 Structure and content

Once you have your title, or working title, Figure 10.1 will help you to see that a presentation is really just a way of communicating, orally, what you already are learning to communicate,

[2] Bradbury, N. (2016). American Physiological Society. *Attention span during lectures: 8 seconds, 10 minutes, or more?* Available at: https://www.physiology.org/doi/full/10.1152/advan.00109.2016.

in writing, by answering a problem or essay question. Consider, as a starting point, whether your presentation resembles more:

- an oral presentation of the answer to a problem question ('problem style' presentation), (for example, you have certain specific facts such as names, places, dates, and events and are expected to *apply* the law to the facts in your presentation), or

- an essay question ('essay style' presentation) (for example, you are asked for critical *analysis* of an area of law, such as one which is new, controversial, ripe for reform, or the subject of several inconsistent judgments, but you do not have a detailed fact pattern to which you can apply the law, other than any familiarity you may already have with whoever is in the audience).

If the former, Figure 9.1 (problem-solving) will help you with your preparation. If the latter, you can use Figure 14.1 (essay-writing). Figure 10.1 assimilates them both into a strategy you can use for any presentation.

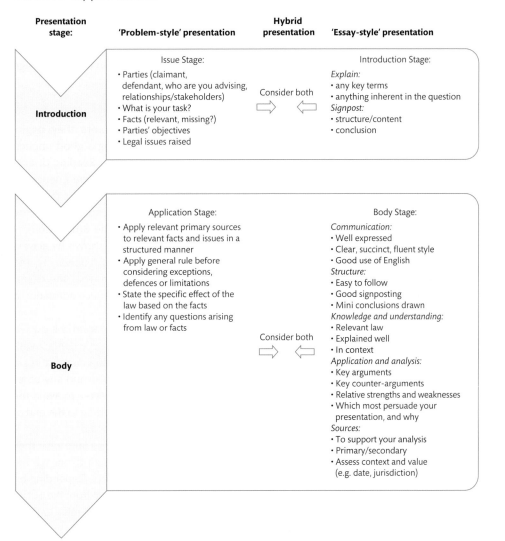

Figure 10.1 Structuring the content of a presentation

Persuasive oral communication and presentations

Chapter 10

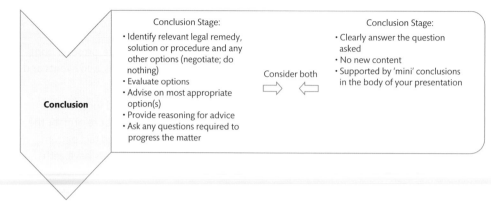

Figure 10.1 *Continued*

10.1.3.6 Communication of your presentation

When you have completed all of the preparation above, you can progress to thinking carefully about how best to communicate what you want to say. Ensure you plan to allow enough time for this important stage of preparing your presentation.

Introduction

Even experienced and professional presenters can feel nervous before they begin. However, a veneer of confidence will increase your chance of making a good impact. Chapter 15 and the two articles by Johnson and Tsaousides in Further Reading discuss effective techniques to control nervousness, and you are encouraged to experiment with these now, to discover what works best for you. Be patient with yourself, and be prepared to make mistakes, and to expect an element of discomfort. It is all part of the learning curve (see Adams, Further Reading, Chapter 11). In their article for the British Council (see Further Reading), Ros and Neil Johnson observe the nervousness shown by actress Emma Watson, in her presentation to the UN on women and leadership at university, and the techniques she uses effectively to stop her nerves detracting from what she has to say. Note, however, that a little nervousness is a good thing as it will produce adrenalin to enhance your performance.

You must do your best to establish good rapport with your audience from the outset. Employ good body language, smile, hold yourself confidently, and make eye contact with everyone in the room if possible. Remember that people like to mirror, so you must begin positively if you want your audience to react positively. Introduce yourself, and any other presenters, very clearly. Now is the time to check that everyone can hear you, to avoid the embarrassment of someone asking later if you can speak up, or, worse, getting to the end of your presentation only to discover that no one has heard a word you have said.

The best presentations are interactive; think of the needs of your audience (and what they do not need, including to be bored by your monotonous reading of a script), engage the audience and make them active contributors rather than passive observers. Depending on the size and nature of your audience, you may wish to set the interactive tone from the outset by asking them to introduce themselves. It can be very impressive if you can refer to them by name when you interact with members of your audience during your presentation. If in doubt, ask your lecturer in advance about their expectations of you in terms of interacting with your audience in any assessed presentation.

For clarity, share how your presentation will be structured (in general terms) with your audience. This is a technique known as **signposting**. You let your audience know what is in store. It is good practice to refer to the title and the specific aims of your presentation, including what the intended outcome is for your audience. Your lecturers are likely to do this at the beginning of a seminar or lecture, by referring to 'learning outcomes' (typically based on Bloom's Taxonomy, see Further Reading). The SMART model (see 18.2.5.2) will also help you to structure and articulate the aims of your presentation.

Body

This is where you will deliver the bulk of the content of your presentation. You need to use all of the communication skills discussed in this chapter to keep your audience engaged during this period. Be confident, clear and succinct, continue to use effective body language, and provide examples that are tailored to and will appeal to your audience. Again, make sure your audience is aware of the structure of the body of your presentation. If you were communicating in writing, and there are obvious headings and subheadings which would clarify your answer, then also make these clear in your presentation. (First, we will consider . . . Let's move now to examine the second requirement under section one . . .). You can also underscore the structure of your presentation in your visual aid (see 10.1.3.7), making it even easier for your audience to follow your chosen structure.

Having tailored the content of your presentation to your audience, you should consider how else to appeal to them. Address your audience directly. If you are asked to present to an audience of (during your studies, imaginary) employers, say 'You, as employers, will need to bear this cost' rather than, say, 'This cost is borne by employers'. You are looking to produce 'light bulb moments'; when what you say truly resonates with your audience. Involve your audience at this stage wherever possible. Ask them questions. Ask their opinions. Give them a short time to discuss something with the person next to them. Do anything and everything to keep them engaged. Just as varying the tone of your own voice can add interest, a change of presenter can also renew your audience's enthusiasm. Think about whether there is a timely point in your presentation when a change of presenter might be well received. In a world where attention span is reportedly decreasing due to technology, paying attention to how you can focus your audience's attention is important.

Broadcasters and politicians are trained to identify and summarise concisely for themselves the key points which they want to make, in order to be certain that they will both remember and deliver them (regardless of whether they answer any question asked). Make sure you follow suit and have identified and are very familiar with the key messages of your own presentation, so you can be certain that you will deliver them. As a rule of thumb, any more than three is likely to be unwieldy. You will need to reiterate your key messages, too, so that you can be certain your audience will hear them. The maxim 'say what you're going to say; say it; then say it again' is a good one (see Chapter 14 for its application in your written communications). As a minimum you should deliver your key message three times: Signpost in the introduction what you intend to say. In the middle, say it, then, at the end, summarise what you have said.

Relax, be your best authentic self, and enjoy the experience. Your audience will 'catch' your enthusiasm (and vice versa).

Conclusion

You must draw everything together. Identify and summarise the key points of your presentation (which will refer back to your presentation's title). Remind your audience of the aims or learning outcomes of your presentation and check whether they have achieved those aims, in an interactive way if possible. Leave the audience with a good lasting impression. Ask if they have any questions. If they do not, do not end your presentation there; it comes across as a damp squib. Instead, wrap up the presentation properly and enthusiastically, signposting clearly that it has come to an end. If appropriate, ensure everyone has your name and your contact details and make clear you are available for questions afterwards. It is common for audience members to be shy about asking questions in front of others, but relish the chance to speak to you one to one, so make sure your audience know exactly where and when you will be available for questions after your presentation ends. When you do face questions, the good news is that, unlike with advocacy, they are not certain to be calling into question what you have just said (although they may do so). They may also be checking their understanding, asking for further information, or thanking you. Feel curious (not afraid) of their questions. In all cases, allow your questioner to feel heard. Repeat the question so that everyone in the audience has heard it. Thank them for their question (unless it really is inappropriate). Resist the pressure to answer any question to which you do not know the answer. Do be prepared for questions, though. They will test your own understanding of your presentation, and it will become immediately clear (if it hasn't already) if you are delivering a script you have learned by rote.

10.1.3.7 Visual aids

Typically you will be given the option of preparing visual aids. Visual aids have several advantages. They can help to focus your audience, add interest, act as your prompt, and give the audience something else to look at other than you. Used well, they can add impact to a presentation. However, you are encouraged to use them with caution. Many presenters use slides poorly, and 'presentation' is frequently misinterpreted as a 'slide show'. While PowerPoint remains popular in university lectures, and indeed among lawyers, it is not without its critics, so be sure to use it wisely (see articles by Noah and Microsoft in Further Reading). Remember to use slides to supplement what you say, not to replace it. The human brain is wired for storytelling (Noah) so use your visual aid to engage your audience with narrative, not replace it. These are the hallmarks of a *poor* presentation, and they may already be familiar to you:

- put everything you want to say on the slides;
- create lots of slides;
- fill each slide with as many words as you can;
- do not provide handouts;
- do not allow enough time for your audience to copy down the slide either;
- add some token clip art or randomly chosen stock photographs;
- choose your favourite colours, regardless of whether they are easy to read;

- fail to proofread your slides properly;
- do not leave enough time to familiarise yourself with the projection equipment;
- progress too many slides at once and leave your audience hanging while you work out how to go back one slide, engaging them in a one-way dialogue about every step of this process;
- read out the slides, and read from the screen so that your back is facing the audience and they cannot see or hear you.

Example 5 explores this further.

> ## ⊘ Essential explanation
>
> People learn in lots of different ways, and these ways are referred to as **learning styles**. If you prefer to read a book rather than listen to a presentation on the same topic, like lecturers to use slides or write on a whiteboard rather than just speak, and find it helpful to distil information into a mind map or diagram, then your preferred learning style may be **visual**. If conversely you would much rather attend a lecture to listen to a speaker, or download a podcast, then your preferred learning style may be **aural**. If you prefer to write down what you are learning, in order to learn it, or learn best while doing a repetitive activity like walking, or gardening, then your preferred style might be **kinaesthetic**. There are other learning styles on which further reading is suggested at the end of this chapter. A good presentation will contain a mixture of elements which appeal to the full spectrum of learning styles. This is one of the reasons why visual aids, to supplement what you are saying, can be helpful in having your message heard.

Example 5

Compare the two slides at Figure 10.2. They both convey the same messages in the same basic font and colour, and neither are wonderful. However, we can use these basic tools to explore our thoughts about visual aids. The first slide needs an injection of colour, creativity, and interest, but as a starting point, it is a better visual aid than the other figure. It captures key points and lets the audience know what is to come. It has been proofread properly. This slide needs a good presenter to embellish these key points with an engaging narrative.

The second slide is a disaster, but may feel familiar, because slides are frequently used poorly. It attempts to convey the entire message in full sentences. You will need to read it out, because the audience towards the back of the room will not be able to read it. The rest of the audience will not be listening to you while they are reading the slide, of course. This will probably not be a problem however, because you will not be audible as you will be facing the screen, to read the slide. As they will be focusing all of their attention on this slide, the audience will notice your inconsistent use of full stops, your erroneous comma, and your misspelling of reliant.

Which slide do you prefer, as a starting point, if you had to choose? From the audience's perspective, the written content of the first slide is clear, readable, and prepares them to listen to the presenter. The written content of the second slide could be a good note to take away (if corrected), but the presentation is likely to add little to it.

From your perspective as a presenter, the second slide does provide a safety net for you, in terms of content. However it will actually detract from your ability to use all the communication skills set out in this chapter to influence your audience. The first slide provides a decent prompt for you, but will encourage you to become more familiar with, and to understand, the content of your presentation and to employ effective communication skills to engage and inspire your audience with your narrative.

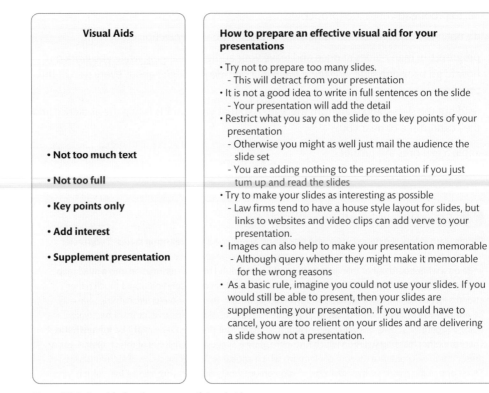

Visual Aids	How to prepare an effective visual aid for your presentations

• **Not too much text**
 	
• **Not too full**
 	
• **Key points only**
 	
• **Add interest**
 	
• **Supplement presentation**
	• Try not to prepare too many slides.
	  - This will detract from your presentation
	• It is not a good idea to write in full sentences on the slide
	  - Your presentation will add the detail
	• Restrict what you say on the slide to the key points of your presentation
	  - Otherwise you might as well just mail the audience the slide set
	  - You are adding nothing to the presentation if you just turn up and read the slides
	• Try to make your slides as interesting as possible
	  - Law firms tend to have a house style layout for slides, but links to websites and video clips can add verve to your presentation.
	• Images can also help to make your presentation memorable
	  - Although query whether they might make it memorable for the wrong reasons
	• As a basic rule, imagine you could not use your slides. If you would still be able to present, then your slides are supplementing your presentation. If you would have to cancel, you are too relient on your slides and are delivering a slide show not a presentation.

Figure 10.2 Considering the purpose of visual aids

10.1.3.8 Notes

The second slide in Figure 10.2 is attempting to fulfil not only the role of slide, but also of script and notes. As a good presenter, you should not rely on a script, and a slide is not the ideal way to provide notes for your audience either. If you would like your audience to have a note to take away, then prepare a separate note for them. Most software packages have a function to allow you to prepare and print notes next to the slides, and for you to have your notes available only to you, on a separate screen to that which the audience can see, while you present (see Microsoft article, in Further Reading).

10.1.3.9 Scripts and prompts

Reading from a script will severely inhibit your ability to use the effective communication skills discussed in this chapter, including eye contact and body language, and is bound to detract from your presentation and your ability to influence and have your message heard. Your audience, certainly, will notice this. They are, though, unlikely to notice, or be too concerned, if you omit to mention one esoteric point because you were not reading from a script. On balance, the risks of reading from a script far outweigh the risks of jettisoning a script and being prepared for a few minor omissions. Never just read out a pre-prepared, scripted presentation if you are expecting to influence your audience.

The best presenters do not use separate prompts either. It is of course a good idea for even the most experienced presenter to have a prompt (remember Ed Miliband forgetting to mention the key issue of the deficit, to his detriment[1]), and it will be particularly important for you if your assessment is being assessed and there is content you absolutely must remember to cover. However, as discussed, it is best to rely on a basic prompt from the visual aids you have prepared for the benefit of the audience. If you really cannot do without a more detailed prompt, restrict yourself to bullet points on cards or to using the software's presenter notes facility.

10.1.3.10 Developing your skills

Think about someone—a lecturer, a colleague, or someone on television who you think presents well. Watch them. What are they doing (or not doing) that makes them so good? Do not make the mistake of thinking what they are doing is spontaneous. That is unlikely. To be a good presenter takes rigorous practice. It is not by chance that television presenters stand in the correct place, look at the correct camera, and deliver an effortless joke which is absolutely suitable for their target audience. Talented presenters practise. They also improve with experience. Now think of someone who you consider to be a poor presenter. What are they doing (or not doing)? Why do you think they continue to do this, even as a professional? As with most performance skills, observation, reflection, and practice will show you what works and what does not. The Practical Exercises at the end of this chapter provide links to three presentations in very different contexts (one by Lady Hale in the Supreme Court; one by Professor Jeanette Winterson, delivering the annual Richard Dimbleby speech in the House of Lords; and a third by Emma Watson, delivering a speech to the UN), which you can enjoy watching and critiquing, to inform and inspire your own practice.

10.2 Oral communication skills and presentations: in practice

Once again, you can feel reassured that what you have learned from 10.1 in terms of the skills you need during your studies, are highly relevant for practice (and units designed to prepare you specifically for practice). There are various ways you will be required to use good oral communication skills in practice, and Chapter 11 will help you with interviews and meetings, Chapter 12 with negotiation and mediation, and Chapter 13 with advocacy. These skills, even advocacy, have generic qualities that are transferable. That is, they can be employed in contexts and careers other than law (see Chapter 16). Indeed the requirements or job specification for most professions and careers will stipulate 'excellent communication skills'. Once you are in a graduate role, providing advice and services as a professional, you will be communicating with a wide range of people, including clients or customers, other employees, suppliers, officials of public bodies, and/or other professionals. You will need to deploy your good communication skills in diverse situations, such as interviews, meetings, telephone calls, negotiations, presentations, and court appearances. The rest of this chapter provides guidance specifically about how to use what you have learned about good oral communication in order to deliver effective presentations in practice. At the end of 10.2 we will consider Example 6 to illustrate how you can assimilate the learning in this chapter. It uses a business law example, concerning directors' duties and insolvency. Other examples might include advising partners in a partnership about the effect of running their business as a company, or advising a board on corporate manslaughter, or updates to employment law. You can transfer the learning from the example to other scenarios relatively easily, such as advising the police on the latest thinking regarding domestic violence and coercive control legislation, or providing information about the trends in environmental prosecutions to a local authority.

10.2.1 **Oral communication skills in practice**

You may be surprised to consider how a client receiving legal advice might be likely to assume (not necessarily correctly) that every lawyer has learned what they need to know about the current law, and would deliver the same advice as you (just as you might assume that doctors have learned what they need to know about medicine, and would recommend the same treatment). This means that, while a client might not actually spot immediately if your advice is below par, or plain wrong, they are much more likely to judge you rather quickly, and decide whether to remain loyal to you, on *how* you deliver your advice. So, in practice, your verbal communication is very important, and will influence whether a client instructs you again. You should pay particular attention to the techniques set out so far in this chapter which will help you establish rapport, provide clarity in your advice, and allow you to be at your most persuasive, through what you say and how you choose to say it. The articles in the Further Reading section will help you to develop these techniques for practice.

10.2.2 **Presentations in practice**

10.2.2.1 Purpose

There are several reasons why you might need to deliver a presentation in legal practice. One is to pitch for new work. In effect this presentation is to sell the firm to a client, and the stakes are high as a good presentation can secure high value work from a reliable client over a sustained period of time (see the Essential explanation which follows). Other reasons are to deliver training or advice, either internally to trainees, your peers, or other departments in the firm, or externally, to clients. In this type of presentation you need to convey your message clearly, succinctly and persuasively, in a way which will appeal to your audience. Finally, you may be delivering a presentation in order to recruit new trainees for your firm, for example, when presenting to a law school, in which case your presentation needs to fulfill both the selling and training functions. As earlier, thinking about your audience is paramount, and key to your preparation and delivery of an influential presentation with impact.

> ### ⓘ Essential explanation
>
> Larger clients will put their legal work out to competitive tender, which is sometimes referred to as a **beauty parade** (because it involves law firms showing how attractive they are in order to win the competition). Usually the beauty parade involves a panel of people from each firm having to present to a panel of people from the client as to why they are the best firm for the job, and this presentation is known as a **pitch**. Lawyers and members of the firm's business development team will invest a significant amount of time preparing the pitch and tailoring the selling message to the client.
>
> Law firms will visit university careers fairs to advertise their graduate vacancies, with a view to recruiting the best candidates to work for them. This was known as the **milk round**, to reflect the atypical position that the employers are delivered to the students at their universities, just like milk is delivered to people at their homes. Most firms no longer recruit directly in the milk round, but instead will advertise why they are a good place to work as a lawyer and encourage students to apply using their centralised and uniform (often online) application process.

10.2.2.2 Structure and content

As with for presentations during your studies, Figure 9.1 will provide essential help in preparing the content and increasing the effectiveness of any problem-style presentation, and

Figure 14.1 of any essay-style presentation. You will recall that Figure 10.1 amalgamates the two, and this is likely to be particularly helpful to prepare presentations for practice, which are likely to be a hybrid of the two styles. This is because, however much the presentation you have been asked to give may seem to resemble the essay style, unlike in your studies, in practice you are likely to know at least some facts about the recipient, your client, and so will be expected to apply the relevant law to any facts you do know, however basic.

10.2.2.3 Persuasive communication

During your studies, you may end a problem-style presentation (as with an answer to a problem-question) with a conclusion that identifies a cause of action and a remedy, and leave it there. Similarly, you may conclude an essay-style presentation with a definitive conclusion, based on your own view informed by critical analysis. Chapters 9 and 14 explain that, in both cases, in practice, there is more to do at the conclusion stage. You may need to help the client evaluate options, manage their expectations, and, in some cases, persuade them of the merits of seeing sense, if they have their head in the sand. Example 6 illustrates this point. In order to do this, you will need to be as interactive as possible in your presentation.

10.2.2.4 Ethics

You need to keep in mind relevant professional ethical matters and the SRA's Codes of Conduct, such as not mentioning confidential matters about other clients (see 6.4).

10.2.2.5 Practical considerations

During your studies, you may have little control over the environment in which you deliver your presentation. As you enter practice, or practice-focused units, this is something you will be expected to consider. The following guidance will help you.

Setting up your room

Consider this from the audience's perspective. The layout of the room can make a difference to your presentation.

Will your audience be able to hear you?

Test the acoustics. Consider whether there is likely to be any background noise. Check if there is a microphone you can use. If the audience is struggling to hear, they will switch off. Always ask the audience at the beginning of the presentation if they can hear, and encourage them to let you know if they cannot. Also remember to ask the audience to turn off their mobile telephones, and always remember to switch off your own. As a presenter, there should not be a need to switch your telephone to silent mode, and switching it off is a better solution. However, if you are in the audience and you must leave your telephone on, then make sure it is set to silent mode and that your silent mode settings do not allow the telephone to vibrate.

Will your audience be able to read your slides?

We have discussed what you can do to make your slides readable at 10.1.3.7. However, the layout of the room may prevent the audience from reading even the best slides. Check if there is anything impeding the audience's view, or whether people at the back are too far away, and change the layout of the room accordingly. Take hard copies of the slides with you in case you cannot overcome any problems with audience members being able to read the screen. Do not obstruct their view yourself by standing in front of the screen.

Will your audience be able to interact with you?

The best presenters engage with their audience. This can be difficult to do if you are far away from them, or on a stage. Do what you can with the room to make it as intimate as possible. When you have exhausted the possibilities for this, then there are other steps you can take to allow you to interact with your audience. If they have all sat at the back of the room, encourage them to come to the front just before you start. If you are on a platform or stage, it can be very effective to leave it from time to time and walk among your audience. You will need to have a cordless microphone and mouse to do this most effectively, so that the audience can still hear you and you do not have to return to the stage to progress your slides.

Do your audience need anything?

It is usual to leave at least a pen and some paper for each member of the audience, in case they arrive unprepared for taking notes. Law firms often have branded pens and paper for this purpose, which will also help with business development. You should have prepared a handout for use during the session, so it is helpful to put this out in advance too, and to leave copies on spare chairs for any latecomers. If you have prepared further notes to take away, consider whether you want to give these out at the beginning or the end. Consider whether you should leave anything else on chairs for business development purposes (such as business cards, brochures, or other branded materials). You should also check whether the room will have WiFi. If not, then make sure you take screenshots of any webpages you intend to show instead of using hyperlinks.

Do you need anything from your audience?

You may wish to capture the audience's contact details for networking or marketing purposes. If so, you will need to think about how to capture this information lawfully, in accordance with data protection laws such as The Data Protection Act 2018 (the UK's implementation of the General Data Protection Regulation (GDPR)).

Delivering off-site

If you are delivering a presentation at someone else's premises, do not assume you have no control over the layout. If you can show that you are putting the needs of your audience first, then your enquiries are likely to be well received by the person who has control of the room. Always arrive well in advance of your presentation too. You want to spend the time before your presentation welcoming your audience as they arrive, networking and generally making a good first impression. You will not be able to do this if you are setting up your presentation on your laptop. As a general rule, aim to arrive at least an hour before you are due to begin. You need enough time to get lost on the way, go to the toilet, check your appearance, greet your host, set up (sometimes completely rearrange) the room, wait for IT to fix any glitches with the technology, write up any information on a whiteboard or flip chart, check you have all the equipment you need, and then be ready to network before you begin.

Equipment

Often you will be asked what equipment you need, or told what equipment will be available. The following list of equipment is a good guide as to what you might need.

- laptop or tablet;
- back up copy on a memory stick or in cloud storage;

- projector and screen;
- cordless mouse;
- cordless microphone;
- flipchart;
- whiteboard;
- marker pens;
- pens/pencils for the audience;
- paper for the audience;
- handouts;
- name cards or badges.

10.2.2.6 Commercial awareness

Make sure you are aware of what is going on in the world around you and your target audience. Read newspapers, read Part III of this book, and pay particular attention in the run up to your presentation not only to developments in the legal field but also to issues which are close to the heart of your audience.

10.2.2.7 Visual aids, notes, scripts, and prompts

You might imagine that your approach to visual aids, notes, scripts, and prompts in practice might differ to that during your studies, because the law and events you are dealing with are more complex. This is not so. You should continue to use what you have learned from 10.1.3.7–10.1.3.9, which is best practice whatever the context. Whether during your studies, in practice, or in a wedding speech, a script will not enhance the audience's experience. In addition, all of your visual aids and notes must meet a professional standard, and follow your firm's house style (see 14.2.1.3) which will include font, colour, and design. You should be referring to the client company and directors by name, and applying the law to any facts you have about the company, rather than using a 'one size fits all' set of slides.

Example **6**

A presentation in practice

Read Example 3 in Chapter 15, which explains what happened to Patisserie Valerie in 2018/19.
Imagine you are invited by Juke Lonson, CEO, to deliver to the board of directors of Café Catherine a 'refresher presentation' about insolvency law and director's duties, as a follow up to that which you delivered three years ago. The title is, 'Insolvency and Directors' Duties: a refresher for Café Catherine'.

Purpose and Title

Have a curious mind about why the board has asked you to present on this subject, and why they have asked you now. Has the board recently changed, or is there a possibility the company is in financial difficulty? Resist making assumptions. In practice, you can ask. In practice assessments, look for clues in the question about context, and prepare for any eventuality.

(Continued)

Research and commercial awareness

The title has given you the relevant law: insolvency and directors' duties. You would use the skills set out in Chapters 7 and 8 to find and read the relevant law (here, legislation and case law), using the research strategy at Figure 8.1. Before reading the primary sources, you would use a decent secondary source to both identify the primary sources and provide commentary about what you might expect to find in them. Now that you are researching the law for practice, an electronic database, such as Practical Law or Lexis®PSL, will be particularly helpful, because they will include commentary which is specifically practice-focused. They will make clear, for example, the draconian effect of the sanctions that directors can face in theory, and make the link to a domino effect that can lead from corporate insolvency to personal insolvency. They will also provide important information about the extent to which those *theoretical* sanctions have been used *in practice*, and any current trends or imminent reform. You should also refresh your relevant commercial awareness. What is happening in the economy and the client's sector. How are its competitors? Has the client, its competitors, or the sector been in the news recently? What announcements have they made?

Timing

You need to check how long they are expecting the presentation to last, and tailor your content, or otherwise manage the client's expectations if they are unrealistic. The board will have other events scheduled into their day, and so your timing is as important as for any assessment during your studies. As discussed in 20.1.7, costs are also calculated by reference to time, among other things.

Client Matters and Professional Ethics

- Cost. You would need to consider costs generally, and discuss them with the client in good time before you begin your presentation, so you are all in agreement. Are you charging for this presentation, and if so, how much is your hourly rate, and how long will your presentation take? Will you be charging for travel, in terms of tickets, petrol and/or time taken? (You might like to consider the following ethical issue: if you are travelling by train to see one client, and do some work while on the train for another, can you charge both clients for that same time?). What effect might the particular topic of your presentation have on your decisions about costs, if at all?

- Acting in the client's best interests. Sometimes this involves having a difficult conversation with the client (see 6.4.3, and 'Persuasive oral communication' later in this example).

- Conflict. If this is a new client, you would need to conduct a conflict check to make sure your firm does not have to refuse to act for conflict reasons. (You would also have to comply with anti-money laundering guidance.[3]) See 6.4.3

- Confidentiality. You need to comply with the SRA's confidentiality requirements in its Codes of Conduct (see 6.4.3). What will be your response if the client discloses something to you about their adverse financial position?

Structure and content

If you were answering this in writing, would it most resemble a problem question, or an essay? There are elements, here, of both, because you have information about the client, and will be able to access some facts about the company, however it is not as specific as a title such as 'What to do now you have discovered the issue of fraud in your accounts' . . . and so in some ways this resembles an essay

---

[3] Solicitors Regulation Authority (2020). 'Money Laundering'. Available at: https://www.sra.org.uk/solicitors/resources/money-laundering/money-laundering/.

question, where you will have to outline the law and provide examples, not based in any fact provided, by way of illustration. As such, using Figure 10.1, we will use the hybrid model to prepare an effective presentation.

Practical considerations

Where will the presentation take place? Do you have a choice, and what is your preference? You should run through the list at 10.2.2.5 to ensure that you have thought about what you need, in advance.

Visual aids, notes, scripts, and prompts

You should prepare these to a professional standard, using your firm's house style, well in advance, to give you plenty of time to proofread, and familiarise yourself with the content. The more you practise your presenting skills including, for example, the summarising key issues, the more you will be able to cope to assimilate and present information effectively on the occasion you are not given as much notice as you would have liked.

Persuasive oral communication

You would use the techniques set out at 10.1.3.6, bearing in mind that there is likely to be more scope for, and indeed more expectation of, interaction using the techniques described than there might be during your academic studies:

- Engage the board; address them by name, apply the law to the facts you know about the client company and the board. Consider the impact of hearing 'you, as directors, have a duty' rather than 'company directors have a duty'.
- Use open and closed questions (see 11.1.8) and silences to fill in any remaining gaps about the purpose of your presentation. Is there something specific, and timely, informing their request?
- As explained, you may need to draw on your powers of persuasion in this practical context, compared to during your studies. For example, discussing remedies and sanctions for breach, including:
  - personal liability, (fines, prison, and disqualification from working as a director)
  - the effect on the company (the end of the company; loss of jobs (including those of the directors))
  - loss of income profit by way of dividend for shareholders (including directors who are shareholders)
  - the likely loss of their capital investment (being bottom of the list for return of capital)
  - needing to honour any personal guarantees

  works very persuasively, as you might imagine, to focus the mind and pull any heads out of any sand in which they may be buried.
- Conversely, if you omitted this detail from your presentation, then the outcome of it might be to convince the board that the situation is not as concerning as they thought it might be, and nothing too awful is likely to happen.
- Compassion and empathy are also important. If you anticipate that the effect of your presentation might be to bring your client out of a state of denial and into a state of awareness, you need to anticipate the emotional impact too, and adjust your tone accordingly. Make sure they feel heard.
- Conversely, is the client reacting in a way which suggests they have not heard your message, for example, are they preoccupied with calling a board meeting to discuss their next pay rise? Are all directors acting similarly, or not? What are they telling you, by their verbal and non-verbal communication? How will you bring up the subject of fraud in your presentation, and how do you anticipate you might feel when you do that?

(Continued)

- Having some flexibility in your approach will help you to reach your goal, if your preferred approach is not working (see 12.1.5.1).
- Consider what follow up activity is necessary, and have you addressed this so your client is clear about what will happen next. For example:
  - do you need to arrange a meeting to provide further advice (see Chapter 11)?
  - how are you going to respond to any questions you may have been asked but need to look up?
  - will you be following up with an email?
  - do you have any notes to leave the client or will you be emailing them?
  - do you need the client to do anything as a follow up to the meeting?
  - what, specifically, are the next steps?

Summary

- Oral communication comprises both verbal and non-verbal communication.
- There are ways to address issues with non-verbal communication; self-awareness is the key.
- Confidence can be practised.
- Recognise and take every opportunity to practise oral presentations during your studies, however informal (for example, speaking in class).
- Adopt an inclusive practice; the needs of your audience are key.
- Think carefully about your visual aids, and their purpose.
- In practice, practicalities such as setting up the room are important aspects reflecting your attitude to client care.

What the professionals say

As technology continues to evolve in such a way that clients can now obtain legal advice and insight through a wider variety of media than ever before (including webinars, podcasts, videos, blogs, Tweets, and other social media as well as by Skype, letters, emails, and telephone calls), the skill of being able to communicate effectively has never been more important for a career in law.

I first practised these skills during interviewing practice on the Legal Practice Course. I remember having reams of notes with me, but suddenly realising that being a solicitor meant so much more than knowing and understanding the law: I needed to be able to think on the spot, select the most relevant points from my legal knowledge and then articulate them to a layperson in a simple and meaningful way. My notes were actually nothing more than a safety net and the real skill lay in being able to explain complex legal concepts to someone with little or no legal knowledge.

Since then, I've continued to develop and adapt my communication skills throughout my career. As an employment solicitor, I regularly advised HR professionals and business owners with limited legal knowledge, but would take a slightly different approach to advising experienced in-house employment counsel. Frequently, I'd be negotiating with other employment solicitors on the other side of a case/issue, which requires a different approach again and I'd also attend at the Employment Tribunal to conduct advocacy, where a more formal and procedural style is appropriate. Finally, I was fortunate to spend time with a client on secondment, where I was advising a wide variety of people within the business on the day-to-day management of legal matters and even presenting to large groups of employees to up-skill them in certain areas. Now, in my current role, I am responsible for training both clients and the solicitors in our team on employment law matters. I do this in a variety of different ways, including face-to-face training sessions, producing written or video articles, and posting about employment law issues on social media. Communication is key for all of these aspects to my role and I think it always will be. So, for anyone considering a career in law, my advice would be to start practising early!

Helen Almond, 2001 LPC student and Senior Knowledge Lawyer in the Employment, Incentives and Immigration Group at Addleshaw Goddard LLP.

Practical exercises

Consider how you would answer these questions. Reflect on how your reading of this chapter has informed or changed how you might answer them. How might you use what you have learned in an interview or exam situation?

1. What do you do in terms of body language that you need to pay attention to? What effect might this have on your communication skills?

2. What is your preferred learning style? What would you do in a presentation to make sure you appealed to those in the audience who have a different learning style from you?

3. Who do you admire for their communication skills? Can you articulate precisely what it is that they do that you admire? Is this transferable into what you do now, as a student, or will do later, as a professional?

4. If you can, find and watch all or some of the The Richard Dimbleby Lecture 2018, presented by Professor Jeanette Winterson (referred to in Further Reading), which is 45 minutes long. (For example, if you have Box of Broadcasts, at the time of writing you can find it here: The Richard Dimbleby Lecture 22:45 06/06/2018, BBC1 London, 45 mins. https://learningonscreen.ac.uk/ondemand/index.php/prog/1165D976?bcast= 126849762.) Reflect on the effectiveness of Professor Winterson's communication skills to influence and have her message heard. What does she do to engage and inspire her audience? How is she remembering the content of her presentation? What else about her presentation strikes you, having read this chapter?

5. Watch Lady Hale delivering her summary of the Supreme Court's judgment in the *Miller* case (which you read in Chapter 7) available on the Supreme Court website (https://www.supremecourt.uk/watch/ uksc-2019-0192/judgment.html). Reflect on the effectiveness of Lady Hale's communication skills to influence and have her message heard. In what way does Lady Hale's presentation style differ from Professor Winterson's, and why might this be?

6. Watch, and reflect on, Emma Watson's presentation to the UN, on women and leadership at university, via an interesting article on the British Council website (https://www.britishcouncil.org/voices- magazine/how-overcome-fear-public-speaking). What can you learn from this? In what way does her presentation style differ from Lady Hale's, and Professor Winterson's, and why might this be?

7. Read and reflect on Luke Johnson's reaction to his business' collapse (see Unwin, Further Reading). How, if at all, does this inform your chosen approach to making presentations in practice as a lawyer?

 *Visit the **online resources** for the authors' reflections and to check your progress.*

Further reading

Bridge Group (2018) *Socio-economic background and early career progression in the law.* Available at: https://static1.squarespace.com/static/5c18e090b40b9d6b43b093d8/t/5cd180d73cfb160001436429/1557233888333/03+Research+2018+Progression+law.pdf
—Working with eight global law firms and the Sutton Trust, this study examines the correlation between background characteristics and early career progression in the legal profession. The research includes the analysis of data relating to over 2,800 early career professionals and interviews with current and former employees. It provides a compelling evidence base to drive a shift in mindset, and to boost firms' efforts to increase socio-economic diversity and inclusion in the legal sector.

Eswaran, V., 2019. The business case for diversity in the workplace is now overwhelming. *World Economic Forum.* Available at: https://www.weforum.org/agenda/2019/04/business-case-for-diversity-in-the-workplace/
—An article which references multiple studies to argue that diversity has a positive financial impact in the workplace.

Gorman, C.K. (2011) Forbes. *The Art and Science of Mirroring.* Available at: https://www.forbes.com/sites/carolkinseygoman/2011/05/31/the-art-and-science-of-mirroring/#761fda3c1318
—This article explains the concept of mirroring ('limbic synchrony') and how you can use it to establish rapport and build good business relationships.

Honey, P. and Mumford, A. (2006) *The Learning Styles Questionnaire.* Maidenhead: Peter Honey Publications Limited
—A useful source of further information on learning styles.

Johnson, R. and Johnson, N. (2016) British Council. *How to overcome your fear of public speaking.* Available at: https://www.britishcouncil.org/voices-magazine/how-overcome-fear-public-speaking
—An interesting article analysing the public speaking techniques used by Emma Watson in her presentation to the UN about leadership and women in university.

Kurt, S. 'Using Bloom's Taxonomy to Write Effective Learning Objectives: The ABCD Approach' in *Educational Technology*, April 24, 2019. Available at: https://educationaltechnology.net/using-blooms-taxonomy-to-write-effective-learning-objectives-the-abcd-approach/
—A quick guide to writing learning outcomes that you can use to inform your presentations in the classroom.

Microsoft. *Create a Presentation in PowerPoint.* Available at: https://support.office.com/en-gb/article/create-a-presentation-in-powerpoint-422250f8-5721-4cea-92cc-202fa7b89617
—A link to PowerPoint training on the Office website. Learn how to create presentations from scratch or a template, add text, images, art, and videos, select a professional design with PowerPoint Designer, add transitions, animations, and motion, save to OneDrive, to get to your presentations from your computer, tablet, or phone, and share and work with others, wherever they are.

Noah. A. (2018) Presentation Panda. The Pros and Cons of Amazon's 'No PowerPoint' policy. Available at: https://presentationpanda.com/blog/the-pros-and-cons-of-amazons-no-powerpoint-policy/
—A blog post discussing how Jeff Bezos, CEO of Amazon, banned PowerPoint in meetings in favour of narrative, and what we can learn about visual aids as a result.

Public speaking, overcome the phobia and get charisma (2015) YouTube video, added by NLPLife. Available at: https://www.youtube.com/watch?v=qZ99UQWGims

—In this short video, Dr Richard Bandler, the co-creator of neuro-linguistic programming, gives his tips for charismatic and inspirational public speaking.

Smith, L. (2019) 'Why we need to tackle discrimination at work'. Available at: https://uk.finance. yahoo.com/news/accent-bias-why-we-need-to-tackle-discrimination-at-work-115900839.html

—An article exploring research findings that employers make discriminating decisions based on regional accents.

Social Mobility Business Partnership (2019) *Social Mobility Business Partnership*. Available at: https:// smbp.org.uk/

—Provides opportunities and support for students from less privileged backgrounds, to break down psychological 'fitting in' barriers.

Solicitors Regulation Authority (2019) 'The business case for diversity'. Available at: https://www.sra. org.uk/risk/risk-resources/risk-business-case-diversity/

—This paper is about the business benefits of a diverse and inclusive legal profession. It provides practical examples of the actions firms can take and what the SRA are doing to support firms.

Tsaousides. T. (2017) Psychology Today. *How to Conquer the Fear of Public Speaking: Are you ready for a standing ovation?* Available at: https://www.psychologytoday.com/gb/blog/ smashing-the-brainblocks/201711/how-conquer-the-fear-public-speaking

—A neuropsychologist advises how you can train your brain to overcome the most common phobia, the fear of public speaking.

Urwin, R. (2019) 'I felt like fleeing UK, says Patisserie Valerie boss Luke Johnson', *The Times*, 9 June. Available at: *https://www.thetimes.co.uk/edition/news/i-felt-like-fleeing-uk-says-patisserie-valerie-boss-0tb70z5zx*

—The former chairman of Patisserie Valerie reveals that his ego took such a battering after his business collapsed that he considered fleeing the country, developed chronic insomnia, was despairing, rarely ventured out and felt ashamed that he had brought such difficulties upon his family.

Winterson, J. (2018) *The Dimbleby Lecture: 'Don't protect me, respect me'*. The House of Lords. BBC. 6 June 2018

—A hundred years on from the first women in the UK securing the right to vote, and 60 years since women could be members of the House of Lords for the first time, Professor Jeanette Winterson in her Dimbleby Lecture engages her audience in examining the recent campaigns promoting the equality of women and explores what can be learnt from the Suffragette movement a century ago.

 *For the authors' reflections on the practical exercises, additional self-test questions, sample interview questions and a library of links to useful websites, visit the free **online resources** at www.oup.com/he/slorach4e.*

11 Client interviews and meetings

Learning objectives

After studying this chapter you should be able to:

- Consolidate your understanding of why you need good oral communication skills as a student and a professional.
- Practise and develop these skills during your legal studies and in everyday life.
- Understand and use Figure 11.1 to conduct an effective interview (or first meeting) with a client during your studies.
- Understand how effective professionals communicate with their clients face to face (in interviews and meetings) and by telephone.

Introduction

This is the second of five chapters on communication skills. Chapter 10 discusses generally what constitutes good oral communication skills, and helps you understand the essential foundations for oral communication to be persuasive and influential. It then explores specifically presentations. You should read that chapter before you read this one. Chapter 12 considers negotiation and mediation, Chapter 13 mooting and advocacy, and Chapter 14 communication in the form of writing and drafting.

This chapter gives helpful guidance about the process of 'interviewing a client'. This is common terminology used during your studies and refers to the first time you meet a client, to take instructions. In practice, some lawyers will refer instead to 'meeting a client' from the outset (for example, corporate lawyers) and others will move on to referring to 'meetings' after the first interview where they have taken initial instructions. Remain flexible, therefore, about terminology. The oral communication skills in Chapter 10 and in this chapter continue to apply to subsequent client meetings as well as the more structured first interview/meeting.

Clients will come to see you when they have a problem, actual or potential, and so all that you learned about case and matter analysis for problem-solving in Chapter 9 (including the strategy at Figure 9.1) are vital for the interviewing process.

Whether you are in the classroom, attending an interview, undertaking work experience or a placement, or volunteering at a law clinic or other pro bono scheme, during your studies you are likely both to observe these skills, and also have to demonstrate some of them yourself. 11.1 provides what you need during your studies. 11.2 makes clear that these face-to-face encounters require skills which are the foundation of the majority of professional relationships, and provides some further context about interviews specifically in practice, and some additional guidance about meetings and telephone calls.

11.1 Interviewing skills

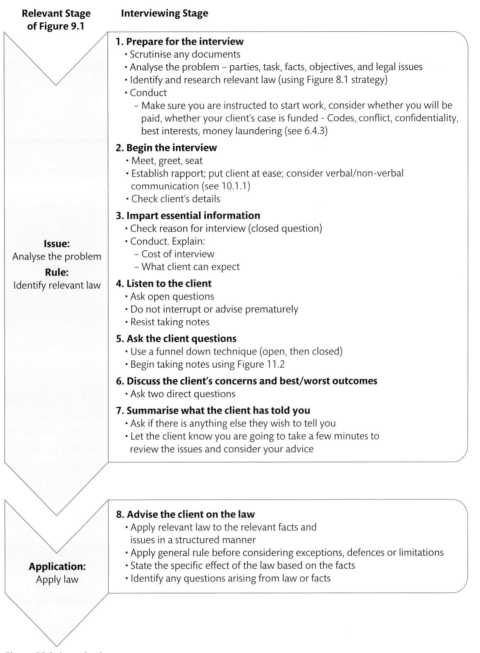

Relevant Stage of Figure 9.1	Interviewing Stage

1. Prepare for the interview
- Scrutinise any documents
- Analyse the problem – parties, task, facts, objectives, and legal issues
- Identify and research relevant law (using Figure 8.1 strategy)
- Conduct
   - Make sure you are instructed to start work, consider whether you will be paid, whether your client's case is funded - Codes, conflict, confidentiality, best interests, money laundering (see 6.4.3)

2. Begin the interview
- Meet, greet, seat
- Establish rapport; put client at ease; consider verbal/non-verbal communication (see 10.1.1)
- Check client's details

3. Impart essential information
- Check reason for interview (closed question)
- Conduct. Explain:
   - Cost of interview
   - What client can expect

Issue:
Analyse the problem

Rule:
Identify relevant law

4. Listen to the client
- Ask open questions
- Do not interrupt or advise prematurely
- Resist taking notes

5. Ask the client questions
- Use a funnel down technique (open, then closed)
- Begin taking notes using Figure 11.2

6. Discuss the client's concerns and best/worst outcomes
- Ask two direct questions

7. Summarise what the client has told you
- Ask if there is anything else they wish to tell you
- Let the client know you are going to take a few minutes to review the issues and consider your advice

8. Advise the client on the law
- Apply relevant law to the relevant facts and issues in a structured manner
- Apply general rule before considering exceptions, defences or limitations
- State the specific effect of the law based on the facts
- Identify any questions arising from law or facts

Application:
Apply law

Figure 11.1 Interviewing strategy

Client interviews and meetings

Chapter 11

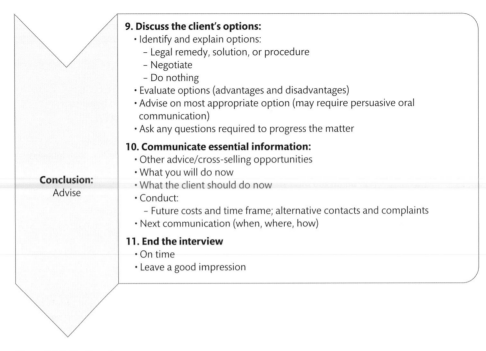

9. Discuss the client's options:
  • Identify and explain options:
    – Legal remedy, solution, or procedure
    – Negotiate
    – Do nothing
  • Evaluate options (advantages and disadvantages)
  • Advise on most appropriate option (may require persuasive oral communication)
  • Ask any questions required to progress the matter

10. Communicate essential information:
  • Other advice/cross-selling opportunities
  • What you will do now
  • What the client should do now
  • Conduct:
    – Future costs and time frame; alternative contacts and complaints
  • Next communication (when, where, how)

11. End the interview
  • On time
  • Leave a good impression

Conclusion:
Advise

Figure 11.1 *Continued*

11.1.1 Structure: using the interviewing strategy at Figure 11.1

When practising this skill during your studies, you will need to follow a structure, to ensure that you remember everything you need to do while you are with your client. This will free you from worrying about 'what comes next', so you can concentrate on listening to your client, establishing vital rapport, and communicating well with them. Figure 11.1 gives you all you need to conduct a successful interview during your studies. It breaks down the interview process into manageable sections, helping you to structure it logically and feel in control of the process. You will want to annotate it to tailor it with your own notes and questions, and take it into the interview. You can do this by photocopying it and annotating it by hand in the margin, or by typing your annotations into the electronic version on the online resources and printing that.

The following commentary will help you to understand and use it well, encouraging you to consider how you can best use what you learned about good oral communication at 10.1, to communicate most effectively at each stage.

As with any skill, the more you practise, the more you will work through the learning curve until you will no longer need to look at Figure 11.1. This is optimum, because you will know from Chapter 10 that non-verbal communication, including body language and eye contact, is vital to succeed in your interview, and while you are looking at Figure 11.1 you cannot be using these communication tools to engage your client. In one sense, then, you should see using a hard copy of Figure 11.1 during your interview as a crib sheet, an essential crutch, the advantages of which significantly outweigh the disadvantages when you are a student. You will know when the strategy has entered your unconscious competence (and you have become unconsciously skilled; see Adams, Further Reading), and are ready to put it to one side.

11.1.2 **Purpose**

During an interview, you will advise a client with a legal problem. You will need:

- excellent **case/matter analysis and problem-solving skills** (from reading Chapter 9);
- to be able to **find, read, and understand the relevant law** (from reading Chapters 7 and 8);
- excellent **oral communication skills**, including an ability to establish quickly a good rapport with your client (from reading Chapter 10 and this chapter).

Rather than seeing interviewing a client as an entirely different set of new skills to learn, then, you are encouraged instead to see the process simply as learning a new way of blending together and developing skills (referred to above) that you already have.

During your studies, you may be given a problem-question scenario in class, and asked to interview and advise one of the parties. Your lecturer may role play the client and you may conduct one interview in front of the class, or perhaps all students will pair up, one role play the client and the other the solicitor, and then perhaps you will swap over. It is illuminating to role play the client, to inform your own practice when you come to role play the solicitor.

Assessing client interviewing skills is increasingly popular in undergraduate programmes, (and has been done for some time in professional programmes), because they provide a means by which you can evidence you have all of these skills through completing one, short, assessment. Such assessments are not designed to intimidate you. Indeed, they are incredibly useful evidence you can use to your benefit in applications and interviews to show that you both know the skills that graduate employers need and will value, and that you have them. However, because the assessments might be recorded and/or your assessor will be in the room with you, (as, or as well as, someone role playing a client, with whom you must interact on the spot), it is easy to understand why they might feel more pressurised even than traditional examinations. The techniques to control any nervous feelings (discussed in Chapters 10 and 16), using Figure 11.1, and practice will all help you to feel you are in control of this process.

11.1.3 **Prepare for the interview**

Preparation is essential for any professional interview. Any failure on your part to understand either the client's objectives of the interview, the legal issues involved, and/or the subject matter in question, will become very obvious to any other party and impede any rapport (which Chapter 10 makes clear is key to effective oral communication).

- Scrutinise any documents upfront, at 'stage 1 – prepare for the interview' of Figure 11.1.
- Analyse the case (contentious) or matter (non-contentious) using the guidance in Figure 9.1:
  - identify the parties (their roles, who you are advising, relationships and other stakeholders), your task, the relevant and any missing facts, the parties' objectives and any legal issues raised (the Issue stage);
  - identify the relevant law, cause of action and the necessary elements of that law (the Rule stage).

(You should re-read Chapter 9 if these concepts are not yet familiar to you.)

- Use what you learned in Chapter 7, about how to read, assimilate, and summarise information efficiently. Ask yourself what is relevant material, but avoid assumptions. Consider, for example, a client who mentions he has come to see you about a partnership. It is impossible to pre-empt what the client wants at this stage. He may want to set up a partnership, exit from a partnership, or even enter into a civil partnership.

- Chapter 14 will help you analyse the drafting of any document (for example, in identifying clauses granting rights, or imposing obligations).

- During this preparation stage, you may be able to populate some areas of Figure 11.2, that is, the notes you intend to take into, and supplement during, the interview (see 11.1.9).

In practice, you will also need to check conduct issues such as checking you are instructed to start work, consider fees, whether you will be charging for the first interview, and whether your client will be self-funded. You can read more about this at 6.4.3 and 11.2.1.4.

11.1.4 Begin the interview

As with a presentation, the beginning of any interview is crucial. It is at this stage that you will set the tone for your entire interview, and establish rapport. The client will form an immediate impression and you want it to be a good one.

11.1.4.1 Meet

- You may need to meet the client at reception and take her to your meeting room, or you may be in the meeting room and the client will be shown in.

11.1.4.2 Greet

- Introduce yourself clearly, stating your name, and your status or role.
- Shake hands and make clear what the client can call you.
- Address the client and establish how she would like you to address her.

11.1.4.3 Rapport

- The client may be nervous at this stage, so do what you can to put her at ease. A question about her journey to your office, or the weather, and taking time to listen to her answer while using appropriate body language, can help her to settle into what may be an unfamiliar or even intimidating environment for her.
- Be your best, authentic self.
- Anticipate that it might feel difficult to judge how formal or informal to be with clients before you know them well. As a general rule, start on the more formal side. It is easier to do this, then become more familiar, than to start off in a way the client considers to be over-familiar and then have to recover from that position. Apply this to how you address the client, initially.

11.1.4.4 Seat

- Show the client where to sit and offer any refreshments.

11.1.4.5 Check client's details

- When you are both seated, check the client's full name (spelling) and address.

11.1.4.6 Oral communication

Pay attention to your verbal and non-verbal communication, including tone and body language (see 10.1.1), and ensure it is appropriate and encourages your client to participate.

11.1.5 Impart essential information

There are a few essential pieces of information which you must deal with at this very early stage of the interview.

11.1.5.1 Double-check the client's reason for the interview

Usually when clients book their first appointment they will give whoever they are speaking to at the firm an idea of why they need an appointment. However, misunderstandings can occur at this stage and so, despite your preparation where you carefully analysed anything you had been told by your partner or secretary, it is always worth checking why the client is there. The potential downside to this is that the client might take this as a cue to tell you absolutely everything about the issue she has come to see you about. Manage this risk by closing your question (see Chapter 13). For example, 'I understand you have come to see me today with a view to setting up a business, is that right?' is a good question to ask here. By structuring your sentence in this way, you are encouraging the client to answer simply 'yes' or 'no' and avoiding the need to interrupt, which would damage rapport at this early stage.

11.1.5.2 Explain cost of interview

In practice, you will need to consider cost, of the interview itself and future cost implications of any advice you give. You can read more about this at 11.2.1.6.

11.1.5.3 Explain what the client can expect to happen in the interview

While you will have a clear idea of what will happen in the interview, based on Figure 11.1, the client will not. Reassure your client, and build essential rapport, by providing a brief outline at the outset. Put the client at ease as far as you are able. For example, you will:

- listen to what she has to say;
- ask a few questions;
- consider the issue;
- give some advice which you will follow up in writing.

You may need to:

- delve into an area of questioning that they find uncomfortable (See Urwin, Further Reading, Chapter 10);
- play devil's advocate, for example to test your client's key concerns and best and worst outcome.

The client will not need to:

- decide whether to go to court;
- make any final decision.

> ⓘ **Essential explanation**
>
> Asking open questions followed by closed questions is known as the **funnel down** technique. Conversely asking closed questions followed by open questions is known as the **funnel up** approach.

11.1.6 Listen to the client

You are now ready to listen to the client's issue. It is a good idea to use the funnel down technique for this (see 'Essential explanation'). As discussed in Chapter 10, lawyers can be inclined to pre-empt what a client is about to say, and interrupt. This is not helpful, because you must give accurate, tailored advice on the client's actual issue, rather than the issue you think the client has. Remember that everyone likes to be listened to, so giving your client the opportunity to explain their issue fully to you, and feel heard, is likely to increase your rapport. In contrast, if you interrupt your client, at best, you will come across as rude; at worst you may stop the client from telling you a pivotal fact. If, on reflection, you think that you have a tendency to interrupt, then resisting the urge to do this is something you can practise now in your conversations with friends and family.

Prepare a good open question to begin your process of listening. For example, 'Now, please do tell me all about the issue you want to discuss with me today', will signal to the client that this is his cue to tell you everything. You can think of your own version of this wording, if you prefer. Remember you can annotate Figure 11.1, so it is tailored specifically to your own developing practice. Use your active listening techniques, discussed in Chapter 10, to encourage the client to continue to speak. You may need to practise your 'poker face', as clients can sometimes disclose information at this stage that is unexpected, salacious, or downright alarming, but you must maintain a professional demeanour at all times.

11.1.7 Ask the client questions

When the client has answered your initial open question, you will need to ask further questions. Following the funnel down technique, you should continue to ask open questions to begin with, and then move on to closed questions.

The 'Issue stage' of Figure 9.1 refers to parties, stakeholders, relationships; let this guide you as to the type of questions you should be asking to fill in any gaps in what the client has said. Your client is unlikely to be the only person involved in the issue. Remember to ask questions about other people, who they are, whether they are in a position of strength or weakness, and how they might affect your client's position. Be inquisitive and explore all aspects of what the client has told you.

Good open questions are:

'Could you tell me some more about . . .?'
'What in particular is the problem with . . .?'
'How does everyone else feel about . . .?'

The reason the funnel down approach is recommended is that it captures more information. For example, if you ask the closed question, 'Are you worried because of X?', then a client may say yes. However, if you had asked the more open question, 'Why are you worried?', the client may answer 'X, Y, and Z'. The closed question did not reveal the existence of Y and Z, but the open question did. Y and Z might be absolutely crucial in determining the advice to give.

Practise this skill now, in your everyday life, by asking questions of people rather than talking about yourself (which many lawyers are guilty of). You may be surprised by the results.

11.1.8 Taking notes

You are likely to feel you want to take notes from stage 4. Consider why this is, and the intended purpose of any notes you make. During your studies, your notes are likely to help you when you reach stages 7–9 of your interview. Do not take notes just to keep yourself occupied. In fact, doing so may prevent you from properly digesting what the client is saying (think of taking notes in a lecture and not knowing what you have written about until you read them through after the lecture). Consider also what you learned in Chapter 10, about the importance of eye contact. If you are taking notes, you will have to sacrifice this effective communication tool, at least to some degree. Depending on the complexity of the information being imparted at this stage, the best interviewers resist taking notes at the very start, particularly if this is the first meeting with a new client. Explore how it feels to tell your client that you will not be taking notes just yet, so you can properly hear and take in what she has to say. Ask the student role playing your client for feedback at the end, as to how this felt for them. If, on consideration, you decide you absolutely must take notes from the very start, then take care to think how you can do that while minimising the communication problems doing so may create.

You should, however, start to take notes at stage 5 (Ask the client questions). 14.1.10.2 provides some guidance as to how to take good notes. You should give some thought to how to do this in the context of a client interview. One effective method is to divide your page into quarters. You can then use each quarter for a different purpose. For example, one quarter to record information about the parties, their concerns and objectives, one to record information about the facts of the problem, including any missing facts or further questions you may want to ask when the opportunity arises, one to record legal issues and the relevant law which occur to you that you must include in your advice. This can help you to see the wood from the trees, when you get to stages 7–9, more easily than with a handwritten block of text in chronological order. You can then use the final quarter to record the options you discussed and evaluated, and the next steps for you and/or your client. Figure 11.2 illustrates how you might do this, and you can print it from the online resources and take it into your interview.

Parties:	Facts of the problem:
- client's role: (eg, claimant, buyer)	-
	-
- other side's role: (eg, defendant, seller)	-
	-
- client details:	-
- relationships/stakeholders?	-Missing facts/ other questions (ask at appropriate time):
- objectives (include client's main concern)?	-
	-
	-
Legal issues raised:	**Options discussed and evaluated:**
-	Legal remedy, solution, procedure:
-	
-	Negotiate:
Relevant law:	
	Do nothing:
	Next steps:
	Solicitor:
	Client:
	(answer any remaining questions?)

Figure 11.2 Contemporaneous note-taking for problem-solving template

11.1.9 Discuss the client's concerns and best and worst outcomes

When you have finished asking the client about his issue, you should have a good understanding of his concerns. However, it is an excellent idea to ask the client two very direct questions, as follows:

> 'It seems to me your concern here is X. Do you agree? Do you also have other concerns?', and
> 'What would be your ideal outcome here? And your worst outcome?'
> (Or your own, preferred wording for direct questions about concerns and outcomes.)

Do not just rely on assumptions you have made, without testing them. What you might consider to be a serious risk from your personal perspective (for example, in terms of a potential financial liability) might not, actually, worry a very wealthy client at all (and vice versa). This type of question really shows that you are thinking from the client's perspective, and the client will appreciate it. It is also vital information for you if you are to help the client reach the best solution, so do not worry that asking this type of question is somehow an admission that you do not know something you should know.

11.1.10 Summarise what the client has told you

You will have received a lot of information in a relatively short time. Be prepared that it may well feel somewhat laboured to you, but rest assured you should summarise to the client at this point all they have told you in the interview. This is because it will be useful in three specific ways. It allows:

- you some much-needed time to digest the facts of the client's issue before you advise on it (you are not expected to be a robot; you will need this time to process information and to think);
- the client a chance to check you have understood everything correctly, and correct any misunderstandings;
- the client to identify anything he has forgotten to tell you or which you have not remembered.

After summarising, it is a good idea to ask the client if there is anything else they would like to tell you before you start to advise them. This gives the client a final chance to disclose information to you, and shows that you recognise that the facts, and what the client knows and feels, are crucial to your ability to identify the correct solution for them.

The next stage involves using your legal knowledge and case/matter analysis for problem-solving skills (see Figure 9.1) to apply the relevant law to the facts of the client's issue. This can be complex, and so it is advisable, to say: 'Thank you. I'm now going to spend a few minutes reviewing all you have told me, so I can consider the issues and how best to advise you.' If there are more refreshments, now is a good time to offer some.

Students can feel that this is somehow cheating, or not expected, because they are under the misapprehension that advising on the law is about immediately bestowing their legal knowledge upon the client. If you have not realised by now, then take notice that, in fact, advising clients on the law is about applying legal knowledge to the facts of a client's problem. This requires careful case/matter analysis of the parties, the client's problem, the relevant law, and, most importantly for the client, the effect of the law on that problem. Therefore, do not worry about a short period of silence while you carry out this important analysis. It may seem interminable to you, but rest assured that, having answered all of your questions, the client will be very happy to have a short rest.

11.1.11 Advise the client on the law

Once you are ready to advise, consider how you can do so in a way which is best for the client. Remember the value clients place on clear communication (see London Economics, Further Reading). You are likely to be nervous while you are inexperienced, so practise the effective communication skills you learned in Chapter 10 to engage the client:

- Make sure you advise in a way that is not only accurate but is clear to the client. If you do anything else but prioritise the client's need for clarity of communication, then regardless of the quality of your advice, they will leave less impressed with your performance than if you had done so.
- Provide clarity in your language, use clear English and avoid unnecessary jargon (see 10.1.2.2). Clients can find jargon intimidating, and it impedes the clarity that we know they want and will judge us by.

- Pay particular attention to:
    - —your eye contact;
    - —other body language;
    - —the tone, pace, and clarity of your voice.

11.1.12 Discuss the client's options

As referred to at 9.2.4.1, when solving legal problems the client's options tend to fall within three general categories, namely:

1. Use your legal remedy, solution, or procedure (litigate, end the business, get divorced, sue, make a payment, comply with a procedure).

2. Negotiate another option and consider bargaining power.

3. Do nothing.

In answering problem questions during your studies, sometimes the expected focus is exclusively on legal remedies (1) at the expense of considering the more commonly chosen options of negotiating or doing nothing (2 and 3), often for reasons such as cost and time. 9.2.4.1 explains how the options may differ depending on whether the work is contentious (such as a dispute) or non-contentious (such as a corporate transaction, drafting a will, or selling a property). If in doubt as to what is required at this stage in terms of the latter two options, ask your lecturer. In practice, they are essential: see 9.2.4.1–9.2.4.4 and 11.2.1.10 for further guidance.

11.1.13 Communicate essential information at the end

11.1.13.1 Can your firm help with anything else?

During your studies, this stage may not be required. In practice, because the law firm is a business (see Chapter 20) it is essential, and you can read further guidance at 11.2.1.11.

11.1.13.2 Let the client know what will happen next

You will always follow up the first client interview with an email (or letter, although this feels increasingly outdated and is becoming limited to clients who may not have access to, or wish to use, email). In this email you will:

- confirm the advice you gave in the interview;
- follow up anything else you promised to deliver; and
- remind the client of anything you need from them.

Even though you will include this in your email, also remind the client now of:

- what you will do next; and
- what they need to do next, with particular focus on anything they need to do as a matter of urgency.

You know that clients want their lawyers to communicate better (London Economics, Further Reading), so this will both reassure and impress your client.

11.1.13.3 Conduct

In practice, you will need to consider the future cost implications of any advice you give, and give an alternative contact and inform the client about the complaints procedure. You can read more about this at 11.2.1.11.

Discuss your next meeting or communication

It may be that the client has decided to do nothing further for the moment. Otherwise, now is a good opportunity to be proactive and discuss when, where, and how a follow up might be appropriate. Consider whether you need to meet face to face, and if so in person, or using technology, or whether a telephone call or email will suffice.

11.1.14 End the interview

Just as it is important to create a good first impression, it is also important to leave the client with a good lasting impression.

- Bring the interview to an end within your estimated time frame.
- Be clear, both verbally ('Thank you. You will be pleased to hear that I have all I need for today, and we can bring our meeting to a close.') and non-verbally (for example, with your tone and body language), that the interview is coming to an end.
- Give a firm handshake, make good eye contact, and walk with your client back to reception.
- Part with a closing comment about how pleased you are to have met the client, and make sure he has your name and contact details.

11.2 Interviews, meetings, and telephone calls in practice

11.2.1 Interviews in practice

In December 2019, the Law Society published a report on skills in the profession (see Further Reading). It was based on interviews with private practice firms, in-house legal teams, and individual solicitors, and revealed that the most prevalent skills gaps identified concerned problem-solving, client-handling, and planning and organisation. Interviewing, of course, combines all of these skills, and so remains a challenging skill for junior lawyers.

Interviewing is a vocational subject, and so Figure 11.1 and the guidance on it at 11.1 will be equally helpful to prepare for a practice-focused unit, and beyond, for practice. The guidance already given makes clear that there are a few additional steps in Figure 11.1 which lecturers on some traditional academic units may not require you to deal with, but which will be needed as you turn your attention to preparing for practice. The following guidance will help you to identify those steps, and how to deal with them with relative ease.

11.2.1.1 Terminology

While 'interviewing' is terminology that has been used in both undergraduate and vocational legal education, traditionally, in practice, some consider this a little unhelpful in encouraging good practice. It can project the wrong message about the balance of power between lawyer and client, who should be speaking and who listening. For that reason, while interviewing is used in some areas of practice (for example, criminal law), in other areas, the process of following Figure 11.1 might be referred to as the 'first meeting with a client' rather than 'interviewing a client'. The skills you have learned in Chapter 10 about effective oral communication, and in this Chapter 11, apply equally to first and subsequent meetings as they would to the first interview. Be prepared that subsequent meetings will be more iterative and less formulaic, however. You can manage this to some degree by preparing and circulating a meeting agenda.

11.2.1.2 Using the interviewing strategy at Figure 11.1

As you prepare for practice, the complexity of the problems clients wish to discuss, and the extent to which you need to use your skills to draw out information from your client, is likely to increase. Therefore you may find you wish to continue using Figure 11.1 as a crutch, until you feel confident enough to leave it behind and explore how you can make the most of the increased scope for sustained eye contact and other non-verbal communication.

11.2.1.3 Purpose

Meeting the client face to face has significant advantages, particularly when this is a new client you are meeting for the first time. For example, you might be interviewing:

- your client from Chapter 8, who has been charged under s. 4 of the Public Order Act 1986, and who you are meeting to explore whether you can run an argument that she did not commit this offence, by reason of her having committed a lesser offence; or
- the CEO of Stentor Limited, from Chapter 9, who wants to meet to discuss his company's liability for the substandard brass buckles and locks, and whether it can provide a replacement and avoid the other legal remedies that Britbag plc is seeking; or
- Jack, again from Chapter 9, who wants to meet you to discuss whether he can seek compensation for the money he has paid the garage, and any other loss, arising from the contaminated petrol he bought from the supermarket; or
- Juke Lonson, CEO of Café Catherine, from Chapter 10, who wants to meet you to discuss a specific incident, which he has become concerned may constitute a criminal offence, following your colleague's recent presentation to him and the rest of the board entitled, 'Insolvency and Directors' Duties: a refresher for Café Catherine'.

Chapter 10 explained the importance of establishing rapport with clients. During face-to-face communication, you can employ the full range of verbal and non-verbal oral communication, to establish excellent rapport from the outset, and build a relationship where you are a trusted adviser to whom your client will feel loyal. After that relationship has been established, then written (see Chapter 14) and telephone communication (see 11.2.3) can continue to cement your good relationship, but it is not a substitute for face-to-face contact. Even if your client is not nearby, modern technology means your first meeting can still be face to face, on screen, using apps such as Skype, FaceTime, Zoom, Google Hangouts Meet, or your firm's conference call facilities. (Helpful during the Covid-19 lockdown in 2020.)

11.2.1.4 Prepare for the interview

Initial instructions

In practice, the initial instructions may come directly to you, through an existing contact you have met while networking, and indeed generating new work through these channels will be expected of you as you progress (see chapter 20 on law firms as businesses). While you are junior, though, it is more likely that the initial instructions will come to you from a partner (or their secretary), perhaps by email, or in person, indicating who the client is and what the client wants to discuss. They may also give you documents such as an agreement which is in dispute (contentious work), the key terms of a proposed business deal (non-contentious work) or a will (which could be either contentious or non-contentious work). These, together with any covering email, are the documents you will scrutinise at Stage 1 of Figure 11.1 (see 11.1.3).

Conduct and professional ethics

You should ensure that the client has instructed you to act, and that you have undertaken all necessary money laundering, conflict and other conduct checks as required by professional conduct rules (see 6.4). You should also consider what arrangements have been made about the cost of the interview because you will have to explain these at the beginning of your interview. You will already have sent your client care letter to your client, in advance of your interview. It will set out the standards that they can expect from you and your firm, including information about who has responsibility for the conduct of their case or matter, and the basis of how it is being funded (see the SRA guidance on client care letters, Further Reading).

> **Essential explanation**
>
> The **Solicitors Regulation Authority**, which regulates the profession, publishes standards and regulations, including seven **Principles** and two **Codes of Conduct** (one for solicitors and one for firms), which provide a framework for ethical and competent practice. You can read the Codes on the SRA website (see Further Reading at the end of this chapter) and 6.4 provides further guidance on them.

Practicalities

When you are in practice, you will have more control of practical issues such as the room in which you conduct your interview, and refreshments, and you should consider in advance what arrangements you need to make in this regard, in particular to help with rapport (see 11.2.1.5) but also to comply with the SRA's rules on conduct.

- Consider a seating plan which reflects an equal relationship between client and lawyer (for example, sitting side-by-side at a table in a meeting room, rather than behind a desk).
- Confidentiality requirements (see 6.4.3) also mean the meeting should be somewhere other than your desk, where there is a risk that a client might be able to see or hear information about other clients. Most firms do not permit clients into the area where solicitors work, but also bear this in mind when using video conferencing facilities.

Documents

You should consider whether you want the client to send you any documentation to read in advance (which will have costs implications), or bring them to the meeting.

11.2.1.5 Begin the interview

Rapport

You should arrive on time and be professional and confident from the outset, to reassure the client that they are in good hands and have chosen their adviser wisely.

This preliminary part of the interview is particularly important in practice, because this is a key opportunity to put your client at ease and establish rapport, both of which will increase the likelihood that your client will remain loyal and provide repeat business. For some clients, the prospect of meeting with their legal adviser is a daunting experience. Some clients will only come to see you at difficult times in their lives, when they are facing a problem.

There are advanced communication techniques you might enjoy learning more about as your skills develop, and which you can practise during your everyday life (when it is safe to do so). Gorman (Further Reading from Chapter 10) explores mirroring, for example.

11.2.1.6 Impart essential information

In addition to the information at 11.1.5, the following are considerations in practice.

Conduct: Explain the cost of the interview

Some firms will not charge for a first interview. Others will charge a fixed fee, or on the basis of an hourly rate. Make clear the cost, upfront, so the client can make an informed decision whether to proceed, or not.

You may feel embarrassed talking about costs at all, particularly so soon after meeting the client. It is a common concern for lawyers, who want to avoid giving the false impression that they are only concerned about money and not about helping their client with the law. In fact, the client will want and expect you to discuss from the outset what the interview will cost (see 20.2.3.3 and London Economics, Further Reading). One of the most common complaints made to the Legal Ombudsman is about a lack of clarity around costs (see Further Reading), so do not hesitate to address costs matters confidently, knowing that clients will appreciate you doing so. Ask a question such as 'This firm charges £X per hour for my time. I have set aside thirty minutes for this interview, so this interview will cost £X/2. Are you happy to proceed on this basis?'. Then, assuming the answer is positive, do make sure you complete your interview on time.

What the client can expect

During a role play, your client will have been instructed to give you information if you ask for it, and receive information readily. In practice, you cannot rely on your client doing this. They may feel nervous, be shy, or not understand that the information they hold is important to inform the legal process. If a client is worrying about what is coming next, they will not be able to be as open with information as you need them to be. So putting them at ease from the outset is in both your interests.

Outline clearly at this stage what they can expect, including the information set out at 11.1.5.3, and ensure they understand how key their role in the interview is, in terms of imparting information about the case or matter. Be prepared to check they have understood correctly what you are telling them, and to repeat information and/or ask the same question more than once, if required.

11.2.1.7 Listen to the client

As with 11.1.6, avoid premature note-taking at this stage, even in practice. It is very important that you listen, hear, and digest what the client is telling you, so remain focused throughout.

11.2.1.8 Note-taking

As explained at 11.1.8, note-taking at this stage may be useful during your studies, to help you digest the facts while you are in the interview. Figure 11.2 provides a helpful template to help you do this effectively. In practice, usually you will need to do something with your contemporaneous note after the meeting has finished. First, you will need to create an attendance note of the meeting. In turn, you may use your attendance note as the basis of some other work, for example, a letter to the client, or for some legal research.

You may think that you will remember all the information until you return to your desk, but frequently you will be diverted into something else on the way back, and by the time you do return to your desk your head will be full of other information. For that reason, the template at Figure 11.2 remains helpful, to enable you, as soon as possible after the meeting, to prepare an attendance note which contains enough information to fully brief anyone reading the note for the first time.

> **⊙ Practice tip**
>
> If you are asked to sit in to observe an interview, in the absence of any express instruction always assume that you should take a contemporaneous note of what is being said. Professionals often expect that the most junior person in the room will take a note, so they do not have to, but sometimes they are not very good at telling them this in advance.

Attendance note

To be useful, an attendance note will record:

- When and where the interview was held, and who was in attendance.
- The parties, facts, client objectives, and legal issues (see 'Issue' stage of Figure 9.1).
- A summary of the main points covered in the interview.
- Any actions or next steps, who is responsible for them, and timescales.
- Enough information to fully brief anyone reading the note for the first time.

Figure 11.3 will help you. Note that this is not a new skill:

- Figure 11.3 uses the same general memorandum template as for the Research Report at Figure 8.1.
- It collates information you will be familiar with, from your reading about case and matter analysis for problem solving in Chapter 9. So, you are already well prepared to use this template to create an effective attendance note which includes case/matter analysis of your interview with your client.

- Chapter 14 provides a useful insight into the type of written communication you will be using your attendance note to create. So, while the attendance note is for internal use (unless, for example, you find yourself the subject of a negligence claim and it is produced as evidence), the more care you take with the structure and clarity of your attendance note, the more you can use this as a basis for other written communication such as an email or a letter.

ATTENDANCE NOTE

CLIENT:	Jack Clark ('JC')
MATTER:	Contaminated petrol bought from Saldi Supermarkets ('S')
FILE REFERENCE:	5678-1234
DATE:	1 November 202X

PARTIES AND KEY FACTS

Summarise the facts set out at Example 5 in Chapter 9, using the guidance provided at 9.2.1.3.

CLIENT'S OBJECTIVES

Summarise your list of Jack's known objectives, using the guidance at 9.2.1.4.

LEGAL ISSUES

Summarise the legal issues, using the guidance at 9.2.1.5.

PRELIMINARY ADVICE

Summarise:
- what you told the client about how the law applies to the fact (see 9.2.3.1);
- the options you discussed with the client (see 9.2.4.1, 9.2.4.2, and Figure 9.5)
- how you and the client evaluated the options (see 9.2.4.3)
- which option you and your client identified as the most appropriate option (see 9.2.4.4)

NEXT STEPS

Summarise here what you agreed (i) Jack needs to do next; and (ii) what you need to do next.

CONDUCT ISSUES

Make sure your note deals with any conduct issues that have arisen, such as what was agreed about fees, funding, confidentiality and/or conflict.

TIME TAKEN

You will remember that in practice this would be required to be recorded to assist time management and be used in calculating the overall cost of the matter for the client. (See Chapter 6 for more detail on the costs of legal services.) It will be helpful, then, to break down the time you have spent into preparation time (for example, 10 minutes), interview time (for example, 25 minutes) and attendance note time (for example, 25 minutes), which will mirror the activities against which you will need to record your time.

Figure 11.3 Attendance note template

11.2.1.9 Advise the client on the law

Make sure you avoid feeling pressurised to give premature advice. In this early stage of the first interview, it is unlikely you will have all of the information you need from the client in order to apply the law to the facts fully and be in a position to advise. You may well only be able to progress the matter at this stage. You can do that by identifying the missing facts and clarifying the further information you need from the client, before you can apply the law to the facts fully and discuss and evaluate the options.

11.2.1.10 Discuss the client's options

Remembering the three general categories at 11.1.12 (from the 'Conclusion stage' of Figure 9.1) will help you to think on your feet and to formulate some options for the client to discuss during the interview. With each category, you need to:

- explain the options carefully (see 9.2.4.1, 9.2.4.2, and Figure 9.5); and
- evaluate the options: be clear about the advantages and disadvantages of each option (see 9.2.4.3 and Table 9.1).

Only then can you help the client to choose the option that suits him best. Figure 9.1 will help you with all of this.

Evaluating the options

During your studies, the focus may be on legal remedies, but in practice, clients may consider the option that lies outside of a legal remedy, solution or process, to have the most advantages for them. Example 1 illustrates this type of evaluation.

Example 1
Contentious work

Your client may want, simply, an apology rather than a legal remedy. This may be for good reason, for example, any of the following:

- The person who has wronged your client has no money and so a legal remedy, say for damages, would not help.
- Your client has a specific time frame that prohibits them from starting a lengthy litigation process.
- Your client needs to maintain a good business relationship with the other side going forward, because they are a key customer.
- Your client cannot afford the costs of pursuing a case through court.

Non-contentious work

Your client is selling a property, and the parties are apart on the price by £X. Your client may:

- agree to proceed, because the risk of not selling outweighs £X;
- consider they have sufficient bargaining power to negotiate about the price;
- walk away from the deal ('do nothing'), because the lack of agreement on the price is 'a dealbreaker'.

Persuasive oral communication

Sometimes a client will respond to one option with particular hostility, or act as if they have not heard it. If this is not in their best interests, you will need to engage in some persuasive oral communication so that they do hear and can evaluate all of the viable options. This concept was described in Chapter 10 with reference to Example 6. It concerns the work you might need to do as a lawyer to ensure a client does not put their head in the sand, but instead clearly hears and understands your advice. It is further illustrated with reference to Example 2 here.

Example 2

Contentious work

Imagine instead that your client in Example 1 is strongly discounting one option. For example, they could be ignoring the pursuit of a legal remedy, and focused instead on accepting an inauthentic apology, *solely* out of what appears to be a fear of conflict. Or, they could be focused on litigation and unwilling to entertain an authentic apology from a longstanding key customer, *solely* out of anger. Ultimately, of course, the client is best placed to choose the best option for them, and you cannot decide for them how they should proceed. However, you do need to have done your best to ensure they understand the reality of the evaluation of their options and are making a properly informed decision. You will need to use persuasive oral communication to help them to remove whatever obstacle is preventing them from considering an option. For example:

- Have they considered the risks of *not* acting (for example, can they bear the financial burden of their loss if they do not seek a financial remedy; conversely, can they bear the potential loss of a key customer if they do seek a remedy against them)?

- What, specifically, is making them discount an option? For example, do they fully understand the process, or the costs involved?

- Is their focus on one option well-founded (for example, the cost of pursuing a claim they may not win, or the maintenance of a key business relationship), or is it based on misconceptions or assumptions (for example, based on watching a court scene from a recent television drama, or an assumption that the other side will act in a certain way)?

- Are they focused on the option they had already decided to take regardless of your advice (for example, have they understood how a negotiation, or perhaps mediation (see Chapter 12) might allow them to pursue a financial solution while maintaining the relationship and without going to court)?

Non-contentious work

Imagine your client from Example 1 is selling the property because of an urgent need for the proceeds of sale (perhaps because the court has ordered them to settle a debt, or to pay a financial settlement on divorce). You may need to use persuasive oral communication to reveal to this client that:

- walking away is not a viable option (for example, if this is the client's only way of raising funds to make the court-ordered payment);

- their bargaining position is weak (for example, if the buyer knows your client's vulnerable position, and has set the price with reference to it).

This is an advanced skill, and it will improve with practice. Reading about the GROW coaching technique, which uses open questions to encourage people to think about their **g**oals, **r**eality and **o**ptions to inform what they **w**ill do next (see Further Reading) will help to give you some ideas as to how you can develop this skill for all oral communication, including presentations and interviewing, negotiation and mediation.

11.2.1.11 Communicate essential information

Once again, you need to remember to impart some information towards the end of the interview for practical, ethical, or regulatory reasons. The advice at 11.1.13 applies equally here, and some further guidance is provided below.

Can your firm help with anything else?

Chapter 20 explains that a law firm is a business, and you should recognise that having a new client in front of you is a business development opportunity. This is a key chance, if appropriate, to 'cross-sell' the services of another department, or to obtain some further work from the client for your department.

 Practice tip

Firms are very keen to encourage **cross-selling**. This is where a solicitor in one department in the firm identifies and takes opportunities to promote to clients the work done by solicitors in other departments of the firm. Historically, partners' profit-sharing arrangements did not motivate partners to do this, as a partner in one department would see no personal benefit if a partner in another department brought in more fees. In fact, sometimes this could jeopardise a partner's position, as by promoting the success of a colleague, the partner risked looking less productive. Unbelievably, this led to situations where, for example, a large insurance company client of the property team may not have even been aware that the firm had expertise in advising on insurance law. However, cross-selling is now encouraged and often incentivised.

Conduct

Discuss future costs and time frame In practice you will need to link future costs and time frame back to the options you discussed earlier in the interview (at stage 9 of Figure 11.1). It is unlikely that the client will have selected a firm option at this stage, but if he has, you can tie your time frame and costs estimate into that (see 20.2.3.3). If the client has yet to choose a way forward, then go through each option and give your best estimate. If you do not have enough information to come up with a meaningful estimate at this stage, remind the client of your hourly rate and that you will keep him up to date with the costs incurred in the meantime.

Alternative contact and complaints procedure In light of how highly clients rate good communication, make sure they have an alternative person to contact in your firm if they cannot reach you, who will be familiar with the matter. Also make clear your firm's complaints procedure, that is, what they can do if they are unhappy with the service they receive, and who they should contact and how (see 20.2.3). Take care to clarify that you are not suggesting this will be required, and that they should feel free to give you feedback immediately if they have any concerns or worries.

11.2.1.12 End the meeting

In practice, if the interview overruns, this will have cost implications, so employ good time management. If this is something you struggle with, then begin to practise good habits now.

11.2.2 Meetings in practice

Lawyers will have external meetings (with clients, see 11.2.1.1) and internal meetings (with their colleagues). All that you learned in Chapter 10 about good communication will be useful for both types of meeting.

11.2.2.1 Internal meetings

While, initially, you may have limited opportunities to attend internal meetings, and even less opportunity to change how meetings are run, you are encouraged to read the material on the online resources, considering further how meetings can run most effectively, because meetings constitute such a considerable part of a lawyer's day.

11.2.3 Telephone calls in practice

Much of the guidance in Chapter 10 about effective oral communication applies equally when communicating by telephone. However, it is worth giving some thought specifically to the skills required to develop a professional telephone manner.

11.2.3.1 Why telephone skills remain important

Messaging, social media, and email have overtaken telephone conversations as a way of communicating in your personal life, and the internet enables you to make bookings that previously you would have made by telephone. It is interesting to consider how this trend will affect law firms in the near future, as they become staffed by, and serving clients who are, millennials who have used voice calls differently to their predecessors (see Hyde and Wiest, Further Reading). There is a debate, currently, as to whether the lawyer's role as trusted adviser will be replaced by equally empathetic, but more efficient, artificial intelligence in the future (see Mwardi and Rose, Further Reading).

For the present, it remains important for you to hone your telephone skills to develop your professional relationships; for now, they are skills you require for practice. In light of this, take every opportunity now to practise your professional telephone manner.

Email or telephone call?

You have just learned how to conduct the first interview face to face. However, after that you will progress cases and matters primarily through a mixture of meetings, telephone conversations, sometimes involving conference calls, and emails, and in a small but growing number of firms, by text message (see Lemzy, Further Reading). Hyde (see Further Reading) reports research (by a case generation company) that suggests a trend towards clients favouring email over telephone conversations, on the basis that it keeps costs down. If this continues, you will have to take the lead as to when, specifically, a telephone call with the client is needed rather than an email.

Delivering difficult messages

One of the key reasons clients complain is the failure of lawyers to update them (see London Economics, Further Reading). Lawyers tend to be most reluctant to update when the news is difficult to deliver. The guidance below will help.

- Email may feel like an easy way of avoiding confrontation, or having to think on your feet, but some matters are better handled by speaking to a client.
- Unpalatable messages, such as missing a deadline, making a mistake, or enquiring why your client has not paid, are exactly the kinds of messages that you may be tempted to deal with by email.
- Email will allow you to avoid dealing with the client's immediate reaction, but they can also be misconstrued and if the subject matter is delicate this can be exacerbated.
- You will find it easier to avoid errors in tone by telephone.
- By calling a client to deliver an unpalatable message, you demonstrate that you are an honest, confident and resilient professional with good communication skills. Research suggests that most clients will appreciate this.

Next time you make a complaint by telephone, enjoy making your point clearly, firmly yet politely, and pay careful attention to any response which is effective, and any which is not. You are also encouraged to read guidance from the Legal Ombudsman (see Further Reading) about effective language, including structure, pace, and tone, for diffusing difficult conversations.

11.2.3.2 Listening skills

The importance of active listening skills is set out at 10.1.1.1. As with all non-verbal skills, it is more difficult to demonstrate this over the telephone.

Do:

- show you are listening with the occasional 'yes', 'okay', or 'mm-hmm', provided it is not obtrusive.

Do not:

- interrupt the client;
- listen solely to respond.

11.2.3.3 Tone

We have already explored the effect of first impressions. On the telephone, your voice will be the thing you are judged on, so consider what impression you want to give, and make sure your tone conveys this. A flat tone can sound indifferent, bored, cold or even hostile, none of which will develop your goal of being 'trusted adviser'.

11.2.3.4 Clarity

Ensure you pace your speech carefully and avoid jargon. Mobile telephones can also present problems in this regard. If the caller comes in and out of range, and you cannot hear properly, do not be embarrassed to say that you really cannot hear her. This is one instance where it is professional to interrupt.

11.2.3.5 Taking a telephone message

If you do pick up a telephone for colleagues, take care about what you might imply about them. Saying that they are still at lunch, or you do not know where they are, or that they have not arrived at the office yet, may be true but the caller may draw adverse inferences. It is standard practice simply to say, 'I'm sorry, X is not at his desk at the moment, can I help you or would you like to leave a message?' If you take a message, make sure you include in your note:

- the caller's full name (ask her to spell it if necessary);
- the capacity in which she is calling;
- her contact details;
- the time she called; and
- establish what she is expecting in terms of a response and by when.

If the client opts to ask you to help instead, do not be afraid to say that you do not know something, but you can find out.

11.2.3.6 Call processing skills

How adept you are at using the features of a telephone will impact on how professional the caller perceives you to be. Dropping callers while transferring them is particularly frustrating for them. If you do not know how to operate the telephone system, ask someone to show you as soon as possible. As a minimum you should learn how to pick up a call that is not being answered, how to transfer a call, and how to join another caller into a conference call.

Summary

- The first interview, when you meet a client for the first time, is key to develop the rapport necessary for a good, continuing relationship with your client.
- In any interview you will be applying the skills you have already learned about problem solving (Chapter 9) and oral communication (Chapter 10).
- Until you are more experienced, taking in and following Figure 11.1 will be a useful crutch to help you conduct a first interview, especially if you are aware of, and take steps to minimise, the risk of compromising your non-verbal communication.
- It is important to take a good, contemporaneous note in the interview, and Figure 11.2 will help you with this.
- In practice, you will write up your contemporaneous note into an attendance note (see Figure 11.3), which you will then use as a basis for all further related work, such as composing a letter or email to the client (see Chapter 14) or a research report (see Chapter 8).

What the professionals say

What do I value in a lawyer? As a client I expect all of our professional advisers to understand our business and to use their expertise to provide advice tailored to us and our strategic vision. I'm looking for the ability to listen, to work together to solve problems and create solutions, and to advise clearly and concisely in a way that resonates with me and on which I can act. For lawyers particularly to become 'go to' trusted advisers, they not only have to know the law, that's a given, but they also need the skills to deploy that knowledge effectively. It shouldn't be a chore to speak to a lawyer or to understand what they are advising, and if it is, clients will vote with their feet.

Chris Morris, CEO, Citation Limited

Practical exercises

Consider how you would answer these questions. Reflect on how your reading of this chapter has informed or changed how you might answer them. How might you use what you have learned in an interview or exam situation?

1. Watch the recording of interviews available at https://www.youtube.com/watch?v=9wG9Pzx27ZQ and https://www.youtube.com/watch?v=VZY3SF8WBGY&feature=youtube to appraise the interviewer's performance. Make notes on any:

   (a) positive points;

   (b) points that can be improved.

2. Remind yourself of the introductory information about Jack in Example 5 of Chapter 9 (maximum 10 minutes). Pair up with someone who can role play Jack. Let them read through Example 5 as their preliminary brief. Use Figure 11.1 to interview Jack (maximum 25 minutes), take a contemporaneous note using Figure 11.2, and write up an attendance note using Figure 11.3 (maximum 25 minutes). Ask your client for feedback.

3. Reverse the roles at 2 above. Reflect on how your experience of role-playing a client will inform your interview practice going forward.

Visit the **online resources** for the authors' reflections and to check your progress.

Further reading

Adams. L., *Learning a New Skill is Easier Said Than Done*, **Gordon Training International.**
Available at: **https://www.gordontraining.com/free-workplace-articles/learning-a-new-skill-is-easier-said-than-done/**
—A short article demonstrating the four stages of competence or ('conscious competence') learning model, developed by GTI in the 1970s. The model reveals the psychological states involved in the process of progressing from incompetence to competence in a skill. It makes clear that a period of discomfort is a necessary stage to master any skill. Let it motivate you to persevere and practise your interviewing (and any other) skills, to reach the stage when you become unconsciously skilled.

Chartered Institute of Legal Executives, CILEx (2019) *Finding and using a lawyer: A guide to choosing a lawyer.* **Available at: https://www.cilex.org.uk/about_cilex/about-cilex-lawyers/cilex-practitioners-directory/finding-and-using-a-lawyer**

—A useful article to encourage you to see the interview from the client's perspective. Information for clients on the CILEx website, including what they can expect when meeting their lawyer for the first time, and how to compare lawyers.

Engels, J. (2007) Delivering Difficult Messages. *Journal of Accountancy*. Available at: https://www.journalofaccountancy.com/issues/2007/jul/deliveringdifficultmessages.html
—An article which discusses tools to tackle dreaded conversations.

Hyde, J. (2019) Clients prefer online contact to speaking with lawyers, research finds. *Law Gazette*. Available at: https://www.lawgazette.co.uk/news/clients-prefer-online-contact-to-speaking-with-lawyers-research-finds/5070115.article
—An article reporting that research (albeit by a case generation company) found that 83 per cent of current and future consumers prefer to deal with law firms online, believing this to be the best way of keeping costs down. Just over half of those surveyed (55 per cent) still want face-to-face contact with lawyers, with just 29 per cent wanting to communicate over the telephone.

The Law Society (2019) *Improving your time management.* Available at: https://www.lawsociety.org.uk/law-careers/career-progression/soft-skills/time-management/
—The Law Society's recommendations about how you can improve you time management skills.

The Law Society (2019) *Research to inform workforce planning and career development in legal services: Skills, training, workplace changes and job quality in the solicitors' profession.* Available at: https://www.lawsociety.org.uk/support-services/research-trends/research-to-inform-workforce-planning-and-career-development-in-legal-services/
—The Law Society's report on the current state of skills and training for solicitors, for use by individuals in career planning and by firms in workforce planning.

Legal Ombudsman (2017) *The Language of Complaints.* Available at: https://www.legalombudsman.org.uk/wp-content/uploads/2014/09/Language-of-complaints-Report-.pdf
—A report which provides some useful in-depth analysis of verbal communication, including language, tone, structure, and pace and their effectiveness in complaints handling. The skills transfer equally into other difficult conversations.

Lemzy, A. (2019) *3 ways to improve client care at your law firm—The Law Society*. Lawsociety.org.uk. Available at: https://www.lawsociety.org.uk/news/blog/3-ways-to-improve-customer-care-at-your-law-firm/
—An article discussing client care skills, including using emotional intelligence, and using text messages for updates.

London Economics (2017) *Research into the experience and effectiveness of solicitors' first tier complaints handling process.* Available at: http://www.legalombudsman.org.uk/wp-content/uploads/2017/11/FINAL-First-Tier-Complaints-Report.pdf
—Research commissioned by the Solicitors Regulation Authority and the Legal Ombudsman, which concluded that customers want clear and timely communication, and information about legal work and costs at the start and end of the work and at appropriate intervals throughout the work. Like the Bellwether Report (see Further Reading, Chapter 9), it reveals a disconnect between what lawyers think clients want, and what clients actually want.

Mwardi, A. (2019) *Aspiring lawyers shouldn't lose sight of the basics*. Legal Cheek. Available at: https://www.legalcheek.com/lc-careers-posts/aspiring-lawyers-shouldnt-lose-sight-of-the-basics/
—In a world of coding and AI, this article concludes that soft skills to build rapport remain paramount.

Performance Consultants (2019) *GROW Model|Sir John Whitmore's GROW Coaching Model Framework—Performance Consultants.* Available at: https://www.performanceconsultants.com/grow-model
—The GROW model has become a popular coaching model for problem-solving and goal-setting. Your personal tutor may have used these techniques when they met you during your studies. Familiarity with the model can help you practise techniques and identify questions you can ask to improve your own persuasive oral communication.

Rose, N. (2018) *Susskind: Machines will replace lawyers if they deliver better outcomes— Legal Futures*. Legal Futures. Available at: https://www.legalfutures.co.uk/latest-news/susskind-machines-will-replace-lawyers-if-they-deliver-better-outcomes
—An article which discusses Susskind's argument that clients are focused on outcomes and would choose a machine if it could deliver the same outcomes more efficiently. It also discusses Flood's counter-argument, that 'the single most important aspect of the professional . . . is the role of the trusted advisor . . . such people don't deliver outcomes. They present views, interpretations, they make connections, they produce ideas from left field . . . Without this we would be impoverished.'

SRA (2019) *Client care letters*. Available at: https://www.sra.org.uk/solicitors/guidance/ethics-guidance/client-care-letters/
—Guidance from the SRA about client care letters, which your firm will send out before the first interview.

SRA (2019) *SRA Code of Conduct for Firms*. Available at: https://www.sra.org.uk/solicitors/standards-regulations/code-conduct-firms/
—The SRA Code of Conduct for Firms, in effect from 25 November 2019.

SRA (2019) *SRA Code of Conduct for Solicitors, RELs and RFLs*. Available at: https://www.sra.org.uk/solicitors/standards-regulations/code-conduct-solicitors
—The SRA Code of Conduct for solicitors and overseas lawyers in effect from 25 November 2019.

SRA (2019) *Guidance: Money Laundering*. Available at: https://www.sra.org.uk/solicitors/resources/money-laundering/money-laundering/
—Guidance from the SRA about obligations on solicitors and firms and how to comply with them. Paragraph 7.1 of the Code of Conduct for Solicitors, RELs and RFLs, and paragraph 3.1 of the Code of Conduct for Firms require individuals and firms respectively to make sure they keep up to date with, and remain aware of, their responsibilities under any new legislation as and when it is introduced. Case studies are also provided here: https://www.sra.org.uk/solicitors/guidance/case-studies/money-laundering/.

SRA (2019) *SRA Principles*. Available at: https://www.sra.org.uk/solicitors/standards-regulations/principles/
—Sets out the SRA's seven principles it requires solicitors to comply with on a continuous basis, including honesty and integrity.

SRA (2019) *Standards and Regulations resources*. Available at: https://www.sra.org.uk/solicitors/standards-regulations-resources/
—Resources and guidance, including videos, on the new SRA Standards and Regulations, which replaced the SRA Handbook on 25 November 2019.

Stanley, G. (2019) *Client Service Awards; What clients really want*. Legal Business. Available at: https://www.legalbusiness.co.uk/analysis/client-service-awards-what-clients-really-want/
—A new research project from *The Legal 500* has set out to identify those making the best impression with clients. This article contains interviews with the top-performing law firms for client service, including Stewarts, Mishcon de Reya and Weil, and Gotshal & Manges, who provide answers to questions including 'How is technology changing the way you meet client needs?' and 'What do you think clients value most from their law firms'.

Wiest, B. (2019) *Millennials Hate Phone Calls, And They Have A Point*. Forbes.com. Available at: https://www.forbes.com/sites/briannawiest/2019/11/04/millennials-hate-phone-calls-they-have-a-point/#1f8701d8517e
—An article discussing the reluctance of millennials to make phone calls, and arguing the benefits of using either face-to-face meetings or email in their place.

 *For the authors' reflections on the practical exercises, additional self-test questions, sample interview questions and a library of links to useful websites, visit the free **online resources** at* www.oup.com/he/slorach4e.

Client interviews and meetings

Chapter 11

12 Negotiation and mediation

Learning objectives

After studying this chapter you should be able to:

- Appreciate why you need good negotiation and mediation skills as a student and a professional.
- Identify your own approach to conflict, uncertainty and negotiation, and develop more flexibility in your approach.
- Understand what a BATNA is, and why it matters.
- Prepare effectively for a negotiation.
- Practise conducting well-structured and confident negotiation and mediation.

Introduction

The right of access to courts is 'an absolutely fundamental ingredient of the rule of law', as Lord Neuberger has highlighted (see Further Reading), and he has made clear his view that mediation 'must not be invoked and promoted as if it was always an improved substitute for litigation'. However, he also observes that 'ordinary people, average citizens, and ordinary businesses' would likely experience problems obtaining access to justice, and mediation might be particularly suitable for their legal disputes.

Negotiation and mediation are both methods of alternative dispute resolution (ADR), and they are essential skills which you can use for both contentious cases and non-contentious matters. In its Final Report, the Civil Justice Council's ADR Working group found that 'there must be a further and more complete embrace of ADR in law faculties and professional training and disciplinary codes'. (Arbitration is the third form of ADR. It has more similarities to litigation in that a third party, the arbitrator, can impose a settlement on the parties in the absence of agreement between them.)

After hearing the very sad case of Charlie Gard, Mr Justice Francis concluded his judgment with a plea for more use of mediation. Mr Justice Cooke, granting Peter Hook permission to continue his derivative action against his New Order ex-bandmates, nevertheless urged the parties to enter into negotiations rather than proceed to trial. The author has previously set out her recommendation that negotiation and mediation become more widely integrated into legal education, and her encouragement of institutions which offer students the opportunity to train as mediators (see Shephard, Further Reading). This chapter will ensure that you are ahead of this emerging trend.

12.1 provides helpful guidance on the skill of negotiation. The main guidance on the skill as you might encounter it during your studies is set out at 12.1.1–12.1.6. Some additional practice perspectives are included at 12.1.7. Guidance on the skill of mediation is covered at 12.2.

This is the third of five chapters on communication skills and you are encouraged to read it in conjunction with Chapter 9 (problem-solving) and the other chapters on communication (10 to 14) for the following reasons.

- These are both methods of solving legal problems, and so you will need a good understanding of Chapter 9 and Figure 9.1.

- You will also require a good working knowledge and understanding of the essential foundations for oral communication to be persuasive and influential, discussed in Chapter 10.

- Chapter 11 discusses specifically client interviews and meetings, which may reveal facts that lead you and the client to conclude that negotiation or mediation is the way forward.

- Chapter 13 discusses mooting and advocacy, which may be required if negotiation and mediation does not succeed to a solution acceptable to all parties.

- Chapter 14 discusses communication in the form of writing and drafting, which will be required in the process of any negotiation and mediation.

12.1 Negotiation

Traditionally, law programmes have favoured mooting, to develop advocacy skills (see Chapter 13) over negotiation skills. As explained in the Introduction, there are now increasing demands to incorporate negotiation skills too. To date, the focus in practice units has been to assess the preparation stage, perhaps asking you to write up your negotiation plan. 12.1.4 and Figures 12.1 and 12.2 will give you what you need to succeed with this. Increasingly, students are being encouraged to use their problem-solving skills (see Chapter 9) and oral communication skills (see Chapter 10) to practise the conduct of the negotiation itself, rather than just the preparation stage. While this is not widely assessed at the time of writing, there are an increasing number of student negotiation competitions, through participation in which you can set yourself apart from your peers and take advantage of excellent networking opportunities (see 15.7). For that reason, 12.1.5 and Figure 12.3 will help you to begin practising effective negotiation skills.

12.1.1 What is negotiation?

The authors of *Getting to Yes* (see Further Reading) define negotiation as 'back-and-forth communication designed to reach an agreement when you and the other side have some interests that are shared and others that are opposed'. It is a process which can help parties arrive at a mutually satisfactory solution to a problem or dispute, without walking away (for example, if the matter is non-contentious, such as a merger or acquisition) or going to court (if the case is contentious, such as a dispute over payment). Reaching agreement is the key aim.

12.1.2 The challenges

Preparation is key to a successful negotiation. However, no matter how well prepared you are, the outcome of a negotiation will be uncertain. This uncertainty and lack of control can feel uncomfortable, because lawyers tend to enjoy feeling in control. You may also find that practising your negotiation skills reveals you feel uncomfortable around conflict.

Before you begin to learn strategies for successful negotiation in this chapter, it will help you to remember that daily interactions, such as with your family and friends, in job interviews, and while returning goods you have bought, are likely to have already provided you with opportunities to work through conflict and uncertainty, to negotiate a solution on which all parties can agree, and will continue to do so. Any parents reading this might enjoy remembering daily negotiations with younger children too (and reflect on what a very powerful negotiating position our young children have).

12.1.3 **Context**

Negotiation is a key skill whatever area of law in which you wish to specialise. Example 6 provides further information, with examples of when you will need this skill in different practice areas.

12.1.4 **Preparing for a negotiation**

Detailed preparation is essential for successful negotiation. Figure 12.1 sets out the steps that will help you to prepare effectively, and further guidance is set out in the following sections.

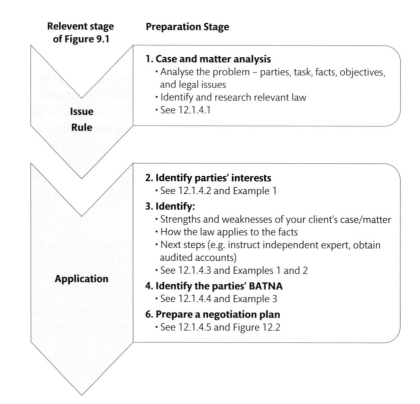

Relevent stage of Figure 9.1

Preparation Stage

Issue
Rule

1. Case and matter analysis
• Analyse the problem – parties, task, facts, objectives, and legal issues
• Identify and research relevant law
• See 12.1.4.1

Application

2. Identify parties' interests
• See 12.1.4.2 and Example 1

3. Identify:
• Strengths and weaknesses of your client's case/matter
• How the law applies to the facts
• Next steps (e.g. instruct independent expert, obtain audited accounts)
• See 12.1.4.3 and Examples 1 and 2

4. Identify the parties' BATNA
• See 12.1.4.4 and Example 3

6. Prepare a negotiation plan
• See 12.1.4.5 and Figure 12.2

Figure 12.1 Steps to prepare for a negotiation

12.1.4.1 Case and matter analysis

To begin your preparation, you need a thorough knowledge of all the key facts and the applicable law. Again, this is not a new skill. Figure 9.1 will be very helpful to you here. Use the case/matter analysis guidance at the Issue and Rule stages to conduct a thorough analysis of the parties, task, facts, objectives and legal issues and then identify and research the relevant law, for any particular case or matter, be it contentious or non-contentious.

Examples 1 and 2 illustrate how to do this.

Example 1

Contentious case

Client (C), a business with an excellent reputation in the antiques sector, has bought goods from another business (OS). Inspection after delivery revealed that the goods were damaged. C has asked OS to return the deposit C paid, at which point C will return the goods. C will refuse to pay the outstanding balance now due. C claims it told the other side (OS) how vital it was that the goods arrived in the pristine condition in which OS described them to be in, given their value as antiques. OS, the seller, is a new entrant to the sector. It maintains it has photographic evidence that the goods were not damaged when they were delivered. OS's position is that the goods must have been damaged after delivery. OS wants C to keep the goods, OS will keep the deposit, and C to pay the outstanding balance in full.

Parties:	C (Client, buyer, good reputation, potential defendant)
	OS (Seller, potential claimant, new entrant)
Task:	Negotiate, on behalf of C, to reach agreement with OS in their dispute about a sale of goods contract.
Relevant facts:	OS sold goods to C. C made pre-contract representations to OS about the required purpose (antiques) and quality (pristine, as described by OS). C paid OS a deposit. OS delivered the goods and took photograph on delivery. On inspection after delivery, C discovered the goods were damaged. The goods remain with C. The deposit remains with OS. The balance is now overdue from C to OS.
Missing facts:	What evidence is there of: (i) C's pre-contract representations to OS? (ii) OS's photographic evidence? What happened between delivery and inspection? Why did C not discover damage on delivery? Did C inspect on delivery? Was there a delay in inspection? What condition are the goods in? Where are parties in the negotiation process to date, and are they willing to go to court?
Objectives:	C: Return goods without paying outstanding balance to OS. Receive deposit back from OS.
	OS: Receive outstanding balance from C.
Legal issues raised:	Is there a valid contract between the parties?
	If so, has OS breached the terms of the contract by delivering damaged goods?
	If not, has C breached the contract by failing to pay for the goods?
Relevant law:	Contract law.
Cause of action:	Breach of sale of goods contract (business to business).
Necessary elements:	Contract formation (offer, acceptance, certainty of terms, consideration); Enforceability (implied terms as to correspondence with description, satisfactory quality and fitness for purpose under ss. 13 & 14 Sale of Goods Act 1979).

12.1.4.2 Identify parties' interests

You have considered under 'objectives', in Example 1, *what* the parties want. Here, you consider *why*. When considering the options available to the client, Chapter 9 made clear that it is not just the legal remedies, solutions, or procedures that you should be considering. Other issues, such as time, funds, or the desire to continue a relationship may well be key to inform the client's options. In negotiation, these matters can help inform your understanding of the parties' interests.

It can help to think of an iceberg, the majority of which is hidden underwater. Focusing on the area that is visible (the *what*) is important, but it will have limited use in informing your understanding of the whole, until you reveal the *why*, which may well be submerged.

The *why* may be emotional, related to how the parties feel, and will be powerful in driving the behaviour of the parties. It might include wider, longer-term commercial or personal goals. This stage will involve conjecture, and you will have the opportunity to clarify, supplement, and confirm the interests and needs you have identified now, before (see Figure 12.2) and during (see 12.1.5.4) the conduct of the negotiation.

Example 1 is continued now, to illustrate how to do this for this contentious case.

Example 1
Contentious case (cont'd)

Identifying parties' interests in a negotiation

Interest	C	OS
Experience	Excellent.	None. New entrant
Future relationship	May not be important . . . need to check any prior relationship between parties, and C's financial position.	Likely to be important, to establish new business.
Publicity and reputation	May be fine . . . but . . . why was damage not discovered on delivery? Was this a mistake? Is C professionally embarrassed?	Risk of bad publicity at vulnerable time (start-up business).
Anything else?	To be confirmed	To be confirmed

12.1.4.3 Identify parties' strengths and weaknesses, how the law applies to the facts, and next steps

Next, you will need to consider:

1. The strengths and weaknesses of your client's case (contentious work)/matter (non-contentious work). The interests you have identified at 12.1.4.2 are likely to have either a strengthening or weakening effect on bargaining position; assimilate them into this step accordingly, together with your case/matter analysis from 12.1.4.1.

2. How the law applies to the facts; and

3. Next steps. This includes obtaining independent evidence. Objective, independent standards, such as an expert's report or audited accounts, can be persuasive and so valuable to support your client's negotiating position. Identifying the need for these now will help you to secure specifically the expert you want to instruct, rather than whoever is available.

Example 1 continues now, to illustrate this step for the contentious case. Example 2 follows it, which illustrates this step for a new non-contentious matter.

Example **1**

Contentious case (cont'd)

1. The strengths and weaknesses of C's case

Strengths include:

- Experience: C is a respected name in the industry; OS is a new entrant to the market.

- Future relationship: OS may need C more than C needs OS?

- Publicity and reputation: Risk for OS as crucial to establish reputation of new business. Potential for C to enhance reputation if seen to handle dispute well.

- Description: C and OS appear in agreement about the OS's description of the goods pre-contract, as pristine.

- Pre-contract representations: C claims it made pre-contract representations to OS about the importance of the goods being delivered in the pristine condition they were described as being in, for use as antiques.

Weaknesses include:

- Experience: Why did experienced C not discover damage on delivery?

- Future relationship: C may need OS?

- Publicity and reputation: If mistakes on both sides, risk of 'supporting the underdog'.

- Contract: Clear evidence of a contractual relationship between C and OS.

- Delivery: OS delivered the goods under the contract.

- Evidence of damage: OS claims it has photographic evidence of an examination of the goods which does not reveal any damage on delivery.

- Pre-contract representations: No written evidence, yet, about pre-contract representations by C to OS. OS claims it cannot recall hearing any pre-contract representations from C.

2. How the law applies to the facts of C's case

- Relevant law is contract, breach of contract, and sale of goods (business to business).

- Validity: Parties acknowledge contract. No suggestion not valid.

- Enforceability:

  - C could seek to rely on claim that OS has breached terms implied into the contract by sections 13 & 14 Sale of Goods Act 1979. This would be on grounds that the goods did not correspond to their description, and/or were not of satisfactory quality and/or fit for purpose. Parties appear to agree on how OS described the goods, and that the goods are damaged. Need evidence of pre-contract representations. Key question in dispute is who bore the risk; did damage occur before or after delivery?

(Continued)

- If C cannot rely on breach of implied terms, then OS could seek to claim C is in breach of contract for failure to pay the balance now due under the contract for the goods delivered.

3. Next steps

- Obtain C and OS's consent to inspection of the goods by a jointly-appointed independent examiner, to assess condition of the goods and further investigate allegations of damage.
- Ask OS for photographic evidence.
- Ask C for evidence of pre-contract representations.
- Then reconsider the range of options that will be available to the parties.

Example 2

Non-contentious matter

Client (C) is a company director who has been approached by a new company (OS), currently flourishing due to the rising popularity of veganism, with an offer of a directorship in marketing. C is excited at the prospect, as a vegan herself, but is worried about the risk of moving from her current, stable company, into this new company. She has asked for a comprehensive suite of incentives, including a *Bushell v Faith* clause to enhance voting rights on any resolution to remove her, a shareholding exceeding 25 per cent, and a long-term service contract of three years. OS has said it cannot agree the *Bushell v Faith* clause, as even its CEO doesn't have one.

1. The strengths and weaknesses of C's matter

Strengths include:

- Relationship: Possibly OS needs C more than she needs OS. OS approached C. OS needs a marketing director. C can remain in her current job in a stable company.
- Fit: C is a vegan, so particularly well-suited to this business and helps marketing message?
- Agreement: C and OS appear in agreement over C's requests about her shareholding and service contract. Sign of strong negotiating position?

2. *Weaknesses include:*

- Relationship: OS may have approached other candidates for the post? C may not be first choice?
- Fit: OS is currently flourishing. C is excited by the prospect of working for OS.
- Agreement: OS can use concessions, in agreeing to provide C with protection through her level of shareholding and the service contract, as evidence of its reasonableness in negotiation.

How the law applies to the facts of C's matter

- Relevant law is that director can be removed by ordinary resolution of shareholders under s. 168 of the Companies Act 2006, or by a term in their service contract linked to fundamental breach. Director can seek protection by (i) seeking long term service contract (providing financial disincentive to removal), (ii) shareholder agreement not to vote against the director on any s. 168 resolution; and (iii) *Bushell v Faith* clause, increasing directors' vote so cannot be removed under s. 168.
- Service contract: It is within C's control whether she breaches these terms. Long term, and so financial disincentive to removal already agreed.

- Over 50 per cent of OS shareholders could vote by ordinary resolution to remove C as a director.
    - The shareholders' agreement could give C a right to sue the other shareholders if they vote to remove her. However: (i) cost and time implications for C in bringing a case, and (ii) shareholders may not have means to pay even if C was granted a remedy.
    - A *Bushell* v *Faith* clause would prevent OS shareholders achieving over 50 per cent to remove C in the first place. This is not agreed and so this risk remains.

3. *Next steps*

- Obtain further information about the OS shareholders, their percentage shareholdings, relationships (to reveal any block voting), and financial position.
- Obtain further information about the role and OS's financial information.
- Then re-consider bargaining power and whether OS's desire to have C as a director exceeds its reluctance to commit to a *Bushell* v *Faith* clause.

12.1.4.4 Identify the parties' BATNAs

Before you begin to negotiate, you will need a clear view of your client's best and worst outcomes in reaching agreement through the negotiation. The book *Getting to Yes* (see Further Reading), uses the acronym BATNA to introduce a third outcome, namely the Best Alternative To A Negotiated Agreement. This refers to the minimum your client would be prepared to accept as an alternative course of action, if the negotiation fails.

Why the BATNA is helpful

The BATNA will clarify the exact point at which your client will choose to reject any offer and instead embrace an alternative to a negotiated agreement. A BATNA is 'a defence against an inferior agreement' (see Hewlin, Further Reading) and can focus all parties' minds on the advantages (and disadvantages) of doing a deal and reaching agreement.

Bargaining power

Your BATNA must be credible. It may be that your client has no credible BATNA at all, in which case, it is dependent on reaching agreement and has a poor bargaining position. If the other side are convinced by your client's BATNA, and believe that your client would indeed sacrifice their pursuit of a negotiated agreement in favour of it, that can strengthen your client's bargaining position. However, even a convincing BATNA is not guaranteed to do this. For example, your client might have an excellent BATNA, but the other side's could be better still. Conversely, if your client's BATNA, while acceptable to them, is poor or risky, and your client will suffer if they fail to agree a deal, this can weaken your client's bargaining power and strengthen the other side's position with the result that they will compromise less. For this reason, you should do your best to determine the other side's BATNA.

Example 3 illustrates this. Practical exercises at the end of this chapter encourage you to identify and evaluate BATNAs used by candidates on *The Apprentice* television series and by the government in Brexit negotiations.

Example 3

When Apple launched Apple Music, it gave users a free three-month trial. The terms of Apple's suggested deal with artists was that it would not pay them for any music streamed by users in the free trial period, but instead pay artists (what Apple described as) a higher royalty rate for music streamed once the trial period had concluded. Taylor Swift (see BBC News, Further Reading) did not agree with these terms. In an open letter to Apple, Swift made clear that she wanted Apple to agree to pay artists during this period, and if they did not agree, then she would refuse Apple any right to stream her album '1989'. Swift's letter persuaded Apple to pay artists during the trial period, and keep the negotiated, higher royalty rate. They took seriously her BATNA of walking away from the proposed terms of Apple's deal, and not have her album streamed through Apple Music, rather than agree to them.

12.1.4.5 Prepare a negotiation plan

Having completed all the previous preparation, the next step is to assimilate it into a useful negotiation plan. It has three main purposes:

- In the negotiation itself, as a crib sheet (see 11.1.1), without compromising too much the non-verbal communication detailed in Chapter 10 as essential for rapport (for example, eye contact).
- To clarify your understanding of the negotiating position.
- In turn, to help you explain the negotiating position to others (the client, your supervisor, other lawyers in your firm). Your client may allocate to you responsibility for negotiating a successful outcome (regardless of the strengths and weaknesses of the case or matter) and blame you if the negotiation does not achieve the outcome they want. The plan will help you to manage from the outset their reasonable expectations about their negotiating position. However, stop short of sharing verbatim the plan itself if it would prevent you from stating the issues as directly as you need to for it to be an effective crib sheet.

Figure 12.2 provides a helpful structure for you and illustrates how you would assimilate into a plan the preparation work for the client at Example 2. It uses the same general memorandum template as for the Research Report at Figure 8.2 and the Attendance Note at Figure 11.3. It also follows the advice for good legal writing in Chapter 14, in that it captures necessary detail but is succinct, avoids verbosity and unnecessary repetition, and focuses exclusively on relevant information.

You will be able to refine your plan as it informs your understanding of your client's BATNA, the interests of the other party, and any required independent, expert evidence. By this stage, your preparation has become an iterative process. You will move back and forth between stages.

NEGOTIATION PLAN

CLIENT:	C
MATTER:	Dispute about sale of goods contract
PARTIES:	C (Buyer), OS (Seller)
FILE REFERENCE:	1234-5678
DATE:	Today

1. Objectives

(a) C

- Receive deposit (£X) back from OS.
- Return goods without paying outstanding balance (£Y) to OS.
- Prepared to defend (any claim for non-payment) and counterclaim (for return of deposit) if necessary.

(b) OS

- Persuade C to hand over the goods to a jointly agreed expert for further investigation about the alleged damage.
- Receive outstanding balance (£Y) from C.
- Protect OS's future business reputation within the business community.
- Maintain a working relationship with C in future.

2. Interests

Interest	C	OS
Experience	Extensive. Confident and bullish as result.	Accepts vulnerability here but photographic evidence conclusive.
Future relationship	Potential, willing to mentor, if good outcome here.	OS needs more than C
Publicity and reputation	Sees potential for excellent PR, arising from fair handling of this dispute. Wants to be seen as rescuer, not pushover. Failure to inspect on delivery was oversight: sensitive, keep quiet.	OS needs more than C. Start-up, but not financially vulnerable. Left job in the City to pursue dream job in antiques.
Anything else?	Reputation as 'best in business' very important. Business doing well. Genuinely passionate about antiques.	Extremely wealthy. Does not need to work or pursue this claim. Genuinely passionate about antiques.

Figure 12.2 Example negotiation plan

3. BATNA

(a) C

Pay for goods, for display in own home.

(b) OS

Drop claim in hope of re-establishing business relationship with C in time.

4. Key relevant legal issues

(a) Contractual liability

- Can the terms of the contract to buy the goods be enforced?
- What was the condition of the goods at the time of sale and/or delivery to C?
- If the goods were damaged, is it possible to prove when the damage occurred? Consider the use of expert evidence.

(b) Correspondence with description

Arguments for C

- Parties agree about how goods were described.
- Disputes goods correspond with that description

Argument for OS

- Damage must have occurred after delivery.

(c) Satisfactory quality and fitness for purpose

Arguments for C

- Disputes this.
- Goods are damaged and not fit for purpose as antiques.

Arguments for OS

- Photographic evidence on delivery.

5. Evaluation

Issue (a) contractual liability

- Not in dispute.
- Facts evidence elements of valid contract.

Issues (b) correspondence with description, and (c) satisfactory quality and fitness for purpose

- Investigation: By jointly agreed expert as to when and why damage might have occurred.
- Photographic evidence: Not seen. Could shift burden onto C to prove the goods were damaged at the time of delivery.
- Pre-contract representations: No evidence found, yet. Evidence of C notifying OS, about its need for goods in pristine condition for use as antiques, would strengthen C's case.

Figure 12.2 *Continued*

12.1.5 **Conducting the negotiation**

Your preparation, culminating in your negotiation plan at Figure 12.2, will have clarified what you know, and what you do not know. During the negotiation itself, you will have the opportunity to ask further questions and fill any gaps in your knowledge. This section will first introduce you to the concept of conducting a negotiation, and then give you a helpful strategy you can follow at Figure 12.3.

12.1.5.1 Different approaches to negotiation

In deciding how best to approach your negotiation of a case or matter, it is important to observe ethical standards and control your emotions. The most successful negotiators are the most flexible, not anchored to one approach, but able to be intuitive to the changing positions during any negotiation and adapt appropriately to achieve the best outcome. This section will help you to reflect on your own practice, and how you might increase your flexibility by learning about and practising other approaches.

Table 12.2 Advantages and disadvantages of different personal styles, for negotiation

Style	Advantages	Disadvantages
1.	● Friendly ● Good listener ● Constructive ● Emphasises similarity not difference ● Constructive ● Open ● Confident ● Patient ● Supportive ● Trusting	● Difficulty saying 'no' ● Difficulty putting own interests first ● Avoidant of conflict at all costs ● Trusting ● Deferential ● Weak ● Can't cope with pressure ● Dislikes responsibility
2.	● Assertive ● Controlling ● Pro-active ● Decisive ● Takes the lead ● Rises to a challenge	● Autocratic ● Impatient ● Overbearing ● Poor listener ● Critical ● Lacks creativity 'take it or leave it'
3.	● Logical ● Detail oriented ● Persistent ● Prepared ● Risk averse ● Follows rules ● Confident ● Evaluative	● Lacks intuition with people ● Lacks creativity ● Uses logic not emotion to persuade ● May over-analyse ● Predictable ● Stubborn ● Resistant to change ● Literal
4.	● Socially charming ● Avoids offence ● Flexible ● Creative ● Persuasive ● Articulate ● Can think on feet ● Seeks opportunities	● Seen as pushy or fawning ● Can come across as insincere ● Talks too much ● Poorly prepared ● Surface listener (listens to respond).

How your own characteristics inform your approach to negotiation

You may already have a good idea, from your exposure to negotiations in daily life, about whether you are naturally inclined towards a competitive, cooperative, or collaborative negotiating style. Table 12.2 sets out the advantages and disadvantages of four different sets of characteristics, based on Dr Lesley Stolz's work on negotiation while at Johnson and Johnson (see Allen and Stolz, Further Reading). Enjoy using it to identify your natural style(s), what its strengths and weaknesses are, and to learn about other styles you would like to have.

Note that in academic texts, a subtle difference is drawn between negotiation styles (the way in which a negotiator communicates) and negotiation strategies (the approach the negotiator takes). For your introduction to this vocational subject in this chapter we have conflated them into 'approaches', reflecting our view that an integrative approach is to be encouraged, where you can explore areas of disagreement and agreement effectively and flexibly. Articles and links given in the Further Reading will provide what you need to explore any academic subtleties, should you so wish.

Adversarial approach (also known as positional bargaining, win/lose, zero-sum)

As the name suggests, parties take up (and depending on bargaining position), then give up a sequence of positions. It can feel like watching a tennis match as the parties knock the issues between them back and forth until they reach agreement. One party's gain is the other party's loss. The aim of each party is for the agreement to more closely reflect their own starting position. This tends to encourage a competitive strategy, but it can also be associated with a cooperative strategy, or soft approach, where a negotiator willingly moves away from their opening position.

While it may superficially signal an initial show of strength, with extreme high or low opening demands, this style of negotiation is unsophisticated, lacks nuance, and can be unsuitable depending on the context. It can strain important relationships between the parties and provides little opportunity for the parties to understand why they have taken up the position they have. However, it can be effective if the other side is not confident enough to handle this combative style, and capitulates. If they are equally confident and competitive, it can lead to deadlock. In theory, this style can succeed for both parties where they have a similar style and the outcome is purely financial (or if trying to understand the 'why' might actually make the relationship worse).

Example 4 illustrates positional bargaining. It also shows that even financial outcomes can involve a relationship that might be better preserved, and in any event it is usually worth exploring 'why' the parties need the financial outcome they say they do. In Example 4, the

Example 4

Following an annual service where the engineer failed to tighten a seal, Robyn's hot water tank leaks and causes water damage to the ceiling in their living room below. The engineer's company, EnergyWise Limited, offer to pay for the painting over of the water-damaged patch, taking 30 minutes, with white trade paint costing £18 per tin. Robyn does not agree, saying the entire ceiling needs to be repainted with two coats of the existing paint (designer) so the entire ceiling looks even, taking a total of 3 hours over two days, and that is should be repainted with the existing designer paint costing £60 per tin.

The possibilities are:

- Paint out patch with trade paint (labour £50) = £68
- Paint out patch with designer paint (labour £50) = £110
- Paint entire ceiling (2 coats) with trade paint (labour £300) = £318
- Paint entire ceiling (2 coats) with designer paint (labour £300) = £360

> £292 difference between Robyn and EnergyWise's preferred outcomes. For every £1 Robyn wins, EnergyWise will be £1 worse off (and vice-versa)

two parties appear to have an existing relationship ('following an annual service . . .') which could continue if they succeed in negotiating without falling out. Robyn does have a reason to explain the difference in their opening position of £360, compared to EnergyWise's of £68. Robyn has used designer paint throughout their house, and also has concerns that simply painting over the patch will not provide an even coverage. While EnergyWise might remain unconvinced, revealing and discussing the 'why' is likely, at least, to prevent EnergyWise assuming that Robyn is simply seeking to exploit them. The authors of *Getting to Yes* (see Further Reading) do not believe that positional bargaining will produce the best agreement. Nevertheless, positional bargaining remains the go-to tactic for some lawyers, and perhaps it is the most widely depicted in TV dramas and films about lawyers.

If you adopt a competitive strategy here, you will see the negotiation as a win/lose situation where any gains you will make will be at the expense of the other side. To use it successfully, you will need to be confident, with a clear expectation of an outcome favourable to your client. You will present a strong opening position, from which you may make few concessions, and concentrate on your client's objectives rather than those of any other party.

If you adopt a cooperative strategy here, you must be convinced that it is possible to conduct your negotiation in an open, trusting, and constructive manner. You will need to be prepared to make concessions, with the belief that that they will help progress more easily towards a satisfactory outcome. Your goal would be agreement rather than victory. While one school of thought is that the other side are more likely to say yes to the requests of someone they like, the counterargument exists that this style can make you vulnerable to those willing to adopt more aggressive tactics.

It would be difficult to couple a collaborative strategy with an adversarial style.

Problem-solving approach (also known as principled, collaborative, or win/win negotiation)

Fisher, Ury, and Patton founded the Harvard Negotiation Project in 1979 to improve the theory, teaching, and practice of negotiation so people could deal more constructively with conflict. They later collaborated to form the Program on Negotiation (see Harvard Law School Further Reading). The Harvard program advocates this approach, which:

- is evaluative, involving 'no tricks, no posturing';
- is creative, open to considering a range of possibilities;
- is collaborative, where parties take a reasoned, intellectual approach to negotiation;
- focuses on the problem, separating it from the people and their personalities;
- avoids making assumptions;
- encourages revealing and sharing the parties' interests (the *why*—see 12.1.4.2);

- acknowledges the possibility that the parties may have aims which are not in conflict (unlike positional bargaining);
- encourages parties to come to a mutually beneficial agreement.

Example 5 illustrates aspects of a problem-solving negotiation style.

Example 5

The Smiths are divorcing, and negotiating where their dog, Burley, should live.

- Mr Smith's lawyer asks for him to have sole custody of their dog, Burley.
- Mrs Smith is upset about this, and so her lawyer advises she could demand joint custody.
- Mr Smith is upset about this, and his lawyer offers instead that Mrs Smith can have him for three days each week, the specific days to be agreed at the beginning of each month.
- Mrs Smith is upset about this, too.

The lawyers, perplexed at the upset caused by their attempts to 'divide up the pie', are flexible enough to move from a cooperative but positional bargaining style into a problem-solving style. They ask *why* Mrs Smith and Mr Smith are upset (exploring the interests as at 12.1.4.2).

- They discover that Mrs Smith is actually allergic to Burley, who was Mr Smith's pet. This explains why Mr Smith was upset by what he perceived as a threat that Mrs Smith would seek joint custody.
- Mrs Smith explains she is happy for Burley to live with Mr Smith. However, her grandson Jim loves Burley. Mrs Smith can take medicine to control her allergy to a bearable degree, and she and Jim share lots of happy memories of time spent with Burley. Mrs Smith is upset at the thought that this chapter of her life, too, will be ending. She would like Burley overnight specifically from Friday evening until Saturday lunchtime, every other week, which is when Jim visits her. This reveals why Mrs Smith was upset when given access to the dog for three days of every week. It was not more time, but the specific time, that she wanted.
- Mr Smith is happy for Mrs Smith to have Burley when Jim is with her. He had been worried he would not be able to continue to play sport on a Friday evening and Saturday morning, because he did not want to leave Burley alone in an empty house. He had assumed Mrs Smith would not want to have Burley to accommodate his sport, or anything else for that matter. Knowing Burley and Jim can enjoy this time together, for half of the weekends of the year at least, is a good outcome for him, Mrs Smith, Jim, and Burley. You will recall that achieving a mutually beneficial agreement is an aim of this problem-solving approach to negotiation.

12.1.5.2 The advantages and disadvantages of your medium

It is commonly assumed that negotiations are best carried out face to face with the other side.

However, there are a number of media through which negotiations can occur. While during your studies you are unlikely to be able to choose, in practice you may have more latitude, and 12.1.7.3 explores this further.

12.1.5.3 Body language and listening skills: Persuasive oral communication

The skills you read about in 10.1, for effective oral communication, apply equally here. You are encouraged to pay particular attention to how your tone of voice, pace of speech, and eye contact might be affected when you are confronted with a situation that is uncertain, or with conflict. Practical exercise 5 at the end of this chapter will help you with this.

Body language may be inadvertent and construed negatively (such as jiggling your leg, fiddling with your hair, or crossing your arms), but some negotiators also employ deliberate body language. Steepling (hands up, fingers together), in particular, is an expression of confidence (see Navarro, Further Reading).

The skills of active listening and effective questioning, discussed in Chapter 11 in relation to interviewing, will help you succeed as a negotiator too. You can also help yourself to enjoy this skill by paying attention to your attitude. Optimism and self-confidence are important for negotiators.

Once you begin to feel comfortable with the basic structure and content of a negotiation, you will be able to enjoy learning and practising tactics to extend your influence and power of persuasion, and spotting when the other side is doing the same (see various articles in Further Reading). Not all tactics have integrity, so choose yours with care.

12.1.5.4 Structuring your negotiation

The negotiation process typically follows a pattern. The more familiar you are with the process, the more you can plan accordingly. Few negotiations are completely straightforward, so keep your client's objectives front of mind, and be alert to any changes you perceive in the agenda and the issues. Figure 12.3 sets out the stages of the negotiation, to help you. While you are inexperienced, you are likely to find it helpful to take into your negotiation with you, together with your negotiation plan at Figure 12.2. Bear in mind the advantages of a crib sheet, outlined at 11.1.1, balanced against the disadvantages in terms of interrupting non-verbal communication such as eye contact and rapport, and that it will not reflect the iterative nature of a negotiation and how you will need to think 'on your feet'. You will know when you feel able to negotiate without this crutch.

Preliminaries

During the early stages, you will explore each other's starting positions, to understand each other's concerns and objectives. As you get to know the other side's negotiating styles and strategies, the issues can be identified. As you become more experienced, you can experiment more with what information you choose to share, and when (within the confines of professional conduct, at 12.1.7.2). In negotiation, information is power.

Offers, counter-offers, and bargaining

By this stage, the issues should have been identified. Differences with the other side must be narrowed as you work towards a negotiated agreement. You will begin to move towards each other's position through the exchange of information and the process of persuasion.

You will need to apply what you learned in Chapter 11 to ask effective questions and uncover additional or new information through good active listening skills. The oral communication skills you learned in Chapter 10 will also be valuable to establish rapport and develop trust with the other party, to encourage information sharing and arrive at mutually acceptable solutions.

At the preparation stage, you considered the parties' interests (see 12.1.4.2 and Figure 12.2) and you will need to clarify, add to, and confirm them here.

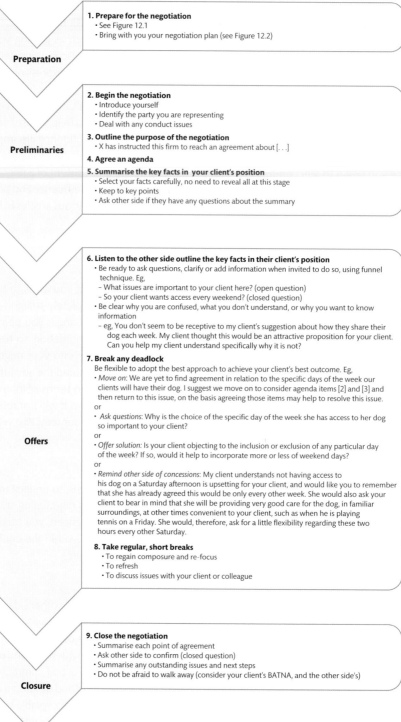

Preparation

1. Prepare for the negotiation
  • See Figure 12.1
  • Bring with you your negotiation plan (see Figure 12.2)

Preliminaries

2. Begin the negotiation
  • Introduce yourself
  • Identify the party you are representing
  • Deal with any conduct issues

3. Outline the purpose of the negotiation
  • X has instructed this firm to reach an agreement about [. . .]

4. Agree an agenda

5. Summarise the key facts in your client's position
  • Select your facts carefully, no need to reveal all at this stage
  • Keep to key points
  • Ask other side if they have any questions about the summary

Offers

6. Listen to the other side outline the key facts in their client's position
  • Be ready to ask questions, clarify or add information when invited to do so, using funnel technique. Eg,
    – What issues are important to your client here? (open question)
    – So your client wants access every weekend? (closed question)
  • Be clear why you are confused, what you don't understand, or why you want to know information
    – eg, You don't seem to be receptive to my client's suggestion about how they share their dog each week. My client thought this would be an attractive proposition for your client. Can you help my client understand specifically why it is not?

7. Break any deadlock
  Be flexible to adopt the best approach to achieve your client's best outcome. Eg,
  • *Move on*: We are yet to find agreement in relation to the specific days of the week our clients will have their dog. I suggest we move on to consider agenda items [2] and [3] and then return to this issue, on the basis agreeing those items may help to resolve this issue.
  or
  • *Ask questions*: Why is the choice of the specific day of the week she has access to her dog so important to your client?
  or
  • *Offer solution*: Is your client objecting to the inclusion or exclusion of any particular day of the week? If so, would it help to incorporate more or less of weekend days?
  or
  • *Remind other side of concessions*: My client understands not having access to his dog on a Saturday afternoon is upsetting for your client, and would like you to remember that she has already agreed this would be only every other week. She would also ask your client to bear in mind that she will be providing very good care for the dog, in familiar surroundings, at other times convenient to your client, such as when he is playing tennis on a Friday. She would, therefore, ask for a little flexibility regarding these two hours every other Saturday.

8. Take regular, short breaks
  • To regain composure and re-focus
  • To refresh
  • To discuss issues with your client or colleague

Closure

9. Close the negotiation
  • Summarise each point of agreement
  • Ask other side to confirm (closed question)
  • Summarise any outstanding issues and next steps
  • Do not be afraid to walk away (consider your client's BATNA, and the other side's)

Figure 12.3 Negotiation strategy

Offers will be made at this stage, and responses to offers. Parties will modify and review their positions informed by their objectives. New issues or unforeseen problems may arise at this stage, and you may need to take steps to avoid, or break out of, deadlock. Be clear in the negotiations when you encounter a 'dealbreaker' or a 'must have' but beware of using empty threats which might weaken your position, and the credibility of your BATNA. Figure 12.4 provides a helpful visual depiction of the zone ('offer zone', 'bargaining zone' or 'zone of possible agreement'), where an agreement can be met which both parties can agree to.

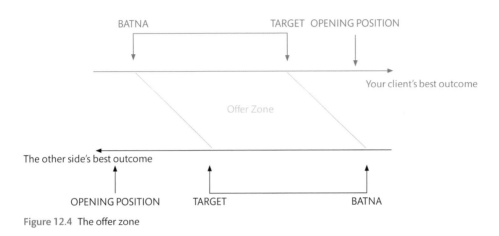

Figure 12.4 The offer zone

Closure

The key aim of a negotiation is for all parties to reach agreement. However, this is not always possible. It may be that a satisfactory closure is one where the parties agree to disagree, rather than agree what is, for one party at least, an inferior agreement. Remember, your client's BATNA (See 12.1.4.4) will inform you as to when any negotiated agreement would be inferior to their best alternative.

12.1.6 Reflection on your negotiation

Like any skill, your ability to negotiate with success will improve with practice. Following any negotiation, adopt a reflective practice, using the following criteria taken from *The Essence of Negotiation* (see Further Reading).

1. Are you satisfied with the outcomes? Why/why not?
2. What concessions were made? By whom?
3. Were the concessions necessary?
4. Who was the more effective negotiator? Why?
5. What strategies and actions helped most?
6. What actions hindered the progress of the negotiation?
7. Did you trust the other party? Why/why not?
8. What factors influenced the feelings between you and other side the most?
9. How well was time used? Could it have been used better?

10. How well did you listen to each other? Who talked more? Why?

11. Were creative solutions suggested? What happened to them?

12. Did you fully understand the other's underlying issues and concerns? Why/why not?

13. How adequate was your preparation? How did this affect the negotiation?

14. What were the strongest arguments put forward by the other side?

15. How receptive was the other to your arguments and ideas?

16. What were your main learning points in this negotiation?

17. What will you do differently next time?

12.1.7 Negotiation in practice

12.1.7.1 Context

Negotiation is a key skill whatever area of law in which you wish to specialise. All lawyers, for example, will need to be prepared to negotiate their own fees with their own client. Negotiations can be in contentious areas of law such as dispute resolution, where the parties are negotiating by reason of circumstance. These negotiations can involve highly emotional issues, such as arrangements about where a child should live following a divorce. Equally negotiations may be in non-contentious areas of law, where the parties are choosing to negotiate, for example to close a deal. Example 6 provides a sample of the variety of contexts in which you may be required to negotiate.

Example 6
Business law

Negotiate:

- the terms of a sale and purchase agreement in relation to your client company, which is selling assets (with the buyer's lawyer);
- share rights for a new class of shares to be issued to your angel investor client, for insertion into the company's articles of association (with the company's lawyer).

Civil litigation

Negotiate:

- a settlement (with insurers);
- an extension of time for the service of documents (with the party's lawyer);
- whether to arrange for mediation to seek agreement in the matter (with your own client).

Criminal litigation

Negotiate:

- a plea bargain, in exchange for your client pleading guilty to a lesser offence (with the Crown Prosecution Service);
- whether to issue proceedings (with your own client).

Property

Negotiate:

- the terms of a commercial lease on behalf of your client (with the landlord's lawyer);
- the completion date on the purchase of a second home (with the seller's lawyer).

12.1.7.2 Professional conduct and ethics

As set out in Chapter 6, as a lawyer, you must always act ethically and in accordance with the SRA principles and codes of conduct. Negotiation can raise some potentially grey areas where you need to exercise careful professional judgement.

Act in the best interests of your client

SRA Principle 7 requires you to act in the best interests of each client. 6.4.3 explores this further. You may be negotiating with quite a small group of professionals, depending on the geographical and legal area in which you practice. It is worth giving some thought to the balance you wish to seek in terms of maintaining a good, professional working relationship with fellow professionals, and also act in the best interests of your respective clients.

You will encounter a range of personalities and approaches to negotiating. Some may be aggressive; some may be rude. Develop your own practice, and your ability to avoid being drawn into reciprocal behaviour. Integrity (now reflected in SRA Principle 5) and courtesy are hallmarks of the best negotiators. Keep front of mind your role, to represent your client and negotiate to reach an agreement if possible and make this clear to the other side. You can refuse to accept unacceptable tactics and behaviour, and practise enjoying staying calm when invited to feel otherwise.

Conflict and confidentiality

You should consider what the Principles and Codes of Conduct say about conflict of interest and confidentiality. (You can find them in the Further Reading section of Chapter 11.)

Weaknesses in your client's case or matter

You need to avoid professional misconduct. You must not lie to or mislead the other side (see 6.4.3). However, you are under no duty to volunteer information which may go against your client's case or matter. You must weigh up any advantages in taking this position against the risk that, if you cannot answer a direct question put to you by the other side, you reveal the weakness in your client's position and the other side can take advantage.

If the other side makes an offer which your client has indicated is at the bottom end of what they would accept, you are under no professional obligation to accept it immediately because it is within range. You could instead remind the other side that it is low, giving persuasive reasons to support your argument.

Act on your client's behalf

You can only act with your client's authority. You must be clear about the scope of your instructions (Codes of Conduct, para. 4.1 (firms); 3.1 (solicitors)). You must also ensure that your advice takes account of your client's attributes, needs and circumstances (Codes of Conduct, para. 4.2 (firms); 3.4 (solicitors)). Remember that you are negotiating on behalf of your client. When you have been working on a case or matter for a long while it can be easy to lose sight of this fact. Your objectives must be based on what your client requires. Your preparation should ensure you fully understand your client's objectives, interests, needs and priorities, and during the negotiation you will clarify, add to, and/or confirm them.

12.1.7.3 The advantages and disadvantages of your negotiating medium

It is commonly assumed that negotiations are best carried out face to face with the other side.

However, there are a number of media through which negotiations can occur, and in practice you may have control over choosing the best medium for your client. If so, you are likely to use more than one, as the case or matter progresses.

If it is not within your gift to choose where and how your negotiation takes place (for example, because you are conducting your negotiation in the context of a practice competition where the medium is chosen for you), then it will help to be alert to the advantages, and take appropriate steps to avoid the disadvantages, of the medium chosen for you. Of course, negotiations can also take place at the last moment, in court, or at the door of the court, and by third parties you have instructed, such as a barrister.

The most common negotiating media are set out in Table 12.3 together with their main advantages and disadvantages.

Table 12.3 Advantages and disadvantages of different negotiating media

Medium	Advantages	Disadvantages
Face-to-face	<ul><li>immediate</li><li>ample opportunity to explore issues thoroughly</li></ul>	<ul><li>risk of other side interpreting as a strength or weakness unintended non-verbal communication (body language, silences, tone of voice, and demeanour).</li></ul>
Telephone	<ul><li>immediate</li><li>quick</li><li>lower risk of misinterpretation of non-verbal communication</li></ul>	<ul><li>silence can be inferred as a strength or weakness of your client's case or matter</li><li>the lawyer making the telephone call is held to be in a stronger psychological position than the receiver</li><li>scope for misinterpretation</li></ul>
Written correspondence	<ul><li>easier to avoid hasty or ill-prepared decisions</li><li>particularly appropriate for negotiating complex cases or matters</li></ul>	<ul><li>can lead to delay</li><li>might be more difficult to obtain concessions from the other side</li></ul>

12.2 Mediation

At the time of writing, mediation remains something of an outlier in legal education, although there are some positive signs of bringing it into the fold, including student competitions (see Further Reading). As mentioned in the Introduction, however, our legal system appears to be moving towards encouraging parties to mediate. The chapter will give you what you need to understand the process, discuss its merits and challenges, and introduce you to the process. Further detail is available in the Further Reading section, and *Practical Law* also has a very good set of mediation documents and commentary, if your school subscribes.

12.2.1 What is mediation

Mediation is 'an informal, voluntary, confidential process in which parties to a dispute can, with the help of an independent intermediary, meet to work out a settlement'.[1] It is similar to negotiation, in that they are both forms of alternative dispute resolution (ADR) with the aim of helping parties reach agreement. It differs from negotiation because the process involves an independent intermediary, called the mediator, and the process tends to be confined to resolving disputes (while negotiation can also be used to reach agreement in non-contentious matters). The definition refers to mediation as a voluntary process, yet in some cases even reasonable refusal to mediate can have costs implications (see 12.2.3).

12.2.2 Advantages of mediation

As referred to in the introduction, mediation is not a universal panacea, but it can offer some advantages over litigation as a means of dispute resolution, specifically in terms of cost, time, the parties' wellbeing, and the possibility of achieving a solution generated by the parties and with which they can all agree. Lawyers can attend mediation meetings with their clients and/or check the contract resulting from any settlement agreed in mediation, so mediation offers them a new income stream. One significant advantage is the freedom to create whatever solution you like. As a mediator, you are able to see the full picture for party A and the full picture for party B, which offers a unique perspective. The opportunities for client (and your own professional) satisfaction are significant too. The legal system is linear and, as illustrated in Example 7, the remedies available will not always satisfy the client. Mediation is more iterative, and theoretically you can achieve any outcome provided it is not ultra vires and the other side will give it to you. Mediation remains unregulated; the closest the sector has to a regulator is the Civil Mediation Council, and there is also a voluntary European Code of Conduct (see Further Reading). If you have insurance and an entrepreneurial mind (see Crockett, Further Reading), you can make a success of mediation. However, mediators can be sued for negligence.

---

[1] Walker, S. and Smith, D. (2013) *Advising and representing clients at mediation.* Simmonds and Hill Publishing.

Example 7

One of the parties in your mediation, Anais, is being bullied at work by three of her work colleagues based on her looks. She has been advised by her lawyer that she has the right to compensation from her Employer, X. When you speak to her, however, you understand that what she actually wants is to be able to enjoy going to work without being bullied. She wants respect and a genuine, authentic apology. When you speak to X, it is clear they want to avoid a court case, and also that there is genuine remorse on the part of Anais' three colleagues, a wish to right their wrong, and a willingness from them to apologise with feeling and start a respectful relationship with Anais on new terms. A court cannot order that. Mediation would offer the possibility of this solution to her, the repair of her working relationships, and the opportunity for everyone to start afresh.

12.2.3 The legal framework

Our legal system is moving towards encouraging parties to embrace the benefits of mediation. There is already a rich legal framework in which mediation takes place. In 2013 the Jackson reforms introduced measures with the aim of encouraging parties to reduce costs[2] and Jackson LJ's aim, of encouraging parties to make realistic attempts to settle, is now documented in a handbook.[3] Recent judicial decisions show that the courts are advocating using mediation to achieve this aim. In *Halsey v Milton Keynes NHS Trust* the Court of Appeal established the courts have power to impose costs penalties on parties who unreasonably refuse to mediate (and set out guidelines as to what constitutes reasonableness).[4] Following this, even parties who consider they have reasonable grounds to refuse now risk costs if the judge applies the guidelines differently and does not agree. The Court of Appeal expressly followed *The Jackson ADR Handbook*'s guidance to hold that simply ignoring an invitation to mediate is in itself an unreasonable refusal to engage in mediation (even if there would have been other reasonable grounds for refusal).[5]

An initial Mediation Information Assessment Meeting (MIAM) is now mandatory in the family courts,[6] and, with all parties under pressure to resolve disputes and to pay their own legal costs whether or not they win their case, there is anticipation that the civil and commercial courts will follow suit. There are EU directives on mediation, and parts of the Civil Procedure Rules also refer to it. HM Courts and Tribunals Service has a small claims mediation service.

12.2.4 Satisfaction rates

Research undertaken by James Rustidge reported findings that 94.4 per cent of those surveyed said they would use the mediation service again and 95.4 per cent were satisfied or very satisfied with their opportunity to participate and express their views; 79.8 per cent reported their cases had successfully settled.[7] Interestingly, even among those whose cases did not settle, the responses remain positive, with 85.9 per cent saying they would use the

---

[2] Jackson, R. (2009) *Review of Civil Litigation Costs: Final Report.* [online] Judiciary.uk. Available at: https://www.judiciary.uk/wp-content/uploads/JCO/Documents/Reports/jackson-final-report-140110.pdf (accessed 26/11/2019).

[3] Blake, S., Browne, J., and Sime, S. (2016) *The Jackson ADR Handbook.* 2nd edn OUP.

[4] *Halsey v Milton Keynes NHS Trust* [2004] EWCA Civ 576.

[5] *PGF II SA v OMFS Company 1 Ltd* [2013] EWCA Civ 1288.

[6] Children and Families Act 2014.

[7] James Rustidge, *Analysis of Qualitiative Data; Small Claims Mediation Service; April 2011–March 2012* (2012).

service again and 88.4 per cent reporting they were satisfied or very satisfied with their opportunity to participate and express their views. (In contrast, in *Cameron v Boggiano and another*, the Court of Appeal described 'suing and being sued . . . is a stressful experience . . . the lawsuit could have unwanted long-term consequences that a sensible compromise might have avoided'.)[8]

The high success rate for settlement of disputes in the small claims mediation service appears to reflect a general capability of mediation to succeed in reaching settlement. The 336 mediators who responded to the Centre for Effective Dispute Resolution's (CEDR) Seventh Mediation Audit in 2018 reported that 74 per cent of their cases settled on the day, with 15 per cent settling shortly afterwards.[9] The UK National Family Mediation statistics suggest that 70 per cent of their cases reach full or partial settlement.[10]

12.2.5 The challenges

The CEDR Audit estimated the mediation market in England and Wales to be around 12,000 cases in 2018, excluding small claims mediations. This is 20 per cent more than the 2016 estimate, representing a market which continues to grow, albeit more slowly than anticipated; a group of 200 mediators undertake the majority of all mediations (about 40 cases each per annum).[11] In *Halsey* the Court of Appeal considered which cases were unsuitable for mediation, including where a point of law has to be resolved, there is a need for a precedent, or there are issues involving human rights.[12] However, the majority of cases are suitable for mediation.[13] In light of mediation's potential, the question arises why the market is not growing more quickly.

Research from 2007 reminds us that personal dislike for the other side drove 47 per cent of respondents to choose litigation; and human nature must be factored in to this equation. For some, there is no substitute for a day in court and a judgment being handed down.[14]

Parties will have concerns about mediation that you might need to manage. Some concerns are valid. Confidentiality and without prejudice are key tenets for trust in the process, and yet exceptions exist which impede the ability to give an absolute assurance on the issue.[15] The emergence of med-arb, where mediation will be followed by arbitration in the event of a failure to settle, can also impede parties from making freely, during mediation, the disclosures which are often so key to finding agreement.

However, you will be able to address most concerns. Common misconceptions include that mediation is: a sign of weakness; unnecessary because lawyers can negotiate directly; doomed to failure if negotiations using lawyers have already failed; simply paying a

---

[8] *Cameron v Boggiano and another* [2012] EWCA Civ 157.

[9] CEDR, *The Eighth Mediation Audit: A survey of commercial mediator attitudes and experience* (2018). Available at https://www.german-resolver.de/resources/The_Eighth_Mediation_Audit_2018-2.pdf.

[10] Family Mediation Survey 2017 (2018). Available at: https://www.familymediationcouncil.org.uk/wp-content/uploads/2018/01/Family-Mediation-Survey-Autumn-2017.pdf.

[11] CEDR, *The Eighth Mediation Audit: A survey of commercial mediator attitudes and experience*.

[12] *Halsey v Milton Keynes NHS Trust* [2004].

[13] Walker and Smith, *Advising and Representing Clients at Mediation*.

[14] Randolph, P. (2010) 'Litigation v Mediation' *New Law Journal*. Available at https://www.newlawjournal.co.uk/content/litigation-v-mediation.

[15] Civil Mediation Council, ' Guidance Note No 1: Mediation confidentiality' (2009) https://www.clerksroom.com/downloads/286-Confidentiality-Guidance-Note.pdf =.

'messenger'; impossible until full disclosure; a waste of money if settlement is not achieved; and, finally, simply delaying the progress of litigation.

It may be that there is a greater need for lawyers to take an active role to dispel these misconceptions, promote the benefits of mediation, and provide validation and reassurance to the public. So far, they appear reticent to do so. Rustidge reports that 65.6 per cent of respondents found out about the small claims mediation service from the court itself.[16] The 2018 CEDR Audit did indicate a slight reversal from the trend away from lawyer-mediators to non-lawyer mediators, yet given lawyers' professional proximity to mediation, the previous trend, and the reversal from that trend being described as 'slight', is worth some reflection. The potential for new income stream for law firms from mediation has already been established. The question arises then why the profession seems reticent to endorse mediation in a way which would encourage it to flourish.

You will recall that Lord Neuberger[17] concluded that there were advantages to mediation precisely because it operates unfettered by constitutional restraints, and that as 'ordinary people, average citizens, and ordinary businesses' would likely experience problems obtaining access to justice, mediation might be particularly suitable for their legal disputes. These are important observations, and access to justice will be front of mind for you as a law student rigorously educated about the rule of law.

Which brings us to consider briefly where you might encounter mediation during your education. 'Ten years ago almost no professional school offered courses on negotiation; now they are all but universal' stated Harvard's Fisher and Ury in 1999.[18] In fact, in England & Wales, it will only be with the introduction of the proposed new Solicitors Qualifying Examination (SQE) that *negotiation* formally appears on the syllabus for students undertaking professional examinations to qualify as solicitors (assuming it progresses as intended at the time of writing). *Mediation* is absent from the SQE syllabus. It is conspicuous by its absence too, generally, in undergraduate law programmes in England and Wales, which traditionally have favoured mooting, to develop advocacy skills (see Chapter 13), over negotiation. You may, however, choose to participate in a mediation competition. The following will help you to prepare well for that, which in turn will help you decide whether you might wish to train as a professional mediator.

12.2.6 **Structuring your mediation**

As with negotiation, the mediation process typically follows a pattern. It begins with the mediator's opening statement, in a joint session with both parties present, and Figure 12.5 sets out a helpful ready reckoner you can use to create an effective opening statement of your own. Following this, the mediation will divide into individual sessions with each party, unless and until the mediator can see there is scope for agreement. At this point, the individual meetings will shape the offers and any counter offers. There will follow a joint meeting to sign the settlement agreement and/or close the mediation. Figure 12.6 gives you a helpful framework to guide you through this process which follows the opening statement. As with Figure 12.5, you can annotate it and take it with you into any mediation competition or role play.

---

[16] See fn 7.

[17] Lord Neuberger, 'Keynote Address: A View from On High ' (Civil Mediation Conference 2015).

[18] Fisher, R., Ury, W., and Patton, B. (1999).*Getting to Yes: Negotiating an Agreement Without Giving In*, Random House.

1. Introduction
- Introduce yourself
- Introduce parties
- Clarify how everyone would like to be addressed
- Thank everyone for attending
- Check parties have authority to settle, that everyone capable of influencing the outcome is in the room
- Check everyone has signed the agreement to mediate

2. Ground rules
- Aim: to reach an agreement that is satisfactory to all
- Confidentiality: everything is confidential; ask parties to keep it so. Nothing must leave the room without the parties' express permission.
- For parties to come up with agreement
- Discussions will be non-binding until reach agreement
- Without prejudice in the event no agreement is reached
- Voluntary: door is always open
- Any questions?

3. Clarify your role as a mediator
- Not a judge and will not impose a judgment
- Will reality-check offers
- May need to play devil's advocate and ask difficult questions to help your understanding
- Will guide discussion.

4. Outline structure
- This is the opening statement
- Soon will invite both parties to present their position statements
- Avoid interruption
- There will follow private individual meetings
- Those meetings are confidential
- When agreement is reached, it will be formalised at a joint closing session, put in writing and signed
- Everyone will take a copy.

5. Position statements
- Invite position statements from both parties
- 'It is a general principle that whoever is bringing the claim speaks first, and on that basis I would like to invite Party 2 to present your understanding of the case first.'
- Avoid interruption

6. Closing
- Thank parties for their position statements
- Remind that aim is to reach agreement
- Questions?
- Confidentiality reminder
- 'You may remember Party 2 gave their position statement first. In the interests of fairness, with your agreement, I'd like to invite Party 1 to the first individual session with me now.'

Figure 12.5 The Opening Statement

1. Open the mediation in a joint session
- See Figure 12.5

⇩

2. Factfinding Session with Party 1
A. <u>Preliminaries</u>
- 'Thank you for giving me your opening statement. Is there anything you want to add to that, that you didn't feel you could say in joint session?'
- Confidentiality reminder: 'Everything you say is confidential, and nothing you say will leave the room without your express permission.'
B. <u>Obtain facts and feelings</u>
- 'Can you tell me in your own words why you are here today?'
- Open questions, extenders, empathy, summarise
C. <u>Get to the heart of the matter and summarise the party's priorities and needs</u>
- 'I'm hearing you say that your main concern is X, is that correct?' 'Do you have any other concerns?' 'Who else might be affected by this decision?'
- Acknowledge emotions: 'You've told me you're feeling . . .', 'How are you feeling about this?'
- 'What are the obstacles to agreement?'
D. <u>Exit</u>
- 'We have discussed the issues which are important to you. While you are waiting outside, could you consider what are the key issues, in order of importance to you?'
- Confidentiality reminder

⇩

3. Factfinding Session with Party 2
- As above, but in individual session with Party 2

⇩

4. Cost Benefit Analysis Session with Party 1
A. <u>Preliminaries</u>
- Confidentiality reminder
- 'I told you in open session I would need to play devil's advocate, to give you a better understanding of what is going on here'.
- 'I asked you to think about what your key priorities were'
B. <u>Visualise dispute continuing</u>
- 'How will it impact on you if this matter doesn't settle today?'
- Reality check costs, time, prospects of success
C. <u>Visualise conflict-free future</u>
- 'Imagine you wake up tomorrow and this matter has been resolved. How would you feel?'
D. <u>Exit</u>
- Set task eg 'What needs to happen now to prepare to enjoy the future you've just imagined'
- Confidentiality reminder

⇩

5. Cost Benefit Analysis Session with Party 2
- As above, but in individual session with Party 2

⇩

6. Negotiation Session with Party 1
A. <u>Preliminaries</u>
- Confidentiality reminder
  Summarise previous session (4) –'Is that correct?'
B. <u>Offers</u>
- 'I asked you to consider what needs to happen next to move forward. Have you clarified the terms of any offer?'
- Clarify terms of any offer
- SMART test offer: Measurable, Achievable, Realistic, time-bound (see 18.2.5.2)
- 'How do you think the other party might respond to . . .?'
- Refine and exchange offers if required
C. <u>Exit</u>
- 'Thank you . Can you think about your offer and what if anything you might like to add, or how you might amend it, and we can discuss in our next private session'.
- Confidentiality reminder

⇩

Figure 12.6 The Mediation Process

---

7. Negotiation Session with Party 2
  – As above, but in individual session with Party 2

---

8. Refine and make a note of Party 1's offer
A. <u>Preliminaries</u>
  – Confidentiality reminder
  – Remind of aim – to reach an agreement satisfactory to both parties.
  – 'You are now at the stage where I can take your offer to the other side if you feel ready'
B. <u>Refine offer</u>
  – Recap offer from session 6.
  – 'At the end of the last session, I asked you to think about your offer and what, if anything, you
    might like to add, or whether you would like to amend it in any way'
  – Amend or add to offer
    SMART test changes (see 18.2.5.2)
C. <u>Make a note of offer</u>
  – In full
  – Ensure understand rationale behind offer, including figures
  – Obtain authority from Party 1 to disclose to Party 2
D. <u>Exit</u>
  – Confidentiality reminder – covers everything except authorised disclosure of offer

---

9. Convey Party 1's offer to Party 2 and make note of any counter offer
A. <u>Preliminaries</u>
  – Confidentiality reminder
  – Remind of aim – to reach an agreement satisfactory to both parties.
    'I have been asked to put to you an offer from Party 1. I appreciate you will want to to discuss this, and I am bound
    first to disclose the offer to you, then you can discuss your reaction.'
B. <u>Put offer</u>
  – Do not take a counter-offer first
  – Gauge reaction
C. <u>Formulate counter-offer</u>
  – SMART test counter-offer (see 18.2.5.2)
D. <u>Make a note of counter-offer</u>
  – In full
  – Ensure understand rationale behind counter-offer, including figures
  – Obtain authority from Party 2 to disclose to Party 1
D. <u>Exit</u>
  – Confidentiality reminder – covers everything except authorised disclosure of counter-offer

---

10. Close
  – Thank parties
  – Make clear that any agreement reached in the mediation will not be binding until it is in writing
    and signed by all of the parties
  – Draft and ensure everyone signs the Settlement/ Mediation Agreement
  – Confidentiality reminder

Figure 12.6 *Continued*

12.2.7 Essential skills and characteristics for mediation

The oral communication skills referred to in Chapter 10 as essential skills for lawyers are also essential for mediators. Active listening (providing subconscious prompts), effective body language and excellent eye contact are key. Your ability to solve problems, discussed in Chapter 9, are also key (and creative mind maps—see 9.2.1.3 and Figure 9.3—can be a particularly helpful way to work through issues with the parties).

In addition, the following are particularly valuable for mediators, in the following specific ways.

12.2.7.1 **Rapport and trust**

Mediation requires a very different set of skills than for advocacy, as it is a non-adversarial process. Indeed, as a student seeking to learn the skill of principled negotiation (the evaluative method advocated by Harvard and involving 'no tricks, no posturing' described at 12.1.5.1) you might feel positively hindered by much of what you have learned about advocacy and persuasion. Ironically, learning about non-contentious practice such as advising on acquisitions (where a buyer wants to buy and a seller wants to sell, although they will likely have some disagreement about matters such as price and liabilities on the way) appears to have more potential to nourish mediation skills than would learning about contentious dispute resolution practice such as litigation. If you are leaning towards a career in non-contentious law, or away from law altogether, do not write off the prospect that mediation can inform, or form part of, your career. Rapport and trust are key to success. You must be approachable. Your body language (posture, tone of voice, eye contact, avoiding folding your arms) is particularly important here, as is a warm handshake on arrival. Getting refreshments and the WiFi password is also part of our role, and will help with rapport.

Before arrival, speak to all parties by telephone. Make sure to ask if there is anything they are concerned or worried about, and whether there is anything you should know, such as whether they need any adjustments for access. Speaking before you meet will help them to relax when they do meet you.

12.2.7.2 **Empathy**

It is very important to recognise the parties' emotions. Lawyers can be poor at this. Recognising emotions, such as fear, is essential in resolving a dispute successfully. To clarify the issues between the parties and find any potential points of agreement, you need to separate the facts of the dispute from the emotions of the parties. Parties may begin from an emotional perspective, where any unknown facts are filled in by emotion. For example, one party may have interpreted the other party's action as a threat, and so be feeling fear. The mediation process may reveal to you no intention of any threat, which will assuage the fearful feelings of the other party, and allow them to see past this emotion to find a solution on which both parties can agree.

Jonathan Haidt's analogy of the elephant and the rider is a good analogy to explain how turning down the volume of emotion will allow the rational brain to exert influence (see Further Reading). If the elephant is emotionally charged, its human rider has no hope of exerting influence over it. When the elephant is calm, the rider can steer it relatively easily.

Note that your role as a mediator is to provide empathy, not sympathy. That is, 'I can see that you're struggling with this and it is difficult for you' rather than, 'What an awful thing they have done to you'. Listen to the parties. Do not bring your own experiences into the room. You are a neutral third party with no stake in the outcome. For this reason, you should also avoid using 'we'. Avoid passing judgement, for example, say, 'I can see you are excited about that prospect'.

However, you must avoid supporting abuse of power. It is important to be alert to parties who are hoping to avoid the consequences of their behaviour by using tactics such as offering a fake apology or blaming the other party. For this reason, further training is required for a family mediator, over and above that provided for a civil-commercial mediator, because failing to spot these tactics by a perpetrator in a family context can result in the mediator unwittingly perpetuating one party's abuse of the other.

12.2.7.3 Perspective

Your role as a mediator is to look at the situation through fresh eyes. How can the parties deal with their differences? In his TED talk (see Further Reading), William Ury states that the secret to peace is the surrounding community—us. As mediator, you are the third side of the conflict and can play an incredibly constructive role as you remind the parties of what is really at stake. You are in a place of perspective. Ury refers to this place as 'the balcony'; the parties are at an intersection is a road, and you can bring conflict down by taking them with you to the balcony, where they will see the same thing, but from a calmer perspective.

12.2.7.4 Curious and encouraging

The following can help you to help parties, who may be feeling nervous, to engage with the process.

- Extenders—'oh I see, please go on . . . what else?'
- Silence.
- Positive reframing—e.g. 'are you feeling trust issues?'
- Curiosity. Who is the person in front of me and what is their conflict? Be curious about the parties' relationships, personalities, values, beliefs, for example:
  - 'I didn't quite get that—could you help me to understand that a little better?'
  - 'What was most surprising to you about that?'
  - 'How did it affect you /what impact did it have on you?'
- Summarising
- Tone of voice. Use:
  - positive vocabulary;
  - an upbeat tone;
  - a professional tone and volume.

You can read further examples in *The Mediation Process* (see Further Reading).

12.2.7.5 Motivating

Being honest (new SRA Principle 4), genuine, and straightforward will help you keep the process moving forwards. Build in time for the parties to decompress. Set practical deadlines but be flexible. Bear in mind at all times that any deadline must not come from you, it has to come from the parties. Make sure the parties feel in control. For example, 'The door is always open. If at any point today you wish to bring it to a close, that is always possible. However, give me 15 minutes to talk it through with you before.'

12.2.7.6 Resilience

Parties can feel the need to vent during the process of mediation. They may blame you. You will need to bear in mind it is unlikely to be personal, and let it go. In his TED talk (see Further Reading), Ury reports saying the following statement, which might be helpful for you to use in your learning of mediation, and beyond, 'I appreciate your criticism . . . and I take it as a sign we are among friends and can talk candidly to one another. And we are not here today to talk about . . . we are here to discuss . . .'.

12.2.8 **Practicalities**

12.2.8.1 Timing

In practice, you will need to set aside an entire day for your mediation, together with one day to prepare. Afterwards, you need to build in time to answer emails, and also to decompress. For that reason, professional mediators will advise not scheduling more than one mediation per week. In terms of preparation, remember you are not a judge, and you will not be forming a view or imposing an opinion on the parties in mediation. You will be reading so you can follow the conversation, no more. Consider asking the parties to condense their case down to, say, 20 pages and ask them to tab any pages that they consider are essential, or ask them for a position statement.

12.2.8.2 Who will be present?

Potential attendees include:

- The parties, who have authority to settle the case. Check this—if one party cannot settle until he checks with his wife, then she should be there.
- Lawyers. Not all parties will have lawyers, but some will insist on their lawyers being present.
- Family or friends. Some parties will want to bring someone to support them.

Ensure everyone present is included in and has signed the agreement to mediate, before the mediation begins (see 12.2.9).

12.2.8.3 Venue

You will need to think carefully about a location. It needs to be fair, accessible to all parties, and open long enough should the mediation take longer than you expect. Check how long you can have the room, and whether parties will be able to get home if there is a late finish. If not, consider using a room in, or near, a hotel. It is a good idea to stagger the arrival time of the parties, so they will not all arrive at the venue together.

The space needs to be safe. You will need to have separate break out rooms for each party, so they can meet in private. Think carefully about how sound might travel; you need to maintain confidentiality. Consider a sign on your meeting room door to indicate when parties can enter, and when they cannot. You do not want to be speaking to one party about something confidential, only for the other party to burst in. Make sure you arrive early, and certainly earlier than the parties. Set a clear time for the opening session.

12.2.8.4 Setting up the room

Body language is important, and the parties are in control, so set up the room in a way which reflects this. You need to make sure that you are not seen to favour one party over the other. If lawyers are also attending, it is best for you to sit closer to the parties than their lawyers. One common set up is for you to sit between the parties, and then the party's lawyers will sit next to their respective client and opposite each other, then friends and family next to their respective lawyer, and so on.

12.2.9 **The agreement to mediate**

This document (not to be confused with the agreement recording any settlement, often referred to as the Settlement or Mediation Agreement) sets out the ground rules for the mediation process, and must be sent out, read, and signed before the mediation begins. It will set out key issues such as the parties, a confidentiality and without prejudice clause, your fee, the venue, and who will pay costs of the venue and refreshments. It will also make clear that any agreement reached in the mediation will not be binding until it is in writing and signed by all of the parties. Note that while the detail of arbitration is beyond the scope of this chapter, clients may be inhibited from airing their dirty laundry despite the confidentiality clause in the agreement to mediate, in case the information they disclose is then relied on in subsequent arbitration or court proceedings. The mediation itself, though, is confidential and parties bear the consequences of any breach. A specimen agreement to mediate is available from the resources section of the CEDR website (see Further Reading).

12.2.10 **The opening statement**

The opening, joint session is key. You, as mediator, give your opening statement and then invite other parties to make their position statements. Whoever is bringing the claim usually is given the opportunity to speak first. When you speak to the parties individually, you can ask if there anything they would like to add to their opening statement that they did not feel they could share in the joint session.

12.2.11 **Confidentiality**

You should top and tail every session with a reminder of confidentiality, for example, 'Nothing you say will leave the room without your express permission.'

12.2.12 **Factfinding sessions**

In this first set of private sessions your aim is to obtain a clear sense of what the parties' priorities are. You will work with curiosity to draw out what has been happening, to whom, and what the impact on them has been. When you think you have all you need, you can ask a 'catch all' to be sure, such as 'Is there anything else which is important to you which we haven't yet had a chance to discuss?'. You can then ask this question again if they answer it. If the party is showing little sign of drawing breath, you can ask them to pause, to agree a summary of what they have said so far.

This early session is important for building rapport. Ask open questions throughout, and summarise. There should be no closed questions, and no judgment. If you hear something you want to challenge, make a note for the sessions which will follow. Aim to establish the party's best outcome, and who else might be affected. Setting follow-up tasks can help the party focus their attention on something productive while they wait for you to complete the individual session with the other party. Here, it could be to consider and rank priorities.

As ever, take care to balance your note-taking with plenty of time for effective eye contact.

Finish with a confidentiality reminder. Everything remains confidential. You will not take anything to the other side without the party's express agreement. The burden is therefore on the party to highlight what can, rather than what cannot, be disclosed. Remember to remain neutral throughout, and that this is not about you advising on the law at all.

12.2.13 Cost benefit analysis sessions

At the end of the factfinding session, you summarise all that the party had told you. You do not need to repeat that here, but you can very briefly summarise, for example, 'Last time you told me about your [. . .]. I asked you to think about your priorities, what are your thoughts on that?' Remember that in the previous session, you will have set the party a task, and you can ask them about that as a preliminary.

The key point in this session is that you will be helping the parties by acting as devil's advocate, to reality test whether they truly want to reach agreement or continue their dispute. Use as ammunition things they have told you are important to them, such as money, time, and stress, to make this an effective and worthwhile exercise. For example, you can ask questions such as, 'How would it impact on you if you had to go to court? What are the costs of continuing? What would be the impact on your time?'. In the opening statement, you will have already prepared the client for this. Remember that you are not cross examining anyone. Use a neutral and open voice, and remind the party, for example, 'I told you in my opening session that I might need to play devil's advocate, to allow you to gain a better understanding of what is going on here.'

12.2.14 Negotiation sessions

At this session, you are not yet taking offers, but the party will be thinking about forming offers that meet their interests and needs. You will be SMART testing any such hypothetical offers (see 18.2.5.2). Be strategic with this testing, and use it where needed. For example, if you paid this, would you still be able to afford your rent (Realistic)? Would it help to pay in instalments (Time bound)? Remember you need to be helpful to both parties to reach agreement, and are not cross-examining, so obtain a good balance between testing and being too harsh. Close by making clear you will not be taking offers yet. Encourage your client to think about their offer and what, if anything, might need to be added to it.

12.2.15 Sessions conveying offers and counter-offers

Confidentiality is key, so check what you can share. Ask whether you have permission to disclose the offer as you have summarised it and remind the party that everything else will remain confidential. Listen for potential apologies and take particular care over whether they feel genuine and authentic.

In the first of these sessions you will be taking the offer from one party. In summary form, refer to the offer you discussed last time, and ask if the party wants to add anything to it. Check you have permission to reveal the rationale behind the figure. Consider where the party stands with an authentic, genuine apology. If there is one, where and when will it be made? Then repeat the offer to them verbatim as you would communicate it to the other side. When you have agreed the wording, write it down, obtain consent, and time stamp and sign the written record.

In the second of these sessions, you will be disclosing the offer to the other party. Make sure you do it verbatim, as recorded in your signed written note. Take good care to remind yourself whether you have permission to disclose the rationale behind any figure. Or just the figure itself, so that you do not breach any confidentiality obligations.

Make clear you intend to disclose the offer first before you will receive a counter-offer from the other party. For example, 'Thank you for waiting, this is all confidential, I do have an offer from the other side that I would like to give to you now and gauge your reaction'.

12.2.16 Closing: The Settlement or Mediation Agreement

The mediation process is non-binding until agreement is reached. When the parties do reach agreement, you need to arrange for the agreement to be written up and signed by all parties. A specimen agreement (Settlement Agreement) is available on the CEDR website (see Further Reading). As with negotiation, do not assume the process has failed if agreement is not reached. Not all disputes will lend themselves to a mediated agreement, and an effective mediation will have value in informing the next step, even if it does not close with an agreement with which both parties are satisfied.

12.2.17 ODR—online dispute resolution

The increasing availability of online mediation removes geographical, time, and cost barriers, allowing parties to mediate even if they are in different continents or time zones. It can also be cheaper, for example because a venue and refreshments are not required.

12.2.18 Networking and learning opportunities

The following organisations offer opportunities for you to learn more about mediation, and to network. Many of them have links, events, useful documents, and other information on their websites (see Further Reading for more details).

- ADR-ODR International;
- CEDR—Centre for Effective Dispute Resolution;
- Civil Mediation Council;
- Family Mediation Council;
- IDRC—International Dispute Resolution Centre;
- London School of Mediation;
- The TCM Group.

Part II

Legal Skills

Summary

- Negotiation and mediation are both forms of ADR (the third form being arbitration).
- Negotiation has always been a key skill for practice, and is now beginning to feature in both academic and professional legal education.
- The legal system is encouraging mediation, although to date the profession and legal education have been relatively slow to respond.
- Good preparation is important for a successful outcome.
- Our crib sheets (such as Figures 12.2 and 12.3 for negotiation and Figures 12.5 and 12.6 for mediation) will help you succeed.
- The most successful negotiators are flexible to adopt a different approach to achieve the best outcome.

Practical exercises

Consider how you would answer these questions. Reflect on how your reading of this chapter has informed or changed how you might answer them. How might you use what you have learned in an interview or exam situation?

1. Watch the annual negotiation task on *The Apprentice* (see Further Reading) and reflect on the negotiating mistakes Karen Brady observes (for example, in 2019, regarding the candidates' purchase of the quant, the mortar board, and the book by Lewis Carroll (eg, 'We *need* to purchase this hat, what are you going to charge us?'). What is their BATNA? How do you think they could they have increased their chances of success in negotiating a better price for these items? What could they learn from the sellers of these items, in terms of negotiation strategy?

2. The European Union made clear they would prefer the UK to remain, and not Brexit.[19] Prime Minister Boris Johnson made clear that his BATNA was a no-deal Brexit, saying 'We are tabling constructive and reasonable proposals . . . the alternative is no deal'.[20] Parliament, however, voted against the possibility of no-deal.[21] Analyse this, not from a political perspective, but in terms of negotiation, the BATNA and its effect on the government's ability to succeed with its mandate to negotiate with the European Union a Brexit deal for the UK. Then consider, what was the effect of the Conservative Party's landslide victory in the General Election in December 2019 on the Prime Minister's BATNA?

3. If you have not done so already, consider Table 12.2. Identify which of the four styles you identify with most closely. Are there any of the styles which you feel do not come easily to you, and which you would like to practise, and why? Consider safe ways to practise these styles in your everyday life (for example, saying 'no').

4. Find out the details of this year's negotiation and mediation competitions (see Further Reading) and consider applying, and enquire whether your institution offers accredited mediation training for students.

[19] Boffey, D. (2019). *Donald Tusk's message to UK voters: don't give up on stopping Brexit. The Guardian.* Available at: https://www.theguardian.com/politics/2019/nov/13/donald-tusks-message-to-uk-voters-dont-give-up-on-stopping-brexit.

[20] BBC News (2019) *Johnson: No-deal only alternative to Brexit plan.* Available at: https://www.bbc.co.uk/news/uk-politics-49906702.

[21] Woodcock, A. (2019) *Law to stop no-deal Brexit passed by Parliament.* The Independent. Available at: https://www.independent.co.uk/news/uk/politics/brexit-no-deal-bill-vote-house-lords-boris-johnson-law-parliament-latest-a9094741.html,

5. Ask your friends to say three statements about themselves, and make three statements about yourself, on the basis that two must be true, and one false. Emotions show on your face. Evaluate your friends' 'tells', and your own, when what is being said is untrue (for example, eye movement, tone, and pace of voice), to hone your non-verbal negotiation and communication skills.

*Visit the **online resources** for the authors' reflections and to check your progress.*

Further reading

ADR-ODR International. Available at: https://www.adrodrinternational.com/
Provider of dispute resolution and professional training, including in online dispute resolution.

Allen, D. and Stolz, L., 2020. [online] Bio.org. Available at: https://www.bio.org/sites/default/files/ legacy/bioorg/docs/Negotiation%20Preparation_Lesley%20Stolz%20&%20Debbie%20Allen.pdf
—A PowerPoint presentation on negotiation strategies, including information about individual negotiating styles.

***The Apprentice: Oxford and Cambridge Discount Buying, Series 15 Episode 5.* (2019) BBC One Television. 30 October 2019. Available (with a Box of Broadcasts subscription) here: https:// learningonscreen.ac.uk/ondemand/index.php/prog/14BB94E0?bcast=130612032 or, at the time of writing, on iPlayer, here: https://www.bbc.co.uk/iplayer/episode/m0009vkr/ the-apprentice-series-15-5-oxford-and-cambridge-discount-buying**
—The annual negotiation task on *The Apprentice*. (You can find the episode for previous years on iPlayer if this one is no longer available.)

BBC News (2015) *Apple Music in Taylor Swift backdown*. Available at: https://www.bbc.co.uk/news/ entertainment-arts-33220189
—An article describing Taylor Swift's willingness to walk away as a successful negotiation strategy with Apple.

CEDR. Available at: https://www.cedr.com/
—CEDR is a leading ADR service provider specialising in mediation and alternative dispute resolution (ADR), an independent non-profit organisation and a registered charity. Its vision is 'Better conflicts result in better outcomes leading to a better world'.

CEDR (2019) *National Student Negotiation Competition—CEDR*. Available at: https://www.cedr.com/ foundation/currentprojects/negotiatorcompetition/
—This competition pits pairs of law students from across universities in England, Scotland, and Wales against each other, to negotiate a series of challenging fictional scenarios. There are initial regional finals of the competition and then those winners progress to the national finals. The winning team travels to an international championship. CEDR offer the winners of the regional finals a one-day negotiation skills training course.

Civil Justice Council ADR Working Group (2018) *Final Report*. Available at: https://www.judiciary.uk/ wp-content/uploads/2018/12/CJC-ADRWG-Report-FINAL-Dec-2018.pdf
—A report reviewing the way ADR is encouraged and positioned within the civil justice system.

Civilmediation.org (2019) *Civil Mediation Council—The no. 1 information resource for civil, commercial and workplace mediation in England and Wales*. Available at: https://civilmediation.org/
—The CMC is a charity which aims to promote the resolution of conflicts and disputes by encouraging the use of mediation and other dispute resolution techniques and methods and to advance the education of the public in matters related to this.

Crockett, Z. (2014) *How Southwest Airlines Settled a Legal Dispute with Arm Wrestling*. Priceonomics. Available at: https://priceonomics.com/how-southwest-airlines-settled-a-legal-dispute/
—Article with video detailing the 'Malice in Dallas', a creative negotiation between two US companies, commended by then-President George H.W. Bush for their win-win solution.

Davies, N. (2019) *Influence, Persuasion and Negotiation*. Available at: http://www.reallygreattraining.co.uk/course-influence-persuasion-and-negotiation.html
—A small PDF that reminds of some of the main aspects involved in influence and persuasion.

Facebook.com (2019) *UK Student Mediation Competition 2019*. Available at: https://www.facebook.com/pg/UK-Student-Mediation-Competition-2019-306240663500952/posts/
—Information about the UK Student Mediation Competition.

Ec.europa.eu. *European Code of Conduct for Mediators*. Available at: https://ec.europa.eu/civiljustice/adr/adr_ec_code_conduct_en.pdf
—The website of the European Commission contains various documents relating to mediation, including this voluntary European Code of Conduct for Mediators.

Europeanresolution.com. *European Institute for Conflict Resolution—European Institute for Conflict Resolution*. Available at: https://www.europeanresolution.com/en/european-institute-for-conflict-resolution/
—A private, not-for-profit, organisation with a mission that includes promoting mediation and training in mediation.

Family Mediation Council (2019) *Home—Family Mediation Council*. Available at: https://www.familymediationcouncil.org.uk/
—The FMC is a not for profit organisation that maintains a professional register of family mediators.

Fisher, R., Ury, W., Patton, B., and Boutsikaris, D. (2011) *Getting to Yes*. New York: Simon & Schuster Audio, 3rd edn
—Fisher, Ury, and Patton founded the Harvard Negotiation Project in 1979, which with collaboration then developed into the Program on Negotiation (see Harvard Law School). This 3rd edition of their book about principled bargaining advocates four fundamental principles of negotiation, namely (i) separate the people from the problem, (ii) focus on interests, not positions, (iii) invent options for mutual gain; and (iv) insist on objective criteria. William Ury also discusses these issues in his TED talk, here: https://www.ted.com/talks/william_ury_the_walk_from_no_to_yes?language=en.

Goulston, M. (2018) *Just Listen*. New York: AMACOM, 2nd edn
—Psychiatrist and business coach Mark Goulston reveals simple techniques you can try, to move people from resistance to consensus.

Haidt, J. (2016) *The Rider & the Elephant—Jonathan Haidt on Persuasion and Moral Humility*. Youtube.com. Available at: https://www.youtube.com/watch?v=24adApYh0yc
—Jonathan Haidt, Professor of Ethical Leadership at New York University's Stern School of Business, discusses persuasion and the role of emotions, using the metaphor of the elephant and the rider (where the rider represents consciously controlled processes and the elephant represents automatic processes).

Hamilton, D. (2015) *Calming Your Brain During Conflict*. Harvard Business Review. Available at: https://hbr.org/2015/12/calming-your-brain-during-conflict
—An article which will help you to identify when you, a client, or party to a mediation, is responding to conflict with a fight or flight response, and how to move from there into a more effective state of mind for dispute resolution.

Harvard Law School (2019) *Program on negotiation; daily blog*. Available at https://www.pon
.harvard.edu/blog/
—The Program on Negotiation (PON) is a consortium program of Harvard University, Massachusetts
Institute of Technology, and Tufts University dedicated to developing the theory and practice of
negotiation and dispute resolution in a range of public and private settings. This blog examines past and
current negotiations from many fields including business, government, education and law. Read the blog
daily and you will learn how to improve your skills at the negotiating table. It includes free reports and
articles, for example, the article on hardball tactics here: https://www.pon.harvard.edu/daily/batna/10-
hardball-tactics-in-negotiation/ and the article on the BATNA here: https://www.pon.harvard.edu/
freemium/batna-basics-boost-your-power-at-the-bargaining-table/ and you can subscribe to the blog
here https://www.pon.harvard.edu/free-reports/get-report/?freemium_id=19594.

Hewlin, J. (2017) *The Most Overused Negotiating Tactic Is Threatening to Walk Away*. Harvard
Business Review. Available at: https://hbr.org/2017/09/the-most-overused-negotiating-tactic-
is-threatening-to-walk-away
—An article which explores that the BATNA as a negotiator's primary source of relative power can
range anywhere from significant to non-existent. Includes helpful examples of students' relative
power in job interviews.

Hiltrop, J. M. and Udall, S. (1995) *The Essence of Negotiation*. London: Prentice Hall
—A concise, expert guide to learning the negotiating skills that are critical to business success.

Hyde, J. (2019) *Ombudsman ditches mediation scheme after just 4% success rate*. Law Gazette.
Available at: https://www.lawgazette.co.uk/news/ombudsman-ditches-mediation-scheme-after-
just-4-success-rate/5102255.article
—An article describing how the Legal Ombudsman has scrapped plans to extend a pilot to use
mediation to settle disputes between lawyers and their clients. The 2019 pilot found limited take-up
from both legal services providers and complainants—and even then, just half of cases going to
mediation were settled.

ICC—International Chamber of Commerce (2019) *Mediation Competition application process—
ICC—International Chamber of Commerce*. Available at: https://iccwbo.org/dispute-resolution-
services/professional-development/international-commercial-mediation-competition/
mediation-competition-application-process/
—This international competition is open only to students who do not yet have full-time work
experience (except internships) in law, business, or otherwise. The competition is open to students of
all disciplines, but only law students may take the role of counsel in the sessions. Accordingly, at least
one member of each team must be a law student.

IDRC—International Dispute Resolution, Mediation and Arbitration Centre. Available at: https://
www.idrc.co.uk/
—Offers arbitration rooms, conference facilities, and mediation rooms. You can arrange a visit if you
are interested in this field. They also offer the Michael Mustill student essay prize (for which certain
postgraduate students are eligible to apply).

Laborde, G. Z. (1995) *Influencing with Integrity—Revised Edition: Management Skills for
Communication and Negotiation*. Carmarthen: Crown House Publishing, 2nd edn
—A book on the psychology of communication. Dr Laborde uses techniques derived primarily from
neuro linguistic programming to create a set of state-of-the-art skills which you can use to improve
any interaction.

London School of Mediation. Available at: https://www.londonschoolofmediation.com/
—Provider of mediation training and networking events.

Lord Neuberger (2015) *Keynote Address: A View From on High*. Civil Mediation Conference 2015. Available at: https://www.supremecourt.uk/docs/speech-150512-civil-mediation-conference-2015.pdf
—An informative, balanced speech about mediation, considering its advantages and disadvantages.

Moore, C. (2014) *The Mediation Process: Practical Strategies for Resolving Conflict*. San Francisco, CA: Jossey-Bass, 4th edn
—A comprehensive work in the field of mediation and conflict resolution. Contains useful guidance about different types of questions you can use in a mediation.

Navarro, J. (2019). *Body Language*. Available at: https://www.jnforensics.com/blog-1/categories/category-1
—Written by a former FBI counterintelligence expert, and now one of the foremost authorities on non-verbal communication.

Shephard, C. (2017) *Raising awareness of the benefits of mediation | Solicitors Journal*. Available at: https://www2.mmu.ac.uk/news-and-events/news/story/6263/
Shephard, C. (2018) *Justice Week: Mediation Deserves Consideration in Legal Education—Part One*. Available at: https://www2.mmu.ac.uk/law/about-us/news/story/?id=8655;
Shephard, C. (2018) *Justice Week: Mediation Deserves Consideration in Legal Education—Part Two*. Available at: https://www2.mmu.ac.uk/law/about-us/news/story/index.php?id=8667;
—Three short articles by author Catherine Shephard about mediation and its role in legal education.

The TCM Group (2019) *Conflict & Change Management News and Blog—The TCM Group*. Available at: https://thetcmgroup.com/news-and-blogs/
—Helping HR professionals, managers, and leaders to embed a mediation-friendly culture.

University of Oxford, Faculty of Law (2018) *Horst Eidenmueller proposes that the Brexit negotiations should be mediated*. Available at https://www.law.ox.ac.uk/news/2018-10-19-horst-eidenmueller-proposes-brexit-negotiations-should-be-mediated
—Horst Eidenmueller is Freshfields Professor of Commercial Law at the University of Oxford. This article, with links to his academic paper and later newspaper article, describes his argument that Brexit should be mediated. This is based on the premise that all European citizens are affected by Brexit and so should have the right to expect that the negotiating parties use all means which professional negotiators use day by day in divorce, neighbourhood and commercial conflicts, including mediation.

Walker, S. *Stephen Walker Mediation*. Available at: http://swalkermediation.com/
—A rich resource of helpful videos, books, and blogs about mediation, by Stephen Walker, a civil and commercial mediator, visiting lecturer, and former litigator.

The Worshipful Company of Arbitrators (2019) *Mediation Skills Competition—The Worshipful Company of Arbitrators*. Available at: https://www.arbitratorscompany.org/education-pupillage/mediation-skills-competition/
—This competition is open to universities, law colleges, and junior members of the profession throughout the UK. It is intended to assist in training law students and junior lawyers to better understand the skills needed to be effective in negotiation and mediation, and to give them the opportunity to exhibit and develop their problem-solving skills.

 *For the authors' reflections on the practical exercises, additional self-test questions, sample interview questions and a library of links to useful websites, visit the free **online resources** at www.oup.com/he/slorach4e.*

13 Advocacy and mooting

Learning objectives

After studying this chapter you should be able to:

- Appreciate what constitutes good oral and written advocacy.
- Prepare effectively for a moot and a criminal advocacy competition.
- Appreciate the need for good communication skills as a student and a professional.
- Practise and develop these skills during your legal studies and in everyday life.

Introduction

To be a successful advocate, you will need to be able to find and read relevant primary sources of law (Chapters 7 and 8), use case analysis to solve problems (Chapter 9), and be persuasive and influential with your oral and written communication (Chapters 10 and 14). This chapter provides you with what you need to learn the other skills specifically required for the art of oral and written advocacy.

Advocacy is a vocational subject and so your study of it will be focused particularly on preparing you for practice, but it can also help you to develop other transferable skills such as team-working, research, time-management, and good oral and written communication skills.

The main guidance on the skill is set out at 13.1. Specific and helpful guidance is provided as to what you will need during your studies for mooting (13.1.4) and criminal advocacy competitions (13.1.5). Some additional practice perspectives are included at 13.2.

13.1 Advocacy skills

13.1.1 What is advocacy?

Advocacy is the art of written and oral persuasion. It involves:

- preparation (see 13.1.2) and performance (see 13.1.3) using various skills, written and oral, with the aim of persuading a court (or other forum) towards a specific conclusion, finding, remedy, procedure, or course of action;
- case analysis, to establish that specific legal principles or rules should be applied or followed, because of the existence of specific facts (see 13.1.2.1);
- the use of evidence (see 13.1.2.2 and Chapter 3) and precedent (see 13.1.2.1 and Chapter 5);
- in appeal cases, arguing that the law has not been properly applied.

13.1.2 **Preparation**

As with a talented presenter, a successful advocate will make the task before them look entirely spontaneous, but it will not have been. Preparation and rehearsal, so that you are familiar with all aspects of your case analysis, is essential if you are to assimilate and process information quickly while on your feet in the mock court. There will of course be occasions where an opponent raises something that takes you completely by surprise, and you will have to react spontaneously and think on your feet. However, this should be the exception and not the rule.

13.1.2.1 **Case analysis**

Figure 9.1 provided you with a problem solving strategy, expanding the IRAC model to incorporate case/matter analysis and your legal research strategy. This will help you with your case analysis for advocacy. Case analysis is vital for advocacy, in order to identify the key aspects of any dispute. You will have to establish what you need to prove, and how you can prove it. If you have not already done so, you should read Chapter 9, and in particular Figure 9.1, Example 4 and all related guidance, to understand in more detail how to use this strategy. Guidance follows as to how you can then use Figure 9.1 specifically for advocacy.

The Issue stage

As an advocate, you will need to analyse the facts of your client's case well. Use the Issue stage of Figure 9.1 to identify:

- parties (claimant, defendant, who you are advising, any other relevant relationships or stakeholders);
- what is your task;
- the relevant facts (for example, what is the loss that has been suffered?) and any missing facts;
- the parties' objectives; and
- the legal issues raised.

The Rule stage

As Figure 9.1 reveals, at this stage you will need to use your reading, legal research, and problem-solving skills (see Chapters 7, 8, and 9) to identify:

- the relevant law (e.g. contract, tort);
- the relevant cause of action (e.g. if tort, is it nuisance, trespass, negligence?); and
- the necessary elements of that law (e.g. if negligence: duty of care, breach of duty, and causation).

For advocacy specifically, at this stage note the following:

- You will be interested not only to find the relevant law which will help you, *but also any relevant law which your opponent may seek to rely on.*

- Part of case analysis for advocacy involves *anticipating your opponent's arguments* and *planning how you would answer them* in favour of your client. This is similar to analysing the key arguments and counter-arguments in a legal essay (see Figure 14.1). So, while researching your own submissions, when you encounter points which may support your opponent's position, make a note of these. This will help to familiarise you with them and anticipate how to respond when your opponent raises them.

- Detailed knowledge of the relevant primary sources (cases or legislation) likely to be referred to in court is vital.

- For case law:

  - Be sure to read the whole authority, and not just the headnote, in order to build a persuasive argument. This is critical in advocacy, because the judge or your opponent may highlight passages of a judgment which are less helpful to your client, and you must be able to deal with this.

  - Present authorities which are binding on the court you are in. For example, if you are in the Court of Appeal, a decision by the House of Lords or the Supreme Court will bind the court, but a High Court decision will not. There is further guidance about precedent at 5.1.

  - Focus on the following in particular:

    - be prepared to summarise the facts of the case;

    - be able to explain which *principle* of law the case establishes, and why you consider that the case should be followed or distinguished;

    - focus your legal research efforts on finding a case which establishes or distinguishes a similar legal *principle*; students can get distracted by focusing too hard on finding a case with similar *facts*. There is further guidance about this at 8.1.6.

The Application stage

Figure 9.1 explains that here you need to:

- apply relevant primary sources to relevant facts and issues in a structured manner;
- apply the general rule before considering exceptions
- state the specific effect of the law based on the facts; and
- identify any questions arising from the law or facts.

The Conclusion stage

As mentioned, when you practise advocacy during your studies you will be preparing your conclusion in expectation of a response which immediately disputes it (unlike when you are answering a problem question, or making a presentation). To accommodate this, modify your approach to the conclusion stage at Figure 9.1 as follows:

- present factual *evidence* to the court (or other forum) in support of your client's case;
- present legal argument to satisfy the court that *as a matter of law* your client is entitled to a *remedy*; and
- give your reasoning by explaining how the *relevant law* applies to the *relevant facts*.

To help develop your understanding, Example 1 provides an illustration of how to do this.

Example 1

There has been a breach of contract (details of which are not provided here) and one party to the contract, C, a company, considers that it has suffered a loss of around £500,000 due to the breach by the other party, D. C seeks legal advice on the matter, and its solicitor, S, advises that it has an excellent chance of recovering this amount if they sue D. D then offers C an out-of-court settlement of £300,000. C refuses. The matter goes to court and the court awards C just £100,000 in damages, and also orders C to pay some court costs.

C now wants to know whether it has a case against S for damages based on S's negligent advice.

You can use Figure 9.1, in conjunction with guidance and modifications advised above, to prepare for advocacy as follows.

The Issue stage

- *The claimant* in this negligence action is C. C was the claimant in the original breach of contract action, that had suffered a contractual loss and sought advice from its solicitor, S, on how to recover the loss.
- *The defendant* is the solicitor, S, who advised on C's chances of success in litigating the breach of contract.
- You are *advising* the claimant, C and *your task* is to evaluate whether C should pursue a negligence claim against S.
- *The loss* C has suffered can be estimated from the *relevant facts* as the difference between the £300,000 it was offered to settle (but rejected in the belief that it would receive more by going to court) and the £100,000 (less court costs) it eventually received.
- C's *objective* is to find out whether it can recover its loss through pursuing a case against S for damages based on S's negligent advice.
- The *legal issue* is whether C can recover this loss from S in law.

The Rule stage

- The *relevant area of law* is the law of tort.
- The *relevant cause of action* is negligence.
- The *necessary elements of that law* are duty of care, breach of that duty, and causation.

The Application stage

- You would then apply this *relevant law* to the facts and issues in a structured manner, to establish and explain whether:
  - the defendant, S, owed the claimant, C, a duty of care;
  - S breached this duty with the advice given to C; and
  - if so, did the breach of duty actually cause C to suffer the loss identified.

The Conclusion stage

Here you would:

- present C's factual evidence to the court (to satisfy the court that S did *in fact* advise C to litigate against D on the basis of what S described as C's excellent chance of recovering its loss); and
- present legal argument to satisfy the court that *as a matter of law* the claimant is entitled to a *remedy* in the law of tort, because:
    - the defendant (S) owed the claimant (C) a duty of care;
    - S breached that duty of care by advising that C had excellent prospects of recovering its entire loss through litigation;
    - S's advice to litigate caused C to suffer the loss identified.

13.1.2.2 Evidence

Evidence, key in both criminal and civil cases, is 'the information or material, whether oral, documentary or real, that may be presented to the court to prove a fact in dispute and to enable the court to decide the issues of fact in a case'.[1] It can include, for example, a blood sample or a witness statement. There are rules of evidence covering such matters such as relevance and admissibility. See Chapter 3 for further information and examples.

13.1.2.3 Rehearsal

Malcolm Gladwell suggests it takes 10,000 hours of practice to become expert at something (see Further Reading). As with any skill, your advocacy will improve with practice and you should expect mistakes and not let them deter you. While you may understand the theory of advocacy very well, there is a difference between intellectual understanding and the skill development (see Long, Further Reading), and rehearsal will help you bridge that gap.

13.1.3 Performance

During your legal studies you will use advocacy to:

- present *evidence* to a mock court (witnesses can provide evidence in written form or they may attend in person to give oral testimony);
- present the *relevant law*, as it applies to that evidence (referred to as *legal submissions*). Typically, this involves inviting the mock court to apply the law as it was found to be in previously decided cases where the principles are similar to the present case; and
- ask the mock court to find in favour of your client.

[1] McMullen, J. (2019) 'Admissibility of evidence in civil proceedings' *Practical Law*. Available at: https://uk.practicallaw.thomsonreuters.com/5-562-4665.

We will now consider some of the detail you need to know specifically in the context of performing your advocacy.

13.1.3.1 Courtroom etiquette

This is the name for the series of conventions that have developed over time regarding how advocates should present their case in court. They should not detract from your communication skills: but you will need to learn and adhere to these conventions as you practise advocacy during your studies.

Language

As an advocate you represent your client, but you are not the client. Your role is to submit the relevant law and evidence to the mock court, not to offer a personal view on the case. Take care that when you make submissions to the mock court you do not use language which suggests that you have adopted the client's case as your own. In particular, avoid subjective language such as 'I think', 'in my case', and 'in my opinion' and instead learn to adopt objective phrases such as 'it is submitted' and 'it is the claimant's case that'.

How to address the court

How you address the judge will depend on the type of judge who is sitting. For example, you should address a District Judge who sits in the county court as Sir or Madam. Typically, you should address a High Court or Court of Appeal judge as My Lord or Lady. The website of the Judiciary of England & Wales explains in detail how to address judges (see Further Reading).

You should address other advocates as 'my friend' or 'my learned friend'.

Dress

Professional advocates wear dark suits, and it is usual for lecturers to ask you to replicate this in any advocacy assessment.

13.1.3.2 Presenting a persuasive argument in court: persuasive oral communication

How you present your winning argument can be just as important as being technically correct (Bennion, Further Reading). A significant part of your role as a successful advocate is to persuade the judge (and jury if appropriate) to decide in favour of your client. They need to be able to hear, understand, and feel sufficiently confident in what you are saying in order to agree with you. This is *why* you need to learn the skill of persuasive oral communication.

The power of persuasion is often discussed as if it is an inherent talent. To some degree this is correct, and you can reflect whether you are naturally adept at persuading others to see your point of view. If you are, then this is a good foundation on which to build in order to be a successful advocate.

However, the power of persuasion is really a skilful combination of good communication and presentation skills together with the effective case analysis, preparation, and knowledge of courtroom etiquette you have read about in this chapter, all of which you can practise and hone.

The guidance in Chapter 10 about effective, persuasive oral communication, and presentation skills is highly relevant in the context of advocacy. There are, of course, some key differences between presenting and being an effective advocate. For example, questions during or after a presentation tend not to be adversarial (although they can be). With advocacy, however, you can expect someone to be ready to dispute or call into question what you have argued.

As an advocate you will use both verbal and non-verbal skills to communicate with your client, the judge, other advocates and, in some cases, a jury. You are encouraged to read the guidance below and the articles in the Further Reading section to give you some ideas as to *how* to be persuasive.

- Read Chapter 10, if you have not already done so, and consider how you can use to best effect your physical presence, eye contact, voice, tone, volume, and pace.
- Express yourself clearly and concisely.
- Avoid padding and needless repetition.
- As with presentations, reading out notes will neither engage nor inspire confidence, so learn from the outset not to depend on notes.
- You can use notes effectively in other ways; populate a page with a list of points made in evidence on which you hope to rely, so your strengths are all to hand, at a glance, when you need to refer to them.
- Memorable phrases can be powerful (for example, 'in the wrong place at the wrong time').
- More can be less. Too many points might dilute your argument, so evaluate which are your strongest and make them the focus of your argument.
- Know when to stop. Finish on your strongest point. For example,
  - To a judge: making clear reference to authority which supports your case will invite them to think about their own decision being appealed.
  - To a criminal jury: ending with a reminder about the burden of proof can switch their focus, from what your client might have done, to the topic of reasonable doubt . . . and in turn its link to a not guilty verdict.
- Consider your audience (the judge—and jury if appropriate). Pay attention to their non-verbal cues and respond appropriately.
- Create trust and rapport. Be credible.
- Use structure and signposting (for example, 'turning to the second issue . . .').

13.1.3.3 Confidence

Advocacy requires confidence, and confidence can be built (see Bhaiwala and Dow, Further Reading).

- Life gives you lots of opportunities to practise advocacy. Are you influential in convincing your friends or family where to eat, or which film to watch? You can start with something as simple as speaking up and having your voice heard in the debate about this weekend's plans.
- Other activities, such as acting and debating, can also develop the skills you need to succeed as an advocate.

- Read as much as you can about advocacy. The Further Reading list is an excellent starting point.
- Visit court and watch others practise advocacy (see 13.1.3.4)
- Practice. Mooting and criminal advocacy competitions provide excellent opportunities for you to do this, and 13.1.4 and 13.1.5 will help you learn what you need to enjoy participating during your studies.

13.1.3.4 Visiting court

In practice, the advocacy employed in most courts and other dispute resolution forums is rarely of the type often portrayed in television and film courtroom dramas. To improve your understanding of the skills required of you during your studies, and assist you in developing your own advocacy skills, a visit to a court is highly worthwhile.

The vast majority of our courts are open to the public and you should visit at least one during your studies to enhance your understanding of how the law works in practice. Court visits offer you a valuable insight into what practising advocates do on a daily basis. You will be able to observe how lawyers use the law and apply it to the facts of the case, how a judge reaches a conclusion, and the court procedure generally.

You should take care to comply with the rules of the court that you visit. There is a link to a helpful guide to visiting court in the Further Reading section at the end of this chapter. The reception staff and court ushers will be happy to help you when you arrive at the court. Explain that you are a law student and would like to observe the court proceedings.

Technology also afford further opportunities to learn from watching others practise advocacy. Chapter 7 made clear that you can watch online the hearings of the Supreme Court (see Further Reading). The Young Legal Eagles documentary (see BBC, Further Reading) illustrates a criminal trial at the Old Bailey, with commentary and feedback from barristers and other experts.

13.1.4 Mooting

13.1.4.1 What is a moot?

A mooting competition, referred to as a moot, is a fictitious court hearing. Generations of law students have used mooting to help them develop both their knowledge of the law and their advocacy skills. It involves presenting to the court the legal arguments that relate to a particular written problem provided to you in advance. Typically, moots are presented as appeals, so you present to an appellate court. This requires you to accept the *facts* and *issues* as they are presented in the written problem and focus exclusively on presenting legal *arguments* (also known as *submissions*). Mooting therefore helps you develop your skills of critical thinking and analysis (see 14.1.3).

You should aim to participate in a moot during your studies (for example, as part of a team in a competitive moot such as the Oxford University Press National Mooting Competition) so you can demonstrate to a prospective employer that you have developed the skills referred to in this chapter. The City University Law School have produced a list of annual moots (see Further Reading). The process of mooting will also reveal to you whether you enjoy contentious work (see 7.2 and 13.2.3).

Example 2

Example 1 (about the negligent solicitor, S) could be presented as a moot problem. You would be given the facts of the problem in writing. Appeal cases are based on an *error on a point of law* and you will be told what the *grounds for the appeal* are. Imagine that S, the defendant, successfully defended the negligence case against him, and that C, the claimant, has appealed.

In the appeal, if you are told to represent C, the claimant, note that they will now be referred to as the *appellant*, because it is bringing the appeal. You need to persuade the Court of Appeal that the judge at first instance made an *error in law* and should have found in favour of your client, the appellant.

Alternatively, if you are told to represent S, the defendant, note that they will now be referred to as the respondent, because he is responding to the appeal. You need to persuade the Court of Appeal to the contrary, that the judge at first instance did not make an *error in law* and their finding in favour of your client, the respondent, should stand.

13.1.4.2 How a moot is structured

You will receive the written moot problem in advance of the moot, and you will be told whether you represent the appellant or the respondent. In most national competitions there will be two grounds of appeal, so your team would comprise two people who take one ground each, and you will need good team-working skills (see 15.4). There will be moot rules which you need to observe carefully. They will include rules about how long you have to make your submissions and the maximum number of legal authorities on which you can rely.

You and your partner will then undertake your case analysis and preparation, as described in 13.2.1. You will research the moot problem and prepare your legal submissions either to support or oppose the grounds of appeal. This will involve deciding which authorities you wish to rely on and why you say they are relevant and binding.

Some moots require you to present a written summary of your submissions (known as a *skeleton argument*) in advance of the moot (see 13.1.4.3 and Figures 13.1 and 13.2). You may be asked to take to the moot copies of the authorities referred to in your skeleton argument for use by the judge and your opponent.

The structure is as follows:

1. The team representing the appellant present their submissions first and answer any questions that the moot judge may have arising out of those submissions.
2. The team representing the respondent make their submissions.
3. The team representing the appellant will often be given a very short amount of time to reply to the submissions for the respondent.
4. The moot judge will then give a judgment on the law and, in a competitive moot, declare the team whose submission the court found most persuasive to be the winner.

13.1.4.3 Mooting skills

The judge will be judging your mooting skills, which include:

- case analysis (including the grounds of appeal);
- teamwork;

- time management;
- effective presentation of your submissions;
- structuring your arguments;
- responding appropriately to judicial intervention;
- using court etiquette.

Be reassured that it does not necessarily follow that the team that succeeds in the appeal will win the moot. It may be clear to you that the other team have the advantage of the law on their side (for example, because the application of legal precedent very clearly favours their client's position). While this may help them to succeed in the appeal itself, the judge remains free to declare your team the winner of the moot if you have demonstrated superior mooting skills despite your weaker starting point from a legal perspective.

Case analysis

Case analysis is key in mooting and you should familiarise yourself with the guidance about case analysis for problem solving generally in Chapter 9 and Figure 9.1, and for advocacy in particular at 13.1.2.1. Pay particular attention to case analysis , which can be challenging. Use the guidance at 13.1.2.1 to show that this is a particular area of strength for your team, and you will have a distinct advantage.

Dealing with judicial intervention

During the course of a moot, the judge may intervene and ask you a question. Typically, students become anxious at the thought of 'questions from the bench' and find judicial intervention difficult to deal with. It will help to consider this simply as an instance where the judge wants assistance with a point, and to view this as your opportunity to demonstrate how well you understand your legal argument and supporting authority. There may, of course, be an instance where you do not understand a question or cannot answer. It is perfectly acceptable to ask the judge for a moment to consult your notes for further clarity if you do not understand. However, if you still cannot answer, then 'My apologies, I cannot assist your Lordship with that particular question' is an appropriate response. More importantly, stay calm. A judge may test you with a question precisely to see how you handle a little pressure. Learning to respond well to judicial intervention is a transferable skill (see 16.4.3) which will prepare you well to deal with the unexpected in a variety of scenarios, including interruptions to presentations and questions in job interviews.

Written advocacy: the skeleton argument

It was noted at 13.1 that advocacy can be written or oral. As explained at 13.1.4.2, in the course of a moot, your written advocacy will be assessed in the context of a skeleton argument, which will be taken in and marked. A skeleton argument is exactly what the name suggests. It is the bones of the argument, and you will put the flesh on those bones through your skilful advocacy in the moot. Typically, a skeleton argument will comprise one page that details your basic submissions and the cases or other authorities that you will rely on.

The skeleton constitutes a permanent record of your argument, so you must take care to ensure not only that you have researched and applied the correct law, but also that you have presented it clearly in a way that a judge can follow. The guidance on good writing and drafting in Chapter 14 will help you with this. Figure 13.1 provides an example of a skeleton argument for the respondent, and Figure 13.2 an example of a skeleton argument for the appellant, which you can feel free to use as templates when preparing your own. Practically, it can be useful to draft and save your own 'core' word-processed skeleton argument, which you can then adapt for each moot. To help you, a soft copy of Figures 13.1 and 13.2 are available for you to download in the online resources.

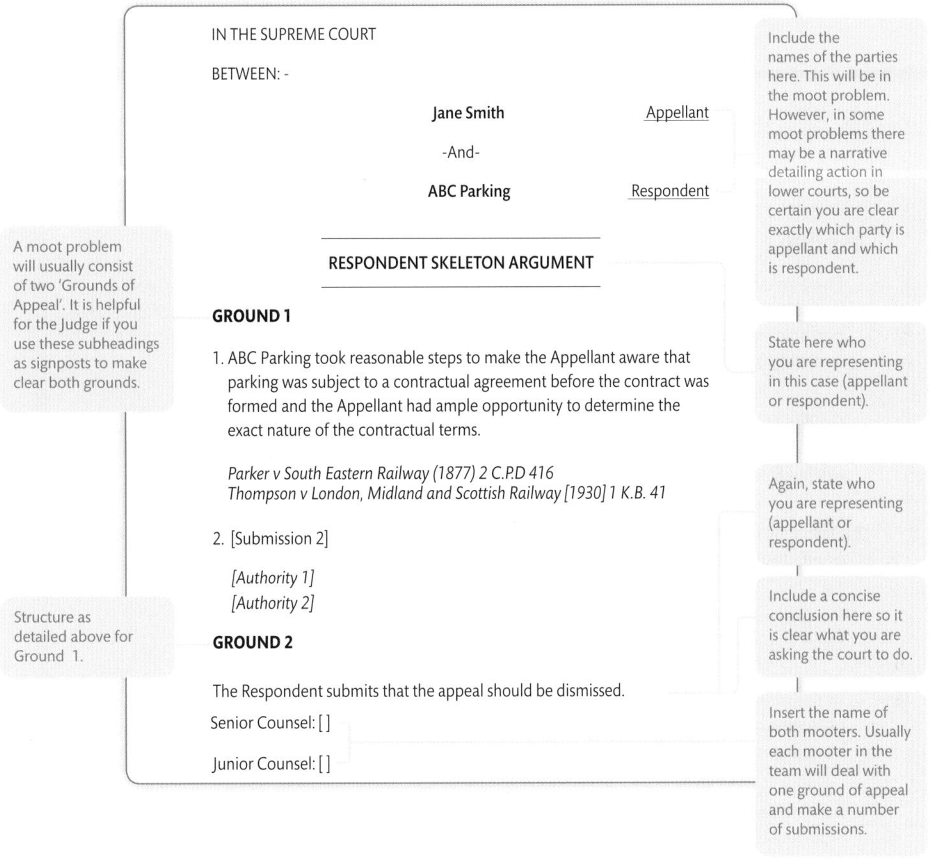

IN THE SUPREME COURT

BETWEEN: -

Jane Smith	Appellant
-And-	
ABC Parking	Respondent

RESPONDENT SKELETON ARGUMENT

GROUND 1

1. ABC Parking took reasonable steps to make the Appellant aware that parking was subject to a contractual agreement before the contract was formed and the Appellant had ample opportunity to determine the exact nature of the contractual terms.

Parker v South Eastern Railway (1877) 2 C.P.D 416
Thompson v London, Midland and Scottish Railway [1930] 1 K.B. 41

2. [Submission 2]

   [Authority 1]
   [Authority 2]

GROUND 2

The Respondent submits that the appeal should be dismissed.

Senior Counsel: [ ]

Junior Counsel: [ ]

Callout annotations (left side):
A moot problem will usually consist of two 'Grounds of Appeal'. It is helpful for the Judge if you use these subheadings as signposts to make clear both grounds.

Structure as detailed above for Ground 1.

Callout annotations (right side):
Include the names of the parties here. This will be in the moot problem. However, in some moot problems there may be a narrative detailing action in lower courts, so be certain you are clear exactly which party is appellant and which is respondent.

State here who you are representing in this case (appellant or respondent).

Again, state who you are representing (appellant or respondent).

Include a concise conclusion here so it is clear what you are asking the court to do.

Insert the name of both mooters. Usually each mooter in the team will deal with one ground of appeal and make a number of submissions.

Figure 13.1 Example respondent skeleton argument

Creating a case bundle

As part of a moot it can be customary to prepare a 'bundle' of authorities. This is simply a ring-binder containing, in printed form, the authorities on which you intend to rely. The rules of the moot will detail how many bundles are required, but as a minimum one should be prepared for the judge and available for the actual moot. A moot judge will be very impressed with a well-presented bundle and an efficient advocate who can skilfully navigate their way through a bundle of cases. You will save yourself and the judge valuable time and create a professional image. Conversely, an untidy bundle which is difficult to navigate may ensure the judge is not as receptive to your oral submissions as she could be.

IN THE SUPREME COURT

BETWEEN: -

Primarni Couture Fashion Ltd   <u>Appellant</u>

-And-

Manchester Fabrics   <u>Respondent</u>

APPELLANT SKELETON ARGUMENT

GROUND 1

1. The aim of an award of damages is to put the claimant in the position which he would have been in had the contract been performed according to its terms. In cases of defective performance a claimant is entitled to calculate loss as the cost of cure to ensure expectation under the contract is fulfilled.

   Golden Straight Corporation v Nippon Yusen Kubishka Kaisha (The Golden Victory) [2007] A.C. 353
   Ruxley Electronics and Construction Ltd v Forsyth [1996] A.C. 344

2. Damages in this case are not punitive or disproportionate nor do they inhibit the principle of efficient breach. They are merely the reasonable cost of reinstatement.

   Radford v De Froberville [1997] 1 W.L.R. 1262
   Dean v Ainley [1987] 1 W.L.R. 1729

3. In the alternative it is recognised that a party to a contract may have an interest in performance, which is not readily measured in terms of money. Furthermore, the courts have been willing to recognise this 'consumer surplus'.

   Ruxley Electronics and Construction Ltd v Forsyth [1996] A.C. 344
   Attorney General v Blake [2001] 1 A.C. 268

GROUND 2

1. The case falls firmly within the principles laid down, namely that an account of profit is, in exceptional cases, an appropriate remedy.

   Senior Courts Act 1981, S50
   Attorney General v Blake [2001] 1 A.C. 268
   Wrotham Park Estate Co Ltd v Parkside Homes Ltd. And Others [1974] 1 W.LR. 798

Figure 13.2 Example appellant skeleton argument

2. An account of profits is an equitable remedy, an instrument to mitigate the unjust enrichment of the Respondent.

Lake v Bayliss [1974] 1 W.L.R 107
Penarth Dock Engineering Co v Pounds [1963] 1 Lloyd's Rep 359
Reading v Attorney General [1951] A.C 507

The Appellant submits that the appeal is allowed.
Senior Counsel: [ ]
Junior Counsel: [ ]

Figure 13.2 *Continued*

The starting point for the bundle is your skeleton argument. As your skeleton argument details all of the authorities on which you intend to rely, it serves as a list of exactly what should be included in your bundle. Therefore, your first practical step would be to obtain a printed copy of each of those authorities from the relevant electronic legal database, such as Westlaw UK or Lexis®Library (see 8.1.3.2). For example, for the skeleton argument for the respondent at Figure 13.1, you would need to include in your bundle a copy of both cases.

You should arrange the copies in the order they appear in your skeleton argument. It can be particularly helpful for the judge if you place a numbered file divider between each authority. Then, during the moot, you can refer to, for example, 'tab 2 of the bundle' and the judge can quickly and easily locate the authority to which you refer. Once you have directed the judge to the authority, you should then direct him to the specific point.

It is worthwhile including a copy of your skeleton argument at the front of the bundle, together with a copy of the moot problem. Place all of the documents in a plain-coloured ring-binder (black or blue is best) and the bundle is complete. The judge then has everything he needs to hand.

Dealing with an opponent's skeleton argument

As part of a moot it is usual practice to exchange a skeleton argument with your opponent. Usually the date, time, and method for doing so is outlined in the rules and is specific to each competition. Typically, there is a day or two between the exchange of skeleton arguments and the actual moot, and the exchange takes place by email. This provides you with some time to review their submissions and prepare to deal with them before the moot itself.

This is the first opportunity you will have to discover your opponent's line of argument. As explained at 13.1.2.1, while researching your own submissions, you are likely also to encounter points which support your opponent's position. This will help you to be familiar with these points already, when you see them in your opponent's skeleton argument. Therefore, while conducting your case analysis, keep a note of such points. However, from time to time an opponent may surprise you with cases or other authorities which are new to you. Take time to read carefully the submissions and authorities in detail. What you are looking for is a weakness in your opponent's argument. For example, your opponent may rely upon a case which was heard in the High Court, however your authority may have been heard in the Court of Appeal and be more persuasive. If an opponent's case cannot be distinguished in this way, then you can analyse whether it is factually relevant. Make a note of any and all weaknesses you are able to identify, and keep this to hand to use in the moot.

During the moot, if representing the appellant, you may wish to deal directly with your opponent's skeleton argument even before your opponent has given their oral submissions. This approach requires a real command of the authorities and is a gamble. It is a real risk to anticipate what your opponent is going to say purely on the basis of their skeleton argument. Your opponent may present their submissions in a manner you did not expect. Therefore, if you are not feeling this confident, a safer approach is to deal with their submissions during the appellant's 'right to reply' at the end. However, as you become more experienced and confident, you can combine both approaches to great effect.

Note that there is no risk in this regard if you are the advocate representing the respondent, who always has the benefit of hearing oral submissions by the appellant before having to respond.

Regardless of your approach, respond you must. There are valuable marks available for dealing with your opponent's submissions and an effective response is the hallmark of a promising advocate.

13.1.5 Criminal advocacy competitions

13.1.5.1 What is criminal advocacy?

Another way of developing your advocacy skills as a student is through a criminal advocacy competition, such as Blackstone's National Advocacy Competition. Criminal advocacy comprises an oral presentation in a mock criminal court, and it requires a different approach to mooting. To succeed, you need to prepare thoroughly by reading the court papers carefully and deciding on a case strategy. At 8.2.2.1 you were advised not to begin writing your legal research report until you had finished your library research and had identified a definitive answer. Similarly, with criminal advocacy, before you start to construct your argument you should know the angle you would like to adopt. You should consider yourself a storyteller, and you need to know the ending before you start telling the story. In other words, what is your perspective on the issues to be decided by the jury?

13.1.5.2 How criminal advocacy is structured

A typical mock trial running order is as follows:

- Opening speech for prosecution.
- Examination-in-chief of any prosecution witnesses.
- Cross examination by defence counsel.
- Re-examination of prosecution witnesses if necessary.
- Reading of any agreed witness statements.
- Examination-in-chief of any defence witnesses.

- Cross examination by prosecution counsel.
- Re-examination of defence witnesses if necessary.
- Closing speech for the prosecution.
- Closing speech for the defence.

You should familiarise yourself with this structure; observing a case in a criminal court will help you with this. The documentary 'Young Legal Eagles' is a good starting point (see BBC, Further Reading). The following guidance will help you to deliver your criminal advocacy effectively.

The opening speech

As a courtesy you should introduce yourself, and your opposition, to the jury. As a bare minimum you should explain the charge to the jury, the facts of the case, and the burden of proof required. A more sophisticated opening speech will include *your* version of events and outline exactly the theory on which you have based your case.

Examination-in-chief

The purpose of examination-in-chief is to provide the witness with an opportunity to tell his story and provide his evidence for the court. However, you must avoid asking leading questions. A *leading question* is one which includes facts which have not been established (for example, 'Was Mr Smith holding the gun in his left or right hand?', when it has not yet been established from the witness there is any evidence Mr Smith had a gun in his hand at all). The exception to this is where facts are not in dispute.

Cross examination

The purpose of cross examination is to discredit the witness' version of events and to further your own case. You may ask leading questions. However, cross examination does not need to be hostile and you should always avoid an argument with the witness. Using the closed questioning technique (see Essential explanation) will help with this. Remember, 'honey catches more flies than vinegar'.

> **Essential explanation**
>
> A *closed question* is one that can be answered with the word 'yes' or 'no'. In the context of cross examination they can be used to control the witness. For example, 'You drove the stolen car on the 18th January, didn't you?'
>
> An *open question* is exactly what the name would suggest, a question which leaves it open to the person being asked the question as to how to answer it. These are typically used during examination-in-chief to allow the witness to tell their story in their own words. For example, 'What were you doing on the 18th January?'

The closing speech

The purpose of the closing speech is to persuade the jury of your version of events. Use this opportunity to deal with any weaknesses and strengths in your case and remind the jury of the burden of proof. You should aim to do this in language the jury will understand, so it is best to avoid using legal terms and jargon.

13.2 Professional advocacy

Advocacy is a vocational subject and so what you have learned in 13.1 about preparation, including case analysis, and performance will continue to be helpful. In practice you will be able to conduct advocacy in a much wider range of forums (see 13.2.4).

There follows some guidance designed to prepare you for some of the more practical changes, in context and environment, you can expect to find when you move from studying to professional advocacy practice.

13.2.1 Barrister or solicitor

A professional advocate can be a barrister or solicitor, who appears in court (or other forum) to argue her client's case before a judge. Table 13.1 summarises some of the key differences between a barrister and a solicitor. The article by Chambers Student (see Further Reading) provides further detail. There are currently more barristers practising in the higher courts than solicitor advocates, although solicitor advocates are increasing in number, which has not gone unnoticed (see Bowcott, Further Reading). The amount you can expect to be paid can also differ considerably between barristers and solicitors (see Prospects, Further Reading) and between different practice areas (see 13.2.2). The careers brochure co-authored by the Bar Council (see Further Reading) provides more detail about life as a barrister, including information about, and contact details for, all the bodies referred to in Table 13.1, and a jargon buster. Further information is included at 6.3.

13.2.2 Areas of practice

Legal work can be categorised as *contentious* or *non-contentious* work. Contentious work involves the resolution of disputes, some of which may result in proceedings in court (or other dispute resolution forums), and non-contentious work does not. An advocate's work is contentious work. As you progress in your studies, it is usual to find that you prefer one type over the other, however some lawyers do not discover this until they have progressed quite significantly through their training (and some not even by then).

Some areas of law, such as crime and family law, involve regular advocacy. In civil cases, as explained in Chapter 12 many claims are settled out of court, and so there is less advocacy. Non-contentious areas of law (for example, corporate law), will involve little advocacy in court, but barristers may specialise in this area and work in providing legal opinions or the negotiation process (see Chapter 12). Other areas of law (for example, employment law) will involve some contentious work and advocacy (for example, in an employment tribunal), and some non-contentious work (for example, drafting a director's service contract). Segregation is increasing between those who work in criminal, legal aid or state-funded cases and those who take cases for better-paying commercial or private-sector clients.[2]

---

[2] Bowcott (see Further Reading).

Table 13.1 Some of the key differences between a solicitor and barrister

	Barrister	Solicitor
Rights of audience	Can practise in all courts.	Can practise in the lower courts unless they have acquired their Higher Rights of Audience to become a Solicitor Advocate, when they can practise in the higher courts. This qualification includes submitting a portfolio and practical tests (see SRA, Further Reading).
Where (majority) practice	Chambers, where self-employed barristers share staff, overheads, premises, and a corporate identify.	Law firm, but some in-house, for example, in industry.
Employment status (of majority)	Self-employed, but some are employed, e.g. by the Government Legal Service, the Armed Forces, and in private practice.	Employed by law firm (until promoted to equity partner/owner).
Role	Advocate (represent clients in court, draft court documents, provide opinions).	Advocate and solicitor (represent clients and do most of the work outside court). Potentially more scope for continuity with the client.
Representative, regulatory, and other bodies	The General Council of the Bar, known as the Bar Council) (representative body); Bar Standards Board (regulatory body). The four Inns of Court (Lincolns Inn, Inner Temple, Middle Temple, Gray's Inn) have the role to educate and train barristers, and have the exclusive right to call barristers to the bar.	The Law Society (representative body), Solicitors Regulation Authority (regulatory body).

13.2.3 **Advocacy activities**

What you learned in 9.1.1, about using Figure 9.1 to help you with case analysis for problem solving, will help you in practice. You will continue to solve problems by proving your client's case, using facts, to argue persuasively for a remedy under, or compliance with, primary sources of law. Clarity and structure will remain very important, whatever the complexity of the case. You will still encounter both written and oral advocacy.

However, in practice (and on vocational programmes), you will be exposed to a much wider range of advocacy activities than during your undergraduate studies. You will continue to argue about substantive rights and remedies, of varying complexity. However, you will also be arguing about more mundane issues such as process, procedure, admissibility, interlocutory hearings, and mitigation. You can expect to work on some or all of the following, under supervision early in practice:

- plea in mitigation, to persuade the court to provide the most lenient sentence possible. For example, arguing that a custodial sentence is not appropriate (see Barnard, Further Reading);
- bail application (see CPS, Further Reading);

- opening speeches (see BBC, Further Reading);
- application for strike out for abuse of process;
- submissions of no case to answer.

13.2.4 Courts, tribunals, and judge in chambers hearings

The Courts and Tribunals Judiciary website produces helpful structure charts of:

- the courts, showing the routes taken by different cases as they go through the courts system, and which judges deal with each; and
- the tribunals system (see Courts and Tribunals Judiciary, Further Reading).

Table 13.1 refers to the different rights of audience between barristers and solicitor advocates on the one hand, and solicitors on the other. You need to ensure that you have the appropriate right of audience to appear (see Hilborne, Further Reading). Generally speaking (the rules are nuanced), the lower courts include the Magistrates Court (criminal), County Court (civil) and Tribunals (such as the Employment Tribunal) and the higher courts include the Crown Court (criminal), High Court (civil), Court of Appeal, and Supreme Court. Before qualification (for example, as a paralegal), you may have rights of audience in the small claims court, some tribunals and, provided you are representing your solicitor or qualified litigator employer, in some interim application hearings and hearings in Chambers.

> ### ⊚ Practice tip
>
> A reference to *court* may conjure up a specific image in your head. The layperson often thinks of a court as comprising a judge—in full wig and gown—and a jury, all sitting in a room with wooden panels. However, in practice, this is not always the case. Serious criminal offences will be tried before a judge and jury, while less serious offences and most civil cases are heard before a judge sitting alone. Court dress differs depending on the court in question, with full wigs retained mainly for ceremonial purposes. Tribunal judges and magistrates generally wear suits. Many courtrooms are now more modern in decor.

13.2.5 Dress

Professional advocates wear smart, professional dark suits. In criminal courts you must wear a wig and gown, but this is not the case in all courts. You would not require a wig in family court proceedings, and increasingly judges are allowing advocates to remove their wigs during civil cases (especially in the summer months). Lady Hale has made public her views about the wearing of wigs in court (see Peacock, Further Reading).

13.2.6 Conduct and ethics

As you will no doubt be aware from watching television dramas, your role as a professional advocate will be to persuade the court to find in your client's favour. However, as an advocate you must be aware at all times that although you represent your client, you do so as an officer of the court. This means that you cannot mislead the court to help your client (e.g. by presenting evidence which you know is untrue, or providing a positive defence for a client you know to be lying). You must be ethical, maintain professional standards, and have appropriate expertise to act. The Bar Standards Board regulates barristers in England and Wales, and the Solicitors Regulation Authority performs the regulatory role for solicitors. For further information see 6.4 and Moorhead et al, Further Reading.

Summary

- You will need good communication skills as an advocate, when mooting or participating in a criminal advocacy competition.
- Practising advocacy as a student will help you to develop other transferable legal skills (for example, teamworking skills).
- Effective case analysis is a vital component of successful advocacy.
- Advocacy can be oral or in writing.
- Visiting court is a must for students studying advocacy.

What the professionals say

Opportunities to take part in mooting and advocacy activities are invaluable. They provide a safe environment in which you can test your ability to stand on your feet and present a persuasive legal argument. You get a feel for what it is like to represent a party in court, which can be exciting. Everyone feels nervous. However, it gets easier and will increase public speaking confidence considerably. It is not just for those who wish to pursue a career at the Bar. Public speaking is an important skill for any career. Perfection is not necessary, every lawyer has 'a bad day in court'. The key is resilience, keep going.

Sarah Cook, Kenworthy's Chambers and former Winner, Blackstone's National Criminal Advocacy Competition

Practical exercises

Consider how you would answer these questions. Reflect on how your reading of this chapter has informed or changed how you might answer them. How might you use what you have learned in an interview or exam situation?

1. Where is your nearest court and when might you be able to attend to observe proceedings?
2. What mooting and criminal advocacy competitions does your university participate in?
3. Watch the advocacy in the *Miller* case, which you considered in Chapter 7 (https://www.supremecourt.uk/cases/uksc-2019-0192.html) and make a note of how you might adapt what you have seen into your own practice.

4. What would you say is the main difference between conducting advocacy and making a presentation? Are there any similarities?

5. From your studies to date, would you describe (or expect) your preference to be towards contentious or non-contentious areas of law, and why?

6. Can you construct an argument against an issue you would usually agree with?

 Visit the **online resources** for the authors' reflections and to check your progress.

Further reading

Barnard, D. (2014) *The Plea in Mitigation in the Crown Court*. Graysinn.org.uk. Available at: https://www.graysinn.org.uk/sites/default/files/documents/members/Plea.pdf
—Ten Do's and Don'ts for students and pupils presenting a plea in mitigation in the Crown Court, prepared by David Barnard of Grays Inn with help from colleagues at the bar and on the bench.

Bar Council (2019) *Your Career as a Barrister*. Available at: https://www.barcouncil.org.uk/
—Co-authored by the Bar Council, the Council of the Inns of Court and the four Inns of Court. This useful document also contains the social media and web addresses of all the Inns of Court, and a jargon buster.

Bar Standards Board (2019) *The BSB Handbook—Code of Conduct*. Available at: https://www.barstandardsboard.org.uk/the-bsb-handbook.html?part=E3FF76D3-9538-4B97-94C02111664E5709&audience=&q=code+of+conduct
—The Code of Conduct includes the ten Core Duties which underpin the *Bar Standards Board's* entire regulatory framework, as well as the rules which supplement those Core Duties. Compliance with both the Core Duties and the rules is mandatory. The Code of Conduct also contains details of the outcomes which compliance with the Core Duties and the rules is designed to achieve.

Bar Standards Board (2019) https://www.barstandardsboard.org.uk
—Official website of the regulator of barristers in England and Wales. Includes information about how to qualify as a barrister.

BBC (2019) *BBC Two—Young Legal Eagles—Clips*. Available at: https://www.bbc.co.uk/programmes/b01j71s0/clips and, through the Box of Broadcasts subscription, in full at https://learningonscreen.ac.uk/ondemand/index.php/prog/029985EF?bcast=115547308
—With unprecedented access to in the inside of a courtroom at the Old Bailey, this ground-breaking documentary explores the British legal system. Young people from UK state schools and colleges take on the roles of barrister, defendant, witness, jury, court reporter, court artist, forensic scientist, and court usher. Presided over by Baroness Scotland QC, barristers and other experts in the field teach them the skills of oration and debating, details about crime investigation and what to expect in cross-examination, so that they are ready for their day in court.

Bennion, J. (2015) 'Why Lawyers Are So Bad At Persuading', *Above the Law*. Available at: https://abovethelaw.com/2015/05/why-lawyers-are-so-bad-at-persuading/
—An article from the US reminding lawyers that how you present your winning argument can be just as important as being technically correct. It recommends that lawyers need to unlearn focusing exclusively on being right, and law schools need to teach them how to be persuasive (and right).

Bhaiwala, N. (2019) 'Increasing your self-confidence at work', *The Lawyer | Legal insight, benchmarking data and jobs*. The Lawyer. Available at: https://www.thelawyer.com/increasing-self-confidence-work/?nocache=true&adfesuccess=1
—Some 'quick-win' actions, as well as some longer-term habits, to help build self-confidence.

Bowcott, O. (2019) 'Barristers, solicitors and paralegals urged to join single trade union'. *The Guardian*. Available at: https://www.theguardian.com/law/2019/apr/20/barristers-solicitors-and-paralegals-urged-to-joinsingle-trade-union
—An article supporting a single trade union to unify the profession, in which, it argues, segregation is increasing between those who work in criminal, legal aid or state-funded cases and those who take cases for better-paying commercial or private-sector clients.

Chambers Student (2019) *What kind of lawyer do you want to be?—Chambers Student Guide.* Available at: https://www.chambersstudent.co.uk/where-to-start/what-kind-of-lawyer-do-you-want-to-be
—An article providing information to inform your decision as to whether you would like to practise as a barrister or solicitor.

Courts and Tribunals Judiciary (2019) *The Structure of the Courts.* Available at: https://www.judiciary.uk/wp-content/uploads/2012/08/courts-structure-0715.pdf
—Structure diagram showing the routes taken by different cases as they go through the courts system, and which judges deal with each.

Courts and Tribunals Judiciary (2019) *Tribunals Organisation Chart.* Available at: https://www.judiciary.uk/publications/tribunals-organisation-chart/
—Structure diagram showing the tribunals system.

Courts and Tribunals Judiciary (2019) *What do I call a judge?.* Available at: https://www.judiciary.uk/you-and-the-judiciary/what-do-i-call-judge/
—A useful resource for students who wish to learn more about court etiquette, including how to address judges.

Crown Prosecution Service (CPS) (2019) *Bail | The Crown Prosecution Service.* Available at: https://www.cps.gov.uk/legal-guidance/bail
—Crown Prosecution Service guidance on bail, to consult when preparing a bail application.

Dow, M. (2019) 'Self-Confidence—A Key Legal Skill', *LawCareers.Net.* Available at: https://www.lawcareers.net/Explore/BlogPost/Matthew-Dow/Self-Confidence-A-Key-Legal-Skill
—An article discussing the role of confidence for, among other lawyers, advocates, for example when a witness abruptly pivots position, a case lands on their desk mere minutes before the trial, or missing documents suddenly become pertinent evidence.

Gillespie, A. and Weare, S. (2019) *The English Legal System.* Oxford: OUP, 7th edn
—Visit this book's online resources at http://global.oup.com/uk/orc/law/els/gillespie7e/and click 'Student Resources'— 'Activities'— 'Visiting Court' for useful tips that you can use in planning your first court visit.

Gladwell, M. (2013) *Outliers: The Story of Success.* New York: Back Bay Books
—Gladwell explains that reaching the '10,000-Hour Rule', which he considers the key to success in any field, is simply a matter of practicing a specific task that can be accomplished with 20 hours of work a week for 10 years.

Gray's Inn (2019) *Resources.* Available at: https://www.graysinn.org.uk/education/students/resources
—A selection of articles taken from Graya News and aimed at students, pupils, and barristers new to practice. They are written by highly experienced practitioners and offer concise, practical guidance on some of the fundamentals of advocacy. They include articles about cross-examination, skeleton arguments, and mooting.

Higdon, M. (2008) 'Oral Argument and Impression Management: Harnessing the Power of Nonverbal Persuasion for a Judicial Audience', *Kansas Law Review*, 57(3). Available at: https://papers.ssrn.com/sol3/papers.cfm?abstract_id=1270979

—An article, again from the US, which applies social science research, on non-verbal communication, specifically to the area of oral advocacy.

Hilborne, N. (2018) *Barrister suspended for High Court advocacy before and during pupillage. legalfutures.* Available at: https://www.legalfutures.co.uk/latest-news/ barrister-suspended-for-high-court-advocacy-before-and-during-pupillage
—An article describing how a barrister was suspended for six months by a Bar disciplinary tribunal for acting as an advocate in the High Court before and during his pupillage.

Langford, S. (2018) *In Your Defence: Stories of Life and Law.* London: Doubleday
—True life courtroom stories told by Sarah Langford, a barrister practising in criminal and family law.

The Law Society (2019) *Advocacy—The Law Society.* Available at: https://www.lawsociety.org.uk/ practice-areas/advocacy/
—News and advice for solicitor advocates from the Law Society on civil, family, and criminal advocacy issues.

Learnmore (2019) *Get Mooting: Rundown of Competitions.* Available at: https:// learnmore.lawbore.net/index.php/Get_Mooting:_Rundown_of_Competitions
—A list of mooting competitions complied by the City Law School.

Long, J. (2016) *The Importance Of Practice—And Our Reluctance To Do It—Harvard Business Publishing.* Harvard Business Publishing. Available at: https://www.harvardbusiness.org/ the-importance-of-practice-and-our-reluctance-to-do-it/
—An article which explains why you might avoid practice, and how it is essential to practice, whether you aspire to 'pretty good' or 'expert' (10,000 hours?).

McPeake, R. (2018) *Advocacy.* Oxford: OUP
—An introductory text about the skills and techniques required to be an advocate. Coverage includes guidance on making opening and closing speeches; planning and delivering examination-in-chief and cross-examination; questioning witnesses; as well as examples of specific questioning techniques which may be employed in practice. It also highlights the ethical boundaries and rules within which an advocate must work.

Middle Temple (2014) *Advocacy Guide | Middle Temple.* Available at: https://www.middletemple.org .uk/advocacy-guide
—The Middle Temple guide to advocacy skills.

Moorhead, R., Denvir, C., Sefton, M., and Balmer, N. (2015) *The Ethical Capacities of New Advocates.* UCL Centre for Ethics and Law. Available at: https://www.icca.ac.uk/wp-content/uploads/2019/07/ The-Ethical-Capacities-of-New-Advocates.pdf
—Research commissioned by the Inns of Court College of Advocacy (ICCA) into the ethical capacities of new advocates. It revealed that there was a tendency for advocates to re-frame ethical questions as tactical questions. It concluded, 'An advocate that better understands his or her own values may better understand and improve their own decision-making. An understanding of the subjective elements of ethical decision-making may merit inclusion in ethical training'.

Morley, I. (2015) *The Devil's Advocate A Spry Polemic on How to Be Seriously Good in Court.* 3rd edition. London: Sweet & Maxwell
—A best-selling advocacy manual bringing a fresh approach to the Do's and Don'ts of good advocacy. Written with humour and style, the title explains clear techniques, taking the reader through the practical application of advocacy step by step.

Peacock, L. (2014) Britain's most senior female judge, Baroness Hale: 'My biggest fear . . . When am I going to be found out?', *The Telegraph,* 18 April. Available online at https://www.telegraph.co.uk/

women/womens-business/10773941/Britains-most-senior-female-judge-Baroness-Hale-My-biggest-fear-...-When-am-I-going-to-be-found-out.html

—Lady Hale admits she grapples with the fear of 'being found out' and discusses impostor syndrome, what really goes through her head in court and why the legal system should ditch 'silly wigs'.

Pope, D. and Hill, D. (2015) *Mooting and Advocacy Skills*, 3rd edition, London: Sweet & Maxwell

—A helpful, short mooting and advocacy guide.

Prospects.ac.uk. (2019) *How much do lawyers earn?* | *Prospects.ac.uk*. Available at: https://www.prospects.ac.uk/jobs-and-work-experience/job-sectors/law-sector/how-much-do-lawyers-earn

—Discover how your location and specialism can affect your salary.

The Secret Barrister (2018) *The Secret Barrister: Stories of the Law and How It's Broken*. London: Picador

—A junior barrister's view of our criminal justice system, addressing questions such as, 'How can you defend a child-abuser you suspect to be guilty?', 'What do you say to someone sentenced to ten years who you believe to be innocent?', and 'What is the law and why do we need it?'.

SRA (2019) *Higher rights of audience*. Available at: https://www.sra.org.uk/solicitors/accreditation/higher-rights-of-audience

—Solicitors are granted rights of audience in all courts when they are admitted or registered. However, they cannot exercise those rights in the higher courts until they have complied with additional assessment requirements. Here the SRA provide information about higher rights, including a link to their Higher Rights of Audience Competence Standards. Reading the Standards will give you an excellent understanding of the skills you need for practice.

The Supreme Court website at https://www.supremecourt.uk/decided-cases/index.html

—Official website of the Supreme Court, where you can watch recordings of hearings of cases decided in the last year.

University of Oxford. Mooting: what is it and why take part? Available at https://www.law.ox.ac.uk/current-students/mooting-oxford/mooting-what-it-and-why-take-part

—Includes some reasons to moot, tips, and footage taken at a mooting competition. Features brief interviews with participants who explain what mooting is and talk about their experiences of mooting at Oxford.

Vaughan, S. (2010) Persuasion is an Art ... but it is also a Valuable Tool in Advocacy. *Baylor Law Review*, 16(2). Available at: https://www.baylor.edu/content/services/document.php/116809.p

—An interesting and well-structured article (again from the US) designed to provide advocates with a systemic study of the tools and techniques of effective written and oral advocacy that can be used in representing clients.

For the authors' reflections on the practical exercises, additional self-test questions, sample interview questions and a library of links to useful websites, visit the free **online resources** *at* www.oup.com/he/slorach4e.

Advocacy and mooting

Chapter 13

14 Writing and drafting

⦿ Learning objectives

After studying this chapter you should be able to:

- Understand the legal writing skills required during your studies and beyond.
- Use Figures 14.1 and 14.2 to write an essay which succeeds in meeting assessment criteria.
- Use OSCOLA to reference your work and avoid plagiarism.
- Use Figures 14.5 and 14.6 to write a letter and email of a professional standard.
- Understand and develop drafting skills.

Introduction

You may consider that, to get to this stage in your education, you have mastered the skill of writing. However, your legal studies will require you to develop your writing and drafting skills further, and graduate employers demand good written communication skills of those they recruit. As we shall see, there is a significant difference between simply being able to write, and being able to communicate effectively in writing.

This chapter will help you to develop your writing and drafting skills as you develop your understanding of the law. While new methods of assessment, such as presentations and posters, are becoming increasingly common, traditionally law programmes have used essays to assess your legal knowledge and intellectual skills, and many continue to do so. 14.1 will consider approaches to writing good essays which communicate effectively the quality of your knowledge and skills. 14.2 will consider the importance of writing and drafting skills in legal practice and professional life generally.

14.1 Writing essays

In this section, we will concentrate on the development of your writing skills in the context of a legal essay. However, the approaches discussed apply equally to other types of writing you might be asked to produce, such as reports, discussion documents, pieces of coursework, and undergraduate dissertations. Chapter 9 considers in detail how to write effective answers to problem-solving questions.

Writing is like any other skill in terms of development: improvement requires conscious consideration of its fundamental elements. With practice, these become part of your subconscious and you will be able to write to a high standard with relative ease (see Adams, Further Reading, Chapter 11). Before you achieve this, you must first go through the stage of conscious thought and practice.

14.1.1 **An effective essay-writing strategy**

Figure 14.1 provides a helpful essay-writing strategy that shows the structure of your essay, the content that is required at each stage, and how you can write in a way that you can be confident will fulfil all of the typical assessment criteria against which your essay will be

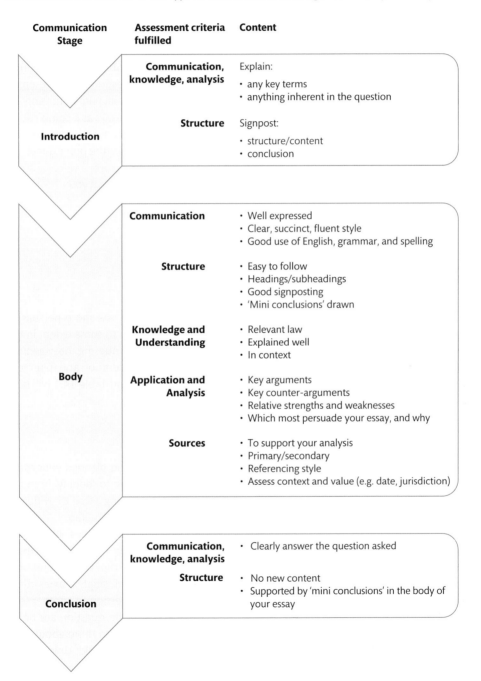

Communication Stage	Assessment criteria fulfilled	Content
Introduction	**Communication, knowledge, analysis**	Explain: • any key terms • anything inherent in the question
	Structure	Signpost: • structure/content • conclusion
Body	**Communication**	• Well expressed • Clear, succinct, fluent style • Good use of English, grammar, and spelling
	Structure	• Easy to follow • Headings/subheadings • Good signposting • 'Mini conclusions' drawn
	Knowledge and Understanding	• Relevant law • Explained well • In context
	Application and Analysis	• Key arguments • Key counter-arguments • Relative strengths and weaknesses • Which most persuade your essay, and why
	Sources	• To support your analysis • Primary/secondary • Referencing style • Assess context and value (e.g. date, jurisdiction)
Conclusion	**Communication, knowledge, analysis**	• Clearly answer the question asked
	Structure	• No new content • Supported by 'mini conclusions' in the body of your essay

Figure 14.1 Essay-writing strategy

marked. The first column encourages you to structure your essay into three stages, namely an introduction, body, and conclusion. The second column reveals the opportunities for you to fulfil assessment criteria within each stage. The third column provides guidance about the content, relevant to any essay topic. This chapter continues to provide guidance as to how you can use it for essay-writing success.

14.1.2 The general purpose in setting an essay question

In contrast to a problem question, which is based on a set of facts describing particular events, and asks you to 'advise' a particular party (see Chapter 9), an essay question either presents a proposition for critical analysis, or an instruction or question to be dealt with in the context of a particular statute, case, or topic. You might be tempted to view essays as a combination of a necessary evil and a rite of passage, producing 'essay crises' as deadlines loom. Rest assured, understanding the underlying purpose of a legal essay will make the process feel less daunting for you, so let us explore that further now.

The general purpose of a legal essay is to enable you to demonstrate that you:

- *know* the relevant law and its *sources*;
- *understand* the law;
- can *analyse* the pertinent arguments and counter-arguments;
- support your analysis with reliable *sources*; and
- conclude which sources most persuade your essay, and why.

The more effectively you *communicate* and *structure* your writing, the more persuasive your own argument will be. The italicised words are likely to feature to some extent in the assessment criteria against which your essays will be marked. Remembering these general purposes, and the related assessment criteria, will make your consideration and fulfilment of the specific purpose of any essay much easier. 14.1.3 to 14.1.6 and Table 14.1 will help you with this.

14.1.3 Preparation: analysing the question

You should begin to write only when you have properly prepared and planned your essay, and this process begins with analysing the question. You will be able to identify, from the question or title of the essay, the specific intellectual skills you are being asked to evidence. Underline or highlight the key word (or words) which indicates the skill required.

Table 14.1 sets out some basic guidance about common words in essay titles, all of which invite critical thinking, and the same basic approach to critical thinking. In some cases, there are some nuanced differences in approach intended by using one of the words rather than another. Mostly, they are used interchangeably, and sometimes confusingly if assessment criteria refer to one set of intellectual skills (e.g. analyse) and the question to another (e.g. evaluate or discuss). If in doubt, ask your lecturer if the words in the question are being used interchangeably, or if there is an intended difference. You can read more about critical analysis in the Further Reading section (Chatfield, University of Sheffield, University of Manchester).

Table 14.1 What is the essay question asking you to do? (Critical thinking)

Analyse (or evaluate)	This indicates that you should be examining the subject matter in depth and in a logical, structured manner. Your structure might be chronological, if you are analysing the development of law, or involve you breaking down the constituent parts of the proposition. Your analysis should identify and weigh up (evaluate) arguments and supporting evidence relating to the subject matter, and then the counter-arguments, drawing a reasoned conclusion as to which most persuade your essay, and why.
Compare (or Contrast or Distinguish)	You are being asked to identify and discuss, in relation to the subject matter, those elements which are common and those which differ. You should discuss the importance and impact of the differences.
Consider (or Examine)	This is asking for your view or opinion on a particular statement, proposition, case, or piece of law. You will need to support your view with argument and evidence from reliable sources. You should also demonstrate knowledge and understanding of contrary views or opinions (counter arguments).
Discuss	This requires an essay that structures a discussion of different views, reasons why those views were held, arguments for and counter arguments against the proposition and suchlike. If you proffer only one viewpoint, there is no discussion. You should indicate which viewpoint you favour, and why. This will help you to avoid a dry, factual account of a topic, limited to description only.
Evaluate (or Assess)	To evaluate a particular statement, proposition, case, or statute, you should examine the importance and effect of the item in question, weigh up related arguments and evidence, and come to a reasoned conclusion.
Explain	This appears straightforward, requiring you to set out an account of what is meant by a particular term or what is the effect of a particular law. However, such a narrow interpretation risks producing a dry, factual, descriptive essay which demonstrates *knowledge* but not *understanding*. Instead, think beyond dealing with *what*, and consider *how* and *why* too. For example, *why* did Parliament enact the statute, *how* has the meaning of a word been interpreted over time, *why* has the case or statute been important?

14.1.3.1 Critical thinking

The requirement to demonstrate critical thinking is often made explicit in the title, for example 'Critically analyse (or "Critically evaluate") the statement that . . .', but you should treat it as an implicit requirement in every essay. To think critically is not the same as to criticise. Critical thinking is an approach, not simply an action. It involves you:

- identifying the proposition in the question;
- demonstrating *understanding* of its meaning and importance;
- considering objectively the *arguments which support* the proposition, and the *counter-arguments* which undermine the proposition (this demonstrates that you understand not only that differing views are held but *why* they are held);
- *evaluating the supporting evidence* for those arguments, by referring to reliable primary and secondary sources of law (see 8.1.5 and 8.1.6); and
- reaching a reasoned *conclusion* which *answers the question* and makes clear which of the *arguments* or *counter-arguments* most persuade the essay (*what* you have concluded from the process of producing your essay), and *why*.

14.1.4 **Planning: drafting a skeleton essay**

Essay title: There has been a noticeable increase in delegated legislation. Discuss the proposition that the advantages of delegated legislation outweigh any disadvantages.

SKELETON ESSAY PLAN

INTRODUCTION

Explain:

• key terms: what is delegated legislation (DL)

• anything inherent in the question:

  – that there has been a noticeable increase

  – that there are both advantages and disadvantages

  – that it is reasonable to explore the notion that the advantages outweigh the disadvantages

Signpost:

• structure/content

  – this essay will discuss first, the history of DL to date, including its purpose, how it operates, its effect, and how and why it has increased

  – it will then analyse the advantages and disadvantages of DL

• conclusion

  – this essay will conclude that the advantages do/do not outweigh the disadvantages [for the key reason that/ for the reasons set out below].

BODY

1. The history of DL

Demonstrate *knowledge* and *understanding* of DL here, including the rationale for the increase:

  a. The purpose of DL (*Sources*: texts.)

  b. How DL operates, and its effect (*Sources*: texts and examples of delegated legislation to illustrate.)

Figure 14.2 Example skeleton essay plan

c. How and why the use of delegated legislation increased (*Sources*: texts; and search for statistics to illustrate.)

  • The practical implications (*Sources*: as above plus journal articles.)

2. **The advantages and disadvantages of DL**

Demonstrate *analysis* here: the intellectual skill of discussion, with critical thinking:

a. The advantages of delegated legislation (*Sources*: texts; journal articles; cases.)

  • Why they are perceived as advantages (*Sources*: as above, primarily journal articles.)

b. The disadvantages of delegated legislation (*Sources*: texts; journal articles; cases.)

  • Why they are perceived as disadvantages (*Sources*: as above, primarily journal articles.)

c. Do the advantages of DL outweigh the advantages of DL? (*Sources*: texts; journal articles; cases.)
  • Which sources discuss this?

  • Is there a consensus of support, one way or another?

  • Explore the context and value of those sources, and any bias (e.g. date, jurisdiction)

  • Of those arguments, which most persuade this essay, and *why*?

CONCLUSION

Answer the question asked: this essay is/ is not persuaded that the advantages of DL outweigh the disadvantages of DL [for the key reason that/ for the reasons set out above].

Figure 14.2 *Continued*

Producing an essay which is a well-structured and argued piece of writing which meets all of the assessment criteria at the grade descriptor you are aiming for (for example, first class) requires planning. Figure 14.1 provides a helpful structure which you can follow to make sure your essay meets all of the assessment criteria, whatever the topic. You are encouraged to use it at this stage, not to write out your entire essay, but instead to create a skeleton plan of your essay. The skeleton will:

- set out what you will be including in your introduction, body, and conclusion;
- use headings, subheadings, and bullet points;
- outline structure and content you intend to deal with at each stage;
- allow you to check that you will be fulfilling all the criteria against which your essay will be marked.

Figure 14.2 is a worked example to show you how to create a skeleton essay plan. The benefit of preparing this skeleton is that you can easily re-arrange your headings and related content around, until you are content it will communicate your ideas well and is structured for optimum clarity. If you had already written out your essay in full, without preparing a skeleton, the process of re-arranging content would feel much more complicated and cumbersome. You are less likely to do it, and your ability to meet the *structure* and *communication* criteria would suffer as a result.

Drafting a skeleton of your essay allows you to plan for your preparation and provides an outline structure for your essay itself. This shows the importance of thinking about the purpose of the essay: by doing so, you can create much of your skeleton without detailed knowledge of the subject area. Then you can refine your skeleton as you use your legal research skills (see Chapter 8) to locate material within the various sources you have identified. Highlight or note the material relevant to each of the elements in your plan. As you do so, think how you might use the material, what it might illustrate, and how you can best present it within your structure. An important consideration is the relevant intellectual skill: in this case, 'discuss'. You should, as part of your preparation, collate and begin to order the material that will form the basis of the discussion. You could also summarise each of the main arguments as you find them, which will help you when you come to write up your essay. As explained at 14.1.8 you should also, at this stage, make a note of the information about the source material you have used, so you can properly reference your writing. You will note that the skeleton essay plan makes no reference to lecture notes as sources, because it is noting sources that you can reference in your essay when you write it. While, of course, your lecture notes will inform what you write, you would not reference them as they are not a reliable secondary or primary source of law (see 8.1.5 and 8.1.6).

14.1.5 Performing: writing up your essay

General guidance as to how you can demonstrate good writing skills is set out at 14.2.1.11. There follows here some useful techniques to inform your writing of essays in particular.

14.1.5.1 Avoid needless repetition and restatement

Compare the following excerpts from the introduction of the same essay title considered in the skeleton at Figure 14.2, one by student A, and one by student B.

Example 1

- **Student A**. 'The fact that there has been a noticeable increase in the amount of delegated legislation means that it is important to discuss the advantages and disadvantages of this form of law.'
- **Student B**. 'In the three years from 2010–12, 89 UK Public General Acts were enacted. In the same period, 9,429 UK Statutory Instruments were made, an average of over 3,000 pieces of such delegated legislation per year. Yet, in the ten years to 2012, that average was under 2,000. The prevalence and growth of delegated legislation raises important questions, and this essay will discuss first, the history of issue of DL to date. . .'

Student A is simply restating the proposition in the essay title. Student B is immediately demonstrating research and analysis of the issues, and is likely to fulfil the assessment criteria at a higher level.

Take a similar approach in the body of your essay, demonstrating analysis, which requires more than simply stating the law. 14.1.5.2 provides further detail specifically about the conclusion.

14.1.5.2 A reasoned conclusion

As Figure 14.1 makes clear, your conclusion should answer the question asked. The body of your essay will contain the detail of the arguments and counter-arguments, and mini conclusions you have reached, on the key areas for discussion. You therefore do not need to restate the detail of all your previous analysis, nor should you introduce new material. Your conclusion should instead bring together the threads of your essay in a clear, reasoned manner. There should be a link to the intellectual skill aspect of the essay's purpose. If it was a discussion essay, then conclude where you stand on the debate, and *why*. If you were asked to evaluate a proposition, then give your conclusion on the extent to which the proposition is valid or correct, and *why*. The 'and *why*' will clarify which mini conclusion(s) most persuade the essay, and will ensure that your conclusion will be reasoned.

14.1.5.3 Point, evidence, analysis

You have already been encouraged to consider the purpose of your essay before you write, and as you write, have the question in front of you and remind yourself, 'what is the point?' This is not a deeper philosophical question, but rather a means of analysing specifically what each piece of your writing is adding to your essay. It may help to think of this using the 'PEA' model: Point; Evidence; Analysis. That is, what point are you making; what objective evidence do you have to support it; what is your analysis of that evidence? The following example is annotated to show application of the PEA model.

> ### Example 2
>
> In an essay on duress (a concept in contract law) you might need to demonstrate your *understanding* of the relevant law by showing that you *know* that there is a difference between someone entering into a contract under (i) duress; and (ii) legitimate commercial pressure. Consider:
>
> (P) There is a distinction between duress and legitimate commercial pressure. (E) In *Pao On* v *Lau Yiu Long* (1979), Scarman LJ held that, for there to be duress, there must be the presence of some factor 'which could in law be regarded as a coercion of [his] will so as to vitiate his consent' to the contract. (A) This requirement of coercion suggests that, for duress to be found, it would not be enough that a party held a stronger bargaining position and used that commercial advantage to bring pressure on another party to enter into a contract on particular terms.

(Note that, in relation to the evidence element, a case is cited as a source. You must reference sources of evidence correctly. Different law schools, and even different tutors, may adopt variations in approach to citation. You should receive guidance on the preferred approach that you should follow; see further guidance about this at 14.1.8).

14.1.5.4 Narrative and flow

It would be highly unfeasible—and result in a rather odd essay—to have a body that comprised only repetitions of the PEA model. You will need introductory, linking, and concluding sentences for paragraphs and sections, to ensure a smooth narrative which flows well and which your reader can follow. A good narrative is easier to read and understand, and, as such, is a demonstration of good writing skills. A useful test of narrative is to check that, certainly within a paragraph or section, you can point to a clear link between a particular sentence and those that precede and follow it. See how this works in the continuation of Example 2, where there has been added an introductory (I) and a linking (L) sentence. (Once you have done this, if minded, you could re-read this paragraph to assess the links between sentences and hence the smoothness of the narrative.)

Example 2 (cont'd)

(I) To understand fully the concept of duress, it is beneficial to consider it in the context of commerce. (P) There is a distinction between duress and legitimate commercial pressure. (E) In *Pao On* v *Lau Yiu Long* (1979), Scarman LJ held that, for there to be duress, there must be the presence of some factor 'which could in law be regarded as a coercion of [his] will so as to vitiate his consent' to the contract. (A) This requirement of coercion suggests that, for duress to be found, it would not be enough that a party held a stronger bargaining position and used that commercial advantage to bring pressure on another party to enter into a contract on particular terms. (L) To determine whether this is the case, it is helpful to compare the facts of the following cases where duress was alleged.

- I links to P by introducing commerce, which is picked up in P by the reference to commercial pressure.
- P refers to a distinction between duress and legitimate commercial pressure, which is picked up in E by the reference to what must be present for there to be duress.
- The requirement of coercion in E is picked up in A and analysed.
- The initial conclusion reached in A is then picked up in L, which describes how that conclusion will be tested.
- You can now imagine what the first sentence of the next paragraph would be, taking a lead from L.

Avoid using linking words (e.g. 'Many academics believe . . .') which are unsupported allegations and raise issues of evidence. 14.1.9.3 discusses this further. Examples of useful linking words are included in the University of Manchester's academic phrasebank (see Further Reading). Headings and subheadings can be incredibly helpful for flow and narrative structure, because they so clearly signpost to your reader that you are changing topic, either to a new topic (using a new heading) or a related topic (using a subheading). Let your reader know which is which by formatting consistently. For example, you might use a number, and bold underlined font for main headings, a letter and bold font for sub-headings, and a roman numeral and non-bold underlined font for sub-sub-headings. Consider how this text has used formatting for a consistent style, so you can follow its structure. Sometimes, lecturers will have a preference not to use headings, perhaps specifically because they want to encourage you to use narrative and linking words, and not rely on the help that headings can give in this regard.

14.1.6 **Polishing: a hard edit**

If your essay is in word-processed form, you have no reasonable excuse for not carrying out this final element of producing a good quality essay. (Consider that previous generations of students had to physically rewrite their essays at this stage.) If you are writing an essay under timed exam conditions, then the reduced scope for this polishing stage will likely be reflected in the marking scheme, with slightly more latitude given for misspellings or referencing style.

You will achieve the best results if you make an early start and manage your time, so leave a period of time between completing your first draft and the 'polishing' element. Divide this final element into two stages, a check of content and approach; then a final edit.

14.1.6.1 **Checking content and approach**

Here you will check aspects that have already been discussed. Ask yourself the following questions *and* only answer them positively if, *on a fresh reading*, you can see sufficient evidence in your essay to support that answer:

- Knowledge and understanding: Have I consistently demonstrated *knowledge*, but, more importantly, *understanding* of the required area of law, and how?
- Application and analysis: Have I consistently demonstrated *application*, *analysis*, and/or any other intellectual skills required by the essay, including *critical thinking*, and how?
- Structure: Is there an identifiable introduction, body, and conclusion? (Note, the headings in your draft skeleton plan at Figure 14.2, 'Introduction', 'Body', and 'Conclusion' would not feature in your final essay, but these elements would certainly remain in your essay, in terms of structure and content.)
- Communication: Does my introduction not only inform readers, with clarity, but also interest and motivate them to read on, and *how*? Is my conclusion clear, reasoned, and aligned with the required intellectual skill? Have I consistently demonstrated the characteristics of good legal writing (see 14.2.1.11)?
- Sources: Within the body of the essay, have I supported each point with evidence (properly referenced) and followed up with my analysis of that evidence (the PEA model)?

Be honest in your self-assessment of your own work. Consider also swapping an essay with a colleague to obtain their feedback (you must avoid the risk of plagiarism, see 14.1.7).

14.1.6.2 **A final edit**

It is very important that you check and proofread your work (see 14.2.2.4 for further guidance). Deal with any outstanding legal writing points and make sure your writing is clear and concise.

Word count

You may have been set a word limit or target to encourage you to achieve this; even if you have not, writing concisely is wise. This means communicating clearly what you want to communicate, using as few words as necessary, and avoiding unnecessary verbiage (unlike this sentence, as we shall see). This skill takes time to develop but is invaluable. Consider the versions of the sentence before last in Example 3.

Example 3

A. This means communicating clearly what you want to communicate, using as few words as necessary, and avoiding unnecessary verbiage.

B. This means communicating clearly using as few words as necessary.

In Example 3, version B uses nine, almost 50 per cent, fewer words to communicate the same information. It has been shown that readers prefer plain language (see Trudeau, Further Reading). Therefore, even if your eyes are on a word count target, do not meet that target by using longer sentences than you need or, worse still, padding out sentences. It is a false economy as it will affect the content, quality, and clarity of your essay, and so, ultimately, your mark.

If you have exceeded the word count, you must edit out the excess. Experience dictates that it is likely you have (i) included irrelevant material, (ii) been too verbose; and/or (iii) used needless repetition, so let this list help you with your edit.

14.1.7 Plagiarism, academic honesty, and academic misconduct

 **Essential explanation**

Plagiarism

In her *Handbook for Deterring Plagiarism in Higher Education* (see Further Reading), Jude Carroll defines plagiarism as 'passing off someone else's work, whether intentionally or unintentionally, as your own for your own benefit'.

Academic honesty and academic misconduct

In *Academic honesty, Plagiarism and Cheating: A Tutorial for New Undergraduate Students* (see Further Reading), Jenny Moon defines academic honesty as 'the adoption of habits that meet agreed academic conventions and that thereby avoid the various forms of academic misconduct' and academic misconduct as the 'abuse of academic conventions unfairly to one's own advantage. The term includes examination cheating, plagiarism and collusion'.

When you are asked to produce a piece of writing as part of your studies, you should also be given clear guidance as to what will be viewed as plagiarism and the penalties that can result. Read this carefully and, if in doubt, seek clarification because, as the definition indicates, plagiarism can result from negligence, carelessness, or misunderstanding, as well as from deliberate action (such as buying student essays online or cutting and pasting from Wikipedia). Honesty and integrity are two of seven principles comprising the fundamental tenets of behaviour that the SRA, as regulator of the profession, expects all those it regulates to hold. As set out at 15.1.3, if you are planning a career in legal practice, be aware that during the application process the SRA will ask questions to determine your honesty, including specifically about academic offences (see SRA, Further Reading). So, committing plagiarism will have serious consequences for you (more than for, say, your housemate studying the history of art—provided he is not planning to practise law). It is, therefore, important to understand what plagiarism is, and how to avoid it. Of course, a significant part of your learning will result from consulting the work of others: that is how you will develop your knowledge and views on a subject. However, you must then ensure that you employ academic honesty and do not attempt to obtain marks by passing off the work of others as your own for your own benefit. Table 14.2 introduces some common examples of plagiarism, and how you can avoid them.

It is common now to submit written coursework electronically through Turnitin. This allows tutors to provide feedback and award a mark which you can then view electronically, and it also provides an originality report, checking for textual similarity against its database, to detect plagiarism. The good news is that, usually, you can submit as many drafts as you wish using Turnitin. If this is the case at your school, you should use Turnitin in advance to check your own work to detect anything which it perceives might constitute plagiarism, and revise any draft accordingly as required, before you submit your final draft.

Table 14.2 Common examples of plagiarism and how to avoid them

Example of plagiarism	How to avoid
Using the words of others in your work as if they were your own.	If you cite a source verbatim, use quotation marks to make clear this is a direct quote.
Failing properly to acknowledge words, ideas, and facts that you have obtained from the work of others.	Acknowledge all of your sources in the text and in your reference list and/or bibliography (according to the reference style you are using).
Presenting the ideas of others in your work as if they were your own.	Even if you are not citing a source verbatim, you must both acknowledge the source of the ideas and also take care with paraphrasing. If your wording is similar to the original source text, this is bad practice, even if you acknowledge the source, as you are not demonstrating understanding, which is likely to be one of the criteria against your written work is marked. Instead, focus on key words only and seek to express the idea in a way which shows you understand it and have been able to critically evaluate it.

14.1.8 Referencing

It is important that you cite and reference all the sources you refer to in your writing, and acknowledge the work of anyone to whom you have referred, not only to avoid the serious offence of plagiarism, but also to enable anyone reading your written work to find the sources to which you have referred. By being transparent and disclosing what you have read of the ideas of others, you can then enjoy taking credit for the quality of your own evaluation of those ideas.

A referencing style is a set of rules which specify exactly how to set out your reference for different sources, such as books, articles, and electronic sources. Your school should provide you with guidance on its specific referencing requirements at the start of your studies. The criteria against which your written work is marked typically will include the quality of your referencing. If you are asked to reference your work in a certain style, and you do not do this, academics will notice and you will not be awarded marks which, in fact, should be easy to achieve because following a referencing style really is quite formulaic.

It is important to digest early in your studies the rules of the referencing style you must use. Electronic referencing tools such as EndNote and Cite This For Me (see Further Reading) can help you to create an electronic database of references which you can then automatically insert into your word-processed work. If you choose to use one of these electronic referencing tools, then early adoption will help you take the most benefit from it. Once you are familiar with the information you need to provide a complete reference, you can also adopt the good practice of taking an appropriate contemporaneous record of that information as you go, so that referencing does not become a mammoth additional task you need to undertake once you have completed your written work. (Not having enough time to properly reference is another common reason students fall foul of the plagiarism rules, as well as misunderstanding what it is and how to avoid it.)

There are numerous referencing styles, although the most popular in law schools is the OSCOLA style (where citations are provided in footnotes—see the example at Figure 14.3) and

The Legal Education and Training Review Report[1] ('LETR Report') contemplates the nature of legal services and seeks to establish a framework to support and facilitate provision of these services. The market is experiencing 'a time of unprecedented change with consumer demands, technology and the regulatory system fundamentally changing the way that legal services are delivered'[2]........ Part 1[3] proposed the authors' theoretical model, which recorded their observations that change management in the public sector can be categorised into three strategies.......

You will see that the full reference is inserted by way of a **footnote**. The OSCOLA style guide (see Further Reading) will dictate layout, and you can see that the titles of the reports take italics but the title of the journal article does not; it is within quotation marks.

[1] LETR Independent Research Team, *Setting Standards: The Future of Legal Services Education and Training Regulation in England and Wales* (LETR 2013).

[2] Solicitors Regulation Authority, *Training for Tomorrow: Ensuring the Lawyers of Today Have the Skills for Tomorrow* (Solicitors Regulation Authority 2013).

[3] Catherine Shephard and Ian Anderson Todd, 'Strategies for Managing Change and the use of Paraprofessionals: a Cross-sector Study for the benefit of Post-LETR Providers of Legal Services, Part 1' (2016) 67 Northern Ireland Law Quarterly 99.

Figure 14.3 Example of a journal article referenced in OSCOLA Style

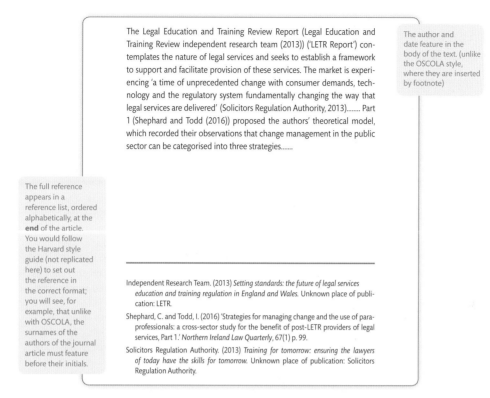

The author and date feature in the body of the text. (unlike the OSCOLA style, where they are inserted by footnote)

The Legal Education and Training Review Report (Legal Education and Training Review independent research team (2013)) ('LETR Report') contemplates the nature of legal services and seeks to establish a framework to support and facilitate provision of these services. The market is experiencing 'a time of unprecedented change with consumer demands, technology and the regulatory system fundamentally changing the way that legal services are delivered' (Solicitors Regulation Authority, 2013)........ Part 1 (Shephard and Todd (2016)) proposed the authors' theoretical model, which recorded their observations that change management in the public sector can be categorised into three strategies.......

The full reference appears in a reference list, ordered alphabetically, at the **end** of the article. You would follow the Harvard style guide (not replicated here) to set out the reference in the correct format; you will see, for example, that unlike with OSCOLA, the surnames of the authors of the journal article must feature before their initials.

Independent Research Team. (2013) *Setting standards: the future of legal services education and training regulation in England and Wales.* Unknown place of publication: LETR.

Shephard, C. and Todd, I. (2016) 'Strategies for managing change and the use of para-professionals: a cross-sector study for the benefit of post-LETR providers of legal services, Part 1.' *Northern Ireland Law Quarterly*, 67(1) p. 99.

Solicitors Regulation Authority. (2013) *Training for tomorrow: ensuring the lawyers of today have the skills for tomorrow.* Unknown place of publication: Solicitors Regulation Authority.

Figure 14.4 Example of the journal article at Figure 14.3, this time referenced in Harvard Style

in business schools, the Harvard style (where the name and date is put in the text, and the full reference in the reference list at the end—see the example at Figure 14.4). If you compare Figures 14.3 and 14.4 you will see that the references look quite different, even though they are in the same article and referencing exactly the same sources. Note, then, that if you are seeking to copy a reference you have found online or in hard copy, it will only be possible to cut and paste it if it uses the same referencing style as the one your school has asked you to use. If not, you will need to manipulate the information, from the reference you have found, into the format required by the style you have been asked to use.

14.1.8.1 OSCOLA

You should now read the Quick Reference Guide for OSCOLA online (see University of Oxford, Further Reading). While this guide is quite clear, experience suggests students accessing it for the first time appreciate some further explanation of how to use it. Examples 4–6 will guide you as to how to reference a hard copy book, a journal article, and a case. You will find it useful to access the full standard (using the link at Further Reading—it is in its 4th edition at the time of going to press) and read about how to reference these specific sources as you read the examples below, because you will see that it provides further detail which may be vital for your particular reference. Figure 14.3 illustrates how you should use footnotes to include your OSCOLA references in your written work.

Example 4

Referencing a book using OSCOLA

You will see from the opening pages of this book that it has an ISBN number. As such, whether you are reading it online or in hard copy, you should reference it as a hard copy book.

The required style is:

author, *title* (additional information, edition, publisher year).

So this book would be referenced in the OSCOLA style as follows:

Scott Slorach and others, *Legal Systems and Skills* (4th edn, OUP 2020).

Authors: You will note that, because there are more than three authors of this book, sadly Embley, Goodchild, and Shephard do not get a mention in the OSCOLA style reference of their book; they are relegated to 'and others', it is Scott Slorach, as the first mentioned author on the cover page, who receives the namecheck. (Note the Quick Reference Guide does not provide this information; you would have had to consult the full standard to obtain this.) In a footnote, the first name or initial precedes the surname, and as the name Scott, not just his initial, is used in this publication, so it appears in the reference. If it appeared in this book as S. Slorach instead, then that is how it should appear in the reference. The name is followed by a comma.

Title: The title of the book is italicised. The first letter in all major words in the book title should be capitalised, but minor words (such as 'and') should not, unless they begin the title.

Additional information: There is no further additional publication information required for this book. This can include information such as an editor or a translator.

Edition: As the first edition of this book was published in 2013, the second in 2015, and the third in 2017, the reference must make clear that you are referring to this fourth edition, published in 2020, because, while the basic format has remained the same, the text has been updated and added to significantly in the seven years since first publication.

Publisher and year: This reference shows that OUP published this book in 2020. There is no need to include Oxford as the place of publication.

Parts, chapters, pages, and paragraphs: If you wanted to refer to a particular part, chapter, page, or paragraph of this book, you would insert this at the end of the reference, after the final bracket. Use 'pt' for part, 'ch' for chapter, and 'para' for paragraph; page numbers stand alone and do not take 'p' or 'pp'. The footnote is then closed by a full stop.

Example 5

Referencing a journal article using OSCOLA

The required style is:

author, 'title' (year) volume journal name or abbreviation first page of article.

So, one of Catherine Shephard's journal articles would be referenced in the OSCOLA style as follows:

Catherine Shephard and Ian Anderson Todd, 'Strategies for Managing Change and the use of Paraprofessionals: a Cross-sector Study for the benefit of Post-LETR Providers of Legal Services, Part 1' (2016) 67 Northern Ireland Law Quarterly 99.

Authors: As there are not more than three authors, both Catherine and Ian are referred to in the reference, by their full names as they appear in the article itself. The names are followed by a comma.

Title: The title of a journal article is placed in single quotation marks. Note that this is a different format than is required for the title of a book (which takes italics).

Year: This is placed in round brackets because there is a separate volume number for this journal. If there has only been one volume in 2016, then the year, because it would identify the volume, would have been placed in square brackets.

Volume: The reference makes clear that this is volume 67. In fact, it was in issue number 1 of volume 67, but because the page numbers of issue number 2 do not begin again, but carry on from issue number 1, it is not appropriate to include the issue number (but if it had been, then the reference would include 67(1)).

Journal name or abbreviation: This shows that Catherine and Ian's article was published in the Northern Ireland Legal Quarterly (which is published by the School of Law, Queen's University, Belfast).

First page of article: This shows that their article begins on page 99. If you wanted to refer to a particular page of the article, you would still cite the first page number, then insert a comma and then the number of the page you wished to pinpoint. (So, 99, 101 would pinpoint page 101.) The footnote is closed by a full stop.

Example 6

Referencing a case using OSCOLA (using the cases from Chapter 7)

The required style for a case from before 2001 is:

Case name [year, where year identifies volume] OR (year) volume and first page of the relevant law report (court).

Donoghue v Stevenson [1932] AC 562 (HL Sc).

For cases after 2001 with a neutral citation, include the neutral citation after the case name, then continue as above, separated with a comma. As the neutral citation includes the court, this is not needed at the end.

R (Miller) v The Prime Minister [2019] UKSC 41, [2019] 3 WLR 589.

If you provide the name of the case in the body of your writing, you can omit the name from your footnote (e.g. [1932] AC 562 (HL Sc)).

14.1.9 Pitfalls to avoid

Following the guidance at 14.1.1 to 14.1.9 will mean that you avoid most of the pitfalls. However, if you find yourself indulging in any of the following, take corrective action.

14.1.9.1 Using the title as the introduction

There is no need to repeat verbatim the title or question of the essay in your introduction. The person who set the title knows it; and, in any event, it should be at the top of your essay, before the introduction. Worse still is the introduction that rephrases the title into an expanded sentence or series of sentences. Figure 14.1 and the guidance at 14.1.5 and Example 1 provide some ideas for a more influential introduction to your essay.

14.1.9.2 Journalistic style

Avoid relying on 'exciting' language to convey the strength of your argument, e.g. 'the court's disgusting and appalling treatment of the victim in this case'. Instead, seek to present strong arguments (supported by evidence from decent sources) using more temperate language, e.g. 'the court's treatment of the defendant in this case fell short of the standard that her family felt she deserved, has been widely criticised, and prompted swift reform'.

14.1.9.3 Unsubstantiated assertions

Example 7

'This was a landmark case, the facts of which raised a series of interesting questions about the important issue of the measure of damages in tort, and resulted in a major change in the law.'

If you are going to use adjectives like these, then you should be able to substantiate *why* it was a landmark case; *why* the questions were interesting; *why* the measure of damages in tort is important; and *how* the change in the law was a major one.

Other common examples of unsubstantiated assertions include, 'Clearly. . .', 'Many academics believe. . .', 'It is obvious that. . .'. Resist the temptation to use words like this in a legal essay. While you are likely hoping they add flow to your narrative, simultaneously they raise issues with evidence, because you are not supporting what you are saying. Instead, read 14.1.5.4 and consider other more effective means to introduce flow and a smooth narrative to your work.

14.1.9.4 The 'case list'

Most legal topics will involve you in referring regularly to cases and legislation in your essays. They are primary sources and, as such, are valuable points of reference and evidential material. However, you should not refer to a specific case or statute unless it is clear from your narrative *why*. A statement of the law as decided in case A followed by 'as has subsequently been applied in case B, case C and case D' fails to do any more than give dry, factual, descriptive information. Explore, instead, what is the significance of those subsequent applications? Were the facts of those cases similar or different? Does this show that case A provided a wide or narrow definition? Merely listing lots of cases only demonstrates that you have *knowledge*, or have found, lots of cases on the subject. However, without demonstrating that you have read them, thought about them, and understand their significance, you will not be able to demonstrate the understanding, application, or analysis required for a higher grade. 8.1.6 provides some helpful guidance about how to use primary sources to illustrate your argument.

14.1.9.5 Lengthy quotations and regulatory extracts

This follows from the previous pitfall. As well as showing that you understand the significance of a case or regulation, you also need to pinpoint the *specific* aspect of it that makes it significant. Therefore, if a single sentence in a judgment provides a legal definition, you do not need to include the entire paragraph which contains that sentence. Similarly, if the crux of a case is the interpretation of one word in a statute, you need only include sufficient wording to place that word in context. Be selective, relevant, and concise.

14.1.9.6 The conclusion sitting on the wall

> #### Example 8
>
> 'Thus it can be seen that this is both an important and interesting area of law which has promoted a great deal of discussion, with some legal academics claiming that it has had a wider effect than originally intended by Parliament.'

There is a strong case for saying that the previous sentence is not even a conclusion at all: it is merely a loose combination of fact and opinion, offering neither a viewpoint nor any evidence of critical thinking. See 14.1.5.2 for guidance as to how to draw a reasoned conclusion.

14.1.9.7 Overly focused on knowledge and sources

Students can tend to focus on knowledge and sources (for example, showing how many cases you know) at the expense of the other criteria (for example, analysing the impact of the most important cases, supported by reliable sources, including journal articles providing the views, and opposing views, of academics). If you and your friend consider you submitted essays based on the same law, but your friend received a mark in a better grade band, the likely explanation is that your friend paid more attention to the other assessment criteria than you did. Feedback that your work 'is too descriptive' would be consistent with this explanation. Seek feedback specifically on the strengths and weaknesses of your essay with reference to the assessment criteria.

14.1.9.8 Avoiding or ignoring formative feedback

Feel curious not fearful in your approach to feedback. If you do not understand feedback, ask. It is unlikely you are doing everything poorly, particularly as you have taken time to read the guidance in this chapter. Re-read this chapter, ask your lecturer, and use all the support and resources from your school (such as writing courses, or a seminar on critical thinking) so you can be certain to improve and enjoy delivering your best performance in the summative.

14.1.10 Developing your writing skills during your studies

Now that you understand what you will need to write, we will consider two things you can be doing now, as a student, to develop and practise these skills.

14.1.10.1 Reading

The more legal writing you read, the more examples of good and bad writing practice you will be able to draw on, avoid, or experiment with in your own written work. So, read as much and as widely as possible, including other students' work and as many examples of legal writing as you can. Good journal articles will display many of the features essential to a good essay, and will familiarise you with referencing styles.

14.1.10.2 Note-taking

You can develop your writing skills by practising effective note-taking. An important skill for all professionals is the ability to summarise. Consider the following good practice:

- Be present, engage, and understand what is being said in lectures, rather than take a verbatim note of all that is said.
- Use your reading, or electronic lecture capture, to consider the detail and produce a more comprehensive note.
- You can then annotate this note during subsequent class work, consolidation, and revision.
- Structure your notes effectively.
- Use headings and bullet points to order your notes logically.
- If you are not word processing your notes, consider writing on alternate lines so that you can supplement your notes later without rendering them illegible.
- You do not have to write in full sentences.
- Use technology to your advantage.
- Type notes into slides your lecturer will provide electronically.
- Capture images, for example on the whiteboard, using your mobile phone.

14.1.10.3 Characteristics of good writing

You are encouraged to read the advice at 14.2.1.11, which will apply equally during your studies and in practice.

14.2 Writing and drafting in practice

The expectation that graduates should have good writing skills is directly related to the commercial requirements of professions and businesses, which operate in an increasingly competitive market and need to be effective and efficient in carrying out their operations. A significant factor in this is communication: both internally within the organisation, and externally with clients and customers, who will make a judgment about an organisation based on the quality of its professional communications. These communications need to be clear, concise, precise, in plain English and, above all, directed to the particular requirements of the recipient (e.g. another lawyer, your client, a third party, expert, or the court). You may be writing a variety of documents, such as a case note, briefing paper, or an email to the client. Increasingly, you may be tasked with blogging or writing a social media post (see 15.10).

This section on writing and drafting examines these skills in the context of professional practice. Written skills are transferable (see 16.4.3), that is, once developed, they can be applied in a different context. Therefore, the majority of information and suggested approaches provided in this section are equally applicable to any graduate career, whether in professional or public services, finance, manufacturing, or any other industry. You can also apply many of them when dealing with questions on your law programme that require you to advise. In all cases, the requirement for quality of communication does not vary. Whatever your career path, you can distinguish yourself through your written skills.

14.2.1 **Writing in practice**

14.2.1.1 Why professionals advise in writing

Professionals need to commit their advice to writing for several reasons:

- they advise on relatively complex issues, so recording advice in writing can help a client to understand that advice by:
  - setting out clearly what has been said;
  - providing a record which recipients can read in their own time and at their own pace;
- the recipient can show the written advice to others;
- written advice creates a permanent record in the event of a query, misunderstanding, or complaint.

14.2.1.2 Formats for professional writing

Professionals use a variety of formats to communicate their advice in writing, including the most common:

- a letter (see Figure 14.5);
- an email (see Figure 14.6);
- an internal memorandum (see Figures 8.2, 11.3 and 12.2);
- a contemporaneous note (see Figure 11.2);
- an attendance note (see Figure 11.3);
- a research report (see Figure 8.2);

as well as other documents including briefing papers, summaries (see, for example, in Chapter 7, the summary of the *Miller* judgment prepared by the Supreme Court), and case notes. Which format is chosen will depend on a number of factors, including whether it is an internal or external communication, who the recipient is, the subject matter in question, and the formality of relationship between the writer and recipient. The overriding factor is the requirement of the recipient: therefore, in the same way that the content must be relevant to the recipient, the format must be appropriate both for the content and the recipient.

14.2.1.3 Writing a letter

Figure 14.5 is a template to help you write a professional letter which you can start to practise as a student. Download it from the online resources and save it for use whenever you write,

Writing and drafting

Chapter 14

adapting it to your own style and preferences as you go. As it explains, when you join a professional firm, they will likely have their own house style, including font, spacing and colour, which they have chosen to reflect their own image and brand.

Ensure you read the content in the body of the template, as well as the annotations. Both contain useful guidance to help you identify and avoid common errors. Let it help you with structuring your writing, give you guidance as to the content and purpose of your letter, and suggest how you can tailor your letter for different recipients. Expressing yourself in writing in a professional manner, for example when applying for jobs and work placements, will set you apart as a student and junior professional.

Letter template

This should be in longform, e.g. 28 April 202X.

If you are not sure how familiar to be, err on the side of caution and choose Mr/Mrs/Miss/Ms/Mx. If you are writing in someone else's name, check the file to see how that person has addressed the recipient in previous correspondence.

The most contemporary way is not to follow this with a comma. However, if you choose to use a comma here, you should be consistent and use a comma after 'Yours sincerely' (or faithfully) too.

Make sure the heading is not visible through any envelope window. If the matter is very sensitive, use a non-sensitive heading or dispense with a heading altogether. This is not a good way for a husband to discover his wife is divorcing him. 'Re:' has fallen out of use in larger, commercial firms. Consider, what does it add?

Firm's headed notepaper
Name of firm
Address

Recipient
Name
Address

Ref: 1234/5678
Date

Dear Recipient

Heading

The letter should begin with an opening sentence, explaining what it is about. You may need to remind the client why you are writing, for example if you are advising this client on several other matters. Consider the needs of the recipient you are writing to when deciding whether to include jargon, technical detail and citations, and the tone you wish to take.

Make your letter as clear and as easy to follow as possible. Layout and structure will help with this. Short sentences are easier to follow and also easier to write. Consider using paragraphs of an appropriate length, subheadings, and bullet points. Bullet points will be introduced with a colon:

- as a general rule
- consider whether they will help the recipient
- to understand what you are saying
- and decide whether you will
- begin each bullet with upper or lower case
- and end each bullet point with or without a full stop.

Some lawyers do not like to see bullet points in a letter. You will get to know the preferences of the person you are working for, but bullets points can add clarity when used appropriately. Do not just use them in order to write in shorthand.

Firms have their own 'house style' which will be reflected in all of their precedent documents to provide a uniform brand. This means that fonts, colour style, and layout will have been chosen for you.

If your firm does not have a house style, or if you are writing before you join your firm, use a professional looking combination. Arial or Verdana size 10 are good contemporary choices and are used by larger, commercial firms. Times New Roman size 12 is more traditional.

This is the client's file and matter reference. In practice, each client will be given a reference number (e.g. 1234), and each matter will be given a separate reference number (e.g. 5678). It is helpful to include these references here (e.g. 1234/5678) so it is clear where to file the letter and to ensure that any time spent on this letter, e.g. proofreading it, can be recorded to the correct file.

Figure 14.5 Letter template

1. Consistency

   If you do use headings or numbering, check they too are consistent.

2. Orphan headings

A 'hanging' or 'orphan' heading is one left at the bottom of the page with its related paragraph on the next page. You should ensure headings are on the same page as their related paragraph.

The text in this letter has been justified, which means that the text spreads uniformly from left to right. This looks modern, gives clean lines, and complements the use of contemporary fonts such as Arial. You can justify text quickly by highlighting it, then pressing the justify button. You can highlight all the text in a letter at the same time by pressing 'control' (or 'command') and 'a' together.

This paragraph has not been justified. It is aligned to the left, so you can see the difference. It is written in Times New Roman font. It looks less contemporary, however it is still used in house style by some, often smaller, firms.

You may wish to indent text. If so, always use the tab key for consistency, not the spacebar.

If you are asking a client to consider several options, it is helpful to list them at the end of the letter so that the client can identify them and refer to them easily. Similarly, if you need the client to send you anything then you should list it clearly at the end of the letter. This is an example of using a good structure and clear language to make your own life easier. The clearer your instructions as to what you need the client to do, the more likely the client is to follow those instructions.

Your letter should end with an appropriate closing paragraph. Leave the recipient with a good impression.

Kind regards.
Yours sincerely/ faithfully

Name of lawyer or firm
Status

This is a professional way to close a letter, but it acknowledges your familiarity with the recipient. Note the lower case 'r' in regards. Some lawyers prefer not to use the word 'kind', and simply to write 'Regards'. Whichever you choose, with formal letters it is recommended that you follow it with a formal closing too (as here) as this looks professional and sufficiently formal if the letter ever needs to be produced in court proceedings.

If you have addressed the letter to the recipient by name, you should use 'sincerely', and note that it takes a lower case 's'. If you have not used a name, but have written a 'Dear Sir' or 'Madam' letter, you must use 'faithfully' with a lower case 'f'.

The most contemporary way to do this is not to follow with a comma. However if you choose to use a comma here, you should be consistent and use a comma after 'Dear X' too.

Some letters will be signed on behalf of the firm, and it is the firm's name which should appear here. In this case, you should write the letter using 'we' not 'I' throughout.

Other letters you will sign personally, and it will be your own name that features here. In this case, you should write the letter using 'I' throughout.

If you are signing your own name, check house style. Some firms include your status, others do not.

Figure 14.5 *Continued*

> ### ⊕ Practice tip
>
> In practice, a senior lawyer may delegate the writing of a letter to a more junior lawyer (see 15.5). She will then read, check, and make any amendments to the letter before she signs it. In other words, you *ghost write* the first draft of the letter to be sent by someone else.
>
> This is a specific skill in itself. It involves you having to write in the style, manner, and tone of someone else. For example, if you would usually address the client as Miss Shephard, but the partner in whose name the letter will be sent out is on first name terms with the recipient, then you should write, for example, 'Dear Catherine' as the salutation in the letter rather than 'Dear Miss Shephard'. You should not leave any clues for the recipient that the person who read, checked, then signed the letter did not actually write it.
>
> Your aim is to write the letter so well that the senior lawyer will be able to sign and send it without having to amend it substantially first.

14.2.1.4 Writing an email

The guidance set out in the letter template at 14.2.1.3 applies equally here. You should write your email in the same professional manner as you would write a letter. They have the same status, and both could be scrutinised in court. Use tone, rather than shorthand, to convey your sentiments.

Email can discourage you from paying as much attention to your writing as you would if you were writing a letter, and it is very easy to send a message without checking it first. Prepare the body of your email in a word-processing package, print, and check it. You can then cut and paste the text into your email.

If your email is quite long, consider whether it would be better to write a letter and attach it to an email instead. Bear in mind that if the recipient is reading the email from a smartphone, opening an attachment can sometimes present problems. You can enquire about this when you ask clients how they would prefer to receive letters.

Figure 14.6 provides a template which will help you with the structure, style, and content of any email. It includes an excerpt of some sample advice to a client about a sale of goods issue, to give you an idea of how the content might look. (You will find it helpful to remind yourself of Example 1 in Chapter 12.). Note that this advice is for learning purposes only and does not constitute legal advice. You will see that it is structured, with headings that reflect the content of Figure 9.1. You can also see that if you draft your research report well (using Figure 8.2), then this will pay dividends because you can use excerpts from it (including headings) in your letter. Remember, however, that unlike with your report, which you will be sending internally to your supervisor, the recipient of your letter will be an external client, who is not likely to be a lawyer, and so you may need to make some amendments in terms of jargon and detail, for clarity. Note also that, once you have written one letter on sale of goods, then that letter will also form a useful precedent for any future letters you need to write to different clients, but note that while the relevant law is the same, the facts are (and therefore the advice is) likely to be different.

Email template

From: trainee@lawfirm.com
To: client@xltd.com
CC:
BC:
Date: 1 December 202X
Subject: Recovery of £X plus VAT from Y

Dear [*Recipient*]

I trust that you are keeping well and that business continues to be busy. In consultation with my supervisor, *[...]*, I have now had an opportunity to consider the present position in your case. I am writing to explain this position, as I said I would when we last met.

Your instructions

On [*date*] you instructed us to act on behalf of your company, X Limited ('X'), to recover from Y Limited ('Y') the sum of £Z plus VAT, arising out of a contract where X would manufacture and sell [*goods*] to Y.

According to my instructions the chronology of the case is as follows:

[*...omitted for the purposes of this work*]

Your objective

X is seeking to recover in full from Y the sum of £Z plus VAT.

The legal issues

There is a valid contract between X and Y. The legal basis of X's claim against Y is breach of that contract, as the amount to be paid to X by Y under the contract remains outstanding. However this position must be considered against the reason Y has put forward for its refusal to pay, namely that the [*goods*]:

1. did not correspond with the description that you had given during the pre-contract representations
2. were not of satisfactory quality, and
3. were not fit for purpose.

I will now consider each in turn each of these grounds.

Writing and drafting

Chapter 14

Figure 14.6 Email template

The relevant law and how it applies to the facts of the problem

1. Correspondence with description

Y maintains that the [*goods*] which X delivered to it did not correspond with the description that X had given during the pre-contract representations. The law (s13 Sale of Goods Act 1979) requires that goods sold in the course of a business must correspond with the description that you, as Seller, gave to Y, as Buyer.

I note that in your sales literature you claim that the [*goods* ...]. This may be significant in determining the understanding and intentions of Y during the negotiations with X, about the precise suitability of the [*goods to* ...], before X and Y entered into the contract.

2. Satisfactory quality

Y also maintains that the goods were not of satisfactory quality. The law (s14(2) Sale of Goods Act 1979) states that where the goods are sold in the course of business there is an implied condition that the goods are of satisfactory quality. The key issue is what is regarded as satisfactory quality. The assessment is made objectively, so it is based on what a reasonable person, rather than Y itself, would consider to be satisfactory quality, taking into account the description of the goods, the price and all other relevant circumstances. For example, more expensive goods should be of higher quality than would be expected of cheaper alternatives.

There is an expert report providing [...'s] guidance about whether the [*goods*] were of satisfactory quality. [...*omitted for the purposes of this work*]

3. Fitness for purpose

Finally, Y maintains that the goods were not fit for purpose. The law (s14(3) Sale of Goods Act 1979) requires that goods sold in the course of a business should be reasonably fit for the purpose for which the buyer (Y) intended.

Once again, the representations made by both X and Y in the negotiations before they entered into the contract will be relevant. If Y can evidence it made clear to X the precise purpose for which it intended to use the goods, then X may find it difficult to dispute this. The expert report appears to support that Y's argument would have some weight if the matter proceeds to litigation.

Conclusion and advice

Any and all representations that may have been made by X to Y before entering into the contract for the sale of the [goods] is emerging as a key issue. It will be helpful if we can meet to discuss this further, and also your view as to how X might be able to argue against the three reasons Y has given for its refusal to pay, or not.

Figure 14.6 *Continued*

In light of those reasons Y has put forward, I would advise that it is not in X's interests to consider issuing court proceedings against Y right now.

Next steps

1. We need to arrange a further meeting to discuss this case further. I am free Monday and Tuesday of next week. Please let me know which you prefer, or suggest a few alternative dates in the following week.
2. Before we meet, can you give some thought to the pre-contractual representations, and in particular send me any evidence of them you can find.

I look forward to discussing this matter further with you when we meet.

Kind regards.
Yours sincerely

Name of Lawyer
Firm
Firm's address
Telephone number
Website

This information is usually contained in an auto signature, in house style if available, which you can prepare and arrange to be added to an email automatically when you send it. It may also include logos and references to social media pages, but beware attaching anything that will annoy the recipient in terms of the amount of hard drive space it takes up.

Figure 14.6 *Continued*

14.2.1.5 Writing a research report

Figure 8.2 sets out a template you can use, and Chapter 8 provides further guidance on legal research.

14.2.1.6 Writing a contemporaneous note

Figure 11.2 sets out a template you can use, and Chapter 11 provides further guidance on note-taking specifically in the context of interviewing, but which is transferable to other circumstances when you might need to take a note.

14.2.1.7 Writing up an attendance note

Figure 11.3 sets out a template you can use to convert your contemporaneous note into a formal attendance note, and Chapter 11 provides further guidance about this, again specifically in the context of an interview, but which is transferable into other scenarios when you may wish to write an attendance note.

Familiarising yourself with these templates and guidance for professional writing will help you to develop good writing skills which are valuable wherever your career may lead. There follows some advice on the specific considerations that apply when advising in writing.

14.2.1.8 Quality of advice

Quite simply, the advice you deliver as a professional has to be right. The first step is to ensure full understanding of the elements in Figure 9.1, including the facts, the client's objectives, the relevant law, and how it applies to the client's situation (and these areas are reflected in the headings in Figure 14.6). Without this understanding, it is impossible to give advice tailored to the client. If you do not understand the law, you will be unable to make it clear to clients. If clients do not find the advice clear, they will, at best, be unhappy with the professional service being provided, and may not engage that lawyer again. As Chapter 20 explains, lawyers rely on repeat business from clients, so failure to impress with quality work could lead to losing a client to a competitor. At worst, the advice could be incorrect and, being written, it is in the form of permanent record which could be used in court in the event of a negligence claim (see Chapter 13, Example 1). You will find guidance on problem-solving questions in Chapter 9. The characteristics of good writing (see 14.2.1.11) apply equally to written legal advice.

14.2.1.9 Tone

You should aim to use a tone which is both personal and professional, but neither over-familiar nor too terse.

Tone should be relatively measured in order to convey professionalism. Recent graduates often find it difficult to know how they should express emotion in their professional writing. Everyone is different, and some people express their feelings more than others, however you need to avoid sounding 'over the top'. For example, if writing to a recently bereaved person, it is of course appropriate to express condolences, but 'You really must be absolutely devastated and I just cannot find words to express my absolute sympathy for your dreadful loss' might come across as a little disingenuous if there is no personal link to either the client or the deceased. Similarly, there should be no scope for exclamation marks in written advice to clients, no matter how alarming their predicament may be.

Once an ongoing professional relationship has been formed with clients, then it is easier to use a specific tone appropriate for them. Until that point, the best advice is to use a measured, professional tone, which still conveys approachability.

You should avoid the use of abbreviations such as 'shouldn't', 'won't', and 'haven't', even if using email. The use of instant messaging has also introduced new problems with abbreviation. To state the obvious, using message-speak such as '2' rather than 'to' or 'B' instead of 'be' is wholly inappropriate. Alarmingly, however, this practice is creeping into student emails, essays, and assessments on an increasingly frequent basis (see Yale Repository, Further Reading).

14.2.1.10 Jargon or 'legalese'

It may be appropriate to use legal terms without explanation when writing to another lawyer or a professional with some knowledge of the law in a particular field.

> #### Example 9
>
> A practising business lawyer will often be instructed by a company secretary. A company secretary is often a lawyer or, if not, will be familiar with areas of company law. This is an example when it may be appropriate to use jargon when writing to a client.

Advice should always be in language understandable to the recipient. If you must refer to jargon, for example because your recipient will need to be familiar with it when reading some documents, or appearing in court, then you should decipher it for them. Overall, give consideration to just how much legal detail it is essential to provide. While it is important for you as a *professional* to understand the background behind advice, the recipient *client* may not need or want to know the specific detail that supports it.

While undoubtedly lawyers used to enjoy showing how clever they were by peppering their sentences with Latin and using as many words as possible that a non-lawyer would find difficult to understand, there has been a significant move away from this practice relatively recently. Increased competition within the profession has seen law firms market themselves on putting the client first. Everyone appreciates plain English (see Trudeau, Further Reading).

Similarly, a client is unlikely to be impressed by the use of needless legalese, even such as 'vendor' or 'offeror' when 'seller' would convey the meaning perfectly well. The best lawyers are able not only to understand legal complexities, but they have the additional skill, which not all lawyers have, to break down those complexities and explain them in a way which a non-lawyer can understand.

The point is not that a client would be tempted to start looking for a new lawyer simply because his lawyer used the word vendor. However, if that client happens to come across one of these better lawyers who can and does use the same language that the client does, do not underestimate how impressed that client will be, and how it will increase rapport.

14.2.1.11 Characteristics of good writing

Legal concepts are often complex and, whether in the context of legal studies or professional practice, the ability to communicate difficult concepts clearly and concisely in writing in a way that is easy to understand is a valuable and transferable skill (see 16.4.3).

Before considering the fundamental characteristics of good writing, note that no-one can write well without sound knowledge and understanding of the subject matter. You should never begin writing until you understand what you are writing about. When you do start writing, you must consider each of the characteristics set out below and ensure high standards. If you do not, then, at worst, you will fail to communicate what you actually mean which can result in lost marks (in practice units) and, in practice itself, lost integrity. At best, you will appear careless. Note that we have used the word 'expectation' in relation to writing skills at 14.2. They are expected of you. Therefore, you will not receive great plaudits for getting them right: however, you will lose credibility if you get them wrong. While there is not necessarily a correlation between the two, a reader may well conclude that if you make errors in your writing, then your knowledge, understanding, and advice may not be completely sound either.

We will now examine the main criteria against which a recipient of your written work is likely to judge you, together with guidance as to how you can make sure you are judged positively. Common mistakes are also discussed, on the basis that the more familiar you are with the potential errors you could make, the less likely you are to make those errors.

Spelling

Good spelling is essential. While most spelling errors will be picked up by a spell-check facility, an amount sufficient to be noticeable will not. Some words are easily confused with others which sound alike. Common examples include 'complimentary/complementary', 'there/their/they're', 'were/we're', and 'its/it's'. So if, for example, you say 'X did not accept that there goods were faulty', a spell-check facility will not identify that 'there' should be spelled 'their'. Another common example is 'judgment/judgement'. In a legal context, the correct spelling is 'judgment', however the spell-check will not know that you are discussing the law and so will not detect this error. You will need to learn to identify these errors. If this does not come naturally to you, consider keeping your own checklist of words like this to remind you what to look out for, or invest in a book to help you such as *i before e (except after c)* (see Parkinson, Further Reading).

In addition to the standard words that can evade a spell-check, there will be legal terminology and proper nouns, such as case names, which you should take care to spell correctly.

Punctuation

You need to be familiar with how and when to use punctuation, including capital letters, full stops, exclamation marks, question marks, colons, semicolons, commas, and apostrophes. Your sentences should be properly punctuated, as punctuation can change the entire meaning of a sentence. Lynne Truss refers to some excellent examples in her book about punctuation called *Eats, Shoots and Leaves: The Zero Tolerance Approach to Punctuation*. This example of hers illustrates the point very effectively.

Example 10

How would you punctuate this sentence?

A woman without her man is nothing

You may have used some commas, to this effect:

A woman, without her man, is nothing.

However, consider the entirely different meaning if you had punctuated differently:

A woman: without her, man is nothing.

You should always pay particular attention when using an apostrophe, as this tends to be the most commonly misunderstood and misused punctuation mark. If you struggle to put apostrophes in the right place, or simply do not use them at all (which is becoming increasingly common), you must address this.

You should also make sure you use punctuation consistently. For example, you may choose whether to put a full stop after a bullet point. However, if you choose to use the full stop, make sure you do so after each bullet point.

If punctuation is something you find difficult, then Truss's book is a good place to start, as is the BBC adult literacy website (see Further Reading). Your school may also provide writing clinics or programmes. As ever, the earlier you begin, the more time you will have to practice, and enjoy making mistakes when they do not matter.

Grammar

Your sentences should be grammatically correct. As with spell-check, the grammar-check of your word processing software can help (as can an application such as Grammarly—see Further Reading) but they are not infallible. You must write sentences in prose and they must contain a verb. Do not write in note form. You should not start sentences with conjunctions such as 'and' or 'but'. Make sure you do not write as you might speak, for example writing 'could of' and 'should of'. These are common errors. The correct grammar is 'could have' and 'should have'.

You should also pay attention as to how you structure your sentences. It is possible to write an active sentence, 'I opened the door', or a passive one, 'The door was opened'. In certain scenarios, using the passive can be quite helpful. Consider, for example, how the passive sentence, 'It appears that a mistake has been made', can have a conciliatory effect compared to the active 'It appears that you have made a mistake'. However, in law, as a general rule you should avoid the passive. This is because, in law, it is very important to identify where obligations and liabilities lie. If you fail to do so, you risk ambiguity, which can be read as not being confident about a viewpoint or piece of advice. Compare the following examples.

Example 11

Passive:	The goods were not delivered on time.
Active:	X did not deliver the goods on time.
Passive:	Liability could arise for failure to take steps to prevent accidents.
Active:	Y could be held liable for failing to take steps to prevent accidents.
Passive:	The form must be filed at Companies House within 14 days.
Active:	The company must file the form at Companies House within 14 days.

In writing generally, and in professional correspondence specifically, you should take care with reflexive pronouns, as they are increasingly misused. 'Yourself' and 'myself' are not more sophisticated versions of 'you' and 'me'. It is perfectly correct to use 'you' and 'me' in a sentence in a professional context. 'If you have any questions, please contact me' is correct. In contrast, 'If you have any questions, please contact myself' is not. 'You and Jack must attend the meeting' is correct. Again, 'Yourself and Jack must attend the meeting' is not. 'Yourself' and 'myself' have a specific grammatical use as reflexive pronouns, which means they must refer back to an earlier pronoun in the same sentence, such as 'I cut myself'. They can also be used correctly as intensive pronouns, to provide emphasis, 'You, yourself, knew this at the time'.

Structure

You do not want the recipients of your writing to find reading your work a difficult task. Therefore, your writing should follow a logical structure which enhances clarity. Consider how you will structure your writing before you start to write. When you are quite new to professional legal writing it helps to sketch out a skeleton plan of relevant headings and content before you start (as with your skeleton essay plan at Figure 14.2), and we have provided templates for all of the forms of writing you will encounter as a junior lawyer, or as a student on a practice unit, to help you (see 14.2.1.2).

Generally, short sentences are both easier to write and easier to follow than long sentences. Write as concisely as you can, without losing essential detail. Avoid tautology such as 'In my opinion I think that', or padding such as 'It has frequently been thought that'.

That said, in law, scenarios and issues can be complex, and even if you write succinctly your interpretation and advice may be lengthy. Very long paragraphs can be off-putting and difficult to follow, so you should subdivide a long paragraph into several smaller paragraphs, and consider whether headings and subheadings would help the recipient to read your writing. For example, if you were writing about remedies in contract law, you might use paragraphs headed 'damages', 'rescission', and 'specific performance', rather than write about everything in one unwieldy paragraph. This would help the recipient both to identify the main remedies available and also to locate information easily about any one remedy in particular. With more lengthy pieces of writing, where you need to cross-refer to different paragraphs within the body of that work, consider numbering the paragraphs, so you can refer to 'paragraph 4' rather than, for example, 'the paragraph about damages'.

Clarity

You must write clearly and in the way that best promotes the recipient's understanding. Write in a way which shows you live in the modern world and avoid affecting an archaic writing style, reminiscent of a Dickensian courtroom. Words and phrases such as 'henceforth', 'hereinbefore mentioned', and 'of even date' pepper poor work. There is no real advantage to be gained by trying to make writing look or sound like this, and it can inhibit clarity of expression.

Choose language carefully. Generations of students have used ambiguous language in essays to get round difficult issues they do not fully understand. Equally, passive language (see Example 11) can cause unintentional ambiguity. Ambiguous language is, by definition, unclear and you will not prosper if a lecturer considers that you have not evidenced understanding. *Levicom v Linklaters* (see Further Reading) shows the potential effect of ambiguity in legal practice. In this case, the court held that two letters of advice sent by lawyers to their client (about the client's likelihood of success in litigation proceedings) were negligent, not because of the views the lawyers held, but because the lawyers did not set out their views sufficiently clearly. Therefore, make sure not only that you understand the point you are making, but also that you state your point clearly and unambiguously so that anyone else reading it will also understand it.

14.2.2 Drafting

14.2.2.1 Why lawyers draft

There is considerable overlap between writing and drafting. Drafting involves writing, but while the examples of writing we have considered are communications of information, the term drafting tends to be used specifically to describe the task of creating a document. This could be anything from form-filling, to drafting company meeting documentation, to creating a written contract setting out legally binding rights and obligations. These documents can be a single page through to several hundreds of pages long, and range from the very simple to the very complex.

Lawyers frequently need to draft documents in order to give legal effect to their clients' instructions, and these documents must comply with all legal and procedural requirements. For example, you cannot circumvent the law on murder simply by drafting a document whereby a client agrees in writing that someone can kill her (as the ongoing public debate surrounding euthanasia has highlighted). So, as with legal writing, drafting must be underpinned by a sound knowledge and understanding of the relevant law and procedure. However, again as with legal writing, to draft within the law in a way which effectively and unambiguously carries out a client's instructions, calls for a skills requirement in addition to knowledge of the law.

During your training or as a paralegal, you are likely to be working on a range of different client matters, and drafting different documents for different people. Be prepared to draft an entire document, but equally, be prepared to draft a discrete clause for inclusion within a document. There is more than one way to draft to achieve the same legal effect, so make sure you understand what you are drafting, and that one supervisor might like you to use one terminology (e.g. 'chairman') and another a different one (e.g. 'chairperson').

14.2.2.2 Drafting a contract

Lawyers draft contracts for all sorts of different reasons. However, most contracts follow a similar structure. Figure 14.7 sets out the common structure and parts found in most contracts.

Contract template

You should define terms which you intend to use frequently in the contract. Then make sure you refer consistently to these terms in the body of the contract. Definitions should be in alphabetical order.

It does not matter whether 'the' is inside or outside the quotation marks, or whether the quotation marks are single or double, but you must be consistent.

This is an example of an active sentence. It makes clear who is granting the rights in a way that a passive sentence such as 'X is granted the following rights' would not.

The discussion in 7.1.3.2 about language which grants 'rights, obligations and prohibitions' in a statute, will help you with your drafting for this clause 3, clause 4, and clause 7.

AGREEMENT

Dated: [   ]
Parties: (1)
 (2)

THIS AGREEMENT is made the day of BETWEEN

(1) [Name] of [Address] (the '[defined term]'); and
(2) [Name] of [Address] (the '[defined term]').

IT IS AGREED as follows:

1. DEFINITIONS

In this agreement:
1.1 the ' ' means [ ];
1.2 the ' ' means [ ]; and
1.3 the ' ' means [ ].

2. OPERATIVE PROVISIONS

This is where the clauses granting rights and imposing obligations will feature. You will structure the document so perhaps one clause grants rights, the next imposes obligations, the next deals with any payments, and so on.

3. GRANTING OF RIGHTS

The [   ] gives the [   ] the following rights subject to the provisions of this agreement:
3.1 to do X;
3.2 to do Y; and
3.3 to do Z.

Ensure numbering is consistent and sequential.

4. OBLIGATIONS

[   ] must do A on or before [   ].

5. PAYMENT

[   ] must pay to [   ]:
5.1 a deposit of £ [   ] on or before [   ] pm on [   ]; and
5.2 a further sum of £ [   ] on or before [   ] pm on [   ].

6. OTHER CLAUSES TO REFLECT THE CLIENT'S SPECIFIC INSTRUCTIONS

You must make sure that your drafting carries out all of the client's instructions.

7. RESTRICTIONS

[   ] must not:
7.1 do A;
7.2 do B; or
7.3 do C.

Figure 14.7 Contract template

Ensure cross-references are accurate.

8. BOILERPLATE CLAUSES

At the end of every agreement, whatever the context, you will find similar clauses referred to as boilerplate clauses. They include the following clauses.

9. LIABILITY AND INDEMNITY

[   ] must indemnify [   ] against [   ].

10. TERMINATION

The rights granted in clause 3 will end:

10.1 immediately on [   ]; or

10.2 on not less than [   ] month's notice expiring at any time given by either party to the other.

11. ASSIGNMENT

The benefit of this agreement [is] [is not] assignable.

12. NOTICES

All notices given by either party under any provision of this agreement must be:

12.1 in writing; and

12.2 addressed to [ ] at [ ] and served:

    12.2.1 by hand; or

    12.2.2 sent by registered post; or

    12.2.3 sent by recorded delivery; or

    12.2.4 sent by email to [. . .], provided that a confirmatory copy is delivered by hand or sent by registered post or recorded delivery on the same day.

SIGNED by [   ])
in the presence of)
SIGNED by [   ])
in the presence of)

Be clear by using 'or' or 'and' whether provisions are in the alternative.

You must choose the correct signing (or **attestation**) clause. Some documents need to be signed as a deed, others do not. Obtaining a witness is always helpful in any event, for evidentiary purposes. You should ensure that the signing clause is suitable for the person signing. If it is a company, consider how it will be signing—by company seal, or one or more of its officers? Once the document is signed, no amendment should be made (see Hyde, Further Reading).

Figure 14.7 *Continued*

14.2.2.3 Characteristics of good and bad drafting

The characteristics of good writing set out at 14.2.1.11 apply equally here. There are also the following additional considerations particular to drafting to examine.

Using and adapting a precedent

Law firms tend to maintain precedent banks of documents for their lawyers to use as a basis for their drafting. These precedents are drafted in general terms and must be adapted to suit the situation of individual clients. For example, a simple precedent licence may be adapted to suit any type of licensing, perhaps with some guidance notes about legal issues to be borne in mind depending on the situation (e.g. if the sale of alcohol is involved). Where a firm does not have its own precedents it may subscribe to other resources such as the electronic resources Practical Law, Lexis®PSL, or the *Encyclopaedia of Forms and Precedents* (see Chapter 8 and Further Reading, Chapter 14).

Lawyers may also refer to a different type of 'precedent', namely the use of a document prepared by the firm previously that recorded a similar situation to that which a client needs. For example, a document drafted to grant a licence for the hire of a hall for a private event may then be amended by another lawyer to grant a licence to hold a festival in a field.

Precedents have significant advantages in that they promote efficiency (and so can help to keep costs down and allow firms to charge competitively) and they allow know-how to be passed on within a firm. However, they can have disadvantages too. First, the law is constantly changing, and so it can be a full-time job to make sure the firm's precedents are kept up to date. Indeed it is common for larger firms to employ *professional support lawyers* to do this job. If precedents are not kept up to date then they need to be treated with caution. The second disadvantage is that precedents can encourage and perpetuate poor drafting. Using a precedent which has been used before and appears to have worked can inhibit a lawyer from changing anything in it, even if it is not drafted as clearly as it might otherwise have been. Both of these disadvantages can be overcome if you use precedents responsibly. Your reader's needs, as ever, are paramount and should inform your drafting, which generally should be in clear English. However, caution must be exercised in changing wording, as in some cases words have been specifically chosen for maximum benefit under the law: if the wrong deletion is made, the intended effect of the agreement may be reduced or even negated. A good precedent bank will contain explanatory or guidance notes to deal with issues like this.

Consistency

It is common for many items to be repeated frequently within the body of any contract. It is important that any reference to the same item is consistent throughout the contract to avoid any ambiguity as to the intent of the parties. The use of definitions (seen in Figure 14.7) is a common means of ensuring consistency. The proofreading example below sets out common inconsistencies that can appear in a contract in error.

Cross-referencing

Within contracts, clauses will often refer to other clauses for interpretation or meaning. Cross-referencing by clause number is a standard approach to ensure that the correct clause is referred to. This too must be consistent and, given that many contracts go through a number of drafts with many amendments to both the substance and number of clauses, it is good practice, on a final proofread (see Example 13), to check that each cross-reference refers to the correct clause.

Clarity

As a contract sets out legal rights and obligations, clarity is particularly important. In fact, there is a specific rule of law about contract interpretation, known as the *contra proferentem* rule, which reinforces this (see DLA Piper, Further Reading, and 4.4.3 for other rules of interpretation).

Contracts commonly impose deadlines or timing provisions, and, as Example 12 illustrates, it is common to see examples of poor drafting in this regard.

Essential explanation

The *contra proferentem* rule

This rule provides that anything which is unclear or ambiguous will be construed against the party who included it in the contract.

Example 12

Consider the following clause:

1. The Buyer must pay a deposit to the Seller of £1000 within 7 days.

The clause is unclear as to when the 7 days start to run. If this clause was in a contract signed on 1 September, could the deposit be paid on 8 September? The wording could be improved as follows:

1. The Buyer must pay a deposit to the Seller of £1000 within 7 days beginning with the date of this agreement.

Another example is:

2. The Buyer must pay a deposit to the Seller of £1000 before 22 December.

This can be improved as follows:

2. The Buyer must pay a deposit to the Seller of £1000 on or before [5pm on] 21 December.

14.2.2.4 Checking work: proofreading

A final stage in drafting, which is equally applicable to all pieces of legal writing, is to ensure before you send it out that the work looks exactly as intended. This checking requires the skill of proofreading.

Whatever your skills as a writer, you must take time to ensure no errors have crept into written work during the document production process. Many pieces of writing fall at this hurdle, as the practical processes of dictation (see 14.2.3) and word processing afford ample opportunity for unexpected errors to be incorporated. These are often referred to as 'typos' (short for *typographical errors*), which conveniently sounds if as the error is with the word processing system rather than the person with responsibility for checking the document. Turner (Further Reading) offers a cautionary tale of the dangers of typographical errors.

Generally, proofreading benefits from time and attention, which can be difficult when working under pressure. However, it also benefits significantly from practice. If time allows, putting work to one side for a while before proofreading it can be helpful.

⊙ Practice tip

Proofreading changes made to larger documents is a common task for trainees in legal practice. One technique is that one trainee reads from the hand-amended 'marked up' document, and another checks that everything has been incorporated properly into the newly typed draft. Some firms draw up a 'checking rota' to make sure the burden is spread among all trainees regardless of which seat they are in.

Example 13 helps to illustrate some common proofreading errors.

Example 13

You are asked to test your existing proofreading skills by marking, in pencil, any errors on this draft section from a document granting a licence to store wine in part of a warehouse.

1. DEFINITIONS

In this Licence:

1.3 the 'Warehouse' means the building at Unit 4 Pickstock Industrial Estate, Pickstock, Yorkshire PK6 9NW edged green on the plan annexed to this licence.

1.4 "the Plan" means the plan attached to this agreement;

1.5 the 'Licence Period' means the period from and including the date of this license until and including the date on which the Hirer's rights under Clause 1 are terminated in accordance with Clause 4;

1.6 the 'Licence Fee' means £800 including VAT; and

1.7 'the Storage Area' means the the area shown edged red on the Plan;

2. THE LICENCE

The Licensor gives the Hirer the exclusive right for the Licence Period to use:

2(a) the Storage Area (or such other area as the Owner may allocate by written notice to the Hirer;

2(b) the designated parking space for parking one car or van; and

2(iii) The entrance hall and corridors edged blue on the Plan for access to and from the storage area

How did you do? Set out below are the errors from Example 13, together with some practical steps to improve your proofreading skills.

Spelling

If you dictate a draft, or mark it up for amendment illegibly, this may result in spelling errors. Alternatively you may also be checking the work of another fee-earner who is not as good at spelling as you.

As described in this chapter, the on-screen spell-check facility can help here, but it will not identify some errors. For example, in clause 1.5, 'licence' (the noun) was spelled as 'license' (the verb) in error. The spell-check facility would not identify this as a spelling error.

Punctuation

As with spelling, punctuation errors may find their way into a draft. For example, clause 1.3 ends with a full stop rather than a semi-colon; clause 1.7 with a semi-colon rather than a full stop, and clause 2(iii) is missing a full stop.

Layout

Layout should be consistent. Here a double space was used in error between clause 1.6 and 1.7, and clause 2 is aligned differently to clause 1.

Numbering

It is common for word-processing software to lead to errors in numbering and cross-referencing. Here the numbering began with 1.3, and 2(c) had become 2(iii) in error. There also appears to be a cross-referencing error in clause 1.5; the cross-reference to the clause giving rights to the Hirer should be to clause 2, not clause 1.

Defined terms

Defined terms present several opportunities for error. First, if a term is defined, the defined term should be used throughout. Here clause 1.3 refers to the 'plan annexed to this licence' rather than the defined term 'Plan'. Second, ensure consistency. Here some definitions use single inverted commas, some use double; some include 'the' within the definition, some do not. Third, consider whether there is a need to define a term. There is no need to define a term which is used only once, but any term used several times should be defined. This document refers to 'Licence', 'licence', and 'agreement' when it should use one, clearly defined, term.

The 'find' function in word processing software can help here. Use it to find each defined term throughout the document, and check the defined term is used consistently and looks the same throughout. There is no 'correct' format for a defined term; look to the firm's house style for guidance as to whether to use single or double inverted commas and whether to include 'the' within the definition.

General typographical errors

In this draft, clause 1.7 repeated 'the' in error, clause 2(a) did not close brackets, and clause 2(iii) begins with a capital letter.

14.2.3 **Dictation**

You are probably aware that many lawyers and other professionals use dictation to record written communications and, in some cases, elements of drafting. Many find this a more efficient process, particularly if they cannot type at an appropriate speed. Dictation is the process of speaking into a dictaphone voice recorder (or voice recognition software) what you want to write (see Example 14). A secretary, or the software, will then transcribe your dictation for you to review. This process can be awkward when you start. Unless you use voice recognition software during your studies, your first attempt is likely to be either during work experience or at the start of your graduate career. You may be sharing an office, or in an open-plan environment, so your performance will be relatively public (although Covid's arrival may change this). At first it can be very hard to think as you speak, structure your work properly, and also give appropriate instructions to the transcriber. With dictation, you must speak everything that you wish to find on the page, so you need to dictate punctuation, paragraphs, heading, fonts, capitals, spelling, and so on. A kind secretary may plug the punctuation gaps for you, but it is something of a rite of passage to be presented with your first effort at dictation consisting of one long, useless, unpunctuated paragraph. If this happens to you, do not worry. You are not the first person this has happened to, and you will not be the last.

When you first begin to learn dictation, you may struggle to see how it could ever be a more efficient process than simply typing your own work. However, you should persevere, because although it may initially seem completely alien and inefficient, with practice it will suddenly click and, in retrospect, you will wonder why you found it so difficult in the first place.

Example 14

This is what you would have to dictate for the first few lines of the document used in the proofreading exercise at Example 13:

(Bold heading)(figure) one (all capitals) definitions (new line, capital I) in this (capital L) licence (colon, new line, figure) one point one the (open inverted commas, capital W) warehouse (close inverted commas) means the building at (capital U) unit (figure) 4 (capital P) pickstock (capital I) industrial (capital E) estate (comma) . . . and so on through to . . . (full stop).

⊕ Summary

- Legal writing is a fundamental skill and your school will test it against assessment criteria.
- Through legal writing, you should be able to demonstrate understanding of the law and specific legal intellectual skills: use Table 14.1 to determine what the title is asking you to do.
- When writing a legal essay, follow the strategy set out at Figure 14.1 and begin by drafting a skeleton using Figure 14.2.
- Dry, factual, descriptive essay writing will attract a poorer mark than writing which includes critical analysis.
- Writing and drafting skills are a core part of the work of lawyers and other professionals.
- Figures 14.5 and 14.6 will help you to write effective letters and emails.
- Figure 14.7 will help you to understand the basics of contract drafting.
- In both academia and practice, considered and careful review of written work before submission or sending is vital.

What the professionals say

You soon realise that everything you write is either on the clock, against the clock, or both. That pressure, combined with the need to ensure everything you write is effective in the eyes of others and can withstand being crawled over with a fine tooth comb if it is ever scrutinised in court, soon instils a respect for legal writing skills that you didn't expect you would ever have.

Stedman Harmon, Legal Counsel, Aviva plc

❓ Practical exercises

Consider how you would answer these questions. Reflect on how your reading of this chapter has has informed or changed how you might answer them. How might you use what you have learned in an interview or exam situation?

1. Think about your own writing skills. What are your strengths and weaknesses? What can you start doing now to address your weaknesses in good time before you start to apply for, or begin, graduate employment?

2. When reading a newspaper, try to read one article critically for proofreading errors. Did you find any? If so, what steps would you take to prevent such errors in your own writing?

3. Reflect on an instance where correspondence (which you either wrote or received) did not go as you had planned. Analyse what went wrong and how it was, or should have been, corrected.

4. Do you think it is fair for clients to expect a lawyer's written work to be entirely free from any proofreading errors? What are the arguments for and against? Which are you most persuaded by?

 *Visit the **online resources** for the authors' reflections and to check your progress.*

Further reading

BBC adult literacy website. **Available online at: http://www.bbc.co.uk/skillswise/english**
—This site contains a great set of one minute videos to help you brush up on your grammar and writing skills.

Carroll, J. (2007) *A Handbook for Deterring Plagiarism in Higher Education.* **Vol. 2. Oxford: Oxford Centre for Staff and Learning Development**
—This book defines plagiarism and discusses how to combat it. It is written as a guide for teachers in HE. An introduction for students, which references Carroll's work, can be found in Jenny Moon's book, also in this reading list.

Chatfield, T. (2018) *Critical Thinking.* **London: SAGE Publications Ltd**
-A guide to help you with your critical analysis, to deliver clear and confident written analytical assignments.

Cite This For Me (2019) *Save Time and Improve your Marks with CiteThisForMe, The No. 1 Citation Tool.* **Available at: http://www.citethisforme.com/**
—An app and web page to help you format and generate citations in various referencing styles, including OSCOLA and Harvard.

DLA Piper (2015) *Back to Basics. . . Contractual Interpretation.* **Available at: https://www.dlapiper .com/en/uk/insights/publications/2015/11/contractual-interpretation/**
—A corporate update from law firm DLA Piper explaining, in clear English, how the courts will interpret a contractual provision if the parties to the contract dispute its meaning.

Encyclopaedia of Forms and Precedents. **LexisNexisUK. Available online at: http://www.lexisnexis .co.uk/en-uk/products/encyclopaedia-of-forms-and-precedents.page**
—An electronic precedent resource. Subscription access.

EndNote (2019) *EndNote|Clarivate Analytics.* **Available at: https://endnote.com/**
—An electronic research and reference manager.

Grammarly.com. (2019). *Write Your Best with Grammarly.* **Available at: https://www.grammarly.com/**
—An online writing assistant that can improve your writing by helping with grammar, tone and spelling.

Hyde, J. (2018). Trainee barred from profession over document cover-up. Law Gazette. Available at: https://www.lawgazette.co.uk/news/trainee-barred-from-profession-over-document-cover-up/5101474.article.
—Article describing how a trainee solicitor was removed from the profession after trying to pass off a faulty document as having been replaced.

Levicom v Linklaters **[2009] EWHC 812 (Comm)**
—A useful case for showing the potential effect of ambiguity in legal practice.

Lexis®PSL available at https://www.lexisnexis.com/uk/lexispsl/pslhome
—A popular electronic practitioner resource featuring precedents and know-how. Subscription access.

Moon, J. (2006) *Academic Honesty, Plagiarism and Cheating: A Tutorial Unit for New Undergraduate Students*. Available online at: https://www.keele.ac.uk/media/keeleuniversity/lpdc/downloads/Academic%20Integrity%20Guide.pdf

—This short article is useful reading regarding the issues of plagiarism and referencing discussed at 14.1.7.

Morrison, L. (2017) *The True Importance of Good Spelling*. BBC Worklife. Available at: https://www.bbc.com/worklife/article/20170807-the-true-importance-of-good-spelling

—An article discussing how poor spelling is likely to make you look less credible and intelligent than you are.

Parkinson, J. (2007) *i before e (except after c)*. London: Michael O'Mara Books Ltd

—This text contains plenty of useful memory tools for remembering grammatical rules.

Practical Law. Available online at: uk.practicallaw.com

—Another popular electronic practitioner resource featuring precedents and know-how. Subscription access.

Royal Literary Fund, (2019). *Essay Guide*. Available at: https://www.rlf.org.uk/resources/writing-essays/

—The RLF's online guide to everything you wanted to know but were afraid to ask about writing undergraduate essays, including guidance on common areas of difficulty such as understanding the question and creating a logical structure. Includes the Alex Essay Writing Tool, a step-by-step guide to writing an essay complete with an app you can download and a list of further helpful resources you can read and watch.

Rylance, P. (2012) *Writing and Drafting in Legal Practice*. Oxford: OUP

—An 'at a glance' guide for common writing and drafting problems.

SRA (2019) *Client Care Letters*. Available at: https://www.sra.org.uk/solicitors/guidance/ethics-guidance/client-care-letters/

—Guidance from the Solicitors Regulation Authority (SRA) about client care letters, which your firm will send out before the first interview (see Chapter 11). Includes practical information about what the SRA considers to be the hallmarks of good legal letter writing skills.

SRA (2019). *Student information*. Available at: https://www.sra.org.uk/students/resources/student-information/

—Information about the character and suitability screening process you must complete before entering the profession. Includes a link to a form which asks a question specifically about assessment offences that amount to plagiarism or cheating.

Trudeau, C., 2012. The Public Speaks: An Empirical Study of Legal Communication. *Scribes J. Leg. Writing*, 14, p.121-152. Available at: https://works.bepress.com/christopher_trudeau/1/.

—A study providing empirical data to support the principle that the public prefers clear, understandable communication.

Truss, L. (2003) *Eats, Shoots and Leaves: The Zero Tolerance Approach to Punctuation*. London: Profile Books Ltd

—This entertaining book is a useful resource for sharpening up your punctuation skills.

Turner, C. (2015) 'Government in £9 million payout after single letter blunder causes business to collapse'. *The Telegraph*. 27 January 2015

—An article highlighting a case which shows the importance of avoiding typos and spelling mistakes. In the case of Taylor & Sons in the High Court, a judge found Companies House liable for the demise of the company, after they mistakenly recorded that it, rather than Taylor & Son, had been wound up.

University of Manchester (2019) *Academic Phrasebank*. Available online at http://www.phrasebank
.manchester.ac.uk/

—A general resource for academic writers. It aims to provide you with examples of some of the
phraseological 'nuts and bolts' of writing.

University of Oxford, Faculty of Law *OSCOLA: The Oxford University standard for citation of
legal authorities* (4th edn, Hart Publishers). Available online at: https://www.law.ox.ac.uk/
research-subject-groups/publications/oscola

—The OSCOLA referencing style is edited by the Oxford Law Faculty, and this website includes useful
guidance, including a link to a quick reference guide, FAQ sheet, and downloads to import this style
into EndNote and other electronic referencing systems.

University of Sheffield (2019) *Critical Thinking*. Sheffield.ac.uk. Available at: https://www.sheffield
.ac.uk/ssid/301/study-skills/everyday-skills/critical-thinking

—Resources, including a video, to help you engage with all levels of the Bloom's taxonomy of learning
model, including the higher critical skills of analysing, evaluating and creating, to work towards
achieving higher grades.

Yale Repository (2017) *Is Texting Eroding Good Writing Skills Among Young Students?*
Available at https://campuspress.yale.edu/perspective/is-texting-eroding-good-writing-skills-
among-young-students/

—An article which explores the trend for text-speak and its effect on students' writing skills.

*For the authors' reflections on the practical exercises, additional self-test questions, sample
interview questions and a library of links to useful websites, visit the free **online resources** at
www.oup.com/he/slorach4e.*

Employability and Commercial Awareness

It is a reality of life that all students, whatever their intended career path, need to consider employability and developing their commercial awareness at an early stage in their studies, and law students are no exception. This section is designed to assist students in developing a better understanding of the requirements of employers, and to provide guidance on how best to demonstrate knowledge, skills, and commercial awareness.

An employability skills chapter introduces law students to the skills and competencies valued by all professional employers, including those in the legal services sector. The following chapters consider a range of areas which are essential elements of commercial awareness, a crucial requirement when applying for work in the legal and many other sectors. They not only provide students with guidance on how to develop commercial awareness, but also show them how to demonstrate this awareness to potential employers.

Supported by a number of business case studies, sample interview questions, and activities, students are challenged to reflect on and actively improve their commercial awareness. They are encouraged to engage with the wider business environment in which the law operates, and are introduced to law firms and the individuals and businesses that have recourse to the law. The section includes guidance as to how best to demonstrate required competencies to prospective employers when applying for roles, through application letters and CVs, and in interviews and other selection processes.

15 Making yourself more employable

> ◉ **Learning objectives**
>
> After studying this chapter you should be able to:
>
> - Appreciate the skills professional firms are seeking in prospective graduate employees.
> - Recognise the importance of commercial awareness.
> - Begin to develop these skills and your commercial awareness.
> - Understand the concept of transferable skills.

Introduction

Chapters 7 to 14 consider the essential legal skills which all lawyers need, whether they are in practice or not (and of course several of them are essential skills for practice as a professional generally). This chapter focuses on the *additional* skills you will require if you intend to embark on a career in the *practice* of law, or indeed any other profession into which law graduates typically and successfully progress (including accountancy, banking, finance, the civil service, the police, government, the armed forces, management, journalism, publishing, recruitment, and academia). It is important to recognise, before you read this Part III, just how important it is that you develop your employability skills now, and how these skills will help you. Historically, accountants have been much better than lawyers at celebrating and indeed marketing their qualification as a 'gold standard', a hallmark that they possess a suite of skills which are eminently transferable and which equip them well for a career in whichever profession they choose. Accountants have tended to be much more open minded in their approach to future careers, and consider that their education and training clearly equips them well for more than simply being an accountant. This is an attitude you should be encouraged to adopt in relation to your legal education and training. You should consider the skills you learn during this process to be eminently transferable and of value wherever your career takes you. This is explored further in Chapter 16.

In today's competitive marketplace, employability skills are key. Law students tend to prioritise the acquisition of knowledge over the acquisition of skills, but this is not a good idea. This is because employability skills play a pivotal role in distinguishing a good professional from an average one, from both an employer's and a client's perspective.

The term 'solicitor' is an umbrella term to describe professionals who practise all areas of that broad and diverse subject known as law. You cannot possibly arrive at a law firm on day one of your training contract or qualifying work experience armed with a comprehensive knowledge of the specific area of law you intend to practise. Law firms (and, similarly, other graduate employers) understand this and will help you to supplement your existing knowledge as they train you on the job for practice in a particular area or sector. Clients, rightly or wrongly, will assume you have the requisite knowledge. But although there is a limit on how much you will impress your employer or the client with your knowledge on day one, it is possible to impress on day one with polished employability skills. By learning these skills early, you can stand out from your peers when you enter the world of professional practice. It is quite a transition between being a student and being a professional. This chapter will help to ease that transition for you when it comes, by showing what you can be doing now to prepare for professional life.

The term 'employability skills' includes all those skills which make you a covetable employee. Of course, it includes technical competence, which in turn requires the skills covered in this work (for legal practice, namely being able to read and understand the law, undertake legal research, solve legal problems, draft competently, and communicate effectively, both orally and in writing). However, effective professionals, including lawyers, deploy a host of other skills which we will consider in this Part III. This chapter considers the personal characteristics and interpersonal skills you will require to be a covetable employee, and how to showcase them in the application process for a professional role. This Part of the book sets out topics of which you will need a decent working knowledge and, again, which you will need to be able to demonstrate during an application process. It may be difficult to appreciate this in the current stage of your education, but consider this; employers will consider *every* law graduate to have acquired subject 'knowledge', demonstrated by their degree. They are unlikely to seek to test this again; rather, their application processes are likely to focus on the untested areas which are important to them, and it is regarding these areas where Chapters 15 to 20 will help to put you ahead of your competition.

15.1 Personal characteristics

Effective professionals share similar characteristics. They have a positive attitude to their work, approach work in a business-like manner, act with professionalism, and reflect on their work to develop their practice. These characteristics come more naturally to some than others, however the good news is that they can be learned and improved with practice, like any other skill. As a first step it is important simply to appreciate that they are vital components of a good professional. Eventually, most find they can demonstrate the following qualities when things are going well. However, working as a professional in any area tends to be not only rewarding but also demanding, and law is no exception to this. It involves working under pressure, often during long and sometimes unsociable office hours. A really good professional will be able to show the same qualities when things are not going as well.

Employers will be looking for evidence of these characteristics when they consider your application and during the interview process. Let's explore further what they are and how you can show that you have them when you apply for a job. Work experience (see 15.3.3) is excellent in terms of really bringing these points home. Spending time in any professional environment is a great idea at this stage, and will demonstrate clearly the points set out in this chapter.

15.1.1 **Attitude**

It is important to demonstrate that you have a positive attitude to your work. One of the most important things to show is enthusiasm, even (particularly) when you are given something to do which is relatively mundane. Taking responsibility for your own work, being proactive in identifying other work that might be required and being willing to do that work and showing commitment to your work are also examples of taking a professional approach. The key point is that you must show that you are someone with whom other people would want to work. Lawyers work closely together and the hours can be quite intense. Being flexible, approachable, and having a sense of humour even when things are going wrong will count significantly in your favour. Do not underestimate how the personality of work colleagues can affect life in the office. If you present yourself as someone who would enhance the experience rather than detract from it, you will make yourself a covetable employee. Adopt good habits now, by recognising when you are tired, stressed, or just cannot be bothered, and making a particular effort to try your best at these times. Try out different coping mechanisms to get you through these difficult periods, and find what works for you. Something as simple as going for a walk, listening to music, or taking a coffee break can make a difference. Talk to others; too many students isolate themselves when they feel overwhelmed. Everyone has concerns; some are just better at dealing with them than others. You can learn from your fellow students; consider who has an attitude you admire and would like to emulate, and talk to them about their coping strategies. Ask your tutors if they have any advice regarding any issues you are facing; they are likely to have advised many students with similar problems. You will continue to experience these feelings in professional life; there are just never enough hours in the day, so start now to discover what will help you through.

15.1.2 **Approach**

You must approach your work in a business-like manner. Examples of behaviour which evidence this are being organised, demonstrating a high capacity for work, being resilient under pressure, self-aware, diligent, and paying attention to detail. In other words, you need to show that you are 'a safe pair of hands'. Of course, what you are doing right now, being a law student, lends itself to evidencing that you have these skills, but the fact is that some students are much more adept than others at organising their work. This is something you can improve now. Time management is crucial. You must be able to multi-task and achieve a balance between your work and social life, and this is no less true once you are a professional. It is not sustainable in the long term simply to work all the time at the expense of a social life. You can help yourself by being familiar with your timetable; importing it into your smartphone is best, so you always have it with you, but if this is not possible at least stick a copy on the fridge. Maintain a 'to-do' list; again you can do this on a smartphone so it is always with you. Set alerts to make sure you do not forget key events or deadlines. Ask your lecturer how many hours a week the course demands of you, and timetable that into your diary, allocating blocks of time for non-timetabled activities such as preparation, consolidation, and revision, so you can then also clearly ring-fence some leisure time. Start your work early, so you have time to look over it with a fresh perspective before the deadline. Know what you have to do, where you have to be, and when.

15.1.3 **Professionalism and ethics**

There is an understanding that professionals behave in a certain way. This behaviour includes being polite, approachable, reliable, honest, dependable, punctual, and dressing and behaving in an office-appropriate manner.

If anyone helps you, say thank you. This is equally the case if the help is by email. It is increasingly common for students and trainees simply not to reply to tutors and colleagues who respond to their queries by email. A brief reply to say thank you will never be a waste of anyone's time.

All professionals should demonstrate reliability, honesty, and dependability, but these are particularly important qualities for those working in the legal profession where professional ethics are held in high regard. Section 6.4 explored the area of professional ethics. You will appreciate that clients may need to disclose quite sensitive information to you so they must be able to trust you. Indeed the Solicitors Regulation Authority (see 6.3), which regulates the profession, may not admit you as a solicitor at all if you have in your record certain matters which suggest that you are dishonest. Further information on this is set out in their Suitability Test which they publish on their website (details of which are set out in the Further Reading section at the end of this chapter). It is important to realise that anything you do now which suggests dishonesty could impact quite seriously on your ability to join this profession, where honesty is valued above all else. So, for example, if you are found guilty of plagiarism, or are caught on a train without a valid ticket, this is likely to have more serious consequences for you than for, say, your housemate studying the history of art (provided he is not planning to convert to law).

As Chapter 20 explains, traditionally a solicitor has charged on a time basis (see 20.1.6). Where this continues, a client will not tolerate a solicitor taking longer than necessary over work, or keeping the client waiting unnecessarily. If you are a student who tends to be late to lectures on a regular basis then take heed and adopt good habits sooner rather than later.

In terms of dress, it can be difficult to pre-empt what is office-appropriate if you have not been inside a professional working environment before. Bear in mind that they tend to be relatively conservative places, and law firms are at the conservative end of the professional spectrum. You have a working lifetime to express yourself through your clothes once you are more familiar with the firm and its culture. Initially however, as a rule of thumb it is a good idea to err on the side of formality if you are at all unsure. It is better to be too formal at first, and become less so, than to be too casual and have to smarten up. The look you are aiming for is that of a polished professional. The following guidelines may help:

- sober black, grey, or navy blue suits will never be out of place;
- for men, shirts should be light-coloured and long-sleeved, preferably without a pocket;
- women have more latitude in terms of colour, but should avoid anything too revealing;
- shoes should be polished;
- men should be cleanly shaved;
- hair should be clean and tidy;
- avoid anything 'novelty', including ties, socks, cufflinks, and jewellery;
- it is a good idea to wear your suit in the house for a practice run first, to identify any scope for a wardrobe malfunction.

Bear in mind that you will meet professionals during the course of your studies. They will visit your university and you will meet them at law fairs, while doing pro bono work and on vacation schemes. You should think carefully about how you can demonstrate that even at this stage you have the attributes of a professional. Like it or not, you will make an impression when you meet these people, and you need to give some thought as to what impression you want to make, then dress and act accordingly. Think carefully before making any permanent alterations to your appearance, such as having a visible tattoo or stretching the holes of your pierced ears. Something that you will feel comfortable sporting in the student union may make you feel very uncomfortable when you speak to lawyers at a law fair or enter a law firm for a vacation placement. Nor should you worry about your friends' reactions, for example, if you choose to wear smart clothing to a law fair. Have the confidence to be guided by your own instinct.

That said, law firms are not looking for clones and you should not be afraid to let your personality come through in your dress, provided you still fall within the description of a polished professional.

15.2 Reflection and personal development

Professional firms are constantly looking for ways to improve, so that they can beat the competition. As an employee you will be expected to operate a *reflective practice*, which means that you should reflect on your work at regular intervals and learn from your experiences, good and bad, to inform your practice going forward. This involves taking responsibility for your own learning and development, reflecting on your performance and learning from mistakes, seeking and accepting feedback and advice, and being willing and able to learn new skills.

Generally your employer will be understanding if you make a mistake once, however she will be considerably less understanding if you make the same mistake again. The skill is to learn from your mistakes. This is one reason why it is important to secure a role with an employer who will provide lots of practical experience. The sooner you are free to make mistakes, the sooner you will learn from them, and you will be a more impressive professional at an early stage in your career.

Reflective practice is something you can start to develop now, as a student. Analysing our own mistakes is never a comfortable exercise, but it pays dividends.

15.2.1 **Feedback**

When asked for their views, it is common to hear students say they would like more feedback on their work. However it can be that students who receive a poor mark find this so disappointing that they are tempted to file the work away without paying attention to the feedback provided. No matter how painful it may be, you must try to read feedback objectively, and discuss anything that you do not understand with your lecturer. If you change your perception and view this as a positive process, from which you can learn, it can help. Remember that it is feedback, not failure.

15.2.2 **Professional development planning**

It can also be useful to keep a reflective log, which might be referred to in practice as a personal development plan (PDP). It is not uncommon for undergraduates to identify towards the end of their degree that during their degree they have not focused as clearly as they might have on their career goals and what is really required to achieve those goals, and as a result have not engaged as fully as they might with the help and resources available to them at university. A PDP can help practically to structure your reflection on your learning, performance, and achievement and use this reflection to help you to (i) articulate these more clearly in an employment application and interview process, and (ii) identify and address any issues which require attention in advance of that process.

The starting point of any PDP is self-evaluation of your current position. You should record your academic and work skills and experience to date and your short-to-medium term (say, five year) career goals. It is also helpful to undertake a SWOT analysis. As explained further at 18.2.6, this involves identifying your strengths and weaknesses and also the external factors which might create opportunities and threats for you. It might, for example, identify that you would struggle to evidence one or more of the skills we have identified you will need in professional life. It is likely you will also need to undertake some research to enhance your commercial awareness (see 15.3) of current opportunities and threats regarding your chosen career path (for example, that increasing delegation to paralegals of the more process-driven areas of law constitutes a potential threat to seeking a career as a solicitor in that area of practice, or that an employer stating it will recruit solely from candidates with a minimum 2:1 constitutes a clear threat if you are currently predicted a 2:2). Reflecting on your SWOT analysis will help you to set your short to mid-term career goals and establish an action plan to achieve them. For example, if your analysis reveals you are struggling to demonstrate teamworking skills, your action plan will be to seek out teamworking opportunities to provide clear evidence of this skill which you can use on your CV. You might identify that you can achieve this by applying for a pro bono activity offered by your university or by taking a part-time job.

The final stage, of course, is putting your PDP into action and then reflecting on what you have done. This reflection may identify further action which is required and so the cycle continues. The simpler your PDP, the more likely you are to use it, so you could condense it to a simple notes page on your smartphone highlighting areas of concern and how you are addressing them, which you can reflect on and update to chart your progress. A resource to help you to structure your PDP is set out in the Further Reading section at the end of this chapter (your university may provide its own materials for this).

Example 1

The following example might help you to understand why law firms value the characteristics discussed in this chapter, but it is equally relevant to any other work experience you might undertake, such as working at a magazine publishing house (although the copying may be of slightly more glamorous documents).

Imagine you are a solicitor. It is 6pm. You are going to be working late and you have cancelled your plans for the evening. You ask your trainee, James, if he can copy the 150-page document which you will need to append to the document you will be drafting later in the evening. James' body language suggests he is not overly impressed with your request. He replies, 'OK, although I warn you I do have to leave by 7 pm latest to meet my girlfriend'. You leave your office for a while and return to find a pile of papers on your desk, and that James has left for the evening. The papers appear to be the photocopied document.

At 11.30pm, after several hours of drafting, you finish your document. However, when you try to append the copy document to your draft, you find that pages 148–50 are not in the pile of papers on your desk. You look for the original document, but it is not with the papers on your desk. You find it on James' desk, next to a half-finished cup of coffee. Unfortunately pages 148–50 are also missing from the original document. You go to the photocopier and find that the lights on the copier are flashing to indicate a paper jam. You open the photocopier and fish out the original pages 148–50. You reset the copier. The copier is out of paper. You refill the copier. Finally you are able to add the photocopies of pages 148–50 to the appendix, email it to its destination, and go home at midnight.

As the solicitor in this scenario, what is your opinion of James? Consider again the personal characteristics which law firms value. Has James demonstrated any of them? Which ones has he definitely not shown? Analyse specifically what you would have liked him to have done differently. Now read the following:

Imagine you are a solicitor. It is 6pm. You are going to be working late and you have cancelled your plans for the evening. You ask your trainee, John, if he can copy the 150 page document which you will need to append to your document when you have finished drafting it. John looks up from his work, smiles and replies, 'Yes, of course'. You leave your office for a while and return to find two piles of papers on your desk, one with a label 'copy' and one with a label 'original', along with a cup of coffee. He explains that he has counted the pages and two pages appear to be missing, so he is going to find them. Ten minutes later John returns with the two missing pages and puts them into the appropriate piles in the right place, explaining that he had just won a battle with the photocopier.

If both John and James were looking for a job in your department, it is likely that you would recommend John over James. John has made your life easier than James did. It is interesting to note what John did to earn your support. He was pleasant, did not complain, made you a coffee, checked the copying, and extracted two documents from the photocopier. None of these things in isolation is particularly burdensome. However it is these little things which can make a big difference to someone who asks for your help. Note that you did not have to do any of John's work. In contrast, it would probably have been more efficient for you to have done the copying yourself rather than give it to James. James runs the risk that you will not trust him again, and as a result he will not gather the same level of experience during his training that John will.

15.3 Commercial awareness

It should be clear to you now that if you think that your career will *just* be about passing on to clients the knowledge you have learned at university, then that career will be short lived. Lawyers, like everyone else involved in business of any sort, need to show commercial awareness. Let's explore now what commercial awareness is and why you need it if you are aiming to be involved with the law, or any other profession. Chapters 17 to 20 look at law firms and their clients and the relevance of these issues for lawyers, introducing you to the fundamentals of commercial awareness: business structures and organisation, basic economics, financial markets and banks, accounts, and insolvency. You may wonder why any of these are relevant. At the beginning of your career, you cannot be expected to have the same commercial understanding as a partner who has been practising for 20 years. However, commercial awareness is an essential aspect of your professional development, and it is never too soon to start developing this knowledge. Commercial awareness is crucially important when applying for graduate jobs.

15.3.1 What is commercial awareness?

Unfortunately there is no neat definition. The term means different things to different people. If you think for a minute about what it means to you, you may come up with something along the lines of 'Commercial awareness is understanding how businesses work'. That is fine as far as it goes, but for lawyers, it means a bit more than this. Lawyers will have clients which are businesses, companies, partnerships, or sole traders; however, they will also have clients who are individuals and who come to them for advice on matters unrelated to business, for example buying a house or getting a divorce. Businesses are run by individuals: the directors of the company, or the partners in a firm. Businesses also have employees, customers, or clients. These are the people with whom lawyers will deal on a day-to-day basis.

You will be faced with typical concerns of those clients, both individuals and businesses: personal, financial, and legal. Understanding those concerns is the first step towards commercial awareness. Then there is one more step. Whether the clients are businesses or individuals, they will be affected by the same external factors. All matters will be affected by what is going on in the world: in other words, by the wider context within which the client operates, whether it be economic, political, social, or financial. So commercial awareness is about understanding businesses and the business and wider environment, which Chapter 18 aims to help you to do, but is also about all of these other factors: your clients' personal concerns, the financial implications, and the wider environment in which they are operating.

You have seen in Chapter 9 that problem-solving requires a lawyer to work through several stages before advising the client. The first thing that you will do is establish the facts (why they have come to you) and then establish the main issues and the client's concerns (what are the client's objectives?). Usually, the client will tell you what she thinks are the relevant facts, what her concerns are, and what she is hoping to achieve. (These are her expectations.) The problem is that this will never be quite the whole story.

Once a client has outlined the matter about which she is consulting a lawyer, and explained her objectives, the next considerations will generally be financial: how much will the matter cost, what will be the financial consequences, and how can the client raise the finance needed to proceed? Once you start to dig a bit deeper, you will find out there are other relevant facts or concerns that the client has not told you about, which may change her objectives. Clients have 'latent' (or hidden) concerns and objectives, often based on facts that they have not even thought about. If you are commercially aware, you should be able to spot them.

The flowchart in Figure 15.1 shows the underlying considerations which lawyers should take into account when advising a client, and how they fit into the problem-solving model that you were introduced to in Chapter 9.

Figure 15.1 Commercial awareness steps

Consider this straightforward example (Example 2).

Example 2

You are instructed by a client who tells you that he manages a shop in your local high street. A customer owes £2,500 for goods purchased on credit. The client wants to sue the customer for the amount owed.

The objective appears clear. He wants you to issue proceedings to reclaim the £2,500. You advise the client how to make the claim.

You are instructed by a client who tells you that he manages a shop in your local high street. **The shop is part of a national chain of retailers, making annual sales of over £10 million a year. An important corporate customer owes £2,500. The customer places regular orders, and there have never been any problems over payment before.** The client wants to sue the customer for the amount owed.

So, the stated objective is the same, but who is your client? The manager instructing you, or the national chain of retailers who owns the shop? What is best for that company? These are factors you should consider and discuss with the manager, including specifically:

1. The corporate customer owes a relatively small amount. Does the national chain of retailers need to sue to recover it?

2. Litigation will be expensive and must be weighed against the amount likely to be recovered. If litigation costs will amount to, say £1,500, is it worth it?

3. The corporate customer places regular orders. Is the recovery of £2,500 worth ruining this relationship? Might it simply be an oversight or a temporary blip? Might the national chain of retailers expect a significant income stream from this corporate customer in the future?

4. Has the national chain of retailers run a credit check on its corporate customer? It would be good practice to do so regularly.

None of this is legal advice (although point 2 is based on knowledge of a legal process). It is based on understanding the client's financial position, the environment in which he is operating, common sense, and experience. All of this is commercial awareness.

However, things are not always as clear as they first appear. Let's consider that, using an effective listening and questioning technique (see Chapter 11), you uncover some further facts, shown emboldened in Example 2 (continued). You can see that these facts, together with your commercial awareness, might alter your advice.

15.3.1.1 How is commercial awareness tested at interview?

As a general rule, legal interview questions divide into categories: personal questions, legal questions, questions about the legal profession, questions about the firm, and questions to test your level of commercial awareness. An employer will want to test at interview in particular that you have commercial awareness, as it is difficult to ascertain that you have this from your CV. They tend to do this by asking questions that you cannot anticipate specifically, and will observe how you think on your feet, your level of general knowledge, and how well you understand and can explain the commercial issues underpinning the headline event. Therefore there is not, by definition, a technique to anticipate the specific questions you might be asked to test your commercial awareness. 15.3.3 provides guidance as to what you can do to best prepare for these types of question. However, it will be helpful to consider some examples of the kind of questions that would test commercial awareness, and the underlying general areas of commercial knowledge and understanding that you can demonstrate in answering such a question. You know from your legal research reading (see Chapter 8) that the time it takes between writing and publishing a textbook, even one updated as regularly as this one, means that it is an impossible task to set out here a question on a current event you might be asked during a forthcoming interview. 15.3.3 will help you with techniques to find current issues that will be 'live' in the lead up to any interview you have managed to secure. However, the good news is that, just as your skills are transferable (see Chapter 16), so you can learn how to dissect one question to show commercial awareness in your answer, and transfer this skill to any question on a current event.

Let us first consider, then, two examples of commercial awareness questions (Examples 3 and 4), and how you can answer in a way that shows a prospective employer that you have both the required knowledge and understanding that they are looking for. You can also access a recent example, on Brexit, via the online resources.

Once we have analysed these two questions, you will see why Chapters 15 to 20 are so important. You can then use these examples to practise how you can extrapolate the same analysis into examples that have featured in the recent press (at the time of writing, leaving Brexit aside, examples would include the young activists campaigning for the environment, political advertising on social media, or the use of medicinal cannabis). This is essential pre-interview preparation (see Chapter 16).

Example 3

In October 2018, the well known café and cake chain, Patisserie Valerie, almost ceased trading following the discovery of a 'black hole' of £94 million in its accounts as a result of fraud and false accounting. Its biggest shareholder and chairman, entrepreneur Luke Johnson, advanced £10 million of his own money, and the company issued new shares to raise further capital, effectively bailing it out. It continued trading and narrowly avoided being wound up by HMRC for unpaid tax. However, the rescue was short lived as its financial situation was found to be significantly worse than first thought. Profits and cash flow had been overstated and were 'materially below' figures announced in October. In January 2019, it collapsed into administration with the loss of 900 jobs, when talks with its bankers to raise further finance failed. The company was subsequently bought out of administration by an Irish private equity firm, Causeway Capital Partners (CCP) for £5m, which kept 96 outlets open.

Part III

Employability and
Commercial Awareness

You may wonder why you are being asked to consider this case study. Recent years have seen the collapse of several well known companies, including in the retail sector House of Fraser, and in the construction industry Carillion plc or in the leisure industry, the tour operator, Thomas Cook. The answer is that there is more to the collapse of Patisserie Valerie than meets the eye, and you can use this event to test your commercial awareness skills, by asking whether you can summarise the impact and analyse the issues arising out of this event. As explained earlier, 15.3.3 will help you to identify what you can do to stay abreast of current issues, so for the purposes of Example 3, we are going to focus on unpicking the facts of the scenario to reveal the underlying commercial awareness issues you can use to your advantage in interview.

The company

The first opportunity is to demonstrate your knowledge and understanding of the *company* as a legal entity. Patisserie Valerie Ltd, a private company, was a subsidiary of Patisserie Holdings plc, its parent, or holding, company. Patisserie Holdings was a public company. You have seen that it was bought by a private equity firm who are now running it as a going concern, keeping the Patisserie Valerie name. To do this, you need to know how to explain these corporate relationships.

1. What is the difference between a public and a private company?
2. What is a holding company?
3. What do private equity firms do?

Corporate governance

Second, you can also show you understand the fundamentals of how companies are run and managed, which is referred to as 'corporate governance' (see 18.2.3). Patisserie Valerie's collapse was the result of 'significant, and potentially fraudulent, accounting irregularities'. The legal consequences were that in 2018, the Finance Director was arrested (and subsequently bailed). At the time of writing, the Serious Fraud Office was carrying out criminal investigations into five people and Patisserie Holdings plc was put into administration.

What is surprising is that a company as well known as Patisserie Valerie could collapse as quickly as it did without its board of directors being aware of its difficulties. Its chairman, Luke Johnson, said that he was unaware that there were any problems until the CEO told him that the company's bank accounts had been frozen.[1] It is even more surprising that it was unaware that HMRC had issued proceedings to put it into liquidaton. In a Parliamentary Committee, MP Rachel Reeves, said the administration 'raises grave corporate governance concerns'. So, you will impress if you can show you understand:

1. What is the role of the board of directors of a company?
2. What is the role of a CEO?
3. What is the role of a chairman?

---

[1] Johnson, L., 'My very public disaster with Patisserie Valerie', *Sunday Times*, 9 June 2019. Available online (with subscription); https://www.thetimes.co.uk/article/luke-johnson-on-his-very-public-disaster-with-patisserie-valerie-9p5xbwph8 (accessed 13/07/2019).

Finance and accounts

You saw that Patisserie Valerie collapsed when it was unable to raise further loans from its banks, despite having been lent £20 million in unsecured interest free loans by its chairman, Luke Johnson. Without further finance, it was insolvent and unable to continue trading. Subsequent forsenic investigations into Patisserie Valerie's accounts show that the profit and loss and balance sheet of its accounts had been significantly manipulated and its cash position was overestimated by £54 million, with thousands of false entries on its ledgers. The fraud had seemingly been going on for years, but the cover up was so successful that the annual accounts were given a clean bill of health by Patisserie Valerie's auditors, Grant Thornton, a top six accountancy firm, who 'had the wool pulled very comprehensively over its eyes'.[2] Grant Thornton is currently being investigated by the Financial Reporting Council, the regulatory body for accountants and auditors (the accountancy equivalent of the SRA). This raises further opportunities for you to demonstrate understanding of the following commercial issues:

1. How do companies raise finance?
2. What is the difference between a secured and an unsecured loan?
3. When is a company insolvent?
4. What is the difference between administration and liquidation?
5. In the accounts of a company, what is the purpose of the profit and loss account and the balance sheet?
6. What is the role of a company's auditors?

The stock markets, shares, and ownership

Although not listed on the Main Market of the London Stock Exchange, Patisserie Holdings was listed on the Alternative Investment Market (AIM) and in the four years up to 2018 its share price had increased by 155 per cent. It seemed a good investment. When the news of the fraud came to light, its shares were suspended. The collapse of Patisserie Valerie meant that shares in a company which had been worth over £450 million became effectively worthless, and shareholders did not recover their investment. It is estimated that two-thirds of Luke Johnson's wealth was invested in Patisserie Valerie. His shareholding was worth £170 million at the time that the fraud was discovered and he will recover very little of the unsecured loans made to the company.

1. What do you know about shares?
2. What is a stock market?
3. What do we mean by 'wealth'?
4. Why are share prices important economically?

The sector

Research into the hospitality industry shows that recent years have been hard, particularly in the restaurant sector. In 2018 over 1,200 restaurants and cafés shut down and there have

---

[2] Ibid.

been a number of high profile casualties, e.g. Jaimie Oliver's chain of restaurants or Prezzo, both of which went into administration. There are both macro and micro economic reasons for this. Although inflation at the time was low and levels of employment high, the economic and political uncertainty at the time together with interest rate rises meant that consumer confidence was low and demand had consequently dropped. There are also social and environmental issues to consider, e.g. a trend towards healthy eating and a developing consumer preference for local restaurants and cafés sourcing local produce in the interests of sustainability. Further questions are:

1 What is an industry sector?
2. What is the difference between micro and macro economics?
3. Why are supply and demand so important?
4. What is inflation?
5. Why do interest rates have an effect on the economy?

How did you do? It does not matter if the answer is 'Not very well'. The point here is that one event (that is, Example 3), which appears on the face of it to be mainly about legal issues, gives rise to a large number of underlying issues covering economics, financial markets, business structures and organisation, accounts, and insolvency, and raises the sort of questions which you may face at interview. It does not matter how well you analyse the legal issues; if you do not know some of the basics of the topics in the headings above (the company—management—valuation—the stock markets and ownership—the sector), you will not stand out. Memorising these headings will help you to transfer the 'chunking down' technique we adopted, to use this example to show your commercial awareness, and will allow you to do the same to good effect in relation to any similar scenario (e.g. the collapse of Thomas Cook).

If you are not considering corporate practice, you may be thinking that none of this has any relevance to you. This is not the case. As Chapter 20 explains, law firms are themselves businesses and you will be expected to know how they operate from the structure they have adopted. You will be working for a business and so you will be expected to understand the fundamentals of business, regardless of the client base of the firm. You can easily let yourself down at interview with any firm, by something as simple as calling a partnership a company, or not knowing why a company is public or private.

We will now consider a second example of a question (Example 4) which will test your commercial awareness.

Example 4

In 2018, it emerged that the data analytics firm, Cambridge Analytica, had collected the personal information of up to 87 million Facebook users without their permission, using an app in the form of a quiz. The data which they harvested was detailed enough for Cambridge Analytica to create psychographical profiles. These were allegedly used to help Donald Trump win the 2016 election and were then sold to Brexit campaign group 'Leave.EU' during the 2016 EU referendum campaign. Facebook was subsequently fined $5 billion in the US for violation of consumer privacy. Cambridge Analytica, which was set up by Robert Mercer, the data billionaire and CEO of the hedge fund, Renaissance Technologies, went into liquidation following the scandal in May 2019. When the scandal

(Continued)

broke, the value of Facebook's shares plummeted. At the annual general meeting, shareholders demanded changes to its corporate governance and other reforms, accusing Mark Zuckerberg of 'corporate dictatorship'.

The legal issues here relate to data privacy, but, together with issues of corporate governance, this scandal also raises social, ethical, and political issues that go far beyond these legal issues.

Again, you can use this example to test your commercial awareness skills, by asking whether you can summarise the impact and analyse the issues arising out of it. You are seeking to provide an analysis that sets you apart by showing knowledge of the world around you, that you can think on your feet, and that you understand the commercial awareness issues which underlie the headline facts. Chapters 15 to 20 are intended to help you to analyse some of these issues. You may not need the information all at once, but at some point either during your studies, during the application process, or when you start a job, you will. As your career develops, you will need to adapt your knowledge for different clients, different firms, and as the world changes. The topics covered in this chapter are a starting point. If you look at some of the 'Practical exercises' at the end of these chapters, they will give you an opportunity to practise this sort of analysis once you have read these chapters. Reading the *Guardian* article[3] will also help you to answer the specific questions asked in the following sections.

What threats are posed by social media?

1. Summarise the ethical issues raised by the Cambridge Analytica scandal.

2. Do you think that Facebook's corporate structure and governance contributed to the problem?

3. It has been argued that social media poses a threat to democracy. Do you agree with this?

4. 'Data is the new oil'. Do you consider that this statement accurately reflects the value of data to governments, businesses, and other organisations.

5. What is meant by 'Big Data'?

6. See if you can guess the how many emails or texts are sent or Google searches conducted every minute. (Then find the Visual Capitalist article by Jeff Desjardins, *What happens in an Internet Minute in 2019?* (13 March 2019)[4] and see how near to the correct numbers you were.)

7. What is 'data analytics'?

8. How would you explain the purpose of the EU General Data Protection Regulation to someone who is not a lawyer?

9. What legislation is in place to protect personal data in the UK?

10. What does the Information Commissioner's Office do?

---

[3] Wong, J.C. (2019) 'The Cambridge Analytica scandal changed the world – but it didn't change Facebook' *The Guardian*, 18 March 2019. Available online: https://www.theguardian.com/technology/2019/mar/17/the-cambridge-analytica-scandal-changed-the-world-but-it-didnt-change-facebook, accessed on 21/08/2019.

[4] Available online at: https://www.visualcapitalist.com/what-happens-in-an-internet-minute-in-2019/.

Once more, you can usefully analyse the 'chunking down' technique we adopted (social media–data–privacy–data protection–political issues–ethics), and employ it to give you a structure to reveal the commercial awareness issues in any similar scenario or debate (e.g. whether political advertising should be banned on all social media).

15.3.2 Why you need it

Building up commercial awareness cannot begin too early. Having a level of commercial awareness as a student can help to contribute to your understanding of various areas of black letter (academic) law.

Example 5

Take contract law: it is sometimes said that 'Contract follows the money'. If you look at some contract cases, you can see that an understanding of the economic context at the time throws light on these. In the 18th century, Britain's wealth was based on its maritime trade: many 18th-century cases involve ships. Until the 20th century, a person's main asset was often his horse: there are a huge number of cases involving horses. In the 19th century, the advent of the railway transformed Britain—leading to a number of railway cases. In the latter part of the 20th century, the introduction of computers in the workplace transformed the economy: suddenly, computers became the subject of some very important cases.

Commercial awareness will also help you stand out when you apply for a graduate role. Employers will want to know that you are tuned into the wider world, that you have the ability to meet your clients' expectations and add value to your advice. They will expect you to know the law, but you have to show that 'edge' which sets you apart from other applicants. Let's consider this from a commercial perspective.

1. The first hurdle is your application, where you will need to evidence your commercial awareness. You have already analysed two examples (Examples 3 and 4) which illustrate the sort of commercial understanding you need to demonstrate. How can you highlight that you have this understanding, in your application, in a way which will help to make your application stand out?

2. Once you get to an interview or assessment day, the questions will take this a little further, as explored in the two commercial awareness examples (Examples 3 and 4).

3. Finally, you will be expected to have an insight into the firm itself, its structure, its position within the market, and who its clients are, and their position within the market in which they operate, so you will need to do some detailed research before you go. We will look at the sort of information you are looking for in this Part of the book.

Chapter 16 considers the application process further.

15.3.3 How to get it?

So how do you develop (and show that you are developing) commercial awareness? Much of this has been covered in Chapter 6 and Part II, but we are now going to put a commercial slant on this.

15.3.3.1 Skills

Commercial awareness is often about your clients and managing their expectations. The skills set out in Part II are designed to help you to develop successful professional relationships as well as improve your ability to give effective advice.

15.3.3.2 Research

It is not just legal research (see Chapter 8) which is going to further your career. You need to know about economic, social and political, and technological, as well as legal issues. You should:

- Read the quality daily broadsheets (*The Guardian, The Independent, The Times*, and *The Telegraph*), particularly the financial pages.
- Watch the television news. Listen to news items on the radio. As understanding develops, progress onto reading *The Financial Times* and *The Economist*, and watching and listening to programmes which analyse economics and finance, like *Newsnight* or the *Today* programme.
- Be aware of what is going on in the legal press. *The Lawyer, Lawyer2B* (for students and trainees), and *Legal Business* magazines are excellent sources of legal news, and help you to understand law firms as businesses, and the context within which they are operating. Websites such as Legal Cheek[5] provide legal 'gossip' and comment on law firms (including the salaries they pay) and the legal profession and can be a useful source of information and insight into topical issues, such as LawTech (and see 20.1.10)

15.3.3.3 Work experience

However much anyone reads, there is no real substitute for working in a commercial environment. Vacation placements in law firms or pro bono work with organisations such as the Citizens Advice Bureau show commitment to the legal profession, and will inevitably help to develop commercial awareness. However, it is not just legal jobs which help to improve commercial know-how. Working for any business gives an insight into how businesses work, how they deal with money, and gives experience of working as part of a team as well as client/customer relationships. If you think about it, a job in a local supermarket teaches all these things in the same way as a job in a City bank. Law firms recognise such skills as transferable: provided you can demonstrate that you have acquired these skills, and how, they are less concerned about the context in which they have been acquired. Transferable skills are explained further at 16.4.3.

15.3.3.4 Networking

Networking (see 15.7) is a crucial skill. Use any contacts who have worked in some sort of commercial environment as a resource to help you to find out what the trends are within

---

[5] Available online at: http://www.legalcheek.com.

Part III

Employability and
Commercial Awareness

their businesses, what factors are influencing their business decisions, their customer/client experiences, and what contributes to success or failure.

15.3.3.5 Opportunities

Usually colleges or universities will arrange seminars and talks on subjects that are relevant to commercial awareness. There will be clubs and societies which help to develop this. Social media and blogs also offer opportunities to develop your commercial awareness (see 15.10). Students should always make the most of these opportunities. It can all go into a CV (see 15.2.2 and 16.4).

15.4 Team-working

In the past, the image of a lawyer was perhaps of a professional sitting alone in an ivory tower, bestowing knowledge of the law onto grateful clients. Those days are gone. To be a good lawyer, or indeed any other professional, in the modern world you need to have good people skills and be able to work well with others. This includes working with those with whom you do not have a natural affinity. This is especially pertinent for trainee lawyers, who will work in at least four different departments of a firm during their two-year training contract.

> **Practice tip**
>
> Trainees sit with different departments during their training contract of two years. The time spent with one department is referred to as a 'seat', and when a trainee moves to a different department, this is called a 'seat move'. The majority of firms offer trainees four seats each lasting six months, but some firms offer more seats over the two-year period. Arranging seat moves can be a stressful time, as several trainees may indicate an interest in the same seat, and not all will obtain their first choice. It is important to give your best performance in all seats, even if you are not seeking to qualify into that department. Do not forget that the partner in your current department may well be acquainted with the partner in the department you want to go to next, and a positive or negative referral from one partner to another, however informal, may be pivotal in deciding whether you secure your first choice of seat move or not.

Most candidates who apply for any kind of employment refer in their CV to good team-working skills. It is useful to give some thought as to what this actually entails.

15.4.1 What is team-working and why is it important?

You should be able to identify some examples where you have worked as part of a team. Playing team sports, being a member of a committee, or working as part of any other team, be it during work experience in a law firm or waiting tables, will all help you to give context to demonstrate that you are a good team player. If you have not done so already, use the PDP technique referred to at 15.2.2 to examine your CV for any gaps you need to fill in terms of team-working, and undertake activities now to plug those gaps. For example, you may need to take part in some extracurricular activities such as joining a sports team or society (law-related, such as mooting, or otherwise). However when, having read Chapter 16, you grasp the concept of transferable skills, you may also be able to use examples you had not thought of to date as 'team work', such as working in groups during your face-to-face teaching, or setting up your own study group and establishing ground rules to help it work effectively.

A common question asked of prospective trainees at the interviewing stage is what exactly team-working involves. This list highlights some of the vital skills, in the order 'ABCDEF' to help you to commit them to memory.

- **A**cknowledging the contributions of others in the team.
- **B**uilding good working relationships.
- **C**ontributing to the team.
- Being able to **D**elegate, and be delegated to, **E**ffectively.
- Knowing how to **F**unction well as a team, including in team meetings.

We will explore these skills further in this chapter, and you can reflect on which component skills you may already have, and which you may be able to develop.

15.4.2 **Roles within a team**

It is worth spending some time reflecting on the role you like to take in a team, whatever team that may be. Most people have a preferred role that they find themselves adopting over again. Consider the scenarios in which you have worked as part of a team to date. Are you dominant or do you prefer to work away from the spotlight? Do you help the team to stay focused and on task, or are you a constant source of diverse creative ideas? Do you like detail, or do you prefer to think strategically but leave the finer detail to others?

There are several assessment tools available to determine how you can work to your full potential in a team, including *Belbin Team Roles*, which analyses the team role which would suit you best, and the *Myers-Briggs Type Indicator*, which analyses your personality type. It is common for employers, including law firms, to use these assessment tools as part of staff team-building days, to analyse how they might deploy their employees' skills to maximum advantage. Both of these assessment tools require a fee to be paid, however they also have some useful free information available on their websites and the addresses are set out in the Further Reading section at the end of this chapter.

Whatever your preferred role, an employer will expect you to be aware of the strengths and weaknesses of that role. For example, if you are a dominant team member, you will have no problem in demonstrating that you contribute fully to the team, but are you aware that you may inhibit a valuable but quieter member of the team from contributing to the discussion? If you can both (i) identify the potential disadvantages of your personality type and also (ii) devise steps to address them, you are demonstrating high-level team-working skills. Graduate employers will also be looking for employees with leadership potential. Regardless of the role you tend to adopt within a team, it is possible to show that working in any role within a team has allowed you to develop your own leadership skills. Team-working provides opportunities to reflect on your own strengths and weaknesses, and those of others, and to devise strategies and develop communication skills which allow team members to participate in the team inclusively and in a way which plays to their strengths. It affords opportunities for you to practise how to identify a goal and work towards that goal effectively, and how to learn from the successes and mistakes you or others may make. If you can show that you have recognised these opportunities and learned from them, you will be able to demonstrate leadership potential, as they are all essential characteristics of a good leader.

15.4.3 Who might be in your team?

It is worth considering what teams you consider yourself to be working in at the moment. The number may surprise you. Team-working is an important skill for a lawyer because at any one time you might be working in several different teams. Let us consider the example of a trainee working in the commercial and corporate department of a law firm. What teams might she be working in? This is precisely the sort of question you may be asked at an interview. Simultaneously the trainee might be working in all of the following teams:

- **Team 1: trainee team.** The trainee may be one of an intake of several trainees. The trainees will support one another as peers and may work together in the same department or across other departments.
- **Team 2: department team.** The trainee is spending a finite period of time in the commercial/corporate department. During this time she must work effectively with the other trainees, fee-earners, partners, and secretaries in that department.
- **Team 3: transaction team.** The entire commercial/corporate department will not be advising on the same transaction (or 'deal'). Instead, a transaction team will be selected from the department to work on one particular transaction. Depending on the size of the transaction, this team will comprise one or more partners, fee-earners, and trainees.
- **Team 4: client team.** The transaction team may be advising a client which is a company. There will be a team of individuals at the company who are involved in putting the deal together, such as the company secretary (often a lawyer), the directors (who manage the company), and possibly a team of senior managers who are not directors. The trainee must be able to work with these people as part of a team.
- **Team 5: advisory team.** Typically the client will need other advice, in addition to legal advice, in order to complete the transaction. For example, the client's advisory team might consist of accountants, bankers, stockbrokers, and public relations professionals.

It is important to realise that you will not always have a natural affinity with those in your team. Nevertheless you will be expected to work seamlessly with these people as well as those towards whom you would more naturally gravitate. Law tutors may help you to develop these skills by encouraging you to sit with people other than your friends during workshops and seminars, and perhaps to adopt a role that would not be your first preference. This can help you to develop your team-working skills and will also help to prevent you always adopting the same role within a team (which you have been encouraged to identify). As part of the self-reflection process, and to work on the problem-solving skills referred to in Chapter 9, it is good to consider any problems you have or might experience while working as a team, and how you tried or might try to solve these problems. For example, you may come across someone who does not contribute to your group work. This may be for a number of reasons:

perhaps he has not prepared, is shy, is reluctant to interrupt a more dominant group member, lacks confidence, does not understand the work, is tired, genuinely has a more pressing problem distracting him, and so on. How might you encourage this person to contribute? Should you? Does the reason that he is not contributing make a difference? How would you find out the reason? Should you? Get into the habit of learning from your experiences, and do not be afraid to admit that you handled a situation in a way you would not repeat. This is all part of your learning as a student, as much as reading *Donoghue* v *Stevenson*.

15.5 Delegation

For a team to work most effectively, each member of the team should be working to their highest level. This involves the team members working together in a structured way, sharing the workload efficiently between them according to their training and experience. This is not restricted to law firms; consider, for example, why you have blood taken by a nurse but your appendix removed by a surgeon. It is particularly important however that lawyers work at an appropriate level, because, at least historically, clients pay each lawyer a different rate calculated specifically by reference to experience (see 20.1.6). If a senior lawyer with a high charge-out rate is doing basic legal work, there is a danger that the charge would be so expensive that the client would not pay it. Rather than 'write off' this time, which would adversely affect the firm's profits, it is better for more senior members of the team to delegate less complex tasks to the more junior members. (Note that, as Chapter 20 explains, in the new, deregulated legal market firms are slowly beginning to acknowledge the need to revise their thinking about how they charge clients for their work, but many firms continue to use this model.)

Example 6

In Shephard & Son, a partner charges £360 per hour, an associate £150 per hour, and a trainee £50 per hour. A client, Emma, has asked the planning team whether she can cut down a tree in her garden. The team needs to research the issue then provide some advice to Emma in writing.

The partner could do this. It would take her 15 minutes to research the law, and 10 minutes to draft the letter. The cost to the client would be £150 (£360/60×25).

Alternatively, the partner could delegate some of the task to the trainee. Let's assume that it would take the trainee 30 minutes to research the law and 30 minutes to draft the letter. The partner could then check and amend the work in 10 minutes. The cost to the client would be £110 (£50 + (£360/60×10)).

Effective delegation has allowed the firm to charge more competitively for the work for Emma, has freed the partner's time to work on a more complex problem for another client, and has given the trainee valuable experience.

It can be very frustrating for both the person delegating and the recipient of the delegated task if this delegation is not done effectively. Unfortunately, poor delegation is very common. The following are common signs of poor delegation:

- Leaving a task until it is urgent before delegating it.
- Not giving enough thought about who to delegate to.

- Failing to give clear instructions as to what needs to be done.
- Not agreeing a deadline.
- Not being available to answer essential questions.
- Not passing on new information.
- Giving no feedback, or negative feedback with no scope to allow for learning from mistakes.

Why is poor delegation common? There are several contributing factors and understanding them can help you to be better both at delegating and being delegated to. Looking from the delegator's perspective, he may simply be too busy to have given enough thought to how to delegate effectively. Sometimes a delegator may feel too inhibited to delegate properly. He may be embarrassed at having to ask for help or worried about burdening other people. In some cases, there may be something on the file which the delegator would prefer others not to see, such as a complaint or a long delay on his part. From the delegatee's perspective, she may be inhibited and respond negatively to the delegator due to the fact she is already overloaded, or because of previous negative experiences of delegation, or simply because the work is not at the right level for her to take on.

Good delegation can avoid these problems, but it requires planning and forethought. The flowchart at Figure 15.2 will help you, as a guide to what to do if you are in the role of delegator, and to help you ask for appropriate guidance if you are a delegatee. As a student you may consider that you are more likely to be the delegatee, and this is true in terms of the role you will have while on work experience, or a vacation scheme. However, if you think carefully you will probably be able to identify some times where you have taken, or should have taken, the role of delegator. For example, if your lecturer gives you a group assignment to complete, how have you decided who is doing what and when? If you have held a charity cake sale, who has decided who will bake, who might sell some raffle tickets, and who might be in charge of the money? On what basis were these decisions made? Whether you knew it or not, someone was delegating, and if you are going to be a good delegator it helps to realise this.

15.6 Client care

All businesses need to care for their customers, but some do this better than others. It is much more efficient to keep an existing, good client content than to lose that client and have to find another, but this is not always put into practice. For example, you might have experienced the frustration, as an existing customer of a bank or mobile phone company, of discovering that new customers are being offered better rates.

Without clients, businesses are nothing, and in an increasingly competitive marketplace all businesses, including law firms, need to keep their clients happy. When asked, law firms would say that they expect their employees to provide a good level of customer care, but anecdotally it would seem that many are yet to incorporate customer care into their training and development programmes. In the absence of any formal customer care training, the best guide is to consider the service you provide from a customer's perspective. This is good practice whatever the nature of the business. There are things you can be doing now to increase your understanding of customer care. If you have any experience of working in a

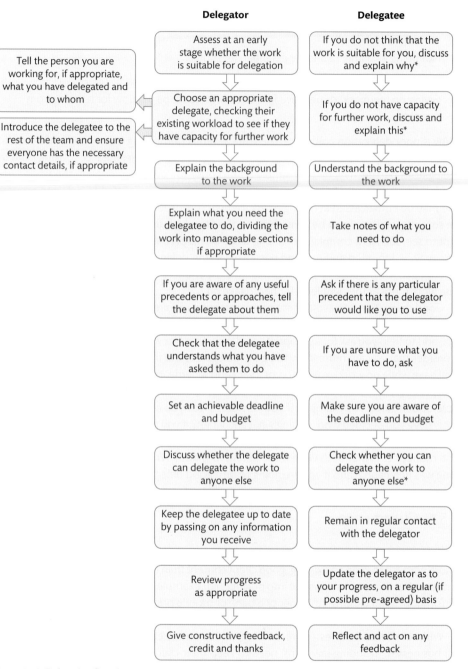

Figure 15.2 Delegation flowchart

*Take a cautious approach here. As a lawyer, you must be willing to take on challenging work in order to develop, and you must be willing to work hard. However, part of being a professional is also being able to manage your workload effectively, and knowing when to ask for help. If, for example, a supervisor mistakes you for someone else who is more senior, it would be appropriate to discuss that you are, say, a trainee. If you have been told by one supervisor that you should not take on any further work until you have completed a task for him, then again you would need to discuss this with the delegator. As ever, your tone and body language will be important here to make sure you do not come across as defensive, or simply saying 'no'.

service industry, such as in a shop, bar, or pro bono clinic, you will have a better understanding of what you can do to improve the customer's experience. Reflecting on this will help you to develop this skill now, and you will be able to showcase it on your CV (see Chapter 16).

15.6.1 Common complaints (and how to avoid them)

Let's now consider some of the most common complaints made by law firm clients, together with guidance to help you avoid being the lawyer they complain about. Again, this is exactly the sort of question that might arise in a law firm interview, but be aware that these complaints are not confined to law firms. Be alert to items in the news about customer care, and consider how they might transfer into areas relevant to your career.

15.6.1.1 Fees

Not surprisingly, bills can be a source of frustration for a client. A frequent complaint is that they are too high, but other complaints include that the bill arrived unexpectedly, contained obvious errors on its face, appeared to refer to work which was unnecessary or on which too much time had been spent, or included charges for disbursements (see Essential explanation) that seem very high or were unexpected.

> **Essential explanation**
>
> A *disbursement* is a payment that the law firm has made on behalf of the client for goods or services. Examples include photocopying charges and fees paid to the Land Registry for land searches. They can amount to a significant proportion of a client's bill.

A good lawyer can help to avoid this by managing a client's expectations well. The bill should not come as a surprise to the client, nor should there be any surprises in the bill itself.

15.6.1.2 Jargon

Lawyers can become so used to using jargon or 'legalese' between themselves that they forget that a client will not understand what they are saying. Chapters 10 and 11 explain that all communication between lawyer and client should be clear and as succinct as possible. Clients will become frustrated if they cannot understand the advice they are paying for. A good lawyer can understand difficult legal concepts, but it takes a very good lawyer to be able to communicate those concepts clearly in a way that a non-lawyer can understand.

15.6.1.3 Listening

Everyone likes to be listened to and clients are no exception to this. Lawyers, like many other professionals, can be poor listeners, with a tendency to interrupt clients or make assumptions about what they think. As Chapter 10 sets out, this can have a catastrophic effect on the appropriateness of the work which a lawyer produces, but it can also leave the client feeling neglected and not valued. Asking lots of open questions, and listening to the answers without interruption, can help a client feel satisfied with your work. Chapter 10 explores this further.

15.6.1.4 Manner

It does not matter how technically brilliant you are if you have no interpersonal skills when it comes to delivering your advice. You need to develop a good 'bedside manner' with clients that is neither too patronising nor too abrupt. This will not be the same for each client. Once you know your clients and the work you will be doing for them, you can and should tailor your manner to suit. For example, advising a recently bereaved person may require a different manner to advising a company director on a multi-million pound deal. However, even this will depend on the individual concerned.

15.6.1.5 Keeping the client updated

Clients should not have to call you to find out what is happening with their matter. It is much better if you are proactive, and take the initiative to contact them, even just to convey a brief message that nothing has happened. It is particularly important to contact clients if they have tried to contact you. Failing to return a call is a common complaint: reflect on how you would feel if you tried to contact your lecturer to arrange a meeting to discuss a problem and your call was left unanswered. Admittedly as a lawyer it can be a difficult step to call a client to deliver an unpalatable message, such as your work is going to be late, or you have made a mistake in some way. However, experience dictates that clients will always appreciate an early and honest call rather than the alternative which is for them to wait, eventually call you and finally, when pressed, for you to confess to the delay or the error. Lawyers who covet the role of trusted adviser must develop good habits in keeping clients informed of everything they need to know, good and bad.

15.6.1.6 Poor-quality work

Chapter 10 explained that clients will judge you on the standard of your writing and drafting (often more so than the quality of your legal advice, which they will presume is accurate in the absence of any obvious error). Clients will complain about work which is clearly deficient in terms of spelling, grammar, and punctuation. Some errors which are undetectable using spell-check can actually cause offence. Consider the impact of 'Dear Gut' instead of 'Dear Gus', or 'See you shorty' rather than 'See you shortly'. Common complaints surround poor use of punctuation (particularly the apostrophe) and sentence structure (particularly long letters with no paragraphs).[6] While lawyers can argue that the work was actually of satisfactory quality given the circumstances in which it was done, for instance if they had to dictate a letter very quickly over the telephone, or draft a clause in the middle of the night, you can

---

[6] For an amusing example of a mistake made by a law firm, see https://www.legalcheek.com/2019/10/clyde-co-seeks-paralegal-with-excellent-attention-to-detials/, accessed 02/11/2019.

see that from the client's perspective these errors can be perceived as reflecting a generally substandard service.

15.6.1.7 Lack of continuity

Law firms are busy places and lawyers will be working for several clients at the same time. Client matters can also take a long time to resolve and even lawyers need holidays. It is a business reality therefore that from time to time you will have to pass work for one client to one of your colleagues. Most clients will understand this if the process is managed properly. However all too often, due to time pressure, the client is the last to know that someone else has taken over the work on his file, or will discover that the new lawyer may not have been brought fully up to date as to the progress on the file. Again, you might be able to reflect on your own experience; anyone who has had the experience of trying to contact a business only to find themselves passed from one person to another, having to explain the same issue to several different people, will appreciate how annoying this can be. Factor in that as a client of a law firm you are often paying by the minute for these repeated explanations and you will appreciate why this is a common client complaint. A few simple conversations, with the client and the lawyer you are handing over to, can remove these aggravating factors.

15.6.2 Managing clients

The key to good client relationships is to manage the client's expectations. For example, if a client is calling several times a day to check your progress, you clearly need to explain to her that you will provide a regular update and this will be a more cost-effective way for her to monitor your progress. Similarly, a client who expects you to be available to her or deliver work at unsociable hours needs to understand that this may be either unnecessary or may warrant a higher fee. The best time to discuss and establish all of this is at the outset, before the client instructs you.

15.6.3 SRA Standards and Regulations 2019

You have read at 15.1.3 that lawyers must be aware of ethics. The Solicitors Regulation Authority, which regulates the profession, issued a new set of Standards and Regulations in November 2018 which creates two Codes of Conduct, one for firms and one for solicitors. Both Codes describe the standards of professionalism required of solicitors and firms, and the regulations are underpinned by a revised Enforcement Strategy (see Chapter 6).

15.6.4 Feedback

It is good practice to seek feedback from any customer when you complete work for them. You may already have provided feedback to your university, for example on your course materials or the teaching you have received. This is so that the university can listen to your opinion, address any issues you raise, and ensure it continues to do everything that receives positive feedback. Thinking carefully about how you provide such feedback will develop your employability skills. For example, it is likely that you have been able to provide feedback anonymously to date, which has benefits in terms of freeing you to give your honest opinion, but has the drawback of allowing you to say things that you would not say to someone's face. When you enter the professional world your feedback will be attributable, so it is worth developing now the skill of providing feedback in a way that is constructive and which you would feel comfortable delivering face to face. As a professional, you will not just receive feedback but you will also have to give feedback to your colleagues and delegates, for example. Some businesses, including law firms, have formal procedures in place for this. Everyone likes to be asked their opinion, and indeed if business clients request feedback in their own business they may think it strange if you do not ask their opinion of your work at the end of the process.

15.7 Networking

Networking is a key skill for professionals, and although lawyers may have been relatively slow to embrace the need for this skill, it is now accepted that networking is part of a lawyer's job. Networking involves building new business relationships in order to generate business opportunities. Some people are very comfortable approaching and speaking to new people, and actively enjoy it, and to those people this skill will come more naturally. However for many professionals, junior and senior, it is one that can take them outside their comfort zone. As ever, the keys to mastering this skill are preparation and practice.

There are networking opportunities everywhere and accomplished networkers will not only be able to identify these opportunities, but also work them to their advantage. As a student, you may encounter face-to-face networking opportunities through work experience, pro bono work, sitting in on court hearings, attending talks and law fairs, and also simply by socialising with your peers, who one day may be prospective and sought-after clients or employers. Social media such as Twitter and Facebook and the practice of blogging have also opened up networking opportunities online.

When you meet potential clients or employers, as the case may be, you want them to remember your name. If you have been given a name badge, wear it. It will be most prominent if you wear it on the side of your body you shake hands with. If you do not have a name badge, you need to develop another strategy to make sure the people you wish to secure as business contacts remember your name. If you have a business card, you can give them your card. Ask if they have a card, as not only do you want them to remember your name, you also need to remember theirs. If you are attending an event, it is helpful if you can see the attendee list in advance. Some event organisers are very good in this regard, and will send the attendee list, either directly to you or to the person in your organisation who has arranged your attendance. It is worth asking if one is available in advance. If it is not, there is often a sign-in sheet at the door of the event, and a quick glance can reveal whether there is anyone attending who you already know or who you would specifically like to make a business contact.

Then you need to start speaking to people. This is sometimes referred to as 'working the room'. It can be difficult to approach people, but remember that they too will be open to networking opportunities and are likely to welcome you. Use your communication skills, including good eye contact and body language, to signal to someone that you would like to join them.

Once you have the attention of the person you would like to meet, you need to be able to engage them. You can prepare in advance what you might be able to say if the conversation does not flow naturally from the outset. Remember that the other person is not privy to your preparation, so do not decide to talk about something so esoteric that, while impressive, will not allow the other person to participate in the conversation. The morning's headlines, or even something as simple as the good old weather, will be enough for most people to start the flow of conversation.

Another skill you will need is to be able to exit from a conversation. A good networker will seek to circulate as much as possible. Do not be inhibited about doing this (indeed the person you are speaking to will also want time to speak to others), but obviously there is a technique to exiting in a polite fashion. Classic techniques include excusing yourself to go to the toilet. Clearly however you cannot use this too many times. Going to get a glass of water or sandwich can also help you to exit in a polite fashion.

If you have been attending a talk, do not underestimate the value of staying behind to thank the speaker. Most attendees file out immediately, yet the five minutes after the talk can be an excellent opportunity for networking. Speakers will feel at ease, and will be happy to hear some feedback and answer questions which show that you have listened to and enjoyed what they had to say.

Remember to follow up the contacts you have made. Sending a short follow-up email, or, if appropriate, a short telephone call to say how you enjoyed meeting them, is a good idea. Social media, for instance the LinkedIn platform, can also be helpful to secure an ongoing contact. Use your instinct and skills to determine what it is appropriate to say in this follow-up communication. Depending on the individual concerned, and how your conversation went, sometimes it is not appropriate to do anything other than say thank you, while at other times a suggestion that you meet for coffee, or an expression of interest, such as in work experience or mentoring opportunities, can be appropriate and pay dividends.

Even reading this paragraph may have made your toes curl. To the uninitiated, networking can sound embarrassingly like you are trying to secure a date. In practice, take comfort from the fact that you will not be the only one in the room to be networking. It is now generally accepted that everyone in the room will be, or should be. Also appreciate the fact that most people will also feel a little out of their comfort zone. The more polished your networking skills, the more people will want to talk to you because, conversely, *you* will help to put *them* at ease.

Be aware that networking does not necessarily have immediate rewards. Do not feel frustrated if you attend an event and leave empty-handed, or people do not respond to your email. Networking will deliver benefits in the long term. It may only be after meeting someone for the fourth time, for example, that you feel comfortable in inviting that person to connect with you on LinkedIn, or to suggest you meet for a coffee. The only thing you can say with certainty is that if you do not attend events at all, you will definitely not extend your network.

You can practise your networking skills now. No matter how early a stage you are at in your career, you will already have a network you can access. Although they are likely to have no influence on getting you a training contract or other career just yet, your fellow students are excellent contacts as in the future they will go on to become lawyers and other professionals. The person you are sitting next to now might be the CEO of a company a law firm would love to bring in as a client in 15 years' time. Following the guidance in this work you can extend your current network to include alumni of your university and other legal professionals.

15.7.1 **Law fairs**

Law fairs offer a valuable opportunity to meet many firms under one roof. Many students choose to attend them, but often find themselves wandering rather aimlessly up and down many aisles of stands, perhaps managing to gather a few branded freebies on the way. Few students exploit their full potential.

At a law fair you will be able to speak to employees of many firms. Typically firms send a mixture of recruitment personnel, trainees, and other fee-earners. This is a huge expense for a firm, not least because the trainees and fee-earners are not fee-earning while they are at the fair. So think for a moment about why they bother to attend. They are hoping to attract good-quality candidates for training contracts. From this perspective, then, law fairs have the potential to be mini interviews where the firms have done all the work and come to meet you in one place. Put this way, it should be clear that no student considering a legal career should pass up the opportunity to attend a fair.

As many firms recruit years in advance, you should attend law fairs even in your first year of study. Although firms pay considerable sums to consultants to draft a set of values and to create a website which they feel reflects them uniquely, it is a common student observation that 'they all say the same thing'. The fairs offer a forum to meet and talk informally to firms and to get a real feel for their true culture and values.

The firms will be interested in meeting you. They will also expect you to be interested in meeting them. You need to prepare to make sure you leave the firm with a good impression of you and what you have to offer.

15.7.1.1 Preparation

The organisers of a law fair will circulate a list of attendees and a floor plan in advance of the fair. You need to study this to plan who to target, as the fairs are often so large you are unlikely to stumble across the firms you are looking for by accident. For example, if you are interested in working in a mid-sized regional firm which has a strong intellectual property presence, you need to work through the list in conjunction with a legal directory such as *Chambers and Partners* or the *Legal 500* and access to the firms' websites, and highlight those firms you would like to visit. Alternatively, if you have not yet narrowed your preference to that degree, you may like to make a varied selection of firms, from boutique practices to the largest Magic Circle firms, to start this process. Wherever you are in recognising where you want to practise, your aim should be to be able to produce a shortlist based on your experiences at the fair and feed this into your PDP (see 15.2.2).

15.7.1.2 Presentation

Having drawn the conclusion that the fair offers an opportunity not unlike a mini interview, it follows that you should present yourself well. You will be making an impression on the law firms that you meet, and you should dress to convey the impression you would like to make. There is guidance at 15.1.3 about how to dress professionally. You may feel more comfortable dressing in something a little more relaxed than a suit, however the guidance about general presentation in terms of your hair, shoes, and so on is just as applicable for law fairs.

15.7.1.3 Execution

Once you are at the fair, with a plan of action, you can expect to feel a little nervous. Take courage though, that the firms will appreciate that you might find the prospect of speaking to them quite daunting. If you can appear polite, well informed, and work on developing a veneer of confidence, this is all you need. The firms will want to speak to you, but this is easier for them if they have some information about you. Introducing yourself by name, shaking hands and telling them what you are studying, where, and what you are enjoying will help to start a conversation and strike up a rapport.

You should not ask questions you should already know the answer to. These include anything you could reasonably be expected to find on the firm's website. If you have prepared in advance you should already know the basics. This is not to say asking questions is wrong, far from it, but you should prepare questions which help to give you the edge in any subsequent application to the firm. For example, do not ask where the firm is based, or whether it has a property department (both of which you should have researched already), but, for example, you might ask whether the firm is planning to expand, geographically or strategically. Subtly show the firm that you have done your homework about them. Tell the firm what you are enjoying, and sound enthusiastic. Ask what you can be doing to impress in this area, give examples of what you are already doing, and what in the area has taken your interest.

After the fair, use the experience to prepare a shortlist of firms which you liked, and make a note of anything you learned which could help your application to that firm. A well-placed tweet can be helpful in putting a marker in the sand that you spoke to the firm, but be selective as the firms will be able to see who else you are tweeting.

15.7.2 **Mentors**

Having a mentor is a long-established and valued process by which you are guided by someone who has reached the place you are aiming for. The process has benefits for both the mentor and the mentee, and you will find that practising professionals are often keen to take on the role of mentor. There are various ways of finding a mentor, and most universities have formal schemes which you can join. This is another valuable way to gain an insight into the profession, and learn valuable wider lessons about being a professional. Increasingly universities are harnessing their alumni network to help with mentoring current students, so this is a route you may be able to explore. Social networking may also lend itself to a more informal version of mentoring. Finally, do not forget the value in mentoring, and being mentored by, your fellow students. You will all have different skills and experiences to share and learn from, and appreciating at this early stage that you have something worthwhile to share will help you with your PDP, to reflect and identify your own individual strengths that you can showcase at interview.

15.7.3 **Work experience**

Employers will expect to see that you have sought and found work experience. Work experience will help you to develop your employability skills as well as give you an opportunity to impress those you are working with and learn what goes on in a law firm, chambers, or other professional organisation. Mini-pupillages, vacation schemes, law tasters, opportunities to work as a paralegal, and other informal work experience are therefore things you need to seek out actively, and the sooner you do this, the better. An increasing number of firms are recruiting trainees solely from their pool of paralegals.

15.7.4 **Pro bono**

Pro bono means 'for the public good' and pro bono initiatives provide a superb opportunity to provide advice to real clients while helping members of society to access legal advice which they could not otherwise afford. There are numerous initiatives, covering the full spectrum of legal work. Universities often run law clinics in partnership with practice or charities, and there are also other external pro bono schemes, such as the Innocence Network UK. LawWorks is the Solicitors' Pro Bono Group, together with the Bar Pro Bono Unit and the CILEx Pro Bono Trust, it forms part of the National Pro Bono Centre in Chancery Lane. Further information on pro bono is available online, for example on the website of ProBonoUK and on the Law Careers website. Further details are provided in the Further Reading section at the end of this chapter.

15.8 Marketing

Most businesses realise that they have to market the goods they are selling or the services they are providing, but some businesses will be more naturally adept at marketing than others. Lawyers do not tend to be natural salespeople. However, the market is now so competitive that everyone in the firm is expected actively to market their firm and bring in new business. In order to do this effectively, you need to understand the message that the firm wishes you to deliver. Most firms now have their aims, objectives, and/or strategy set out clearly on their website. When you join a firm, further information is likely to feature on the firm's intranet site. The earlier you are familiar with these selling messages, the better you will be at marketing. Of course, the best form of marketing that you can deliver as a lawyer is to provide exceptional client service.

15.9 Information technology

There is no escape, you are likely to need sound IT skills wherever you work in today's world. From multinationals to local services such as your local car wash or gardener, businesses are using IT to increase their public profile and develop client relationships. The good news is that this is an area where youth is most definitely on your side. You are likely to have grown up around so much IT that your skills are well honed. Conversely, some of the partners in a law firm would not have had a single computer in their classroom during school and may have started out as a lawyer before mobile phones and the internet were in common use. You are therefore in a good position to dazzle them with your skills in this regard.

The firms will train you on their individual IT systems, which will include some or all of online time recording, dictation and precedent and information sharing systems. However the better you are with word processing, spreadsheets, email, and typing, the more polished you will look and the more efficient you will be on arrival. Take advantage of the expertise you can tap into at university. Attend any courses you can which will polish your IT skills for the professional world.

15.10 Social media

Law firms are as alert to new business development opportunities as the next business and increasingly they are turning to social media platforms such as Twitter and Facebook to extend their reach. These platforms can also be useful networking opportunities for you as an individual. However, you must use them with care.[7]

15.10.1 A word of caution

Remember that these are very public platforms, and you should not post anything on them which you would not be happy to say or show to a partner's face. Some professionals operate different Twitter accounts, one personal, and one professional. However, given the nature of the legal profession and the general availability of Twitter posts to the public at large, junior lawyers would be best advised to play safe and avoid using Twitter in a personal capacity. It is not uncommon for employers to check a prospective employee's Twitter feed. Clearly it is possible to use your feed to impress a potential employer if it evidences an interest in law or in other ways supports any claims you have made on your application form. However, your holiday snaps, or tweets about your latest big night out, might be best reserved for a more private forum. Facebook can be more private than Twitter, but you must take care to set your privacy preferences correctly, and choose your friends wisely. Again, given the potential for error it is advisable that you post only information that you would be happy for your employer to read. The accessibility of social networking sites works both ways and it is not unknown in some jurisdictions, e.g. the US, for employers to ask interviewees for their Facebook login details,[8] although in the UK the Computer Misuse Act 1990 offers some protection to employees. Example 7 can be a warning to you of the power of social networks, and not getting your privacy settings right.

---

[7] See, for example, Embley, J. and Goodchild, P. 'The Seven Deadly Sins of Social Media – Don't be Tempted'. University of Law (2018) Available online at: https://www.law.ac.uk/about/news/2018/seven-deadly-sins-of-social-media/, accessed 02/11/2019.

[8] Raymond Law Group LLC. (2019) 'Can Employers Request Social Media Account Information?' *Lexology*. 28 May 2019. Available online: https://www.lexology.com/library/detail.aspx?g=17685fc1-1dfa-42b3-b625-088b26172833, accessed on 02/11/2019.

Example 7

After leaving University, Charlotte started looking for jobs as a PA. She had two successful interviews with a leading London property firm. The second interview went well, and she was expecting to be called for a third interview. She heard nothing, and contacted her recruitment agent for feedback. She was told that she had interviewed well, but it was very unfortunate about the Facebook photograph. One of her friends had sent her a photograph of a naked DJ, to whom Charlotte bore an uncanny resemblance. Charlotte had posted this on Facebook, and jokingly changed her profile to 'DJ'. The 'joke' had cost her the job.

15.10.2 Twitter

Twitter can be an effective networking tool if used correctly. By following firms and individuals in whom you have a professional interest, you can extend your professional network and access a wealth of relevant information, including employment opportunities. Tweeting itself improves your ability to summarise and distil information as you must restrict yourself to the limit of 140 characters. You can also increase your commercial awareness (see 15.3) simply by following the right people then reading your timeline. Professionals, including employers and academics, tweet on a range of issues that can help you develop the skills in this work. By re-tweeting or 'favouriting' tweets you can bring yourself to the attention of those you are following. However, if you are to do this you need to make a sustained effort. Several firms currently have a Twitter identity which is not managed on a regular basis, and this is revealed when they are copied into tweets which remain unanswered or are not commented on. If you no longer intend to maintain your account regularly, it is best to shut it down, otherwise you may well become known, but for the wrong reasons.

15.10.3 Blogging

A blog, or web log, is an online diary. There is extensive guidance available on the internet as to how you can create your own free blog. Maintaining a regular blog on a subject you are interested in, legal or otherwise, can help you to practise and improve your written communication skills and raise your profile among your professional network. You can use Twitter and Facebook to link to and promote your blog. Reading other people's legal blogs can also help to increase your own commercial awareness. Again, if you do decide to maintain a blog, take care to ensure the content is suitable for reading by a prospective employer.

15.10.4 LinkedIn

LinkedIn provides a professional social media platform on which you can showcase your CV and capture your professional contacts, and it has been embraced by the legal sector. The process of putting together a profile will help you to focus your mind on your CV, and the earlier you begin to think about your CV the better it will be by the time you come to apply for a job. You will be able to link in to your peers immediately, and having your profile ready means that you are in a better position to capture any contacts you make while networking. The way the site works is that a standard message is sent to the contacts of your choosing, asking if they would like to connect with you. It is possible to personalise this standard message and this can be a good idea with contacts you are hoping to impress. As the site makes clear, however, you should only ask to connect to people you know well. As a rule of thumb, if the recipient will not be able to place you when your connect request arrives, you should probably not be sending them a contact request.

 ## Summary

- Technical ability is important for a lawyer, but as a professional, the modern lawyer needs other skills, which are relevant to all businesses.
- Business skills such as client care, networking, marketing, and using IT and social media effectively are very important.
- Employers are not looking for clones. You need to show how your specific combination of skills will help the business to achieve its goals.
- A good team comprises individuals with complementary skills who work together effectively to achieve a common goal.

 ## Practical exercises

1. What kind of personal characteristics would you like your colleagues to have? Consider ranking these attributes in order of importance, starting with those which you consider essential. Do you think you have these characteristics yourself? If so, are you able to show others that you have them?

2. What role do you tend to take when working in a group? Is this the role you like to take? What other role do you think you might flourish in?

3. If today you unexpectedly happened to meet a lawyer who works for a law firm you want to apply to, what would you say to him?

4. Think of a famous brand. How do you know about it? What did the company do to market its brand so well? What can a junior lawyer do to promote the firm's brand?

5. What current world events might you expect to be asked about at interview?

*Visit the **online resources** for the authors' reflections and to check your progress.*

What the professionals say

What tips would I give a law student about employability? When it comes down to it, you can have the best legal knowledge in the world, but if you can't get on with people, they aren't going to trust you or engage with you. Start the process of learning relationship and influencing skills now. This can be achieved through many different routes but possibly the most rewarding being pro bono work. If you have that on your CV, you have evidence that you've engaged at a human level, benefited society and honed relationship building and influencing skills in a legal context. All of these factors will work in your favour when convincing a future employer that you have the skills to practise law as well as the requisite legal knowledge accumulated during your academic career.

Barry Matthews, SRA Board Member
and CEO LexJam Consulting

With a huge variety of careers in the law, work experience can help you to decide where to focus your job applications. I did several mini pupillages, a vacation scheme with a city firm and a placement with the Government Legal Service before making my decision. I was then able to justify that choice based on my personal experiences when asked at interview.

Getting first-hand experience means you are better-informed about the job you are applying for and whether you are suited to it. When you tell recruiters, 'I know what the work involves and I think I would enjoy it and be good at it', that claim is much more believable when evidenced by relevant work experience. It also shows potential employers that you are committed to their area of practice.

Work experience also gives you material to draw on in the application process. Many application forms and interview questions take the form of 'tell us about a time when you've demonstrated a particular skill or competence'. A placement gives you the opportunity to demonstrate those skills in a professional, relevant environment, which is likely to be more impressive.

Sophia Hurst, Barrister, Serle Court

What advice would I give to mature students? It is easy to convince yourself that age and maturity may be viewed negatively by law firms. From my experience, nothing could be further from the truth. Your life experiences are attributes which will positively differentiate you from many of your legal contemporaries. Many of the skills which you have acquired to date will be transferable to your studies and later on in to practice.

In my first degree (pharmacy), which I studied straight after leaving school, I used to sit silently at the back of the lecture theatre, too unsure of myself to engage with the lecturers. By the time I came to study law several years later, I was determined to maximise the opportunity to learn. I was confident enough to ask questions and interacted with the tutors without fear of embarrassment. As a result, I really engaged with the subject and this undoubtedly came across during my training contract interviews.

During those interviews, I demonstrated to my potential employers how my experience as a pharmacist would benefit their business as a law firm. I already knew how to communicate effectively and behave professionally; I had acquired customer care skills; and I had background knowledge about the pharmacy sector which would benefit the firm's business. The bottom line is that many employers look for positive attributes in candidates which will differentiate them from all the other applicants clutching a 2:1. Work history, maturity, and life experience are all positive differentiators for the mature student. Be prepared to use them confidently to your advantage.

To students who are not mature students, my advice would be to get stuck in to your studies and try not to worry too much about what others think. And invite the mature students to the odd party or two.

Richard Hough, former Pharmacist and Partner at Brabners LLP

Further reading

Belbin. Available online at: http://www.belbin.co.uk. *Myers & Briggs Foundation.* Available online at: http://www.myersbriggs.org

—These websites contain different assessment tools to determine how you can work to your full potential in a team, and are familiar to most law firms.

Cottrell, S. (2010) *Skills for Success: The Personal Development Planning Handbook*. Basingstoke: Palgrave Macmillan, 2nd edn

—This will help you to give you some ideas as to how to structure your PDP.

Innocence Network UK. Available online at: http://www.innocencenetwork.org.uk;
LawWorks. Available online at: http://www.lawworks.org.uk;
National Pro Bono Centre. Available online at: http://www.nationalprobonocentre.org.uk;
Law Centres Network. Available online at: http://www.lawcentres.org.uk/

—These four websites all contain information about pro bono initiatives.

Institute of Paralegals. Available online at: http://www.theiop.org

—If you are considering becoming a paralegal this website is a useful source of information.

Junior Lawyers Division. Available online at: http://juniorlawyers.lawsociety.org.uk/front

—The website formed to be the independent voice of the Law Society for LPC students, paralegals looking for training contracts, trainee solicitors, and solicitors up to five years qualified.

SRA (2019) *Solicitors Regulation Authority*. Available online at: http://www.sra.org.uk

—This website sets out information relevant to the profession including the Suitability Test for prospective solicitors and the Codes of Conduct.

SRA (2019) *Solicitors Regulation Authority Training: Students page*. Available online at: https://www.sra.org.uk/students/

—This website contains information about the SRA's programme of education and training reform.

Tuckman, B. W. (1965) 'Developmental Sequence in Small Groups.' *Psychological Bulletin*, 63(6) p. 384. Available online at: http://dennislearningcenter.osu.edu/files/2014/08/GROUP-DEV-ARTICLE.pdf

—This article provides further reading on team-working, and details a group development model by Bruce Tuckman which is commonly referred to in business.

 *For the authors' reflections on the practical exercises, additional self-test questions, sample interview questions and a library of links to useful websites, visit the free **online resources** at www.oup.com/he/slorach4e.*

Making yourself more employable

Chapter 15

16   CVs, applications, and interviews

Learning objectives

After studying this chapter you should be able to:

- Understand and sell your transferable skills.
- Understand how to highlight your employability in a professional job application.
- Prepare effectively for an assessment day.

Introduction

Life as a law graduate, is competitive. Having read Parts II and III, you will now understand that it is your *skills* (Chapters 6 to 14) and *commercial awareness* (Chapters 17 to 20) that will give you the professional advantage. This in itself is an understanding that not all law gradu-ates possess; many still consider to their cost that *knowledge* is all they need. However, this is a mistake. By requiring that applicants meet a stated minimum academic threshold, graduate employers ensure that *all* candidates come to the application process equipped with knowl-edge. If you have only knowledge, you will have nothing to distinguish yourself from the field. This chapter seeks to harness your understanding that graduate employers covet a blend of knowledge, skills, and commercial awareness in order to give yourself the best chance of suc-cess when competing for professional employment. By choosing to study the law of England & Wales as an undergraduate you have very sensibly opted for an internationally recognised and respected subject. As Chapters 15 and 16 indicated, the academic discipline of studying law will have helped you develop life-long, transferable skills (such as critical analysis and reasoning, evaluation, attention to detail, the ability to distil and summarise information, research, solve problems and communicate well face to face, by telephone and in writing) which graduate employers across the professions will appreciate and covet. Parts II and III of this work encourage you to do as the accountants have always done, and to view your studies as a law undergraduate as progressing towards attaining a hallmark that you possess a suite of skills which are eminently transferable and which equip you well for a career in whichever profession you choose. High-flying law graduates can be found at the top of most profes-sions, including academia, accountancy, the armed forces, banking, the civil service, finance, government, journalism, management, the police, publishing, and recruitment as well, of course, as the legal profession, drawing on the knowledge, skills, and commercial awareness instilled in them as law undergraduates.

This chapter aims to equip you now, as a student, to highlight that you are eminently employable (by evidencing knowledge, skills, and commercial awareness) in a way which will give you the advantage when the time comes to apply for any professional role.

16.1 The application process

One of the reasons it is important to understand the employability skills (in Parts II and III) at an early stage in your studies is so that you will come across well when applying for any graduate role. As far as the application process for solicitors is concerned, you will have read in the Preface that the the Solicitors Qualifying Examination (SQE) is due to be introduced from 2021, with a new system of exams and qualifying work experience (QWE). The proposed changes are unlikely to affect the application which is set out below.

Your careers adviser should have a wealth of information to help guide you through the graduate application process. Wherever you are studying, you should consult a careers adviser, as soon as possible after you start your studies. Take as full advantage of the careers resources as you can. Find out any arrangements in place to contact alumni. Begin your PDP process (see 15.2.2) early, and begin to draft a curriculum vitae ('CV') the minute you start your studies (see 16.4), asking your careers adviser and personal tutor if needed, so that you can identify gaps and issues that you can work on while you are studying. This chapter provides guidance about the application and interview process to help inform that process.

To supplement what you have already read in Chapters 10 and 12, further information is set out in this chapter about presentations, group work, and socialising, because you may encounter them on an assessment day or during a vacation scheme or work experience. It can be startlingly clear to an interviewer which applicants have not been exposed to studying skills in a practical context, and which have. This can put undergraduates at a disadvantage compared to those applicants applying later in life or having completed their vocational stage of training or QWE (although, of course, there are several distinct advantages in applying at this earlier stage). Having read and engaged with Parts II and III of this book, the intention is that you will be in the best position to demonstrate your legal skills and commercial awareness at whatever stage you have reached in your legal career.

16.2 Timing your application

It is common to find post-graduate students who admit they were completely unaware of the fact they could have applied for many graduate roles, law and non-law, at a much earlier stage—when they were law undergraduates—and in some instances even obtained funding from graduate employers for the remainder of their studies. This section aims to inform you that it is never too early to apply for work experience and that application windows for some larger firms open not long at all after that. The time to begin to engage with this process is now. The *Law Careers* website referred to in the Further Reading section of this chapter sets out firm-specific application windows in relation to training contracts and work placements. However, the following will give you a sense of the general timescales of which you should be aware.

16.2.1 Larger law firms

The large law firms recruit two years in advance, so if you wish to apply to work for one of these firms you could be applying for interview in your *first year* of a two-year law degree or in your *second year* of a three-year law degree (hence the need to develop your employability skills now). If you manage to secure a training contract or QWE this way this would mean you could then complete your vocational stage of training or any further training course necessary to pass the SQE Stage 1 examination (possibly funded by your future employer) immediately after your law degree and progress straight into your training contract or QWE.

Applications for both training contracts and vacations schemes tend to open in the autumn term, generally from October to December. Many vacation scheme applications close at the end of January, but some remain open as late as April. Training contract applications tend to close at the end of July. As the vast majority of these firms recruit from their vacation schemes, you should apply for both a vacation scheme and a training contract at a firm. Historically law firms did not take applications from first year students (on a three year degree) for vacation schemes, however this is changing and more firms are introducing what they refer to as 'law tasters' for first year students.

You should look out for announcements that firms are recruiting to meet increased demand, as very occasionally the larger firms will realise they have under-recruited, perhaps as the market expands after recession. Again, your careers adviser, Twitter, and your network of contacts will help in this regard.

16.2.2 Smaller law firms

Smaller firms recruit later, however the earlier you start to hone your employability skills, the better you will come across in any interview further down the line. These firms may recruit 12 to 18 months in advance. You should seek to obtain some qualifying work experience with these firms from your second year onwards. If you are going down the training contract route, bear in mind that these firms often recruit trainees from (sometimes exclusively from) their pool of paralegals. Generally these firms are more open to speculative applications.

16.2.3 Other graduate employers

Law firms are not the only graduate employers with structured graduate recruitment programmes. The lead-in time for the larger law firms means that they tend to arise first in the applications timeline, but you should research carefully any employers outside the legal sector to whom you might wish to apply. For example, the Further Reading section sets out resources giving information on graduate roles in the BBC. Your careers adviser will be a good starting point to help identify other non-law sector-specific resources.

16.3 Your application

Your application is likely to be the first impression you make on a firm, so you need to make it stand out for the right reasons. Usually you will need to show that you have:

- a good academic record;
- good knowledge of the firm and the sector in which it operates (ideally referencing work experience);
- the skills referred to in this work.

16.3.1 Attention to detail

Despite the open acknowledgement that the application process for professional employment is highly competitive, it is all too common to find spelling and grammatical errors in applications. Firms receive huge amounts of applications and need to apply a filter system to identify which ones to reject. Those containing such errors typically will be rejected without further reading. You must not give the firms any easy excuse to reject your application. For firms which still require handwritten applications, it is obviously important that the form is legible and neatly presented. Follow any specific instructions, such as to write in capital letters using black ink. Failure to do so will help the employer narrow down the forms it needs to continue to read.

16.3.2 Strengths

When composing your application, of course you must highlight your strengths, but be aware that law firms remain relatively conservative places and so too many superlatives ('I am excellent at', 'I excel at') might dilute the overall effect. Analyse what you write from an objective perspective. If you are describing your academic results as excellent, consider whether they really are. Just because you describe results as excellent does not render them so. Be honest; identify what you think are your strong points (your PDP should have helped you to do this— see 15.2.2) and make sure your application highlights these strengths. Research the firm's stated objectives or strategy and make clear how your strengths will help the firm achieve its goals. Once you have identified your real strengths, do not be afraid to bring them to the interviewer's attention; it is not 'brash' or 'bragging', and you can be sure that the candidates before and after you will be drawing attention to what they do well.

16.3.3 Weaknesses

It can come as a surprise to those new to the applications process that you also need to scrutinise your weaknesses. Is there anything in your record that stands out as being below your usual standard? If so, then you have two choices. You can either remain silent about it pending confirmation of an interview, or you can address the issue in your application. Whichever route you choose, be ready for an interviewer to ask you about your weaknesses. This is not necessarily a negative. Candidates who can show how they have learned from previous mistakes can make a very good impression. Those who refuse to acknowledge their mistakes will not come across well. Again, a good PDP, discussed at 15.2.2, will help you to have identified your weaknesses at an early stage and given you time to take steps to address them before the application process begins.

16.3.4 **Inconsistencies**

Analyse your application for any perceived inconsistencies, which you may need to explain either in the application itself or later if you are called for interview. For example, if you are applying to a corporate law firm, but your work experience to date has been with a high-street criminal practice, or you have chosen to study personal injury law, be prepared for an interviewer to question you about this. Again, it is not necessarily a negative, but being ill-prepared for what an interviewer considers an obvious question that your application raises will be deemed a negative.

16.4 **Your CV**

Some firms, typically the smaller firms, will ask you to apply by submitting your CV. As explained in 15.2.2, you should start your PDP as soon as possible as a student, and this process should then help you to 'build' an effective CV. By the time you apply for a professional role, you should be familiar with your personal SWOT analysis, and have identified and filled any skills or other gaps. Having taken good care to ensure you actually have what potential graduate employers are seeking, you must then ensure that your CV is effective in highlighting this. You should think of your CV as a document which 'sells' you. The CV template at Figure 16.1 sets out a common structure which you can adapt to suit your needs.

16.4.1 **Format**

Your CV must be succinct enough to read. Remember, if your CV does its job, you will then have an interview where you will have the opportunity to provide further detail. Take a good look at the format once you have finished your first draft and be willing to experiment until it looks polished. Your CV will be sitting in a pile of others and you should pay attention to ensuring it looks attractive to read, as well as having good quality content. As a rule of thumb, most readers would lose interest after two pages, so you must choose your content carefully for maximum impact. You should format your CV in a way which renders it uncluttered and attractive to read. Would key information jump out at someone glancing at it? When you are contemplating whether to include something, ask yourself whether and how it evidences to an employer that you have what they need.

16.4.2 **Focus**

Your CV should really highlight the key points you would like to land with the reader. Avoid being purely descriptive in your application. Consider what a long, chronological list of your employment history achieves. Are you expecting your employer to read between the lines? Could you help them further? If, say, you worked in a bar in Corfu, rather than state what you

Format contact details succinctly; limit to one line if possible. It is imperative that they are accurate. Consider where you are contactable year-round and, if providing a mobile, bear in mind that from now on you may receive calls unannounced from a prospective employer. Also acquire an e-mail address which is reliable, sounds professional and is not inappropriate.

Use reverse chronological order.

Bullet points can encourage clarity and focus. Format bullets so there is a space between the bullet and the start of the sentence.

Focus the reader on key information; do not rely on them taking time to read around to find it.

Make good use of headings and subheadings and ensure your formatting distinguishes between the two by using combinations of formatting (such as bold, underline, italics) and case. Too much underlining can look cluttered. You must insert a space after punctuation. Consider a modern font, like calibri or arial. Review your final draft for orphan headings.

Remember that your CV is to highlight your key strengths. You must be prepared to talk in more detail at interview about anything you include. Employers will test that you can do this at interview, and will also sometimes look for evidence that you have reflected on what went well and what you might do differently next time, and why.

As mentioned, you need to draw attention to the fact that the skills you have acquired in a role outside of the sector you are applying for are useful, valuable skills that you can transfer for use in the role you are applying for. Some readers will make this connection instinctively, but some will not, so it is always better if you do it, expressly, for them.

CURRICULUM VITAE of **LAW STUDENT**

4 Woodstock Street, Bidsdury, Camchester C1 2AB
T: 0111 123 456 M: 01234 567 890 E: Law.Student@email.com

EDUCATION

20XX – date	**University of Camchester,**
LLB (Hons) Law	*Second Year:* Consumer Law, Criminal Law, EU Law, Human Rights Law, Land Law,
	First Year: Contract Law (70%), English Legal System (52%), Public Law (58%), Roman Law (60%), Tort (68%)
20XX-20XX	**Camchester High School**
A levels	English (A), French (A), History (B)
GCSEs	Biology, Chemistry, English, French, German, History, Latin, Mathematics, Physics, Religious Studies (all grade A)

WORK EXPERIENCE

Legal

July 20XX   **Shephard & Son, Camchester: vacation scheme**

- Research regarding contested development of land
- Note-taking at client meeting
- Proofreading sale and purchase agreement

May 20XX   **Pro bono clinic, South Camchester: voluntary legal advisor**

- Advising start up technology clients on business law issues
- Drafting formation of companies documentation
- Promoted an innovative legal helpline to local businesses

June 20XX   **Jackson Court Chambers: mini pupillage**

- Observed contested trials and interlocutory applications and reviewed documentation in personal injury actions

Non-legal

June 20XX   **Primarni, Camchester: part-time retail team supervisor**

- Managed a team of four retail staff which has consistently exceeded its targets
- Responsible for dealing with customer complaints
- Developed leadership, teamworking, client care, negotiation and problem-solving skills

---

Figure 16.1 CV template

Employers and clients want professionals who are rounded individuals, not just workhorses. If the firm is local, evidence of good contacts within the community may also be valuable here. Be brief but specific: if you organise a team, state how big the team is and whether you were elected to the role, if you have raised money, say how much. Personalised detail can stick in the mind of the reader and help sometimes. Unusual hobbies can make you stand out from the crowd. Don't forget to mention proficiency in IT and languages here too.

AWARDS AND SKILLS

- Westlaw UK Advanced Certification
- Lexis®Library Research Certification
- ConversationalFrench
- Proficient user of Microsoft Word, Excel and PowerPoint
- Full, clean driving licence

INTERESTS

- Debating: Vice-Chair of the University Debating Society 20XX; Runner-up, Northern University Consortium Mooting Competition 20XX, opposing 'This house believes that the lawyers make the best managers'; developed good communication and problem-solving skills.
- Trampolining: Competed at the British Championships 20XX; coach adult beginners weekly; developed responsibility and resilience.

REFEREES

Academic: Dr Patricia Anderson, Professor, Faculty of Business and Law, University of Camchester, Foster Building, Camchester C2 3YZ.

Personal: Mr Jack Todd, Manager, Primarni, 123 Cambridge Road, Camchester C1 4GH

See Further Reading section for more information about Westlaw UK and Lexis®Library certification.

Usually academic and personal referees are required. Make sure you ask permission and that they have the information they need to provide you with a good reference (such as a copy of your cv). As an undergraduate, the more you engage with your personal tutor, including sharing your PDP process, the better position they will be in to provide a detailed reference for you.

Figure 16.1 *Continued*

did (served drinks to customers for three months) isn't it better instead to highlight what you *learned* from it and how that will *help the law firm's business needs* (and so at the same time show commercial awareness of the firm's needs), for example that you enhanced your skills in customer service, teamworking, communication, punctuality, and complaints handling. This technique allows you to show that your skills are *transferable*.

16.4.3 **Transferable skills**

The introductions to Chapter 15 and to this chapter have made clear just how valuable it is for you to understand the concept of transferable skills, and to be able to persuade any graduate employer of the value to their business of the skills and commercial awareness you have learned as a law undergraduate. Let us consider this in more detail.

16.4.3.1 Transferring non-legal skills into the legal profession

Part II and III make clear the skills that graduate employers are seeking in their prospective employees. It goes without saying that during the application process you must show you are aware of the skills they value, and evidence that you have those skills. Students with work experience of the specific sector they are applying to work in—for example, legal work experience for those applying to law firms—might achieve this (although this is not recommended) simply by describing *what they did*, because the prospective employer may instinctively 'read in' the *skills they will have learned* through that work, through familiarity with the sector-specific work the student describes. As noted in Chapter 15, it is highly recommended that, as part of your PDP, you seek sector-specific work experience from an early stage of your undergraduate studies. However, if you have come to this advice late in the day, or your search for sector-specific work experience has proved fruitless, then all is not lost. The vast majority of skills referred to in this book as desired by graduate employers are *transferable*. This means that what you learned in one role can help you to add value in another role, even though the context may differ. Your task, then, in your application, is simply to make this very clear on the face of your application. For example, if you have worked in a call centre which fields customer complaints, you would focus in your application on how you have learned about client care and complaints handling. As explained in Chapter 15 these are things in which all graduate employers want their employees to be skilled. Once you learn how to evidence that you have skills which are transferable, you can see that almost every experience you have had can be used to show that you will be valuable to an employer, regardless of the field or sector of the experience or of your potential employer. It is a very valuable technique. There is a question in the Practical exercises to help you with this at the end of the chapter. Figure 16.1 shows how you can signpost your transferable skills in your CV.

16.4.3.2 Transferring legal skills into other professions

Consider also that, similarly, as a law graduate, you will be equipped with a range of skills which will be well regarded by employers in other sectors. As this book makes clear, you will be able to research, draft, write, negotiate, advise, interview, explain complex ideas clearly, analyse, solve problems, think strategically, network, and will be commercially aware. So, if you apply for a graduate role outside the legal sector, have confidence and take care to show that the skills you have acquired to date will be valued highly by your prospective employer. There is a 'thought provoking question' to help you with this at the end of the chapter.

16.4.3.3 Work experience

Think carefully about how to present your work experience. Present it in a way which plays to your strengths. If you have decent sector-specific work experience (that is, in the same sector to which you are applying to work), like the candidate whose CV is set out at Figure 16.1, then it makes sense to highlight it with a heading. However, if you do not, then you could instead use a general heading such as 'Employment History' or 'Relevant Experience', and focus on showing how this has given you the transferable skills which your employer will covet. If you have extensive employment history in various different roles, think flexibly; rather than a long, chronological, factual list, which describes what you did, how could you present the information in a way which shows more clearly what you learned, and why this will help you to add value? You could, for example, consider a 'Skills' heading which is broader than that in Figure 16.1, and which lists the skills covered in Part II of this work, with specific examples of where and how you can evidence that you achieved them. In short, once you have identified the content for your CV, you may need to experiment with different ways of presenting it to find the one which best highlights your particular strengths.

Some students are keen to describe a firm they have worked for as a 'city firm' or 'regional firm' in their CV. Check on the firm's website as to how it describes itself, and remember that household name firms will not need to be described.

16.5 The covering letter

Once you have prepared an effective CV, the role of the covering letter is to highlight your areas of particular strength and, possibly, if you have decided to do so at this stage, explain any inconsistencies or weaknesses (see 16.3.3). The advice provided in Chapter 14 and the letter template at Figure 14.5 (14.2.1.3) will help you to construct a professional letter. Again, make sure you have proofread it carefully. Do not be tempted to use a generic letter for all your applications. While you may have some core content, you must tailor each letter so that readers will be convinced that the application had been made specifically with their firm in mind. Your covering letter should not simply repeat your CV or application form. You should include your motivation for applying for the role, why you want to join that particular firm, any specific areas of practice which interest you, and how you will add value to the firm. Research the firm but put into your own words why you are attracted to working for them. You should familiarise yourself very well with the website of the firm to which you are applying, and in particular the areas to do with careers, areas and locations of practice, partner and client profiles, the firm's strategy, and any mission or values statement. You should also consider the issues which a firm would not deal with on its promotional website, such as who its competitors are and any threats it may be facing. As with your CV, the letter should be clear, concise, and to the point.

16.6 The application form

Many, often the larger, firms will ask you to complete and submit electronically a bespoke application form. The purpose of the form is the same as that of the CV and covering letter, namely to attract attention and to highlight your key strengths and show why you would be a covetable employee. The advice provided in this chapter in relation to the CV and a covering letter is therefore applicable equally to the application form. The STAR technique detailed at 16.8 can help you to provide evidence of your skills and experience in the format required in an application form. Most application forms will allow you to save a copy. You should do this and complete a draft in a word processing package first and then apply a spelling and grammar check before you cut and paste your final draft into the form.

16.7 Psychometric tests

Graduate employers often use psychometric testing to assess candidate's abilities. Practice tests are available online (see Further Reading) and you should practise them in advance of making your application. The results of the practice tests will also help you with your SWOT analysis for PDP purposes (see 15.2.2).

16.8 Interviews

16.8.1 Introduction

If you are called for interview you should feel a sense of achievement. You now have the opportunity to impress face to face. Naturally your communication skills (see Chapter 10) will be key in achieving this. First impressions count, so make sure you offer a firm handshake, look the part, pay attention to your body language and vocabulary, and are polite from the moment you arrive on the premises.

You are likely to feel nervous, but nevertheless you must be able to present with a veneer of confidence, both verbally and non-verbally. Try not to let nerves prevent your personality coming across. It is very easy for personable, enthusiastic individuals to turn unwittingly into overly intense, grim-faced interviewees. Remember that you want to convince the interviewer that she would like to work with you. Try to relax, smile, and make plenty of eye contact from the outset. You need to let your personality shine through the polished version of you that you are presenting to the interviewer. Never try to be someone you are not. It will be obvious to an interviewer and the chances are that the person you actually are is just as, or in fact more, appealing. Remember that you have been selected for interview on the basis of your application, and this details all that *you* have achieved to date.

16.8.2 Preparation

There are some techniques you can use to address the issue of nerves before an interview. Thorough research into the firm and its clients is essential to help reduce your nerves and speak with confidence. Make sure that you arrive in good time. Aim to arrive at least an hour in advance, leaving plenty of time to allow for a late train or getting lost. When you arrive at the firm itself, you will be making an impression from the moment you open the door, so before you do that you may like to factor in some time to have a coffee nearby, where you can read through any notes, go through what you plan to say in your head, and check that you look presentable. If you can do all this 'off-site', the more professional and confident you will look when you arrive at the firm's offices.

Some students suffer more from anxiety than others. A certain level of anxiety can be helpful, as it can enhance your performance. However, if you know that anxiety is a particular problem for you, and can cause you to feel overwhelmed, you need to take steps to address this as it will inhibit your performance at interview. There are things that you can do to help. Regular exercise, relaxation, and talking to friends can all reduce stress levels which can lead to panic attacks, so try not to change your routine or isolate yourself in the run-up to an interview, or spend too much time worrying about it. When you are at the interview, if you feel overcome, buy yourself some time by asking to be excused to go to the bathroom, practise good breathing techniques, and take a small bottle of water with you to sip as this can have a calming effect. Further guidance on how to control anxiety is set out in the Further Reading section at the end of this chapter.

Being an impressive interviewee is a skill in itself, and as with all skills it improves with practice. Seek and take any opportunity to participate in a practice interview, and, if possible, record and review the practice interview yourself. Prepare answers to questions that you could well be asked, for example: 'why law (or other profession)?', 'why this firm?', 'what is your main strength/weakness?'. Generally, you need to be prepared to talk about yourself, your interests, your strengths and weaknesses, challenges you have faced and how you tackled them, your team-working and leadership skills, what you are proud of, and precisely why the firm should choose you over another candidate. Go over your application form as you will usually be asked questions tailored to the form.

16.8.3 The interview

During the interview process employers will be looking for good communication skills and in particular whether you can answer questions clearly, react appropriately, retain your composure, and listen to what others have to say. Your answers need to be fluent, comprehensive, and promote all those skills and experiences which, having read this work, you know that the employer is looking for. A good interviewer will help you to showcase your talents. However some interviewers do little in terms of guiding you through the process and simply ask open questions which leave it up to you to choose what to tell them. You need to be familiar with what you have written in your application and show the interviewer that you (i) understand which skills they want you to have, and why, (ii) actually have those skills, and (iii) indeed can point to examples in your application which prove this.

Do not be afraid of taking a moment to consider your answer before you speak. What can seem like a deafening silence to you is likely to sound simply like a natural pause from an interviewer's perspective. Remember that employers want employees to think carefully before they speak. Some employers will test whether you can do this specifically by asking you a question that you could not possibly have pre-prepared, (for example, see Example 2 at 15.3.1) In fact, the actual answer to a question like this is unlikely to be of great import to the interviewer. Instead they will be looking to see how well you deal with the unexpected. If you did not pause for thought before such a question, your answer is unlikely to be good. You may start to stumble as you realise you need some thinking time, or in the heat of the moment you may simply say you do not know. This is not going to come across well. Instead, a candidate who responds by acknowledging that is an interesting question and requests a moment to think before answering is likely to come across well, even if ultimately his answer is not that feasible. As 15.3.1 and 15.3.3 explain, however, good commercial awareness, and keeping up to date by reading a quality newspaper regularly, certainly in the month or so prior to interview, would give you an advantage in answering this type of question. Conversely, make sure that your answers to any obvious questions, such as 'Why do you want to be a lawyer?' or any question relating to the information on your application form (see 16.6), are fluent and reveal that you have prepared well for the interview.

You may also be asked questions about commercial awareness. Section 15.3 and the case studies and sample interview questions in the online resources for Chapters 15 to 20 will help you to think about how you might tackle these.

For all these questions the STAR technique can help you to structure your answer well:

- Situation—give context.
- Task—describe the challenge, why you were facing it, and the expectations of that challenge.
- Action—describe what you did and how you did it.
- Results—explain what they were and how you quantified them (e.g. did you obtain some recognition, make any savings?).

At the end of the interview, you will undoubtedly be asked whether you have any questions. The answer should not be 'No'. This is an opportunity to show interest in the firm and the role. Prepare some questions in advance, but use these with care. Do not ask about something that has already been covered in the interview or which should have been obvious from the firm's website, although a question based on the firm's website shows that you have done your research: for example 'I see from your website that the firm is involved in pro bono work. What are the opportunities for trainees to participate?'

16.8.4 Feedback

Finally, remember that even if you do not succeed at interview, the process itself will have been a valuable one in terms of improving your interviewing skills for the next time. If you have not been successful, you should always ask for feedback. Study the feedback carefully and make sure you implement any recommendations you are given. Remember you only need to succeed in one application to get into the profession, so stay positive.

16.8.5 Video interviews

Video interviews are increasingly popular for first round interviews, particularly with top firms, as firms seek to streamline and reduce the costs of the recruitment process. There are two types of video interview: a live interview using Skype or FaceTime or a short series of automated, pre-recorded questions answered under timed conditions, with a deadline for completion. For the former, you are sent instructions on how to join the call and for the latter a link to the interview questions, which the firm will review later. Clearly, there are differences between these interviews and a face-to-face interview.

16.8.5.1 Preparation

However, in many ways you should treat a video interview in exactly the same way that you would a face-to-face interview. As with any interview you should practise and prepare thoroughly. Create an organised and professional environment, dressing appropriately as you would for a live interview. Do not leave the interview until the last minute of the deadline. Technical failures can and do happen and you must give yourself time to fix them. Test your equipment in good time to ensure everything is working. Make sure that you are not disturbed: if necessary, put up a notice on the door: 'Do Not Disturb. Video Interview in Progress' to warn your family or friends not to burst in. Position the webcam where there is a clear image—one tip is to put it above your eyeline as you will look better. (Apparently, directors of horror movies position cameras looking up at an actor's face to give a more horrific look.)

16.8.5.2 The interview

Once the interview starts, try to relax and maintain eye contact as you would during a face-to-face interview. Faced with a series of timed questions, you will be under pressure, but firms are looking for lawyers with good communication skills, who can answer questions clearly and concisely under pressure. Look at the camera—not the image of yourself in the corner of the screen. Cover this up if you need to. Do not read from pre-prepared notes as your answers will be stilted and you will lose eye contact; however, if it helps, you can put a series of prompts on post-it notes on your computer screen. The interviewer will not be able to see them. If something does go wrong with the tech, and you are cut off, email or ring the graduate recruitment department who should be able to re-establish the link.

16.8.6 **Presentations**

Chapter 11 considered the skill of presenting, and it is not unusual for an employer to test this skill by asking you to give a presentation as part of the assessment process (including on a vacation or other work experience scheme). This could be sprung on you when you arrive, or you may have been asked to prepare it in advance. The firm may set the title for you, or you might be able to select a topic of your own. Your audience may include other candidates, solicitors, partners, and/or members of the recruitment team.

You will usually be given a target time frame for delivery of the presentation. Practise your presentation to make sure it will not go on too long, and have extra items you can bring in, or items you can cut out, to give you some flexibility to hit the target timescale. Often you will be given the option of preparing visual aids. When preparing these, bear in mind how long the presentation is and keep them to a minimum; a slide show may help to put you in your comfort zone but it rarely makes for a good presentation. The best presenters do not use cards, but if you really cannot do without a prompt, restrict yourself to bullet points on cards and never read out a pre-prepared presentation.

When structuring your presentation make sure that it has a clear beginning, where you signpost the audience as to what is to come, a middle, and a definite end which draws everything together. In delivering your presentation, make sure you use the communication skills outlined in Chapter 11; engage the audience by using effective body language (posture, eye contact, no distracting habits), looking professional (no leaning on the table or rushing around the room), projecting your voice (ask the audience if they can hear you), and trying to relax and smile. If you do not seem to be enjoying your presentation, the audience will really struggle to do so. Humour can be effective, but avoid being flippant and bear in mind you are unlikely to have had time to get to know your audience well. Remember to keep it simple. If you try to include too much detail you are likely to overrun. Include the essential information, and present it succinctly and clearly. Remember to try to relax, be yourself, and smile.

16.8.7 **Group work**

Assessment days can also include group exercises where the firm will test your team-working skills and how you work with others. You should bear in mind everything you have learned from 15.4 and seek to demonstrate you have these skills. Often the firm will have tasked particular employees to watch specific people. So the observer sitting at the back of the room might nevertheless be watching your every move. They will be looking to see what role you play in the group. You absolutely must make a contribution. However you must not be seen to dominate the discussion at the expense of the quieter members of the group. Showing that you have noticed someone who has not had the chance to contribute, and giving her the chance to speak (without putting her on the spot) will work in your favour. If you always take the easy role, such as writing up others' ideas without contributing any of your own, the observers will notice. They will also be looking to see how you handle any disagreements between the group members, and whether you have any powers of persuasion.

16.8.8 **Socialising**

Often lunch or drinks are factored into an assessment day (or vacation scheme) to allow you to meet the people who work there. Do not make the mistake of letting your hair down too much at these events. While they have more of a sociable element than the rest of the day, there is no doubt that you are still being assessed. Enjoy these occasions, certainly, as they represent another opportunity to show how well you fit with the firm, its employees, and culture: However, the clever applicant will use them as an opportunity to find out more information about the firm and its people, particularly information which can be used later in the assessment day. A simple mention in passing of the name of a person who is interviewing you later can often turn up a few useful facts (e.g. 'she is *the name* in corporate at the moment', 'I hope you're a United fan', 'that's him over there', 'he's a man of few words'). Often those attending the lunch or drinks will be asked if anyone particularly stood out, so use your networking skills to your advantage (see 15.7) and circulate, wearing your name badge, making a good impression, to give you the edge over other good candidates who have not yet honed that particular skill.

You can practise this skill now by attending more formal events at university. You will find that drinks receptions after talks are good places to try out these skills.

16.9 Conclusion

You should now have an understanding of how your study of academic law fits into the wider context of professional life, an appreciation of the valuable, life-long transferable skills it instils in you, and confidence in how you can use the knowledge, skills, and commercial awareness you learn during your degree to help you achieve your goals, whatever they may be. Having a degree in the law of England & Wales is something of which you should be rightly proud; our laws are recognised and respected internationally. However, your degree represents much more than the possession of this legal knowledge; it is ripe with potential to be packed also with essential, valuable skills and commercial awareness which will help you make a smooth transition from undergraduate to professional.

 Summary

- Employability skills improve with practice and preparation.
- Skills are transferable: the skills you have learned in non-law environments transfer into valuable skills in the world of legal practice, and conversely the skills which you acquire as an undergraduate law student transfer into and are valued by other professions.
- PDP is essential long-term preparation for any application, and you should begin this process now if you have not already, with a view to identifying and filling any gaps in your experience to date.
- You should have a word-processed, draft CV and regularly review and amend it.
- You should be applying for work experience now.
- If you are seeking a training contract with a larger firm, you are likely to be able to apply in your first year (of a two-year degree) or your second year (of a three-year degree).
- An application form must focus the reader on the key, relevant points you wish them to read.

 Practical exercises

1. Identify the skills you have acquired outside of your study of, and practical work experience in, law. Consider how they would help you to add value to a law firm.

2. Identify the skills you have acquired during your study of, and practical work experience in, law, and highlight those which you think are transferable skills which would be valued by graduate employers in sectors other than law.

3. When is the best time for you to schedule regular time for PDP, and how much time can you devote to it?

4. Identify three gaps in your current CV which you need to address as priority. How do you plan to address them, and by when?

5. When is the earliest time you can apply for the graduate role you are seeking?

*Visit the **online resources** for the authors' reflections and to check your progress.*

What the professionals say

I found that the best thing to do was to research the type of firm I wanted to work for, making sure I was realistic about the size of the firm and the type of work I wanted to be involved in. I realised early on that it was best to choose something I was interested in as firms always pick up on this. Applying early for vacation schemes is a good way of ensuring success; law firms are keen to secure trainees early in the year and applying early is proof of your interest and commitment, so I always tried to do this. The university law fair is a great place to meet different firms and introduce yourself so I always made sure I was there. My advice is to do your homework; knowledge of individual firms is key. Training contract applications can seem incredibly similar but remember that works both ways so you need to make yourself stand out.

Damian McParland, former LPC student, University of Law

As a police officer, my job is one of problem solving and finding the right solution to fit a certain set of facts. This involves a lot of research by looking at case law, statutes and also police policy in order to work out the best way to proceed with a certain scenario. My first real experience of this type of research was during my law degree, being presented with a set of facts and having to research the legal position using a number of different resources, both electronic and print. Although I use a number of new systems now alongside only a few that I used at university, being able to finesse your research skills will benefit you in any career—it is a skill that can be applied almost anywhere. The world is full of vast swathes of information and it really is a skill to be able to select the correct pieces and use them effectively. Concentrate on this, and you won't go far wrong once you graduate.

R Burrell, Police Officer, Metropolitan Police Service and Law graduate

Further reading

Assessment Day. Available online at: http://www.assessmentday.co.uk/
—This website provides aptitude test practice.

BBC, *Trainee Schemes and Apprenticeships*. Available online at: http://www.bbc.co.uk/careers/
    trainee-schemes-and-apprenticeships
—This provides information about graduate roles across the BBC.

Hatloy, I. (2012) *Understanding Anxiety and Panic Attacks*. London: Mind
—A booklet on the causes of anxiety, its effects, and how to manage it. Available online at: https://www.mind.org.uk/media/1892482/mind_anxiety_panic_web.pdf.

Law Careers. Available online at: https://www.lawcareers.net
—A resource for future lawyers, which works with the Law Society. Among other things it publishes information on pro bono and application deadlines, and you can register as a student to receive a weekly e-mail bulletin. There is also a MyLCN feature which allows you to save information on firms you are interested in.

Legal 500. Available online at: http://www.legal500.com
—A leading guide to law firms in the UK and other jurisdictions.

LexisLibrary. Available online at: http://www.lexislibrarycertification.co.uk/
—This website details how to obtain certification in this electronic database.

Psychometric Success. Available online at: http://www.psychometric-success.com/

—This website offers free practice psychometric testing.

Westlaw UK. Available online at: https://legalsolutions.thomsonreuters.co.uk/en/products-services/uk-law-student/get-certified-westlaw-uk.html

—This website details how you can obtain formal certification regarding this electronic database.

 For the authors' reflections on the practical exercises, additional self-test questions, sample interview questions and a library of links to useful websites, visit the free **online resources** *at www.oup.com/he/slorach4e.*

17 Understanding clients: individuals and businesses

Learning objectives

After studying this chapter you should be able to:

- Identify life events that will require individuals and businesses to have recourse to the law.
- Describe how individual wealth is created.
- Explain how businesses finance their operations.

Introduction

Whatever sort of organisation you go into when you finish your studies, at the heart of that organisation are its clients or customers. Throughout the next chapters, we will consider the importance of 'adding value' to the client/customer experience. The starting point for providing this 'added value' element is to understand why someone has come to your organisation in the first place. Anticipation is key to commercial awareness. If you can anticipate the needs of your clients or customers, you can manage their expectations. You will find that this is not rocket science. Most people's needs are based on ordinary life events, and understanding those life events—and the underlying personal, social, financial, or business concerns which arise as a result of those events—will add a further dimension to your commercial awareness.

At any interview or assessment day, you will be asked questions or set tasks designed to test whether you can anticipate, and meet, the needs of that organisation's clients or customers. This applies whether those clients or customers are individuals or businesses.

In this chapter we look at typical concerns of both individuals and businesses. We consider this in a legal context, but much of the information will be relevant to many other professions or occupations. Lawyers rarely act alone in transactions, and other professionals will often be involved in giving advice alongside a lawyer, e.g. accountants may give financial or tax advice. Table 17.2 shows the sort of legal advice which a solicitor will give in relation to various life events and suggests which additional professionals and institutions may be involved at each stage. We also consider some topical issues which will be useful for you to know about whether or not you are looking for a career in the law.

17.1 Why individuals and businesses have recourse to the law

At some point in their lives, most people will need some sort of legal advice, usually as a result of some life event, or change in their circumstances, such as buying a house, marriage, death, divorce, employment problems, or a criminal prosecution. Different life events give rise to different legal rights and duties, on which law firms can give advice. Businesses, like individuals, have a life cycle. They grow and develop, and experience changes in circumstance, for instance buying premises, taking on employees, changing the status of a business from a sole trader to a partnership or company, all of which give rise to equivalent legal rights and duties. Businesses often need the same sort of advice as individuals, it is just that the emphasis is a little different.

In this chapter we are going to use a client case study to explore typical life events in more detail and look at the social and economic circumstances that help to shape those life events. We have seen that commercial awareness is about people, so you need to understand how these bigger issues influence an individual's 'latent', or underlying, concerns. An example is the Cambridge Analytica example (see 15.3.1), which raised a variety of political, ethical, and social issues.

17.1.1 Individuals

In 1967, Thomas Holmes and Richard Rahe, two psychiatrists, conducted a survey to see how stress contributed to illness. They listed typical life events (which they called Life Change Units or LCUs) and gave them a stress score. (The conclusion, although not really relevant for our purposes, was that the higher the score, the more likely the subject was to become ill.) Table 17.1 shows an extract of the top six LCUs (and the lowest scoring one, so that you can make a comparison).

These are all events about which individuals are likely to consult a solicitor. (Number 42, incidentally, is Christmas, which carries 12 stress points. Clearly this is not an event which will send someone rushing to see their solicitor, but, interestingly, more couples consult a

Table 17.1 Extracts from the Holmes and Rahe Stress Scale[1]

	Event	Stress score
1	Death of spouse	100
2	Divorce	73
3	Marital separation	65
4	Jail term	63
5	Death of close family member	63
6	Personal injury or illness	53
...	...	...
43	Minor violations of law	11

[1] Holmes, T. and Rahe, H. (1967) The Social Readjustment Rating Scale. *Journal of Psychosomatic Research* 11(2), p. 213.

solicitor about matrimonial difficulties in the period immediately following Christmas than at any other time of the year.) From Table 17.1, you can see that the most stressful life events all involve a change in circumstances for the worse, and it is undoubtedly true that a lawyer will often be advising clients when they are most vulnerable.

However, the life of a solicitor is not all doom and gloom. Often clients' circumstances change for the better; for example they get married, have children, or buy their first home.

17.1.1.1 Example

Let's look at some clients and think about the sort of legal advice a law firm might provide (see Example 1).

Example 1

Tom Stevens is 29. He works as a procurement (purchasing) manager for a national chain of wholesale wine retailers. He earns £30,000 a year. Tom's fiancée, Anna Evans, is 28. She teaches English and Drama at a local Community Academy. She earns just over £27,000 a year. They live and work in the East of England.

Anna and Tom are planning to marry in July next year. They are both agreed that they would like to have two children. Anna hopes to carry on working once she has had the children. Both Tom and Anna's parents are willing to help with childcare, and there is a good local nursery near where they are looking for a house.

At the moment, Tom and Anna rent an unfurnished flat, but they are hoping to buy a house to move into once they are married, and have saved enough money.

Tom has recently paid off his student loan, and has started saving for the house. Tom's grandmother died a year ago, and left him £10,000 which he will use as part of the deposit. Anna has not yet paid off all her loan, so she will not be able to contribute as much to the house as Tom. They both have credit cards. Tom pays his off every month. Anna tries to do this, but occasionally has a balance outstanding on hers.

Tom and Anna operate their finances separately. They have separate bank accounts and they each pay their share of the rent and split bills equally. Once they are married, they intend to pool their finances and open a joint account, from which they will pay the mortgage and the bills.

Tom has a car as part of his job. Anna drives a ten year old car, which she has had since she was a student, but it is unreliable. She realises that she will need to buy a new one before too long, and it would be sensible to get one which is suitable for children.

Tom is passionately interested in wine, which he regards as his hobby as well as his job. He is hoping to start up his own business as a wine merchant in a year or two's time. He plays golf and football for his local team. He is a bit of a gadget man: he always upgrades to the latest Smartphone and Tablet. Anna loves the theatre and clothes, and reads a lot. She plays tennis and goes to a local gym to keep fit. They like eating out when they can afford it. The both enjoy travelling, and have been on several holidays together, both long-haul and in Europe. They hope to continue taking annual foreign holidays, and family holidays once they have children.

Tom and Anna do not lead particularly exceptional lives. Tom is in management, and Anna is one of the 5.42[2] million people employed in the public sector. They have the same sort

---

[2] ONS (2019) *Statistical Bulletin: Public Sector Employment, June 2019*. Available online at: https://www.ons.gov.uk/employmentandlabourmarket/peopleinwork/publicsectorpersonnel, accessed 12/10/2019.

of hopes and aspirations as many young couples—a family, a house, two cars, annual holidays. They are fairly 'typical' clients who experience 'life events'—events which change their lives to a greater or lesser extent. There will be legal consequences when each one of these events occurs.

17.1.1.2 Legal personality

Each phase of life or 'life event' will bring with it corresponding rights and duties imposed by the law. In legal terms, all human beings are born with a 'bundle' of legal rights and duties imposed by the law which govern every aspect of their lives. For example, at the moment, Tom and Anna are renting a flat. The law gives them a right to live in the property without disturbance, but imposes an obligation on them to abide by the terms of the lease. When they buy their own house, these rights and duties change. They no longer have a landlord to whom they must pay rent, but property ownership brings other obligations, for example if they have borrowed money to buy the property, they will have to pay this back. This 'bundle' of rights and duties makes up what is described as an individual's *legal personality*. The exact extent is determined by each person's status: married or single, employer or employee, house owner or tenant, and so on. Just like human personalities, legal personalities develop as individuals mature.

17.1.2 The role of a lawyer

On the basis of what we know about Tom and Anna so far, let's look at the sort of work a law firm is likely to be able to do for them.

1. **Property work**. When Tom and Anna buy their house they will want legal advice on the property transfer and how to finance their purchase. They may need advice on ending the tenancy on their current flat, for example if they have a problem getting the deposit back.

2. **Finances**. They may need some advice on the implications of pooling their finances, especially as Anna is going to contribute less to the house than Tom. At this stage in their lives, they probably do not even want to consider this, but what will happen if they do not live happily ever after, and the marriage ends in divorce?

3. **Wills**. It is always advisable to make a will on marriage or when you cohabit with someone, so that you can be sure that your partner will inherit your property on your death.

4. **Probate**. When Tom's grandmother died, the people who were responsible for administering her estate (her executors) may have come to the firm for advice about the administration of the estate (the probate).

5. **Contract law**. Individuals make contracts every day of their lives. When Anna buys her new car, she will enter into a sale of goods contract with the seller.

6. **Company/commercial**. When Tom sets up his new business he will want advice on this. We will be looking at this at 17.1.3.

7. **Employment**. Hopefully, Tom and Anna's jobs are reasonably secure, and there will be no problems here. (Employees who lose their jobs often consult solicitors if they

think that they have been dismissed unfairly, or the correct procedure has not been followed.) However, when Tom sets up his own business, a lawyer may need to look at his contract with his current employers to see whether it contains any restrictions preventing him from working in the same area or approaching the company's clients. These are *restrictive covenants* and protect employers against competition from employees once they have left the business.

8. **Welfare and benefits**. If at any time in the future either Tom or Anna is out of work, they may need advice on the benefits to which they may be entitled.

9. **Tax**. At the moment, Tom and Anna's tax affairs are straightforward. Their employers will deduct tax (PAYE) and national insurance (NI) from their salaries and send the correct amount to Her Majesty's Revenue & Customs (HMRC). However, once Tom sets up his own business, he will need more detailed tax advice.

10. **Retirement and pension provision**. Once they have funded the purchase of their home, and paid off their student loans, Tom and Anna will need to think about starting to save for their retirement. This may seem a long way away, but it is still an important consideration.

Most people will not go to a solicitor until they buy their first home. When they do approach a solicitor, the solicitor will advise them about their legal position on their house purchase but, as we can see, if Tom and Anna remain clients of the firm, over the years the solicitor will give advice on a variety of legal rights and duties.

17.1.3 Business clients

We are now going to fast-forward a few years and think about Tom's business as an example. You will remember that Tom wanted to start up business as a specialist wine merchant. Businesses, like individuals, have a life cycle from start-up (birth) through expansion (growing to maturity) to when they cease to trade (death). They employ people, and must look after them (a bit like having children). Businesses merge or acquire other businesses (marriage). In the same way that individuals need somewhere to live, businesses need premises to trade from, which they will either rent or buy. They need money to set up, buy assets, survive, and expand. Like individuals, businesses have certain legal rights and legal duties, which govern their day to day lives. The life of the business is ongoing, and the advice which they need will also be ongoing. Let's look at the sort of legal advice that Tom's business may need:

1. **Company/commercial**. Tom will need advice on the type of business structure which is most suitable for his business, and the legal issues which affect each type (see 18.1). Once it is up and running, although the lawyer will be dealing with Tom, the business will be the client. Businesses do not stay the same forever: Tom will want the business to grow and develop. At each stage of its development, he will need advice.

2. **Property**. Tom will have to decide whether to rent or buy his business premises. In either event, he will need legal advice on the lease or property transfer. If the business expands, it may need to move into larger premises.

3. **Financial**. Tom will have to raise money to start trading, and will need advice on the implications of either putting his own money into the business, or borrowing the money

he needs. Again, as the business expands, it may need to raise more finance. Tom may need advice on the options available and on banking law.

4. **Employment**. Tom may be taking on employees, such as sales staff, so he will need advice on his obligations as an employer, the rights of his employees, and the employment legislation which protects them. He will need to think about their contracts, working conditions, and health and safety, for example.

5. **Tax**. Once Tom starts up his own business, he will be responsible for his own tax and the tax affairs of his business.

6. **Licensing and other regulatory matters**. As Tom is setting up a wine business, there are certain licensing requirements with which he must comply.

7. **Consumer issues**. Apart from basic contract law which affects everyday sales, there is a great deal of complex legislation which protects consumers in relation to the provision of goods, services, and credit, particularly where a business is selling online. In particular, there are *data protection* issues to consider in relation to collating and holding customers' personal details.

8. **Insolvency**. It is a sad fact that many start-up businesses fail. If this is the case, the lawyer may need to advise Tom on the implications of the business becoming insolvent, and, in a worst-case scenario, how this can have a knock-on effect and result in his own *personal bankruptcy*.

As well as economic and political context, there are other factors which influence an individual's choices. Life does not stay the same forever. As their life circumstances change, so will their legal needs, and we have seen that Anna and Tom are making plans for their long-term future together. So next we need to look into the future and consider some of these life events, both for Tom and Anna as individuals and for Tom's business and the legal and financial implications.

17.2 Typical life events: individuals and the law

If Tom and Anna's plans work out, their legal personalities will undergo a series of changes. We now look at some of these developments. We explore the concerns and expectations of the clients at each stage of their lives, the environment in which they are taking place, the financial implications, and then think about the underlying legal issues. You can see how an individual's legal personality develops and the impact of seemingly everyday events. One point that should become clear is that clients are not always primarily concerned with legal issues. Their life plans and often their finances are more likely to be at the forefront of their minds. An understanding of those underlying concerns will help you anticipate your clients' needs.

17.2.1 The wedding

17.2.1.1 Client concerns

Tom and Anna's main concern when planning their wedding will be that everything is perfect on their 'big day'. They will be arranging all the details of the event: the ceremony, the venue for the reception, the food and drink, the photographer, the flowers, Anna's dress, the bridesmaid's dresses, and so on. This is where their attention will be focused.

17.2.1.2 Financial considerations

In 2019 the average cost of a wedding is nearly £32,000.[3] Clearly an important consideration is how to finance this. Traditionally, the bride's parents usually foot the bill for their daughter's wedding, and we will assume that they will do so in this case. Anna's father (who is 62) has said that he will draw down part of his pension fund. This means that he will take a lump sum, say £20,000, out of his pension fund, as a way of releasing some of his savings. This is one way that older people can benefit from a lifetime of saving, but obviously the fund will be worth £20,000 less, and provide proportionately less income when he retires. We will consider pensions in more detail at 17.4.4.

17.2.1.3 Legal considerations

While planning the wedding, Tom and Anna are very unlikely even to think about legal issues. However, underlying all their plans there will be legal implications.

First, and most obviously, the marriage must be valid. It has to be conducted according to the requirements of the Marriage Acts; couples cannot just go and say their vows to each other on top of a mountain and be married. The marriage has to be in a recognised format, in a licensed venue, and properly witnessed. It has to be consummated. So if Tom and Anna have a massive row at the wedding reception and never see each other again, the marriage will be void.

Getting married changes a person's legal status, giving different rights and obligations from those of single people or cohabitees who are not married. There are rights in relation to a spouse's (husband's or wife's) property if they die. If a couple want to end a marriage, they cannot just walk away and be free to marry again. They must either obtain a divorce or show that there is a valid reason for annulment of the marriage. Both of these are court-based procedures, requiring legal advice. The couple's finances are crucial to any settlement that they may reach on divorce or separation.

The moment that a couple get married, any will which either of them may have made previously is automatically 'revoked' (i.e. it becomes invalid). A common mistake that many couples make is thinking that they will automatically inherit each other's property should one of them die. This is not the case. In the absence of a will, there are legal rules which determine who gets what.

As we have seen, the couple must consider their finances carefully, for example if they decide to have a joint bank account. There are tax reliefs which apply on gifts of property between married couples and on death, so a lawyer can advise on the implications of pooling their finances and tax planning.

---

[3] Pye, H,. 'How much does a wedding cost: The UK Average Revealed?', *Hitched*, 15 August 2019. Available online at: https://www.hitched.co.uk/wedding-planning/organising-and-planning/the-average-wedding-cost-in-the-uk-revealed, accessed 12/10/2019. Estimates vary: *The Money Advice Service* puts it at at just over £27,000 (https://www.moneyadviceservice.org.uk/blog/how-much-does-an-average-wedding-cost), but it is still a staggering amount of money.

Then there are the legal implications from the organisation of the wedding itself. Tom and Anna are entering into a series of contracts for the supply of goods and services. If something goes wrong, they have the benefit of consumer protection legislation, which governs the sale and supply of both goods and services.[4]

Unless things go badly wrong it is unlikely that, at this stage in their lives, Tom and Anna will need legal advice, except in relation to their wills (see Table 17.2), so we will now move on and look at a life event which will involve the advice of professionals, the purchase of a property.

17.2.2 **The house**

17.2.2.1 Client concerns

Tom and Anna also want to buy a house. Their main concern will be to find a house which they like, with the right accommodation, in the right area. As they are planning a family, they will probably want to find a suitable family home at a price that they can afford. They will need to make sure that once they have found the right house, there is nothing structurally wrong with it. Once they have bought it, they will need to fit it out and furnish it.

17.2.2.2 Financial considerations

In July 2019 the average house price was £232,710, with house prices rising by 0.7 per cent in 2018–19[5]. In London, it is now nearly £600,000 (although prices have fallen over the last year) and in the South East £376,822. As we have seen, Tom has £10,000 and some savings, but that is not going to cover the cost of a house. The couple will have to borrow some money, that is to say approach a bank or building society for a mortgage.

> ### Essential explanation
>
> A *mortgage* is another word for a property loan. It is a loan which allows you to borrow a large amount of money in order to buy a property. The loan is *secured* against the value of the property, and you pay it back, with interest, over an agreed period of time. The term 'secured' means that if you *default*, in other words fail to make the payments as agreed, the lender has the right to *repossess* your property, in other words to sell it to recover the money which it has lent.
>
> (The word mortgage actually means the security provided for the loan but the term is now used to cover the whole transaction, i.e. the loan and the giving of security.)

Economic factors may also play a role in their decision, for example they may be concerned that following the recession house prices soared. In 2000, the average UK house price was just over £84,620, so house prices have increased by over 175 per cent in nearly 20 years. In times

---

[4] E.g. Consumer Rights Act 2015, Consumer Protection Act 1987, Consumer Contracts Regulations 2013 (SI 2013/3134).

[5] Land Registry (2019) *House Price Index*. Available online at: http://landregistry.data.gov.uk/app/hpi, accessed 12/10/2019. (All statistics in relation to property prices will be from this source unless otherwise indicated.)

of recession, however, house prices tend to stagnate or fall, though historically, once a recession ends, house prices have recovered and outstripped inflation. This is what has happened in the UK during 2013–16. As the country came out of recession, property prices started to rise, with particularly dramatic rises in London and the South East of England, creating a housing bubble. Although property prices stagnated in the uncertainty caused by Brexit, there is no indication at the time of writing that the 'bubble' has burst.

! Essential explanation

A *housing bubble* occurs when house prices rise spectacularly, fueled by demand and speculation. A shortage of housing leads to an increase in demand. Once prices start to increase, property speculators enter the market, hoping to make quick profits from short-term buying and selling, which further drives up demand. As with all economic bubbles, it eventually bursts, as demand decreases, or supply increases, resulting in a sharp drop in prices.

In recent years, there has been a shortage of housing (particularly affordable housing), which has the effect of pushing up house prices and increasing rents for those who cannot afford to buy (for a simple example of how supply and demand works—see 19.1.3.3). In the late 1990's the average house cost 3.55 times the average salary. In June this year, this had increased by nearly 120 per cent to 7.8 times the average salary,[6] making it increasingly difficult for people to buy their own homes.

! Essential explanation

The ratio of house prices to earnings is referred to as the *affordability ratio*.[7]

The shortage and affordability of housing in the UK has been one of the most important social issues of the decade.

Despite attempts by successive governments to encourage house building,[8] the UK has been described as suffering from 'one of the worst housing crises in the democratic world'.

One problem for Tom and Anna is that no bank or building society is going to lend them the whole amount they need for their house purchase, so they will have to put up a proportion of the purchase price as a deposit. The average deposit for first time buyers has risen from £6,793 in 1990 to £43,000 in 2018.[9] Once they have raised the deposit, on these figures, they will have a mortgage of over £280,000 and will have to pay interest on that amount each month. They will therefore have serious concerns about the affordability of buying their own home, and the implications of buying during a housing bubble, possibly at the top of the market. There is also considerable uncertainty at the time of writing about the impact of Brexit on property prices.

---

[6] Collinson, P. 'Boris Johnson and the housing crisis' *The Guardian*, 2 August 2019. Available online at https://www.theguardian.com/politics/2019/aug/02/boris-johnson-and-the-housing-crisis, accessed 12/10/2019.

[7] See ONS (2019), *Housing Affordability in England and Wales: 2018*. Available online at: https://www.ons.gov.uk/peoplepopulationandcommunity/housing/bulletins/housingaffordabilityinenglandandwales/2018, accessed 12/10/2019.

[8] e.g., Housing and Planning Act 2016 or the Help to Buy Scheme.

[9] Moneysupermarket data (July 2019). Available online at: https://www.moneysupermarket.com/mortgages/first-time-buyers/how-to-raise-a-deposit, accessed 12/10/2019.

It is important that the couple should be encouraged to seek independent financial advice as to the timing of the purchase, the security of the investment, and how to raise the money they need.

17.2.2.3 Legal considerations

Starting with their legal personalities, home ownership confers a variety of rights and obligations, which, as we have seen, are different from those which affect someone who is renting a property.

Tom and Anna will need to think about how they want to own the house. Even if Tom is putting more money in than Anna, they could choose either to own the house in equal shares, or, alternatively, in proportion to the amount of money that they have put in: for instance, if Tom puts in two-thirds of the money, he will own two-thirds of the property and Anna will own one-third. This makes it easier if they should ever divorce.

When Tom and Anna agree to buy the house, they are entering into a contract. Contracts for the sale and purchase of property are a particular type of contract. They need to be clear on the terms of the contract and must be made aware that once they have signed the contract, they are committed to the purchase and will be liable if they do not go through with it. They must ensure that they have all their finances in place, including any mortgage, before they sign.

Primarily, their solicitor will deal with the transfer of the ownership, or *title* to the property from the people who are selling to Tom and Anna. However, this raises all sorts of legal issues. The title to the property may be freehold or leasehold.

They will want to ensure that the property does not have any fundamental problems, for example they do not want to find that there is planning permission for 1,000 houses to be built on adjoining land, or that the road that runs past their house is subject to an improvement scheme which will turn it into a motorway, or that it has been built on contaminated land. They must be clear on what exactly is being sold, for example, whether the sale includes the fixtures, such as lights, and fittings, such as carpets and curtains or any items of furniture.

Once the purchase has been completed, Tom and Anna will be able to move into their property. However, there are formalities to be completed. The property transfer, and notice of any mortgage, must be registered at the Land Registry. Stamp duty, which is a form of property tax, has to be paid.

Tom and Anna also need to consider what will happen to the house if one of them dies. If this has not been provided for, they should update their wills.

Furnishing and fitting out the house will involve more contracts for the sale of goods and services.

Bear in mind that when they buy their house Tom and Anna may go to a solicitor, but they may choose to instruct and alternative legal service provider, such as a licensed conveyancer to carry out the legal work, or a will writer to make their wills (see Chapter 6).

17.2.3 The children

17.2.3.1 Client concerns

Tom and Anna want to have children. Again, they will probably not be thinking about the legal implications of this decision. They will consider how many children they want, and when they want to start a family. Their main concern will be that the children are healthy and have a happy family upbringing.

17.2.3.2 Financial considerations

According to figures from the insurer Liverpool Victoria (LV=), the average cost of raising a child from birth to 18 was estimated at £75,233 in 2019. The main cost is childcare and education.[10] Clearly, although a huge amount of money overall, the cost is at least spread over 18 years, and most will be met out of income, but there may be times when Tom and Anna will need to borrow money, either by way of short-term loan or overdraft, or by using their credit cards for exceptional expenses. Using credit cards is fine if they are able to pay off the credit card each month, but failure to pay off credit card debt is one of the most common causes of individuals finding themselves in financial difficulties.

In the wider social and economic context, there are issues that you should be aware of, particularly if you are interested in family, child, or welfare law or other related areas: for example, the charity, The Children's Society Group estimates that four million (or 1 in 3) children in the UK are growing up in poverty, and this appears to be increasing as a result of welfare and benefit cuts[11] (you would do well to research these, and their impact, too).

17.2.3.3 Legal considerations

When Anna becomes pregnant, she will have certain rights in relation to her employment. She will be entitled to maternity leave of up to a year, and maternity pay during her leave. Tom will also be entitled to paternity leave of up to two weeks. Since 2015, parents have also had the option of shared parental leave. Whatever they choose, they have the right to return to their jobs.

Once a child is born, like all individuals, it has its own legal personality. A new-born child has few rights and duties but as the child grows up and assumes more responsibilities these increase. The rights of children are mainly governed by the Children Act 1989, which governs parental responsibility and obligations, as well as providing for situations where parents are unable to look after their children or where children are suffering from abuse.

As a married couple, Tom and Anna will share responsibility for their children and will be responsible for their basic needs. The welfare of children is of paramount importance legally. It is assumed that all children, for example, have the right to health care and education, and the right not to be abused. Most parents take this for granted and provide the best of care for their children. However, where there is evidence that a child is not being properly looked after or is out of control, the child may be taken into local authority care. Family lawyers deal with this sort of work.

Parents do not generally seek legal advice in relation to children unless they separate or divorce. The parents then have to decide who the child should live with, and how to arrange

---

[10] LV= (2019) *How much will it cost to raise a child in 2019*. Available online at: https://www.lv.com/life-insurance/cost-of-raising-a-child-2019, accessed 12/10/2019.

[11] The Children's Society (2019) *What is child poverty?*. Available online at: https://www.childrenssociety.org.uk/what-we-do/our-work/ending-child-poverty/what-is-child-poverty, accessed 12/10/2019.

contact between the child and the absent parent. If the parents cannot decide, these matters may need to be settled by court order. Absent parents are responsible for the child's maintenance, and financial orders may be made if the parents are unable to agree the amount.

These are all worst-case scenarios. However, all families may face certain legal problems, e.g. if they are unable to get a child into the school of their choice, they may need legal advice on the appeals procedure to try and sort this out.

Parents are entitled to certain benefits. Most mothers are entitled to child benefit for each child until it reaches 16, subject to income constraints. Single parents can claim various additional benefits. Welfare and benefits are a highly specialised and topical area of law.

Again, Tom and Anna will probably not be seeking legal advice at this stage, but Table 17.2 shows what sort of advice they may need if things go wrong.

17.2.4 **The car**

17.2.4.1 Client concerns

Anna needs a new car. Again, it is not something about which she will consult a solicitor. Her concerns will be what make and model to buy, its performance, safety features, economy, colour, and so forth. She will have to think carefully about the finance.

17.2.4.2 Financial considerations

The average cost of a new car in 2018 (latest figures available) was £33,559 (admittedly, that takes into account every type of car from a Lamborghini down to a Smart car, and Anna probably will not be spending that much), but even if she buys a second-hand car, the average cost of a family-size used car was approximately £13,000.[12]

Whichever option Anna chooses, she will not be able to pay for this out of her income, so she will have to borrow the money, either by getting a short-term loan from the bank or perhaps from a finance company. Most car dealers have arrangements with finance companies to enable buyers to finance the cost of a new car. The average yearly running cost of a family car with finance in the UK is £388 a month.

17.2.4.3 Legal considerations

If Anna buys a new car from a dealer, she will again be entering into a sale of goods contract, which will protect her as a consumer in the event that the car turns out to be defective. There is, however, less protection if she buys a defective second-hand car privately. In either event, she may find herself involved in litigation and will need legal advice. Her finances will be important in deciding whether or not to sue or whether it is better to settle the dispute.

If she borrows the money or enters into a finance deal, again as a consumer, she will be protected by consumer credit legislation, which is designed to protect individual borrowers from being taken advantage of by loan sharks and other unscrupulous lenders when

---

[12] Based on cap hpi figures https://www.cap-hpi.com/.

borrowing money or entering into contracts for credit. We look at this legislation in more detail at 17.4.5.

As a motorist, Anna has certain obligations to other motorists, such as to obey speed limits and drive with 'due care and attention'. Failure to do so may lead to criminal prosecution under the Road Traffic Act 1988. Over 1 million traffic offences are dealt with by the magistrates' courts each year, including drink driving, careless driving, and use of mobile phones. Punishment for such includes fines and penalty points on driving licences. Serious offences, such as causing death by dangerous driving, can lead to imprisonment. Road traffic offences are a common cause of individuals consulting their solicitors and there are specialist firms of solicitors for this type of work.[13]

All motorists must take out insurance to cover any damage or injuries to third parties in the event of an accident. Driving without insurance is also a criminal offence. An insurance contract is a specialised form of contract.

17.2.5 Holidays and hobbies

17.2.5.1 Client concerns

Tom and Anna hope to take annual holidays, and they both have hobbies and interests which they pursue. This seems innocuous enough, but in reality this will involve more expense and there are still legal implications.

17.2.5.2 Financial considerations

Looking at Tom and Anna's hobbies, although a recent survey by the accountants, Deloitte, shows that in 2019 consumers were spending less on leisure activities in the light of Brexit uncertainty, the fitness market is estimated to be worth £5 billion, an increase of 2.9 per cent on 2017.[14] Holidays are most families' major expense, and the Office of National Statistics (ONS) figures show that 6.8 million people took overseas holidays in June 2019.[15] Hobbies can generally be paid for out of income, but holidays are the sort of expense that many people put on their credit cards or pay for with an overdraft or loan.

17.2.5.3 Legal considerations

Again, contract law is central to holiday bookings and membership of clubs. The main purpose of these types of contract is pleasure and enjoyment, so if something goes wrong, there are additional remedies to compensate for disappointment.

---

[13] See for example, DPP Law (2019), *Driving Offences UK 2019 Statistics.* Available online at: https://www.dpp-law.com/driving-offences-statistics/

[14] Deloitte (2019), *A Passion for Leisure.* https://www2.deloitte.com/uk/en/pages/consumer-industrial-products/articles/passion-for-leisure.html

[15] ONS (2019) *Overseas Travel and Tourism: June 2019 provisional results.* Available online at: https://www.ons.gov.uk/peoplepopulationandcommunity/leisureandtourism, accessed 12/10/2019.

17.2.6 **Old age and death**

17.2.6.1 Client concerns

By now, you will be able to see that with every life event come financial and legal implications. This is true from birth to death. Tom and Anna will probably give little consideration to these 'events' (old age and death) at this stage in their lives. They may have started thinking about saving for their old age, but that will probably be about as far as they have got. Early planning is crucially important. A further consideration is their parents, or other older relatives, who may need care in their old age.

17.2.6.2 Financial considerations

With an increasingly ageing population, individuals who retire in their mid-sixties will have to provide a pension fund to live off for 20 to 30 years or more. Anna, as a teacher, will get a teacher's pension, paid by the government. Tom will have to save for his pension himself. To get £15,000 a year, he would need a pension fund of over £250,000. If he saves £50 a month in a pension fund, he would only have a fund of about £190,000 on retirement.

A Sun Life Direct *Cost of Dying Survey 2018* found that the average cost of dying, including the cost of the funeral, probate fees, and a headstone, is £9,204.[16] People do plan ahead for this, and you will see advertisements for funeral plans, which are savings schemes to finance your funeral (another form of contract), but Tom and Anna will hope to have a few years to think about this.

17.2.6.3 Legal considerations

Pension law is becoming an increasingly important area of law as individuals become more concerned about saving for their old age.

As people get older, they may become ill or infirm and not be able to manage their affairs. We have seen how important it is to make a will at various stages of life. Once individuals lose their 'capacity' to do so, for example as a result of dementia,[17] it is too late. It is also important to make arrangements for someone to manage their affairs if they become unable to do so for themselves. Individuals should take advice on these things both for themselves and for elderly relatives.

During their lives, as we shall see, Tom and Anna will substantially increase their wealth. When they die, this will be taken into account in calculating how much their estates are worth. There are legal formalities which have to be completed before the money in the estate

---

[16] Sun Life Direct (2018) *Cost of Dying Survey 2018*. Available online at: https://www.sunlife.co.uk/press-office/funeral-costs-spiral-to-4271-following-annual-rise-of-4.7but-you-can-hold-a-funeral-for-less-than-half-the-price, accessed 12/10/2019.

[17] The Alzheimer's Society charity estimated that in 2019, 850,000 people in the UK had a form of dementia, with the number set to rise by over 1 million by 2025. Alzheimer's Society (2019) *Facts for the Media*. Available online at: https://www.alzheimers.org.uk/about-us/news-and-media/facts-media, accessed 13/10/2019.

can be released to whoever is entitled to the money. Assets, e.g. property or shares, may need to be sold or transferred. Tax may be payable on the estate. Often, though not always, solicitors will be involved and complete the legal processes on behalf of the relatives. The larger the estate, the more likely it is that a solicitor will be instructed to administer it.

Now consider Table 17.2 for a summary of the advice that a lawyer may provide as a result of Tom and Anna's concerns. If you had thought that the issues raised were only relevant to lawyers, the third column will show you that many non-lawyers will be involved. Law is not the only career where you need to be aware of the underlying concerns of your clients or customers. This table provides a summary of other professionals and advisers who will be involved in the various legal events of an individual's life.

17.2.7 **The context**

So far, we have thought about the client's concerns, and financial considerations and the type of legal advice that might be given. A lawyer should also think about the economic environment and its effect on the client. Over a lifetime, the economic climate will change dramatically. There will be times of economic prosperity and phases of economic downturn, as now. You will look at the *business cycle* at 19.1.4.5

The recession, following the financial crisis of 2008 and the uncertainty as a result of the Brexit referendum, has had a profound effect on most individuals' finances and standard of living. In an article in 2010, the (then) Labour leader, Ed Miliband, referred to people living on average incomes as 'the squeezed middle',[18] that is to say individuals who are seeing their standard of living fall as a result of rising prices, rising taxes, and pay cuts. A report by the think tank the Organisation for Economic Co-operation and Development (OECD) shows that this has persisted[19] and the middle classes are increasingly under pressure to keep up their lifestyles. Tom and Anna could be seen as falling into this category. This has then been compounded by Brexit, which, coupled with the austerity measures implemented by the Coalition and Conservative governments from 2010, damaged household incomes further.[20]

17.3 Typical life events: businesses and the law

Like individuals, each phase of a business's lifecycle will involve its owners thinking about the context in which the business is operating, its long term plans, and finance. The main considerations are commercial, but there are underlying legal issues and practical concerns on which business clients will need advice. Often these will be the same as for an individual. Again, you should anticipate the client's business needs, by having an in-depth understanding of the business and the concerns of the owner(s).

[18] Hennessy, P. 'Ed Miliband: my pledge to the squeezed middle class', *The Telegraph*, 25 September 2010. Available online at: http://www.telegraph.co.uk/news/politics/labour/8025448/Ed-Miliband-my-pledge-to-the-squeezed-middle-class.html.

[19] OECD (2019), *Under Pressure: The Squeezed Middle Class.* Available online at: https://www.oecd.org/social/under-pressure-the-squeezed-middle-class-689afed1-en.htm.

[20] For a discussion of the impact of Brexit, see the online resources.

Understanding clients: individuals and businesses

Chapter 17

Table 17.2 Life events: legal advice, advisers, and institutions

Event	Legal Advice	Other Advisers/Institutions
Property purchase, including finances/mortgage	Different types of property ownership, implications and advantages/disadvantages of each; Searches; Contract; Transfer of ownership; Formalities/registration/tax; Mortgage advice; Legal implications of mortgage; Terms, including effect of default; Registration.	Estate agent Surveyor Licensed conveyancer Mortgage adviser Bank or building society
Wills and tax planning	Drawing up and execution of will; Inheritance tax	Accountant or tax adviser Bank Will writers
Consumer disputes (goods/services/credit)	Consumer protection legislation	Citizens Advice Bureaux Trading Standards Financial Conduct Authority
Divorce	Grounds for divorce; Financial settlement, including division of property; Arrangements for children.	CAFCASS officer (Court welfare officer in event of dispute over children)
Care proceedings	Local authority duties/responsibilities; Care/supervision or emergency care orders.	Social worker Teachers Police Medical professionals (doctors/psychologists)
Employment	Employment legislation; Tax implications; Tribunal work.	Accountant HM Customs and Revenue
Motoring offences	Road traffic legislation; Magistrates' court work.	Police
Welfare	Entitlements	Department of Work and Pensions
Pensions	Pension legislation	Pensions adviser Department of Work and Pensions
Law and the elderly	Powers of attorney; Wills and validity; Residential care.	Medical professionals Social workers
Death	Inheritance law; Probate and the administration of estates; Tax.	Valuer/estate agent Probate Registry HM Customs and Revenue Bank/Building Society Stockbroker

To illustrate the issues that may arise in a business context, we are going to fast-forward a few years and look at Tom's business as an example (see Example 2). Although you will see that some of the issues raised are legal, many are relevant to all types of business.

Example 2

You will remember that Tom wanted to start his own wine business. He has found an empty shop for his business in the high street of a picturesque local market town. He is confident that this is a good location. It is an affluent small town in the commuter belt.

He has conducted some market research and feels that there is a gap in the market for a specialist wine merchant which can offer its customers a wide range of wines, from affordable to top end prices, with specialist advice. He realises that he will not be able to undercut the supermarkets and larger wine retailers, but he has come up with a marketing concept to attract customers. He has a name for his business, The Wine Seller, which he hopes to use to develop its brand.

The business will offer wine tasting 'experiences', accessible advice and education, with regular talks from wine journalists and experts in the wine trade. Customers will have access to an online wine magazine, *Seller's Sips*, with recommendations, and he hopes to develop an app for customers' phones. Using the latest technology, he is hoping to expand to offer a similar online service. Customers will pay a subscription for regular tasting samples, email recommendations, reminders, and the online magazine.

17.3.1 **Start up**

17.3.1.1 **Client concerns**

When he starts up the business, Tom's main concern will be whether this a viable business, and whether he will be able to make a profit.

17.3.1.2 **Financial considerations**

It is essential that anyone starting up a business has a realistic business plan.

> ## ⓘ Essential explanation
>
> A *business plan* is a written document that describes a business, its objectives (what it hopes to achieve), its strategies (how it hopes to achieve them), its products, the market it is operating in, the potential for growth within that market, and, most importantly, its financial forecasts. A business should have a plan at every stage of its development, not just when starting up.

Before the business even opens its doors, Tom will need to spend money to get the business going. He needs suitable premises to operate from, stock to sell, and customers to sell to. There will be expenses like legal fees, marketing materials, doing up the shop, or buying in the wine to sell. He will have to buy assets for the business, such as shop fittings, computers, telephones, cash registers, or wine storage units. He may need to pay rent in advance to his landlord, and put up a deposit (as you have to do when you rent a flat). There are various things that Tom will need to organise, and therefore pay for, before he starts to trade. These are illustrated by Example 3.

Example 3

Tom is hoping to open his business on 7 September. He gives up his job at the beginning of August and starts to prepare for the opening of the business. The following transactions take place:

1 August	Tom transfers £50,000 of his own money to the business bank account.
2 August	He negotiates a loan with the bank for £20,000, repayable in five years.
3 August	He rents premises in the High Street.
	He pays a deposit of £4,500 and the first instalment of rent (£3,000).
	He pays for insurance on the property (£230).
10 August	He buys shop fittings and fixtures, and computers.
12 August	He orders marketing materials, stationery, and business cards.
15 August	He buys wine for £20,000 cash to stock the shop.
16 August	He pays a web designer for designing and setting up the business website.
5 September	He obtains and pays for his licence to sell alcohol (£985).
6 September	He pays the shop fitters who have installed the fixtures and fittings.
	He pays his solicitor (£1,000 plus VAT) for general advice on business set up, licensing, and checking the lease on the property.

Often, clients setting up new businesses tend to underestimate start-up costs, and forget that it will take time to get the business going before it starts to generate income. In our example, all of the money that Tom has paid out between 1 August and 7 September constitutes his start-up costs. This is just a simple example. In reality, the process may take much longer, and involve more money (e.g. to obtain a licence to sell alcohol, the shop owner must attend a training course and sit an exam).

On a personal level, he will need to consider how he is going to pay his everyday living expenses while he is setting up the business.

The best option for Tom is to get independent financial advice. He will need a good accountant and a sympathetic business relationship manager at his bank.

17.3.1.3 Legal considerations

Ownership of a business will change Tom's individual legal personality. The rights and responsibilities which he had as an employee will be replaced by a new set of rights and obligations as a business owner/employer. As a result, Tom may need advice on a range of legal issues.

To begin with, Tom will need advice on the legal structure of the business. From the facts that we have, it looks as though he will be running the business by himself as a sole trader. Tom has full responsibility for the business both financially and legally. There are other types of business structure, such as partnerships or limited liability companies (see 18.1).

Tom is going to borrow money from the bank to fund the business, and will be entering into a loan agreement. The bank may require some form of security to ensure that if the business runs into difficulties, it will get its money back, for instance it may ask Tom for a further mortgage on his house. There are other options for raising finance (see 17.5).

Tom is renting the business premises under the terms of a lease.

> ### Essential explanation
>
> A *lease* of premises is a contractual arrangement which grants the right to occupy the premises for a fixed period, subject to the terms and conditions set out in the lease (e.g. payment of the rent). The lease of business premises may contain restrictions as to the type of business activity which can be carried out on the premises, e.g. it may prevent the sale of alcohol.

Tom is entering into a series of contracts for goods and services with various suppliers, and for the installation of the fixtures and fittings. Like an individual, he has certain rights if any goods or services turn out to be defective. However, as a business customer, he does not have the benefit of consumer protection legislation.

To promote his business, Tom has ordered some marketing materials. He needs to be aware of what he can and cannot say in advertisements and promotional material.

He has arranged insurance. This involves a further type of contract. Running a business exposes the owner(s) to various risks, for example liability should either customers or employees injure themselves on the premises, or if the business sells defective products. Risk management is crucial for every business.

Before he starts up, Tom should get advice on the tax implications of setting up the business and how to minimise his tax. There will be further tax implications once the business is up and running. He should be made aware of these before he starts the business, and be advised to get an accountant to oversee the business finances.

Tom is selling alcohol and will therefore require a licence, and should know about the law in relation to the sale of alcohol.

Tom has a name for the business, 'The Wine Seller'. Before he starts to use the name, he will need to check whether any other business is trading under this name, or he may be infringing that other business's intellectual property rights (e.g. its trade mark). The name will be his brand. It will be one of the most valuable assets of the business (see 17.4.4) and he will need to protect this and other intellectual property rights.

17.3.2 Running the business

17.3.2.1 Client concerns

Once Tom opens the doors of his business, his aim will be to make a profit. He will be concerned with all the day-to-day running of the business.

17.3.2.2 Financial considerations

To make money, businesses have to spend money. Example 4 gives some simple examples, showing the constant expenditure involved in running a business.

Example 4

On 7 September, Tom opens the shop.

7 September	He sells £2,000 of wine to customers who pay cash.
	He sells £3,000 of wine and champagne to a wine bar on a 30-day credit period (i.e. the customer does not need to pay his bill for 30 days).
	He buys champagne for £10,000 from his supplier on a 14-day credit period (i.e. he has to pay his bill within 14 days).
	He pays the next instalment of rent and insurance (£3,230).
8 September	He pays an electricity bill off by cheque.
	He buys a second-hand van for £5,000, and employs a delivery driver.
9 September	He negotiates an overdraft facility with the bank and draws down £5,000 to buy more stock. (He pays the bank an arrangement fee for setting up the overdraft.)
10 September	He pays his phone and internet bill (£850).
	He makes further cash sales of £3,000.

Assume further sales and purchases during the rest of the month

30 September	He pays the van driver's wages (£1,090).
	He pays Mastercard and Visa for use of credit facilities.
	He pays bank charges and interest of £550.
	He employs a cleaner for five hours a week at £10 an hour.

Tom will have to ensure that he maintains his stock of wine. The wine will not sell itself, and he may need to employ sales staff in his shop. At the moment, he is just employing a driver and a cleaner, and selling the wine himself.

Throughout the year, he will be paying rent, rates, utility bills, and other outgoings. All this is fine, provided that he continues to sell the wine. There will be some days when he sells a fair amount, and he should use this to build up a reserve. In our example, on 7 September, Tom has sold £5,000 of the £20,000 worth of wine which he bought to stock up the shop, although he is not paid for all of this immediately. On the same day, however, he has bought £10,000 worth of champagne, but it is possible that none of his customers will want champagne until Christmas. All businesses need to keep a reserve for periods when trade is slow. (A rough guide for a business with start-up costs of £50,000–£70,000 is a reserve of £20,000–£30,000.)

17.3.2.3 Legal considerations

The day-to-day transactions—the sale of the wine—will be governed by contract law. Where Tom is selling to consumers, he will have to bear in mind consumer protection legislation.

Where he is offering credit to consumers, consumer credit legislation offers them further protection. He may also need advice if his customers fail to pay, for example on debt collection.

Once the business is making a profit, there are tax implications. Tom, as a sole trader, will be liable for tax on those profits. In addition, once the total sales (turnover) of the business reach £85,000, he must register for VAT.[21]

---

[21] Rates for the year 2019–20. HM Customs and Revenue (2019) *VAT Registration Thresholds*. Available online at: https://www.gov.uk/vat-registration-thresholds, accessed 13/10/2019.

> **Essential explanation**
>
> VAT is an indirect tax on consumers charged on most goods and services sold by VAT registered businesses. It is not paid by the business itself. It is paid by the customers and the business collects it and passes it on to HMRC.

This means that Tom must charge VAT at 20 per cent on everything which he sells, although he will be able to reclaim any VAT which he has paid on his own purchases. He will have to complete VAT returns for HMRC every three months.

Tom has employed a driver, and it is likely that as the business grows he will take on sales staff. All employees are protected by complex and detailed employment legislation. Employees have rights in relation to their contracts, pay, working hours and conditions, holidays, pensions, and also the right not to be dismissed wrongly or unfairly. They have the right not to be discriminated against on the grounds of race, sex, disability, religion, age, and so forth. Employment protection is not all one-way traffic. The converse is true; the employees should look carefully at their contracts, and understand that they have certain obligations towards their employer, for example to work their contracted hours and not 'moonlight' (i.e. work for someone else at the same time).

Employers are responsible for paying their employees' tax (called PAYE), which they take directly out of their wages and pass on to HMRC (see 17.4.2.1).

The cleaner is more likely to be self-employed than an employee. If this is the case, the cleaner will not have the employment rights which the other employees enjoy, but it is important that Tom establishes the status of all of those working for him before he takes them on.

17.3.3 Expansion

17.3.3.1 Client concerns

Let's assume that Tom's business has been running successfully for five years, and he is considering whether or not to open a second shop. He has the option to buy another wine merchant's business in a neighbouring town.

He is also considering combining his shops (known as the 'bricks and mortar' part of his business) with expansion of the online (e-commerce) part of the business. If he expands, he is thinking about incorporating his business, to raise funds and to give himself the protection of limited liability.

17.3.3.2 Financial considerations

If Tom expands his business, he will have all the same expenses, but on a larger scale. For example, he will have additional premises, and so he will have to pay more rent and his utility bills will go up. He may incur additional marketing costs to promote the business in its new venue or format. There will be legal and other professional fees (e.g. accountancy fees). More storage space will be needed to store more stock, so Tom may have to rent a warehouse, and pay for rent and utility bills for that as well. He may take on more sales staff, and administrative support will be needed. He may need a fleet of vans and so have to employ more drivers.

For the e-commerce venture, he will need to invest in the relevant technology, and the staff to operate this, in particular IT support. Often the result of incurring additional expenses is that profits decrease, especially initially, before the benefit of the expansion takes effect. Once the profits do increase, a further consideration is that there will be extra tax (e.g. VAT).

If all goes well, however, expansion should mean that Tom can achieve *'economies of scale'*. This effectively means that as his business expands, costs per unit sold will decrease, allowing him to make a higher profit, and reduce prices. Instead of buying for one shop, he will now be buying for two and will be supplying his online customers. If he buys more, he may be able to get lower prices. Some of the costs will be spread across all parts of the business, such as advertising, professional, or administration costs. An example of how this works is the big supermarkets. They are able to cut prices as the sheer size of their operations enables them to get lower prices from their suppliers. However, economies of scale tend to work less well for smaller than for larger businesses.

17.3.3.3 Legal considerations

There are various ways that a business can expand, and so Tom should consider the best way of doing it. He can expand by just buying the shop in the neighbouring town (i.e. acquiring a new asset). This means that he will develop his existing business from two outlets. Alternatively, he can buy the business itself as a going concern, with all its assets, thus combining the two businesses. Finally, he could go into business with the owner of the other wine merchant and merge the two businesses.

> **Essential explanation**
>
> An *acquisition* is the purchase of one business by another. This will not result in a new business being formed.
>
> A *merger* is where two businesses merge or combine their existing operations to form a new business.
>
> The main reason for both is to achieve *synergies*, i.e. improving the efficiency of the business by staff reduction, economies of scale, expanding markets and customer base, or acquiring new technologies.

Certainly, if you are interested in corporate practice, you should know the difference. Interviewers would certainly expect that you do.

If Tom decides to buy the business as a going concern, his advisers will carry out a 'health' check on the business by examining all the documentation, financial records, and other material facts relating to the business to ensure that the business is sound and there are no problems that have not been revealed during the purchase negotiations. This process is known as *due diligence*. If he decides only to buy the shop, the solicitor will need to investigate the title to the premises and ensure that ownership is transferred to Tom.

As the business grows, Tom will need ongoing advice on many of the issues that we have already considered, such as contractual and employment issues, tax, and debt collection.

In the light of these considerations, Table 17.3 shows the sort of legal advice Tom will be looking for, and the professionals and other advisers involved.

Table 17.3 Business life cycle: legal advice, advisers, and institutions involved

Event	Legal Advice	Other Advisers

Setting up the business	Type of business structure:
	  – sole trader or company
	  – advantages/disadvantages of each
	  – tax implications of each
		Bank/Small business adviser
		Accountant
		HM Customs and Revenue

– Loan from bank	Terms of loan agreement Security for loan Advantages/disadvantages of debt finance Alternatives for raising money	
– Premises	Leasehold property legislation Terms of lease, including restrictions, e.g. on sale of alcohol	Estate agent Surveyor
– Marketing	Restrictions on advertising/promotions Intellectual property rights	Marketing consultants Advertising Standards Authority
– Supply contracts	Contract law Terms and exclusions of liability	
– Insurance	Terms of insurance contract	Insurance broker
– Brand	Intellectual property rights generally Protecting a brand	Marketing consultants
– Licensing	Licensing regulations Application procedure	Local authority
Running the business		
– Employees	Employment legislation Tax: PAYE/NI	Accountant HM Customs and Revenue Trading Standards
– Sales	Contract law Consumer protection legislation Tax: VAT Debt collection	
Expansion	Merger/acquisition—implications, advantages/disadvantages of each Due diligence Property law Contract law	Accountants Bank/Business adviser
Insolvency	Insolvency legislation Insolvency processes—implications and advantages/disadvantages of each	Accountant Insolvency practitioner

17.3.4 **The context**

Again the final stage is to analyse the commercial factors and the economic environment in which the business is operating. Tom, as a retailer, will need to be aware of all the same factors in relation to his customers as lawyers should consider in relation to their clients. This will give him an insight into the strength of the market in which he is operating, and his customers' expectations.

If Tom decided to start his business at the time of writing, January 2020, i.e. at the beginning of the Brexit transition period, he will be setting up at a time of considerable uncertainty. In addition, export clients and those buying from abroad are very much at the mercy of developments in the currency markets, which are subject to fluctuations as a result of economic conditions both domestically and globally. Tom should also be aware that the wine business relies heavily on imports, particularly from France, and a strong exchange rate for the pound.

Example 5

The importance of economic growth, inflation, imports and exports, and the currency markets to the economy will be considered in Chapter 19. You will see that understanding economic developments and currency fluctuations and the advantages and disadvantages of a strong or weak pound is a crucial part of commercial awareness, and something that you can demonstrate at interviews.

The type of business and the market in which it operates is important to its success. Tom is aiming primarily at an affluent market. ONS figures show that people from higher socio-economic groups are more likely to drink frequently.[22] Whether an increase in alcohol prices would affect these figures remains to be seen.

Another important fact that Tom should bear in mind is that this is a seasonal market, with sales increasing, for example during the period leading up to Christmas and the New Year, and then falling off. This may cause him cash flow problems, so he should run a tight credit policy following up bills and ensuring that they are paid, and it is important to keep reserves for these periods.

17.3.5 **Insolvency**

At each stage of the life of a business, there is always the spectre of insolvency hanging over it. The knock-on effect is very often the bankruptcy of the proprietor of the business. When you look at insolvency, you will see that own business failure is one of the commonest causes of individual insolvency, particularly amongst men (see 19.4.4).The number of insolvencies has increased over the last year, and businesses cannot be complacent.

Start-up companies are particularly vulnerable to the vagaries of the economy. We have seen that Tom will have significant start-up costs before he begins to make any money. Even once he is up and running, he will need to think about how to raise the money he needs to

---

[22] ONS (2018) *Adult drinking habits in Great Britain: 2017*. Available online at: https://www.ons .gov.uk/peoplepopulationandcommunity/healthandsocialcare/drugusealcoholandsmoking/bulletins/ opinionsandlifestylesurveyadultdrinkinghabitsingreatbritain/2017, accessed 14/10/2019. Note that this survey was discontinued after 2017, but drinking habits are not likely to have changed drastically (although the survey does show a small increase in teetotalism).

keep afloat or expand. Although Bank of England statistics show that bank lending to small businesses has improved over recent years, very few start-up businesses become mid-sized. Even if the funds are available, he will need to be realistic. Over-expansion is a further common cause of insolvency.

We have now seen why individuals and businesses have recourse to the law, and the legal and financial impact of everyday events. We are next going to think further about the financial concerns of both individuals and businesses, and how clients of both types raise finance, and the people and institutions involved.

17.4 Forms of individual finance

You have seen that as individuals and businesses progress through their lives, their financial concerns are paramount. In short, everyone needs money. Now we are going to consider how individuals raise finance and what they do with it. We will look at individual wealth, in its broadest sense, thinking about what individuals are worth in terms of their total assets and the effect that this may have on their financial decisions.

17.4.1 Background

To fully understand their clients, lawyers need to be aware of their financial background. There are four main aspects to consider, which taken together represent an individual's wealth:

- how much money your clients earn (*income*);
- how they spend it (*expenses*);
- what property and savings they have (*assets*); and
- how much money they have borrowed (*liabilities*).

Figure 17.1 shows how all of these factors contribute to an individual's wealth.

'Wealth' is a bit of a buzz word at the moment. The annual *Sunday Times* 'Rich List' and the attention which it attracts shows how fascinated people are by the concept of wealth. It shows that if you add up the wealth of the 1,000 richest people in the UK, it comes to nearly £724 billion (the combined wealth of the 40 per cent poorest households is £567 billion.)[23] Top of the list are the Hinduja brothers, who control the Indian conglomerate, the Hinduja Group with a combined wealth of £22 billion.[24] Many law firms no longer have 'private client' departments, they have 'private wealth' departments, which advise clients on financial planning, tax issues, inheritance, wills, and probate. However, this focus on wealth gives a totally false impression of what wealth actually is. Having wealth does not necessarily mean that you are rich. In its true sense, wealth is simply a measure of what you own.

---

[23] The Equality Trust (2018), *UK Rich Increase Their Wealth by 274 billion over Five Years*. Available online at: https://www.equalitytrust.org.uk/wealth-tracker-18, accessed 13/10/2019.

[24] 'Sunday Times Rich List 2019', *Sunday Times*, 12 May 2019. Available online at: *https://www.thetimes .co.uk › article › sunday-times-rich-list-cbxfbprqf* (subscription access needed for full version).

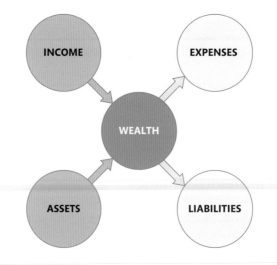

Figure 17.1 Wealth

> ### ⓘ Essential explanation
>
> An individual's *wealth* is what she is worth, taking into account income, expenses, assets, and borrowings. In practice, you will be looking at the impact of a client's 'wealth', whether you are working in a large commercial firm or a small high-street firm.

Most people try to budget carefully. They work out how much income is coming in each month, and what their main expenses are. If anything is left over, they can use the money to reduce their liabilities, buy extra assets, or put the excess into savings, all of which will increase their wealth. In Chapter 19 you will see this is basic accounting (see 19.3). However, there are variables, which will affect their budgets. As well as inflation, we have already seen that typical life events cost money, and sometimes they cost a large amount of money. Not all of an individual's expenses can be met out of income, and generally people will not want to sell assets. One way of raising finance is to borrow money, creating liabilities.

> ### → Practice tip
>
> It is crucial at this stage to realise that, as a lawyer, you will not be giving detailed financial advice to your clients. Most of this information will be background only to your advice to your clients. This is because there are very strict conduct rules which govern what sort of financial advice a solicitor can give. The fundamental principle of the Solicitors Regulation Authority's Standards and Regulations[25] is that solicitors can only advise if they have the necessary skill and expertise to do so. If not, they will not be acting in their client's best interests. Most solicitors will not have financial expertise, but even if they do, they (and all professionals who offer financial advice) are regulated by the Financial Services and Markets Act 2000, which prevents professionals giving specialist financial advice of any sort unless they are authorised to do so. Most solicitors are not authorised, and so would commit a criminal offence were they to do so. This is punishable by a two-year prison sentence and/or a fine.

[25] *SRA Standards and Regulations.* Available online at: http://www.sra.org.uk.

You can give general advice, for example explain the nature of shares or bonds, and that shares are a riskier investment than bonds (we will look in detail at different types of investment in Chapter 19). However, you cannot go on to give more specific advice, such as you think that shares in BP are a investment to make at the moment, because of rising global oil prices. You may be right, but you need to refer your client to an independent financial adviser, like a stockbroker.

17.4.2 Income

1. **Income**. Income is what you earn. Most individuals' income comes from their salaries as employees. The average salary in 2018 (latest figures available at the time of writing) was £29,588 a year (gross) for full-time employees in the UK.[26]

2. **Benefits**. For those who are unemployed or on low salaries, benefits are an important source of income. There are 2.3 million people relying on Universal Credit.[27] The welfare system again is highly topical, because of the problems over the last few years with the introduction of Universal Credit.

3. **Savings**. Individuals may also have savings and investments which earn income, e.g.:

   - interest from savings accounts, or bonds;
   - dividends from investments in shares;
   - rent from property. Individuals may invest in residential or other investment properties which they let out for profit. It is estimated that there are over 4.8 million buy-to-let properties in the UK.

17.4.2.1 Tax

As Benjamin Franklin famously remarked, 'in this world nothing can be said to be certain, except death and taxes'. Most income is subject to tax. An employee is paid a net salary, that is after deduction of tax. Tax on employment income is known as Pay As You Earn (PAYE). The employer calculates the tax due each month and takes it out of the employee's salary before payment. Employees also pay National Insurance (NI) contributions to the government. This is deducted at the same time. NI helps to fund the welfare state, and in particular affects the final amount of an individual's pension.

> ### Essential explanation
>
> *Gross* income is income before tax has been deducted.
> *Net* income is the amount received after the deduction of tax.

[26] ONS (2019) *Employee Earnings in the UK: 2018*. Available online at: https://www.ons .gov.uk/employmentandlabourmarket/peopleinwork/earningsandworkinghours/bulletins/ annualsurveyofhoursandearnings/2018, accessed 14/10/2019.

[27] Department of Work and Pensions (2019), *Universal Credit Statistics: 29 April 2013 to 11 June 2019*. Available online at: https://www.gov.uk/government/publications/ universal-credit-29-april-2013-to-11-july-2019/universal-credit-statistics-29-april-2013-to-11-july-2019.

Understanding clients: individuals and businesses

Chapter 17

The rate of tax depends on the amount which the employee earns. As at April 2019, a tax-payer can earn up to £12,500[28] without paying any tax, but note that these rates change annually. Once someone's income goes above this figure, they start to pay tax. The rates of tax are set each year in March by the Chancellor of the Exchequer in the budget statement, which is the yearly update on the state of the economy. The budget is of vital importance for individuals and businesses alike. It is one of the political events of each year which you should always know about, and be prepared to discuss at an interview.

17.4.2.2 Inflation

You will consider inflation and its impact on the economy at 19.1.4. It is also a vital factor when advising clients, as it impacts on real wages. This is illustrated by Example 6.

> **❗ Essential explanation**
>
> *Actual* wages are wages before taking into account inflation.
>
> *Real* wages take into account inflation.
>
> *Gross* wages are wages before any deductions, e.g. for tax or NI.
>
> *Net* wages are wages after deductions have been made.

Example 6

If an employee's actual wage is £1,000 a month (net), and inflation for that month is 2 per cent, his real net wage is £980.

According to the ONS, after several years during which real wages fell consistently, as wage rises failed to keep pace with inflation, real wages are now beginning to increase slowly, as, on average, pay rises exceed inflation.[29]

17.4.3 Expenses

The most recent ONS statistics show that households spent an average of £572.60 a week in 2018 (latest figures available).[30] Most people's expenses are housing (rent or mortgage payments), utilities (gas, electricity, and water), running the car, and food. They will have to pay

---

[28] GOV.UK (2016) *Income Tax rates and allowances for past and present years*. Available online at: https://www.gov.uk/government/publications/rates-and-allowances-income-tax/income-tax-rates-and-allowances-current-and-past, accessed 14/10/2019.

[29] ONS (2019) *Average Weekly Earnings in Great Britain: July 2019*. Available online at: https://www.ons.gov.uk/employmentandlabourmarket/peopleinwork/employmentandemployeetypes/bulletins/averageweeklyearningsingreatbritain/july2019, accessed 14/10/2019.

[30] ONS (2019) *Family Spending*. Available online at: https://www.ons.gov.uk/peoplepopulationandcommunity/personalandhouseholdfinances/expenditure/bulletins/familyspendingintheuk/financialyearending2018, accessed 17/02/2020.

council tax (tax paid to the local authority) on the property. They probably have other expenses as well, such as their mobile phones. Hobbies cost money. They may be paying interest to the bank on any overdrafts which they have, or on any unpaid balance on their credit cards. The cost of living is influenced by the price of commodities, raw materials and agricultural produce such as oil, gas, minerals, wheat, or coffee. In recent years, commodity prices, particularly the price of oil, have risen, and the ONS figures show that household expenditure is increasing. As we have seen, many middle class families would struggle to maintain their lifestyles, and a report by the charity, the Joseph Rowntree Foundation, shows that many families fall short of the Minimum Income Standard (the income needed to achieve a socially acceptable standard of living).[31]

17.4.4 Assets

An individual's assets are the various items of property which he owns. An asset has a value. It can be sold and converted into cash. Examples include land and buildings, bank accounts, investments, cars, furniture, and electronic equipment. The sum total of an individual's assets is sometimes referred to as his *capital*. Some assets are more easily converted into cash (i.e. are more 'liquid' than others). Cash is the most liquid of assets. You can go to your bank and get all your cash out of your account, but it may take some time, for example, to sell your car.

17.4.4.1 House ownership

In England, 14.8 million people (or 63 per cent of households) own their own home,[32] which will be by far their most valuable asset. Other important assets are savings and investments.

17.4.4.2 Savings

Savings provide individuals with a fund for the future, and in the meantime produce an income. There are various ways that individuals can save.

1. **Savings accounts with banks and building societies**. These are the most common way of saving, as they carry little risk, but the problem for savers is that interest rates are low at the moment so the return on these savings is minimal.
2. **Individual Savings Accounts (ISAs)**. These are tax-free savings schemes. In simple terms, they are ordinary bank savings accounts or portfolios of stocks and shares but which are subject to tax exemptions.

17.4.4.3 Pensions

One of the main ways that many people save is by paying into a pension. A pension is an investment policy which provides income when you retire. Everyone is entitled to a state

---

[31] Joseph Rowntree Foundation (2019) *A minimum income standard for the UK 2008–2018: continuity and change*. Available online at: https://www.jrf.org.uk/report/minimum-income-standard-uk-2018?gclid=EAIaIQobChMIk4Gzupyc5QIViaztCh0BVwNCEAAYASAAEgJHiPD_BwE, accessed 14/10/2019.

[32] Ministry of Housing, Communities and Local Government (2018) *English Housing Survey. Home Ownership 2017–18*. Available online at: https://www.gov.uk/government/statistics/english-housing-survey-2017-to-2018-home-ownership, accessed 14/10/2019.

pension, paid by the government, funded from NI contributions paid during an individual's working life. Following recent reforms to the pension system, the new State Pension for an individual is £168.60 a week (rate for 2019–20),[33] which only gives limited support. It is advisable to supplement the state pension by paying into a private scheme and building up a fund which will provide income for your old age. Pension provision is a complicated area and there are various types of private pension schemes.

Public sector workers, such as doctors, the police, teachers, and civil servants, get a pension funded by the state, and based on their final salary. Outside the public sector, however, government research shows that millions of people are not saving anything at all into private pensions. This has led to large-scale reform of pension law, and from 2016 all employers have been obliged to enrol all their workers automatically into an employer-funded pension scheme.[34]

17.4.4.4 Investments

Investments are a form of saving, in that they provide a fund for the future and an income (e.g. investors receive dividends on shares), but they also have the potential to increase (and also, if you are unlucky or unwise, to decrease) in value. Paying into a pension fund can be regarded as an investment, in that a pension fund should increase in value over the years, whereas cash in the bank or building society is not. In real terms, cash will decrease in value, because of inflation. Investments can take various forms:

1. Bonds, shares, and unit trusts, all of which will produce an income (see 19.2.4).

2. The purchase of a house is also an investment but, unlike other investments, houses do not provide an income (unless bought to let). As we have seen, since the 1980s, house prices have gone up dramatically, and more quickly than inflation, and thus provide *capital growth*.

17.4.4.5 Tax

Some assets are subject to *capital gains tax* (CGT). This means that if an asset is sold or given away, a proportion of any increase in value is subject to tax. In addition, on death, all an individual's assets are added together to form her 'estate'. If the total value exceeds a certain limit, or threshold known as the nil rate band (currently £325,000),[35] then *inheritance tax* (IHT) has to be paid. From 2009 until 2019, the inheritance tax threshold has remained the same. This is an example of what is known as 'fiscal drag'. From 2017, however, allowances have been made for an individual's main residence, which will reduce the amount of IHT payable, and mean that many estates are no longer be liable for IHT.

---

[33] GOV.UK (2019) *The new State Pension*. Available online at: https://www.gov.uk/new-state-pension, accessed 14/10/2019.

[34] Pensions Act 2008, in force from October 2012.

[35] For the year 2019–20. HM Customs and Revenue (2019) *Rates and Allowances: Inheritance Tax Thresholds*. Available online at: https://www.gov.uk/government/publications/rates-and-allowances-inheritance-tax-thresholds/inheritance-tax-thresholds, accessed 15/10/2019.

> **! Essential explanation**
>
> *Fiscal drag* is a term for the situation where inflation, earnings, or asset growth pushes taxpayers into paying more tax, without the government explicitly putting up taxes. An example is the effect of rising house prices, which have meant that many more estates are subject to IHT.

17.4.5 Liabilities

An individual's liabilities are the amounts which he owes (his debts) to his creditors.

> **! Essential explanation**
>
> A *debtor* is someone who borrows, or *owes*, money.
>
> A *creditor* is someone who lends, or is *owed*, money.

17.4.5.1 Borrowing and credit

Since the 1980s, with the rise of consumerism, borrowing and credit have been an important part of the everyday lives of individuals in the UK. As the Money Charity recently reported, households in the UK owed £1.647 trillion (£1,647,000,000,000). The average household owes £59,319.[36]

> **! Essential explanation**
>
> An individual's *credit* is the amount of money which is available for him to borrow. It is called credit because it is based on the trust that the amount will be repaid in the future. Loans, mortgages, overdrafts, and credit cards are all forms of credit.

The provision of credit is very highly regulated in order to protect consumers. Banks and other financial institutions which provide credit to consumers must be authorised by the Financial Conduct Authority (FCA), and follow prescribed guidelines in relation to the information which they give when a credit contract is formed, and procedures to follow during the term of the agreement and when the agreement comes to an end.[37]

17.4.5.2 Credit rating

Knowing about credit ratings is one of the most important bits of financial knowledge that you can have, both for your clients and in relation to your own affairs. The amount of credit available to any individual depends on her credit rating. This is an assessment of her credit-worthiness based on her assets and liabilities, past borrowing, and repayment history.

[36] The Money Charity (2019) *The Money Statistics July 2019*. Available online at: http://themoneycharity.org.uk/money-statistics/, accessed 14/10/2019.
[37] Consumer Credit Act 1974, as amended.

Credit reference agencies collect financial information on individuals, looking at all aspects of their financial lives, such as how many credit cards and mobile phone contracts they have, and whether they have missed payments on those. They then draw up credit reports which they sell to banks and other institutions. When you apply for a loan or a credit card, the bank or card provider will 'score' you, based on how well, (or badly) you have managed your finances in the past. It also looks at non-financial information such as court orders against you, and whether you are on the Electoral Roll.

A poor credit score makes it difficult to get credit. However, anyone can improve their credit rating by taking a few simple steps to demonstrate that they are managing their finances responsibly, such as always paying bills on time, not exceeding overdraft limits, reducing debts, and, perhaps surprisingly, getting a credit card (but you must repay it on time every month).

17.4.5.3 The cost of borrowing

Banks and other commercial lenders make a profit by charging interest on borrowing. Interest rates vary, depending on the type of loan and the risk involved. Lenders may also charge fees when the loan is taken out, and this will put up the cost of the loan. It is sometimes far from clear how much interest is actually payable. Lenders are required by consumer credit legislation to state how much it will cost per year to take out a loan. It is vital to understand this calculation.

> **! Essential explanation**
>
> The *Annual Percentage Rate* (APR) is the annual cost of a loan. It includes the interest on the loan and any associated fees that are automatically included for that type of loan. It is possible that the interest rate is 10 per cent, but the APR is, say, 12 per cent because the costs of the loan put up the APR.

Borrowers should always check the APR before taking out any form of loan, so as to make a comparison between various loans, and see what is being charged for. Many borrowers are unaware of the significance of APR.

17.4.5.4 Secured loans

> **! Essential explanation**
>
> A *secured loan* requires the borrower to put up an asset, or *collateral*, to back the loan. The term secured means that if the borrower *defaults* (i.e. fails to make the payments as agreed), the lender has the right to *repossess* the asset (i.e. to sell it to recover the money which it has lent).
>
> An *unsecured* or *personal loan* does not require the borrower to put up any collateral. The lender relies on the borrower's promise to repay the loan.

17.4.5.5 Mortgages

The most common type of secured, long term loan is a mortgage, where the loan is secured against the value of the property. Banks and building societies offer mortgages and there are also specialist mortgage lenders. The lender is the *mortgagee* and the borrower is the *mortgagor*. The loan is repaid in one of two ways:

- *Repayment* mortgages: the mortgagor makes monthly payments for an agreed period, or *term*. These payments cover the interest and an amount to repay the capital of the loan itself. The usual mortgage term is 25 years.

- *Interest only* mortgages: the monthly payments cover the interest only on the loan. At the end of the term, the mortgagee has to find the money to pay off the capital.

There are a wide variety of mortgage types, and a range of interest rates to choose from. It is essential to advise clients that they should seek specialist mortgage advice to decide which type of mortgage is most suitable for them, how much they can afford each month, and how much they will be able to borrow.

They also need to be aware that because the loan is secured against their house, they could lose the house. The mortgage agreement will give the bank or building society the right to *foreclose* if the mortgagor does not keep up with the payments. The bank will take possession of the house, and sell it to pay off their loan.

This does not necessarily mean that the clients will lose all the money which they have invested in the house. The mortgagee is only entitled to the amount of the loan. If the house is worth more than the loan, then the client keeps the balance. That balance is the *equity* in the house. Consider Example 7.

Example 7

If someone buys a house for £250,000 and borrows £150,000 from the bank, secured by a mortgage, the *equity* in the house is £100,000. If the borrower defaults on the loan, the bank can repossess and sell the house. Assuming that the house is sold for £250,000, the bank will get £150,000 and the borrower (the mortgagor) will get £100,000 (equity) from the sale. If the value of the house has fallen and it is worth less than £150,000, this is described as '*negative equity*' and the bank will not recoup its loan.

17.4.5.6 Unsecured loans

Unsecured borrowing takes a variety of forms. Individuals enter into unsecured loans every day. When you borrow £10 from your friend for a night out, that is a simple form of unsecured loan. Bank of England statistics show that unsecured borrowing, having increased in 2018, fell slightly in 2019.[38]

Without security, unsecured loans are riskier for the lender, and interest rates tend to be higher than for secured loans. The main types are:

1. **Credit and store cards**. The most usual form of unsecured credit is purchases made on a credit or store card. The average family spends £2,609 monthly on credit cards. They are a convenient way of financing purchases, and offer the cardholder a short period of interest free credit, provided that the amount is paid off at the end of each month.

---

[38] Bank of England, *Credit Conditions Survey Q2 2019*. Available online at: https://www.bankofengland .co.uk/credit-conditions-survey/2019/2019-q2, accessed 15/10/2019.

Problems arise if a cardholder is unable to pay off the balance each month. Interest rates are high, depending on the credit rating of the cardholder. For example, the average APR on credit cards is just under 20 per cent and on store cards it can be up to 30 per cent. Some providers also charge late payment and other fees. Interest is added to the balance, and then next month interest is charged on that total (compound interest). Month by month the balance adds up and can lead to serious debt problems. Each day, credit card lenders write off a staggering £4.5 million worth of credit card debt.

2. **Personal loans**. These are a cheaper way of funding smaller purchases than using credit cards. They are generally used to finance the purchases of items between £500 and £25,000, such as home improvements, car purchases, furniture, or domestic appliances. The repayment period is usually set at anything between one and ten years, with the borrower paying an agreed monthly sum to clear the loan.

3. **Hire purchase and conditional sale agreements**. Often stores or dealers offer to arrange finance for their customers to purchase items such as domestic and electrical appliances or cars. The stores or dealers are not providing the finance themselves. They enter into an agreement with a credit provider who buys the goods from them, and then hires the goods to the customer in return for monthly payments over an agreed term, so the customer does not own the goods until she has finished paying for them. If the customer defaults on any of the payments, the credit provider still owns the goods and can take them back.

4. **Overdrafts**. As almost every student will be aware, you go into overdraft when you spend more from your bank account than you have in it. Many people will arrange an authorised overdraft facility with their bank. This enables them to overdraw their account up to a certain limit, in return for an agreed rate of interest or fee, although some authorised overdrafts are interest free. Unarranged overdrafts are considerably more expensive. 19 million people a year use an arranged overdraft and 14 million resort to unarranged overdrafts.[39]

ⓘ Essential explanation

An *overdraft facility* is an agreement with the bank which allows a customer to overdraw his account up to an agreed maximum limit (say £1,000). The customer only borrows (or 'draws down') the money when he needs it. Interest is only paid on the amount actually borrowed, not the full amount of the facility.

Unauthorised overdrafts incur higher penalties and are expensive. The characteristic of an overdraft is that the bank can 'call in', or require the loan to be paid, at any time.

5. **Pay day loans**. For individuals with poor credit ratings it can be extremely difficult either to arrange an overdraft or get credit card or loans from a bank. This can cause problems for people who run out of money for one reason or another in the middle of the month before they are paid. Pay day loan businesses lend money to 'bridge the gap'. Historically, they have charged large fees for loans and very high interest rates, often at a time when

[39] Peachey, K. 'Overdraft woes: "we were one bill away from disaster"', *BBC News*, (18 December 2018). Available online at: https://www.bbc.co.uk/news/business-46590724, accessed 15/10/2019.

poorer people are at their most vulnerable. Although rates have fallen considerably, many companies still quote a maximum APR of over 1,000 per cent.[40] However, from January 2015 the government introduced a cap on interest and fees on such loans to prevent borrowers owing very considerable amounts of money, with no prospect of repaying.

6. **Guaranteed loans**. Somewhere in between the secured and unsecured loans are guaranteed loans. These are unsecured loans where a third party guarantees that it will pay the lender in the event that the borrower defaults. A simple example of a guarantee is when you rent a flat. You are responsible for the rent, but the landlord may require a guarantee from your parents that, in the event that you do not pay, they will be liable for the amount you owe. Your parents are the 'guarantors'. Very often banks or other financial institutions will require guarantees from the directors of the company to which they are lending money (see 17.5.2). These are examples of personal guarantees.

Loans may be guaranteed by a government agency. Examples include your student loan, and types of business start-up loans, e.g. the Enterprise Guarantee Scheme or the 'Help To Buy' scheme. The government provides a guarantee to the mortgage lender in the event of default by the borrower.

17.5 Forms of business finance

Just as individuals need money to finance their ever-changing lifestyles, businesses need to finance their development. Without the requisite funding, a business will fail and have to be wound up. Now we are going to consider how businesses raise money at each stage of development.

There are two main sources of business finance: equity finance and debt finance.

> ### Essential explanation
>
> *Equity* finance is raised from individuals or businesses putting money into a business in return for a share in the business and a share of the profits.
>
> *Debt* finance is money which is lent to the business. Lenders are not entitled to a share in the business or profits, but will be paid interest on the loan. The loan will usually be secured to guarantee repayment.
>
> The money which is put into the business is its *capital*.

You may think that debt and equity finance is about large corporate deals, involving millions of pounds, so this is something you only need to know about if you are going into corporate practice. This is not the case. All businesses raise finance: if you decide to start up a business and your parents help you by investing £5,000 in the business, that is equity finance; if your parents lend you £5,000 for your business, that is debt finance. If a multi-national corporation raises £50 million from its shareholders, that is equity finance; if it borrows £50 million from its bank, that is debt finance. Whether large or small amounts are involved, the terminology is the same.

---

[40] E.g. Satsuma Loans APR in October 2016. Available online at: https://www.satsumaloans.co.uk/.

17.5.1 **Sources of equity finance**

17.5.1.1 Owner funding

Initially, most businesses will be funded by their owners, either using their savings or through borrowing. If you go back to Example 3, this is how Tom financed his business. This initial funding will be the original capital of the business.

Anyone who provides equity finance for a business (i.e. invests in the business) will want some stake or share (equity) in the business, which ensures a return on their investment. The larger the investment, the bigger the share that they will want. The type of stake will depend on the type of business. The different types of business structure are explained in Chapter 18.

1. **Sole traders**. A sole trader will provide all the capital (equity) for the business himself, and so, as the sole investor, will own the business and be entitled to the entire profit of the business.

2. **Partnerships**. If the business is to be run as a partnership, there will be two or more investors, who will each be given a partnership share. This will entitle them to receive a share of the profits. The share in the business and entitlement to the profit should be agreed between the partners and set out clearly in a partnership agreement. The agreement may also entitle investors to interest on their investment. If investors do not want to take part in the management of the business, they may be *sleeping partners*. They would still have a share in the business and be entitled to a share of the profits and interest if agreed, but would not need to participate in the everyday running of the business.

3. **Companies**. If the business is to be run as a company, the original investors will be given shares in the company. There are various types of shares which a company can issue to its investors, in return for voting rights and, generally, dividends, which represent a share of the profit. The most common type of shares in small limited companies is ordinary shares, which do not necessarily guarantee a dividend but do give the holder voting rights. However, if a company fails to pay dividends it is unlikely to attract further investment, and existing investors may pull out.

The original owners of the business may be able to provide enough finance when a small business starts up, but if the business has an ambitious plan or as the business grows, it will need larger sums of money. It will need to look to outside sources. There are a variety of options.

17.5.1.2 Share issues

When a company starts up, shares are issued to the original investors, who are usually the promoters of the company. As the company grows, and seeks to expand, they may wish to raise finance through further share issues. Public companies can issue shares to the public. Private companies can also issue shares, but these can only be offered privately. The disadvantage is that once a company issues more shares to outside investors, more people have a stake in the company and are entitled to dividends, and the company's original shareholders will take correspondingly less and have less control of the company.

Where a company is seeking to expand and raise capital for growth, joining a stock market or the Alternative Investment Market (AIM) is another way to raise finance. A stock market listing is not suitable for small or start-up companies, but for much larger businesses seeking to expand, it is not only a useful way of raising capital but can raise the public profile of the business and attract investment. You will look at stock markets in Chapter 18.

17.5.1.3 Business angels

Business angels are wealthy individuals who invest in high-growth businesses in return for a share in the ownership of those businesses (equity in the business). Examples are the 'Dragons' in the television programme *Dragons' Den*. Not only do they provide funding for the business, but as they are successful entrepreneurs themselves, they have the business experience, management skills, and contacts to help businesses either to start up or expand. The 'Dragons' work with the owners of the business.

17.5.1.4 Private equity

Private equity firms manage private pools of funds for investors. They raise funds from private sources, usually pension funds and wealthy individuals, as well as borrowing. They buy controlling interests in undervalued or underperforming companies which they have identified as having the potential to improve. They then use their controlling interest to turn the company around and sell it on at a profit at a future date, usually within five to ten years. You saw in Chapter 15 that Patisserie Valerie was saved by a buyout by the Irish private equity firm, Causeway Capital. (see 15.3.1.1).

17.5.1.5 Venture capital funds

Venture capitalist firms again provide investment in return for equity in the business. They manage funds on behalf of individual investors who want to invest in businesses with high growth potential. They sit somewhere between business angels and private equity firms. Whereas private equity firms invest in larger businesses, venture capitalists provide funds for start ups and smaller private businesses. They invest larger sums of money than business angels and are often prepared to take on higher risk ventures than either private equity firms or business angels.

17.5.1.6 Technology

Technology is beginning to change the way that businesses raise finance.

⚠ Essential explanation

FinTech (or Financial Technology) describes the technologies used in the financial services sector to deliver financial services or products. They include technology which facilitates, e.g. opening a bank account online or mobile payments and bank transfers, but increasingly technologies are being developed to facilitate businesses to obtain loans or raise funds.

Understanding clients: individuals and businesses

Chapter 17

17.5.1.7 Crowdfunding

Crowdfunding is an example of FinTech. Crowdfunding sites, such as Kickstarter in the US or Crowdcube in the UK, invite investment from the public over the internet. Individuals invest small amounts of money—usually between £100 and £10,000—into a business. The individual investments are then pooled together to help a business reach its funding target. This is a suitable investment option for small, often high-risk innovative businesses, which may have difficulty raising finance from more conventional sources. An early example was Kickstarter, which raised over $3.3 million (£2 million) from 87,142 backers in just over eight hours for a San Francisco company, Double Fine Productions, to develop the computer game 'Double Fine Adventure' ('Broken Age'). Investors do not necessarily get a share in the business. They provide funds solely to enable the business to start up or finance a particular project. The return for a small investment in Double Fine was a copy of the finished version of the computer game.[41]

17.5.1.8 eCommerce Lenders

A recent example is the rise of eCommerce lenders. Many businesses use third-party companies like Amazon or Etsy to market and distribute their products or to manage their payments, e.g. PayPal. They are also starting to fund the businesses which use them. PayPal Working Capital has lent £400 million to UK small businesses and Amazon Lending has lent over $3 billion to companies worldwide. These companies collect significant amounts of data and are in a position to assess the credit-worthiness of the business.[42]

17.5.1.9 Other forms of investment

Although these are the main options for equity finance, there are other possibilities, for example family and friends may be prepared to invest in the business, and initially are an important source of finance for small businesses. Government-backed schemes such as the enterprise investment scheme (EIS) offer tax advantages to small limited companies.

17.5.2 Sources of debt finance

17.5.2.1 Bank finance

Businesses can borrow money in the short term (i.e. it has to be paid back within one year) or long term (an agreed term of over a year). Most loans will come from a bank.

1. **Long-term loans**. Banks or other lenders will usually require some form of security for the loan in the form of a charge over assets of the business. The type of charge will depend on whether the business is a sole trader, partnership, or company. If the business owns its premises, it will be easier to get a loan as this is the best form of security for a

---

[41] Kickstarter (2019). Available online at: https://www.kickstarter.com/projects/doublefine/double-fine-adventure, accessed 15/10/2019.

[42] Deloitte Perspectives, *Three types of SME lenders to watch*. Available online at: https://www2.deloitte.com/uk/en/pages/financial-services/articles/three-types-of-sme-lenders.html, accessed 15/10/2019.

lender, which will take a mortgage over the premises. Companies give different types of charge, known as fixed and floating charges, but the effect is the same. If the company does not keep up its payments, the lender can recover the amount owed from the sale of the charged asset. Limited liability means that shareholders of a company are not personally liable for the debts of the company (see 18.1.1). Unlimited liability means that if the company defaults, the bank will require the directors themselves to repay the loan from their personal assets. The bank may also require personal guarantees from the directors. If a sole trader or partnership does not own its own premises, the bank may require the owners to grant a charge over their own properties.

2. **Overdrafts**. These are the most common form of short-term loan for a business. Businesses will arrange an overdraft facility and borrow money when they need it. Overdrafts are particularly useful when a business is up and running to prevent short-term cash flow problems. Overdrafts can, however, be expensive, as interest is charged on a daily basis.

17.5.2.2 Corporate finance

Public companies can issue bonds and other debt instruments in order to raise capital. Whereas the value of shares is based on the *equity* value of a company, bonds are based on *debt*. These are effectively loans which are not backed by any form of security. The company issuing the bond agrees to repay the amount of the bond at an agreed date (on 'maturity') and to pay interest to the holder of the bond until maturity. For the investors, bonds have the advantage that, like any other investment, they can be sold and the investor gets her money back. The interest will be paid to the current holder of the bond, who will claim the capital sum on maturity (see 19.2.4.3).

17.5.2.3 Other sources of debt finance

Although most debt finance comes from banks, there are other options available, especially if the business has a poor credit rating or has existing high levels of borrowing which make it difficult to raise money. The most obvious example of non-bank finance is borrowing from family or friends, who may charge a lower interest rate or be able to make loans over a longer period than a bank. Other sources are commercial loan providers, which provide financial services like loans and credit facilities, though they cannot take deposits like banks. In addition, the government offers a variety of grants and loan schemes for small businesses, for example Small Business Administration Loans.

17.5.3 **Credit rating for businesses**

Businesses have credit ratings in the same way as individuals do (see 17.4.5.2). Large corporations (and even countries) are credit rated so that investors can decide whether or not to invest in their shares or bonds. Businesses will run credit checks on business customers before offering credit, if they are uncertain whether they are creditworthy.

Business lenders rely on a similar credit scoring system to decide on the risk of lending to a particular business. There are credit reference agencies which report to banks and other lenders on businesses. The main one is Dun & Bradstreet, which issues a *Paydex* score. Unlike individual credit scores, Paydex only takes into account whether a business makes payments on time and meets creditors' payment terms. Businesses are scored from 0–100. If a business scores 80 or above, it means it pays on time. The later the business pays its bills, the lower the score.[43]

> ### Practice tip
>
> Dun & Bradstreet or Thomson Reuters' World Check are examples of information service companies. Such companies provide comprehensive information about businesses (as well as credit ratings) using data and analytics. You should be aware that these agencies are a useful tool in practice to enable you to familiarise yourself with businesses with which you are involved.

17.5.3.1 Government and corporate credit ratings

When buying government bonds, or bonds and shares in public companies, investors will want to know that the investment is safe. The three main credit reference agencies for investment purposes are Moody's, Standard and Poors (S&P), and Fitch IBCA. Their ratings help investors determine the risk associated with investing in a specific company, or indeed, country. Triple A (AAA) is the highest credit rating, and C or D (depending on the agency issuing the rating) is the lowest, which is sometimes referred to as *junk quality*. To give some examples, Germany, probably the strongest of the European economies, has a AAA rating, and Greece and Italy which have struggled with debt within the Eurozone, have ratings between BB and BBB. The UK was downgraded to AA negative at the beginning of 2019 following fears that it would leave the EU without a deal, which made it more expensive for the UK to borrow money on the markets.

17.5.4 Equity finance vs debt finance

Whether debt or equity finance is better depends on the situation of the business. Factors to think about include:

- the type of business;
- the amount of financial capital the owner of the business has to invest;
- whether there are other potential investors, and the amount of capital which they have available to invest;
- tax considerations;
- the relative costs of borrowing or raising equity finance.

A final consideration will always be the environment in which the business and its owners are operating. In this chapter, we have concentrated mainly on social, personal, and financial issues. In the next two chapters we will consider the business and economic environments which influence the decisions of individuals and businesses alike.

---

[43] Dun & Bradstreet (2016) *Paydex*. Available online at: http://www.businesscreditreports.com/documents/guide-to-d-b-ratings-scores.pdf, accessed 6/12/2016.

Summary

- There are a variety of reasons why individuals and businesses will have recourse to the law. Often the need for legal services is triggered by some form of important life event, such as moving house, divorce, or setting up a business.

- All life events, some seemingly mundane, will have a legal and financial impact on individuals and businesses. Lawyers need to anticipate their clients' needs in the light of this.

- 'Wealth' is the term used to describe what an individual owns, taking into account all his financial circumstances, including income, expenses, assets, and liabilities. Lawyers acting for individual clients must be aware of their financial background in order to advise their clients effectively.

- Adequate funding is crucial for businesses not only when they start out, but also for the everyday running of the business and as they expand and grow. Businesses raise funds in a variety of ways. Lawyers acting for businesses should understand the difference between equity and debt finance and the advantages and disadvantages of each.

Practical exercises

1. Think of a life event that has affected you. How did it impact on your finances? What were the legal implications?

2. Calculate your wealth. What could you do now to increase it?

3. Find out how to check your credit rating. What do you think you could do to improve it?

4. What are the main advantages and disadvantages of debt and equity finance?

 *Visit the **online resources** for the authors' reflections and to check your progress.*

Further reading

Follow up some of the websites referred to in this chapter. They will give a useful insight into some of the issues discussed. Much of the information in this chapter is background knowledge that you can acquire by reading quality newspapers on a daily basis. Make sure that you do so.

Aviva Family Finances Report: http://www.aviva.com/search/?q=family+finances+report&section=
—If you are interested in socio-economic factors, this is published bi-annually (summer and winter) and provides useful further information.

Department of Business, Energy and Industrial Strategy: https://www.gov.uk/government/organisations/department-for-business-energy-and-industrial-strategy
—Information on funding for businesses, including a straightforward guide, *Business Finance Explained*, at https://www.gov.uk/business-finance-explained, accessed 30/07/2016.

Office of National Statistics (ONS): http://www.ons.gov.uk
—The national statistical institute of the UK. It collects, compiles, and analyses statistics on all aspects of social, economic, and demographical issues. It provides invaluable information on a variety of topics and is often a useful starting point for research into social and economic factors.

 *For the authors' reflections on the practical exercises, additional self-test questions, sample interview questions and a library of links to useful websites, visit the free **online resources** at www.oup.com/he/slorach4e.*

Chapter 17

Understanding clients:
individuals and businesses

18 Businesses and the business environment

 Learning objectives

After studying this chapter you should be able to:

- Explain the main types of legal business structure, their organisation, and management.
- Explain different markets, sectors, and industries in which businesses operate, and the role of consumers within these markets.
- Understand a simple supply chain.
- Recognise the impact of competition within different markets.

Introduction

Chapter 15 introduced you to the importance of commercial awareness. In Chapter 17 you explored how you can add value to the advice which you give your clients by understanding their 'latent' concerns; in other words, the underlying concerns—social, economic, and financial as well as legal—which they may have as a result of simply living their lives. You saw that when you attend an interview for your first job, you will need to set yourself apart by demonstrating that you can anticipate the needs of your clients. Those clients may be:

- the people who own those businesses;
- the people who work in them;
- the customers or clients of those businesses;
- the people who supply those businesses;
- the people who provide services to those businesses; or
- the people who are responsible for the regulation of those businesses.

The list is endless, but this demonstrates that most people at some point will have some contact with business, even if it does not involve any legal issues. So the next thing that you need to understand is how those businesses work. This is essential not only for lawyers, but for any graduate looking for a job. At any interview, whatever else you are asked and whatever job, legal or otherwise, you are interviewing for, you will be asked, in one form or another, why you want to work for that particular organisation.

You won't be able to answer this unless you understand the organisation itself; what types of individuals or organisations make up its clients or customers; and what is going on within those organisations. In this chapter we look at:

- businesses generally;
- who owns them;
- who runs them;
- what are their motivations and drivers; and
- the significance of the environment in which they operate.

This chapter will also help you to answer some of the questions posed in the Patisserie Valerie example in relation to companies, their organisation and structure (see Example 3 at 15.3.1.1) and to demonstrate that you understand the business environment, and how businesses operate. Our starting point is business structures.

18.1 Types of business structure

There are five main types of legal business structures, which are illustrated in Figure 18.1:

1. Sole traders.
2. Partnerships.
3. Limited liability partnerships.
4. Private companies.
5. Public companies.

Figure 18.1 Types of business structure

In every high street in every town in the country, there is a huge variety of different types of business of various sizes, operating in several sectors: retail, professional services, banking, and hospitality—cafes, restaurants, and bars. We will use the high street as a model for considering the advantages and disadvantages of these different business structures.

It is crucial to understand that not all businesses are companies. The term business covers a wide range of business structures, each of which has its own legal status, which affects its conduct and performance. We will start by looking at some general principles.

> ### ⓘ Essential explanation
>
> Businesses can be either *incorporated* or *unincorporated*.
>
> 1. An *incorporated* business must undergo a formal registration process before it is set up and before it can 'legally' exist. The most common examples are private limited companies, public companies, and limited liability partnerships.
> 2. An *unincorporated* business is not required to follow any formal process in order to be set up. All the owners need to do is open the doors and start trading. Unincorporated businesses include sole traders and partnerships.

18.1.1 **Legal personality**

> ### ⓘ Essential explanation
>
> Legal personality consists of a 'bundle' of legal rights and duties imposed by the law which govern every aspect of the lives of individuals or incorporated businesses. These rights and duties dictate their legal status.

Whether a business has its own legal personality depends on whether it is incorporated or unincorporated.

1. Unincorporated businesses have no legal status of their own. If the business fails, it is not just the business assets, such as the premises, stock, and shop fittings, but the owner's personal possessions, such as her house, car, and savings which may be taken and sold to pay outstanding debts. If she cannot pay, she may be made bankrupt. This is known as *unlimited liability*. In addition, partners have 'joint and several' liability. Effectively, the actions of one partner can mean that the others could lose their house, car, or other assets, and in a worst-case scenario be made bankrupt. There is an old adage that you should 'choose your [business] partner more carefully than your spouse'.

2. Incorporated businesses do have their own legal personality, which gives them an independent legal existence, entirely separate from their owners. If the business fails, the owners lose the money which they have invested in the company, but no more. They cannot lose their personal assets in the same way that sole traders or partners may. This is known as *limited liability*.

In a famous case,[1] Lord Denning compared a company with a human body. Like a person, he described a company as having a brain and a nerve centre—the board of directors—which controls the entire body. The employees are their hands, and they carry out the instructions of the 'brain'.

18.1.2 Sole traders

The smallest, and most common, type of business entity is the sole trader. As the name suggests, this type of business is owned by just one person. Sole traders are the largest group of businesses in the UK. The Department of Business, Energy and Industrial Strategy (BEIS) estimated that, of the 5.7 million private sector businesses there were approximately 3.4 million sole traders (or 59 per cent of the total) operating throughout the UK in 2018.

A sole trader may have a few employees but, according to the BEIS statistics, 4.3 million (or 76 per cent of all businesses) have no employees at all[2] (these are called *class zero businesses*). Most sole traders operate in the service sector: plumbers, builders, small retailers, and professionals. For example, on a typical high street, it is likely that the gift shop, butcher, and perhaps the accountant are run by sole traders. Table 18.1 shows the advantages and disadvantages for sole traders.

18.1.3 Partnerships

For a partnership to exist, two or more people must own the business. For example, a boutique on the high street which is run by two friends will automatically be a partnership (unless they have set up a company). Partnerships are found in the same sectors as sole traders. They are particularly common in the professions. As well as the boutique, firms of solicitors, estate agents, or accountants could be partnerships, and it is equally possible that a gift shop or a

Table 18.1 Advantages and disadvantages for sole traders

Advantages	Disadvantages
Set up: A sole trader can set up with minimum administrative steps (the only thing that he will need to do is to inform the tax authorities (HMRC) for tax purposes).	**Start up costs:** The owner will be solely responsible for the start-up costs.
Regulation: Sole traders are free to run the business as they wish. Day-to-day record keeping is unregulated and comparatively simple.	**Debts:** The owner is personally liable for all the debts of the business.
Testing the market: This is a good way to test the market for the new business.	**Expansion:** The owner must find the funds to expand the business himself.
	Management: The owner is responsible for all management decisions, and will have little support.

[1] *HL Bolton Engineering Co. Ltd* v *TJ Graham & Sons Ltd* [1957] 1 QB 159.
[2] BEIS (2018) *Business Population Estimates for the UK and Regions 2018*. Available online at: https://www.gov.uk/government/statistics/business-population-estimates-2018, accessed 31/07/2018. All statistics on business structures from this source, unless otherwise stated.

Table 18.2 Advantages and disadvantages of partnerships

Advantages	Disadvantages
Set up: Partnerships can be set up with minimum and are formalities and administrative steps (apart from advising HMRC for tax purposes). A partnership agreement is advisable, but not required.	**Profits:** All profits belong to the partners, shared between them.
Regulation: Partners are free to run the business as they wish. Day-to-day record keeping is unregulated and comparatively simple.	**Debts:** The partners will be personally liable for all the debts of the business.
Management: Partners share management decisions, and each partner can specialise in, and concentrate on a particular area of the business, although with too many partners, decision making can be cumbersome.	**Joint and several liability:** If one partner cannot pay his share of the debts, the other partner or partners can be personally liable for that partner's share (as well as their own) from their own personal assets.
Start-up costs: The partners will share the start-up costs.	**Borrowing:** The partners must personally service all loans.
Expansion: With more owners, more finance can be raised so expansion is easier. If more money is needed, more partners can be brought in.	**Uncertainty:** If no partnership agreement has been entered into, this can lead to uncertainty.

butcher's shop could be. The BEIS figures show that there are nearly 405,000 (or 7 per cent of total UK businesses) ordinary partnerships (as opposed to LLPs) in the UK. 72 per cent consist of the partners only with no employees. Compare the advantages and disadvantages of sole traders with those of partnerships, as shown in Table 18.2.

18.1.4 Companies

Again, there is a wide range of company types, both in size and in the services they provide. There are over 1.9 million actively trading companies registered in the UK (or 34 per cent of total UK businesses). The oil companies BP, Royal Dutch Shell, and Exxon Mobil are all examples of large multi-national companies. Most companies, however, are much smaller, employing fewer than four people. 883,000 of all limited companies have no employees, and are managed and run by a sole director. Now compare sole traders and partnerships with the advantages and disadvantages of setting up a company (Table 18.3).

18.1.5 Limited liability partnerships

A limited liability partnership (LLP) is basically a hybrid between a partnership and a limited company. Like a company, it must be incorporated, and as a result, it has its own legal personality separate from its owners. The owners are not personally liable for its debts, but it is run like a partnership. As with a partnership, there must be two or more people. There are approximately 45,000 LLPs in the UK. Many larger LLPs are professional firms (e.g. solicitors or accountants), e.g. Linklaters LLP with over 2,300 employees in 20 countries.[3] These numbers, however, pale into insignificance compared to the global accountancy firms, e.g. PwC LLP

[3] https://www.linklaters.com/en/about-us/our-firm-at-a-glance, accessed 31/10/2019.

Table 18.3 Advantages and disadvantages of setting up a company

Advantages	Disadvantages
Debts: Owners have limited liability so are not personally liable for the debts of the company.	**Setting up:** Companies must register with Registrar of Companies and obtain a certificate of incorporation.
Start-up costs: Finance will be raised by issuing shares or borrowing.	**Profits:** Profits are shared between the shareholders.
Management: Board of directors responsible for day-to-day management.	**Management:** Directors have extra legal duties and may be liable if these are breached.
Expansion: Further finance raised by issuing more shares or borrowing, which will be more readily accessible.	**Regulation:** There are ongoing regulatory requirements which must be complied with, e.g. companies have to file their annual accounts at Companies House, so financial information is made public.
Loans: Shareholders are not personally liable for servicing loans.	

with over 250,000 employees in 157 countries, and which describes itself as a 'powerhouse of a commercial enterprise',[4] or KPMG with over 207,000 employees in 155 countries,[5] which is impressive considering that there are 196 countries in the world today.

Size is not a necessary criterion to become an LLP. It is possible that your nearest high-street solicitors are an LLP.

18.1.6 Private and public companies

> **⚠ Essential explanation**
>
> A *public* company can offer its shares to the public. 'Public' does not mean that it is a nationalised company owned, or partially owned, by the government; these companies are known as *publicly owned* companies. Examples of the latter include Royal Bank of Scotland (which came into public ownership when the government rescued it in 2008/9 to prevent its collapse by taking a 58 per cent shareholding) or Channel 4 (which, although commercially funded, is publicly owned).[6] Conversely, *private* simply means that the company is not public and so it cannot make a public offer of its shares, which must be sold privately.

18.1.6.1 Private limited companies (Ltd)

Most companies in the UK are private limited companies, many being small family concerns, such as hardware stores and hotels.

---

[4] PwC (2018) *Global Annual Review 2018*. Available online at: https://www.pwc.com/gx/en/about/global-annual-review-2018/people.html, accessed 28/07/2019.

[5] KPMG (2018) *Global Annual Review 2018*. Available online at: https://home.kpmg/xx/en/home/campaigns/2018/12/global-review.html, accessed 28/07/2019.

[6] See https://www.gov.uk/government/uploads/system/uploads/attachment_data/file/208096/foi-130687-companies-uk-tax-payer-shareholder.pdf. Although dated 2013, this Freedom of Information Act request gives an insight into the diversity of companies in public ownership (although some, like Royal Mail, have subsequently been privatised).

It is possible for a private company to be owned by a single shareholder and managed by a single director, usually the same person. Equally they can be large national companies. Richard Branson's Virgin Group Ltd is a private company. You can easily spot whether a company is a private company by looking at the name: a private company will have the abbreviation 'Ltd' for 'limited' after its name.

18.1.6.2 Public limited companies (plc)

A company has to comply with various statutory requirements to qualify as a public company. The most important is that it must have a specific amount of share capital, currently £50,000 or more. Again you can tell whether a company is a public company by looking at the name. You will see the abbreviation 'plc', for example, Marks & Spencer plc or Next plc.

A public company may be quoted, or listed, on a *stock exchange* in the UK. Private companies cannot be. There is no obligation on a public company to join a stock market. A company does not start out as a listed company. Companies tend to start small, expand, and once they reach a certain size, reputation, or level of growth, then they apply. To join the Main Market (see 19.2.4.1), a company must successfully complete a time-consuming and complicated procedure, known as a 'flotation' or 'IPO' (Initial Public Offering), but the rewards can be huge. (We will look at how the stock market works at 19.2.4.1.)

Not surprisingly, some of the largest IPOs involve the US stock exchanges, for example the flotation of Facebook in 2012 which valued the company at $16 billion, although the biggest IPO ever is the flotation of the Chinese internet giant, Alibaba, valued at $21.8 billion. By contrast, in the UK, one of the largest was Worldpay, the company which provides payment processing services when you use a credit or debit card, which was valued at £4.6 billion.

18.1.7 Who owns a company?

When a company is set up, the owners buy shares in the company, and become, not surprisingly, the *shareholders* or '*members*' of the company. When someone buys shares, there are two results:

1. She owns a fraction of the assets of the company as each share represents a share of the ownership of the company. Shares also represent a fractional entitlement to the capital value of the company. The more shares owned, the greater the entitlement of that shareholder if, for example, the company was to be sold and its assets distributed to its shareholders.

2. She is entitled to receive a share of the profits. The amount of profit which she will receive depends, again, on how many shares she owns. The payment of profit which each shareholder receives is called a *dividend*.

Note that shareholders are not necessarily *directors*. There is no obligation on a shareholder to be a director. There is a distinct division between the roles and responsibilities of the two groups, which we will look at in 18.2.1, when we consider how companies are managed.

18.1.8 Other classifications

18.1.8.1 Multi-national companies

A multi-national company is a company which trades worldwide and is quoted on more than one stock exchange. Coca-Cola and McDonald's are probably two of the best-known examples. On the high street, HSBC is a multi-national bank with operations in 66 countries, 235,000 employees,[7] and it is listed on the Hong Kong and Bermuda stock exchanges.[8] Starbucks has 24,000 stores in 75 countries,[9] but does not meet the true definition of a multi-national as it only listed on one stock exchange in New York, the NASDAQ.

18.1.8.2 Micro, small, and medium sized enterprises

At the other end of the scale are *micro enterprises* and *small and medium sized enterprises* (*SMEs*). The Department of Business, Energy and Industrial Strategy defines these as businesses which have between 0 and 249 employees. 99.9 per cent of all businesses are within the definition, and with a total turnover of £2 trillion, they account for 52 per cent of all private sector turnover. They include sole traders, partnerships, and companies. Historically, they have been responsible for stimulating the economy and driving competition but they are also an indicator of the health of the economy. The Department of Business, Energy and Industrial Strategy's statistics show that, in 2018–19, with the economic uncertainty as a result of Brexit, the number of small businesses declined by approximately 1 per cent.

18.1.8.3 Groups of companies

Increasingly, companies are formed into groups. There is a *parent* (or *holding*) company and *subsidiary* companies, which together form one single economic entity. The subsidiaries are controlled by the parent. The parent company has a majority shareholding (51 per cent or more) in the subsidiary and a right to appoint its directors. Figure 18.2 shows a typical group relationship.

Examples on the high street include Burton (a subsidiary), which is part of Sir Philip Green's Arcadia Group (parent company), which also includes Top Shop and Miss Selfridge (subsidiaries). In 2018 Costa Coffee was bought by Coco-Cola for £3.9 billion from its parent company the Whitbread hotel and restaurant group (parent). In other words, many successful, better-known companies are part of a larger group.

18.1.8.4 Franchises

A franchise is where a business (the '*franchisor*') allows third parties ('*franchisees*') to use its name, concept, business format, and experience in return for payment. In particular, the

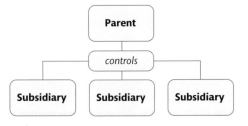

Figure 18.2 A group of companies

[7] https://www.about.hsbc.co.uk/hsbc-in-numbers.
[8] https://www.hsbc.com/investors/shareholder-information, accessed 28/07/2019.
[9] http://www.starbucks.com/business/international-stores, accessed 17/08/2019.

franchisee can use the franchisor's intellectual property rights. Unlike a corporate group, where the parent controls the subsidary, the franchisor does not own the franchisee, but has a contractual agreement which obliges the latter to operate in a particular way.

Franchising is becoming increasingly popular, and you will find franchises in various sectors. Well-known examples include McDonald's, KFC, and the Body Shop. If you go to McDonald's in any city in any part of the world, the restaurant set-up is the same, the food is the same, the price is the same, and everything is sold under the McDonald's brand.

A franchise offers a franchisee a relatively cheap and comparatively risk-free way of opening a business, without starting from scratch. The franchisee is able to use a business concept which has been proved to work and is an established brand. For the franchisor, franchising can also be a way of expanding into new or unfamiliar markets. For example, Next plc has 199 franchises in 32 countries.[10]

18.1.9 Which is best?

The role of the solicitor will be to advise a client who is setting up in business on the advantages and disadvantages of each type of business structure, but it will be up to the client to decide which is best for him, bearing in mind the advantages and disadvantages of each.

Commercial awareness, as we have seen, is not all about law and facts. Before a client makes a decision, it is important that he considers all the practical consequences of starting up a business. Examples of further factors which he should think about are:

1. **The economic climate.** Is this the best time to start up a business? Brexit, for example, has had a profound effect on the economy.

2. **Personal factors.** Setting up a business is stressful and uncertain, not just for the client but for his family. Is he (and are they) ready for this?

3. **Change of lifestyle.** It takes commitment and motivation to get a business up and running. Is he ready to work long hours and weekends?

4. **The financial implications.** How will he manage financially before the business starts to earn money?

5. **The need for a new skill set.** How good is the client at financial planning, managing employees, logistics, marketing, and sales?

6. **Business plan.** Has the client got a business plan? Has he got the support of his bank/ small business adviser?

18.2 Business organisation and management

Your client may be a business, but a business is run and managed by people—they may be very high-powered business executives, like Richard Branson of Virgin, or they may have limited business experience, like a newly qualified plumber starting a small business in a local town.

---

[10] Next plc (2019) *Annual Report, p.38.* Available online at: https://www.nextplc.co.uk/investors, accessed 28/07/2019.

It is often said that vets have highly stressful jobs because not only do they need to be able to treat the animals effectively, but they also need to deal with the concerns of their owners. As a lawyer, acting for a business is similar. Lawyers need to know the law and advise on what is best for the business. However, lawyers are dealing not with the business itself (which, after all, is inanimate), but with a variety of individuals involved in business, such as the directors or managers of a company, or the partners of a firm. These are the people you will be dealing with on a day-to-day basis, and being a successful lawyer involves building good relationships with them. One of the things you need to know is what the people you are dealing with do within their organisation. They will not be impressed if you do not. Again, as we have seen from the Patisserie Valerie example at 15.3.1.1, this background will help you at interviews and assessment days.

In this section, we will look at the management structure of businesses, and how they organise and plan their operations, concentrating particularly on larger public companies. Although management techniques and concepts are outside the scope of this chapter, we will cover some of the more important ones, so that you have an idea of the underlying rationale of company organisation, and understand some of the (sometimes seemingly incomprehensible) jargon used by those involved in management of companies.

18.2.1 Companies

We have already seen that there is a distinct division between the role of directors and the role of the shareholders. Shareholders do not need to be directors of the company and directors do not necessarily have to be shareholders, although often they will be required to do so by the company's constitution.

18.2.1.1 Directors

The directors take the day-to-day decisions on the running of the company at *board meetings*.

Directors have certain legal duties which ensure that they act in the best interests of the company and the shareholders, and do not take advantage of their position for their own benefit. In addition, there are certain things that they cannot do without the consent of a majority of the shareholders, for example, they cannot take a loan from the company. If directors or officers of the company are found to be in breach of their duties, they can be held liable.

There are a number of different types of director who may be involved in the running of the company, and we will consider some of the roles of directors in 18.2.2. You should also be clear on the roles of executive and non-executive directors.

> ### ⓘ Essential explanation
>
> *Executive* directors play an active role in the day-to-day running of the company, and *non-executive directors* (*NEDs*) have a supervisory and balancing role over the activities of the executive directors and the board in general. Private companies may have no NEDs, and in practice they are more relevant for public companies. Companies which are listed on the Main Market of the London Stock Exchange must have a certain number of NEDs. In the aftermath of the 2008 financial crisis, there has been considerable regulation of the role of NEDs within such companies, as poor supervision of the decisions of boards of some companies was perceived as contributing to the crisis.
>
> There is no legal distinction between an executive and non-executive director in terms of their responsibility towards the shareholders of the company. If things go wrong, all directors share potential liability.

Businesses and the business environment

Chapter 18

18.2.1.2 Shareholders

The shareholders, although they are the owners of the company, do not take part in the day-to-day running of the company. In theory at least, they take the more important decisions affecting the company, because they are entitled to attend and vote at *general meetings*. In fact a majority of shareholders, particularly shareholders of public companies, never attend such meetings and take no part in the running of the company.

Public companies, but not private companies, have to hold an annual general meeting to allow the shareholders to elect new directors and question the directors on the annual report. The annual report is a report to the shareholders on how the company has performed during the year, and their plans for the following year. Again, most shareholders do not attend or vote. However, some do, and there are increasing signs of shareholder 'activism'.[11] Directors' remuneration is an increasingly topical issue with more and more shareholders prepared to challenge what they see as excessive pay increases for top executives.

Increasingly shareholders are prepared to challenge poor corporate governance.[12] You saw that Mark Zuckerberg and his fellow directors faced angry shareholders demanding reforms to Facebook's corporate structure in the wake of the Cambridge Analytica scandal (see 15.3.1.1) and a group of institutional investors have brought a legal action against Tesco in the High Court in relation to the losses suffered as a result of Tesco publishing misleading information about its profits.[13]

18.2.2 Differences between private and public companies

Public companies by their very nature have far more complex management structures than private companies.

18.2.2.1 Private companies

Private companies have a board of directors which carries out the day-to-day management of the company. A private company may have just one director (a public company must have at least two). The shareholders of a private company are more likely to be the directors, but this will not necessarily be the case. For example, when a client sets up a company, he may issue shares to both himself and his wife. He will act as a director, but she may play no role in the running of the company.

18.2.2.2 Public companies

Figure 18.3 shows the hierarchy of the management structure for a plc. Like a private company, there will be a board of directors who will be responsible for decisions affecting the day-to-day running of the company.

---

[11] See, for example, PwC Insight, *Shareholder activism: Coming soon to a company near you*, https://www.pwc.co.uk/industries/retail-consumer/insights/the-consumer-global-m-and-a-trends-in-the-consumer-sector/shareholder-activism-coming-soon-to-a-company-near-you.html, accessed 17/02/2020.

[12] BBC News (2018) *Shareholder revolts 'up by a quarter' at FTSE firms*, 29 August 2018. Available online at: http://www.bbc.co.uk/news/business- -45335841, accessed 17/08/2019.

[13] At the time of writing, this action is on-going, see https://www.stewartslaw.com/news/tesco-shareholder-action-case-update/, accessed 1/11/2019.

Part III

Employability and Commercial Awareness

569

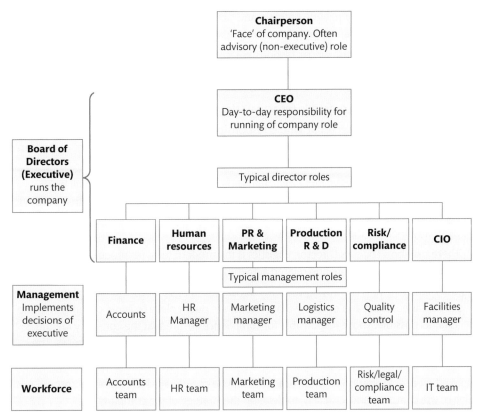

Figure 18.3 Management structure of a public company

Head of the board is the Chief Executive Officer (CEO). (CEO is a US term which is gaining popularity in the UK, and replaces the previously more commonly used term Managing Director (MD).) There may also be a Chairman above the CEO. The Chairman is often a figurehead, and acts in a non-executive or advisory capacity (see 18.2.1.1).

The board is responsible for the management of the company. The directors exercise these management powers by passing resolutions (decisions) at board meetings. Below the board will be the operational managers of the company who are responsible for carrying out the board's decisions, and ensuring that its goals and objectives are achieved, through organisation and planning. In other words, they manage and organise the next level, the workforce, which implement the decisions of the board. This is illustrated in Figure 18.3.

Typical roles within most major companies will include:

- *Finance* Director, who is responsible for all the financial decisions for the company. This is the most important role after the CEO. The *finance* or *accounts* department which she oversees is responsible for everything to do with money, for example the funding of the business, investment, paying suppliers, and ensuring that customers pay.

- Director of *Human Resources* or *People*, who takes decisions in relation to staffing, employment issues, and all other decisions affecting the workforce. His department's responsibilities include payroll, holidays and sick leave, performance, and disciplinary procedures. He will draft and implement company policies.

- *PR* or *Marketing* Director, who is responsible for promoting the company, dealing with customers, promotions, branding, and public relations. The PR department is responsible for dealing with the press and building the company's public profile.
- The *Sales* Director is responsible for actual sales to customers and account management.
- *Chief Information Officer* (CIO), who is responsible for all the information technology. The ICT department deals with communication issues and the functioning of computers, networks, and telephones.
- *Research and Development* and *Production* Director, as the name suggests, will be responsible for the development and quality of products. He has to ensure that products are produced as efficiently as possible and have a technological advantage, putting the company ahead in the market place.
- There may be a *Logistics* Director. Logistics is the modern term for procurement (purchasing), distribution, and related activities.
- *Risk management* is identifying the sorts of risks (or things that can go wrong) in a particular business, and ensuring that systems are put in place to avoid or mitigate these as far as possible. Those responsible for *compliance* ensure that the company identifies regulatory risk and meets all regulatory requirements for that particular business. They are often lawyers. There may be a separate *Legal Director*.

In an efficient organisation all these functions will be coordinated to ensure the smooth running of the company and, crucially, to develop the strategy of the company.

18.2.3 Corporate governance

The separation of the roles of the directors, who are responsible for the day-to-day management, and the shareholders, who are more concerned with their investment, means that there is potential for problems and abuse. Directors may be tempted to run a company in their own interests. Corporate scandals involving fraud by directors in the 1990s and early 2000s, leading to the collapse of multi-national companies such as the Mirror Group or Enron, focused attention on what is now referred to as corporate governance. The corporate governance debate intensified following the global financial crisis of 2007–08 which triggered the deepest worldwide recession in over 70 years. With recent high profile insolvencies, such as Carillion and Patisserie Valerie, corporate governance is an increasingly topical issue.

> **Essential explanation**
>
> At its very simplest, corporate governance means how companies are run and managed. However, it is wider than this: it also includes how a company is performing, how that performance can be enhanced, and a company's accountability to interested parties such as shareholders, employees, and other stakeholders.
>
> *Stakeholders* are any persons or entities who can affect or be affected by a company. They can be internal (e.g. employees) or external (e.g. customers or suppliers or local communities) and society in general.

An example of the wide-reaching effect of poor corporate governance is the announcement of redundancies by the law firm, BLM, following the collapse of the tour operator, Thomas Cook, which was one of the firm's major clients.[14]

Over the years, the government has commissioned reports to produce recommendations for improvement, the most important of which are the Cadbury Report published in 1992[15] and the Walker Review, published in 2009. These have resulted in a various codes, which regulate the behaviour of premium listed companies.[16] One of the most important is the UK Corporate Governance Code, the latest version of which was implemented in January 2019. The purpose of the Code is to promote greater transparency, accountability, and integrity in business. The Code is 'soft law', in that it is not binding on the companies to which it applies, but companies are required to explain in their annual reports whether or not they have complied. Currently, it only applies to premium listed companies although there are proposals for extending corporate governance principles to large private companies.[17]

Closely aligned to this is the increasing focus on ethical behaviour and social responsibility on the part of companies, including respect for the environment. Companies interact with a wide variety of other interested groups: employees, stakeholders, such as customers or suppliers, and the public at large. To an extent, legislation is in place to ensure that companies act ethically, e.g. the Bribery Act, the Modern Slavery Act, and the Money Laundering Act. Increasingly, the public also expects companies themselves to implement policies which encourage ethically, socially, and environmentally responsible behaviour by the company itself and by everyone involved with the company, e.g. employees, suppliers, and customers. Investors when considering where to invest look at what is known as environmental, social, and governance factors (ESG), on the basis that these contribute to the sustainability of the company and thus long-term returns on the investment. The UK Corporate Governance Code now places emphasis on the importance of considering the impact of all these factors as part of the drive towards better corporate governance.

18.2.4 Sole traders and partnerships

We have seen that sole traders and partnerships are managed by their owners, who have the responsibility for the day-to-day running of the business.

In professional partnerships, often the senior partner will have overall management control, and act as the equivalent of the CEO of a company. Traditionally, this role has gone to the longest serving partner, and only became available when a senior partner retired. However,

---

[14] Lock, S. 'UK Firm Begins Reduncancy Round Following Thomas Cook Collapse', *Law.com*, 31 October 2019. Available online on subscription: https://www.law.com/legal-week/2019/10/31/uk-firm-begins-redundancy-round-following-thomas-cook-collapse/, accessed 02/11/2019.

[15] If you are interseted in learning more about this, there is an excellent summary of the report and accompanying explantion in the archives of the Cambridge Judge Business School, available online at http://cadbury.cjbs.archios.info/report, accessed 28/07/2019.

[16] Stock market listed companies subject to highest levels of regulation under LSE rules.

[17] Financial Reporting Council (June 2018), *The Wates Corporate Governance Principles for Large Private Companies.*

as management has become more challenging, length of service has not necessarily provided the necessary skills for the job. Good lawyers are not always good managers.

In law firms, larger partnerships, and LLPs will often have a *managing partner*, who will have overall responsibility for the management of the partnership. The managing partner will oversee all the management roles mentioned earlier in relation to companies, personnel, finance, marketing, and so forth. According to *Legal Business* this is not always an easy task. Lawyers tend not to be easily managed, and are often resistant to change. It has been said that lawyers are difficult to manage because they always think they know best. In 2012, the strategist, Stephen Mayson, who has written extensively about law firm strategy and management, wrote 'Compared to most other forms of large commercial endeavour, law firms are still lagging in terms of effective governance and management'.[18] However, the Law Society reports that over recent years there have been considerable improvements, especially so far as larger firms are concerned.[19]

18.2.5 Strategies and objectives

Once you know how a business works, and who has responsibility for its management, it is important to know what it is hoping to achieve.

18.2.5.1 Strategies

Business organisations, both large and small, should have a strategy.

> **(!) Essential explanation**
>
> A *strategy* sets out a long-term plan of what the business wants to achieve (its *vision*) and how it proposes to achieve it (its *mission*). You will sometimes see strategies referred to as the 'roadmap' for the business or its 'game plan'.

An organisation's vision and mission statements are usually published on its website, for example Google's mission is 'to organize the world's information and make it universally accessible and useful'[20] and Coca Cola, whose mission is to 'refresh the world . . .'.[21]

These statements are closely allied to transparency in relation to the organisation's *values and ethics*. When explaining its strategy, the organisation may state its values and/or culture, emphasising what makes a company unique within a particular market, or what binds it together. Taken together, the statement of values and the vision and mission statement set out *why* the company is in business.

---

[18] Mayson, S. 'Law Firm Partnership: the Grand Delusion', blog posted 9 October 2012. Available online at: https://stephenmayson.com/2012/10/09/law-firm-partnership-the-grand-delusion/, accessed 28/07/2019.

[19] E.g. The Law Society of England and Wales, *The Future of Legal Services*, January 2016. Available online at: https://www.lawsociety.org.uk/support-services/research-trends/the-future-of-legal-services/, accessed 08/07/2019.

[20] Google (2019). Available online at: https://www.google.com/about/, accessed 28/07/2019.

[21] Coca-Cola (2019). Available online at: http://www.coca-colacompany.com/our-company/mission-vision-values, accessed 07/07/2019.

Part III

Employability and Commercial Awareness

Millions of pounds are spent by businesses developing strategies in order to improve their competitiveness within the market in which they are operating. However, there is no point in having a strategy if you cannot get your workforce to buy into it, or effectively communicate this to potential customers. The idea of a strategy is to motivate the workforce, which in turn will bring in customers and investment. In other words, the strategy needs to be effectively communicated and implemented. It is more likely to work in a business where everyone knows *what* they are required to do to achieve the strategy, *how* they are supposed to do it, and *who* is going to ensure that it is done.

If you go back to Figure 18.3 showing the management hierarchy, you can see how this can be achieved by a company.

- *Why*, the vision, mission, and values, is decided by the directors.
- *What*, the objectives, or targets of the business, again will be set by the directors.
- *How*, the tactical decisions how this is to be achieved are made by the management.
- *Who* is the workforce, which implement the tactics.

The relationship between each of the various levels should be clear so everyone knows who is responsible for, and to whom. A business may have an *organogram*, which is a diagram showing the structure of the organisation and the interrelationship between directors, management, and the workforce. Figure 18.3 is a simplified organogram. If you are acting for any organisation, you will often find it useful to see its organogram, as it will clarify the role of the people you will be dealing with.

18.2.5.2 Objectives

> **Essential explanation**
>
> An *objective* is a target. It is different from a strategy in that it is more concrete and immediate.

The target of many businesses is to make or increase a profit, for example increase profit by 10 per cent per year for the next five years, or to achieve 50 per cent return business. In order to ensure that targets are met they have to be achievable. Managers often use the SMART model in relation to objectives. You have already considered this in the context of a presentation (see Chapter 10), but the model has a range of applications, and is frequently used by business organisations. Objectives are SMART if they are:

- **S**—specific (clear and unambiguous);
- **M**—measurable (capable of being measured against objective criteria);
- **A**—achievable (can be accomplished by the workforce);
- **R**—relevant (suitable for and of appeal to the workforce);
- **T**—time-appropriate (achievable within an agreed time frame).

18.2.6 Analysis

A further role of management is analysis of its position within the market place. A variety of management tools are used, which you may also find useful in other situations. For example, if you are preparing for a negotiation, you can use a SWOT analysis to organise the information which you have, or you can use it when you research an organisation when you are looking for a job.

18.2.6.1 SWOT

> **Essential explanation**
>
> SWOT is a management tool used to examine the strengths (S) and weaknesses (W), opportunities (O) available, and threats (T) confronting the business. *Strengths and weaknesses* are factors which are *internal* to the firm or business, whereas *opportunities and threats* relate to *external* factors. The results are usually shown in a grid form (see Figure 18.4).

SWOT can be used for a variety of different applications. Using SWOT provides useful information for managers on the current position of the business and allows them to determine what their future priorities will be. It can be used on the business, its customers, or competitors. It is usually done when some change in business operations is likely, such as bidding for new customers, or expanding into new markets.

18.2.6.2 PESTLE

Just like the professionals who advise them, the owners and managers of companies need to think about the context in which they are operating.

> **Essential explanation**
>
> **PESTLE:** political (**P**), economic (**E**), social (**S**), technological (**T**), legal (**L**), and environmental (**E**) changes that affect commercial activity.

All businesses are affected by changes brought about by these factors. They must take advantage of the opportunities offered and respond to the challenges and restrictions which they may impose. For example, political factors include the stability of the government, and its tax policy, etc. Similarly, economic factors to be considered would include interest rates, the level of inflation, unemployment, projected economic growth or decline. Social factors include population growth rate and demographics, for instance the ageing population, social mobility, and public opinion. Technological issues include new ways of working and communication. Legal issues include trends in regulation and deregulation or employment legislation. Environmental issues are factors such as weather and climate change.

In Chapter 17, we looked at a business case where a client is thinking of setting up an wine shop. There are concerns about binge drinking among young people and the increase in alcohol consumption amongst middle-aged professionals and the ensuing health problems. There is increasing debate about whether or not the government should intervene and legislate to restrict, for example, the opening hours of pubs, clubs, and off-licences in town centres. So a social concern will lead to political intervention and consequent legal constraints. The easiest way to control alcohol consumption is to increase the cost of alcohol by

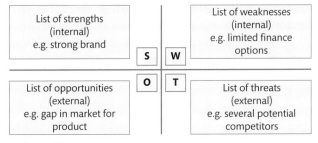

Figure 18.4 SWOT analysis grid

increasing taxes on all types of alcoholic drinks, making this an economic issue as well. All of this is bound to have an effect on the client's business. He will also need to think about the impact of technology.

18.2.6.3 Technology and social networking

In recent years, technology has revolutionised business. The internet, social media, apps, chat-bots, free calling platforms, and new payment methods have opened up global markets. One of the challenges for any business is to harness and drive technology for its own ends. Whereas in the past, businesses had to go out and find customers, over the last three decades, businesses have harnessed the internet as a forum for customers to find them, to promote their products, and to ease communication with their other stakeholders, investors, and suppliers, for example, and enable them to cut costs by outsourcing. Social network sites such as, in order of popularity, Facebook, YouTube, Instagram, Twitter, and LinkedIn, and the use of blogs have opened up important opportunities for businesses. The importance of social networking cannot be underestimated. The marketing potential has been immense. By March 2019, Facebook, the most popular social media platform, had 2.38 billion active monthly users. 1.56 billion people log on to Facebook every day, and its advertising revenue for the first quarter of 2019 was over $14 billion.[22] Social networks have provided infinite marketing opportunities, growing exponentially in the last decade. According to the specialist social media consultancy, Avocado Social, it is estimated that 40 million adults (or 71 per cent) in the UK can be reached using Facebook advertisements.[23]

The accessibility of social networking sites works both ways. Consumers are better informed and, with access to a wider choice of goods and services, price comparison websites, and online reviews as well as social media, are increasingly demanding and critical. This has changed the way that people shop, and businesses are being forced to find ways to manage the expectations of their customers and engage with the demands and criticisms of an increasingly powerful group.[24]

[22] Facebook (2019) *Facebook Q1 2019 Results*, released 24 April 2019. Available online at: https://investor .fb.com/investor-news/press-release-details/2019/Facebook-Reports-First-Quarter-2019-Results/default. aspx, accessed 28/07/2019.

[23] https://www.avocadosocial.com/latest-social-media-statistics-and-demographics-for-the-uk-in-2019/, accessed 17/02/2020.

[24] See for example, PwC (2019) *Total Retail Survey*. Available online at: https://www.pwc.co.uk/industries/ retail-consumer/insights/retail-outlook.html, accessed 28/07/2019.

One of the direct results of new technologies is the huge amount of data that it generates from a variety of sources from emails, texts, social media, audio, financial transactions, and so forth. Apparently 2.5 trillion megabites of data is generated globally each day.[25] This is a good and a bad thing for businesses. Data has, of course, always been collected, stored and used by businesses, but the problem arises as more and more data becomes available. This has given rise to the term 'Big Data'.

> **Essential explanation**
>
> *Big Data* is a term coined by O'Reilly Media[26] in 2005. It simply describes the vast amount of data that inundates businesses on a day-to-day basis, and which is impossible to manage using traditional technology.

Data is a valuable resource. It has been said that 'data is the new oil'.[27] The challenge for businesses is ensuring that they can organise, analyse, and use the data to make better business decisions and build more successful business strategies. However, using data brings new risks which businesses need to understand. As well as the need for effective cyber security and issues of privacy, as you saw at 15.3.1.1, the Cambridge Analytica scandal has focused attention on economic, social, political, and ethical considerations.

Related to this, and of increasing importance, and consequently increasingly topical, is artificial intelligence (AI) which is steadily passing into everyday business use. The accountancy firm, PwC considers AI to be one of the 'biggest commercial opportunities in today's fast changing economy', potentially boosting GDP by 10.3 per cent.[28] It is one of the ways by which businesses can manage data.

> **Essential explanation**
>
> AI is a branch of computer science. It is defined in the Cambridge English Dictionary as: 'the *study* of how to *produce machines* that have some of the *qualities* that the *human mind* has, such as the *ability to understand language, recognize pictures, solve problems,* and *learn*.'[29] There are three types:
>
> 1. artificial 'narrow' intelligence (ANI) which is the ability of a machine to handle one task;
> 2. artifical 'general' intelligence (AGI), which is the ability to learn and cope with any task that is asked of it, like a human brain; and
> 3. articicial 'super' intelligence (ASI), which is the ability to think and cope with tasks which are beyond the scope of the human brain.

[25] Desjardins, J. World Economic Forum, *How much data is generated each day?* (17 April 2019) https://www.weforum.org/agenda/2019/04/how-much-data-is-generated-each-day-cf4bddf29f/, accessed 17/08/2019.

[26] https://www.oreilly.com/, accessed 17/08/2019.

[27] https://www.economist.com/leaders/2017/05/06/the-worlds-most-valuable-resource-is-no-longer-oil-but-data, accessed 17/02/2020.

[28] PwC (2019), *The Economic Impact of artificial Intelligence on the UK economy.* Available online at: https://www.pwc.co.uk/services/economics-policy/insights/the-impact-of-artificial-intelligence-on-the-uk-economy.html, accessed 29/07/2019.

[29] Cambridge Academic Content Dictionary, Cambridge University Press, 2019. Available online at https://dictionary.cambridge.org/dictionary/english/artificial-intelligence, accessed 29/07/2019.

AI is not new. You probably use it every day. ANI—examples of which include speech rec-ognition programs, 'Siri' on an i-Phone, Google's 'Translate', or Facebook's 'Friend' recom-mendations—has been used for some time. It just gets more and more sophisticated. AGI, and certainly ASI, as yet, do not exist, but the race to develop these continues apace.[30] It may be possible by 2050 or more realistically the end of the century.[31] You will look at how law firms are harnessing this technology in Chapter 20.

18.3 The business environment

We now look at another important economic concept: markets and sectors. When we looked at the Patisserie Valerie example (see 15.3.1.1), we saw that Patisserie Valerie operated within the 'restaurant sector'. When we look at law firms, we will talk about the 'legal market'. The very act of selling goods or services creates a market. Businesses sell those goods and services to make money, and to make money they need to get as many buyers, or consumers, of the product as possible. The result is that within any market or sector businesses compete between themselves to be the biggest or the best, so markets and sectors are important because they generate competition. Healthy competition is good for businesses, as it drives growth, and it is good for the consumers of their goods or services, as it means that there will be more goods and services available, and prices will be lower. This section will consider what we mean by sectors and markets, the role of consumers, how products reach those consumers (the supply chain), and the influence of competition in providing goods and services for consumers.

18.3.1 Sectors and markets

The problem here is to define what exactly we mean by these terms, because you will see them used in all sorts of senses.

18.3.1.1 Economic sectors

> (!) **Essential explanation**
>
> An *economic sector* is a part or subdivision of the economy. It describes one of the areas into which the economic activity of a country is divided, and the proportion of the population engaged in particular activities.

There are four economic sectors:

1. **Primary:** extraction of raw material, such as mining, farming, or fishing. This is the oldest sector, as people have been engaged in farming since pre-historic times. Developed

---

[30] See, for example, Waters, R., *Microsoft invests $1 billion in OpenAI effort to replicate Human Brain*, Financial Times, (22 July 2019), https://www.ft.com/content/df752cc6-ac98-11e9-8030-530adfa879c2, or Sender, H., *China's iFlytek raising $350m to invest in AI, Financial Times*, (5 June 2019), https://www.ft.com/content/d4dbbd18-81a8-11e9-b592-5fe435b57a3b, both accessed 29/07/2019.

[31] See, for example, BBC News video, *What exactly is artifical Intenligence?* https://www.bbc.co.uk/news/av/technology-34224406/what-is-artificial-intelligence, accessed 29/07/2019.

economies such as the UK or US will now have comparatively few workers involved in the primary sector.

2. **Secondary:** production, such as manufacture, construction, or refining. There is a logical progression from extraction of raw materials to producing a finished product, like cars, houses, or textiles. The number of workers involved in manufacturing and related industries has declined in the UK in recent years, as more workers have moved into service industries. The decline of manufacturing industry is known as *deindustrialisation*.

3. **Tertiary:** provision of services, such as law, medicine, retail, entertainment, or tourism. This is the most important sector of the UK and other developed economies. As an economy develops, demand for services increases. The majority of workers in the UK are involved in the service sector, which accounts for over 80 per cent of the UK economy.[32]

4. **Quarternary:** research, design, and development, such as pharmaceuticals or computer programs. This is a comparatively new sector, but of increasing importance.

There is also a suggestion that there may be a fifth **quinary** sector, which includes workers who are involved in the highest decision-making processes, for instance top executives in media, culture, education, etc.

These are the main economic categories, but you will see further subdivisions. For example, energy, retail, industrial, hospitality, media, healthcare, financial, and so forth.

18.3.1.2 Public, private, and voluntary sectors

Public sector organisations, as we have seen, are those which are owned, financed, and controlled by the government. They provide services to the public, often free. Obvious examples are the National Health Service, or the BBC. The public sector is far wider than this and includes all central government departments, the central bank, local authorities, and government agencies.

By contrast, the *private sector* is made up of all businesses which are run by individuals and companies for profit, whether they be sole traders, partnerships, or companies. Earlier in this chapter, you looked at the BEIS' statistics for private sector businesses.

Voluntary sector organisations are charities and other organisations, such as clubs, which are not run for profit.

18.3.2 **Industries**

You will also see reference to *industries* and *industrial sectors*.

🛈 **Essential explanation**

An *industry* is a group of businesses that produce the same goods, for example the electrical industry, the retail industry, or the pharmaceutical industry. These are then grouped into wider *industrial sectors*, for example the manufacturing sector, construction sector, or transport sector.

---

[32] House of Commons, Research Briefing (12 July 2019), *Service Industries: Key Economic Factors.*

18.3.3 **Markets**

> **Essential explanation**
>
> A *market* is any place where the sellers of particular goods or services can meet with the buyers who want to buy those goods or services. They can be actual physical markets or they can be 'virtual' markets.

Ever since people started trading, markets have existed. The very width of the definition shows there are going to be lots of different types of markets. If you watch *The Apprentice*, you will see that Lord Sugar tests his candidates by introducing them to a variety of 'market' experiences, and seeing how they cope in each one.

- Actual physical *retail markets* can be any type of market from the local market held each week in any typical market town to large scale markets which cater mainly for business customers. *Virtual markets* exist only online.

- *Geographic markets* range from global markets (where trade takes place with every country in the world) to regional (e.g. the European Union) or local markets (a small defined area within one country). They are hugely important in assessing the competitiveness of a business.

- *Emerging markets* are markets which are experiencing rapid economic, social, and business growth. The main ones, historically, have been Brazil, Russia, India, and China (the BRIC economies). However, growth has now slowed in China and India, Brazil is on the brink of a recession and the Russian economy has stagnated. Some of the faster growing economies are now in Africa.[33]

- Other markets include *product markets*, *labour markets*, and *financial markets* (considered in Chapter 19) and *consumer markets* and *industrial markets*.

We are now going to concentrate on two categories, consumer and industrial markets, and think about how the goods you buy end up in the shops.

18.3.4 **The supply chain**

If markets are about buying and selling, it goes without saying that there have to be goods and services to buy and sell. Someone has to manufacture goods from raw materials, put them on the market, and make sure they reach the people who want to buy them.

> **Essential explanation**
>
> The *supply chain* describes the steps it takes to get goods and services from a supplier to an end user, and includes every company that comes into contact with those goods in the process. Any break in the supply chain will cause shortages, and has the potential to increase prices.

---

[33] Figures from International Monetary Fund, IMF DataMapper, (October 2019) https://www.imf.org/external/datamapper/NGDP_RPCH@WEO/OEMDC/ADVEC/WEOWORLD, accessed 17/02/2020.

Businesses and the business environment

Chapter 18

One possibility is for a manufacturer to sell its goods direct to retailers, or wholesalers, who will sell on to other retailers or direct to the end user. This is, however, not the most usual arrangement, and often a 'middle man' in the form of either a distributor or an agent will be involved. Figure 18.5 shows a simple supply chain.

To look at an example, you may remember that in February 2018, in what the *Financial Times* described as a 'logistics fiasco',[34] KFC had to shut hundreds of its restaurants when it ran out of chicken, having been let down by its new distributors, DHL. It was reported that KFC 'could be' losing £1m a day during the 'chicken delivery meltdown'. Having got over the chicken shortage, two weeks later, it ran out of gravy, but that received slightly less publicity.

At the top end of the chain, the manufacturer will have two concerns:

1. First it has to produce the goods or services, its products, as efficiently and cheaply as possible. One aspect of the manufacturing process is the sourcing of the raw materials, services, and utilities necessary to produce the goods and enable the business to function effectively. Where necessary, materials have to be transported and stored. (This process is referred to as *supply chain procurement* or *logistics*.) As a result, the manufacturer enters into a series of contracts to enable it to produce the goods. These are known as *upstream contracts* (the manufacturer's money is flowing up the supply chain).

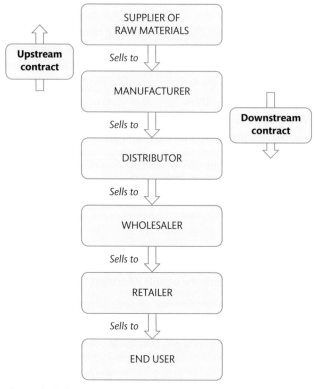

Figure 18.5 A simple supply chain

34 Rutter Pooley, C, *KFC runs out of chicken in logistics fiasco*, (19 February 2019), https://www.ft.com/content/223d4df0-1595-11e8-9376-4a6390addb44, accessed 17/08/2019

2. Next, it has to get the product to the ultimate consumer as cheaply and efficiently as possible. This process is known as *supply chain management*. Here the manufacturer organises a series of contracts to enable it to sell the goods. These are known as *downstream contracts* (the manufacturer passes the products down the supply chain, thus generating income for the business).

We have used a relatively simple supply chain example, where raw materials are being manufactured into a single product, but the logistics can be much more complicated, such as car manufacture. Cars are manufactured from a variety of component parts, such as doors, mirrors, windscreens, engine parts, electrics, nuts, bolts, and so forth. Possibly over 70 per cent of the components will be manufactured by someone else and bought in, often from different countries. A supply chain of this sort can be immensely complex, a 'logistical nightmare' in the true sense.

18.3.5 **Consumers**

At the other end of the supply chain are the consumers.

> ### Essential explanation
>
> *Consumers* are the end users of goods or services. They buy products for their own use, and not to use them in manufacture or to sell them on to other buyers.

They too want to buy the goods as cheaply as possible. Understanding the consumer market is vital for any business wishing to exploit its products successfully.

We live in a consumer society where the economy is highly dependent on consumer spending, and consumers are encouraged to buy material goods. The 1980s saw the rise of consumerism and a change in the way that people shopped. Rather than just buying necessities, people wanted luxury goods, for example designer clothes, mobile phones, computers, electrical goods, or luxury cars. The Office for National Statistics' report on household spending in 2019 shows that the percentage that consumers spend on household goods and services has remained stable in the last year but spending on clothing and footwear has fallen, indicating a lack of consumer confidence.[35]

> ### Essential explanation
>
> *Consumer durables* include vehicles, central heating, white goods such as washing machines or dishwashers, microwaves, mobile phones, satellite receivers, home computers and internet connection.

There has been a consequential rise in the amount of money that people spend, partly as a result of the increasing availability of credit during the 1990s and the first decade of the

---

[35] ONS, *Family Spending in the UK: April 2017- March 2019 (released January 2019)*. Available online at: https://www.ons.gov.uk/peoplepopulationandcommunity/personalandhouseholdfinances/expenditure/bulletins/familyspendingintheuk/financialyearending2018, accessed at 29/07/2019.

21st century. Spending on these items has been encouraged by advertising (and again, consequentially, increased the importance of mass and social media). There is much more emphasis on 'quick fix shopping' and shopping as a leisure activity. This, in turn, has led to a change in the types of shops people use, away from small retailers to supermarkets and national chains located in large shopping malls. Increasingly, during the last decade, consumers are shopping online. Online sales rose by 9.1 per cent between September 2018 and September 2019, totalling 19.1 per cent of all retail sales.[36] Increasingly, consumers use smartphones and tablets to shop.

18.3.6 Consumer protection

Despite their immense power as a group, individual consumers can be vulnerable, particularly at the hands of large producers. The rise of the consumer market has been accompanied by increasing regulation to protect consumers from unscrupulous suppliers. Consumer protection is a vast and specialist area of law, and it is very difficult to summarise. A good starting point is the website of the Citizens Advice Bureau, which tells you the bare minimum that a consumer who buys goods or services can expect,[37] e.g. that defective goods can be returned up to six years after purchase.

18.3.7 Competition

Where two or more businesses operate within a particular market or sector providing the same goods or services, they will be competitors. If we return to the example of the typical high street in 18.1, there are several obvious competitors and some non-competitors within that geographical market.

For example, high-street competitors might include the following examples:

- Costa and Starbucks both sell coffee;
- Waitrose and M&S Simply Food are upmarket supermarkets selling food;
- Next, New Look, and the boutique sell ladies' clothes;
- Barclays, TSB, and Santander provide banking and financial services.

These are competitors because they are operating in the same sector selling similar products. Non-competitors on the high street might include:

- the gift shop, phone store, and hardware store—if there are no others in the high street, they have no competition;
- solicitors, accountants, and estate agents are all operating within the service sector, but the services which they provide are complementary rather than competitive (if someone wants to buy a house, the estate agent may recommend the solicitors to do the property work and the solicitors may recommend the accountants to give any financial advice which their clients may need).

---

[36] ONS (2019) *Retail sales in Great Britain: September 2019*. Available online at: https://www.ons.gov.uk/businessindustryandtrade/retailindustry/bulletins/retailsales/september2019, accessed at 02/11/2019.

[37] The Citizens Advice website is Available at: https://www.citizensadvice.org.uk/consumer/, accessed at 29/07/2019.

The high street illustrates how competition works, but it is only a very small local market. If we expand the geographical market, the amount of competitors will increase. For example, many towns have out-of-town shopping centres, where you will find large supermarkets, such as Tesco or Asda, which would clearly provide further competition for the food stores in the high street. There are likely to be other mobile phone providers. Large supermarkets will sell gifts, so the gift shop will face competition here. There may be a McDonald's or KFC which will increase the choice for fast food. At the other extreme, the two banks operate within a global market, competing for customers throughout the world.

The level of competition is determined by the number and size of the businesses operating in a particular market.

ⓘ Essential explanation

A *monopoly* is where one business dominates the market, such as Microsoft within the global market for computer operating systems.

An *oligopoly* is where a few businesses dominate the market, for example the 'big four' supermarkets, Tesco, Sainsburys, Asda, and Morrisons together have a market share of nearly 70 per cent of the UK grocery market, although they are increasingly being threatened by discount chains such as Aldi and Lidl.[38]

A *competitive market* exists where there are hundreds or thousands of producers, none of which are particularly large or dominant. If you look, for example, in the Yellow Pages for any local area, you will see that there are hundreds of small businesses, such as hairdressers, pubs, or plumbing services, all competing within the same market.

A *cartel* is where two or more businesses join forces to dominate a particular market. An international example is OPEC (Organization of Petroleum Exporting Countries) which dominates the world oil market.

The structure of the market and the market conditions will affect prices. If a business has a monopoly, or is operating as part of a cartel, it will be able to charge more than a business which is operating in a competitive market. This is clearly not a good thing for consumers.

In the same way that regulation exists to protect consumers from unscrupulous suppliers, there is considerable regulation to protect against anti-competitive practices. Competition law (which you may see referred to as *anti-trust* internationally) is designed to promote healthy competition. Understanding this area of law is vital for any business as breaking the law can have very serious financial consequences. For example, between 2017 and 2019, Google has been fined a total of €8.25 billion for anti-competitive behaviour.[39]

18.3.8 Environment

The environment in which a business operates, its markets, its customers, and the competition it faces will influence all of the decisions which the managers of the business make. These factors are also important considerations for lawyers when advising any business. The emphasis throughout this chapter has been on the economic and financial environments, so those are what we will explore in Chapter 19.

[38] https://www.kantarworldpanel.com/en/grocery-market-share/great-britain, accessed 17/02/2020.

[39] http://europa.eu/rapid/press-release_IP-19-1770_en.htm, accessed at 29/07/2019.

Summary

- In order to demonstrate commercial awareness and give effective advice to business clients you need an understanding of the main business structures—sole traders, partnerships, the different types of company—and the advantages and disadvantages of each. This involves understanding how those businesses are run and managed, and by whom and investigating a business's strategy and objectives.

- It is crucial to understand the environment within which a client is operating and take into account the factors that contribute to that environment: political, economic, social, technical, and legal. Businesses operate within a variety of sectors and markets; you need to be able to understand the market in which that client operates, how the client operates within the market, and the competition within that market.

 Practical exercises

1. What are the main reasons why someone would choose to set up in business as a sole trader rather than a limited company?

2. What is an LLP? What are the advantages and disadvantages of these?

3. Research a company of your choice online. What are its vision, mission, and values?

4. What do you think are the main advantages and disadvantages of social media sites for businesses?

5. Research a law firm of your choice online. Use the SWOT analysis to identify one strength, weakness, opportunity, and threat for that firm's business.

 *Visit the **online resources** for the authors' reflections and to check your progress.*

 Further reading

Jones, L. (2019) *Introduction to Business Law.* **Oxford: OUP**
—Contains an accessible introduction to the structure and management of businesses.

Stokes, C. (2014) *Commercial Awareness 2015/16.* **Wendover: Christopher Stokes Ltd**
—Essential reading for information on how companies are run and managed. Aimed more at business people than lawyers, it still provides a unique insight into the subject. A revised version is published each year.

Again, follow up on some of the websites given in this chapter. Technology and innovation are buzzwords at the moment.
The Deloitte Consumer Review, which provides further information and analysis of trends and issues: https://www2.deloitte.com/content/campaigns/uk/consumer-review/consumer/consumer.html

*For the authors' reflections on the practical exercises, additional self-test questions, sample interview questions and a library of links to useful websites, visit the free **online resources** at* **www.oup.com/he/slorach4e.**

19 Essential economics and finance

🎯 **Learning objectives**

After studying this chapter you should be able to:

- Appreciate the importance of micro and macroeconomics in a business environment.
- Explain the role of banks and other financial institutions in the money markets.
- Recognise how the principles of business accounts affect businesses.
- Realise how personal and corporate insolvency may arise and their effects.

Introduction

In Chapter 18 you were introduced to different types of legal business structures and saw how businesses operate and are managed. We have stressed the importance of the environment in which individuals and businesses conduct their affairs. You have seen how the economy shapes the environment in which businesses operate and influences the everyday decisions of individuals. Now we look at the basics of economics, financial markets, and the major players within those markets. We look at the very fundamentals of money and finance: what money is, how to organise and account for it, and what happens when things go wrong.

The obvious question when you see a chapter headed 'Essential economics and finance' is 'Why do I need to know about this?' You may think that economics are for economists and politicians and City financiers. However, *Chambers Student Guide* (which is the law student's bible when looking for a job—see 16.2.1), in a section paraphrasing the well-know adage, entitled 'It's the stupid economy' makes the point that, firms want you to understand 'the journey that the UK and global economy has been on in recent years and how trends in different sectors, and Brexit, may affect their firm.'[1]

This does not just apply to law firm interviews. The economy has had a profound effect on all types of business and organisations, and, indeed, on ordinary individuals. Whether or not you decide to pursue a career in the law, you need, at the very least, a basic understanding of how the economy operates. Andy Haldane, Chief Economist at the Bank of England, argues that 'the economy and economic policy affects most people's lives, every day of their lives. More than that, an improved understanding of the economy and economic policy would

---

[1] *Chambers Student Guide* (2019) 'Trends affecting the legal profession'. Available online at: http://www.chambersstudent.co.uk./, accessed 03/08/2019.

probably help many people when making everyday decisions, big and small'.[2] He goes on to talk about 'financial exclusion' and 'financial illiteracy' and its social consequences, which we will look at later in the chapter when we look at debt (see 19.4.4).

If we go back to our Examples (see 15.3.1), the scenarios raised economic and financial issues which you need to understand.

Bear in mind that any discusson of economics in the UK has in recent years been dominated by Brexit, and no doubt that the impact of Brexit on the UK economy will be felt for some years to come. Although we are not going to look at Brexit in any detail in this chapter, whilst this remains a topical issue, it is a given that you need to understand and competently discuss the issue at interview so you should keep up to date with what is happening. However, to understand economics you need to look a great deal further than just this issue—and outside the UK and Europe.

Globalisation has meant that the impact of the global economy is an increasingly important factor.

> ### ! Essential explanation
>
> In economic terms, *globalisation* is the increasingly deeper integration of markets in the global economy, with the result that national economies have become more inter-connected.

In this chapter, to help you develop your understanding, we will concentrate first on some important economic concepts.

19.1 Basic economics

What is economics? Economics is about wants and resources: the goods and services that individuals, businesses, and governments want, the resources that they have available to buy them, and the choices that are made when buying them. A central tenet is scarcity. No individual, business, or government can buy everything they want: neither goods and services nor resources are unlimited. In principle, and in economic terms, you have *infinite wants*, but you have limited resources with which to satisfy them—in economic terms, you have *finite resources*. The same is true for businesses, and for governments. Economics looks at how individuals, businesses, and governments manage this problem.

To demonstrate commercial awareness, at interview and once you are employed, you need to show that you are familiar with some basic economic issues. As a starting point, see if you can answer the following questions:

1. What is the difference between micro and macroeconomics?
2. What is GDP?

---

[2] *Everyday Economics*, Speech by Andrew Haldane, Chief Economist, Bank of England (27 November 2017). Available online at https://www.bankofengland.co.uk/news/speeches, accessed 03/08/2019.

3. What is a recession?

4. What are the main causes of inflation, and why does it matter?

5. What are the main causes of unemployment, and why does it matter?

6. What is meant by the balance of payments?

7. What is the difference between fiscal and monetary policy?

8. What role does the Bank of England play in the economy?

9. What are the main financial institutions, and what role does the City of London play in the economy?

10. Why are trade deals so important?

11. What is the deficit?

12. Are you aware of what are the current most widely reported economic issues?

As with the Patisserie Valerie example (see 15.3.1.1), it does not matter that you cannot answer all these questions at this stage. A YouGov survey revealed that 25 per cent of the population do not know what GDP is, and that percentage increased to 29 per cent amongst the 18-24 age group.[3] However, that is not a reason to be complacent. What follows will help to improve your commercial awareness.

One of the problems about economic issues for students is that they are so central to our everyday lives that you will find that everyone—your tutors, employers and, when you start work, clients and customers—tends to assume that you know what they are, and why they are important. If you have studied economics, you may do. If not, you need somewhere to find the information. This section is designed to give you some background, and help you with the sort of terminology and jargon which you will hear on the news, and which may come up at interviews. Refer to it when you need it.

For lawyers, an understanding of these issues is vital when advising clients; for students, these are the issues which make the news and which you need to understand when you are applying for jobs, so we are going look at these in more detail.

However, it is not enough that you tick the box and say that you know what these terms mean. Once you understand what is meant, you need to be able to put them into context. It is important that you watch the news and read the newspapers to keep up with economic trends. If you attend an interview, you should be able to relate the impact of economic trends on the firm and the type of client the firm acts for. Using Brexit as an example, in a corporate context, you should have researched whether any of the firm's clients have made any announcement on the consequences for them, or whether is there any indication of the effect on the volume of merger and acquisition transactions; in a real estate context, what is happening to property prices as a result of the impact on the construction industry; or in a commercial context, how currency fluctuations are affecting imports and exports, and how this will impact on the firm's clients.

[3] *Post Crash Economic Society Survey Results*, YouGov plc (2015) Survey conducted in conjunction with the Post Crash Economics Society at Manchester University.

Essential economics and finance

Chapter 19

19.1.1 **Macroeconomics and microeconomics**

Economists divide economics into macroeconomics and microeconomics. At its simplest, 'macro' means big, 'micro' means 'small'.

> **Essential explanation**
>
> *Macroeconomics* is the study of how the entire economy works. It looks at the overall picture. Most television programmes and reports about the economy generally concentrate on macroeconomic concerns, such as unemployment, inflation, tax, or economic growth.
>
> *Microeconomics* is the study of individual businesses and consumers within the economy, and how they make choices about what to produce or how to spend money.

Clearly, there is an overlap between the two. Macroeconomic factors, such as tax and interest rates, affect individuals and businesses, and microeconomic activity is the basis for macroeconomic decisions, taken by the government and central banks. However, economists find it easier to keep the two separate. We will start with some microeconomics and then move on to macroeconomics, but first we need to consider some economic models and concepts.

19.1.2 **Economic models**

The detail of economics is highly complex. We are, after all, looking at the behaviour of governments, businesses, and individuals. Economists attempt to simplify things by making certain assumptions about how people and businesses behave, to produce economic models and theories which concentrate on the central issues. These are based on analysis of data and statistics. You have already seen the importance of data and statistics when we looked at the underlying concerns of clients in Chapter 17, but economists analyse these rather differently.

Models are based on theory, and are subject to criticism. They come in and out of fashion. For example, from about 1935 until the early 1970s, the government adopted a macroeconomic model for economic growth based on the theories of John Maynard Keynes. These fell out of favour following the recession of 1972. Economic policy, particularly during the 1980s, was based on the theories of Milton Friedman (see 6.6.1), known as 'monetarism'. Since then governments have used a combination of the two.

> **Essential explanation**
>
> *Keynsian economics* advocates active government intervention as a way of achieving economic growth and stability. Intervention takes the form of tax cuts and government spending to stimulate growth in times of recession, and tax increases and government cutbacks to control inflation when the economy is healthy.
>
> *Monetarism* is based on the idea that the quantity of money (the money supply) (see 19.2.2) in the economy is what determines economic growth and inflation. Intervention by the government will eventually lead to higher prices (inflation). The role of the government is to control the money supply by controlling the amount of money within the economy, for example by increasing interest rates.

You may wonder why you need to know about economic theories. Interview questions could touch on the government's economic policy.

Bear in mind that such questions are not an opportunity to give a forthright answer based on your own political views. To answer these effectively, not only would you need to know what the government's current economic policy is based on, but also what the alternatives could be.

19.1.3 Basic microeconomics

Microeconomics studies how businesses, workers, and consumers behave within markets, and the influence they have on prices, costs, and profits. We have already looked at several microeconomic issues, such as when we looked at pricing and sectors and markets at 18.3.1. At first glance, these may seem to be issues that are only relevant for businesses, and not necessarily for lawyers. However, they are the issues that underlie the decisions of the owners and managers of businesses, the people who will be your clients. These are examples of the 'latent' concerns of your clients, which you looked at in Chapter 17, and, as a lawyer you need to be aware of them.

19.1.3.1 Resources and production

The starting point when looking at microeconomic issues is to think about what businesses do. Businesses take resources (referred to in economics as *inputs* or *factors of production*) and convert them into a product (*outputs*). These outputs are not necessarily manufactured goods; they may be services. Outputs are dependent on resources. In economic terms, the resources which businesses have at their disposal are divided into four categories:

1. **Land**: includes raw materials, such as oil, gas, minerals, and agricultural produce, and also the weather, geothermal energy, and the electromagnetic spectrum.
2. **Labour**: the ability of individuals to work and thus contribute to production.
3. **Capital**: the physical 'things' which businesses use to produce other products, such as offices, machinery and plant, computers. It includes all sorts of other things like roads, sewers, electrical grids, and the internet.
4. **Enterprise**, or **human capital**: the human factor that transforms and drives the production process. Entrepreneurs are the people who have ideas, take risks, and invest in business. You tend to think about business people such as Richard Branson or Lord Sugar, but in fact, every shareholder who takes the risk of investing in a company is an entrepreneur.

All businesses, whatever their type, convert these resources into products, either goods or services. Law firms are no exception. They are converting the expertise of their solicitors into the legal service which they are providing to their clients, and as a result, the Law Society estimates that law firms will contribute over £27 billion to the UK's GDP [4] (see 6.1.2).

However, businesses are not going to produce goods or services simply because they have the resources to do so. They are not going to produce anything unless they can make a profit from doing so. In other words, they have to be sure of two things:

1. The return is greater than the cost of production. This return will usually, but not always, be measured in monetary terms.
2. There is a market for the produce, in other words that they can sell it.

---

[4] TheCityUk, July 2019. *Legal Services 2019*. Available online at: https://www.thecityuk.com/assets/2019/Report-PDFs/294e2be784/Legal-excellence-internationally-renowned-UK-legal-services-2019.pdf.

Economists calculate returns on production and analyse how consumers behave within the market. Both of these factors will affect the price of the goods or services.

19.1.3.2 Maximising profits

Economists assume that the main objective of any business is to maximise profits. In very simple terms, they do this by ensuring that revenue exceeds costs.

Economists take a different view of profits to that taken by accountants. Accountants simply look at the amount by which revenue exceeds costs. For example, if a car dealer buys a car for £2,000 (the cost) and sells it for £2,500 (the revenue), he will have made a profit of £500. Economists, however, give different meanings to profit, revenue, and costs. Economic profit, for example, takes into account opportunity costs. So in this example, if the dealer could have put the £2,000 in the bank instead of buying the car, and earned interest of £200, then the true cost is £2,200, reducing profit to £300.

Analysis of costs in relation to revenue enables businesses to set prices and work out how, what, and how much to sell to make a profit. In fact, price and output depend on a variety of other factors, such as the way that the business is run, the information which the business has, and the strategy which the managers of the business have decided to adopt. For example, managers may decide that their priority is to maximise the exposure of their brand, as this will give them a competitive edge in the long run. They may therefore, incur high marketing costs in the short term. (Marketing costs are known as *sunk* costs—costs which have been incurred and which cannot be recovered.)

Equally important are the characteristics of the market in which each business operates. We have already considered the effect of competition in Chapter 18. Clearly, the more competitive the market, the less opportunity there is to raise prices.

19.1.3.3 Supply and demand

The behaviour of the consumers who buy or use their products is also crucial to determining price and profit for businesses. This brings us on to one of the most fundamental economic concepts, supply and demand. Thomas Carlyle, a 19th-century economist, famously stated, 'Teach a parrot supply and demand and you've got an economist', reflecting the fact that these are two of the most basic terms in economics.

Essential explanation

Demand at its very simplest is how much of a product people want to buy at a given price. We look at demand from the perspective of a consumer. The law of demand states that as demand for a product increases, prices will increase. If the price increases, demand will decrease. This is shown on a demand curve (Figure 19.1). Note that the demand curve slopes downwards.

Supply is how much of a product is available, that is we look at supply from the point of view of the supplier. The law of supply states that as the demand increases, and prices go up, supply will increase to meet the rising demand. If prices decrease, businesses will produce less, because they will make a lower profit. This is shown on a supply curve (Figure 19.2), which by contrast slopes up.

Thus supply and demand are the key determinants of price.

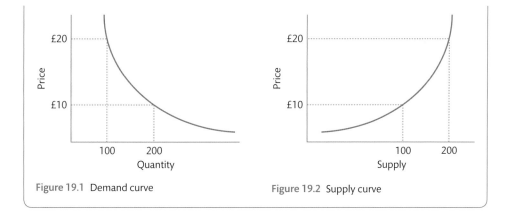

Figure 19.1 Demand curve

Figure 19.2 Supply curve

The essential thing to understand here is the relationship between price, supply, and demand. Normally, in a free economy, markets regulate themselves.

- When demand goes up, prices rise until they 'peak'. People decide that they are paying too much for a particular product and either start to buy something else instead, *substitutes*, or stop buying that product at all.

- On the supply side, businesses will have seen that prices for a particular product are increasing, and high prices encourage production (so supply increases). Once the price 'peaks' there is no further incentive to produce more.

- Eventually, the price will fall to an equilibrium price where consumers are getting exactly the quantity they want at a price which they want to pay, and suppliers are selling exactly the quantity they want to sell at a price which ensures that they make a profit, that is to say everyone is happy. Supply equals demand. This is shown by Figure 19.3.

Example 1

Imagine that there is huge demand for lager, leading to shortages. Prices go up to £7 a pint, way beyond the price of other beers, which still cost £3.50 a pint. Manufacturers notice this and start producing more lager. At the same time, demand for lager will begin to fall because other beers now seem comparatively cheap. Unless lager is the only product people want to buy, they will start to buy other beers. The result is that the price will start to fall to a level where people are prepared to start buying it again. Supply will have gone up so there is now enough to go round. This will keep the price of lager stable at, say £4.00 a pint.

There are of course variables which may prevent this, such as consumer taste, the number and price of substitute goods, the market, and again the amount of competition.

19.1.3.4 Price elasticity

A further factor which businesses need to consider is price elasticity. Elasticity depends on the availability of substitute goods. The more substitutes there are for a product, the more elastic the demand will be, in other words, demand is highly responsive to price changes. Even a small

Essential economics and finance

Chapter 19

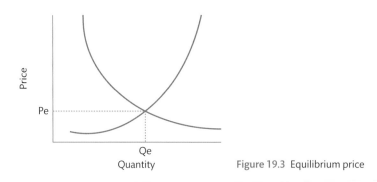

Figure 19.3 Equilibrium price

change in price can lead to a large change in demand. Lager is a good example. There are hundreds of different brands of lager, but other beers can be substituted, depending on taste. So if one manufacturer puts up prices, consumers will start buying another, or a different type of beer. The fewer the substitutes, the more inelastic the demand will be. Petrol is an example. The demand is likely to be inelastic as there is no real substitute. Although raising prices may mean that a few customers are lost, the price change is unlikely to deter a large number of customers.

Historically, it was always thought that professional services, like law and accountancy, were inelastic. Legal services are a necessity at certain times in an individual's life, but the supply of lawyers has been restricted by the monopolistic and anti-competitive structure of the legal profession, which you looked at in Chapter 6. However, this could change with greater competition and deregulation, as discussed in 6.2, thus increasing supply. It is something to bear in mind when considering the threats and challenges to the legal profession.

An understanding of supply and demand is fundamental to your understanding of economics. Wherever you look, you can see that it has practical application. One of the fundamental microeconomic issues over recent years has been volatile oil prices. Oil prices are mainly affected by supply and demand. Oil prices reached a record high in July 2008, but over-supply and stock piling, particularly in the US, drove down demand, resulting in falling prices. The last decade has seen considerable fluctuations.[5] The escalating price of property in the UK (see 17.2.2.2), a direct result of a shortage of housing, is a further illustration of the effect of supply and demand.

19.1.4 Basic macroeconomics

Macroeconomics is the study of how the entire economy works. The main macroeconomic issues are GDP (gross domestic product), inflation, unemployment, and what is called the current account, which is the difference between exports and imports. All of these are controlled to a certain extent by government policy. They are also the factors which businesses and those who manage them will need to consider before making any decisions.

19.1.4.1 Resources and output

We started looking at microeconomics by thinking about resources and output, and how resources need to be allocated to production. In general, in a mixed economy like the economy

---

[5] As at July 2019.

of the UK, market forces will be the most important factor determining what goods and services are produced, but the government does have a considerable influence through legislation, government spending, and welfare. Thus most resources and means of production are owned by individuals and businesses, but the government is responsible for the provision of some goods or, more likely, services, like education, health, and defence. Thus, within the economy as a whole, the government also has to make choices as to how they allocate resources, e.g. whether to spend money on the NHS or funding higher education.

> ### (!) Essential explanation
> #### Types of economy
>
> A *free*, or *laissez faire*, *economy* is one where market forces determine decisions about production, and the government plays a very limited role.
>
> A *planned*, or *command*, *economy* is one where the government plans what is produced and by whom.
>
> In reality, most economies are *mixed economies*, where both market forces and government policy determine what goods and services are produced.

19.1.4.2 Supply and demand

Supply and demand are still important issues, but macroeconomics looks at *aggregate* supply and demand, namely the supply and demand in the whole economy.

> ### (!) Essential explanation
>
> *Aggregate demand* is the total of all consumption, investment, government spending, and net exports in the economy.
>
> *Aggregate supply* measures the volume of goods which can be produced in the entire economy at a given price level, namely the productive capacity available in the economy to *produce* goods and services, taking into account the available resources.

Again, there is a relationship between prices and aggregate supply and demand. If demand rises, prices will rise and, to achieve price equilibrium, supply will also have to increase. Equilibrium occurs when supply equals demand. This time, however, we are not looking at the price of individual items supplied by one business, we are looking at price levels across the whole economy.

When times are good, government, business, and consumer spending and investment (i.e. demand) will be high, which will have the effect of driving up prices. This will not be a problem if supply can increase in tandem. However, aggregate supply depends on available resources, such as the supply of labour or land. In good times, there is likely to be full employment and land will be expensive, so finding a new factory or office, and staffing it, may be difficult and expensive. It will be difficult for businesses to produce any more. Prices therefore continue to rise, resulting in inflation. The economy 'overheats', which is often the first sign that the economy is going into recession. We will go on to consider the causes of recession.

19.1.4.3 Government intervention

In all types of economy, the government will intervene to a greater or lesser extent. Even in a free market economy, there may be reasons why a government might have to intervene. To take an extreme example, if there was no government intervention in the economy, it would be perfectly legitimate to sell Class A drugs (there would be a legitimate supply and legitimate demand), however harmful these may be: So the government needs to legislate on this for the greater good of society. The extent of government intervention in an economy can be measured by looking at the percentage of government spending and investment in relation to GDP, which we will consider shortly.

In the UK, as with all mixed economies, government intervention aims to achieve four main objectives:

- economic growth;
- stable prices/low inflation;
- low unemployment; and
- favourable balance of payments.

Whatever else you might or might not know about the economy, you need to know about these. They are in the news all the time.

These objectives can be achieved by the use of fiscal and monetary policies. Policies which seek to control demand are known as *demand side policies* and, not surprisingly, those that seek to control supply are known as *supply side policies*.

🛈 Essential explanation

Monetary policy involves the use of interest rates to control the rate of aggregate demand, the *money supply*, and inflation. This is the responsibility of the central bank. The Bank of England is the UK's central bank. We will look at this at 19.2.1.

Fiscal policy involves the use of government spending, taxation, and borrowing to control *demand* and therefore economic activity. A 'tight' fiscal policy is where governments limit public spending. The UK government's 'austerity programme', which began in 2010, has been a version of this. The aim is to reduce government debt, which currently stands at over £1.8 trillion (that's £1,800,000,000,000), and amounts to over 83 per cent of GDP.[6]

Government debt (which you will also see referred to as the *national debt* or *public sector debt*) is the total debt owed by the government. Where the government spends more than it can raise in tax, it will need to borrow money by issuing bonds and other securities (see 19.2.4.4). For example, the amount that the government had to borrow in the financial year to 31 March 2019 was £23.5. billion.[7] The annual amount which the government needs to borrow to meet the shortfall is known as the *budget deficit*, and each year contributes to the national debt.[8]

---

[6] ONS (June 2019) *Public Sector Finances, June 2019*. Available online at: https://www.ons.gov.uk/economy/governmentpublicsectorandtaxes/publicsectorfinance/bulletins/publicsectorfinances/june2019, accessed at 13/08/2019.

[7] Ibid.

[8] ONS, *UK Government Debt and Deficit, March 2019*. Available online at: https://www.ons.gov.uk/economy/governmentpublicsectorandtaxes/publicspending/bulletins/ukgovernmentdebtanddeficitforeurostatmaast/march2019, accessed at 21/08/2019.

19.1.4.4 Gross domestic product or GDP

> **Essential explanation**
>
> *GDP* is the equivalent of *aggregate demand*. It is the sum of everything produced in the economy (inputs) less the amount it costs to produce (outputs). It is the sum total of everything that the government and millions of businesses and individuals are contributing, spending, and earning, measured in current market prices. It is measured quarterly (i.e. every three months) based on a huge survey of figures compiled by the Office for National Statistics (ONS). Figure 19.4 shows what contributes to GDP.
>
>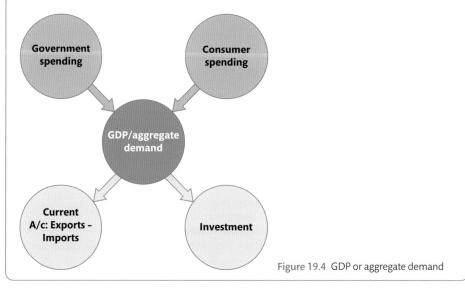
>
> Figure 19.4 GDP or aggregate demand

GDP is important because it is the chief measure of economic growth (i.e. the increase in economic output). It shows how well (or badly) the economy is doing. Ideally, the economy will grow at a consistent rate. In the UK there is no set target for economic growth, but on average, historically, the economy has grown at a rate of between 2 per cent and 3 per cent. At 2.5 per cent, aggregate demand will grow at an equivalent rate to aggregate supply, so there will be low inflation and low unemployment. Slow or negative growth impacts on all sectors of the economy.[9] If growth is too rapid, the economy will 'overheat', as happened in 2007–08.

19.1.4.5 The business cycle

As Figure 19.5 shows growth does not remain constant. There are periods of expansion or boom, recession, depression or slump, and recovery, with peaks and troughs as the economy expands and contracts. These phases are known as the business, or economic, cycle.

---

[9] In August 2019, the Bank of England forecast for 2019 and 2020 is 1.3 per cent. See, for example, https://www.bankofengland.co.uk/inflation-report/2019/august-2019, accessed 04/08/2019.

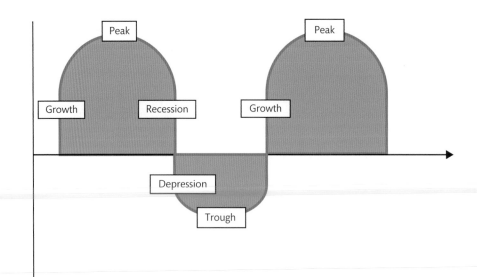

Figure 19.5 The business cycle

> **① Essential explanation**
>
> A *boom* is when the economy grows.
>> A *recession* is when the economy shrinks for two or more quarters.
>> A *slump*, or *depression*, is where a recession is severe and prolonged.
>> *Recovery* occurs when the economy begins to grow after a recession.
>> A *double-dip recession* is when the economy starts to recover, but then falls back into recession (see Example 2).

19.1.4.6 Causes of recession

There are various causes of recession, but the most usual are inflation and 'economic shock'.

1. **Inflation**. As inflation increases, demand falls, and people start to save rather than spend. Businesses produce less, and generally start to lay off workers in order to cut costs.

2. **Economic shock**. An 'economic shock' is a (generally) sudden and unexpected external factor which reduces demand pushes the economy into recession. An example would be a sudden rise in oil prices. In August 2019, in an interview on the Radio 4 *Today* programme, the Governor of the Bank of England described Brexit as an economic shock, but one which impacts on both supply and demand.[10]

Example 2

From 2008, the global financial crisis resulted in one of the deepest and most prolonged recessions on record. The economy began to grow in 2009, but since then recovery has been slow and there were periods during 2010–11 when either the economy showed no growth or shrank. It appeared that the UK economy officially went back into recession when GDP shrank by –0.3 per cent in the final quarter

[10] https://www.bbc.co.uk/news/business-49203426, accessed 03/08/2019.

of 2011 and –0.2 per cent in the first quarter of 2012 (i.e. two quarters of negative growth). However, in 2013 the figures were later revised by the ONS to show that growth was in fact flat (0 per cent) in Q1 of 2012, thereby avoiding a double dip recession. Since then it has improved, but more slowly than expected in the light of slowing global growth and the uncertainty caused by Brexit.

19.1.4.7 Inflation

> **(!) Essential explanation**
>
> *Inflation* is the rate of change of prices for goods and services. There are a number of different measures of inflation, but the ones that you are most likely to see are:
>
> - the Consumer Price Index (CPI); and
> - the Retail Price Index (RPI).
>
> To arrive at a figure, the government tracks the price of a hypothetical basket of over 650 goods each month. The 'basket' includes the things which we use all the time, such as food, drink, fuel, and entertainment. The RPI includes mortgage payments and council tax and is said to be more reflective of real prices than the CPI, which does not include these items. The quicker prices go up, the higher the rate of inflation.

The amount that the basket goes up is calculated as a percentage. If the cost of the basket goes up by 5 per cent over a 12-month period, then the rate of inflation for that 12-month period is 5 per cent. The same goods and services cost 5 per cent more than they did 12 months ago. People will be worth 5 per cent less in real terms, unless their incomes also rise by 5 per cent. High rates of inflation therefore reduce living standards as individuals have less money to spend.

The current target rate of inflation is 2.0 per cent based on the CPI.[11] The Bank of England has the responsibility of ensuring that inflation remains within that target. When inflation misses that target by more than 1 per cent, the Chairman of the Bank of England is required to write an open letter to the Chancellor to explain why this has happened.

There are two main causes of inflation.

1. Demand grows faster than supply. This is known as *demand-pull inflation*. With rapid economic growth in the first decade of the 20th century, China experienced this type of inflation, as the wealth of its population increased and demand for consumer goods rose.

2. Production costs rise, for example the cost of raw materials and labour. Businesses pass these increased costs on to consumers. This is known as *cost-pull inflation*. An example is if the cost of food rises, e.g. in early 2019 food prices increased by 1.9 per cent and reached their highest level for five years as a result of extreme weather in the UK in 2018, and rising grain prices globally. However, the impact on the overall rate of inflation was offset by a fall in some non-food items, such as clothing.[12]

[11] Bank of England (2016) *Inflation and the 2% target.* https://www.bankofengland.co.uk/monetary-policy/inflation, accessed 04/08/2019.

[12] Jackson, G., 'UK Inflation climbs to 1.9% on rising food prices', *Financial Times*, 20 March 2019. Available online at https://www.ft.com/content/152b9150-4af3-11e9-bbc9-6917dce3dc62, accessed 04/08/2019.

Inflation has a number of consequences for both businesses and individuals. As prices rise, resources become more expensive and profits for businesses fall. Wages fall in real terms. Labour becomes more expensive as workers seek wage rises. Forecasting profits and prices becomes more difficult, and businesses cut back, leading to higher unemployment. The knock-on effect will be that the economy contracts.

19.1.4.8 Unemployment

> **Essential explanation**
>
> *Unemployment* measures all those who are willing and able to work, but who cannot find a job. The official level does not include those who are either unable or unwilling to work (e.g. because of disability). The government measures unemployment monthly. In August 2019 the number of people unemployed was 1.3 million in the UK (3.8 per cent of the total workforce), the lowest figure since 1974.[13] These workers are entitled to claim jobseeker's allowance.

There are various causes of unemployment.

1. **Cyclical** unemployment is the most important at the moment. This occurs as a result of a downturn in the economic cycle. As we have seen, if demand within the economy decreases then businesses will lay off workers. Accordingly, it is also referred to *demand-deficient* unemployment.

2. **Structural** unemployment is the result of a particular industry going into decline. Workers who lose their jobs as a result do not have the skills to get jobs in other industries or sectors.

Labour is one of the main economic resources, so unemployment represents the waste of a resource. For the government, fewer people working means less income from tax and the need to pay out larger sums in benefits.

19.1.4.9 Balance of payments and the current account

As well as the situation within the UK, international trade also has to be taken into account when measuring the health of the economy. Businesses export their goods and services to countries outside the UK and businesses and individuals import resources, such as raw materials and products or services, like cars and electrical goods, from outside the UK.

> **Essential explanation**
>
> The *balance of payments* measures the difference between the country's exports and imports, including all financial exports and imports. It measures all money flowing in and out of the country. The *current account* is the difference between exports and imports of goods and services (as opposed to sales and purchases of land or shares and bonds).

[13] ONS (2019) *UK Labour Market overview, May 2019*. Available online at: https://www.ons.gov.uk/employmentandlabourmarket/peopleinwork/employmentandemployeetypes/bulletins/uklabourmarket/may2019, accessed 04/08/2019.

Ideally exports should exceed imports. This is a *trade surplus*. In this case, income from abroad is *injected* into the economy. However, in the UK the reverse is the case; we import more than we export, so the UK has what is known as a *trade deficit*. In March 2019 this stood at £30.0 billion.[14] The UK does have a strong record for the export of services, especially financial services, which is why the City of London is one of the major financial centres in the world, but as manufacturing has declined in the UK, we have imported more goods than we have exported. In recent years, falls in the value of sterling, which have historically boosted exports, have had little or no impact on exports, whilst increasing the cost of imports.[15]

The balance of payments is one of the measures of a country's financial health. It is an indicator of a country's ability to pay its way in the world. A trade deficit will mean that the government has to borrow more. It may also have an effect on the value of the currency.

The nature and extent of government intervention to control these factors will depend to a large extent on the political leaning of the government in power at the time. Conservative governments tend to favour cutting back government spending and borrowing (monetary policy). Labour governments favour increased spending and increasing taxes (i.e. fiscal policy).

The problem for governments is that it is rarely possible to solve all economic problems at one time. Improvements in one area come at the expense of others. For example, since March 2009, the Bank of England has kept interest rates low (0.75 per cent in August 2019) which has helped to stimulate growth and reduce unemployment and levels of inflation. Persistently low interest rates, however, can encourage excessive borrowing, which in turn, as we have seen, can have the effect of creating a housing bubble (see 17.2.2.2). However, if interest rates rise, people cut back on spending. In a fragile economy, this could mean that growth falls back and inflation increases.

19.2 Banks, money, and the financial markets

Chapter 18 shows us that the financial markets are just another type of market or sector of the economy. In the UK, the City of London is the financial district of London. Although it is only approximately one square mile in the centre of London (and thus sometimes referred to as the 'Square Mile'), it is one of the world's leading financial centres, with financial institutions from all over the world based there. UK financial services sector contributes £132 billion to the UK economy, 6.9 per cent of national output and employs 1.1 million people,[16] and in 2016, London's GDP was estimated to be equal to that of Saudi Arabia.[17] It is impossible to underestimate the influence of the financial markets and the City on the economy, and consequently the decisions taken by individuals and businesses. Even today, it is probably

Essential economics and finance

Chapter 19

---

[14] ONS (June 2019) *Balance of Payments, UK January to March 2019*. Available online at: https://www.ons .gov.uk/economy/nationalaccounts/balanceofpayments/bulletins/balanceofpayments/januarytomarch2019, accessed 04/08/2019.

[15] See for example, Strauss, D., *What Is the effect of the falling pound on Brexit Britain, Financial Times*, 30 July 2019, https://www.ft.com/content/0ee55f40-b2c9-11e9-8cb2-799a3a8cf37b, accessed 17/02/2020.

[16] Rhodes, G. *Financial Services: Contribution to UK Economy*, Briefing Paper 6193, House of Commons Library, 31 July 2019. Available online at: www.parliament.uk/briefing-papers/sn06193.pdf, accessed 04/08/2019.

[17] BBC (2016). Available online at: http://www.bbc.co.uk/news/resources/idt-248d9ac7-9784-4769- 936a-8d3b435857a8 accessed 11/07/2016.

fair to say that everyone's lives are still affected by the 2008 banking crisis and its aftermath.[18] In Chapter 17 we looked at how individuals and business raise finance, and some of the difficulties they face. In 2018, the major banks lent a total of £477 billion to UK businesses, and nearly two-thirds of the public have purchased their homes with the aid of a mortgage.[19] As a lawyer, whether you are acting for a young couple buying their first home, or for a corporate client involved in a large-scale corporate acquisition, you need to be aware of what is going on in the City, as it affects their ability to raise finance.[20]

19.2.1 Banks

Ever since the financial crisis of 2008, the influence of the banks within the financial markets and the economy has remained a topical issue. If you are going to understand the financial news today, you need to understand about banks and the banking system.

19.2.1.1 The central bank

The Bank of England is the central bank in the UK. It is not a bank in the usual sense as you cannot go and open an account there. Rather, it has overall responsibility for the rate of inflation, and is responsible for the implementation of monetary policy. It sets interest rates and issues bank notes. It issues money into the economy through the banking system and acts as a banker for the government and other banks. Unlike ordinary banks, the central bank does not lend money directly to either the banks or the government. It does so through the use of *financial instruments* such as stocks, bonds, and gilts (see 19.2.4).

19.2.1.2 Commercial and investment banks

Other than the central bank, banks are categorised into *commercial* (retail and wholesale banks) and *investment* banks.

1. **Commercial banks** take deposits from and lend to customers. They borrow money from other banks and the money market. They make their money by borrowing at one rate of interest and lending at a higher rate. There are two types of commercial bank:
   - **Retail banks** who lend to consumer customers and small businesses. They also offer financial services both to individuals, such as investment advice or providing foreign currency for holidaymakers, and to small businesses, for example a start-up business can get advice from a small business manager who will help it through the basics of setting up and running the business.

---

[18] Bruce, A., 'Britain's lasting scars from the financial crisis', *Reuters*, 17 September 2018 available at https://uk.reuters.com/article/uk-britain-economy-crisis-graphic/britains-lasting-scars-from-the-financial-crisis-idUKKCN1LX0FY, accessed 05/08/2019.

[19] TheCityUk (May 2019) *Key Facts about UK Financial and Related Professional Services*. Available online at: https://www.thecityuk.com/research/key-facts-about-uk-based-financial-and-related-professional-services-2019/, accessed 05/08/2019.

[20] The Bank of England's website provides useful explanations and short videos of many of the topics discussed in this section. Go to https://www.bankofengland.co.uk/ and use the Search facility.

- **Wholesale banks** operate in the business-to-business market. They take very large deposits and arrange very large loans, both for other banks and for large corporate and commercial institutions.

2. **Building societies** perform the same role as retail banks, but they specialise in lending for the purpose of buying property. However, many have been taken over by banks, for example the Abbey National Building Society is now part of Santander.

3. **Investment banks** are not involved in the lending and borrowing process like commercial banks. Their customers are governments and large corporations. They deal with bond issues for the government and large companies and also organise takeover bids, flotation of companies, and issues of shares by companies.

Figure 19.6 shows the interrelationship between the banks.

Although some of the larger banks, like Barclays, or HSBC, do have an investment section, individuals and small businesses are unlikely to have dealings with this part of the bank or other investment banks, which are mainly located in major financial centres, like the City of London or New York. The retail sections of the banks, and the building societies, are based on most high streets.

The deposits which customers make enable banks to lend to other customers. When the economy is working well, the savings that one person makes are injected back into the economy in the form of loans.

Most people trust their banks and are happy to leave their savings in the bank. However, if confidence in the bank falls for one reason or another, customers withdraw their money. A panic will lead to a 'run on the bank'. Long term loans cannot be called in to raise the cash needed to pay all the customers who are demanding their money, and the bank will technically become insolvent. This is what happened when Northern Rock collapsed in 2007, presaging the banking crisis of 2008–09. It was subsequently rescued by the government, and was bought by Richard Branson's Virgin Group.

There have been a series of scandals involving the activities of investment banks in the period following the financial crisis, e.g. manipulating interest and foreign exchange rates, breaching international sanctions, and money laundering. The global banking industry is estimated to have paid over $320 billion in fines between 2008 and 2017. Deutsche Bank alone was fined a total of £14.5 billion between 2011 and 2018 and faces further fines

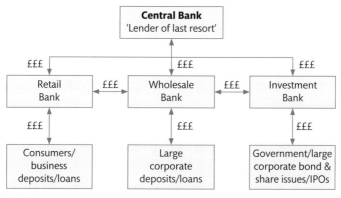

Figure 19.6 The banking system

and prosecutions for involvement in a £20 billion money laundering operation by Russian criminals.[21]

The government has now implemented measures aimed at greater regulation of banks to protect consumers and taxpayers when things go wrong, e.g. greater supervision of banks, the separation of investment and retail banks (ring fencing), criminal sanctions for reckless misconduct,[22] and the introduction of minimum capital requirements.[23]

19.2.2 Money and the money supply

19.2.2.1 What is money?

It is often said that 'money makes the world go round'. Money is central to the economy: the government, the banking system, individuals, and businesses alike. You probably think you know what money is, but in reality it has a variety of functions.

1. Money is a *medium of exchange*. It enables you to buy things. If there was no money, we would have to barter (i.e. swap goods or services for other goods or services, say two pairs of shoes for a handbag). Even early societies found this did not work well. As early as 700 BC, the Chinese developed a system of money, based on metal coins, and about 118 BC introduced paper notes, which were easier to carry around. Gradually, all countries developed their own systems of notes and coins, which have been refined over the years. These are the *currencies* of each country, such as pounds and pence in the UK, dollars and cents in the US, and euros and centimes in most of the countries of mainland Europe.

2. As money is the unit of exchange which we use to buy things, it is also used to set prices. All goods are given a monetary value, so money is said to be a *unit of account*.

3. Money also has a value. If you have a £10 note, you do not need to spend it immediately. You can keep it or save it. Paper notes used to be based on the value of gold, so you could swap your note for the equivalent amount of gold at a bank. This is no longer the case, but notes are now backed by the central bank, which guarantees payment. Money is also therefore a *unit of worth*.

19.2.2.2 The money supply

> **① Essential explanation**
>
> The money supply is based on statistics compiled by the Bank of England. It is the total amount of money in the economy at a given time. It consists of notes, coins, money held in bank and building society accounts, and M4 lending (i.e. loans from banks and building societies).

---

[21] Harding, L. 'Deutsche Bank faces action over $20 billion Russian money-laundering scheme' *The Guardian*, (17 April 2019), accessed 05/08/2019.

[22] Banking Reform Act 2013. For further detail, see the government's policy update, *Government completes banking reforms*. Available online at: https://www.gov.uk/government/news/government-completes-banking-reforms, accessed 05/08/2019.

[23] Capital Requirements Regulation (SI 575/2013), implanting CRD IV Directive (2013/36/EU) and Capital Requirements (Amendment)(EU Exit) Regulations 2018.

So money is not just cash in hand. Individuals and businesses also deposit money in banks and building society accounts (digital money). Those banks and building societies then lend money to other individuals and businesses. The money supply is made up of all these.

19.2.2.3 The money multiplier

Because the money supply takes into account loans, in reality not all money actually exists. Banks are continually 'creating' money by lending out the funds which customers have deposited with them. When a customer deposits money with a bank, the bank is required to keep a 'reserve' (i.e. a percentage of that deposit), but it can lend out the rest. The result of this lending is to expand the money supply. Next is a very simple example (Example 3).

> **Example 3**
>
> Bagit Ltd, a designer handbag company, sells ten handbags for £1,000 cash. It deposits this money with its bank. The bank keeps a reserve of, say, 10 per cent, just in case Bagit does want to withdraw some money, and lends out the rest (i.e. the bank keeps £100 and lends out £900 to nine customers). Each customer borrows £100 and decides to buy a handbag from Bagit. So £900 of Bagit's money flows back into the economy. Bagit deposits this £900 in the bank, and the process starts all over again. The bank lends out £810 and so on. Bagit thinks it has £1,900 in the bank, but in reality most of that money is working outside the bank to increase the amount of cash in circulation.

Clearly, the higher the reserve requirement, the less money there is in circulation (i.e. the money supply is 'tight'). In Example 3, if the reserve was 25 per cent, the bank could only lend out £750 from a deposit of £1,000.

Understanding the money multiplier makes it easier to see how interest rates can control the money supply. When interest is high, people tend to save rather than borrow, so consequently there is less money flowing back into the economy. A tight money supply reduces demand, and economic growth, and can cause inflation to fall below the 2 per cent target. This can be resolved by the Bank of England injecting money into the economy, a process which is referred to as 'quantitative easing'.[24]

> ⓘ **Essential explanation**
>
> *Quantitative easing* is where the central bank buys financial assets from banks and private sector businesses with new, electronically created money. The purpose of injecting money into the economy is to stimulate activity and growth within the economy. It has been used when conventional monetary policy, namely lowering interest rates, is not possible because they are already low (0.75 per cent at the time of writing).

A further problem arises where banks are unwilling to lend, which was the case after the banking crisis of 2008–09. Again, this reduces the amount of money in circulation.

---

[24] Bank of England (2019) *What is Quantitative Easing?* Available at https://www.bankofengland.co.uk/monetary-policy/quantitative-easing.

Essential economics and finance

Chapter 19

19.2.3 **Interest rates**

We have looked at interest rates in the context of individual and business borrowing and credit, but now we are going to consider how these rates are arrived at.

! Essential explanation

Interest is the cost of borrowing or the reward for saving. The *official Bank Rate*, or *Bank of England Base Rate* is the most important rate in the UK on which *market rates* are based.

---

1. The Bank of England's Monetary Policy Committee (MPC) sets the *official bank rate* eight times a year. This is the rate which it charges to lend to other banks. We have seen that the Bank of England uses the official rate to regulate growth and control inflation. At the time of writing interest rates are set at 0.75 per cent. The banks then set their base rate, which will generally follow the official bank rate.

2. *Market rates.* However, the official rate is not the rate at which banks lend to or borrow from their customers. When you look at the financial pages, you can see that there is a very wide variation in the interest rates offered to customers. Banks borrow at a rate which will attract customers and lend at a premium which will ensure that they make a profit. This premium is based on a number of factors, the most important of which are:

   – Risk. With any loan, there is always a risk of default. The greater the likelihood that a customer will default, the higher the interest rate it will have to pay.

   – The rate at which the banks can borrow from each other.

19.2.4 **Financial markets**

! Essential explanation

A *financial market* is a market where traders come together to trade financial instruments, such as shares, bonds, or currencies.

There are various types of financial market, so now we will consider some of these and the main investors in these markets. The starting point is the *capital* markets, made up of the stock (equity capital markets) and bond markets (debt capital markets).

19.2.4.1 **Stock markets**

Shares in public companies, and other stocks and securities, are normally bought and sold on a *stock market*, or *stock exchange*. The London Stock Exchange is an example.

The London Stock Exchange (LSE)[25] is effectively like a supermarket, where everyone who wants to trade in shares can go to buy and sell. With advances in technology, there are now few actual physical market places. Trading is conducted through dedicated computer network systems, such as the National Association of Securities Dealers Automated Quotation (NASDAQ) system in the US.

There are two main markets in the UK: the London Stock Exchange Main Market and the Alternative Investment Market (AIM). This means that the LSE has a 'two tier' system.

1. Larger companies join or are *listed* or *quoted* on the London Stock Exchange Main Market. About 1,400 companies from 70 countries are listed on the Main Market. According to the LSE's *Guide to Listing on the London Stock Exchange*, the combined assets of these companies amount to £3.7 trillion.[26]

2. AIM is a sub-market of the stock exchange. It was set up in 1995 so that investors could trade in shares which are not suitable for the Main Market. It is targeted at smaller companies which are hoping to grow in size, and is also popular with international companies. There are over 950 companies listed on AIM.[27]

19.2.4.2 Share prices

Share prices are not fixed. Once a company has joined a stock market, its share price will be determined by the market (i.e. by supply and demand from investors). For each listed company, there is a fixed number of shares in circulation. Prices will rise when large numbers of people want to buy shares in that company and fall when they want to sell.

The fickle nature of market forces makes share prices volatile, and very difficult to predict. Any number of forces—social, political, economic, technological, or sometimes apparently inexplicable trends—can push share prices up and down. BP's share price crashed following the explosion on its Deepwater Horizon rig in the Gulf of Mexico in 2010, one of the worst environmental disasters of the century. This is a good example of a combination of political, economic, social, and ecological factors acting in tandem. Others are far more random, e.g. the price of shares in WH Group, the world's largest pork producer fell by 33 per cent, following an outbreak of porcine diarrhoea in China.[28] Sometimes the fluctuations are based on rumour and sometimes on fact. You may have seen the terms 'bull market' and 'bear market'. These relate to the performance of the markets.

Essential economics and finance

Chapter 19

---

[25] The London Stock Exchange's website provides useful explanations and short videos on many of the topics discussed in this section. Go to https://www.londonstockexchange.com/home/homepage.htm and click on the 'Education' section.

[26] London Stock Exchange (2019) *A Guide to Listing on the London Stock Exchange*. Available online at: http://londonstockexchange.com/home/guide-to-listing.pdf, accessed 14/07/2016.

[27] London Stock Exchange (2019) *AIM Guide for Entrepreneurs*. Available online at: http://www2 .londonstockexchangegroup.com/AIM-guide-for-entrepreneurs, accessed 05/08/2019.

[28] P. Saefong, M., 'Hog prices poised to soar as deadly swine disease emerges in China', *MarketWatch*, 31 August 2018. Available at https://www.marketwatch.com/story/hog-prices-poised-to-soar-as-deadly-swine-disease-emerges-in-china-2018-08-31, accessed 05/08/2019.

> ### 🛈 Essential explanation
>
> A *bull market* occurs when prices rise, confidence is high, and investors anticipate that prices will continue to rise for a consistent period.
>
> A *bear market* occurs when prices are falling, investors are pessimistic and anticipate that prices will continue to fall for a consistent period.

19.2.4.3 Indexes

To find out what a share is worth, and evaluate its performance, you consult an *index*. An index tracks a 'basket' of shares over a period of time (a bit like the RPI tracks the price of a typical basket of goods). In the UK, there are several indexes, the best known of which are those produced by the *Financial Times*, for example the FTSE 100 ('Footsie') which tracks the performance of the largest UK companies. If the share price of one large FTSE 100 company, like BP, falls sharply, this will bring down the FTSE, as we are looking at average prices.

Traditionally, the London Stock Exchange has been one of the leading stock markets in the world, although not necessarily the biggest. This has given the City of London a leading role in the international financial markets. There are other important markets such as the New York, Hong Kong, and Japanese stock markets. Each has its own index, such as the US Dow Jones Industrial Average (referred to as the Dow Jones, or simply the Dow) or the Hong Kong Hang Seng Index.

19.2.4.4 Bonds and the bond markets

The government and companies issue bonds and other debt instruments in order to borrow money (see 'Corporate finance' at 17.5.2.2). Government bonds are known as gilt-edged securities, or simply gilts. Public, but not private, companies can issue bonds as well as shares, and bonds are an important source of finance for public companies. Bonds can be bought or sold by investors. They are traded on the bond market.

When investors buy government bonds, they are lending money to the government and when they buy corporate bonds, they are lending money to a company. Bonds are generally considered to be the safest type of investment. Investors get a fixed rate of interest, and at the end of a specified period, they get their money back. As bonds are a relatively risk-free investment, the rate of return is relatively low.

19.2.4.5 Other financial markets

Investors do not just invest in shares and bonds. There are numerous other investment opportunities, which tend to be higher risk, but which also offer higher returns if investors get it right. There are markets for each of these types of investment.

1. **Currency markets** are global markets for foreign exchange (*Forex*), such as dollars, euros, yen, sterling, etc. Businesses need foreign currencies to trade abroad. Governments buy and sell currencies. Currencies can also be held as an investment. The price depends on supply and demand. Each day the financial news will report whether the pound has gone up or down in relation to other currencies, for example as against

the dollar or the euro. The strength or weakness of the pound is crucial for both the government and businesses.

2. **Commodity markets** are markets where raw materials such as gold, oil, wheat, coffee, or cotton are traded. Commodity prices can be very volatile, namely going up or down very quickly depending again on supply and demand. The escalation in the price of oil is a current example.

3. **Futures markets**. Contracts to purchase currencies or commodities at a future date are sold on the futures market. Here there is no physical delivery of the commodity. The speculator simply buys the paper (futures) contract and takes on the risk of price fluctuations. If the price goes up before delivery he has made money; if it goes down, he has lost it. This type of investment is highly speculative.

4. **Derivatives markets**. Derivatives are investments the value of which is based on the performance of an underlying investment. When an investor buys a derivative, he is betting on the value of another investment. A futures contract, for example, is a derivative, as its value is based on the price of the underlying commodity. There are even 'weather derivatives' (which is effectively betting on weather conditions).

> ### Essential explanation
>
> Currencies and commodities can either be traded on a *spot market*, where traders buy for immediate physical delivery, or they can buy *forward* for physical delivery at a specified date in the future.

19.2.4.6 Who invests in the markets?

The individual (or retail) investor is a rarity. Not all investors are confident about investing in the markets. It is, after all, risky. Investors may be lucky, but generally they need a certain amount of knowledge and expertise. In addition, there are trading costs on deals, which can be very high. Usually, investors rely on professional advice. The result is that the main investors are institutions, which manage over 80 per cent of the overall value of UK company shares. As they are the main players in the financial markets, we are now going to look at some of these.

1. **Investment funds**. An alternative to DIY for individual investors is to use the services of an investment, or managed, fund. Investors pay a management fee, but gain the benefit of a professionally managed fund and access to a far greater range of investments, and reduce the costs of investment.

2. **Hedge funds**. A hedge fund is simply another type of managed fund, but they are mainly used by wealthy individuals or institutional investors, rather than small investors. Investors pay a management fee, but the managers also take a percentage of the profit, which can be very high. Hedge funds invest in everything from shares, futures, currencies, bonds, commodities, and property down to 'weather derivatives'.

3. **Pension funds and insurance companies**. Paying into a pension is the main way that people save for retirement. The money which investors have paid into pension schemes is managed by the pension funds. They are the biggest institutional investors, way ahead of the investment and hedge funds, insurance companies, and private equity.

> ### ⓘ Essential explanation
>
> *Hedging* is off-setting investments, so that, at its very simplest, for every high-risk investment (with the potential for making high profits, or return), the investor holds a low-risk investment (which will yield a far lower return). The gamble is that the high-risk investments will more than compensate for the low yields on the 'safe' investment.

You should now have a clearer idea about who is doing what in the City, which will help you to understand how the finances of both individuals and businesses work.

19.3 Business accounts

The key to understanding business finance is an understanding of the accounts of a business. We saw with Patisserie Valerie (see 15.3.1.1) that to understand what happened and how the value of the company collapsed, you would need to look at its accounts. However, entering the world of accounting can seem like entering a parallel universe with mysterious rules and incomprehensible jargon, and students tend to assume that accounts involve complicated maths. Nothing could be further from the truth. Accounts simply involve some basic arithmetic; accounts are logical. They follow the same structure, whether they are the accounts of a small business or a multi-national plc. Once you understand the basics, you are in a position to understand and interpret even the most complicated set of accounts.

19.3.1 What are accounts?

> ### ⓘ Essential explanation
>
> *Accounts* are summaries of financial information. They serve two purposes:
>
> 1. They are a record of the day-to-day financial transactions involved in the running of a business.
> 2. They are summaries of the financial performance of the business over a given period.

Not every set of accounts is exactly the same. There is some degree of both national and international regulation of accounts. This means that the information presented in any set of accounts will be consistent, but businesses and companies present their accounts using different conventions, layout, and terminology. However, the structure will always be the same. If you know the basic rules, you should always be able to extract the information you need.

19.3.2 Why study accounts?

Typically, students ask: 'If I'm not going to be an accountant, why do I need to study accounts?' The answer is that accounts provide essential information about both individuals and businesses, and about the organisation in which you are working. We will consider this from the point of view of a lawyer, but many of the points in this section apply whatever sector you are working in. Often the accounting practices of well-known organisations are the subject of media attention, and a serious accounting scandal can lead to the involvement of lawyers as well as accountants. The Patisserie Valerie scandal (see 15.3.1.1) is an example.

19.3.2.1 Individual clients

Individuals need to know what their financial situation is in order to decide how to proceed with a variety of matters.

1. **Property**. Where clients are buying a house, their financial situation and creditworthiness will affect their mortgage application.
2. **Matrimonial**. In a family law context, where there is an acrimonious divorce, you may have to advise a client whether one of the parties is trying to hide their true wealth.
3. **Probate**. Where a client has died, and you are dealing with his estate, you will need details of his finances to advise how much the family will inherit.
4. **Tax**. You may need to give a client tax advice.
5. **Insolvency**. A client in financial difficulties may need advice on possible bankruptcy.
6. **Litigation**. The client's financial position is often crucial in deciding if, or when, to proceed with an action.

In all of these examples, you would get the information you need from their accounts. Even if they do not keep formal accounts, most people use basic accounting principles without realising it, by adding up income and deducting their expenses, and using these figures to prepare a budget. These everyday financial records kept by individuals are crucial to all areas of practice.

19.3.2.2 Business clients

Business clients need to know how the business is performing, and whether it is well managed.

1. **Owners, executives, and managers**. Everyone involved in the running of any business from the chief executive officer (CEO) of a multi-national corporation down to a small service business will use the accounts to make informed decisions about that business, either long-term business decisions, for example whether to expand the business, or everyday management decisions in relation to pricing, staffing, finance, and so on.
2. **Investors and lenders**. No one is going to invest in or lend to a business unless they know it is profitable and solvent. Investors will want to know that they will receive a return on their investment, and lenders that the loan will be repaid.
3. **Employees**. A business's employees will want to know that their jobs are secure and whether or not they have any prospects for a pay rise.
4. **Her Majesty's Revenue & Customs (HMRC)**. The tax authorities will look at accounts to ensure that the correct amount of tax is paid.
5. **Economists and analysts**. As we have seen, economists look at accounts of businesses in various sectors to forecast trends and growth and to analyse what is happening in the economy.

19.3.2.3 Law firms

1. **Solicitors' accounts**. Lawyers are required to deal properly with client's funds, and comply with the Solicitors Accounts Rules. Solicitors' accounts are simply a slightly more specialised and regulated form of accounts.

2. **Performance**. Law firms, as we will see, are primarily businesses, so if you become a partner in a firm, you will need to understand your firm's business accounts so you know whether the firm is making a profit (and how much your partnership share is likely to be), and whether it is maintaining liquidity and solvency.

19.3.2.4 Students

Again, this is not an area that you can safely ignore. If you attend an assessment day with a potential employer, it is possible that you may be asked to do a numeracy test. This may be a straightforward test to see whether you have basic numeracy skills, but it may be based on a set of sales figures and you might be asked to calculate profits. This section will help you to know how to do that.

19.3.3 **Accounting definitions**

Figure 19.7 shows the main accounting definitions which are the basis of business accounts. These are all terms which you have met before. In Chapter 17 you looked at how income, expenses, assets, and liabilities contribute to the creation of individual wealth, and saw how businesses raise capital. Accountants define these terms more precisely.

In Chapter 17, we introduced a case study involving a client, Tom Stevens (see 17.1.1), who was setting up in business as a wine merchant. We considered the finance the business needs and how it gets it. We can use this as an example to look at the activities of a business and consider what happens in accounting terms. Its entire financial life will be recorded, and form the basis of its accounts. Here is a summary of some of the transactions into which the business enters.

Example 4

1 September	Tom transfers £50,000 of his own money to the business bank account.
2 September	He negotiates a loan with the bank for £20,000, repayable in five years.
3 September	He rents premises in the High Street and pays the first instalment of rent (£3,000).
4 September	He buys shop fittings and fixtures, and a van.
5 September	He buys wine to stock the shop for £20,000 cash.
9 September	He buys £10,000 worth of champagne from a supplier on credit.
10 September	He opens the shop.
	He sells £5,000 worth of wine to customers for cash.
	He sells £6,000 worth of wine and champagne to a wine bar on credit.
11 September	He pays an electricity bill by cheque.
12 September	He negotiates an overdraft facility with the bank and draws down £5,000.

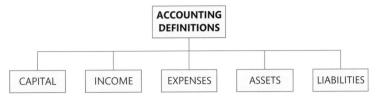

Figure 19.7 Basics of accounts

The first thing to bear in mind when looking at accounts is that all transactions will be considered from the point of view of what is happening to the *business* (not Tom). We will look at the entries in the order that they appear in the example.

19.3.3.1 Capital

 **Essential explanation**

Capital is the amounts owed to the owner(s) of the business.

The money which Tom has provided for the business is the capital of the business. It is money owed by the business to the owner. If Tom suddenly decided not to go ahead, or sold the business at a later date, the business would pay the capital back to him. This is a narrower definition than that used by businesses to describe their working capital (see 17.5).

19.3.3.2 Income

Essential explanation

Income comes from receipts of a recurrent nature.

When Tom sells the wine, he is earning income for the business. Income is what the business earns, either as a result of the labour of its owner and/or employees or as a result of investment of its capital, interest from bank accounts, or rental from property.

- Where you have a trading business, like Tom's, income will come from sales.
- Where you have a service business, like a firm of solicitors, income will come from professional charges.

You may also see these referred to as turnover, revenue, or gross revenue.

19.3.3.3 Expenses

> **Essential explanation**
>
> *Expenses* are outgoings of a recurrent nature, the benefit of which is used in the short term.

Expenses are the outgoings of a business, the benefit of which is used in the short term, and so will recur at regular intervals. Examples are rent, wages, electricity and other utilities, stationery, business rates (local taxes payable to the local authority), or bank interest. Expenses are necessary to maintain the earning capacity of the business. Tom's expenses were the rent, the electricity, and the purchase of his stock.

19.3.3.4 Assets

> **Essential explanation**
>
> *Assets* are resources owned by the business and used for its future benefit.

The cash that Tom has put into the business is an asset of the business. From our example, you will see that it has been used to buy other assets, such as the van and the fixtures and fittings, and it will also be used to buy stock and pay the expenses of the business. In other words, that cash is working for the business.

When Tom sold the wine and champagne to the wine bar on credit, the business incurred another asset, a debt. The wine bar (the *debtor*) owes him money. Debtors *owe* money *to* the business. The debt is an asset because the wine bar will have to pay Tom at an agreed time in the future. In accounting terms, debtors are also referred to as *receivables*.

Assets are the product of expenditure by the business, either by spending cash or incurring a liability. They are an asset, as they are acquired for the long term (or future) benefit of the business. Assets are divided into categories:

- **Fixed assets**, such as premises, fixtures and fittings, vehicles, computers, furniture, and the like.
- **Current assets** are assets which are circulating in the business, such as cash and debtors.

The purchase of assets (which produces a long term result) is not the same as the payment of expenses (which produces a short term result).

There are three particular types of asset which need further explanation.

19.3.3.5 Intangible assets

A business will often be sold for a great deal more than the total value of its physical assets. This is because a purchaser is paying for the goodwill of the business and its intellectual property rights.

> ### ⓘ Essential explanation
>
> *Goodwill* is the value of a business over and above its (physical or tangible) asset value. It reflects the value of intangible assets such as a strong brand name, good customer relations, good employee relations, and any patents or other intellectual property rights.
>
> *Intellectual property rights (IPRs)* are intangible property rights. They are often the most valuable asset of the business. The main ones are:
>
> - **patents**, which protect inventions, either products or processes;
> - **trade marks**, which protect names, brands, or logos;
> - **copyright**, which protects creativity, for example literary, artistic, and dramatic works, and forms of media, like films and computer programs;
> - **design rights**, which protect artistic, industrial, and product designs, both two dimensional (e.g. wallpaper designs) and three dimensional (e.g. furniture).

All these have a value to the business, and they can be bought and sold. They are therefore assets, and appear in the accounts of a business as intangible assets.

19.3.3.6 Cash and cash flow

Do not make the mistake of thinking that cash is income. Cash is an asset. Remember from Example 4 that some of the sales (the income) were cash sales, but others were on credit—no cash was received at that stage, but the business has still earned income by making the credit sales. So income can be represented by cash, but the cash itself is a current or *liquid* asset. As we have seen, it works for the benefit of the business. It is the most liquid (i.e. easily realisable) of a business's assets. The other current assets are *debtors* and *stock*.

The essence of a successful business is having enough cash. It is perfectly possible to have a business which is profitable, and owns lots of assets, but which does not have any cash. Obviously, with no cash, a business is going to have problems paying its immediate expenses—in other words it has cash flow problems.

> ### ⓘ Essential explanation
>
> *Cash flow* is the amount of money going through the business.

Cash flow problems are the commonest cause of business insolvency, particularly for start-up businesses. If a business cannot pay its debts as they fall due, it is insolvent and it may only be a matter of time before one of its creditors takes action and pushes it into either liquidation or administration.

We will now consider how this could happen. With Tom's business, you have seen that he has raised cash and has started buying and selling stock. Although some of his customers will pay cash, some, particularly business customers, will want a *credit period*, say 30 or 60 days

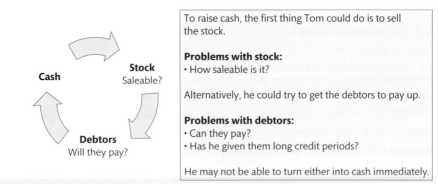

Figure 19.8 Cash flow

to pay. Until they pay, they are debtors of the business. Figure 19.8 shows the relationship between the cash, debtors, and stock, and the problems which may arise.

If Tom has immediate liabilities (lots of bills to pay) and not much cash, he will have to try and come up with some solutions. He could run some promotions, or offer discounts on the stock to try to sell it more quickly. He could offer the debtors incentives to pay quickly. He could try to sell his debts. This is called *factoring*, and there are companies which specialise in the purchase of debts. Tom would not get the full amount of the debt, but it would raise some cash. In the short term, he could use his overdraft facility, but in the long term, that would increase his liabilities.

To raise cash, the first thing Tom could do is to sell the stock.

Problems with stock:

- How saleable is it?

Alternatively, he could try to get the debtors to pay up.

Problems with debtors:

- Can they pay?
- Has he given them long credit periods?

He may not be able to turn either into cash immediately.

19.3.3.7 Stock

Stock is a particular type of *expense*. The purchase of stock is one of the expenses which a business has to incur on a recurrent basis in order to make the sale—in simple terms, if a business does not have any stock, it has not got anything to sell and it will not earn any income. For Tom's business the wine is the stock. However, we have also referred to stock as an asset, so you may wonder what is going on. The answer is that not all stock will be sold in one accounting period. If, at the end of an accounting period, stock is left over, it becomes an *asset* of the business, referred to as *closing stock*, which will be sold in the next accounting period.

You may also see stock referred to as *inventory* or *inventories*.

19.3.3.8 Liabilities

> **ⓘ Essential explanation**
>
> *Liabilities* are amounts owed by the business to either the owner or outside creditors.

The bank loan has also injected cash (more assets) into the business, but this will have to be paid back in the future: in this case, in five years' time. Tom's business has incurred a liability as it owes money to the bank (its *creditor*). Creditors are *owed* money by the business. They are also referred to as *payables*.

Tom has also bought the champagne on credit. Again, the business will have to pay for this in the future. His supplier is a *trade creditor*, and Tom will have been given a *credit period*, say 30 days. Liabilities are, therefore, sums owed by the business, and incurred for the long-term benefit of the business. They are also divided into categories:

- *Current liabilities* are liabilities which must be paid within 12 months, such as trade creditors or overdrafts.
- *Long-term liabilities* are those which are due after 12 months, such as the bank loan.

Note: *capital* is also a liability, as it is owed to the owner of the business.

19.3.4 **Final accounts**

At the end of each accounting period a business will produce a set of final accounts. These are the summaries which give information about its financial performance, its assets, and its liabilities. The final accounts consist of two parts:

1. a profit and loss account (sometimes called an income statement) which lists all the income, deducts all the expenses, and shows how profitable the business is; and
2. a balance sheet which lists all the assets, deducts liabilities, and shows if the business is solvent, both in the short term (liquidity) and in the long term (solvency).

Figure 19.9 shows the basic format of a set of final accounts. The accounts are often accompanied by a cash flow statement, which shows how much cash is available within the business. This is not part of the accounts, but gives a clearer view of the cash position.

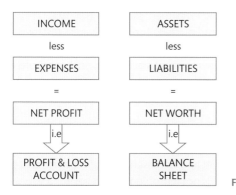

Figure 19.9 Simplified format of a set of accounts

Essential economics and finance

Chapter 19

19.3.5 **Interpreting accounts**

A set of accounts on its own is not very useful unless you know what to look for. Anyone looking at accounts will be asking the three same questions:

1. Is the business making a profit (*profitability*)? You look at the profit and loss account to see whether the business has made a profit.
2. Can the business pay its bills as they fall due (*liquidity*)? You look at the balance sheet to see what the total of the business's current assets are and whether they exceed its current liabilities. This will reflect the cash flow position.
3. What is the business worth (*solvency*)? You look at the balance sheet to see whether the business's total assets exceed its total liabilities. If liabilities are greater the business is insolvent in the long term.

Accountants make comparisons with the performance of the business over previous years and with other businesses. This puts the accounts in context, and provides realistic assessment of the health of the business. They analyse the information which they have by calculating percentages and ratios to work out trends and patterns, from which they can see how efficiently the business is operating.

19.3.6 **Audits**

Companies face greater regulation of their accounts than sole traders and partnerships. One of the more important company law requirements is that medium and large sized companies must have their accounts audited.

An audit is an independent report to a company's members as to whether the company has prepared its accounts and other financial statements in accordance with company law and the accounting standards, and that the accounts provide a 'fair and true view' of the company's finances. That means that the audited accounts are materially accurate and can be used to make informed decisions. If the auditors are unable to confirm this, the company's accounts should be treated with extreme caution.

Recent high profile corporate collapses, including Patisserie Valerie and the construction company, Carillion plc, where the auditors, Grant Thornton and KPMG respectively, failed to spot signs of insolvency and/or fraud, have directed the spotlight on poor auditing practice. The 'Big Four' accountancy firms, Deloitte, KPMG, PwC, and EY have effectively been criticised as forming an 'oligopoly' (see 18.3.7). There are calls for for their audit and non-audit divisions to be separated, in the same way that the banks have split their retail and investment sections[29] (see 19.2.1).

Understanding accounts will help you understand our next topic: insolvency. Just like individuals, businesses that do not manage their income, expenses, assets, and liabilities will soon find themselves in difficulty. The ultimate outcome, sometimes of bad luck, but more often of bad financial management, is insolvency.

19.4 **Introduction to insolvency**

Borrowing money and using credit is a widespread and necessary part of modern, and particularly business, life. Debt, if sensibly managed, is not a problem. However, for a variety of

---

[29] Rutter Pooley, C, 'Grant Thornton and PwC criticised for substandard audits', *Financial Times*, (10 July 2019). Available online at https://www.ft.com/content/cca803ca-a24d-11e9-a282-2df48f366f7d, accessed 05/08/2019.

reasons, individuals and businesses may find themselves in financial trouble. Insolvency is therefore an important part of the work of solicitors and other professionals. Insolvency statistics are an indication of the health of the wider economy, so it is worth knowing where to find them, and what they indicate. We now consider why individuals and businesses become insolvent and the effect. The insolvency rules for companies and individuals are different, so we look at each separately.

> ### ! Essential explanation
>
> People tend to use the terms insolvency and bankruptcy interchangeably, but this is not correct.
>   *Companies or individuals* who are unable to pay their debts are *insolvent*.
>   *Bankruptcy* is a process. It is one way that an *individual* deals with debts that she cannot pay. It does not apply to companies in the UK (although, confusingly, in the US, companies do file for bankruptcy).

19.4.1 **Corporate insolvency**

There are two legal reasons for a company being insolvent.

1. The company is unable to pay its debts as they fall due (often referred to as the 'cash flow test'). This is the most common cause of insolvency for any business. The business is simply unable to raise the cash to pay its bills.

2. Its assets are less than its liabilities (often referred to as the 'balance sheet test'). This will be obvious from the accounts of the business.

In 2019, 17,196 companies entered into insolvency, the highest level since 2013 and statistics for the final quarters of 2019 show that these numbers are decreasing.[30] This was indicative of the uncertain economic climate, with factors such as the lead up to Brexit, lower consumer confidence, and slow national and global economic growth playing a part.

19.4.1.1 **Insolvency procedures**

Insolvency means that the company is not viable in its current form and something needs to be done. It does not automatically mean that the company has to be wound up. This may be necessary, but it may also be possible to rescue the company. There are various options open to the company or its creditors, namely:

- liquidation;
- appointment of a receiver;
- administration;
- company voluntary arrangement (CVA).

Some of these, liquidation and the appointment of a receiver, may lead to it being wound up, and some, administrations and CVAs, are designed to rescue the company.

Essential economics and finance

Chapter 19

---

[30] Insolvency Service (2019) *Insolvency Statistics October–December 2019*. Available online at: https://www.gov.uk/government/statistics/company-insolvency-statistics-october-to-december-2019, accessed 02/07/2020.

Staying within the restaurant sector, a recent high profile example is the failure of Jamie Oliver's restaurant chain. He initially attempted to enter into an arrangement with its creditors (a CVA), ploughing £12.6 million of his own money into the business, to give time to restructure the business, but the chain was forced into administration in May 2019 with, reputedly, debts of £75 million.[31]

If you are interested in a career in insolvency and restructuring, you should research these procedures and their effects.

19.4.2 Insolvency of partnerships and sole traders

If a partnership is unable to pay its debts, all the partners become personally liable for those debts, and may have to pay the partnership debts from their own personal assets. Partners are jointly and severally liable for the debts of the partnership, which means if one partner is unable to pay, then the creditors can recover the debt from any of the other partners, either jointly or individually. If a sole trader's business becomes insolvent, then he is personally liable. Insolvency of the business which is run as either a partnership or sole trader is likely to lead to personal insolvency of the owners.

Partnerships can offer their creditors a *partnership voluntary arrangement*, which is the equivalent of a company voluntary arrangement to give them time to settle their debts.

19.4.3 Knock-on effects of insolvency

The collapse of any business is likely to have a knock-on effect for its suppliers, employees, landlord (if it is renting property), and others, who may find themselves in financial difficulties as a result. The insolvency of a large company can have a considerable impact up and down the supply chain. It is likely that a solicitor may be asked to advise clients who have been affected by the insolvency of a business, and who want to know how much they may be able to claim. Clearly the answer depends on how much is raised from the disposal of the assets of the business, the number of claims that are made, and what type of creditor the client is. Most creditors will not get back all of their money.

Trade creditors, the suppliers or customers to whom the business owes money, are generally unsecured creditors (see 17.4.5.6). They will be paid after the secured creditors and after the liquidator, administrator, or trustee in bankruptcy have taken their money and so will only get a (generally very small) percentage of what is left over. This is called a *dividend*. Example 5 shows how a dividend is calculated.

Example 5

Bagit Ltd, our handbag company, goes into liquidation owing £30,000 to its unsecured creditors. It owes £10,000 to its leather suppliers (LS Ltd) and £100 to Caroline who ordered a handbag which was not delivered before the company was wound up. After paying the secured creditors, his own fees and employees, the liquidator has £6,000 left. The liquidator divides the amount left (£6,000) by the amount owed (£30,000). Each unsecured creditor will get a dividend of 20 pence in the pound. LS Ltd will receive £2,000. Caroline will get £20.

---

[31] See, for example, Eley, J., 'Jamie Oliver's restaurant chain falls into administration', *Financial Times* (21 May 2019). Available online at https://www.ft.com/content/f4b81e9a-7bb5-11e9-81d2-f785092ab560, accessed 05/08/2019.

Employees may be owed some or all of their wages. Although employees are preferred creditors, which means they can claim for unpaid wages up to a statutory maximum; holiday pay; and any unpaid pension contributions.[32] Although they are paid before the unsecured creditors, there may not be enough money to pay all employees in full. They are entitled to be paid any shortfall by the Redundancy Payments Service (RPS), a government body which makes immediate payments to employees up to set limits. In addition, if a business is wound up, all its employees will be made redundant. Even if a buyer can be found for the business, it is likely that many will still be made redundant in order to restructure the business as a viable concern.

19.4.4 Individual insolvency

An individual is insolvent if he is unable to pay a debt of over £5,000, or has no reasonable prospect of being able to pay such a debt in the future. There were 122,181 individual insolvencies in England & Wales in 2019, the highest level since 2010.[33] Again, this appears to be indicative of the uncertain economic climate. The insolvency professionals trade body, R3, reports that 28 per cent of UK households spend more than they receive in income each month, and a 'large minority' have no savings at all.[34] You saw in Chapter 17 that what is sometimes described as 'financial illiteracy' causes people to seek out high cost loans, leading to a cycle of debt and default. Interestingly, R3 report that women are more likely to become insolvent than men, and that the causes of male and female insolvency differ. For men, own business failure is the most common cause of insolvency, whereas for women it is consumer debt.[35]

19.4.4.1 Personal insolvency procedures

An individual's insolvency does not automatically mean that she will become bankrupt. This may be necessary, but as with corporate insolvency, there are various options open to the individual or her creditors, namely:

- bankruptcy;
- individual voluntary arrangements;
- debt relief orders (DROs);
- debt management plans (DMPs).

Again, if you are interested in insolvency, you should research these procedures.

There are a number of non-legal organisations where individuals and (to a much lesser extent) businesses can go to get help and advice with debt problems, e.g. the Citizens Advice Bureau (CAB), or the charity, the Debt Advice Foundation.

[32] GOV.UK (2019) *Your rights if your employer is insolvent.* Available online at: https://www.gov.uk/your-rights-if-your-employer-is-insolvent, accessed 05/08/2019.

[33] Insolvency Service (2019) *Insolvency Statistics October–December 2019.* Available online at: https://www.gov.uk/government/statistics/individual-insolvency-statistics-october-to-december-2019, accessed 17/02/2020.

[34] R3 News Room Article (May 2016) *R3 comments on Q1 2016 Insolvency Service statistics.* Available online at: https://www.r3.org.uk/index.cfm?page=1114&element=26826&refpage=1008, accessed 12/07/2016.

[35] R3, Insolvency Landscape Series (June 2016) *Closing the Gap. Gender and the Changing Demographics of Insolvency* Available online at: https://www.r3.org.uk/what%2Dwe%2Ddo/policy%2Dand%2Dpublic%2Daffairs/policy%2Dand%2Dbriefing%2Dpapers, accessed 05/08/2019.

You may know about debt management companies, as they advertise extensively on day-time television. Debt management became big business as individuals struggled with debt during and after the economic crisis. These companies charge a fee for help with debt problems. Clients should be advised to choose a company with care. They are regulated and have to be authorised under consumer credit regulation, but, historically, there have been examples of debt management companies misleading the public and failing to comply with regulatory guidelines.

19.4.4.2 Effect of bankruptcy

Examples of well-known bankrupts in the last few years include in 2018, former international and West Ham footballer, Carlton Cole; in 2017, former Wimbledon tennis star, Boris Becker;[36] and Katie Price, who was declared bankrupt in 2019 when she failed to meet the terms of an agreement to repay her creditors. The result of a bankruptcy order is that the bankrupt is discharged from her debts. Often, after months of considerable financial stress, it comes as a great relief that someone is managing her affairs on her behalf and dealing with her creditors. However it can have serious consequences. The individual can lose her home. Certain jobs are prohibited until the individual is discharged. An undischarged bankrupt cannot, for example, practise as a solicitor, as she will not be entitled to a practising certificate. If she does continue working, any income which she earns may be used to pay off her debts. While she is bankrupt she cannot apply for credit of over £500. Banks may freeze her bank accounts, and might also refuse to open a new one in the future. After discharge, her credit rating will be very badly affected. She will have trouble getting credit and may have to pay higher interest rates when borrowing. Credit reference agencies keep details of bankruptcy orders for six years.

19.4.5 Law firms

Insolvency will not just be relevant for your clients. Over the years, there have been some high-profile casualties.

In terms of indebtedness, the collapse of the US firm Dewey & LeBoeuf, which filed for bankruptcy in the US in May 2012, is still the biggest law firm failure ever. It employed 1,300 lawyers, and had offices in 15 countries throughout the world including London and Paris. In 2009, trainees in London were paid £40,000 in their first year and pay went up to £75,000 on qualification, together with performance-related bonuses. It collapsed with debts of $300 million, causing the loss of thousands of jobs. In 2014, four of its top executives were indicted in the US for fraud. The importance of understanding accounts can be seen from the remarks of the District Attorney. 'Fraud is not an acceptable accounting practice, . . . The defendants are accused of concocting and overseeing a massive effort to cook the books at Dewey & LeBoeuf.'[37]

---

[36] Becker's bankruptcy was extended by 12 years in 2019 after it was discovered that he had concealed £4.5 million of assets.

[37] FBI New York Press Office (2014) *Chairman, CFO, and Executive Director of Dewey & LeBoeuf Indicted on Grand Larceny Fraud Charges*. Available online at: http://www.fbi.gov/newyork/press-releases/2014/chairman-cfo-and-executive-director-of-dewey-leboeuf-indicted-on-grand-larceny-fraud-charges, accessed 05/08/2019. The first trial ended in a mistrial in October 2015, but in 2017, following a second trial, its chief financial officer was given a £1 million fine and 750 hours of community service, and the firm's executive director was acquitted.

The collapse into administration in 2017 of KWM Europe was the UK legal sector's largest-ever example. In 2013, the silver circle UK firm SJ Berwin merged with KWM to create a billion dollar, self-styled 'global elite' firm with 2,700 lawyers and 30 offices across Asia, Australia, and Europe. However, as one lawyer remarked, 'big is not always beautiful and big is not always safe'. Three years later, the European part of the firm went into administration reputably owing $30 million, seemingly as a result of poor management, partner exits, and lack of funding.[38]

In the UK, a firm which finds itself in difficulty may be put into intervention by the SRA to protect clients' interests. This is aside from the insolvency process, which may follow.

(!) Essential explanation

The SRA has statutory powers of *intervention*. Where the SRA intervenes the firm will be closed down immediately, its accounts are frozen and an agent appointed who takes control of all files and client money. Client money held by a firm belongs to the client, and will be returned to the client. It will not be available to creditors of the firm as part of the insolvency proceedings.

In 2018, the number of law firm insolvencies increased by 70 per cent to an all-time high of 39. To an extent, the economic climate will have contributed to this, with less work coming in (lower income) and rising costs (higher expenses) resulting in lower profits. However, there are other factors at play in the legal sector, e.g. the cuts to legal aid, and over-borrowing, which puts them at risk of insolvency, particularly in a difficult economic climate.[39] To survive, law firms must now find ways to ensure that they run their practices as successful businesses. This is what we will look at in Chapter 20.

(+) Summary

- An understanding of some basic economic concepts is essential to understand the economic environment in which businesses and individuals operate. Lawyers need to appreciate the distinction between macroeconomics—the study of how the entire economy works—and microeconomics—the study of business activity within the economy—and the most important economic principles in relation to each.

- The City of London is an international financial centre. The role of the central bank and commercial and retail banks is central to the money supply and the domestic economy. It is important that lawyers should know how the financial markets work and the role of other key financial institutions in the City of London in order to understand the issues faced by business clients and individual investors.

- The accounts of a business record its day-to-day financial transactions, and provide a picture of its financial health. An understanding of the basics of business accounts is also essential to analysing and assessing a business's financial circumstances, strengths, and weaknesses.

- In an uncertain economic climate, insolvency is a threat for both individuals and businesses. Clients in financial difficulties may need legal advice on their options, requiring an understanding of the main insolvency procedures and their consequences for both companies and individuals.

[38] See, e.g., Thompson, B. 'KWM Europe and how not to run a law firm', *Financial Times* (4 September 2017). Available online at https://www.ft.com/content/93f8487c-80d6-11e7-a4ce-15b2513cb3ff, accessed 05/08/2019.

[39] Rose, N. 'Law firm insolvencies hit new high amid "loan stacking" warning', *Legal Futures* (10 April 2019). Available online at https://www.legalfutures.co.uk/latest-news/law-firm-insolvencies-hit-new-high-amid-loan-stacking-warning, accessed 05/08/2019.

Practical exercises

1. Can you now answer all the questions raised by the Patisserie Valerie case analysis (see also Chapter 15) and the questions on Basic Economics (see 19.1)?

2. Do you think a knowledge of economics is important for lawyers? Be prepared to justify your answer.

3. Why do you think share prices are so important for the economy?

4. Using the financial pages in a quality newspaper, track the FTSE 100 for a few weeks to see whether **it** goes up or down. Analyse why you think this is happening.

6. Why do you think cash flow is so important for businesses?

7. Do you think it is justified that bankrupts should be discharged after one year?

*Visit the **online resources** for the authors' reflections and to check your progress.*

 Further reading

Bank of England, *KnowledgeBank: The economy made simple.* **Available online at:** https://www .bankofengland.co.uk/knowledgebank

—A useful pamphlet published by the Bank of England on its role which is worth looking at to get a further insight into the role of the Bank in the economy, the banking system, and the regulatory regime which has been set up following the financial crisis. The website also has an 'Education' section, where you can find further information about the bank and the economy.

Gillespie, A. (2013) *Business Economics.* **Oxford: OUP, 2nd edn**

—A comprehensive guide to economics in a business context, explaining why economics are so important for business clients, with insights from business practitioners.

London Stock Exchange, *A Guide to Listing on the London Stock Exchange.* **Available online at:** http:// www.londonstockexchange.com/home/guide-to-listing.pdf

—A useful starting point to learn about the stock market.

Rice, A. (2015) *Accounts Demystified: The Astonishingly Simple Guide to Accounting.* **Harlow: Pearson Education Ltd, 7th edn**

—A straightforward guide to the fundamentals of accounting, aimed at readers who do not necessarily have a financial background

Smith, D. (2008) *Free Lunch.* **London: Profile Books**

—One of the most readable (and entertaining) summaries of economic issues. It has a useful glossary of economic terminology. Bear in mind that this was written before the full effects of the financial crisis of 2008–09 had been felt and well before Brexit, but it does help you to understand basic economic issues.

Vaitilingam, R. (2011) *Using the Financial Pages.* **Harlow: Pearson Education Ltd, 6th edn**

—A comprehensive guide to the City that gives a clear insight into who does what, and contains useful chapter summaries.

Useful websites include:

The Economist explains blog: http://www.economist.com/blogs/economist-explains. Click on the 'Economics' tab. There is no need to subscribe. You can register for a number of free articles a week.

*For the authors' reflections on the practical exercises, additional self-test questions, sample interview questions and a library of links to useful websites, visit the free **online resources** at www.oup.com/he/slorach4e.*

20 Law firms as businesses

Learning objectives

After studying this chapter you should be able to:

- Recognise that, as well as providing legal services, law firms are businesses.
- Explain the different types of law firm and their clients.
- Understand the competition and challenges which law firms face.

Introduction

The last few chapters have introduced you to commercial awareness and its importance. You have seen that commercial awareness is an addition to all the other employability skills that you need to find a job. Now we are going to look at the next stage: once you have found that job. When you finish your studies, if you decide to move into practice, the first thing you need to understand is that the organisation you are working for is, first and foremost, a business. In March 2017, Law Society forecasts estimated that by 2020 the total value of legal services to the economy would be over £30.5 billion and the sector contributed over £4.6 billion in exports.[1] So law firms are part of the modern economy in the same way that every other business is.

A television documentary, *The Briefs*,[2] followed lawyers from the successful criminal legal aid practice, Tuckers, in Manchester,[3] as they defended criminal clients. You might imagine that such lawyers would see their role primarily as helping vulnerable clients. However, its senior partner, Franklin Sinclair, ended the programme by stating:

> firstly, let me point out that we are a business, and if we don't make any profit, we won't survive, and there won't be any criminal law firms defending anybody. And as a senior judge recently said, nobody else protects the vulnerable as well as criminal lawyers do.

Like any other business, law firms 'sell' a product—legal services—and the object of doing this is to make money. Being a successful lawyer is, therefore, not just about knowing the law and advising clients; it is also about understanding what makes a law firm a profitable business. In other words, whichever area of practice you work in, you will need to be both a lawyer and a businessperson.

---

[1] Law Society (2018) *Legal Sector Forecasts 2017–2025*. Available online at: https://www.lawsociety.org.uk/support-services/research-trends/legal-services-sector-forecasts/, accessed 19/10/2019.

[2] Sinclair, F. *The Briefs*, ITV, 2 August 2012.

[3] http://www.tuckerssolicitors.com/.

Lawyers, as we shall see, have to make money for their firms and manage the expectations of their clients, whoever they may be. Now we take that a little further and consider the business environment in which you will be working. We look at law firms, their clients, and the business skills that will be required of students once they are in practice. Many of these skills are not unique to lawyers. They will be relevant for all students, whether you hope to be involved with the law, or any other profession or industry. From the beginning of your studies, you should take every opportunity to enhance your business skills. Never forget that when you go for an interview, it is a two-way process. You want to find out what the business can offer you if you decide to take the job. However, you will not be offered the job unless you can show that you can make a valuable contribution to that business.

20.1 Law firms in a business context

Law firms within the commercial sector differ vastly, as we shall see at 20.2.1. At one end of the spectrum are the massive City firms with hundreds of partners, dealing with multinational corporate clients, and at the other end are high-street firms with perhaps one or two partners, who deal mainly with individual clients or small local businesses. However, large or small, law firms have the same financial motivations and pressures as any other business.

- They need money (*investment*) to set up, and then to survive and grow.
- They must earn money (*income*) from their clients and convert this into *profit*.
- They need to attract customers (*clients*).
- They need to stay ahead of other law firms (*compete*) in an increasingly difficult market.
- They need to consider the impact of the *environment* in which they are operating.

You will need to understand where this investment comes from, and how law firms make a profit, how law firms attract and retain their clients, and the nature of the competition which law firms face in doing so. All businesses operate within an economic, political, social, legal, and technological environment which will influence their commercial performance and decisions. Law firms are no different, so you will be thinking about the effect of all of these factors on your firm.

20.1.1 Investment

Athough law firms are moving away from the traditional partnership model towards incorporation (see 6.6.2), over a third are still partnerships or limited liability partnerships, and there are 2,277 sole practitioners practising in the UK.[4] The owners, the sole practitioner or the partners, will provide the funding when the firm is set up by investing a lump sum and sometimes assets, such as premises. The average amount of a partner's capital account (their upfront investment in the firm) is £164,000.[5]

[4] SRA (2019) *Breakdown of solicitor firms.* Available online at: https://www.sra.org.uk/sra/how-we-work/reports/statistics/regulated-community-statistics/data/solicitor_firms/, accessed 19/10/2019.
[5] Cook, L. 'Partnerships: The reward/risk dilemma', *The Financial Times* (18 May 2018). Available online at: https://www.ft.com/content/59dc5968-576c-11e8-806a-808d194ffb75, accessed 19/10/2019.

Part III

Employability and Commercial Awareness

Once a firm is set up, it may need more money to expand and grow. If the firm is facing financial difficulties, more money may be needed to tide it over. A sole practitioner will have to provide the finance herself. Where there is a partnership, the partners can each put in an additional lump sum. For example, in 2016, before it collapsed into administration, KWM asked its partners to contribute between £80,000 and £240,000 each (depending on seniority) as part of a recapitalisation plan.[6] The problem here is that the partners may not be able to predict when such additional finance is needed, and they may not have the money readily available. To avoid having to find substantial amounts of money at unknown intervals, partners may agree that they will pay a certain amount into the firm each year. Often this contribution will be taken out of their earnings. This means that once they have been practising for a period of time, they will have a considerable amount of money invested in the partnership. Usually, where a firm is taking on additional partners, these partners will also be required to put a lump sum into the partnership or to contribute annually. This will also add to the amount of funding.

The partners' overall investment, or total of all their capital accounts, is known as the *equity* in the firm and the partners who have contributed to the investment are known as equity partners.

20.1.2 **Borrowing**

Not all funding will come from the owners of the business. Realistically, they cannot be expected to put their hands in their pockets for every eventuality. Some of the funding for the firm may come from borrowing, either by getting a long-term loan, such as from a bank, or borrowing in the short term, such as by way of overdraft. Borrowing is a necessity for most businesses, and law firms are no exception. Law firm borrowing increased by 24 per cent in 2018 as law firms sought to expand, retain lawyers, and, increasingly, invest in new technology.

Borrowing as a source of finance is dealt with in detail in Chapter 17.

20.1.3 **Other methods of raising finance**

PwC's 2018 *Law Firms' Survey* showed that larger law firms are also considering funding from external sources. For example, since 2015, five firms, including DWF, have floated on the London Stock Exchange's AIM market, raising between £10 and £15 million. Private equity investment is another option. As you will see in 20.1.9 mergers continue as a route to expansion.[7]

20.1.4 **Profit**

When you looked at business accounts in Chapter 19, you saw that businesses make a profit if their income exceeds their expenses. Like any other business, a law firm makes its profit by earning as much income as possible and managing its expenses as efficiently as possible.

---

[6] Ibid. This failed to save the firm from insolvency, and it entered into administration in January 2017. See 19.4.5.

[7] https://pwc.blogs.com/industry_perspectives/2018/12/considering-alternative-funding-time-to-weigh-up-the-options.html., accessed 17/02/2020.

Law firms earn income by charging their clients fees for providing a service. The most successful and well known are those that earn the most money (their income or revenue). Their main expenses will be the wages of their staff. Like any business, the more efficient the firm, the better they manage their expenses, and the higher their profit margin, so there will be more profit to share between the partners. Partners are not paid wages, like employees, but take a share of the profits each year. They can agree amongst themselves the amount of profit which they take out of the business. The amounts which each partner takes out are known as drawings.

Law firms have league tables, just like schools and universities. Some of these tables are based on how much income (revenue or turnover) they earn each year, while others are based on the size of the firm (i.e. the headcount or number of partners and lawyers), profit per partner, or the number and size of deals. Each year, in September, the details of the revenue of the top 200 UK firms are published in the legal press, for example *The Lawyer* or *Legal Business*, together with details of how much profit each of the equity partners is getting.

> ### Essential explanation
>
> The amount of profit which each equity partner in a law firm receives annually is known as *profit per equity partner* or *PEP*. Despite slow economic growth, by 2019, the average earnings of partners at UK firms was over £200,000, up 7 per cent from 2018.[8] It is one, but by no means the only, measure of the financial performance of law firms. Historically, most firms operate a *lockstep* system, where partners share profit from a single profit pool, with the amount of profit a partner receives being based on seniority within the partnership, although this model is beginning to change (see 20.1.8).

The firms in Example 1 give you an idea of the scale of revenues at the top.

Example 1

In 2018, DLA Piper, which is ranked number one in the UK listings, showed a revenue of over $2.8 billion (over £1.9 billion), with profits per equity partner (PEP) of approximately $1.87 million. Clifford Chance reported a revenue of just over $2.2 billion (£1.7 billion), with PEP of nearly $2.12 million (£1.6 million).

Clearly, no firm will be a successful business if it cannot attract and retain clients, so the next consideration is how law firms can do this.

Bear in mind that this is an average. It will be inflated by the very high PEP in large City firms.

20.1.5 Marketing and business development

A business trying to compete in the modern market will not be able to get clients without an effective marketing strategy. Marketing is based on an understanding of client relationships. For solicitors, it is about finding ways to provide services that your clients want, promoting these services so that your clients and prospective clients know that you can meet their expectations, and ensuring that the firm meets those needs profitably. To achieve this, businesses need to understand the 'marketing mix' or 4 Ps.

---

[8] https://www.hazlewoods.co.uk/news/law-firm-partner-pay-breaks-through-barrier, accessed 17/02/2020.

> ### 🛈 Essential explanation
>
> The 'marketing mix' or the 4 Ps:
>
> 1. **Product** (producing a product which people want).
> 2. **Placing** (ensuring that product is available for the people that want it).
> 3. **Promotion** (making those people want to buy it).
> 4. **Price** (striking a balance between incentive and profit).

Marketing is a little different for law firms than some other businesses. First, marketing is highly regulated by the SRA.[9] Most important is that the unique nature of legal services requires a different strategy. Most marketing is aimed at promoting a product, but when a client comes to a solicitor he has generally decided what product it is that he wants. For example, someone buying a house knows that he wants a property lawyer to do his conveyancing. There is no need to 'sell' him the product. What solicitors must do is show why clients should come to that firm, and not the firm down the road, so the firm needs to stand out.

A firm must attract clients, but once it has, it cannot then relax and think that these clients will always come back to the firm. Marketing and business development (often referred to as BD) are two distinct but complementary functions, and, in any firm will be ongoing processes which should not only bring in clients but also encourage client loyalty (see 20.2.2). When you start in practice you will find that one of the roles of any solicitor, from a trainee to the partners, is to help with marketing and business development, either directly or indirectly. An SRA research report states that a third of those providers surveyed thought that marketing is the third most important factor in helping to grow their business, after technology and networking.[10] This is something that you should be aware of when you go for an interview, and any sales or marketing experience which you may have had will be an invaluable addition to your CV.

The role of marketing is to establish the firm's brand, 'putting out' the message to clients and potential clients what the firm has to offer for them. Digital marketing has changed the way that law firms do this. Example 2 shows the type of activities that marketing departments of law firms will undertake.

Example 2

- Work on the firm's brand and strategy.
- Update the firm's website.
- Maintain databases with lists of key clients. Use this information for cross-referrals (*cross-selling*) within the firm.
- Use social media, such as Twitter and LinkedIn and blogs and vlogs, to raise the firm's online presence and thus the profile of the firm.
- Manage firm advertising and sponsorship.
- Liaise with public relations (PR) agencies to publicise high profile cases and ensure that the firm's experts have articles published in both the legal and national press (e.g. if a national newspaper runs an article on tax planning, one of the firm's solicitors contributes the legal background as an 'expert').

---

[9] See, for example https://www.sra.org.uk/solicitors/handbook/code/part3/rule8/, accessed 19/10/2019.
[10] SRA (2019) 'Research and analysis: The changing legal services market'. Available online at: https://www.sra.org.uk/search-results/?q=changing+legal+services+market&_t_dtq=true, accessed 19/10/2019.

Business development is about networking, forming relationships and connections in order to exploit the brand (created by the marketing department) and bring in new clients. Example 3 shows the sort of activities that come within the business development role within the firm.

Example 3

- Developing lists of professional referral sources and of prospective clients.
- Following up on marketing campaigns via email or phone calls.
- Using social media to follow up on prospective and existing clients.
- Organising in-house seminars on updates to the law for key clients and other lawyers and professionals.
- Producing newsletters for clients with legal updates.
- Organising networking events, for example, entertaining clients at external hospitality events such as sporting events, or in-house social events such wine-tasting or quiz evenings.
- Joining trade associations.

Marketing and business development must be tailored to the appropriate audience. There is no point in a small firm trying to attract large corporate clients. In any event, smaller firms are unlikely to have large marketing budgets. Large firms on the other hand have dedicated marketing departments. The purpose of their marketing activities, however, is the same for all firms: to develop a reputation or *brand* within your own market.

> ### Essential explanation
>
> A *brand* represents a business's image. Its purpose is to create an association in the minds of customers and potential customers which persuades them to 'buy in' to a product or idea. It may be a word, a sentence, or a logo. The best-known (and most valuable) brand in the world is 'Apple', worth $234,241,000,000.[11]

Each law firm needs to develop a brand that will represent the firm's identity and values. It does not need to spend a fortune on developing a sophisticated brand. A simple sentence or 'tagline' could produce this result. For example, a long established high street law firm uses the tagline: 'Excellent through experience.'[12] Larger firms will have developed sophisticated brands, based on established reputations. Many of the large City firms appear in the Superbrand ratings of the top 500 UK business brands, but none appear at the top.[13] Each year, the market analysts, Acritas, produce the 'UK Law Firm Brand Index' which in 2019 was headed by Eversheds Sutherlands, followed by Pinsent Masons. The Magic Circle firms, however, still dominate the top places.

---

[11] Interbrand (2016) *Interbrand's 15th Annual Best Global Brands Report*. Available online at: http://interbrand.com/best-brands/best-global-brands/2015/ranking/, accessed 15/08/2016.

[12] Copleys (2019). See https://www.copleys.net//.

[13] See http://www.superbrands.uk.com/, accessed 19/10/2019.

20.1.5.1 Advertising

Traditional, as opposed to online advertising still plays a role in building a brand. However, solicitors were not allowed to advertise until 1986, and, as we have seen, ever since then the content of legal advertising has been strictly regulated, first by the Law Society and now by the Solicitors Regulation Authority. The result has been that solicitors have tended to use advertising with caution, and rely on their reputations. This means that, historically, law firms had minimal 'brand recognition'. This has changed in the last decade with UK lawyers beginning to follow the example of their American counterparts. For example, in 2019, First4Lawyers introduced a new television advertising campaign.[14] These advertisements are still restrained by comparison with the US. It is worth, for example, contrasting this with the advertisements of the so-called Texas Law Hawk, a criminal defence lawyer, whose over-the-top offering became a huge internet trend—his following was such that he even appeared in a commercial at the American Super Bowl.[15]

20.1.6 **Pricing**

Pricing is an integral part of marketing and it is important to get it right. The SRA reports that clients consider the cost of legal services as the most important factor in choosing a legal service and will shop around to find the most cost effective option.[16] However, there is no point in a firm providing a spectacular level of service to a client, if this cannot be done at a profit. Law firms earn income by charging their clients in the form of fees. The amount of those fees is crucial. Charge too much and clients will go elsewhere; charge too little and the firm will sacrifice its profits. It may seem that clients and businesses are looking at prices from opposite ends of the spectrum. In fact, when you look at what professional businesses consider when setting a price, and what clients think about when deciding whether or not to accept, often you will see that they are not that far apart.

- Clients want value for money. This does not necessarily mean getting the cheapest price. Clients will look, for example, at the level of service provided, the experience of the person providing the service, the choice of providers at that level with that experience, and the importance of the matter. The more important the matter, the more a client will be prepared to pay. Experienced business clients understand that an excellent service commands high prices, and a compromise on price could mean a compromise on service. In other words, they know that they 'get what they pay for'. Hence the City firms can command very large fees.

- For the business, making a profit does not necessarily mean charging the highest price. Factors to consider include the importance of the client, the potential for future work with that client, and the complexity of the matter. Sometimes it is better to forego some profit to ensure that the client comes to the firm, and stays.

---

[14] https://www.first4lawyers.com/about-us/our-tv-adverts/, accessed 17/02/2020.

[15] https://www.youtube.com/watch?v=cWpkmXQbZV0, accessed 17/02/2020.

[16] SRA (2019) *Changing Legal Services Market*. Available online at: https://www.sra.org.uk/search-results/?q=changing+legal+services+market&_t_dtq=true, accessed 19/10/2019.

Both sides have to accept that all matters carry a degree of risk; that is, they have the potential to go wrong. The matter may take longer than anticipated or the outcome may not be exactly as planned. Acting for a client is no different from any other business deal: the firm must allocate this risk between the parties. To an extent this is done using different fee structures.

20.1.7 How law firms charge

Lawyers use a variety of pricing structures. The main ones are:

- hourly rates;
- fixed fees;
- contingency and conditional fees ('no win, no fee' arrangements);
- retainers.

20.1.7.1 Hourly rates

As the name suggests, solicitors are charged out at a rate per hour, depending on their seniority. These rates vary considerably, depending on the type of firm and, historically, there has been a lack of transparency surrounding these. In 2016, Jim Diamond, the renowned costs expert, writing for the Centre for Policy Studies, reported that for Magic Circle firms the average hourly rate for partner time was £850, and between £350 to £500 for a newly qualified to year post-qualified solicitor. He also reported that 'a top London firm' has been charging £1,000 for partner time.[17] A high-street firm would typically charge up to £250 for partner time. One boutique City firm, Humphries Kerstetter, has recently published its hourly rates in the interests of transparency,[18] and more firms are likely to follow suit.

Where the firm charges an hourly rate, the risk is on the client. If the matter takes longer than expected, clearly the client will end up paying more. Clients therefore dislike hourly rates as being too open-ended and not providing an incentive for the solicitor to work efficiently. Over the past decade, there has been evidence that clients are increasingly seeking alternative fee arrangements.

20.1.7.2 Fixed fees

A price is fixed at the outset of the matter. Here the risk is on the firm. There is no margin for error: if the matter overruns, the firm will not be able to charge more. These are popular with clients because they know where they stand from the outset and by 2018, PwC's annual Law Firm's Survey showed that fixed fees are now widely used.[19]

---

[17] Centre for Policy Studies (2016) 'The Price of Law'. Available online at: http://www.cps.org.uk/publications/reports/the-price-of-law/, accessed 17/02/2020.

[18] https://www.humphrieskerstetter.com/charges/, accessed 17/02/2020.

[19] PwC (2018) 'Law firms survey overview', https://www.pwc.co.uk/industries/business-services/law-firms/survey/transcript-2018-law-firm-survey-overview-david-snell.html, accessed 17/02/2020.

20.1.7.3 Contingency and conditional fees

The client does not have to pay unless there is a successful outcome for the case. They are mainly used in litigation matters, for instance personal injury or employment claims. There is a difference between the two:

- **Contingency fees:** if the client wins, he pays the solicitor a percentage of the damages which have been awarded.
- **Conditional fees:** even if the client wins, he does not have to pay his solicitor anything. (This is usually because the solicitor will be able to recover the fees from the losing side.)

Clients have access to legal advice and representation with minimum risk, and without having to pay out large sums of money while the matter is unresolved. If things go wrong, they do not have to pay anything at all. The risk is on the solicitor.

20.1.7.4 Retainers

Particularly for larger firms, an increasing amount of fee income is generated from being appointed to the legal panels of the largest global and UK companies, e.g. the global oil company, BP has 12 top City firms on its UK panel,[20] including those which are retained for its UK legal work.

Retainers create an ongoing relationship. The client pays up front for work carried out over a certain period or for future services—often with firms making solicitors available for a set number of hours a week. Retainers reduce the risk of non-payment and aid profitability, because the costs of doing the work have already been met. These arrangements require trust between the client and the firm. They would not be suitable for new clients.

20.1.7.5 Scale of fees

There is a very wide difference between fees charged by the leading City firms and those charged by a high-street firm. This is because there is a variety of ways in which a firm can maximise its fee income.

> #### ! Essential explanation
>
> Professional work types fall into three categories, known as the three Es:
>
> 1. **Expert work** (high cost/high fees).
> 2. **Experience work** (mid-cost/competitive fees).
> 3. **Efficiency work** (low cost/often fixed fee).

At one end of the scale, the City firms offer a high level of expertise to a relatively small number of corporate clients. The work is highly specialised and will be carried out by partners or

---

[20] These include Linklaters, Herbert Smith Freehills, Ashurst, Simmonds & Simmonds, and Addleshaw Goddard.

Law firms as businesses

Chapter 20

highly skilled lawyers. This type of work is known as *expert* work. The result is that these firms can charge high fees, and the clients expect to pay this as they know that they are getting value for money. In economic terms, this type of work is price inelastic. Example 4 illustrates this point.

Example 4

In September 2008 the investment bank Lehman Brothers collapsed, leading to the global banking crisis. Seven years later *Legal Week* reported that the total costs paid to lawyers, accountants, and other professionals as a result of its insolvency amounted to £3.43 billion. Lehman's insolvency was described by a US bankruptcy judge as 'the biggest, the most incredibly complex, the most impossibly challenging international bankruptcy that ever was'. Linklaters acted for the European administrators, PwC, with a team of over 100 lawyers and 20 partners, earning £77 million in the first six months of being instructed, and in the US legal and professional fees are still averaging £3 million a month.[21] It seems a huge amount of money, but there are few firms which would have the expertise to undertake this type of challenge.

At the other end of the scale, smaller firms carry out a high volume of work for a large number of clients, but they charge much less than the City firms. The idea is to attract enough low-value work to bring in a high level of profit. The work is far less specialist and requires less expertise, and so will be carried out by lower paid, often unqualified staff, such as paralegals, who are a growing force in the legal market. This type of work is known as *efficiency* work. An example is the sort of property work carried out by licensed conveyancers which is described at 20.1.9.5. In economic terms, this type of 'commoditised' work is highly price elastic.

In between is what is known as *experience* work. This sort of work is not highly challenging and does not require a high level of expertise. Once a lawyer has carried out one or two transactions, she learns what she needs to do, where to find suitable precedents, and to appreciate the various pitfalls. Most lawyers can do this type of work with practice. Drafting commercial contracts or leases would come into this category. Clients will still be prepared to pay a premium price if the firm offers a particular type of service or a relationship with the client. However, technology, particularly the use of AI and machine learning, is revolutionising this type of work. One of the challenges for law firms is that, increasingly, clients will be unwilling to pay for a service which can be done more cheaply and effectively using technology.

20.1.8 Targets

To maximise the income coming into the firm, law firms need to ensure that their fee earners are working at full capacity, in other words, they are fully utilised. One way of doing this is to set targets.

---

[21] Cash, J. 'Legal fees on Lehman collapse still top £3m a month as total hits £343m', *Legal Week*, 3 June 2015. Available online at: http://www.legalweek.com/sites/legalweek/2015/06/03/legal-fees-on-lehman-collapse-still-top-3m-a-month-as-total-hits-343m/, accessed 20/10/2019.

20.1.8.1 Chargeable hours

All fee earners will be given a number of target hours per day which they must charge to a client. It is important to realise that during a working day, a fee earner cannot spend the whole day on chargeable matters. He will need to take rest breaks or make a cup of coffee; some time will be spent working on non-chargeable matters such as marketing, management, training, etc. Most solicitors will probably be able to record one and a half chargeable hour for every two that they spend in the office. Each chargeable hour will be recorded on a time sheet, which will be used for the purposes of working out the client's bill. It is therefore absolutely essential that fee earners complete their time sheets accurately. The PwC 2019 *Law Firms' Survey* survey shows that in the top ten firms, trainees on average recorded 1,142 chargeable hours annually, an small decrease from 2018.[22]

20.1.8.2 Billing

The firm must also ensure that it gets paid as quickly as possible. The problem for professional firms is that clients do not generally pay up front; they pay when they are sent a bill. Work which the fee earner has done for a client, but has not yet billed, is called *work in progress* or *WIP*. To maximise profits, firms need to ensure that clients are billed promptly, and they are not left with large amounts of unbilled (and therefore unproductive) WIP.

> **Essential explanation**
>
> The length of time it takes a firm to produce a bill from when the work has been done until being paid by the client is known as *lock up*, as the firm will not make any profit until payment is received. Reducing lock up thus increases the profitability of the firm.

Fee earners will also have a billing target. They have to put in bills totalling a certain amount every month or three months. The amount will depend on the firm.

Targets are sometimes tied into bonuses. To offer further incentives, fee earners who exceed their targets may receive a bonus based on a percentage of the amount of the bills that they have delivered in a specified period.

Targets are based on how much each fee earner costs the firm. As we have seen, income has to be turned into profit. All the expenses of the firm have to be paid for out of fee income, so if expenses are very high, profits will be reduced. The main expense for a law firm is its staff, and the more qualified and experienced they are, the more expensive they will be. For each fee earner, there is the expense of support staff, for example secretarial, accounts, and IT. A further expense is the cost of the premises.

- In a small law firm, a fee earner needs to earn income of three and a half times her salary to cover the expense of employing her. (It is said that one-third covers the cost of employing her, one-third covers the overheads, and the rest is profit for the firm.)

---

[22] PwC (2019), 'Law Firms Survey 2019' https://www.pwc.co.uk/industries/business-services/law-firms/survey/transcript-2018-law-firm-survey-overview-david-snell.html, accessed 17/02/2020.

- In a larger firm it will be six times her salary to meet the higher costs of, for example, larger premises, higher marketing costs, and more support staff.

Bonuses are not just used to incentivise more junior fee earners. There are indications that firms will move away from a traditional lockstep system (see 20.1.4) where partners share profit in order of seniority from a single profit pool, to systems (sometimes described as 'eat what you kill') which reward high earning partners, e.g. introducing bonus pools. City firms Clifford Chance, Linklaters, and Ashurst and, more recently, Freshfields Bruckhaus Deringer have reformed their lockstep model.[23]

20.1.9 Changes in the provision of legal services

As you have seen in Chapter 6, fundamental changes continue to take place in the way that legal services are provided. These changes reflect the demand from consumers and businesses for more accessible and cost effective legal advice. The SRA reports that there is significant unmet legal need. Fifty per cent of people encounter some legal problem each year, but only one in three consult a solicitor. It is estimated that there is an untapped market for 'instant' legal advice worth between £15 and £24 billion.

20.1.9.1 Globalisation

The globalisation of business is one of the most important trends of the 21st century. As business is increasingly conducted in an international marketplace, large law firms need a global presence in order to meet the expectations of their international clients. The Law Society reports that UK law firms are winning an increasing share of the global market, and hence contributing to net exports.[24] In terms of size, two of the largest Global 100 law firms (Dentons and DLA Piper) are from the UK, and UK law firms account for 10 per cent of global law firms' revenue of over £25.7 billion.[25]

This has created a new and related trend which began in earnest in 2011: law firm mergers, e.g. Hogan Lovells, Freshfields Bruckhaus Deringer, or Herbert Smith Freehills or Dentons. In 2013, 28 Top 100 firms merged or entered into the Top 100 as a result of a merger, although if you look at the annual list of UK Law Firm Mergers produced by the consultants, Jomati, the pace of 'merger mania' has slowed in subsequent years and more recently has tended to involve acquisitions of smaller firms.[26] There are domestic reasons for merging, but for larger firms, the most compelling are the need to build up a global presence to keep up with the 'Global Elite', and the opportunity to acquire international clients, or create greater brand

---

[23] For a history and analysis of the lockstep model in the US and UK, see, Fontella-Khan, J., Indap, S., and Thompson, B, 'The dawn of the superstar lawyer', *Financial Times* (9 April 2018). Available online at: https://www.ft.com/content/b9c96d04-376c-11e8-8eee-e06bde01c544, accessed 20/10/2019.

[24] Law Society (2016) *Economic Value of the Legal Services Sector*, March 2016. Available online at: http://www.lawsociety.org.uk/support-services/research-trends/a-25-billion-legal-sector-supports-a-healthy-economy/, accessed 10/12/2016.

[25] TheCityUK (2016) *UK Legal Services 2016*. Available online at: https://www.thecityuk.com/research/uk-legal-services-2016-report/, accessed 23/08/2016.

[26] Jomati Consultants LLP. 'UK Law Firm Mergers'. Available online at: http://jomati.com/uk-mergers, accessed 21/10/2019.

recognition. A recent example is Berwin Leighton Paisner's merger in 2018 with the US firm, Brian Cave, creating Brian Cave Leighton Paisner. These objectives can be achieved more quickly and efficiently by merger. The merger trend has changed the structure of the legal profession. Clearly there are fewer firms operating in the market, and the size and scale of many of the Top 100 firms measured by revenue has increased at an unprecedented rate (see 20.1.4).

Globalisation has influenced the way that some of the largest global firms are organised, away from the traditional LLP model to the Swiss verein model, where various international offices have financial and regulatory independence from each other. Examples include Dentons, DLA Piper, and Norton Rose Fulbright. For firms operating in multiple jurisdictions, with different regulatory requirements, there are advantages to the verein system but such firms can lack the cohesiveness and common purpose of an LLP and the collapse of KWM (see 19.4.5) is a cautionary tale for firms looking to operate under this model.

In the context of expansion, you may also see references to 'lateral hire', where partners or very senior associates join a new firm with a client following. This can prove to be a risky strategy. An example was the failed US firm, Dewey & LeBoeuf (see 19.4.5), which brought in 22 lateral hires from other firms, awarding them top salaries, bonuses, and other perks, including guaranteed pensions.[27]

> ### ⓘ Essential explanation
>
> There is no exact definition of *lateral hiring*, but within the legal profession it refers to the hiring of talent at senior level, partners or senior associates, from other firms who move into a position at the same level as the one which they have just left.

20.1.9.2 The Global Elite

You have seen that in the UK, there are various league tables ranking law firms in relation to revenue, size, PEP, etc. (see 20.1.4). The ultimate ranking, however, is global ranking. As well as the UK Brand Index, each year Acritas publishes a 'Global Elite Law Firm Brand Index', based on law firms with 'Truly global footprints, aligned value propositions and strong leadership'.[28] In 2018 (latest figures available), the US firm Baker & McKenzie came out top. Four of the UK Magic Circle firms (see 20.2.1.1) featured in the top ten: Clifford Chance was second and Linklaters and Allen and Overy were fifth and sixth respectively with Freshfields Bruckhaus Deringer ninth.

20.1.9.3 Outsourcing

Legal outsourcing, or legal process outsourcing (LPO) is an increasing trend within the legal services sector. LPO providers can be based either on-shore or off-shore, but the majority are based in India. Globalisation and ever improving technology and 'connectivity' has provided

[27] Stewart, J. B. 'The Collapse: How a top legal firm destroyed itself', *The New Yorker*, 14 October 2013. Available online at: http://www.newyorker.com/magazine/2013/10/14/the-collapse-2, accessed 23/08/2016.
[28] Acritas (2018) *Global Elite Law Firm Brand Index 2018.* Available online at: https://www.acritas.com/global-elite-law-firm-brand-index-2018, accessed 20/10/2019.

opportunities for law firms to cut costs, by outsourcing not only administrative functions, like secretarial, IT, and accounting support, but also legal work that has traditionally been done by junior fee earners and paralegals, from contract review and research to due diligence and litigation support. For example, in 2009, the mining company Rio Tinto employed an Indian LPO provider, making savings of $8 million a year on legal costs.[29] On the other hand, LPO providers pose a threat for some firms whose profits have depended on repetitive, high volume work.[30]

20.1.9.4 Technology

You have looked at the importance of the development of technology for businesses and finance in Chapters 18 and 19. Legal Tech offers considerable advantages for the legal profession to improve efficiency, add value, and meet the challenges of a changing consumer market. Many larger firms now have digital strategists and most have for some time embraced digital knowledge management to win and keep business and to increase efficiency and effectiveness.

> **ⓘ Essential explanation**
>
> *Legal Tech* or legal technology quite simply means technology which is used to provide or aid legal services. It tends to be associated with the larger law firms who are developing and applying internal legal tech capabilities and with technology start up companies, particularly those who are sometimes described as *digital disruptors*, i.e. those that create the technology to change the way that law firms operate, or enable people to have access to legal services without the need for lawyers.
>
> Legal Tech is a vast and ever developing area and a topic with which you should familiarise yourself with. Firms expect their trainees to be digitally aware. The 2018 PwC Law Firms' Survey reportd that 80 per cent of Top 10 firms view technological change as their key challenge over the next 2–3 years, and the 2019 Survey indicates that the adoption of technology is a high priority with all firms, so you could well be asked a question about this topic at interview.

Firms are now embracing new technologies in a way that they have not done before. Professor Richard Susskind identified two benefits of technology for law firms: the first is to optimise pre-existing practices and the second is to innovate to provide new ways of delivering professional services.[31]

If we look at the first: optimisation. AI, blockchain, and other technologies are being used to provide greater efficiency in various fields. An example is cloud-based case management systems which reduce inputting time and errors. These systems enable lawyers to work from home and many allow clients 24/7 access to their matters so that they can review how they are progressing.

---

[29] Solicitors Regulation Authority (2016) *Research and analysis: The changing legal services market*. Available online via: https://www.sra.org.uk/SearchResult.aspx?id=72&searchtext=changing+legal+services+market, accessed 10/12/2016.

[30] Ibid.

[31] Susskind, R. and Susskind, D. (2015) *The Future of the Professions*, Oxford: OUP.

> **Essential explanation**
>
> *Case management systems* are based on computer software which allows every aspect of a firm's practice to be stored in one place. The essence of the system is a shared database of all client and case information with a facility for document storage and, in many cases, document generation. Anyone involved in a matter can access all relevant information and documentation relating to that matter at any time and from anywhere.

Legal databases, e.g. Lexis®Library or Practical Law, with which you will be familiar from your studies, provide an online know-how service that enables lawyers to work faster and more efficiently. A further example which you looked at in Chapter 19 is the use of information services to research information relevant to clients and companies that lawyers are involved with. Dun and Bradstreet, for example, uses Big Data and data analytics. By subscribing to these services, lawyers can find the information they need quickly and efficiently. There are also products which offer 'legal analytics', for example Lex Machina, which helps lawyers decide on litigation strategies. AI is used to navigate and search complex documents or series of documents to extract information, and in automatic contract generation where bespoke contracts are created by simply filling in relevant fields and answering a few questions. These are a few examples of the technology which is being used to optimise existing practice methods.

Increasingly, the emphasis is on innovation. As we have seen in 18.2.6.3 with the growth of digital platforms, the way people shop for goods and services is changing. Clients are using technology and the internet to find the right firm and are shopping around to find the best deals and are looking to law firms which not only are using technology to optimise the service that they provide to clients and drive down costs, but also to innovate in ways that benefit them. Law firms cannot afford to ignore advances in technology. As Professor Stephen Mayson put it: 'We would be horrified if hospitals continued to use old technology when something modern was available.'[32] The same is expected of law firms.

There are a growing number of online providers of legal services. In the UK examples are Keystone Law and DAS Law, which provides online legal documents, forms, and templates for both individuals and businesses. In addition, by the very nature of online services, the competition may not necessarily be based in the UK. Several US online legal providers have launched in the UK, e.g. San Francisco-based Rocket Lawyer.[33] Chatbots such as DoNotPay (which gives advice on how to avoid paying parking tickets) or LawBot (which offers free initial advice to victims of crime) are further examples of how technology is opening up the legal market.[34]

Larger firms are harnessing new technologies, using, for example, legal tech incubators. For example, in 2015 Dentons launched NextLaw Lab 'to develop a suite of technologies that will fundamentally change the practice of law'. Several of the City firms have followed suit, e.g. Allen & Overy's 'Fuse' or more recently, Slaughter and May's 'Collaborate'. There has been an

---

[32] https://www.lawgazette.co.uk/people/interview-stephen-mayson/5053768.article.

[33] See http://www.rocketlawyer.co.uk/, accessed 24/08/2016.

[34] For further Information on 'digital disruptors', see for example, Goodman, J '10 top legal disruptors'. Available at https://www.raconteur.net/risk-management/10-top-legal-disruptions, *Raconteur*, (23 March 2017), accessed 17/02/2020.

increasing trend amongst law firms to host and sponsor legal hackathons to promote innovation, e.g. Ashurst's Legal Hackathon in Frankfurt in May 2019.[35]

> **! Essential explanation**
>
> *Legal Tech incubators* are usually set up by and within City firms, which work closely with tech start-ups to enable them to develop and test technology services and products. The start-ups have access to the firm's lawyers, and client and expert panels to help them arrive at new tech-enabled solutions, focusing on the particular challenges faced by the firm. A *hackathon* is a gathering of computer programmers, who collaborate on code to achieve solutions to problems.

Professor Susskind argues that the 2020s are 'the decade when many of the radical tech-led programmes being designed now will really come to life: namely artificial intelligence and online courts. These will replace our old ways of working.'[36]

Exciting as these developments are, the use of technology poses risks and challenges for law firms. Law firms hold significant amounts of client money and also a great deal of sensitive information. They need to protect themselves from data breaches and comply with data protection legislation. They, and their clients, are increasingly under threat from cybercrime, cyber attacks, and scams. The SRA reported that in 2016–17, over £11m of client money was stolen due to cybercrime. In 2017–18, 60 per cent of law firms reported an information security incident—almost a 20 per cent increase from the previous 12 months.[37] One scam recently has been for hackers to clone solicitors' emails and when a transaction is nearing completion, email the client to tell them that the transfer details of the firm have changed, and the money should be sent to a different account. The client sends the money—to the scammer's account—and, sadly, it is never seen again. Most solicitors now put a caveat on the end of their emails to warn clients not to make changes of this sort without speaking to someone in authority in the firm.

20.1.9.5 Competition and deregulation

To survive as a successful business, law firms must stay ahead of the competition, and they are operating in an increasingly competitive environment, with increasing choice for consumers both at home and globally. Firms have always faced competition from other firms operating in the same areas and providing the same expertise, but nowadays other law firms are just the tip of the competition iceberg.

[35] https://www.ashurst.com/en/news-and-insights/news-deals-and-awards/hackathon/, accessed 17/02/2020.

[36] Quoted in Botsford, P. '2020s is the decade of legal change, says Richard Susskind', *Legal Cheek*, 23 May 2019. Available online at https://www.legalcheek.com/2019/05/the-2020s-is-the-decade-of-legal-change-says-richard-susskind/, accessed 15/11/2019. See also Susskind, R. (2019) *Online Courts and the Future of Justice*. Oxford: OUP.

[37] The Law Society (2019) 'Cybersecurity and scam prevention'. Available online at: https://www.lawsociety.org.uk/support-services/practice-management/cybersecurity-and-scam-prevention/. More recent figures from the Cyber Security Breaches Survey 2019 show that 32% of all business (not just law firms) had experienced cyber security breaches in 2018–19. Available online at: https://www.gov.uk/government/statistics/cyber-security-breaches-survey-2019, accessed 15/11/2019.

You have looked at deregulation of the legal profession following reforms introduced by the Legal Services Act 2007 and the development of multi-disciplinary practices, alternative business structures and other providers at 6.6.2, so we are not going to consider these in detail in this chapter. Legal services provided, by for example, licensed conveyancers and will writers are regulated by SRA approved regulators, but there are also many unregulated providers of legal services, e.g. claims management companies. The SRA estimate that there are nearly as many people providing unregulated legal services (around 130,000) as there are solicitors (around 150,000). In 2016, research from the University of Leeds indicted that these posed a threat to the traditional partnership model, and could come to dominate high volume areas, such as personal injury. Since then a further threat has come from the establishment of the 'Big Four' accountancy firms as alternative business structures (ABSs) which now offer legal services. PwC, for example, now employs 3,600 lawyers worldwide, more than any of the Magic Circle firms, and provides a 'one-stop' for clients seeking to get all their professional advisers under one roof. A recent report by Thomson Reuters shows that 23 per cent of large firms surveyed said that they had lost expected clients to the Big Four.[38]

Clearly this does create competition, but deregulation has often led to problems for consumers. There have been recent reviews of the regulatory system, in 2016 by the Competition and Markets Authority and in 2019, the UCL 'Independent Review of Legal Services Regulation' led by Professor Stephen Mayson.[39] The Law Society's response, whilst admitting that 'the current regulatory framework is not perfect', argues that legislative reform is unnecessary and improvements can be made within the existing framework.[40]

20.1.9.6 Diversity

Following #MeToo, there is greater public interest in diversity within businesses and law firms are no exception, so this is a topical issue and something about which you could well be asked at interview. The legal profession has always been perceived as the bastion of white, middle class males. On the face of it, this is changing: you have seen in Chapter 6 that there are now more female than male solicitors and the PwC 2019 Law Firms Survey reports that the trend towards increasing female representation at partner level is continuing amongst the top law firms. Of the top ten law firms, 83 per cent said that they had a strategy in place to address gender and BAME (Black Asian Minority Ethnic) imbalances. The now established Apprenticeship Scheme as a route into qualification, and, importantly, the new Solicitors Qualification Examination (SQE) with the introduction of innovative routes into the profession due to be introduced from 2021 (see Preface), are intended to improve diversity by reducing the cost of accessing the profession and creating greater opportunity for social mobility and diversity.

However, Women in Leadership in Law hosted a series of round table discussions which show that whatever is happening in the top firms, there is still considerable room for improvement overall. The profession is still predominately led by men, there is significant pay

---

[38] Brudner, A. (Blue J Legal) 'Law in the Age of Artificial Intelligence'. Available online at: https://www.jdsupra.com/legalnews/law-in-the-age-of-artificial-54008/, accessed 20/10/2019.

[39] https://www.ucl.ac.uk/ethics-law/publications/2018/sep/independent-review-legal-services-regulation.

[40] Law Society (2019) 'UCL review of legal services regulation – Law Society response'. Available online at: https://www.lawsociety.org.uk/news/stories/ucl-review-legal-services-regulation-response/.

disparity between men and women who perform similar roles, and a lack of flexibility and unconscious bias which remain barriers to career progression.[41] Independent research by the SRA confirms this and shows that BAME, disabled solicitors, and solicitors who went to state schools are more likely to work in small firms, the prospects of becoming a partner are higher for white men in all types of firm, and BAME women are particularly disadvantaged in progressing to partnership level.[42] In October 2019, *Legal Week* reported that nearly half of Magic Circle partners were educated at elite, Russell Group universities, and half of Slaughter and May's partners were privately educated.[43]

Arguably, there is a need for cultural change. Between January and August 2019, 43 cases of sexual harassment were reported to the SRA, down from 70 in the previous year in the wake of the publicity surrounding the #MeToo movement, but nevertheless a significant number. In September 2019, at a hearing widely reported in both the legal press and the national media, the Solicitors' Disciplinary Tribunal fined a Freshfield's partner, Ryan Beckwith, £35,000 for sexual misconduct after he inappropriately took advantage of a junior female colleague who was too drunk to know what she was doing. He resigned as a partner. Consequently, Freshfields set up a conduct committee and partners may be fined up to 20 per cent of their annual profit share for inappropriate behaviour. Its senior partner, Edward Braham has said that the firm is 'committed to improving behaviour and inclusiveness. For more than a year we have been running a global behaviours programme to drive culture change.'[44] The publicity surrounding this case, the amount of the fine, and Freshfields' response are indicative of increasing client pressure on firms for greater transparency in their approaches to diversity. You will find that if you look on the websites of most law firms, they will have a section on diversity and inclusion.[45]

20.1.9.7 Legal aid and public funding

A further threat to small firms over the last few years has been government cutbacks in legal aid as a result of the Legal Aid, Sentencing and Punishment of Offenders Act 2012 (LAPSO) in an effort to cut the (then) £2.2 billion legal aid budget, which has now been reduced to £1.6 billion. Most of the cuts to date have been in the fields of social welfare, immigration, clinical negligence, and private family law, one of the mainstays of smaller firms.[46] Proposed cuts to criminal aid funding of £220 million were abandoned, in the face of unprecedented

[41] Women in Leadership in Law, (March 2019) *Influencing for Impact: the need for gender equality in the legal profession*. Available online at: https://www.lawsociety.org.uk/support-services/research-trends/gender-equality-in-the-legal-profession/, accessed 27/10/2019.

[42] SRA (2019) *Diversity in the profession*. Available online at: https://www.sra.org.uk/risk/outlook/priority-risks/diversity/, accessed 27/10/2019.

[43] Lock, S. 'Magic Circle Partnerships' Oxbridge and Private School Bias Exposed', *Law.Com*, 29 October 2019. Available online at: https://www.law.com/legal-week/2019/10/29/magic-circle-partnerships-oxbridge-and-private-school-bias-exposed/, accessed 31/10/2019.

[44] Slingo, J. 'Freshfields threatens to fine partners for inappropriate behaviour', *Law Society Gazette*, 21 October 2019. Available online at: https://www.lawgazette.co.uk/news/freshfields-threatens-to-fine-partners-for-bad-behaviour-/5101882.article, accessed 27/10/2019.

[45] See for example, https://www.linklaters.com/en/about-us/responsibility/diversity-and-inclusion, accessed 11/11/2019.

[46] Other factors have also contributed to a decrease in family law work, e.g. the effects of the Children and Families Act 2014.

opposition. The Law Society's review of the impact four years later shows that the result has been that large numbers of people, including children and those on low incomes, no longer have access to legal aid when they need it, those who are eligible find it hard to access, and in many areas of the UK, the reforms have created 'legal aid deserts' where legal aid is minimal or non-existent.[47] The government has been reviewing legal aid, partly as a result of the Law Society's 'Access to Justice Campaign', and has now produced a report on its approach to legal support: *Legal Support: The Way Ahead*, which states its commitment to increasing legal aid.[48]

This has led to a further trend, which has impacted on law firms: unbundling, which is prevalent in family, probate, employment, and immigration matters.

⚠ Essential explanation

Unbundling is where the client and the solicitor share the work involved in a transaction, rather than the solicitor doing everything from start to finish. The client will undertake the more straightforward work himself, and comes to the solicitor to complete only part of the work, usually the more technical parts of the transaction.[49]

This is clearly cheaper for the client, but significantly reduces the profit of the firm, particularly in areas of law like family and probate, which have always been the mainstay of smaller firms.

20.1.10 Environment

Like all other businesses, law firms need to consider the environment in which they are operating, in particular the political, economic, social, technological, and legal context (PESTLE).

At 18.2.6, you saw that all businesses are affected by changes brought about by these factors. They must take advantage of the opportunities offered and respond to the challenges and restrictions which they may impose. Law firms are no exception. They are subject to all these factors themselves, but they also need to be aware of the impact of these factors on their clients, both individual and commercial.

A clear example is the political and economic climate. Never think that knowledge of what is going on politically and economally is irrelevant to you. As we saw in Chapter 16, whatever type of job you are applying for, you will be expected to show an awareness of political and economic issues for the business and its clients or customers. At the time of writing, all attention is focused on Brexit and were you to be interviewed today (21 October 2019), you would undoubtedly be questioned about it. Had you been interviewed on 21 October 2009, you would undoubtedly face questions on the impact of the economic crisis. If you are

[47] Law Society (2017) *LAPSO 4 years on: Law Society review.* Available online at: https://www.lawsociety.org.uk/support-services/research-trends/laspo-4-years-on/, accessed 27/10/2019.

[48] https://www.gov.uk/government/publications/legal-support-action-plan, accessed 27/10/2019.

[49] Law Society Practice Note (2016) *Unbundling civil legal services.* Available online at: http://www.lawsociety.org.uk/support-services/advice/practice-notes/unbundling-civil-legal-services/, accessed 28/10/2019.

interviewed on 21 October next year, there will undoubtedly be different issues. Whatever they are, you need to know about them,

Brexit particularly comes with a health warning: we are moving into uncharted waters. Articles in the legal press point to the short term opportunities for lawyers to advise their clients on the impact of Brexit on their businesses, whilst others are warning of redundancies in the long term.[50] At the time of writing, it is too early to predict what will happen. Keep abreast of developments. And a final warning: whatever you may think, do not use an interview to air your own political views. Employers are looking for a balanced analysis of the issues, both short term and long term.

20.2 Consumers of legal services

As we have seen in Chapter 18, all businesses operate within a 'market'. Within each market there are sellers (producers) and buyers (consumers). We tend to think of buyers and sellers in terms of the sale and purchase of goods, but businesses produce all sorts of products. Some produce goods, others provide services.

Law firms operate within the legal market, producing a product, legal services. The 'consumers' of that product are the clients.

We will now consider who those clients are, and why they chose a particular firm. Clients vary from individuals to multi-national corporations, so it is impossible to generalise. Successful firms have built up a reputation which attracts high-profile, big-spending corporate clients. Smaller firms are looking to attract more local clients and will be concentrating on the consumer market. The lawyers acting for these different clients will have different skill sets to manage the expectations of their respective clients. Lawyers acting for multi-national companies need to understand completely different markets, strategies, investments, and contexts from the lawyer acting for a local plumber.

The fact that clients cannot inspect what they are getting means that they will rely partly on the reputation of the firm which they chose, and we have seen the importance for a law firm of developing a strong brand (see 20.1.5). However, this will not be the only factor in influencing their decision. Law firms must also anticipate and manage the expectations of their clients. The best lawyers provide the sort of service which is tailored to the needs of their clients, so that clients come to the firm and keep coming back (client retention).

Awareness of the different types of law firm and different types of client is essential for students from an early stage. When you are applying for training contracts, you need to show that you know the type of work that a lawyer in that firm will be undertaking, and the type of work the clients bring in, and thus understand the commercial issues at stake. Assessment days and interviews will be based on exercises designed to show that you have done your research and can demonstrate your understanding of the expectations of these types of client.

---

[50] See for example, Segal, D. 'Brexit is Messy. London's Lawyers Are Cashing In', *New York Times* (31 March 2019). Available online at: https://www.nytimes.com/2019/03/31/business/law-firms-brexit.html, accessed 21/10/2019.

20.2.1 Types of law firms and their clients

Our starting point is to think about the different types of firm, and the types of clients which they attract. In July 2019, there were 149,806 solicitors practising in the UK. Solicitors' practices are organised in various ways. The Law Society's statistics show that nearly 22 per cent practise as sole practitioners and 15.5 per cent are in traditional partnerships, and just under 15 per cent are in limited liability partnerships, of various sizes. The last decade has seen a gradual move away from the traditional partnership model, with the majority (over 47 per cent) of firms incorporated as companies. Figure 20.1 shows the breakdown between sole practitioner and partnership practices, based on the SRA's figures. The top 100 firms by revenue make up 1 per cent, but the majority of firms are small firms, with up to four partners or directors.

If you do decide to go into the law and start to look for training contracts, you will need to consider carefully what type of firm you want to work for. To be successful, you should do extensive research into the firms to which you are applying. A useful starting point is *Chambers Student Guide*.[51] The Guide classifies law firms into categories, so we will use their classification to help you understand the main types of law firms.[52] Then we will look at the websites of some typical firms in each category, which gives you a good indication of what sort of clients they act for. This will also be useful knowledge for interviews.

20.2.1.1 Magic circle

This is the name given to the top five 'elite' City firms: Allen & Overy, Clifford Chance, Freshfields Bruckhaus Deringer, Linklaters, and Slaughter & May. These are the firms that earn the most money with massive global revenues. Many of these firms earn more from their

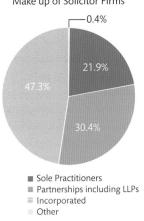

Figure 20.1 Make-up of law firms

Based on SRA (2019) Regulated Population Statistics: Population of practising solicitors, July 2010 to November 2019. Available online at: https://www.sra.org.uk/sra/how-we-work/reports/statistics/regulated-community-statistics/data/solicitor_firms/ © The Law Society

[51] See http://www.chambersstudent.co.uk/, accessed 31/10/2019.

[52] Although there are different classifications. See for example: http://www.chambersstudent.co.uk/where-to-start/different-types-of-law-firm, accessed 31/10/2019.

legal businesses outside the UK than their UK operations. They act for high-profile corporate and financial clients, and deal with a significant number of international clients. Most have offices worldwide. Linklaters, for example, have 30 offices in 20 countries and employ 2,310 lawyers and 5,290 staff overall. Their turnover (revenue) in 2018–19 was over £1.63 billion. They advise 30 of the UK's 100 largest (FTSE 100) companies, including Barclays, BP, and Vodafone. Their website states that they work with companies, financial institutions, funds, and governments to execute the most significant deals and to resolve disputes arising across the world.'[53]

20.2.1.2 Large London commercial

The next ten largest commercial City firms, include the so-called Silver Circle firms, which at the time of writing *Chambers* lists as Ashurst, CMS, Herbert Smith Freehills, Hogan Lovells, and Simmons & Simmons. There is not always a great deal of difference between them and the 'magic circle' firms in terms of the type of work, but their incomes are slightly lower. For example, Herbert Smith Freehills' turnover was £965.7 million in 2018–19. It has 27 offices worldwide. It also advises around a quarter of the FTSE 100 companies, including British Sky Broadcasting Group. It also acted for Sir John Major in relation to the litigation in the Supreme Court over the prorogation of Parliament in September 2019. Its website claims that it is 'one of the world's leading professional services businesses, bringing together the best people across our 27 offices, to meet all your legal services needs globally.'[54]

20.2.1.3 US London firms

There are a significant number of US firms based in London, e.g. Weil Gotshal & Manges and Mayer Brown. Again, they deal mainly with international corporate clients. Weil Gotshal & Manges employs 1,100 lawyers in 19 offices worldwide. Its turnover was nearly $1.45 billion (£1.2 billion) in 2018–19. Weil's website states that it provides 'legal services to the largest public companies, private equity firms and financial institutions for more than 85 years. . . . Weil's lawyers regularly advise clients globally on their most complex Litigation, Corporate, Restructuring, and Tax and Benefits matters.'[55]

US firms have hit the legal press for the eye watering salaries which they are currently paying to newly qualified (NQ) solicitors. The highest is at Kirkland and Ellis: £147,000, £62,000 more than the highest Magic Circle NQ salary.[56]

US firms were in the vanguard of law firm merger activity, as a result gaining significant presence internationally. For example, Lovells merged with Washington-based Hogan & Hartson in May 2011 to create Hogan Lovells, one of the world's ten largest legal practices, with over 2,800 lawyers in 24 plus countries, and Denton Wilde Sapte merged with Chicago-based

---

[53] See https://www.linklaters.com/en/about-us, accessed 21/10/2019.

[54] See http://www.herbertsmithfreehills.com/about-us, accessed 21/10/2019.

[55] See http://www.weil.com/about-weil, accessed 21/10/2019.

[56] University of Law (2019), *Lawyers salaries: what to expect*, Reproduced by 'The Guardian Labs'. Available online at: https://www.theguardian.com/partner-zone-university-of-law/2019/jan/18/lawyers-salaries-what-to-expect, accessed 21/10/2019.

Sonnenschein Nath & Rosenthal, and then the Chinese firm Decheng to produce a combined law firm, Dentons, with 151 offices in 50 plus countries.

20.2.1.4 Other London commercial firms

These fall into two categories:

1. **Mid-sized commercial:** examples are Macfarlanes or Trowers and Hamlins. Again, these firms deal mainly with commercial/corporate clients. However, both have, in addition, long-established private client or 'private wealth' departments. Macfarlanes have resolutely stood out against merger, having made 'a deliberate choice to remain smaller than many of our competitors'. They are best known for their corporate work. They have a turnover of nearly £217 million and PEP of £1.74 million They have one office in London and employ over 273 solicitors and 90 partners. According to their website, they are 'a distinctive law firm' focused on 'delivering excellence in the international legal market'.[57]

2. **Smaller commercial**: examples are Wedlake Bell, with 70 partners and 170 lawyers and support staff or the smaller Collyer Bristow, with 33 partners and 41 solicitors. Both these firms are traditional, long-established law firms. Both deal with a mix of commercial/corporate clients, media and intellectual property, private client, and property work. Both have the same outlook: Wedlake Bell's describes itself as a 'contemporary London law firm, rooted in tradition with a lasting legacy of client service' and Collyer Bristow that they are 'the law firm for those that value individuality, creativity and collaboration'.[58]

20.2.1.5 National and 'multi-site' firms

Chambers uses this classification to cover firms which have offices throughout the UK and are expanding rapidly into the international market. The examples given include Eversheds Sutherland and DLA Piper, both of which have offices throughout the UK and overseas. They have a large number of offices in the UK to serve local businesses, and so are not limited to the City, but the term 'national' disguises the fact that they are also very much international in outlook. The number of offices internationally means that these types of firm are among the largest in the world. Eversheds Sutherland, for example, has 69 offices in 34 countries and 1,600 lawyers worldwide, and a turnover of $1.175 billion (£900 million). It brands itself as a 'global top 15 law practice'[59] and DLA Piper as a 'global law firm', with offices in over 40 countries. DLA's global revenue was over £2.5 billion in 2015. The focus for these firms is still commercial/corporate, but from DLA Piper's website you can see that the emphasis is very slightly different: 'We strive to be the leading global business law firm by delivering quality and value to our clients.'[60]

---

[57] See https://www.macfarlanes.com/who-we-are/about-us/, accessed 27/10/2019.

[58] See https://wedlakebell.com/about-us/ and http://www.collyerbristow.com/about-us/about-us, both accessed 27/10/2019.

[59] See https://www.eversheds-sutherland.com/global/en/who/about-us/index.page accessed 27/10/2019.

[60] See https://www.dlapiper.com/en/uk/aboutus/, accessed 27/10/2019.

20.2.1.6 Regional firms

Regional commercial firms are based outside London and, although some have offices out-side their home cities, they do not have a strong national presence. Examples are the Bristol-based firm Burges Salmon or the Leeds firm, Walker Morris. The larger regional firms still act for large corporate clients, and have the advantage of charging less than the London or national commercial firms. Smaller regional firms tend to concentrate on more local clients, such as Wright Hassall who are based in Leamington Spa, a top-ranked firm of solicitors based in Warwickshire with strong links to the whole of the West Midlands.[61]

Increasingly, however, regional firms are opening offices in London, a recent example being Wilsons, the Salisbury-based private client firm. Regional firms have also leapt on the merger band wagon to gain wider national and international presence, e.g. Newcastle-based Dickinson Dees merged with the southern firm Bond Pearce, and now has offices in London, Bristol, Plymouth, and Southampton as well as its northern offices, and has begun to expand internationally into Germany and the US.

20.2.1.7 Niche or boutique firms

Niche or boutique firms specialise in particular areas of law such as employment, family, media, aviation, shipping, intellectual property, etc. Examples are Actons in Nottingham who specialise in horses (equine law), or larger firms such as Thomas Cooper Partners, an interna-tional firm which specialises in maritime, trade, and finance law. Clearly, such firms will have a select clientele.

20.2.1.8 General practice/high-street firms

There are hundreds of small high-street firms of varying sizes throughout the country. They will have broad-based practices, and act for local businesses and individual clients. They are unlikely to have dedicated commercial or corporate departments, but so-called CoCo de-partments (combined commercial/corporate) will deal with matters such as setting up pri-vate companies or partnerships, and dealing with consumer issues. The emphasis, however, will be on property, litigation, wills, and probate work. The other mainstay of the high-street practices, family law, has been hard hit by the legal aid cuts (see 20.1.9.7).

Figure 20.2 summarises the different categories of law firm and the types of client who instruct them.

20.2.2 Client retention

The vast majority of clients choose a firm based on recommendation, and individuals often return to the same firm throughout their lives. However, bear in mind that not all clients stay with the same firm forever. As their needs change, they may change firms, and 'up-grade'. For example, when a client sets up his first business, he will probably use a local firm which he knows about, for example the same firm that he may have used for his conveyancing. However,

---

[61] See http://www.wrighthassall.co.uk, accessed 27/10/2019.

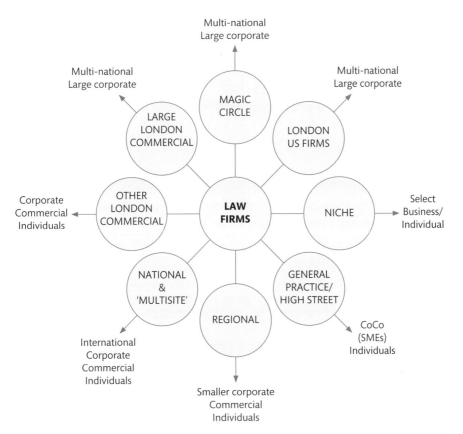

Figure 20.2 Law firms and their clients

as the business expands, he may decide that they no longer have the expertise to cope with increasingly complex business decisions, and he will be able to pay more for legal services.

The converse is true for law firms. As they grow and expand, they will be able to increase their prices, and inevitably, their client base will change. Some existing clients may no longer be able to afford this increase, and the firm will gradually shed less profitable clients, while gaining new and more profitable ones. This is reflected by Acritas findings that the average (business) client works with up to 20 law firms.[62]

However, most law firms work hard to retain their clients. There is a tendency to think that a firm constantly needs to get in new clients to survive. In fact, research shows that it is between five and 12 times more expensive to get a new client than it is to exploit the full potential of your current or past clients. We have seen that business development is an important part of a law firm's activities (see 20.1.5). In terms of business development, clients fall into four categories, depending on their value to the firm. Figure 20.3 shows the different categories of clients.

Figure 20.3 Client retention: categories of client

20.2.2.1 'Hot' clients

Once a firm is established, its most valuable clients are its existing, 'hot', clients. Each firm will have 'core' clients, the important clients who contribute substantially to their income. They are the ones that keep coming back. There is an interesting theory, the Pareto Principle, which helps to explain why your core clients are so important.

> **Essential explanation**
>
> The *Pareto Principle* (or 80-20 Rule/Law of the Vital Few): In any set of circumstances, 20 per cent of causes (inputs) are responsible for 80 per cent of the results (outputs). 80 per cent of profits of a business come from 20 per cent of (core) customers (and, incidentally, 80 per cent of work in a business is done by 20 per cent of the workforce).[63]

Managing customer relationships is essential to ensure that once one matter is concluded, these core clients will use the firm again. If we look at the next two categories, we will see that existing clients are invaluable, not just for the matter in hand, but for the potential which they have to bring in new business. It is thus crucially important to stay in touch with your clients, and nurture the relationship. Little things will ensure that they stay 'on side': while the matter is ongoing you should keep them informed about the progress of a matter—you may know what is going on, but clients will not unless you tell them, so you should ring them before they have to ring you. Be approachable—clients need to be able to talk to you—and avoid bamboozling them with legal jargon. Exceptional client care is central to getting repeat business.

20.2.2.2 'Warm' clients

Existing clients should not 'escape the net' once one matter is concluded. Once a matter is finished, they should not be ignored, and firms need to work hard so that they return. In addition, firms may be 'under-exploiting' the potential of their existing clients. A firm should ensure that a key client who, for example, consults their corporate team, is aware of the service that can be provided by, for example, the private client department so she continues to use the firm for her tax planning, or the property department if she buys a property. You have already seen the importance of 'cross-selling' at 11.2.1.11. It is vital to exploit this potential. Marketing departments have software to help their firms to do this.

---

[63] This is named after the Italian economist Vilfredo Pareto (1858–1923), who put forward the principle in *Manual of Political Economy* (1906).

20.2.2.3 'Lukewarm' clients

A great deal of work for lawyers comes as a result of a recommendation and referrals, which is why your existing clients are so valuable. They are, in effect, the best advertisement for a firm. If existing or past clients are happy with the service, they will recommend the firm to others, and they have the potential to bring in different sorts of work. For example, if a client changes job, he may recommend the firm to his new company, bringing in valuable corporate work. It is therefore important to keep in touch with past clients once a matter is concluded. Again, you have already looked at networking at 15.7. It is a crucial marketing activity for lawyers.

20.2.2.4 'Cold' clients

Firms would quickly stagnate without new clients. However, far harder work, and thus more expense, is required to get in clients who have no connection with the firm at all. Here it is all about marketing, which we considered at 20.1.5. Once a new client comes to the firm, it is essential that the potential value to the firm of that client is carefully assessed. Taking on a new client often involves a significant time investment, in acquiring knowledge of that client's business, business processes, and the sector in which it is operating. Firms have to assess whether the effort will be worth it.

20.2.3 **What happens when things go wrong?**

When consumers buy faulty goods, they can take them back and get a refund. When customers receive a poor level of service, the position is not quite so straightforward. They cannot give a service back. The provision of legal services always carries an element of risk and has the potential to go wrong: for instance, a lawyer may miss a time limit, or fail to include an important provision in a contract. Sometimes the client may simply feel that the solicitor has provided a poor service.

If things go badly wrong, the right to redress lies first with the common law and the tort of negligence. If a poor level of service is provided, the SRA provides a complaints procedure to which all solicitors must adhere.

20.2.3.1 **Professional negligence claims**

> **Essential explanation**
>
> Solicitors owe a *duty of care* to their clients. This means that they must not place their clients in a position where they suffer unnecessary harm or loss. If they do, then they will be negligent. Where a solicitor has not met the duty of care, the client may be able to sue for *professional negligence* (sometimes referred to as *pro neg*) and obtain compensation.

Actions for professional negligence are becoming increasingly common, and a quick search on the internet will bring up hundreds of firms who will advise on this. This is an unfortunate downside of the 'compensation culture'.

The result is that all solicitors are required to take out professional indemnity (PI) insurance to meet the cost of such claims. (In the US, this type of insurance is referred to as 'errors and omissions' (E&O) insurance, which makes its purpose very clear.) In the UK, the SRA regulates indemnity insurance, and solicitors are not allowed to practise without it. This has advantages and disadvantages: it means that solicitors are able to meet the cost of claims, but the premiums are expensive and a significant cost for law firms, especially smaller firms, which have seen their premiums rise by thousands of pounds over recent years, due to an increasing number of claims.

20.2.3.2 Complaints against solicitors

A client cannot bring a professional negligence claim simply on the grounds of poor service, but all firms are required by the SRA to have a complaints procedure, which they must bring to the attention of their clients, and as a last resort clients can complain to the Legal Ombudsman.

Clearly no firm wants a series of complaints about its service. However, a complaint can be used to improve services and does not have to have a continuing negative impact. If acted on swiftly and responsively, it can be an opportunity to demonstrate to a disgruntled client the firm's commitment to client care and retention.

20.2.3.3 Complaints about costs

Solicitors must set out how much the costs of a matter will be at the outset. Where it is not possible to give an exact quotation, a firm should give a 'best estimate'. Statistics from the SRA show that, together with complaints about delay and failure to advise, complaints about costs are amongst the most frequent client complaints.[64] Complaints are likely to arise where the client feels that she has received poor service, or simply has not received value for money. Generally, this can be resolved by negotiation, but as a last resort a client can apply to the court to examine the bill and, if appropriate, reduce it.

20.2.4 Added value

Most importantly, to retain clients, lawyers need to add value. We keep coming back to this point, so why is this so important? The answer is that it is a bit like buying a mobile phone. If you look at this practically, all you need is a device from which you can make phone calls, and you could buy the cheapest phone on the market, but in reality, that is not what you want to buy. Given completely free choice you may well choose to buy the latest iPhone. Why? To many loyal fans of Apple, it has that 'extra something'—its design, its image, its versatility—that creates a 'must buy' urge. Law firms, like any other business, also need to provide that 'extra something'. To do so, their lawyers must stand out. One way they can do this is by demonstrating the sort of commercial awareness that we have explored in these last chapters.

20.3 Conclusion

We started Part III by looking at a couple of topical scenarios as examples of commercial knowledge that you may need. Throughout these chapters, you have seen that commercial awareness is closely tied to employability. It is an important skill. In the same way that you will need to demonstrate, for example, communication or research skills to find a job you will also be tested on commercial awareness.

You can conclude that the last six chapters have given you the commercial background you need. Over the next few years of your studies you can build on this knowledge. When you come to start looking for jobs, you can attend any interview knowing that you can answer questions designed to test your commercial awareness with confidence.

 Summary

- Firms expect their lawyers to be commercially aware. An important part of this commercial awareness is understanding that a law firm is a business, with all the challenges and opportunities faced by every other business. You need to understand how a firm makes its profit, how it attracts its clients, the competition which it faces, and the environment in which it operates.

- Like every business, law firms provide a product—legal services—for their customers—clients—and must tailor their services to their customer base. Commercial awareness involves understanding those clients, why they instruct a particular firm, and their expectations from that firm.

 Practical exercises

1. In order to improve their profits law firms must increase their income and reduce their expenses. Can you think of ways that might help to achieve these aims?
2. What do you think are the main barriers to achieving genuine diversity within the legal profession?
3. How far do you think that the development of technology will affect the traditional law firm model?
4. Choose a law firm and research its website. Explain what sort of clients that firm is trying to attract, identify some of its clients and some high profile cases in which it has been involved.

*Visit the **online resources** for the authors' reflections and to check your progress.*

 Further Reading

Whether you are preparing for an interview or creating your own professional development plan, you may find it useful to access some of the websites referred to in this chapter.

Law Society. Available online at: http://www.lawsociety.org.uk

—Contains comprehensive information on the legal profession, including invaluable information for students, for example on training contracts and 'Top tips for applications'.

In relation to trends within the legal profession, you should particularly look at the Report: *'The Future of Legal Services'* https://www.lawsociety.org.uk/support-services/research-trends/the-future-of-legal-services/

PwC, *Annual Law Firms' Survey.* **Available online at pwc.co.uk**
Published each year, these surveys give a valuable insight into the legal profession and trends over the year. This Chapter refers to the 2019 Survey, but you should concentrate on the current year.

Solicitors Regulation Authority. Available online at: http://www.sra.org.uk
Chambers Student Guide. **Available online at: http://www.chambersstudent.co.uk**
—An excellent starting point for finding out about law firms, their practice areas, and clients. It contains essential information for students when researching and applying to law firms. The 'True Picture' feature gives insight into the life of a trainee at 120 firms.

However much anyone may tell you about an individual firm, it is always best to find out for yourself. Make sure that you look at (at least one) website for each of the categories of firm mentioned.

Susskind, R. (2017) *Tomorrow's Lawyers: An Introduction to Your Future.* **Oxford: OUP**
—An introduction for young and aspiring lawyers to the new legal landscape. Professor Susskind predicts a legal world of virtual courts, internet-based global legal businesses, online document production, commoditised services, legal process outsourcing, and web-based simulated practice. It offers practical advice for those who want to build a career or business in the law.

If you are interested in technological developments, you might watch one or more of his lectures which you can find on YouTube, for example, 'The Future of the Professions', 'Artificial Intelligence and the Law Conference at Vanderbilt Law School', or 'Can Technology Replace Lawyers?'.

For the authors' reflections on the practical exercises, additional self-test questions, sample interview questions and a library of links to useful websites, visit the free **online resources** *at* www.oup.com/he/slorach4e.

Court facts

Statistics taken from *Civil Justice Statistics Quarterly, England and Wales (Incorporating The Royal Courts of Justice 2018), October to December 2018* (Ministry of Justice, 2019) *and Criminal Court Statistics Quarterly, England and Wales, October to December 2018* (Ministry of Justice, 2019).

1. Magistrates' courts

Number of courts	161
Magistrates	Three (sometimes two) sit on the bench. Not normally legally qualified, assisted by a clerk on legal matters.
Number of magistrates	Around 16,000 (with a small number of district judges and deputy district judges).
Criminal jurisdiction	<ul><li>Issue of summonses and warrants for search or arrest.</li><li>Hearing bail applications.</li><li>Trial of summary offences.</li><li>Mode of trial procedure to decide whether a case should be tried summarily in magistrates' court or on indictment in Crown Court.</li><li>Committal proceedings whereby certain cases are formally sent up to Crown Court for trial sentence.</li><li>Maximum jurisdiction (above which magistrates must send trial to Crown Court—six months' imprisonment per offence totalling 12 months). Unlimited jurisdiction to fine.</li><li>Youth Courts.</li></ul>
Civil jurisdiction	Magistrates also have limited civil jurisdiction, e.g. licensing and certain types of family proceedings (as part of the Family Court).
Defendants proceeded against	Around 1.5 million annually (around 150,000 trials)
Average period from offence to completion	24 weeks

2. The County Court

Location	173 County Court hearing centres across the country.
Judges	<ul><li>Circuit judges.</li><li>District judges (a junior appointment; must be legally qualified for seven years).</li></ul>
Civil jurisdiction	General types of work:<ul><li>contract or tort actions;</li><li>equity jurisdiction, e.g. mortgages;</li><li>disputes over wills;</li><li>recovery of land; and</li><li>disputes under the Consumer Credit Act 1974.</li></ul>The County Court does not have any criminal jurisdiction.
Claims	Around 2 million annually.
Trials and small claims hearings	60,165 trials; around half of which annually are small claims hearings.
Time taken from issue of claim to decision	56 weeks (trials); 32 weeks (small claims hearings).

3. The Family Court

Information in this section taken from *Family Court Statistics Quarterly, England and Wales, October to December 2018* (Ministry of Justice, 2019).

Location	Shares buildings with other courts (usually the County Court); Designated Family Centres for each geographical region, with other hearing centres.
Judges	Mainly:

- Circuit judges.
- District judges.
- District judges (magistrates' court).
- Magistrates.

The list of those who, as a result of their office, are judges of the Family Court, extends to 25 categories of judge and magistrate, including:

- The Lord Chief Justice.
- The Master of the Rolls.
- The President of the Family Division.
- Judges of the Court of Appeal.
- High Court judges.

Jurisdiction	General types of work:

- Adoption.
- Divorce.
- Protection of children.
- Violence remedies.

Claims	262,399 in 2018.

4. The Crown Court

Number of centres	77 (across six circuits).
Judges	Depends on the gravity and/or nature of work:

- High Court judge (mainly QBD) or circuit judge or recorder (part-time appointment, e.g. solicitor or barrister).
- Magistrates may sit with judges on appeals.
- Jury for trial.

Criminal jurisdiction	

- Trials on indictment (with jury).
- Committals for sentence from magistrates' courts where the magistrates' sentencing powers are inadequate. (Maximum of six months' imprisonment per offence totalling 12 months).
- Appeals by defendants convicted summarily in magistrates' courts.

Civil jurisdiction	None.
Disposals	66,712 for trial, 33,874 for sentence (i.e. from magistrates), 9,027 appeals from magistrates.
Guilty pleas	66%
Average waiting time	19 weeks (for full trial).

5. The High Court

Location	The court sits at the Royal Courts of Justice, Strand, London ('The Law Courts'); The Rolls Building, Fetter Lane, London; and also at provincial centres (e.g. Manchester). There are 44 district registries.
Judges	Usually one High Court judge will sit alone. If necessary, a circuit judge, senior QC, Lord Justice, or a retired judge, may sit instead, e.g. on appeals from magistrates' courts.
Divisions	The High Court is one court, but it is divided into three divisions.

Queen's Bench Division

Jurisdiction:

- contract and tort actions;
- criminal appeals; and
- contempt of court.

It also incorporates various specialised courts, e.g. the Commercial Court and the Technology and Construction Court.

The QBD also has some appellate jurisdiction, the Divisional Court where two or more judges sit. Of particular interest is the hearing of appeals by way of case stated from magistrates' courts.

The Administrative Court falls within the QBD, and deals with cases of judicial review.

2018 proceedings commenced: 4,439

Administrative Court: 5,180.

Chancery Division

Jurisdiction:

- wills and probate;
- trusts;
- land and mortgage actions;
- company law;
- intellectual property; and
- bankruptcy.

There are specialised courts within the Chancery Division, including the Patents Court and the Companies Court.

2018 proceedings commenced: 13,704 (not including district registries, which annually account for around half of claims).

Family Division

Jurisdiction: A limited category of 'Family' matters, e.g. international child abduction.

6. The Court of Appeal

Location	Royal Courts of Justice, Strand, London
Judges	Usually three, but sometimes five or seven Lords Justices of Appeal.

Amongst those entitled to sit are:

- Supreme Court Justices;
- the Lord Chief Justice;
- the Master of the Rolls; and
- High Court judges as requested.

The majority decision prevails (so an odd number of judges will normally sit).

Jurisdiction	Entirely appellate
Criminal Division	Appeals:

→ Crown Court by the defendant;
→ Attorney General's reference procedure, on a point of law or against an unduly lenient sentence; and
→ referrals by the Criminal Cases Review Commission.

5,101 appeals considered in 2018.

Civil Division	Appeals from:

- High Court;
- County Court; and
- certain tribunals, e.g. Employment Appeal Tribunal.

1,161 appeals considered in 2018.

Procedure	As an appellate court, the Court of Appeal does not receive evidence from witnesses, but reads documents and hears argument.

7. The UK Supreme Court

In 2009, under the Constitutional Reform Act 2005,[1] the Supreme Court took over the functions of the Appellate Committee of the House of Lords.

Location	Parliament Square, Westminster.
Judges	Between three and nine (but usually five) Supreme Court Justices. (Formerly known as the 'Law Lords', Lords Justices of Appeal in the Ordinary.)
Jurisdiction	Almost entirely appellate. It is the final court of appeal not only for England & Wales but also for Scotland (in civil cases) and Northern Ireland.
Criminal jurisdiction	Appeals in criminal cases from:

- Court of Appeal (Criminal Division);
- QBD (Divisional Court); and
- Northern Ireland (not Scotland).

Civil jurisdiction	Appeals in civil cases from:

→ Court of Appeal (Civil Division);
→ High Court ('leapfrog' procedure); and
→ Scotland and Northern Ireland.

Appeals disposed of	78 in 2018.
Procedure	Like the Court of Appeal it does not receive evidence from witnesses but reads documents.

[1] Constitutional Reform Act 2005, s. 23.

8. The Judicial Committee of the Privy Council

Location	Parliament Square, Westminster.
Judges	At least three and (usually five) of: • Supreme Court Justices; • Lord President of the Council; • members of the Privy Council who have held high judicial office; and • Commonwealth judges who are members of the Privy Council.
Jurisdiction	→ Appeals from some Commonwealth countries. → Questions relating to the competences and functions of the devolved authorities in Scotland, Wales, and Northern Ireland.
Procedure	No 'judgment' is delivered; the judges give 'advice' to the Queen. There is one 'opinion' though dissenting opinions are allowed.
Appeals disposed of	44 in 2018.

9. The Court of Justice of the European Union

As a result of the referendum of 23 June 2016, the UK will be leaving the EU in the near future. Any references to the EU in this section should be read with this in mind. For more on the status of EU law, refer to Chapter 2.

Location	Luxembourg
Constituent courts	The CJEU comprises three courts: • The Court of Justice (ECJ), the EU's highest court. • The General Court, formerly the Court of First Instance, There is a right of appeal on matters of law to the ECJ. • The Civil Service Tribunal.
Judges	Judges are appointed by agreement among the governments of the member states (at least one judge from each). The judges are assisted by Advocates General.
Jurisdiction	→ Ensuring European law is applied uniformly in all member states. → Actions against member states to determine whether they have failed to fulfil their obligations under the Treaties. These may be brought either by the Commission or by one member state against another for failure to fulfil its Treaty obligations. → Limited power to deal with actions brought by individuals.
Procedure	In keeping with its 'civil law' traditions, one judgment is delivered. The Advocate General assigned to the case assists the court by presenting an opinion (analysis) and recommendations to the court.
Length of proceedings	In 2018 Art. 234 references took an average of 1 and half years to reach a conclusion.[2]
Completed cases	760 in 2018 for the ECJ and 1,009 for the General Court; both have many more pending.

---

[2] Statistics concerning judicial activity in 2018: new records in terms of productivity and cases brought before the Court of Justice of the European Union: *Court of Justice of the European Union* PRESS RELEASE No 39/19, Luxembourg, 25 March 2019.

10. The European Court of Human Rights

Location	Strasbourg
Judges	Judges are appointed from each of the 47 states which are parties to the European Convention on Human Rights of 1950 (ECHR). These states are members of the Council of Europe.
Jurisdiction	→ Individuals can complain of breaches of the ECHR by member states. → N.B. Convention rights are directly enforceable in UK domestic courts under the Human Rights Act 1998.
Length of proceedings	The Court states that it 'endeavours to deal with cases within three years after they are brought'.[3]
Workload	In 2018, 43,100 applications were made, and the backlog was 9,750 (a substantial decrease). In 2018 there were judgments delivered on 2,738 applications. Since 1959, state violations have been found in 83% of cases. In 2018, the figure was 86%.

[3] The ECHR in Facts and Figures 2018, © European Court of Human Rights, March 2019. More detailed information is available on the Court's website: www.echr.coe.int.

Index

Introductory Note

References such as '178-9' indicate (not necessarily continuous) discussion of a topic across a range of pages. Wherever possible in the case of topics with many references, these have either been divided into sub-topics or only the most significant discussions of the topic are listed. Because the entire work is about 'legal systems' and 'skills', the use of these terms (and certain others which occur constantly throughout the book) as an entry point has been restricted. Information will be found under the corresponding detailed topics. Cross references to the Table of Figures and Tables (available online) has also been provided. Page numbers followed by *f* point to discussion of a Figure in the text, whilst page numbers followed by *t* point to discussion of a Table.